KT-133-162

DONNA WHEELER
CATH LANIGAN
JOCELYN HAREWOOD
ROWAN MCKINNON

# MELBOURNE & VICTORIA
## C I T Y   G U I D E

Mosaic street couch, Fitzroy

Melbourne, like its famed city laneways, is many layered. Brainy and industrious, imaginative and creative; cool and cliquey, welcoming and generous; resolutely urbane and irrevocably suburban. Melbourne's contradictions are worth uncovering.

It's a city that's prolific in architecture, performance, live music and the visual arts. Life buzzes in its beautifully designed interior spaces: 'culture and recreation' (substitute the word fun if you like) is the city's largest industry. Melbourne is also sporty and outdoorsy, with a wealth of wonderful parks and close proximity to stunning beaches and bushland. Melburnians often coquettishly fish for compliments about their city, with a second-city diffidence, but they know they have it good. Their city regularly makes it into the world's 'most liveable' lists.

As intriguing as the city centre is, it's worth taking the time to explore at least a few inner-city neighbourhoods. The main attraction is not going to be a must-see sight, rather it's the quotidian pleasures that the city does so well: shopping, sipping coffee, strolling through a park, catching up at the pub. You'll see what makes Melburnians tick.

Beyond Melbourne's urban attractions, Victoria offers an astounding diversity of landscapes – from the prettily bucolic to the wild and windswept, from the alpine to the arid – all within a relatively small area. Dotted throughout this stunning scenery is a wealth of historic country towns. Outdoor adventure is as varied as the countryside itself: rockclimbing, horseriding, diving, surfing, sailing, skiing, hiking and mountain biking can all be attempted within just a few days.

# CITY LIFE

Melbourne is home to nearly 3.8 million people. It's one of the world's youngest cities yet also one of the longest-inhabited places on earth. If the city's citizens look like a varied bunch, it's because they are: one third of Melbourne's population were born overseas. A long history of migration has enriched the city with fresh and unfamiliar tastes, textures, viewpoints and beliefs. Around 180 languages echo through its streets and over 100 faiths are practiced. Many Melburnians have backgrounds spanning multiple ethnicities and are living symbols of the city's harmony.

Melbourne's mood is often considered serious and bookish. That intellectual image is softened by a sensuality uncommon in Australian cities. People aren't afraid to look each other in the eye, to appreciate details. Street life here has a sexy, celebratory edge. Sartorial style is important, although Melburnians like to appear effortlessly thrown together rather than 'done'.

Locals enjoy an enviable array of top-notch cultural and sporting facilities, and the city is filled with interested chat: what's on, who's in town, how the winner did it. The many bars, cafes, shops and restaurants draw on the best from around the world while retaining an easy-going quintessentially Australian feel. There are tourist traps and purely dollar-driven establishments, but businesses are more usually built on creativity and love. They have soul.

Although economically prosperous, Melbourne also faces great environmental challenges. Melburnians claim to be totally devoted to their trams and bike lanes, but the sprawling city remains car-centric. A long drought and a mild (if somewhat sulky) climate has made it clear what a precious resource water is; after years of below-average rainfall, water supplies sit far below half-capacity. Melburnians have responded to water restrictions with a new-found sense of communal responsibility and drive to live sustainably.

Out of town the pace might be slow and laidback, but regional menus and wine lists, produce shops and markets ooze with a gentle sophistication many big cities would envy. Victorians make time to enjoy the good life too.

*Street art, Melbourne city laneway*

# HIGHLIGHTS

## CULTURE JOLT

*Whatever flag you wave – theatre buff, art snob, rock god, cricket tragic, or footy fanatic – you have a buffet of stimulations to choose from almost every day of the week.*

**❶ Commuters Awaken**
Subversive stencils and well-loved sculptures – it's art in the city (p50)

**❷ Footy Fervour**
Tribal colours at the birthplace of Aussie Rules (p168)

**❸ Aspiring Arts**
The epicentre of Melbourne's cultural precinct (p62)

# RETAIL WONDERLAND

*You want special? You'll find it! Teeming with unique stores selling something for everyone, from handmade toys to one-off designer jewellery pieces, you'll need more than a day to peruse Melbourne's shopping precincts.*

**❶ Back Street Boutiques**
Snap up fresh designer-ware from Melbourne's arcades and laneways (p106)

**❷ Retro Bazaars**
Treasure hunting in retro and antique stores and market stalls (p117)

**❸ Vinyl Revival**
Shop for funky tunes, old faves and rare grooves in speciality music stores (p114)

**❶ Street Party**
Every excuse to dress up and dance: festivals celebrate a diverse city culture (p12)

**❷ Fillies and Fashionistas**
The competition's stiff both on and off the racetrack (p170)

# MAIN EVENT

*Famous for wardrobes filled with black attire, the locals go a bit mad for colour come festival time. Happily almost every month there's good reason to frock up for some major event, from sports to the arts to the plain obscure.*

**❶ Dining Alfresco**
At sidewalk cafes, rooftop terraces or slap bang in Fed Sq (p124)

**❷ Vodkas By The Dozen**
Bars serving top nosh vie with restaurants famous for killer cocktails (p142)

**❸ Sweet Treats**
Stop for a coffee, stay for the pastries (p133)

# DINE AWAY

*Melburnians can be smug about their food options, but who can blame them with world-class dining, fabulous produce markets, and kooky cafes? A disappointing meal is almost unforgivable in this town.*

# VICTORIAN REGIONS

*Forget astronomical airfares and take a holiday in one of Victoria's diverse regions: a sprinkle of Tuscany there, a dash of Northumbria here. And the Great Ocean Road can take on Highway 1 any season.*

**❶ Yarra Valley**
Regional produce from the farm gate and celebrated restaurants (p213)

**❷ Wilsons Promontory**
Tranquil Tidal River snakes down to Victoria's southernmost coastline (p278)

**❸ Great Ocean Road**
Tour lighthouses, surf breaks, and see shipwrecks and limestone stacks (p224)

# CONTENTS

## Donna Wheeler

Born in Sydney, and brought up a fishing rod's flick from the harbour, Donna knew her Darlinghurst days were numbered when she first set eyes upon a fog-clad St Kilda Pier as a teenage art student. There have been stints in New York, London and rural Ireland, but Melbourne's art scene, bands, bars, coffee and wry sense of self has held her wandering eye for almost two decades.

Donna has commissioned food guides and online features for Lonely Planet and has worked as a digital producer, content strategist and art director. She has studied visual arts, English literature and is a graduate of RMIT's Professional Writing and Editing program. She now devotes her time to freelance writing and editing. This is her second book for Lonely Planet.

## Jocelyn Harewood

Jocelyn lives in Melbourne but regional Victoria is her holiday destination. From snow-skiing to water-skiing, bush-camping to lazing by a river, wine touring to gourmet retreats, she always heads north a way. She even sets her teenage-fiction books in Victoria's towns because they provide such interest-ing backgrounds. When she's not writing she's playing with the grandkids (the number keeps increasing) or doing word puzzles and sudokus.

## Cath Lanigan

Cath has lived in East Gippsland for the past eight years and explores Gippsland's national parks, beaches and coastal towns as often as she can with her partner and two children. Cath also lived in South Gippsland for three years, where she worked as a journalist on a local newspaper.

## Rowan McKinnon

Rowan is a freelance writer and musician, and a native Melburnian. He knows that his home town is Australia's greatest city and one of the world's great places to live. He grew up on the outer bayside suburban fringe in the 1970s, but now lives in the inner southeast with his partner and children and a mortgage on a modest weatherboard house. Rowan's worked on many Lonely Planet books including three Australian titles, but mostly works in the islands of the South Pacific.

Don't think you'll have Melbourne all to yourself. It's a favourite destination for sports fans and culture vultures as well as short urban breaks. Hotel prices skyrocket and rooms book out for any major event. Victoria is Australia's smallest mainland state but it boasts an astonishing number of national parks, historic towns and stunning natural landscapes. Getting around is easy, by car at least, and distances between attractions are manageable enough to make combining a night on the town and a day in the country very possible. You can reach most of the state within four hours drive of Melbourne.

## WHEN TO GO

Notorious for its unpredictability, the state's famous 'four seasons in one day' climate can catch travellers unawares. Locals will suggest dressing in layers, so you can rug up or strip off as the weather dictates, but knowing what to pack can be tricky.

Warm summer days and nights attract the crowds from December to February, Victoria's busiest times for tourism. Average summer highs are around 26°C, but it's not uncommon to find the mercury pushing past 40°C and then plummeting to 19°C. December is party time in the city, which can be a blessing or a curse – bars buzz and waits for taxis can be long. There's also a glut of music festivals and concerts. Victorians take to the road en masse for the Christmas holidays, heading for beachside holiday houses, camping grounds and resorts. Accommodation prices rise considerably in the popular holiday hotspots, particularly on the coast, and rooms are often booked out months in advance. Many shops, cafés and restaurants in Melbourne will have a closed sign in the window come the week between Christmas and New Year. There's still plenty for visitors to do and key attractions will be pleasantly quiet.

Autumn brings mild, still days, with the state's gardens and parks bearing all the tints of a European autumn. The Easter school holiday period in early April is another busy time in the coastal regions and the Grampians, so planning and booking ahead is advised.

June and July are the coldest months, with average maximum temperatures nudging 14°C. It's a great time to do as the locals do: rug up and head off to a game of Aussie rules (football), get cosy at the Melbourne International Film Festival or take to the slopes. There are good snowfields within three hours' drive of the city.

Though Victoria's spring weather can be wildly unpredictable, the respite from winter elevates the city's mood and a string of popular festivals and events see everyone out and about again.

## FESTIVALS

Victoria isn't fussy about when it gets festive. Winter's chills or summer's swelter are no excuse, with Melbournians joining like minds at outdoor festivals, in cinemas, performance spaces or sporting venues all year round. Sporting events in particular draw incredibly large crowds; the party often spills out of the stadiums and into the city. Cultural festivals also have enthusiastic audiences, both for the main event and the pre- and after-partying. Summer is celebrated both informally and with festivals that have an obvious emphasis on the outdoors. Regional towns don't miss out, with their own calendar of cultural and sporting celebrations. What follows is a selection; check www.thatsmelbourne.com.au for comprehensive event listings. For a roundup of music festivals, see p33. Public holidays are listed on p350.

## January
### AUSTRALIAN OPEN
www.australianopen.com; Melbourne Park
The world's top players and huge merrymaking crowds descend on the Melbourne Park for Australia's Grand Slam tennis championship. Ground passes make for a grand day out if you're not desperate to see a top seed, otherwise book ahead for arena seats.

### MIDSUMMA FESTIVAL
www.midsumma.org.au
Melbourne's annual gay and lesbian arts festival features over 100 events from mid-January to mid-February, with a Pride March finale. Expect everything from film

screenings to a highly camp rowing regatta, history walks to dance parties.

## BIG DAY OUT
www.bigdayout.com
National rock fest comes to town at the end of January. Big names are guaranteed, but the local Lily Pad bands often steal the show.

## CHINESE NEW YEAR
www.melbournechinatown.com.au; Chinatown, Little Bourke St
Melbourne has celebrated the Chinese lunar new year since Little Bourke St became Chinatown in the 1860s. The time to touch the dragon falls sometime towards the end of January or early February. Eat, drink and dodge the fire crackers.

# February

## ST KILDA FESTIVAL
www.stkildafestival.com.au; Acland & Fitzroy Sts, St Kilda
This week-long festival ends in a suburb-wide street party on the final Sunday. The crowds are large and laid-back, if not as uniformly bohemian as they once were. Live music is a feature, as well as the annual post card show at Linden Gallery.

## ST JEROME'S LANEWAY FESTIVAL
www.lanewayfestival.com.au
Indie kids delight in their natural laneway habitat with a line up of international and local acts loving the intimate atmosphere. It's gone national now, but this is where it all began. Held at the end of February, tickets sell out super fast.

## MELBOURNE FOOD & WINE FESTIVAL
www.melbournefoodandwine.com.au
Market tours, wine tastings, cooking classes and presentations by celeb chefs take place at venues across the city in February and/or March. Chew the gastronomic fat or just eat your fill. Restaurants across town offer a great lunch deal that includes a glass of wine – book ahead if possible.

## A TASTE OF SLOW
www.atasteofslow.com.au
A Taste of Slow counters our frantically paced culture with a series of events that

highlight Slow principles of tradition, community, conviviality, respect and contemplation. Dinners, public talks, workshops, cooking demonstrations and tastings are held in Melbourne and across regional Victoria. There's also Feast on Film, with food-focused documentaries on show.

## HARVEST PICNIC AT HANGING ROCK
www.harvestpicnic.com.au
Simmering sensuality and paranormal phenomena don't get a look-in at this enormous group picnic, held at the base of the famous filmic rock. Stalls sell a wide variety of food and wine and there's live entertainment.

## HARVEST TO TABLE
www.visitmorningtonpeninsula.org
Mornington Peninsula shines the glasses and cutlery for the annual series of parties, picnics and Pinot tastings in Red Hill.

## MOONAH GOLF CLASSIC
www.moonahlinks.com.au
Australasian PGA Tour and Nationwide Tour tournament matches Australian talent against rising stars from the US. The stunning links course has a natural stadium-like setting, great for spectator vantage points.

## PAKO FESTA
www.pakofesta.com.au
Geelong celebrates the diverse backgrounds of its community with a slap-up street party on Packington St and other city-wide cultural events.

# March

## CONTEMPORA SCULPTURE
www.contempora2.com.au
Docklands hosts public art projects along the waterfront from March to April.

## HELEN LEMPRIERE NATIONAL SCULPTURE AWARD
☎ 131 963; www.lempriereaward.com.au; Werribee Park
This is the country's richest sculpture prize and attracts Australia's leading artists, who install their work in the grounds of Werribee Mansion. A picnic on the grass among the contemporary art has become a Melbourne autumn ritual.

## MOOMBA WATERFEST

www.thatsmelbourne.com.au; Alexandra Gardens, Birrarung Marr & Waterfront City Piazza, Docklands
Moomba's had something of a new millennium makeover, with the action focussed around the Yarra and Victoria Harbour. An old favourite is the wacky Birdman Rally, where competitors launch themselves into the drink in homemade flying machines.

## MELBOURNE FASHION FESTIVAL

www.mff.com.au
This week-long style-fest running from the end of February into March features salon shows and parades showcasing established designers' ranges. Join the air-kiss set or get down with the up-and-comings at one of the many off-shoot happenings around town.

## PORT FAIRY FOLK FESTIVAL

www.portfairyfolkfestival.com
Historic Port Fairy is charming at any time of year, but fills to the gills with music fans every Labor Day long weekend. Join them for an impressive line-up of roots acts from around the world. Pints of Guinness are optional, sorting your accommodation well in advance is mandatory.

## AUSTRALIAN FORMULA ONE GRAND PRIX

www.grandprix.com.au; Albert Park
The 5.3km street circuit around normally tranquil Albert Park Lake is known for its smooth, fast surface. The buzz, both on the streets and in your ears, takes over Melbourne for four fully sick days of rev-head action.

## STAWELL GIFT                    Easter Monday

www.stawellgift.com
The central-west town of Stawell has held a race meet on Easter Monday since 1878. The main event is the prestigious 120m dash. It's the richest foot race in the country, attracting up to 20,000 visitors.

## RIP CURL PRO

www.ripcurl.com/?proHome_en
Held each Easter, the Rip Curl Pro is one of the world's great surfing championships. It attracts big crowds as surfers get together for one last tilt at summer. The event is usually held at Bells Beach, but moves to neighbouring beaches depending on the breaks.

## BENDIGO AWAKENING OF THE DRAGON

www.goldendragonmuseum.org
Join the local Chinese community in celebrations with lion dancing, a costume parade and the awakening of Sun Loong with over 100,000 crackers. This festival is unique to Bendigo and they've been making some noise since 1892.

# April

## ANZAC DAY PARADE                25 April

www.shrine.org.au; Shrine of Remembrance
Australians remember the WWI Australian and New Zealand Army Corps (Anzac) defeat at Gallipoli and honour all those who have served in war on 25 April with a sombre dawn service at the Shrine in King's Domain and a veterans parade along St Kilda Rd. The crowd runs the gamut from respectful to jingoistic.

## MELBOURNE INTERNATIONAL FLOWER & GARDEN SHOW

www.melbflowershow.com.au; Royal Exhibition Bldg & Carlton Gardens
The Royal Exhibition Building and the surrounding Carlton Gardens are taken over by backyard blitzers, DIY-ers and plenty of dotty old ladies. The Exhibition Building itself hosts the flower show.

## MELBOURNE INTERNATIONAL COMEDY FESTIVAL

www.comedyfestival.com.au
An enormous range of local and international comic talent hits town with 3½ weeks of stand-up comedy, cabaret, theatre, street performance, film, TV, radio and visual arts. It's spread out across a variety of venues.

## WARRNAMBOOL MAY RACING CARNIVAL

www.warrnamboolracing.com.au
This is Australia's premier regional racing carnival and includes a steeplechase event, the longest thoroughbred race in Australia. It also has the most jumps of any worldwide.

## APOLLO BAY MUSIC FESTIVAL

www.apollobaymusicfestival.com
Ocean views, a laid-back atmosphere and a diverse range of acts make this one of the nicest festivals on the calendar.

## HEPBURN SPRINGS SWISS ITALIAN FESTA
www.swissitalianfesta.com
The area's unique Swiss Italian heritage is celebrated in song and food.

# May
### MELBOURNE JAZZ
www.melbournejazz.com
International jazz cats head to Melbourne and join locals for gigs at venues around town including Hamer Hall, the Regent Theatre and Palms at Crown.

### ST KILDA FILM FESTIVAL
www.stkildafilmfestival.com.au
Australia's first and arguably best short-film festival, with a great grab-bag of genres and talent on show. Opening night pulls local film industry stars (dressed down for the occasion of course).

### GRAMPIANS GRAPE ESCAPE FESTIVAL
www.grampiansgrapeescape.com.au
Gentle gourmet fest with regional food, wine and petanque to ward off the autumn chills. Held in Halls Gap.

### NEXT WAVE FESTIVAL
www.nextwave.org.au
Biennial festival that lets young artists do their thing. There's a small international contingent, and work includes performance, hybrid and new media and visual arts. Events and exhibitions take place in existing arts institutions as well as those that challenge their very existence. The next festival is in 2010.

# July
### MELBOURNE INTERNATIONAL DESIGN FESTIVAL
www.nationaldesigncentre.com
Ten days of exhibitions, forums, design shows, workshops and competitions posit Melbourne as Australia's design hub. The Fed Square design market is a highlight.

### MELBOURNE INTERNATIONAL FILM FESTIVAL
www.melbournefilmfestival.com.au
Midwinter movie love-in brings out black-skivvy-wearing cinephiles in droves. It's held over two weeks at various cinemas across the city in July and August. (The music doco program is a particular treat.) Festival passes and single session tickets are available.

# August
### MELBOURNE ART FAIR
www.artfair.com.au
Biennial art-star gathering, with galleries from across Australia and the Asia-Pacific region setting up shop in the Royal Exhibition Buildings. A party atmosphere prevails for night openings. The next fair is in 2010.

### MELBOURNE WRITERS' FESTIVAL
www.mwf.com.au; Federation Square
Beginning in the last week of August, the writers' festival features 10 days of forums and events celebrating reading, writing, books and ideas. Locals star alongside visiting international authors.

# September
### AFL GRAND FINAL
www.afl.com.au; MCG
It's easier to get a goal from the boundary than to pick up random tickets to the grand final. But it's not hard to get your share of finals fever anywhere in Melbourne. Pubs put on big screens and barbecues (often accompanied by a spot of street kick-to-kick at half time). For the truly devoted, there's also the Grand Final Parade on the preceding Friday.

### MELBOURNE FRINGE FESTIVAL
www.melbournefringe.com.au
The Fringe takes place in September and October and showcases experimental theatre, music and visual arts.

### ROYAL MELBOURNE SHOW
www.royalshow.com.au; Royal Melbourne Showgrounds, Flemington
The country comes to town in September and October for this large agricultural fair. Carnival rides and junk-filled showbags face off against the traditional exhibits. Where else do you get to see the woodchop?

# October

## MELBOURNE INTERNATIONAL ARTS FESTIVAL
www.melbournefestival.com.au
Held at various venues around the city, the festival features an always thought-provoking program of Australian and international theatre, opera, dance, visual art and music. The Famous Spiegeltent, which is pitched in the Arts Centre forecourt, lends the Festival some old-world charm and irresistible late-night glamour.

## LYGON STREET FESTA
Lygon St, Carlton
Italian community festival with music, soccer matches, a food stall and the famous waiters' race.

## SPRING RACING CARNIVAL
www.springracingcarnival.com.au; Flemington Racecourse
Culminating in the prestigious Melbourne Cup, these race-meets are as much social events as sporting ones. The Cup, held on the first Tuesday in November, is a public holiday in Melbourne.

## WANGARATTA FESTIVAL OF JAZZ
www.wangaratta-jazz.org.au
This northeastern town hosts over 350 national and international artists each year at Australia's most important jazz festival. The lineup is often stellar; New York greats make regular appearances. Not to be missed by those that like inventive playing and a hothouse atmosphere. Book accommodation well ahead.

## AUSTRALIAN MOTORCYCLE GRAND PRIX
www.motogp.com.au
Phillip Island's Grand Prix circuit attracts the world's best bike-riders for this three-day event.

# November

## QUEENSCLIFF MUSIC FESTIVAL
www.qmf.net.au
An out-of-town festival that's possible in a day trip, but the great range of local acts will make you want to stay for the weekend.

## BEECHWORTH CELTIC FESTIVAL
www.beechworthcelticfestival.com.au
You'll get a warm *fáilte romhaibh* (welcome) at this celebration of the area's Celtic heritage. Lots of old-school events including pipe bands.

# December

## BOXING DAY TEST
www.mcg.org.au; MCG
Day one of the Boxing Day Test draws out the cricket fans. Crowds are huge and excitable; expect some shenanigans from Bay 13.

## MELBOURNE TO HOBART YACHT RACE
www.orcv.org.au; 27 December
Although it's called Melbourne to Hobart, this exciting race actually starts from Portsea on the Mornington Peninsula. It takes the west coast of Tasmania, while the Sydney-to-Hobart-race lads head down the east.

## NEW YEAR'S EVE                    31 December
www.thatsmelbourne.com.au
Fireworks light up the Yarra at 9pm and midnight.

# COSTS & MONEY
Melbourne is not a cheap place to visit. Visitors from the US are particularly surprised by restaurant and bar prices, especially at the current exchange rates. Those carrying sterling or euros will find it a little more affordable, but the standard of living is generally high. That said, Melbourne does boast some good midlevel accommodation and its more casual dining options can be great value for money.

## HOW MUCH?
Two-hour Metcard $3.50
Short taxi ride $10
Pot of Carlton Draft $3.50
Bottle of drinkable Mornington pinot gris $18
Well-made martini $16
Litre of bottled water $1.75
Café latte $3
Bowl of pasta $16
Souvenir t-shirt you're in the wrong town
Unreserved admission to the MCG $20.30

## ADVANCE PLANNING

**Three months before you go** Book accommodation, especially if your visit coincides with any major events; book a table at Vue du Monde (p128) or the Flower Drum (p129).

**Three weeks before you go** Nab a table at other fine dining restaurants (p124) or if pizza is more appealing, make your reservation at Ladro (p136); look out for what's on at the Arts Centre (p64), Malthouse (p164) or one of Melbourne's many live music venues and book your tickets.

**One week before you go** Read this week's Three Thousand (www.threethousand.com.au) missive, sign up to Michigirl (michigirl.com.au) and see what sales Missy Confidential (missyconfidential.com.au) has discovered; check Ticketmaster for AFL fixtures; browse the *Age* (www.theage.com.au) for new bar and restaurant openings, check the week's weather and pack accordingly; don't forget sunblock, even in winter.

**One day to go** Make sure you return restaurant confirmation calls; check you've packed a couple of extra pieces of clothing – a scarf, a singlet, and a cardie – in case of unexpected hot or cold snaps; stock up on vitamin B for stamina.

Of course, your holiday can be as cheap or as luxurious as your tastes demand. A mid-range traveller who plans to hire a car, see the sights, stay in midrange B&Bs or hotels, and eat well at restaurants, should expect to spend about $150 to $180 per day.

At the low-cost end, if you camp or stay in hostels, cook your own meals, avoid big nights out in the pub and catch public transport everywhere, you could probably manage on $60 per day; for a budget that realistically enables you to have a good time, set aside $80. Of course, these low-cost figures don't factor in sampling the things Melbourne is so good at: food, fashion and bars.

Most accommodation options have cheaper rates for stays of longer than a week and many offer self-catering rooms. Shopping at Melbourne's markets and cooking a few meals can help cut down on food costs and you'll have the added bonus of feeling like a local.

Currency exchange rates are on the inside front cover. See also Directory, p352.

# INTERNET RESOURCES

Melbourne is well-documented online.

**ABC Melbourne Podtours** (www.abc.net.au/melbourne /podtours/default.htm) Great little series of podcasts that get under Melbourne's skin.

**The Age** (www.theage.com.au) Not just the daily news: Melbourne's broadsheet likes to keep up with what's going on in the way of entertainment too. Extraordinarily comprehensive bar and restaurant reviews are a feature.

**Art Almanac** (www.art-almanac.com.au) Stalwart art listings magazine which covers both public and commercial galleries.

**Commonwealth Bureau of Meteorology** (www.bom.gov .au/weather/vic) The BOM do up-to-the-minute information on Victorian weather and warnings.

**Lost and Found** (www.visitvictoria.com/lostandfound) An email newsletter with a focus on creative spaces and events from Visit Victoria, plus a FaceBook page with regular updates.

**Missy Confidential** (www.missyconfidential.com.au) Up-to-date details of all the retail sales.

**Three Thousand** (www.threethousand.com.au) Weekly newsletter with the very hottest tips on music, fashion, bars and other goings on around the city, though you'll need to cut through the sass.

**Parks Victoria** (www.parkweb.vic.gov.au) Excellent site, with extensive profiles on all of Victoria's national and marine parks.

**That's Melbourne** (www.thatsmelbourne.com.au) Easy to use and not overly hyped guide for travellers care of the city council.

**Tourism Victoria** (www.visitvictoria.com) Official state tourism site, with excellent sections on festivals and events, accommodation, restaurants, tours and attractions.

**Stencil Revolution** (www.stencilrevolution.com) Good resource for anyone looking for information on Melbourne's often elusive (though always in your face) stencil art scene.

**Victorian Government** (www.vic.gov.au) Official website of the state government of Victoria, and gateway to information and services in the state.

# SUSTAINABLE MELBOURNE

Given Melbourne's location at the very bottom of the world, there's not a lot a traveller can do to lessen the impact of air travel. A new age of passenger liners might be upon us, but not quite yet. Travelling between Australian cities also involves vast distances, and there are no rapid train services that make rail such an attractive alternative in Europe.

If you're not venturing out of the city, you won't need a rental car – the city's public transport system can get you everywhere you'll want to go and save you on the hassle of parking. Consider hiring a bike (p171) to explore parkland, the bay or the banks of the Yarra.

The drought that has gripped the southeastern states of Australia is an ongoing concern. Even if substantial rains fall, the problems with the city and the state's water supply look like they are here to stay. Mandatory water restrictions are in place for residents, who are forbidden to use hoses or sprinklers to water their gardens or wash their cars. Do your bit by being conscious of your water usage while in the city. Simple measures like cutting down on shower times and ensuring taps aren't left running (while brushing your teeth for instance) can make a real difference. Make sure you take the half-flush option when you flush the loo and rehang your towels in your hotel bathroom so the house cleaning staff don't wash them after every use.

Other things that will score green points are saying no to plastic bags (you'll notice locals use violently green reusable bags sold by supermarkets for a token amount), using refillable water bottles for drinking and making sure all your litter, including cigarette butts, goes in the bin (the correct bin too – recycling bins are often an option). If you stamp butts out in the street, it's an odds-on bet they'll end up in the bay.

## HISTORY
### INDIGENOUS VICTORIA

Australia's first inhabitants made the journey from Southeast Asia between 70,000 years and 40,000 years ago. For the Wurundjeri people who lived in the catchment of the Yarra River, where Melbourne is today, the land and the people were created in the Dreaming by the spirit Bunjil – 'the great one, old head-man, eagle hawk' – who continues to watch over all from Tharangalk-bek, the home of the spirits in the sky.

The Victorian Aboriginal peoples lived in some 38 different dialect groups that spoke 10 separate languages, some were matrilineal, others patrilineal. These groups were further divided into clans and sub-clans, each with its own complex system of customs and laws, and each claiming custodianship of a distinct area of land. Despite this, the British considered the continent to be *terra nullius* – a land belonging to no one.

The Wurundjeri were a tribe of the Woi wurrung, one of five distinct language groups belonging to southern Victoria's Kulin Nation. They often traded and celebrated among the towering red gums, tea trees and ferns of the river's edge with their coastal counterparts the Boon wurrung, as well as other Kulin clans from the north and west.

As the flood-prone rivers and creeks broke their banks in winter, bark shelters would be built north in the ranges. Possums were hunted for their meat and skinned to make calf-length cloaks. Worn with fur against skin, the smooth outer hide was rubbed with waterproofing fat and embellished with totemic designs: graphic chevrons and diamonds or representations of emus and kangaroos. During the summer, camps were made along the Yarra, the Maribyrnong and the Merri Creek. Food – game, grubs, seafood, native greens and roots – was plentiful. Wurundjeri men and women were compelled to marry out of the tribe, requiring complex forms of diplomacy. Ceremonies and bouts of ritual combat were frequent.

In 1835, when British entrepreneur John Batman arrived from Van Diemen's Land (Tasmania), he travelled through 'beautiful land…rather sandy, but the sand black and rich, covered with kangaroo grass about ten inches high and as green as a field of wheat'. He noted stone dams for catching fish built across creeks, trees that bore the deep scars of bark harvesting and women bearing wooden water containers and woven bags holding stone tools. Indigenous people's profound spiritual relationship with the land and intimate knowledge of story, ceremony and season would be irrevocably damaged within a few shorts years.

As European settlement fanned out through Victoria, and the city of Melbourne transmogrified from pastoral outpost to a heaving, gold-flushed metropolis in scarcely 30 years, the cumulative effects of dispossession, alcohol and increasing acts of organised violence resulted in a shocking decline in Victoria's indigenous population. Estimates suggest that before the Europeans arrived, Victoria's Aboriginal population was between 60,000 and 100,000; by the late 1840s it had dropped to 15,000 and by 1860, scarcely 2000 Aboriginal people had survived.

# TIMELINE

| 70,000-35,000 BC | 1803 | 1834 |
| --- | --- | --- |
| The first humans colonise southeastern Australia; the people of the Kulin Nation live in the catchment of the Yarra River, and various other tribes, speaking 38 languages, are spread throughout Victoria. | Victoria's first European settlement is founded at Sorrento. It is an unmitigated disaster, with no available fresh water to be found; the settlers abandon the site after six months and set sail for Van Diemen's Land. | Portland pioneer Edward Henty, his family and a flock of sheep arrive from Van Diemen's Land, marking the first permanent European settlement in the Victoria. |

## ABORIGINAL LANGUAGE

Before European settlement, around 40 languages were spoken in the area now called Victoria. Indigenous Australians at the time could speak around five languages, with tribal diplomats speaking far more.

Within a few years of European settlement, Melbourne's Aboriginal population was decimated. The original inhabitants were dispossessed of their land; large numbers were killed or died from introduced diseases. People were also forced to live in government settlements, prohibiting their traditional way of life. As a result, the transmission of traditional Aboriginal culture, including language, from one generation to the next was profoundly disrupted. Today, no full speakers of any Victorian Aboriginal language remain, and none are used as the main means of communication in any community.

However, many Aboriginal people continue to carefully preserve elements of their linguistic heritage, and words from the traditional Woi wurrung language still echo through the modern city. Melbourne's riverside park Birrarung Marr means 'river of mists', and 'bunyip' is a mythical swamp-dwelling creature, a word commonly used in Australian English. In many communities there's rising interest in traditional languages and culture, and efforts are underway to preserve and maintain the knowledge that remains. The Victorian Aboriginal Corporation of Language (VACL; www .vaclang.org.au) and the Koori Heritage Trust (www.koorieheritagetrust.com) are important sources in the retention of indigenous language and culture, researching and documenting oral histories and vocabulary.

From the earliest days, the colonial authorities evicted Aboriginal people from their traditional homes. By the early 1860s, the Board for the Protection of Aborigines had begun to gather together surviving Aborigines in reserves run by Christian missionaries at Ebenezer, Framlingham, Lake Condah, Lake Tyers, Ramahyuck and Coranderrk. These reserves developed into self-sufficient farming communities and gave their residents a measure of 'independence' (along with twice-daily prayers and new boots at Christmas), but at the same time inflicted irrevocable damage.

Spurred on by the rise of eugenicist thinking and underpinned by economic concerns, the Aborigines Protection Act of 1886 stipulated that only 'full-blooded' Aborigines or 'half-castes' older than 34 years of age could remain in the reserves; others had to leave and 'assimilate into the community'. The act destroyed families and eventually the reserves themselves. By 1923, only Lake Tyers, with just over 200 residents, and Framlingham, with only a handful of people, remained.

By the early 1900s further legislation designed to segregate and 'protect' Aborigines was passed. It restricted their right to own property and seek employment. The Aboriginals' Ordinance of 1918 allowed the removal of children from Aboriginal mothers if it was suspected that the father was non-Aboriginal, which was often the case. Children were still removed from their families until as recently as the late 1960s. In early 2008, the newly elected Prime Minister, Kevin Rudd, made a formal apology to the people known as the Stolen Generations, who suffered under the institutionalised racism of these nation-wide policies.

Despite this brutal and sad history, Aboriginal life in Victoria has endured. Around 25,000 people in Victoria have an indigenous heritage, including around 15,000 in Melbourne and 5000 in the Shepparton region. They continue to live, practice and renew their culture to this day.

## MAPPING THE FUTURE

1803: it wasn't an auspicious start. With a missed mail ship communiqué and a notoriously supercilious British government calling the shots, Surveyor-General Charles Grimes' recommendations that the best place to found a southern French-foiling settlement would be by the

| 1835 | 1837 | 1838 |
|---|---|---|
| John Batman meets with a group of Aborigines and trades a casket of blankets, mirrors, scissors, handkerchiefs and other assorted bibelots for around 240,000 hectares of land. | The military surveyor Robert Hoddle draws up plans for the city of Melbourne, laying out a geometric grid of broad streets in a rectangular pattern on the northern side of the Yarra River. | *The Melbourne Advertiser*, Melbourne's first newspaper, rolls off the presses. |

## INDIGENOUS MELBOURNE

Here are three places where you can connect with Melbourne's indigenous culture:

Koori Heritage Trust Cultural Centre (www.koorie heritagetrust.com) Take a Walkin' Birrarung tour (p354) along the Yarra and explore the vibrant natural and cultural landscape beneath the modern city.

Bunjilaka, Melbourne Museum (p77) See and experience cultural heritage items interpreted by Aboriginal voices.

Royal Botanic Garden's Aboriginal Heritage Walks (p82) Share in the wealth of local plant lore and see the landscape through the eyes of an Aboriginal guide.

banks of the 'Freshwater River' (aka the Yarra) went unheeded. The alternative, Sorrento, was an unmitigated disaster from the get-go. As Lt David Collins pointed out to his superiors, you can't survive long without drinkable water. (For one extremely tenacious convict escapee, William Buckley, it wasn't all bad: he was on the run until John Batman turned up a few decades later.)

Australia's European history had begun with intermittent coastal exploration by Dutch seamen some centuries before. In 1770, Captain James Cook formally 'discovered' Australia and in 1788, the first colony was established at Sydney Cove in New South Wales (NSW). After the failed Sorrento colony it was 20-odd years before explorers made their way overland to Port Phillip, and another 10 before a settlement was founded on the south-west coast at Portland. Also in the early 1830s, NSW's surveyor-general, Major Thomas Mitchell, crossed the Murray River (then called the Hume) near Swan Hill and travelled southwest. He was delighted to find the rich volcanic plains of the Western District. His glowing reports of such fertile country included him dubbing the area 'Australia Felix' (fortunate Australia) and encouraged pastoralists to venture into Victoria with large flocks of sheep and herds of cattle.

## BOLD AS BEARBRASS

'Modern' Melbourne's story also begins in the 1830s. Australian-born John Batman, an arriviste grazier from Van Diemen's Land, sailed into Port Phillip Bay in mid-1835 with an illegal contract of sale. (Britain's colonial claims of *terra nullis* relied on the fiction that the original inhabitants did not own the land on which they lived, and hence could not sell it.) He sought out some local chiefs and on a tributary of the Yarra – it's been speculated that it was the Merri Creek, in today's Northcote – found some 'fine-looking' men, with whom he exchanged blankets, scissors, mirrors and handkerchiefs for a half million acres of land surrounding Port Phillip.

Despite the fact that the Sydney Aborigines accompanying Batman couldn't speak a word of the local language and vice versa, Batman brokered the deal and signatures were gathered from the local chiefs (all suspiciously called Jika-Jika and with remarkably similar penmanship). He noted a low rocky falls several miles up the Yarra where the Queen St Bridge is today. Upstream fresh water made it a perfect place for, as Batman described it, 'a village'. Batman then returned to Tasmania to ramp up the Port Phillip Association.

It's at this point in the historical narrative that things get as turbid as the Yarra itself. Before he managed to return to the new settlement, which he called Bearbrass (along with 'Yarra', another cocksure misappropriation of the local dialect), John Pascoe Fawkner, a Launceston publican, got wind of the spectacular opportunity at hand. He promptly sent off a small contingent of settlers aboard the schooner *Enterprize* who upon arrival got to building huts and establishing a garden.

| 1851 | 1854 | 1854–88 |
|---|---|---|
| Victoria separates from the colony of NSW; gold is discovered in central Victoria and the world's richest gold rush is on. | Gold miners rebel over unfair licenses and other harsh conditions, raising the Southern Cross flag at the Eureka Stockade. Brutally suppressed by soldiers and police, their actions become a core part of Australia's nation-building mythology. | Railway from Flinders St to Port Melbourne opens (1854); water supply turned on (1857); telephone exchange opens (1888). |

On Batman's return, there were words, and later furious bidding wars over allotments of land. Regarded in many varying ways by historians, Fawkner's place in history was sealed by the fact he outlived the syphilitic Batman by several decades. Whatever the interpersonal politics between the wannabe founders, the settlement grew quickly; around a year later, almost 200 brave souls (and some tens of thousands of sheep) had thrown their lot in with the two Johnnies.

New South Wales wasn't happy. Governor Bourke dispatched Captain William Lonsdale in 1836 and dispelled any notion of ownership by the Port Phillip Association. This was crown land; surveyors were sent for to draw up plans for a city. Robert Hoddle, Surveyor in Charge, arrived with the Governor in March 1837, and began to reign in both his unruly staff (they had absconded up river to get drunk or shoot kangaroos one too many times) and the Antipodean topography. For Hoddle, it was all about straight lines. Hoddle's grid, demarcated by the Yarra and what was once a 'hillock' where Southern Cross Station now lies, is Melbourne's defining feature. Land sales commenced almost immediately; surveying continued with little Romantic notion of exploration or discovery. It was, by all accounts, a real-estate feeding frenzy. The British were well served by their *terra nullis* concept; returns on investment were fabulous. The rouseabout 'Bearbrass' was upgraded to 'Melbourne', after the serving British Prime Minister. Various kings, queens and assorted contemporary bigwigs (including Governor Bourke himself) got the nod when naming streets. By 1840 the place, with 10,000 occasionally upstanding citizens, was looking decidedly like a city.

The earliest provincial towns were established along Victoria's coast, around the original settlement of Portland, to the southwest, and Port Albert to the southeast. Early inland towns rose up around self-sufficient communities of sheep stations, which at this stage were still the main source of Victoria's increasing fortunes.

## GOLDEN YEARS

In 1840, a local landowner described the fledgling city as 'a goldfield without the gold'. Indeed, with a steady stream of immigrants and confidence-building prosperity, there had been growing calls for separation from convict-ridden, rowdy New South Wales. By the end of 1850, the newly minted colony of Victoria had got its go-it-alone wish. This quickly seemed like a cruel stroke of fate; gold was discovered near Bathurst in New South Wales in early 1851. Pastoral riches or not, there was every chance that without a viable labour force (many had already succumbed to the siren call CALIFORN-I-A!) the colony would wither and die.

Melbourne jewellers had for some time been doing a clandestine trade with shepherds who came to town with small, illegally got nuggets secreted in their kerchiefs. Wary of the consequences of a gold rush on civic order, but with few other options, the city's leading men declared that gold must indeed be found. A committee was formed, a reward was offered. Slim pickings were first discovered in the Pyrenees and Warrandyte, then a cluey Californian veteran looked north in Clunes. Just over a ridge, in what was to become Ballarat, was the proverbial end of the rainbow. It wasn't long before miners were hauling 60lbs of the magic mineral into Geelong at a time, and the rush was well and truly on.

The news spread around the world and brought hopefuls from Britain, Ireland, China, Germany, Italy, the US and the Caribbean. By August 1852, 15,000 new arrivals docked in Melbourne each month. Crews jumped ship and hotfooted it to the diggings, stranding ships at anchor. Chaos reigned. Even if only for a night or two, everyone needed a place to stay, and, when there was no room at the inn, stables were let for exorbitant amounts. Wives and children were often

| 1856 | 1880 | 1901 |
| --- | --- | --- |
| Stonemasons lead the fight for an eight-hour day (and the need to improve their 'social and moral condition'); by 1860, it became established practice across Victoria, a world first. | The International Exhibition is held at the Royal Exhibition Buildings in Melbourne's Carlton. Over a million visitors come to see the fruits of Empire. | Australia's collection of colonies become a nation. The Federation's first parliament is held at the Royal Exhibition Buildings. |

## THE EUREKA REBELLION

As the easily won gold began to run out, Victorian diggers despaired of every striking it rich, and the inequality between themselves and the privileged few who held the land that they worked stoked a fire of dissent.

Men joined together in teams and worked cold, wet, deep shafts. Every miner, whether or not gold was found, had to pay a licence of 30 shillings a month. The tax was collected by young, sometimes thuggish, policemen who had the power to chain to a tree those who wouldn't, or couldn't, pay until their case was heard.

In September 1854 Governor Hotham ordered that the hated licence hunts be carried out twice a week. A month later a miner was murdered near the Ballarat Hotel after an argument with the owner, James Bentley. When Bentley was found not guilty by a magistrate (who just happened to be his business associate), miners rioted and burned his hotel down. Though Bentley was retried and found guilty, the rioting miners were also jailed, which enraged the diggers.

The Ballarat Reform League was born and called for the abolition of licence fees, the introduction of miners' rights to vote and greater opportunity to purchase land.

On 29 November about 800 miners tossed their licences into a bonfire during a mass meeting and then built a stockade at Eureka, led by an Irishman called Peter Lalor, where they prepared to fight for their rights. A veteran of Italy's independence struggle, Raffaello Carboni, called on the crowd, 'irrespective of nationality, religion and colour', to salute the Southern Cross as the 'refuge of all the oppressed from all the countries on earth'.

On 3 December the government ordered the troopers to attack the stockade. There were only 150 diggers within the makeshift barricades and the fight lasted a short but devastating 20 minutes, leaving 25 miners and four troopers dead.

Though the rebellion was short-lived the miners won the sympathy and support of Victorians. The government deemed it wise to acquit the leaders of the charge of high treason. It's interesting to note that only four of the miners were Australian-born; the others hailed from Ireland, Britain, Italy, Corsica, Greece, Germany, Russia, Holland, France, Switzerland, Spain, Portugal, Sweden, the US, Canada and the West Indies.

The licence fee was abolished and replaced by a Miners' Right, which cost one pound a year. This gave them the right to search for gold; to fence in, cultivate and build a dwelling on a piece of land; and to vote for members of the Legislative Assembly. The rebel miner, Peter Lalor, became a member of parliament some years later. As the then Premier Steve Bracks was to remark at the stockade's 150th anniversary, 'Eureka was a catalyst for the rapid evolution of democratic government in this country and it remains a national symbol of the right of the people to have a say in how they are governed... This means Eureka is not just a story, it is a responsibility and a calling to ensure we stay true to the Stockade's democratic principles and build on its multicultural heritage – because Eureka was thoroughly multicultural.'

dumped in town while husbands continued on to the diggings. Governor LaTrobe despaired of his grand civic vision as shanties and eventually a complete tent village sprung up. Canvas Town, on the south side of the Yarra, housed over 8000 people. Catherine Spence, a journalist and social reformer, visited Melbourne at the height of the hysteria and primly observed 'this convulsion has unfixed everything. Religion is neglected, education despised...everyone is engrossed with the simple object of making money in a very short time.' Over 90% of Australia's £100 million gold haul in the 1850s was found in Victoria. The 20 million ounces found between 1851 and 1860 represented a third of the world's total. That said, relatively few 'diggers' struck it lucky. For a sense of what a gold-mining township was like, tourists visit Sovereign Hill (p249). Adults might find the gold-rush re-creation a bit corny, but kids love it.

The licensing system favoured large holdings, policing was harsh and scratching a living for many proved so difficult that dissent became as common as hope had been a few years before. For some, 1852 was indeed a golden year, but by 1854, simmering tensions exploded in Ballarat.

| 1905-10 | 1923 | 1930 |
|---|---|---|
| The new Flinders St Station built (1905-10); Mebourne Cup declared a public holiday (1910) | Vegemite, a savoury yeast-based sandwich spread, and Australia's most enduring culinary peccadillo, is invented in Melbourne. | Phar Lap, Australia's greatest race horse, wins the Melbourne Cup and a place in the nation's folklore. |

## OUR NED

Victorian bushranger Ned Kelly (1855–80) became a national legend when he and his gang donned homemade armour in an attempt to deflect the bullets of several dozen members of the constabulary. Kelly's story has a Robin Hood–like quality, as well as the whiff of an Irish rebel song. His passionate, articulate letters, handed to hostages while he was robbing banks, paint a vivid picture of the harsh injustice of his time. These, as well as his ability to evade capture for so long, led to public outrage when he was sentenced to death and finally hanged at the Old Melbourne Gaol (p56) in 1880. The enduring popularity of the Kelly legend is evident in a mass of historical and fictional accounts that continue to be written to this day. His life has also inspired a long string of films, from the world's first feature film *The Story of the Kelly Gang* (1906), to two more recent versions, both called simply *Ned Kelly*, starring Mick Jagger (1970) and the late Heath Ledger (2003). Sidney Nolan's series of portraits featuring Kelly in his armour are some of Australia's most recognisable artworks.

Miners burnt their mining licenses and a bloody conflict broke out against British officials at the Eureka Stockade. Under the banner of the Southern Cross, a motley, proudly multinational crew called for democratic reform and universal manhood suffrage, an ultimately quixotic act, but one that changed the face of Australian politics for good. (For details, see the boxed text, p23.)

Brotherhood, sadly, had its limits. The 40,000 miners who arrived from southern China to try their luck on 'the new gold mountain' were often a target of individual violence and, later, systemic prejudice. Regardless, the Chinese community stayed and has continued to have a strong and enduring presence in the city of Melbourne and throughout regional Victoria.

## BOOM & CRASH

Gold brought undreamt-of riches and a seemingly endless supply of labour to Melbourne. Melbourne became 'Marvellous Melbourne', one of the world's most beautiful Victorian-era cities, known for its elegance, as well as its extravagance. Grand expressions of its confidence include the University of Melbourne, Parliament House (p56), the State Library (p57) and the Victorian Mint (cnr William & LaTrobe Sts). Magnificent public parks and gardens were planted. By the 1880s, the city had become Australia's financial, industrial and cultural hub. The 'Paris of the Antipodes' claim was invoked; the city *was* flush with stylish arcades (as well as the odd flaneur, we're sure). The city spread eastwards and northwards over the surrounding flat grasslands, and southwards along Port Phillip. A public transport system of cable trams and railways spread into the growing suburbs.

Regional cities, especially those near the goldfields, such as Ballarat, Bendigo and Beechworth also reaped the rewards of sudden prosperity, leaving a legacy of magnificent Victorian architecture. 'Selection Acts' enabled many settlers to take up small farm lots (selections). Although a seemingly reformist, democratic move, these farms were often too small to forge a real living from and life in the bush proved tough. Grinding poverty and the heavy hand of the law led to some young men turning to bushranging (see the boxed text 'Our Ned' on above).

In 1880, and again in 1888, Melbourne hosted an International Exhibition, pulling well over a million visitors. The Royal Exhibition Buildings were constructed for this event; Melbourne's soaring paean to Empire and the industrial revolution is one of the few 19th-century exhibition spaces of its kind still standing. Sadly this flamboyant boast to the world was to be Marvellous Melbourne's swan song.

| 1956 | 1964 | 1967 |
|---|---|---|
| Melbourne hosts the summer Olympic Games, the first in which athletes mingle at the closing ceremony. Despite this mark of sporting bonhomie, the event is marked with political unrest, due to the Suez crisis and the Soviet invasion of Hungary. | The Beatles visit Melbourne, staying in the Southern Cross Hotel on Bourke St and create city-wide hysteria. | Prime Minister Harold Holt disappears while swimming at Cheviot Beach near Portsea; his body is never recovered. |

## CAPITAL *Kristin Otto*

In 1901 a collection of British colonies – now the states – formed into the Commonwealth of Australia. Melbourne was the political compromise for a temporary capital, while an official site was selected and built upon. Nobody planned on it taking 26 years.

'For the first time in the world's history there will be a nation for a continent and a continent for a nation', said the man who became the first prime minister. In the beginning, he could carry the records of the entire government in his Gladstone bag. Edmund Barton had been one of the founders of the new constitution, writing some of it in the Grand Hotel (now the Windsor, see p183). In the early days, he and Alfred Deakin (the second PM) might boil the billy while sitting up late in an upper room of Parliament House. Barton would occasionally kip there. The third prime minister, Chris Watson, was the first labour leader anywhere to run a country.

Australia was described as 'the social laboratory of the world' and led the way in giving the vote to women, declaring a minimum wage, providing pensions, and having a high standard of living. This nation was born with the 20th century, and in that capital period, the main streams of the modern city appeared: electricity, film, radio, aeroplanes and cars. The first feature film in the world – *The Story of the Kelly Gang* – was made in Melbourne in 1906. Helena Rubinstein began the billion-dollar cosmetics industry in Melbourne when she opened her first salon in the early 1900s.

As a nation, Australia sacrificially blooded itself in WWI, fighting as part of the British Empire. Anzac Day (p14) remains an important commemoration of the fact. John Monash, an Australian reserve soldier with a German-Jewish background, became one of the great generals of that war. His domestic engineering expertise can be seen in the Great Domed Reading Room of the State Library of Victoria, and Morell Bridge near the Botanic Gardens. He managed the electrification of the state, and was a director of Luna Park (p87). A university and freeway are both named after him.

The most fascinating artists and writers worked for Keith Murdoch's *Herald* newspaper group (the Flinders St building is now apartments and restaurants). Murdoch later had a son, Rupert. Walter Murdoch (Keith's uncle), wrote in *The Australian Citizen* of 1912, 'The more civilized a nation is, the greater the number of links by which members of that nation are connected.' This was very true of Melbourne, with its rich layers, and some would say, remains true of how Melbourne works today.

*Extract from* Capital: Melbourne When it was the Capital City of Australia 1901-27 © *Kristin Otto, 2008. Used by permission of Text Publishing.*

In 1889, after years of unsustainable speculation, the property market collapsed and the decades that followed were marked by severe economic depression.

## FEDERATION & EARLY 20TH CENTURY

With Federation, on 1 January 1901, Victoria became a state of the new nation of Australia. Melbourne was the country's capital and the seat of federal government until its eventual move to Canberra in 1927 (see the box text, above). Despite this symbolic honour, Melbourne's fortunes didn't really rally until after WWI, and by then its 'first city' status had been long lost to Sydney.

Australia's loyalties and most of its legal ties to Britain remained firm. When WWI broke out, large numbers of troops from throughout Victoria went to fight in the trenches of France, Gallipoli and the Middle East. The enormity of Melbourne's losses from the 'great war', as well as those from subsequent wars, can still be felt at the Shrine of Remembrance in the Domain (p83).

| 1970 | 1983 | 1988 |
|---|---|---|
| Melbourne's Westgate Bridge collapses during construction, killing 35 workers. | The Ash Wednesday bushfires destroy over 2000 homes and kill 47 Victorians. | The Australian Tennis Open moves from Kooyong to the hard-court venues of Melbourne Park. |

There was a renewed spirit of expansion and construction in Victoria in the 1920s, but this came to a grinding halt with the Great Depression, which hit Australia, and Melbourne in particular, extremely hard. In 1931 almost a third of breadwinners were unemployed and poverty was widespread. During the Depression the government implemented a number of major public works programs and workers were put on 'susso' – sustenance pay. Melbourne's Yarra Boulevard, St Kilda Rd and the Great Ocean Rd were all built by sustenance workers.

One shining light during these gloomy times was a plucky young chestnut gelding called Phar Lap, who won the hearts of the people with an unparalleled winning streak, including the famous Melbourne Cup in 1930. The horse died in mysterious circumstances in the USA two years later, and was mourned by a nation. More than 70 years later, Phar Lap remains one of the most popular exhibits in the Melbourne Museum.

When war broke out once again in 1939, Australian troops fought with the British in Europe and the Middle East. After the bombing of Pearl Harbour, the Japanese threat to Australia became very real. When Britain called for more Australian troops to fight in Europe, Prime Minister John Curtin refused; Australian soldiers were needed closer to home. With the outbreak of WWII, Melbourne became the hub of the nation's wartime efforts, and later the centre for US operations in the Pacific. It was boomtime again, though no time for celebration.

Ultimately, it was the US defeat of the Japanese in the Battle of the Coral Sea that saved Australia from invasion. This event was to mark the start of a profound shift from Australia's traditional allegiance to Britain towards the US.

## MODERN MELBOURNE

Close to a million non-British immigrants arrived in Australia during the 20 years after the war; at first Jewish refugees from eastern and central Europe, then larger numbers from Italy, Greece, the Netherlands, Yugoslavia, Turkey and Lebanon. (With the demise of blatantly racist 'white Australia' immigration policies in the early 1970s, many migrants from Southeast Asia also sought refuge here.) Although the idea that Melbourne had ever been a purely Anglo-Celtic society is an anachronistic fantasy, the fact that a great proportion of migrants chose to live in Melbourne profoundly changed the city's cultural life. Melbourne's streets became vibrantly and irrevocably multicultural during this time and this diversity became an accepted, and treasured, way of life.

Melbourne's Victorian heritage was permanently altered by the postwar construction boom. The city hosted the Olympic Games in 1956 and hectares of historic buildings were bulldozed with abandon as the city prepared to impress visitors with its modernity. Construction continued apace in the 1960s under the Liberal premier Henry Bolte, culminating in the boom years of the 1980s.

## REINVENTION

During the early 1970s a bourgeoning counterculture's experiments with radical theatre, drugs and rock 'n' roll rang out through the inner-city, particularly in the then predominantly Italian neighbourhood of Carlton. By the late 1970s, Melbourne's reputation as a conservative 'establishment' city was further challenged by the emergence of a frantically subversive art, music and fashion scene that launched bands like Nick Cave and the Bad Seeds onto the world stage. Like a hundred years before, land prices rose continuously throughout the '80s and the city boomed, with a thriving restaurant industry and luxury retail stores and enormous nightclubs

| 1988 | 2002 | 2006 |
|---|---|---|
| John Cain's Labor government recommends the liberalising of liquor laws, heralding the era of the small bar. | Federation Square opens – only one year late to mark the centenary of Federation – amid controversy about its final design and cost ($440 million), but to public praise. | Melbourne hosts the Commonwealth Games. |

springing up. Banks were queuing up to lend money to developers; even the worldwide stock market crash in 1987 didn't slow things down. Finally in 1990, the property market collapsed and Melbourne bore the full brunt of the recession.

Recovery was, this time, swift, and over the past decade the city of Melbourne has been transformed; its urban redevelopment has embraced the waters of the Yarra River and Port Phillip Bay as well as the city itself. The current state government has encouraged higher-density living and the city centre has an increasing residential population, including large numbers of international students. The vibrant mix of ethnicities in the community continues to grow, with many recent immigrants from African nations (Victoria has the country's largest Sudanese population) and the Middle East. Many immigrants, particularly those from East Africa, have also settled in regional communities throughout the state.

# ARTS

## VISUAL ARTS Geraldine Barlow

Melbourne has always been a city for artists. A dynamic and ever-changing network of artist-run spaces, experimental events and exhibitions gives the city an exciting production-house edge, and an excellent public infrastructure of major galleries and museums offers travellers visual culture of serious polish and scale.

Melbourne's first visual culture sprang from the traditions of the Kulin Nation tribes who lived from and belonged to the lands we now associate with the Yarra River, Port Phillip Bay, the Dandenong Ranges, the You Yangs and the country beyond. Both the National Gallery of Victoria Australia (NGVA; p50) and the Melbourne Museum (p77) exhibit works of art that predate European settlement, as well as work like that of William Barak and Tommy McCrae that captures the firsthand experience of indigenous life pre- and postcolonisation. The art and artefacts at the Melbourne Museum's Bunjilaka Aboriginal Centre (p77) provide a particularly vivid and intimate picture of Koorie (Victorian Aboriginal) culture.

The grand vistas painted by intrepid Europeans visiting the fledgling colony of Melbourne describe a very different Australian experience. These vast works offer early views of Australia as a colonial jewel. Bucolic pastures and abundant forests represent a land in the throes of colonisation and environmental upheaval, and offer intriguing catalogues of much that was on the precipice of being lost. Eugène von Guérard's works, such as *Mount Kosciusko* (1866, NGVA), seen from the Victorian border, capture the wondrous difference of the Australian landscape to the European eye and reward close study with the delight of their lavish attention to detail.

In the late 19th century a generation of Australian-born artists emerged who are fondly remembered for defining a truly Australian vision of the landscape and cities of the day. The artists of the Heidelberg school took the train down the newly laid railway lines to the bush at Melbourne's fringe and camped together, sketching and working rapidly in oils to capture the bright light and dry elegance of the Australian bush. They created a heroic national iconography ranging from the shearing of sheep to visions of a wide brown land popularly celebrated as offering a chance to all. The most widely reproduced works of Heidelberg school artists such as Tom Roberts and Arthur Streeton are majestic in scale and build grand narratives from the contemporary experience of Australians; other smaller works are surprisingly intimate and impressionistically rendered.

*Lost* (1886, NGVA) by Frederick McCubbin portrays a young girl lost in the bush. The sun shines brightly on the yellowed summer grass, while the repeated vertical staccato of

## MUMA

If you have a particular interest in contemporary Australian art, then a trek out to Monash University Museum of Modern Art (MUMA; ☎ 9905 4217; www .monash.edu.au/muma; ground fl, Bldg 55, Monash University, Wellington Rd, Clayton; ☽ 10am-5pm Tue-Fri, 2-5pm Sat) is worth the effort. It has an inspired collection and promotes Australian work through regularly changing exhibitions and public programs known for their curatorial nous.

It's at least a half-hour journey to get there from the city. Catch a train to Huntingdale Station on the Dandenong, Cranbourne or Pakenham lines. From Huntingdale station, follow the signs to bus stop 630, which will take you to the door.

the gum trees divides the scene, creating a claustrophobic sense through infinite repetition. While portraying an archetypal anxiety, the loss of a child to the land was a particularly poignant concern at the turn of the century. Australians love the landscape, identify with it and take pride in its complexity — its harshness and mysteriousness, its abundance and distinctiveness — and yet it makes us uneasy also; we feel disquiet in the very land that defines us. The disjunction of new peoples arriving in a very old land, and the experience of loss in the landscape, is an abiding anxiety explored in works of art and literature such as the iconic novel and film *Picnic at Hanging Rock* (p34).

Visitors to Melbourne can experience some of the landscapes painted by the artists of the Heidelberg school by catching the train to Heidelberg station and walking across the Yarra River to the rambling gardens of the Heide Museum of Modern Art (below). Heide, former home of the Reeds, played a pivotal role in the development of Australian modernism in the early and mid-20th century. Sidney Nolan's epic series celebrating the bushranger Ned Kelly (see p24) is said to have been painted at the Reed's dining-room table. The early Australian modernism forged at Heide was expressively painted and passionately connected to the emotional, social and intellectual worlds of the artists.

At the same time as the Heide artists were forging newly modern national iconographies, the lyrical watercolours of Aboriginal artist Albert Namatjira were coming to public attention. Namatjira was an innovator who painted his country in vivid jewel-like shades, a radical shift from the traditional ochres of the Arrernte people of central Australia. While he was mission-raised, Namatjira regularly went walkabout, and his highly detailed Western-style paintings describe the landscape he loved: white ghost gums and ochre rock outcrops with shadows of plum and mauve. Animated by myriad possibilities of light, Namatjira's works created an audience for Aboriginal art and for an Aboriginal perspective. More recently, artists such as Emily Kame Kngwarreye and Clifford Possum Tjapaltjarri have created extraordinary bodies of work that establish a bridge between their traditional obligations to culture and country and the development of their own individual artistic language. Likewise, artists of European heritage such as Fred Williams and John Olsen have drawn upon the Australian landscape to create poetic works that newly imagine both representational space and our sense of place.

Contemporary Australian artists are strongly concerned with an Australian sense of place, as well as being actively engaged in the more universal concerns of our contemporary, globalised world. The Melbourne art scene is an energetic and intellectually rigorous one, with a flourishing community of artists, experimental exhibition spaces and events. A good place to tap into this energy is Gertrude Contemporary Art Spaces (p73), where you can see exhibitions by emerging artists and get the low-down on the newest experimental spaces. The Australian Centre for Contemporary Art (p62) generates cutting-edge programs of exhibitions as well as developing large-scale projects with Australian and international artists. The Australian Centre for the Moving Image (p51) exhibits film and multimedia works by contemporary artists in thematic exhibitions that draw upon a rich diversity of moving-image formats, and the Centre for Contemporary Photography (p72) has a strong photo- and film-based program. Melbourne has an active network of university art museums and galleries, among which the Ian Potter Museum at the University of Melbourne (p77) and Monash University Museum of Art (MUMA; p27) offer dynamic exhibition

## HEIDE

Around 10 to 20 minutes drive from Fitzroy, the Heide Museum of Modern Art ( ☎ 9850 1500; www.heide.com.au; 7 Templestowe Rd, Bulleen; adult/child $12/free; ☒ 10am-5pm Tue-Fri, noon-5pm Sat& Sun; ☒ 200) is nestled in sprawling grounds by the Yarra. This area is now deeply suburban, but was once the rural retreat of John and Sunday Reed. The couple nurtured an artistic community here that included Albert Tucker, Sidney Nolan, Arthur Boyd, Joy Hester, John Perceval and Danila Vassilieff. Heide has an impressive collection of modern and contemporary Australian art housed in three galleries and scattered throughout the tranquil gardens. Each gallery is unique: Heide I is the heritage-listed Victorian farmhouse that was the Reed's first home; Heide II, a Modernist beauty designed by David McGlashan in the 1960s, was their second; while Heide III is a purpose-built exhibition space. The Reed's kitchen garden is still lovingly tended and the surrounding grounds are landscaped with a combination of European and native trees.

If you are driving, Heide is signposted off the Eastern Fwy; otherwise, catch bus 200 from outside Melbourne Central on Lonsdale St, or the Hurstbridge-line train to Heidelberg Station, then bus 291.

lonelyplanet.com

BACKGROUND ARTS

28

## WALL TO WALL ART

A stunning black-and-white graphic of a homeless person holding a card: 'Keep your coins, I want change'. A per-petual shadow of a signpost painted on the footpath. A beautiful photo-real representation of 'Animal' – the grumpy Melbourne icon who sits on city street corners drumming on crates and upturned buckets. All arresting examples of Melbourne street art: public nuisance or stimulating element of Melbourne's urban fabric?

Like it or loathe it, Melbourne's graffiti is a beacon for travellers. You'll see many visitors snapping themselves in front of emblazoned alley walls. 'Caledonian Lane attracts more visiting Brazilians, Londoners and New Yorkers than anywhere else in the city,' says Tai Snaith, a local curator and artist. 'Such areas also support thriving and uniquely Melbourne businesses such as St Jerome's (p150), an artistic hide-out.

It's not just the out-of-towners who are flocking to see the city's street art. Wedding parties seeking street cred are recording their special day against the gritty backdrop of Hosier Lane. The National Gallery of Australia is considering ways of incorporating stencil art into its collection of Australian prints. Street art is discussed in art and culture journals, and a world-renowned website on graffiti, www.stencilrevolution.com, comes out of Melbourne.

It wasn't always so universally appreciated. In the lead up to the 2006 Commonwealth Games, the city council intro-duced a zero tolerance policy in an attempt to 'clean up' the streets. It encouraged the public to report broken streetlights in an attempt to counter graffiti. Around the same time there were many condemning the publication of Stencil Graffiti Capital: Melbourne (www.stencilgraffiticapital.com) – a 150-page book documenting Melbourne's stencil-art scene. There were also pressure groups rallying against private and public property being vandalised.

'Street art is a way of artists countering advertising and claiming some of that visual space, which is often sublimi-nally influencing our political ideals,' says Tai. 'The act of graffitiing itself is a political action motivated by aesthetically minded people to make a statement, large or small.'

Does the council's increasing acceptance and its move to allow graffiti in allocated areas mean that the work loses its street credibility and political clout? 'You can see superb sponsored or commissioned work, of course,' says Tai, 'but ultimately work created without pay and often illegally comes from a wilder place.'

It's an exciting time to stroll through Hosier Lane (Map pp52–3; F4), Caledonian Lane (Map pp52–3; E3) and Centre Way (Map pp52–3; E4) in the city, and Canada Lane (Map pp78–9; E7) in Carlton. If you're interested in the artists themselves, *Rash*, a locally produced documentary explores the work and worldview of several key players. It is available on DVD (www.rashfilm.com).

programs of work by contemporary artists, as well as reflecting upon the history of Australian art. Regional galleries throughout Victoria also are very strong.

Melbourne takes pride in being a city for ideas, a city for contemporary art. Only a small slice of the mass of work being produced will be evident at any one time, but between the commer-cial, public and artist-run galleries there is much to discover. The city's strength as a centre for architecture and spatial investigation is reflected in the work of contemporary artists such as Stephen Bram, Callum Morton and Natasha Johns-Messenger. The practice of the making of art and the reflective ricochet between the real and the represented are explored by Melbourne artists Ricky Swallow, Nick Mangan, Christian Capurro, Nadine Christensen and Chris Bond.

The impact of technology upon our lives is a subject of much interest to artists such as Stephen Honegger, Anthony Hunt and Patricia Piccinini, artists who are empowered by the digital world as well as being thoughtfully engaged with the ethical dilemmas it generates. The politics of memory and the borders of empathy are explored by artists such as Susan Norrie, Gordon Bennett, Tom Nicholson and Louisa Bufardeci. Melbourne is also a centre for cross-cultural investigation, with artists such as Kate Beynon, Sangeeta Sandrasegar, Rafat Ishak and Constanz Zikos drawing upon a diversity of cultural perspectives to find their own expressive language.

For a comprehensive guide to the city's galleries get a copy of *Art Almanac* from bookshops and newsagents. See also the White Cube Fever walking tour (p100).

# LITERATURE

Has there been a great Melbourne novel? Melbourne has certainly provided a variety of memo-rable backdrops in literary works from the cult crime fiction of *The Mystery of a Hansom Cab* (1886; Fergus Hume) to the Brunswick backstreets of Chritos Tsoklas' *Loaded* and Steve Carrol's ongoing exploration of cultural shift in outer suburbia. But there's nothing that quite puts the city front and centre.

# VICTORIA IN PRINT

## Fiction

*The Mystery of a Hansom Cab* (1886; Fergus Hume) Marvellous Melbourne–era crime fiction.

*The Getting of Wisdom* (1910; Henry Handel Richardson) Loss-of-innocence story set in a Melbourne girl's school; its simple, direct style ushers in the 20th century.

*Power Without Glory* (1950; Frank Hardy) Barely fictionalised story of crime and dirty politics in WWI 'Carringbush', a suburb closely resembling Collingwood.

*Monkey Grip* (1977; Helen Garner) Tortured love and bohemian life in the inner-city Melbourne of the '70s.

*Loaded* (1995; Christos Tsiolkas) Grunge-era first novel, with sex, drugs and bouzouki. Became the film *Head On,* with Alex Dimitriades as Ari.

*True History of the Kelly Gang* (2002; Peter Carey) This fictional, epistolary account of the life of Victoria's most famous bushranger is told in the vernacular style that Carey is known for.

*Of a Boy* (2000; Sonya Hartnett) This haunting invocation of troubled childhood is one of many books worth seeking out by this prolific Melbourne writer, who also writes for young adults.

*Three Dollars* (1998; Elliot Perlman) A multi-award winning book that's uncompromising in its chronicle of middle-class angst, downsizing and globalisation. It was made into a film directed by Robert Connolly.

*Dead Europe* (2005; Christos Tsiolkas) Tackling the big themes, *Dead Europe*'s central character is a Greek-Australian photographer who leads us through questions of history, belonging and poverty.

*Players* (2005; Tony Wilson) Satirical romp that skewers sporting celebrity and its media handmaidens.

*The Time We Have Taken* (2007; Steven Carroll) Luminous exploration of the radical changes of the '70s and meditation on the rhythms of suburban life.

*Sucked In* (2007; Shane Maloney) The sixth of the Murray Whelan novels, which follow his journey through the ranks of a well-known but entirely fictional Australian political party and takes place firmly in Melbourne, a city he describes as 'on the way to nowhere'.

*The Spare Room* (2008; Helen Garner) The long-awaited return to fiction from one of Melbourne's best writers. A beautifully written but blunt, challenging story of friendship and how we choose to die, set in the familiar streets of inner Melbourne.

Melbourne certainly nourishes writers with its tempestuous weather, richly complex range of cultures and identities as well as its moody architecture, but at the same time it can relegate words and stories to the wings, while sport and social life take centre stage. That said, the city is far from philistine. Publishing companies Black Inc, Text and Penguin are based here and the city produces a host of commercial and 'little' magazines that highlight literature and intellectual life in general. These include the *Australian Book Review*, *Meanjin*, Black Inc's series of 'best' anthologies and *Quarterly Essays*, and the short-fiction collection *Sleepers Almanac*.

There is also a small but vigorous poetry scene. During the 1960s, a group called the 'Melbourne poets' created work that was 'deliberately prosaic... finding their poetry in suburbs and ordinary days'. Chris Wallace-Crabbe is the best known of these and continues to write, and to teach new generations of poets. Dorothy Porter, who is well known for her verse novels, including the *The Monkey's Mask* (1994), which was made into a feature film, is also based in Melbourne.

The Melbourne Writers' Festival (www.mwf.com.au), held at Fed Square, draws crowds each August; its readings and discussions featuring local and international writers often sell out. The State Library of Victoria (www.slv.vic.gov.au) also holds literary events throughout the year (including awarding the lucrative Victorian Premier's Literary Awards), as do bookstores such as Readings (see p116) and Reader's Feast ( ☎ 9662 4699; www.readersfeast.com.au; cnr Bourke & Swanston Sts). The publishers of Sleepers Almanac (www.sleeperspublishing.com) also host 'salons' which feature Australian writers and encourage bookish types to get together and talk literature (see their website for details). The city also boasts some of Australia's most prestigious creative writing courses at RMIT University and the University of Melbourne.

### Memoir

*In My Skin* (2006; Kate Holden) A young woman's story of heroin addiction and prostitution on the streets of St Kilda.

*Unpolished Gem* (2006; Alice Pung) A vivid rendering of immigrant life in the western suburbs and the attendant anxieties of living between two cultures.

*Shadowboxing* (2006; Tony Birch) Linked stories about a working-class childhood in '60s Fitzroy.

### Non-Fiction

*Bearbrass* (1995; Robyn Annear) Melbourne's first decades are brought vividly to life.

*Australian Gothic: A Life of Albert Tucker* (2002; Janine Burke) Mid-century Melbourne through the eyes of its artistic elite.

*The Birth of Melbourne* (2002; Tim Flannery) Includes the voices of a mixed bag of pioneers and travellers, such as John Batman, Mathew Flinders, Marcus Clark and Rudyard Kipling.

*A City Lost and Found: Whelan the Wrecker's Melbourne* (2005; Robyn Annear) The city's history is revealed in this fascinating story of the clash of progress and preservation.

*Yarra: A Diverting History of Melbourne's Murky River* (2005; Kristin Otto) An erudite but rollicking history of Melbourne's main waterway, that tells as much about the city that grew up around it as the river itself.

### Children's & Young Adult Fiction

*Winter* (2000), *The Head Book* (2001), *The Boy You Brought Home (2002)* (John Marsden) Marsden taught generations of Victorian teenagers and is one of the world's most popular young adult writers. His vision can be bleak but his audience adore him.

*How to Make a Bird* (2003; Martine Murray) A country teenager's odyssey through St Kilda and Brunswick in search of the truth about her troubled family and herself.

*Henrietta* (2004; Martine Murray) Murray's illustrated book for younger reader's features the delightfully impish and very modern Melbourne miss, Henrietta.

*Jethro Byrde, Fairy Child* (2004; Bob Graham) This gentle, beautifully illustrated work tells the story of little girl's meeting with a family of fairy travellers. It captures both the rhythms of everyday inner-city life, plus the temper of the times; Graham wrote it as a response to the Howard government's treatment of refugees.

Despite a largely urban, multicultural population, it's still up to a novel with a historical (even mythological) bush setting to claim the 'great' title. Peter Carey's *True History of the Kelly Gang*, set in the central Victorian haunts of Australia's most famous bushranger, took both the Booker and Commonwealth Writers' Prize when it was published in 2002.

For a list of Melbourne's best bookstores, see p107.

# MUSIC

Melbourne's cultural image has involved music since producing two of the most enduringly fascinating talents of the 19th and early 20th centuries. Dame Nellie Melba, opera diva, was an international star who lived overseas for many years, but retained a sentimental attachment to her home town. Percy Grainger, whose innovative compositions and performances prefigured many forms of 20th-century music, was born and brought up in Melbourne. Grainger's eccentric genius extended beyond music to the design of clothing; he was also known for his transgressive sex life. A museum is dedicated to his work at the University of Melbourne – at the time of writing it was closed for restoration until early 2010.

More recently, Melbourne's live music scene exploded in the mid-60s with a band called the Loved Ones, who broke the imitative mould of American '50s rock and roll. The early 1970s saw groups like AC/DC, Skyhooks and Daddy Cool capture the experience of ordinary Melbourne life in their lyrics for the first time. By the end of that decade punk descended; Melbourne's moody weather and grimy backstreets had a natural synergy with the genre. In her book *In The*

*George: St Kilda Life and Times,* author Gillian Upton describes the scene that concentrated around the Crystal or Seaview Ballroom (now the George Hotel):

> Bands could be roughly divided into two camps. One stream of bands, such as La Femme and Chosen Few, grew from skinhead roots…in opposition were the 'art-school' middle-class punks personified by the Ballroom's anointed sons, Nick Cave and the Boys Next Door. The enemy was the moribund culture perceived outside the walls…the so-called Carlton bands playing their American-influenced music across town.

Bands that grew out of this scene included the Sports, the Models, the Johnnys, X, Sacred Cowboys, the Wreckery, Cosmic Psychos, Hunters & Collectors and Paul Kelly. The intervening years have been fast and furious, with too much talent to mention here.

Melbourne is still seen as the live-music capital of Australia, and draws musicians here from around the country, despite an increasing dearth of inner-city venues for them to play in. Current darlings include the Drones, Plug-in City and the Midnight Juggernauts. Although it doesn't have the pulling power of cities like New York or London, for a city so very far away, Melbourne is blessed with a large number of touring acts each year. Pickings are particularly rich during summer. The Drinking & Nightlife chapter (p146) lists live-music venues and gig guides.

Melbourne also has a healthy club and dance music scene. The mega-clubs of the '80s gave way to a more fluid dance party culture revolving around techno and other electronic styles. The 'doof' was born; these festivals, often held in bushland settings over several days, peaked in the late '90s, though still have their devotees. Legendary laneway club Honkytonks took its musical responsibility very seriously and nurtured local DJ talent (and a generation of club kids) through the early years of this decade. Since its demise, venues such as Miss Libertine (p151), Roxanne Parlour (p151) and Brown Alley (p150) have filled the gap. Local electronic artists include Cut Copy, the Avalanches and DJ Digital Primate who works with vocalists such as B-Girls Fabulous. See Drinking & Nightlife (p146) for venues or check out the Melbourne section of national dance website In the Mix (www.inthemix.com.au).

Australian hip-hop is well represented in Melbourne. Listen up for locals True Live and DJ Peril. Hip-hop has also proven enormously popular with young Aboriginal and Islander musicians: the CD *All You Mob* is an excellent compilation of indigenous artists. Other modern indigenous musicians create unique styles by incorporating traditional instruments into modern rock and folk formats. Archie Roach and Ruby Hunter are two well-known and widely respected indigenous musicians based in Melbourne.

Jazz also has a dedicated audience. The heart of the scene is Bennetts Lane (p151), an archetypal up-an-alley jazz club if ever there was one. Its Sunday night A-Live Jazz Series organised by the Melbourne Jazz Cooperative (www.jazzvic.org) features locals, and the venue draws a crowd that knows its hard bop from its bebop. The city is known for its improvisational élan, as well as musicians who cross genres into world and experimental electronic music. Some well-respected Melbourne names include Paul Grabowsky, Paul Williamson, Ian Chaplin, Doug de Vries, Tony Gould, Phillip Rex, Barney McAll, Jex Saarelaht, Sam Keevers, Andrea Keller, Scott Tinkler and Niko Schäuble. Both the Newmarket Music (www.newmarketmusic.com.au) and Jazzhead (www.jazzhead.com) labels were founded in Melbourne. Both are worth checking out for their recordings of local artists.

Ninety years after Nellie Melba was made a dame, classical still has a strong presence in Melbourne. The Melbourne Symphony Orchestra, based at Hamer Hall, performs works drawn from across the classical spectrum from the popular to challenging contem-

## top picks

### SONGS OF THE CITY (AND BEYOND)

- Lygon Street Limbo Skyhooks
- Beautiful People Australian Crawl
- From St Kilda to Kings Cross Paul Kelly
- Leaps and Bounds Paul Kelly
- (Boys) What Did The Detectives Say? The Sports
- Under the Sun Hunters & Collectors
- Throw Your Arms Around Me Hunters & Collectors
- Underneath the Clocks Weddings Parties Anything
- Four Seasons in One Day Crowded House
- Footy Spiderbait
- Melbourne The Whitlams
- Charcoal Lane Archie Roach
- Maroondah Reservoir Augie March

## MUSIC FESTIVALS

**Harvest Festival** (9773 0722) Alternative country and roots music festival held at the Mornington Peninsula's Red Hill in mid-January; includes a film festival and features regional produce.

**Big Day Out** (www.bigdayout.com) Huge line-up of local and international acts, which tours the country. Melbourne's BDO, held at the end of January, attracts about 40,000 people.

**Port Fairy Folk Festival** (www.portfairyfolkfestival.com) This far-west-coast festival has been hosting bluegrass, Celtic, blues and acoustic bands for over 30 years; it's a good one for families. It's held in early March over the Labour Day long weekend.

**Apollo Bay Music Festival** (www.apollobaymusicfestival.com) This community music festival on the west coast has been hosting local and international musos for around 15 years. It's held in March or April.

**Brunswick Music Festival** (www.brunswickmusicfestival.com.au) Held annually in March/April. Attracts around 50,000 people, with stalls and stages featuring world-music acts.

**Wangaratta Jazz** (www.wangaratta-jazz.org.au) Over 350 of the world's finest jazz and blues acts take over Wangaratta for a long weekend at the end of October/start of November.

**Queenscliff Music Festival** (www.queenscliffmusicfestival.com.au) Seaside festival, on the last weekend in November, fostering all-Australian acts from all genres.

**Meredith Music Festival** (www.mmf.com.au) Legendary music festival that's been running annually for almost two decades; it's held over a few days in mid-December in a natural amphitheatre near the small country town of Meredith. Attracts international big-name indie acts.

**Falls Festival** (www.fallsfestival.com) Ten thousand or so revellers head to a 120-hectare property in Lorne on New Year's Eve to hear 50 acts over two days; featuring headliners such as the Go! Team or Black Rebel Motorcycle Club.

**Melbourne Jazz** (www.jazzvic.org) International stars take it out of the clubs and play Crown and the Arts Centre.

porary composition. The Melbourne International Festival has a vibrant music program that features local and international acts, as well as talks and workshops. The independent classical radio station 3MBS (103.5 FM) actively supports local musicians, recording and broadcasting a wide range of concerts and recitals. The 3MBS arts diary (www.3mbs.org.au/arts.html) is an invaluable resource for what's going on. The *Age* newspaper also lists classical performances in its Friday and Saturday editions. See the Arts section (p163) for more details.

## CINEMA

Although Sydney is still considered the centre of the Australian film industry, new production facilities at Docklands, a slightly lower cost of living and generous government subsidies has seen Melbourne wield its movie-making muscle. And Melbourne looks good on the big screen. Filmmakers tend to eschew the stately and urbane and highlight the city's complexity, from the winsomely suburban to the melancholic, grimy and gritty.

Film culture is nurtured in Victoria through local funding projects, education and exhibition. Film making, screenwriting, drama and animation are taught in Melbourne's major universities. Funding for features, documentaries, shorts, digital media and game content is provided by Film Victoria (www.film.vic.gov.au), which also provides mentoring schemes. Federation Square has consolidated a big part of Melbourne's screen culture, housing the Australian Centre for the Moving Image (p51) and the Special Broadcasting Service (SBS).

The prominence of film in Melbourne is evident in the number of film festivals the city hosts. Apart from the main Melbourne International Film Festival (www.melbournefilmfestival.com.au), there's everything from the Melbourne Underground Film Festival (www.muff.com.au) to shorts at the St Kilda Film Festival (www.stkildafilmfestival.com.au) and the Sydney-import Tropfest (www.tropfest.com.au) at the Sidney Myer Music Bowl (p147). Other film-festival genres include foreign-made, seniors, hip-hop, queer and documentary.

Film-focused publications include *Inside Film*, devoted to the creation of screen content and available at newsagents; and *Real Time*, available free from cafés and cinemas. For movie-theatre listings see p162. See p34 for a glimpse of Melbourne's celluloid journey.

## MELBOURNE ON SCREEN

*The Story of the Kelly Gang* (1906) Although only fragments remain of its original 70 minutes, what has survived of the world's first feature film is stylistically sophisticated. Shot in a St Kilda pharmacy and the upper Yarra suburbs of Heidelberg and Eltham, and featuring the actual hand-wrought armour of one of the Kelly gang.

*On the Beach* (1957) Duck-and-cover-era drama with Melburnians facing the end of the world with an unsettling mix of partying and passivity. Sadly, not even Gregory Peck can save us. A train ride to Frankston will never be the same without Ava Gardner waiting at the other end with a horse and cart.

*Picnic at Hanging Rock* (1975) Elliptical, sensual Australian New Wave classic; the rock of the title rises from the plains just beyond Melbourne's outer suburban fringe.

*Pure Shit* (1976) Called 'the most evil film ever made' by the *Herald* newspaper, this ultra lo-fi look at 24 hours in the life of four junkies has great shots of a still-shambolic inner-city as well as hilarious cameos from author Helen Garner, comedians Greg (HG Nelson) Pickhaver and Max Gillies, as well as producer Bob Weiss.

*Mad Max* (1979) Postapocalypse take two: the gangs take over the highways, and the wide-screen anamorphic lens takes in Spotswood, Lara, Williamstown, a stunning car-park underneath Melbourne Uni and the dunes of nearby Fairhaven.

*Malcolm* (1986) Set in the then working class suburbs of Flemington and Preston, a quintessential Melbourne-eccentric story about a tram-obsessive turned petty crim. One of the first in a long line of suburban quirk flicks.

*Dogs in Space* (1986) Shot in the actual house in Richmond where director Richard Lowenstein lived at the end of the '70s. The late Michael Hutchence is joined by a huge local ensemble cast in a swirling, chaotic chronicle of the city's punk past.

*The Big Steal* (1990) Ben Mendelsohn and Claudia Karvan charm in this home-grown teen movie with cars, scams and the good citizens of the western suburbs providing a comic backdrop.

*Death in Brunswick* (1991) Culture-clash high farce with a witless outsider played by Sam Neill, set in a Greek restaurant in prehipster Brunswick. Nice supporting role by satirist John Clarke.

*Romper Stomper* (1992) A much younger Russel Crowe plays a violent, nazi skinhead. Set in the inner city suburb of Footscray, this film has a less-than-subtle depiction of Vietnamese-Australians.

*Love and Other Catastrophes* (1996) Slight but box-office pleasing campus rom-com. Shows the University of Melbourne in all its sandstone-league glory.

*Chopper* (2000) Based on the life of not-so-petty but eternally charismatic criminal Mark Read. Eric Bana's portrayal of Collingwood's most infamous resident proved career-making.

*The Bank* (2001) Bank-bashing paranoid thriller with a rare appearance from corporate Melbourne *and* a Yarra water taxi.

*Harvie Crumpet* (2003) Oscar-winning claymation short made in Melbourne by local film school grad Adam Elliot.

*Ned Kelly* (2003) Uneven but thoughtful depiction of the mythological Ned, adapted from the novel *Our Sunshine*. The late Heath Ledger stars and manages to charm through the period beard. Unlike Tony Richardson's troubled Jagger vehicle, this one was shot in historically accurate locations.

*Salaam Namaste* (2005) Twisted tale of professional Indians abroad was the first Bollywood film shot entirely in Australia. Features loads of shiny city locales and some stunning shots of the Great Ocean Rd (and not forgetting the smash-hit song *My Dil Goes Mmm...*).

*Kenny* (2006) This mockumentary set in the western suburbs takes toilet humour to its logical conclusion and is a feature-length tribute to the vernacular flair of tradesmen.

*Where the Wild Things Are* (2006) Spike Jonze came to town and shot this Maurice Sendak adaptation *his* way in the wet and wild forests of Gembrook. At time of writing, it's not certain it will survive the test audience run-around.

# TELEVISION

There's an enduring affection for police drama and comedy shows in Australia. The barely-ficionalised Melbourne organised crime series *Underbelly* didn't make it to air in the city in which it was set, not because of its tits-and-arse overload, but because it was ruled that its plot lines could prejudice concurrent court proceedings. *Canal Road*, a drama set in a community legal and medical practice is the latest made-in-Melbourne series to be seen at time of writing. It was shot at the Yarra-side warehouse Banana Alley and around Docklands. Beloved local

## LOVE THY NEIGHBOURS *Alan Fletcher*

For many travellers to Australia, particularly those of British origin, Melbourne is a 'must-see' destination because it is home to the internationally renowned TV program *Neighbours*. A trip to Melbourne would not be complete without a visit to the legendary Ramsay St. Pin Oak Ct in Vermont South is the suburban street that has been the home of the show for 23 years.

The best way to see Ramsay St and have a true *Neighbours* experience is by taking the Official Neighbours Tour ( ☎ 03-9629 5866; www.neighbourstour.com.au; $45) It's the only licensed tour and is approved by the residents of Pin Oak Ct. If you're lucky you might see us filming and have the chance to grab a photo and an autograph! Two tours are available: Tour A runs twice daily, Monday to Friday, and visits Ramsay St, Erinsborough High School and includes an exclusive meeting with a *Neighbours* actor; the second, more comprehensive, tour ($65) visits the street, the school and the outside studio sets of the Lassiter's Complex, Lou's mechanics and Grease Monkeys. This tour runs on the weekends and starts at the Neighbours Centre (570 Flinders Street, Melbourne) where you can check out and purchase official *Neighbours* memorabilia.

There are a variety of ways to make the pilgrimage yourself: if you don't have wheels, take the train to Glen Waverley station, then bus 888 or 889 north (get off at Vision Dr near Burwood Hwy). Alternatively, tram 75 from Flinders St will take you all way to the corner of Burwood Hwy and Springvale Rd: a short walk brings you to Weeden Dr and Pin Oak Ct is the third street on the left. If you do make the trip, please remember to respect the privacy of residents. Don't do anything in their street or front yards that you wouldn't be happy with in your own street or home!

The Backpacker King also runs a hugely popular Official Neighbours Trivia Night ( ☎ 03-9629 5866; www.neigh boursnight.com.au; $40; Mon & Fri Nov-Apr) at the Elephant & Wheelbarrow (169 Fitzroy St, St Kilda), where you have the opportunity to rub shoulders and have your photo taken with some of your favourite *Neighbours* stars. The night is full of entertainment and prizes – call the Backpacker King to book. After meeting the stars, fans are entertained with a one-hour concert by my band – The Waiting Room.

*Alan Fletcher has worked in every branch of the performing arts for 30 years. He has played Dr Karl Kennedy on Neighbours since 1994.*

comedies include *Kath & Kim,* a piss-take of nouveau-riche suburban habits and language, and the bitingly satirical *Summer Heights High* – both are available on DVD at ABC shops (http://shop.abc. net.au). And, of course, there's the never-ending froth of soap opera *Neighbours* (see the boxed text, opposite) on Channel 10.

# THEATRE

Melbourne's vibrant theatre scene encompasses a wide spectrum of genres, from blockbuster musicals to intimate experimental productions.

Melbourne's most high-profile professional theatre company, the Melbourne Theatre Company (MTC; www.mtc.com.au), is also Australia's oldest. It stages up to a dozen performances year-round at the Victorian Arts Centre. Productions are often firmly focused on satisfying the company's middle-market subscriber base. It features works by well-known Australian playwrights such as David Williamson and locals Hannie Rayson and Joanna Murray-Smith, as well as international works. The MTC also runs a readings program to promote and develop the works of emerging playwrights.

The Malthouse Theatre (www.playbox.com.au) was established in 1976 and is dedicated to the performance of Australian works. Its program tends to be a little more edgy, nurturing emerging writers and actively promoting its productions in Asia.

Melbourne's numerous progressive fringe-theatre companies not only keep actors in work but challenge theatre's middle ground. The more enduring companies to seek out include Red Stitch Actors Theatre, Hoist, Kage Physical Theatre and Ranters Theatre Ensemble. The Theatre Alive (www.theatrealive.com.au) website has a comprehensive listing as well as news of upcoming performances.

Melbourne's theatrical heritage is evident in the city's remaining Victorian-era theatres: the Princess and Athenaeum. The diminutive La Mama (see the boxed text, p36), in Carlton, is an institution whose humble size and aspect is far outweighed by its place in the heart of the city's theatre scene.

For listings of Melbourne's theatre venues see p164.

## LA MAMA

Founded in 1967 as a theatre for new and experimental plays, La Mama (p164) is literally the mother of independent theatre in Melbourne. If the theatre is the metaphoric matriarch, then Liz Jones – artistic director for nigh on 30 years – is the actual one. La Mama and Liz nurture Australian playwrights and artists by providing the facilities and community necessary to get shows off the ground.

The tiny 40-seater La Mama theatre and its second venue, the Courthouse, stage around 70 performances each year. 'We have five going at a time,' says Liz, who reads 250 scripts a year. 'I'm also considering people who just come up with an idea, a scenario or a group collaboration. Especially for the Exploration season, which is dedicated to non script-based works. It includes a lot of dance and multiple art forms, where people want to really try out new ideas.'

La Mama acts as a production company, of sorts. When it takes on a performance, it provides the theatre space and pays the writer and the director. Actors and others involved in a production split the door takings. Liz spends a lot of time matching writers with directors. 'You might have three or four goes at it before you get a marriage.' La Mama has an illustrious index book of actors, stage directors and set, costume and lighting designers to assist in seeing a script or idea come to fruition.

'If I want to be proactive in this 21st century, I would like to continue to encourage indigenous theatre and ensembles – groups who want to work together,' says Liz. 'When I was travelling through Europe I was really aware how conservative theatrical forms tended to be in the English-speaking countries, and how radical they were particularly in Germany, Spain, Italy and Eastern European countries. I was so much more excited by the theatre I saw in Berlin than the theatre I saw in London. I came home thinking that I did want to try and encourage that. Now, I think the key to that is the ensemble and people working together in a large group trusting each other.'

From an audience perspective, La Mama is intimate and generous. You are invited to chat to those involved in a production after a performance, and you get to participate in the raffle. 'There's such a good chance of winning, which people don't normally have in a raffle,' says Liz. The raffle tradition began in about 1990. 'I edited a book called La Mama – the Story of a Theatre with Betty Burstall (founder of La Mama) and Helen Garner (author). The publisher printed 3500 copies, which were not selling like hot cakes, so Betty said, "Why don't we raffle one at the beginning of each show?" We raffled the entire stock. Then I edited a book of plays, and we raffled the entire stock of that. So, now we just find a worthy book.' Your entry ticket is also your raffle ticket, which is still drawn at the start of each performance.

Seeing a performance at La Mama is a little like a raffle itself. There's a similar anticipation inherent in innovative theatre. And like the raffle, there's a good chance of being rewarded.

# DANCE

The Australian Ballet (www.australianballet.com.au) is the national ballet company and is considered one of the finest in the world. It performs regularly at Melbourne's Victorian Arts Centre, with a program of classical and modern ballets.

Victoria's main contemporary dance company, Chunky Move (www.chunkymove.com), has been pushing the boundaries that define contemporary dance since 1998. Founder and artistic director Gideon Obarzanek studied with the Australian Ballet and choreographs many of the company's shows. Chunky Move is a tidy package of vital choreography, clever concepts referencing pop culture, extraordinary dancers, sleek design and smart marketing. As well as Obarzanek, Melbourne is home to two of Australia's most acclaimed contemporary choreographers. Lucy Guerin, who has been praised by Joan Acocella from the New Yorker magazine, has a small eponymous company and also works with Obarzanek. Shelley Lasica locates her work in nontheatre spaces and collaborates with visual artists and architects, and her works blur the lines between dance and performance art.

Bangarra Dance Theatre (www.bangarra.com.au), though Sydney-based, tours with some frequency. The company presents traditional Aboriginal and Torres Strait Islander dance in a contemporary setting. Stories and characters of the Dreaming are retold through dance. As Bangarra itself puts it, the company is 'one of the youngest and oldest of Australia's dance companies'.

Melbourne-based Dancehouse (www.dancehouse.com.au) is a studio setup that supports and nurtures independents. Supported by the Australia Council, it features a program of lectures and forums, dance classes and workshops, offers rehearsal space and coordinates regular performances. It fosters some truly innovative and beautiful work.

For a list of dance venues see p164.

# ARCHITECTURE

For a planned city, and a relatively youthful one, Melbourne's streetscapes are richly textured. Long considered one of the world's most beautiful Victorian cities, buildings that run the full gamut of that age still survive, from exuberantly embellished Second Empire institutions to hulking former factories that would make Manchester proud. Its built environment has continued to document the highs and lows of its short history. Today its architectural energy comes not from the monumental but from what goes on in between the new and the old, the towering and the tiny. Midcareer practices such as Six Degrees, Cassandra Complex, Ellenberg Fraser and Kersten Thompson create witty, inventive and challenging buildings and interiors that see these spaces spring to life.

Melbourne architect, lecturer and broadcaster Stuart Harrison walks us down the city's spine and loops around its fringe, highlighting prominent buildings that have become landmarks of city life.

## MELBOURNE BY DESIGN Stuart Harrison

Much of Melbourne's excellent architecture is focused in the city centre, along the Swanston St–St Kilda Rd spine and in a loop around the edge of the city grid that was laid down by Robert Hoddle in 1837. Visible down Swanston St, and along St Kilda Rd, is the iconic Shrine of Remembrance (p83). Built to commemorate WWI, it was recently the subject of an excellent contemporary renovation by cutting-edge local architects Ashton Raggatt McDougall (ARM), whose other projects include the controversial (and bright green) RMIT Storey Hall (Map pp52–3; 344 Swanston St) and the redevelopment of Melbourne Central Shopping Centre (p58).

The QV (p58) development takes up almost a whole city block but has used new laneways, emulating the successful shopping lanes that date from late-19th-century Melbourne. QV was also designed by several of Melbourne's best architects. The black QV2 (cnr Swanston & Little Lonsdale Sts) residential 'slug', by McBride Charles Ryan, is perched on the edge of the State Library forecourt, one of Melbourne's best public spaces, a sort of grass beach. The State Library (1856; p57) itself is a fine classical building – the highlight is the glass-domed reading room (1913). The library launched the career of Joseph Reed, who went on to become the most influential Victorian-era architect for Melbourne's skyline.

The Melbourne Town Hall (p56) is another classical institution by Joseph Reed, in French Renaissance mode, featuring a temple-like portico that enters into the spine of the building. The section of Swanston St opposite the Town Hall is a dense urban block, built up to the old 40m height limit imposed by the then government. The Capitol Theatre (Map pp52–3; 113 Swanston St), built in 1924, is the work of Walter Burley Griffin and Marion Mahony Griffin, two Chicago architects who moved to Australia after winning the competition to design Canberra, the nation's new capital. The Capital Theatre's crystalline ceiling is perhaps the most amazing of its type in the world, and a must-see. Featuring a coloured light show, the space is now owned by RMIT University and used for lectures and part of the Melbourne International Film Festival. Free tours run once a month; phone ☎ 9925 1773 for exact dates.

The two corner buildings of this block are by Marcus Barlow; Manchester Unity (1932; Map pp52–3) and the Century Building (1938; Map pp52–3) show the influence of Chicago and New York, with their commercial modern take on the Gothic style. The latter is less decorative, in line with post-WWII principles of abandoning decoration. The former ICI building, now Orica House (Map pp52–3; 1 Nicholson St), on the eastern edge of the city's grid was the city's first purely abstract, glass curtain-wall skyscraper. Finished in 1958, it evaded the 40m height limit by moving just outside the grid. Bates Smart and McCutcheon designed the well-preserved glass slab, which still has the original tropical-feeling garden at ground-floor level.

The Nicholas Building (Map pp52–3; cnr Swanston St & Flinders Lane), designed by Harry Norris in 1926, is a classical *palazzo* (grand building) in terracotta tile. Built as a demonstration of the wealth of the Nicholas family, the building today is full of artists' studios and designers. Having managed to escape being turned into apartments, it's one of the few unrenovated buildings of its type left in the city.

Southward over the Yarra on Princes Bridge and onto St Kilda Rd is the Arts Centre (p64), a suite of cultural buildings dating from the '60s and '70s designed by legendary local architect Sir

Roy Grounds. The National Gallery of Victoria (p63) is his masterpiece. It was recently renovated by Italian Mario Bellini to become NGV International. Key features such as the famous water-wall entry have survived along with the amazing stained-glass ceiling by Leonard French in the Great Hall. Local tradition is to lie down on the carpet in this almost medieval modernist public room and stare up at the ceiling. Nearby are some of the best recent institutional buildings: the Australian Centre for Contemporary Art (ACCA; p62) by Wood Marsh Architects, the exceptional Centre for Ideas at the Victorian College of the Arts (VCA; 234 St Kilda Rd) by Minifie Nixon and the School of Drama (28 Dodds St), also part of the VCA, by Edmond & Corrigan. A trip into the Royal Botanical Gardens will reveal the Sidney Myer Music Bowl (Map pp84–5), a brave work of 1950s' engineering whose 'sound-shell' roof projects sound out to the surrounding lawn.

Buildings on the loop around the edge of the city can be seen from the free city-circle tram (p94). Federation Square (p50) is both part of this circuit and a key point along the spine. It has been the city's main architectural talking point for visitors and locals alike since opening in 2002. Opposite the fine baroque Flinders Street Station (1911; p59) – Melbourne's principal suburban train station – Fed Square was designed by LAB Architecture Studio and features allusions to complex geometry and a desert-like material palette, using Western Australian sandstone in conjunction with zinc, glass and steel. The square itself works incredibly well, serving as the city's lounge room at large events, cramped with people sitting around and watching the giant video screen. Also at this key intersection of Flinders and Swanston Sts is St Paul's (p59), the Anglican cathedral designed by William Butterfield in London in the 1880s. A visit inside will reveal the Italian influence in the polychromatic stonework.

To the east of Flinders Street Station and across the river is Southbank (p62), a 1980s development, the promenade of which extends past the new Freshwater Place and Eureka Tower (p62) apartment complexes and then along past the lavish Crown Casino (p62) to the Melbourne Exhibition Centre (p63), known locally as 'Jeff's Shed' after former Victorian premier Jeff Kennett. Finished in 1996 and designed by Denton Corker Marshall (DCM), the enormous building has a superveranda along the river which provides a flexible exhibition space. The work of DCM is associated with the 1990s Kennett era and Melbourne's architectural and economic recovery.

Further around is Southern Cross Station, formerly called Spencer Street Station, the terminus for interstate trains. It recently had a major upgrade by English architect Nicholas Grimshaw. A waving, complex surface roof covers new facilities and platforms, making a link to the great English railways halls of the 19th century but demonstrating the latest in computer-assisted design and fabrication. The Melbourne Docklands development, a huge conversion of former docks into a commercial, retail and mainly residential space, is separated from the city grid by the Spencer St rail yards. In the last 10 years many people have moved into the City of Melbourne to live, many into the new residential towers of the Docklands (p62). Though not an architectural masterpiece, Telstra Dome has become the heart of the Docklands. The architectural quality is varied at the Docklands; highlights include the Webb Dock Bridge by artist Robert Owen in conjunction with DCM, and the nearby Yarra's Edge Apartments (90 Lorimer St) – a bronzed monolith apartment tower by Wood Marsh.

Along the northern edge of the city grid are the fine Carlton Gardens, and within is DCM's Melbourne Museum (2000; p77). Alongside is the historic Royal Exhibition Building (p77), another by Joseph Reed. It's a large classical show hall that was built for the International Exhibition of 1880 and used for such events since, until the Melbourne Exhibition Centre took over. Now restored, it is the largest exhibit in the museum's collection. The building was used for Australia's first federal parliament in 1901 and the whole park site is now subject to World Heritage listing.

The eastern edge of the grid is formed by Spring St: home to the state government and two fine classical institutions. Parliament House (p56) dates back to 1856 and has never been fully finished; it's a robust classical statement of order at the termination of Bourke St. Further down is the finer Renaissance sensibility of the Old Treasury, designed by 19-year-old JJ Clark in 1857 – the building is now the City Museum at Old Treasury (p58). Behind these two and further east along Macarthur St is the imposing St Patrick's Cathedral (p59), a blending of French and English Gothic tastes by William Wardell; it was consecrated in 1897.

Southeast of the city grid is the Melbourne Cricket Ground (MCG; p67), aka the G, which has been entirely rebuilt in the last 15 years, principally by architect Daryl Jackson. The most recent northern stands redevelopment, completed in time for the 2006 Commonwealth Games, has increased the ground's capacity to just under 100,000. The G is the city's arena, and is the venue for key sporting events such as the AFL Grand Final and Boxing Day Cricket Test. Other great sporting architecture can be seen in the nearby former Olympic Pool, finished for the 1956 Games, which expresses its structural dynamic brilliantly. A proud architectural statement of a city trying to escape its 19th-century heritage, the pool was designed by young architects Kevin Borland and Peter Macintyre; the latter oversaw the building's recent restoration and conversion into the Lexus Centre – the training facility for the hugely popular Collingwood Football Club. This and other buildings around here, such as the Rod Laver Arena (1988), form Melbourne Park (p67).

More information can be found in the excellent *Melbourne Architecture* guide, by Philip Goad, in the National Trust's compact *Walking Melbourne* guide, or on the unrelated website www.walkingmelbourne.com. Also recommended is *Design City Melbourne*, by Leon van Schaik which positions Melbourne as the world's design city du jour.

# ENVIRONMENT & PLANNING
## THE LAND

From a bird's-eye view, Melbourne perches at the top of Port Phillip Bay; it's about 860km south of Sydney by road. At 8806 sq km, compared to Sydney's approximate area of 4000 sq km, metropolitan Melbourne is Australia's largest city per capita and one of the largest in the world.

The CBD comprises only a tiny portion (1.8 sq km). Its flat topography and grid-like planning imbues the city with an ordered and self-contained feeling. The CBD is almost surrounded by a green belt of parks and gardens. Inner-city suburbs cluster around the fringes of the CBD and are often included in the boundaries of the general term 'city'. The Yarra River divides Melbourne geographically and, to some extent, socio-economically. Traditionally, the northern and western suburbs were industrial and working-class, while areas south of the Yarra and to the east have been affluent and professional. With gentrification, these distinctions have become increasingly blurred. The demographic split now lies between the inner and the outer suburbs.

Melbourne's suburbs sprawl in all directions from the city's central core. Highways and bridges duck and weave through outlying Melbourne. New suburbs prop on repurposed land; cul-de-sacs, curving avenues and 'catalogue' homes have moved in where industry or market gardens once resided. A network of highways fan throughout the state to regional centres and beyond.

## GREEN MELBOURNE

Melbourne City Council is committed to reducing the city's greenhouse emissions to zero by 2020. This admirable strategy glosses over Victoria's over reliance on brown-coal-fuelled electricity, although the state government has made some attempt to put the brakes on its rising emissions with research programs into green technologies. Water shortages are an ongoing issue, with restrictions in force at the time of writing. These laws have prompted a complete rethink of the way in which water is used. The days of suburban lawns being pampered by a 24 hour sprinkler system are long gone. Short showers and half-flush toilets have become a way of life for Victorians, and many have also adopted household grey-water systems. Visitors should note that it is seriously uncool to leave taps running. Waste recycling is a success story: public rubbish bins often offer sorting chutes, and all household waste is presorted before collection.

The current state government initiated a bold plan in 2001 entitled Melbourne 2030 which aimed to limit urban sprawl and the growing population's reliance on the car. While no one can doubt the sense of such a project, there has been ongoing problems with its implementation. More than 80% of Melbourne's population growth continues to occur on the outer fringes; many Australians have a deep-seated affection for living in a house on a block of land, something that is hard to discourage by legislation alone. Additionally, given that much of the planned development is slated to take place in existing 'transport hubs' in inner Melbourne, the National Trust of Victoria has expressed concern about the effect on heritage areas, particularly in sensitive suburbs such as Carlton, Fitzroy, Collingwood and South Yarra.

# GOVERNMENT & POLITICS

Melbourne is the capital of the state of Victoria, and the seat of the state's government. The state parliament meets in the imposing neo-classical Parliament House ( ☎ 9651 8911; www.parliament.vic.gov.au; Spring St). There is a Legislative Council – the upper house – and a Legislative Assembly, or lower house. This state, or second-level, government is responsible for hospitals, education, public transport, policing, main roads, traffic management and most major infrastructure projects.

Power is held by one of two main political parties, the centre-left Australian Labor Party and the right-wing Liberal/National coalition parties. The Australian Greens and independents also hold a handful of seats. At the time of writing, the Labor Party is in government, led by Premier John Brumby. Apart from ongoing disquiet among nurses and state school teachers over pay and conditions, and environmental concerns including ongoing controversy about the dredging of Port Phillip Bay, Labor's current tenure has been relatively uneventful. Parliament sessions are open to the public but don't expect high theatre; an architecture and history tour (see p56) when the pollies aren't sitting will be more entertaining for all but the most hardcore wonks and wonkettes.

The City of Melbourne, which takes in the CBD and its immediate surrounds, is governed by the Melbourne City Council ( ☎ 9658 9658; www.melbourne.vic.gov.au). At the time of writing, Lord Mayor John So heads up the council, which sits in what the press have always loved to call 'Clown Hall', in Swanston St. Melbourne's suburbs and the regions are divided up into a network of regional councils which take care of services such as libraries, parks and garbage collection as well as shouldering much of the responsibility for commercial and residential planning.

# MEDIA

The Packer and Murdoch dynasties' global influence is felt nowhere more strongly than in their home country. Australia's media ownership is one of the most concentrated in the world, with most daily newspapers owned by the two organizations, or local player John Fairfax Holdings.

The enormous media empire of the late Kerry Packer, Publishing & Broadcasting Ltd (PBL), owns TV station Channel 9 and Australian Consolidated Press, who publish 60% of all magazines sold in Australia.

Rupert Murdoch's News Corporation has Melbourne's tabloid *Herald-Sun*, the national broadsheet *The Australian*, Sky News, Fox News, Foxtel…the list goes on. The local broadsheet *The Age* is published by John Fairfax Holdings, who are also responsible for the *Australian Financial Review* (universally referred to as the 'Fin Review') and *Business Review Weekly*. See Newspapers & Magazines (p353) for details.

Melbourne's newspapers syndicate many stories from their counterparts in Britain and the US, making by-lines from the *Times*, *Guardian*, *New York Times* or *Washington Post* not uncommon.

The state-funded Australian Broadcasting Corporation (ABC; www.abc.net.au) broadcasts nationally with TV, radio and online services. The Special Broadcasting Service (SBS; www.sbs.com.au) is also a national broadcaster with a special mandate to reflect multiethnic and indigenous communities in Australia. See p33 for more.

Melbourne's independent radio stations are one of the city's most precious assets; see p354 for details.

# FASHION

Melbournians like to look good and fashion plays a big part in the city's self-image. Office clobber may have become more relaxed, and going-out clothes more casual too, but this just gives everyone more opportunities to improvise and layer. Melbourne's fashion needs are catered to by an impressive number of canny retailers who roam widely in search of the world's best as well as showcasing local design talent. And there's lots of that. Rather than adhering to the hierarchy of established studios, many young designers start their own labels straight out of university. This gives the scene an amazing energy and vitality. There are also a large number that have their own flagship shops, where the designer's particular look and personality is writ large and whole collections can be discovered. Vintage is a persisting global trend but one that has flourished in Melbourne, both in the retailing and wearing of vintage pieces and in a general sensibility that pays heed to retro cuts and traditional tailoring.

Melbourne designers are known for their tailoring, luxury fabrics, innovation and blending of global elements, all underscored with a fuss-free Australian sensibility. Those to watch out for include TL Wood and Scanlan & Theodore for smart, lyrical elegance; Tony Maticevki and Martin Grant for demi-couture and dark reworkings of the classics; Ess Hoshika, Dhini and Munk for the beautifully wearable conceptual and deconstructed; Anna Thomas and Vixen for luxuriously grownup looks, both tailored (Thomas) and flowing (Vixen); Gorman, Arabella Ramsay and Obüs for hipster cheek with a delightfully feminine twist; Alpha 60, Schwipe and Claude Maus for clever, urban, pop-culture inspired pieces; Mjölk for precision-cut menswear; and finally, scene stalwarts Bettina Liano for straight-ahead glamour and Alannah Hill for her original girly-girl layers.

One constant is colour, or lack of it. You'll not go long in Melbourne without hearing mention of 'Melbourne black', and it's true that inky shades are worn winter, spring, summer and autumn. Perhaps it's because it works well with the soft light and often grey days, or maybe it's a product of many Melbournian's southern European heritage. It could be the subliminal influence of the city's building blocks of moody bluestone. Some speculate that it's the lingering fallout of the explosive 1980s postpunk scene. The fact is, black clothes sell far better here than in any other city in the country, and it's hard to succeed as a designer if you don't add a little every season. It's never out of fashion.

Where to shop? The city (Map pp52–3) has national and international chains spread out over Bourke and Collins Sts, as well as the city malls of Melbourne Central, QVB, GPO, DFO Spencer St and Australia on Collins. Smaller shops and designer workshops inhabit the laneways and vertical villages of Curtin House and the Nicholas Building. A strip of Little Collins is dedicated to sartorially savvy gentlemen (p106). The length of leafy Collins St lined with luxury retailers, especially towards its Spring St end. Chapel St (Map pp84–5) also has many of the chains and classic Australian designers, as well as some interesting players at the Prahran end. Further up the hill hit Hawksburn Village (p117) or High St Armadale (p120) for bobo chic and fashion-forward labels. Greville St and Windsor do streetwear, the later is also good for vintage shopping. Lygon St, Carlton (Map pp78–9), has some great small shops specialising in European tailoring and local talent, while Brunswick St (Map pp74–5) does streetwear and pulses with the energy of young designers in stores such as the legendary Fat. Gertrude St (Map pp74–5) mixes vintage with the innovators as well as some great menswear. This is just the tip of the well-cut iceberg, with fashion popping up in many other neighbourhoods as well.

## LOCAL LINGO

Victoria was once known as the 'cabbage garden' because of the state's fertile rich soil and prodigious production of fruit and vegetables. Victorians were referred to as 'cabbage gardeners', the implication being that that's all they were good for. Victorians are also described as Mexicans, because from the point of view of New South Wales they are 'south of the border'. Here are some other terms and phrases you're likely to hear:

**Buckley's** No chance at all; refers to the convict William Buckley who escaped from the abortive first Victorian settlement, and lived with Indigenous tribes for over 30 years.

**Doing the Tan** A popular 4km jogging track around Kings Domain and the Royal Botanic Gardens.

**Footy** Australian Rules football.

**Has more front than Myer** Cheeky, not at all shy. Myer is a department store that originated in Melbourne and has a large shopfront presence in the Bourke St Mall.

**Hook turn** A driving manoeuvre that is only done in Melbourne's CBD and terrifies the rest of Australia. To turn right at an intersection, a motorist pulls over to the left of the road and then crosses all lanes of traffic to complete the turn. The hook turn is designed to keep the tram tracks clear of cars waiting to turn.

**Like Bourke Street** Very busy, usually referring to traffic. Bourke St is one of inner-city Melbourne's busiest thoroughfares.

**The Loop** The collective name for the five train stations arranged around the edge of the CBD.

# LANGUAGE

English may be the official and dominant language, but Australians speak over 250 languages other than English, a true reflection of its broad multicultural mix. Surviving Aboriginal languages also contribute to this number. Many Melburnians who consider their first language to be English have family connections that mean they at least comprehend another language. Foreign languages, usually Italian, Chinese or Japanese, are taught in schools from kindergarten onwards.

The 20 most common languages in Victoria are Italian, Greek, Vietnamese, Cantonese, Arabic (including Lebanese), Mandarin, Macedonian, Turkish, Croatian, Spanish, Maltese, German, Polish, Tagalog, Serbian, Russian, Sinhala, French and Dutch. This is also joined by increasing numbers of African languages including Amharic, Tijrinyan, Dinka and Swahili.

The *Macquarie Dictionary* is generally accepted as the definitive source in Australian-English vocabulary and pronunciation. Americanisms are becoming more common in Australian English, though there is gentle resistance to the adoption of US spellings.

Victorians, like all Australians, embrace a plethora of colloquialisms and are particularly fond of shortening words or adding the suffix 'o' or 'y', especially in a social context. The Macquarie Dictionary (http://web.macquariedictionary.com.au) has created an online Australian Word Map that documents regionalisms; for a dictionary product, it's very amusing.

# NEIGHBOURHOODS

## top picks

- **NGVA** (p50) and **NGVI** (p63)
  Arguably the best collection of art in Australia.
- **Chinatown** (p55)
  Discover the 1850s city-within-a-city.
- **Royal Botanic Gardens** (p55)
  A range of plantings grace beautifully designed gardens.
- **Federation Square** (p50)
  Melbourne's piazza, surrounded by cultural heavyweights.
- **Queen Victoria Market** (p57)
  Historic market, fresh produce.
- **Melbourne Cricket Ground** (p67)
  Iconic sporting amphitheatre.
- **Collingwood Children's Farm** (p72)
  Bucolic charm just minutes from town.
- **Melbourne Museum** (p77)
  Slice of local life packed in a postmodern shell.
- **St Kilda foreshore** (p89)
  Palms, a pier and seaside strolls.

What's your recommendation? www.lonelyplanet.com/melbourne

Melbourne is split in two by the turbid, winding Yarra. This divide was once more than a physical one, but blanket gentrification of inner-city neighbourhoods has made north-south class and lifestyle distinctions moot, if not entirely indiscernible.

Melbourne's city centre lies just to the north of the Yarra river, around 5km inland from Port Phillip Bay. Locals do bang on about 'the grid', and the city is indeed a strict matrix of wide, ramrod-straight streets, oriented at an angle to the river. Of course, these are dissected by a tangle of laneways that add an organic dimension to the grand vision and intended order. The city is used by a broad sweep of citizens to work, shop and socialise. There's an ever-changing mix of moods, crowds and venues.

> Melbourne's streets are dissected by a tangle of laneways that add an organic dimension to the grand vision and intended order. There's an ever-changing mix of moods, crowds and venues.

Docklands, a new millennial extension of the city, sits west of the city, beyond the flowing-roofed Southern Cross Station and Telstra Dome. On Docklands' far side are a series of still-working docks and the western suburbs. South of the river, Southbank is home to the city's arts big guns (including the sprawling campus of the Victorian College of the Arts) and a string of hotels, residential apartments, offices and the Crown Casino.

Despite the city's bevy of attractions, and its perpetual pace, Melbourne's character relies just as much upon its collection of inner-city villages. These slices of Melbourne life have distinct and diverse personalities. Sampling at least one of their thriving scenes is a must.

To the east, beyond Fitzroy Gardens, is the sedate residential neighbourhood of East Melbourne, then the outlet strips, Vietnamese restaurants and providores of Richmond. The inner northern suburbs of Carlton, North Melbourne, Parkville and Brunswick blur out from the city fringe, with a laid-back mix of university culture, parklands, shops, cafés and restaurants, many within walking distance of the city. On the northeastern side, right-on but indefatigably fashionable Fitzroy and Collingwood offer a mix of unique shops and cafés, as well as gently bohemian pubs and bars.

The grand tree-lined boulevard of St Kilda Rd is now fringed with office blocks as it stretches its way from the city to the bay. Parkland extends from the Yarra's edge through the Domain, the Royal Botanical Gardens and Fawkner Park to the streets of leafy, upmarket South Yarra and Toorak and their younger, hipper neighbours Prahran and Windsor. Further south, bayside St Kilda is a busy, hedonistic hub. Chi-chi Albert Park, South Melbourne and Port Melbourne share a slice of Port Phillip Bay further to the west. Williamstown, southwest of the city at the mouth of the Yarra River, is an historic maritime town with stunning views of the Westgate Bridge and back to the city.

These are the areas we've chosen to highlight, broken down into nine neighbourhoods. Beyond these, suburbs sprawl down the bay to meet the Mornington Peninsula, to the southeast to meet the Dandenongs, the west to almost meet Geelong and to the north petering out around the airport.

CENTRAL MELBOURNE (p50)

SOUTHBANK & DOCKLANDS (p62)

EAST MELBOURNE & RICHMOND (p67)

FITZROY & AROUND (p72)

CARLTON & AROUND (p77)

SOUTH YARRA, PRAHRAN & WINDSOR (p82)

SOUTH MELBOURNE, PORT MELBOURNE & ALBERT PARK (p91)

ST KILDA & AROUND (p87)

WILLIAMSTOWN (p95)

2 km
1.0 miles

Hawthorn

Kew

Malvern

Alphington

Fairfield

Caulfield North

Armadale

Northcote

Clifton Hill

Abbotsford

Burnley

Toorak

Hawksburn

Richmond

Prahran

St Kilda East

Balaclava

Brunswick East

Fitzroy North

Collingwood

East Melbourne

Windsor

Carlton North

Fitzroy

South Yarra

St Kilda

Brunswick

Carlton

Melbourne

St Kilda West

Parkville

Southbank

South Melbourne

Albert Park Lake

Middle Park

Ponds

North Melbourne

West Melbourne

Docklands

Albert Park

Port Phillip

Flemington

Kensington

Port Melbourne

Hobsons Bay

Ascot Vale

Footscray

Maidstone

Seddon

Yarraville

Spotswood

Williamstown

West Footscray

Kingsville

Newport

Williamstown North

Altona Bay

Maribyrnong

Altona

River Yarra

Yarra River

Port Phillip

# ITINERARY BUILDER

Melbourne's compact city centre and straightforward public transport system make discovering its delights easy in just a couple of days. Do get familiar with a tram map and get your walking shoes on, but resist the urge to overschedule. Melbourne is at its best when you take it nice and slow and leave space for serendipity.

| AREA | ACTIVITIES | SIGHTS | OUTDOORS |
|---|---|---|---|
| | **Central Melbourne** | Federation Square (p50)<br>National Gallery of Victoria Australia (p50)<br>Chinatown (p55) | Birrarung Marr (p51) |
| | **Southbank & Docklands** | Eureka Tower & Skydeck 88 (p62)<br>Australian Centre for Contemporary Art (p62)<br>National Gallery of Victoria Australia (p63) | Docklands (p65) |
| | **East Melbourne & Richmond** | Melbourne Cricket Ground (p67)<br>National Sports Museum (p70)<br>Fitzroy Gardens (p70) | Melbourne & Olympic Parks (p67) |
| | **Fitzroy & Around** | Gertrude Contemporary Art Spaces (p73)<br>Collingwood Children's Farm (p72)<br>Carlton & United Breweries (p73) | Abbottsford Convent (p73)<br>Yarra Bend Park (p73) |
| | **Carlton & Around** | Melbourne Museum (p77)<br>Royal Exhibition Building (p77)<br>Royal Melbourne Zoo (p80) | Royal Park (p80) |
| | **South Yarra, Prahran & Windsor** | Royal Botanic Gardens (p82 )<br>Como House (p83 ) | Herring Island (p86)<br>Fawkner Park (p86) |
| | **St Kilda & Around** | Luna Park (p87)<br>Linden Arts Centre Gallery (p87) | St Kilda Foreshore (p89)<br>St Kilda Botanic Gardens (p89)<br>Elwood Beach (p90) |
| | **South Melbourne, Port Melbourne & Albert Park** | | Albert Park Lake (p91)<br>Station Pier (p94) |

# HOW TO USE THIS TABLE

The table below allows you to plan a day's worth of activities in any area of the city. Simply select which area you wish to explore, and then mix and match from the corresponding listings to build your day. The first item in each cell represents a well-known highlight of the area, while the other items are more off-the-beaten-track gems.

| SHOPPING | EATING | DRINKING & NIGHTLIFE |
|---|---|---|
| Queen Victoria Market (p57)<br>GPO (p58)<br>Christine (p108) | The Press Club (p129)<br>Bar Lourinhã (p131)<br>Cookie (p131) | City Wine Shop (p152)<br>Recorded Music Salon (p150)<br>Transport (p150) |
| NGV Shop (p110) | Guiseppe, Arnaldo & Sons (p133)<br>Tutto Bene (p134)<br>Bhoj (p134) | Alumbra (p152)<br>Bearbrass (p152)<br>James Squire Brewery (p152) |
| Dimmey's (p111) | Minh Minh (p135)<br>Pacific Seafood BBQ House (p135)<br>Pearl (p134) | Der Raum (p153)<br>The Corner Hotel (p153) |
| Douglas & Hope (p112)<br>Vixen (p113)<br>Title (p114) | Ladro (p136)<br>St Jude's (p135)<br>Cavallero (p136) | Gertrude St Enoteca (p155)<br>Caz Reitop's Dirty Secret (p153)<br>Labour in Vain (p153) |
| Readings (p116)<br>Poppy Shop (p117)<br>King & Godfree (p116) | D.O.C. (p138)<br>Abla's (p138)<br>Brunetti (p139) | Jimmy Watson's (p156)<br>Gerald's Bar (p156)<br>Rrose Bar (p155) |
| American Apparel (p117)<br>Chapel St Bazaar (p117)<br>TL Wood (p118) | Borsch, Vodka & Tears (p142)<br>Oriental Tea House (p142)<br>Café Veloce (p142) | Blue Bar 330 (p156)<br>Windsor Castle (p157)<br>Revolver Upstairs (p157) |
| St Kilda Esplanade Sunday Market (p120)<br>Third Drawer Down (p120)<br>Monarch Cake Shop (p120) | Mirka's at Tolarno (p139)<br>Lau's Family Kitchen (p140)<br>Baker Di Chirico (p141) | George Lane Bar (p157)<br>Prince Bandroom (p158)<br>Pause Bar (p158) |
| Avenue Books (p121)<br>Empire Vintage (p122)<br>Nest (p121) | Tempura Hajime (p143)<br>Montague Hotel (p143)<br>St Ali (p143) | Hotel Nest (p159)<br>Lina's Bistro a Vin (p159)<br>London (p159) |

# GREATER MELBOURNE

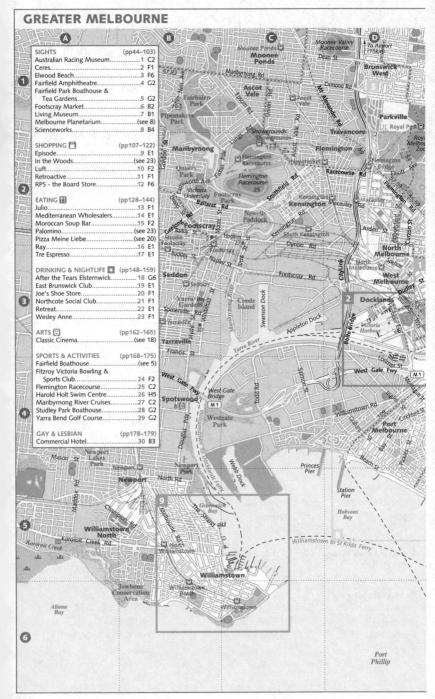

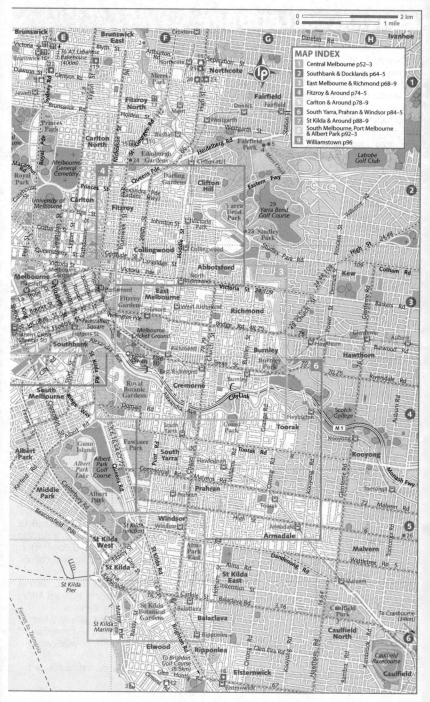

# CENTRAL MELBOURNE

Drinking & Nightlife p148; Eating p128; Shopping p106; Sleeping p182

Melbourne's city centre is unlike any other in Australia. Its wide main streets and legion of laneways pop and fizz day and night, seven days a week. The city's little streets have attracted residents and businesses from as far back as the 1850s, a decade in which Melbourne's population quadrupled. Cheap rents allowed people to build in back lanes, which took on a life of their own with the subsequent sale and subdivision of spacious blocks. Over time, lanes sprouted smaller alleys to provide access for the collection of 'night soil'. The network spread, with alleys bumping into laneways and other thoroughfares, giving rise to bridges and covered arcades. This unplanned labyrinth not only corrupted the city grid but also attracted the seedier side of the 19th-century, prim Victorian city. Romeo Lane (now Crossley St), and Juliet Tce (now Liverpool St) were bursting with brothels, and Vengeance Alley (now Kirks Lane) confirmed the existence of a criminal class. One hundred years on, they are some of the city's most loved, and hyped, attractions.

While many Melbournians still make their home in the suburbs, the city centre has an increasingly large residential population; last estimates were at around 82,000 people. The buildings at the city's heart remain relatively low-rise, lending the main shopping and entertainment areas a human scale and a gentle old-fashioned feel. There are two big ends of town; skyscrapers cluster on the east and west ends of the grid and this is where the city does business. Southern Cross Station sits to the west, with Telstra Dome and Docklands beyond. Opposite the central Flinders Street Station, Federation Square, known to one and all as Fed Square, squats beside the Yarra, and has become Melbournians' favourite gathering place.

## FEDERATION SQUARE Map pp52–3

Fed Sq; ☎ 9655 1900; www.federationsquare.com.au; cnr Flinders & Swanston Sts

Striking Federation Square, despite never-ending debate of its architectural merits, has become the place to celebrate, protest or party. Squatting by the Yarra and occupying a prominent city block, the 'square' is far from square. Its undulating forecourt of inscribed Kimberley stone echoes the town squares of Europe.

The surrounding buildings sport a reptilian skin that takes its cue from the endlessly dissecting lines of the city's grid; within are cultural heavyweights like the National Gallery of Victoria Australia (NGVA) and the Australian Centre for the Moving Image (ACMI). There's also restaurants, the thrumming Transport (p150) pub, and a few select retail outlets. At the square's edge is the subterranean Melbourne Visitor Information Centre (☺ 9am-6pm), a jam-packed resource for travellers. Fed Sq tours depart from here daily, except Sunday, at 11am and 2pm. Bookings are essential and can be made at the information centre gift shop (☎ 9928 0096).

## IAN POTTER CENTRE: NATIONAL GALLERY OF VICTORIA AUSTRALIA
Map pp52–3

NGVA; ☎ 8620 2222; www.ngv.vic.gov.au/ngv australia; ☺ 10am-5pm Tue-Sun

The Ian Potter Centre: NGV Australia was designed as a showcase of the NGV's extensive collection of Australian paintings, decorative arts, photography, prints, drawings, sculpture, fashion, textiles and jewellery.

The gallery's indigenous collection dominates the ground floor; it's given a central position often denied to Aboriginal art in institutions, and seeks to challenge ideas of the 'authentic'. There are some particularly fine examples of Papunya painting, such as the epic *Napperby Death Spirit Dreaming* (1980) by Clifford Possum Tjapaltjarri and Tim Leura Tjapaltjarri.

Upstairs there are permanent displays of colonial paintings and drawings by 19th-century Aboriginal artists. There's also the work of Heidelberg School impressionists and an extensive collection of the work of the modernist 'Angry Penguins', including Sir Sidney Nolan, Arthur Boyd, Joy Hester and Albert Tucker. The permanent collection also has some fabulous examples of the work of local midcareer artists such as Jenny Watson, Bill Henson, Howard Arkley, Tony Clark and Gordon Bennett.

Don't miss the fashion gallery, which highlights both historical and contemporary designers, usually dramatically displayed.

There is also a museum shop located here.

## AUSTRALIAN CENTRE FOR THE MOVING IMAGE Map pp52–3

ACMI; ☎ 8663 2200; www.acmi.net.au; 🕒 10am-6pm

Innovative ACMI is devoted entirely to screen-based culture and houses a screen gallery and two cinemas. Exhibitions range from blockbuster shows that highlight the work of global stars like Pixar to the latest in cutting-edge game and digital design. A new permanent gallery is set to open in early 2009 that will be dedicated to the history and future of the moving image, with a particular interest in the contributions of Australians, as well as how Australians consume and experience screen culture in all its diverse forms.

Cinephiles should look out for great minifestivals of cinema classics that run throughout the year as well as the Melbourne Cinémathèque (www.melbournecinematheque.org) screenings. ACMI's programs for young people, both film screenings and workshops, are also excellent.

## BIRRARUNG MARR Map pp52–3

**btwn Federation Sq & the Yarra River**

Featuring grassy knolls, river promenades and a thoughtful planting of indigenous flora, Birrarung Marr ('River of Mists' in Wurundjeri) is a welcome addition to Melbourne's patchwork of parks and gardens. It's also a scenic route to the Melbourne Cricket Ground (MCG) via the William Barak Bridge; the promenade runs further along to the Melbourne and Olympic Parks sporting precinct. The sculptural Federation Bells perch on the park's upper level and ring out daily (8am to 9am, 12.30pm to 1.30pm and 5pm to 6pm) with specially commissioned contemporary compositions. An old railway building in the park now hosts creative workshops for five- to 12-year-olds: ArtPlay ( ☎ 9664 7900; www.artplay.com.au) gets the kids sewing, singing, painting and puppeteering on weekends and during school holidays.

## COLLINS STREET Map pp52–3

**btwn Spring & Swanston Sts**

The top end of Collins St has long been associated with that most romanticised of European cities, Paris. Lined with plane trees, grand buildings and luxe boutiques (including Bally, Prada and Hermès), the 'Paris end' of Collins St has a certain splen-

# top picks

## FOR CHILDREN

- Children's Garden (p83) With tunnels in the rainforest, a kitchen garden and water-play area, kids and parents love this garden.
- Eastern Hill Fire Services Museum (p70) So they want to grow up to be firefighters? If they don't yet, they will after a visit to this museum.
- Collingwood Children's Farm (p72) Old MacDonald has nothing on this farm.
- Luna Park (p87) Fairy floss will fuel the hysteria of the Ferris wheel and scenic railway.
- Scienceworks (p96) Explains the mysteries of the physical world through interactive displays.
- Melbourne Zoo (p80) Sleepovers in the historic Elephants' Enclosure are offered. Roar 'n' Snore packages include three meals (BYO tent, sleeping bag and pillow) and take you behind the scenes.
- ArtPlay (left) and National Gallery of Victoria Australia (NGVA; opposite) Have art programs that often take their cues from the current show if you can't get them interested in that iconic piece of modern art.
- National Sports Museum (p70) Just walking in will get your junior champion's heart rate up.
- Ceres (p80) Kids are encouraged to participate in their environment, either through playing with the animals or via the interactive education programs on offer.
- Melbourne Museum (p77) The Children's Museum has hands-on exhibits that makes kids squeal (especially the creepy-crawly 'Bugs Alive!' exhibit).

dour, but is as much a mini 5th Avenue as a *grand boulevard*.

Straddling Russell St are two of Melbourne's historic churches. Scots' Church (www .scotschurch.com; 140 Collins St), the first Presbyterian church in Victoria, was built in the decorative Gothic style (1873); opposite is St Michael's Uniting Church (p59).

At 188 Collins St, the Athenaeum (p165), dating back to 1886, has undergone many a face-lift. The Greek goddess of wisdom, Athena, sits atop the façade, imbuing the theatre with classical gravitas. Across the road, the opulent Regent Theatre (p165) was considered one of the most lavish theatres of its kind when it was built in 1929 with the advent of the talkies. Destroyed by fire and then restored in 1945, the Regent had fallen into disrepair by the 1990s. After a

# CENTRAL MELBOURNE

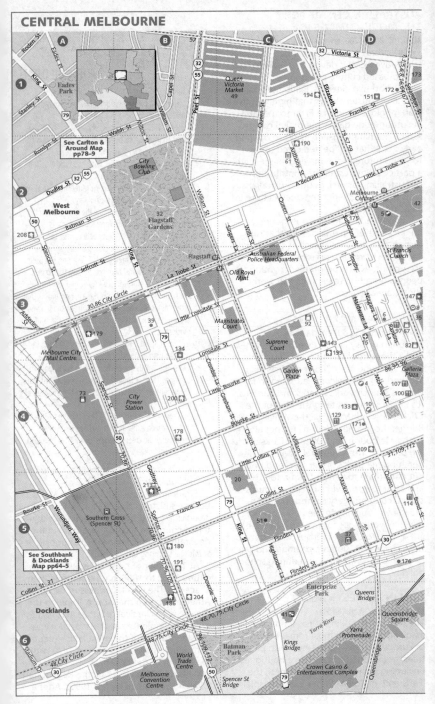

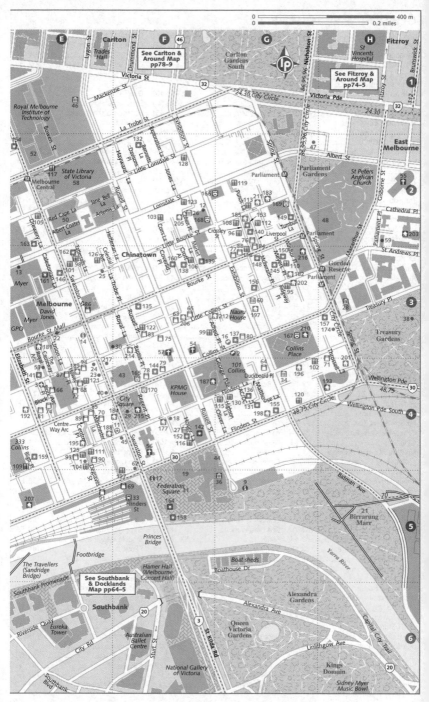

See Carlton & Around Map pp78–9

See Fitzroy & Around Map pp74–5

Carlton

Fitzroy

Carlton Gardens South

St Vincents Hospital

East Melbourne

Royal Melbourne Institute of Technology

State Library of Victoria

Melbourne Central

Chinatown

Parliament Gardens

St Peters Anglican Church

Parliament

Gordon Reserve

Parliament

St Andrews Pl

Treasury Pl

Treasury Gardens

Melbourne David Jones

Myer

GPO

Bourke St Mall

KPMG House

City Square

Centre Way Arc

Block Arc

Nauru House

Collins Place

101 Collins

Duckboard Pl

Wellington Pde

Wellington Pde South

333 Collins

Federation Square

Flinders St

Princes Bridge

Batman Ave

Birrarung Marr

The Travellers (Sandridge Bridge)

Footbridge

Hamer Hall (Melbourne Concert Hall)

See Southbank & Docklands Map pp64–5

Southbank

Southbank Promenade

Riverside Quay

Eureka Tower

Boat sheds

Boathouse Dr

Yarra River

Alexandra Gardens

Alexandra Ave

Australian Ballet Centre

City Rd

Southbank Blvd

Queen Victoria Gardens

Linlithgow Ave

National Gallery of Victoria

Kings Domain

Sidney Myer Music Bowl

0        400 m
0        0.2 miles

major refurbishment it reopened in late 1996 and is now used mainly for block-buster stage shows.

A number of Melbourne's ornate arcades lead off from Collins St. The Block network, comprising Block Pl, Block Arcade and Block Ct, was named after the 19th-century pastime of 'doing the block', which referred to walking the city's fashionable area. The Block Arcade, which runs between Collins and Elizabeth Sts, was built in 1891 and features etched-glass ceilings and mosaic floors. It houses an interesting mix of old-school and

## TRANSPORT

Flinders Street Station is the main metro train station connecting the city and suburbs. The City Loop runs under the city, linking the four corners of town.

An extensive network of tram lines covers every corner of the city, running north–south and east–west along all major roads. Trams run roughly every three minutes Monday to Friday, every 10 minutes on Saturday, and every 20 minutes on Sunday. Also worth considering is the free City Circle tram (see the boxed text, p94), which loops around town.

If you're driving and you don't luck out on a metered parking space, there are plenty of public lots available (see p345), with good after-5pm and weekend deals usually available.

contemporary retailers. Nestled between Block Arcade and Little Collins St, Block Place keeps city kids fuelled with coffee and café food. Weave your way further south through Centre Way Arcade and Centre Place, pausing to take in the street art, maybe some noodles, a drink, or a browse through a boutique.

It's down to business along the western end of Collins St. The city's financial sector begins across Elizabeth St, but the area also has some of Melbourne's best-preserved old buildings. Bankers and stockbrokers call this area home, and it's where you'll find the Australian Stock Exchange (530 Collins St).

## CHINATOWN Map pp52–3

**Little Bourke St, btwn Spring & Swanston Sts**
Chinese miners arrived in search of the 'new gold mountain' in the 1850s and settled in this strip of Little Bourke St, now flanked by traditional red archways. Many of the original 19th-century shops and warehouses remain, and you'll find an interesting mix of discount shops, streetwear retailers, bars and restaurants, including one of Melbourne's best (see Flower Drum, p129). Come here for *yum cha* (dim sum) or explore its attendant laneways for late-night dumplings or cocktails. The Chinese Museum ( ☎ 9662 2888; www.chinesemuseum.com.au;

22 Cohen Pl; adult/child $7.50/5.50; ✆ 10am-5pm) has a temple in the basement and displays of artefacts from the gold-rush era. Chinatown hosts the city's vibrant Chinese New Year celebrations (see p13).

## PARLIAMENT HOUSE Map pp52–3
☎ 9651 8911; www.parliament.vic.gov.au; Spring St
This government building's beautiful classical lines and exuberant use of ornamental plasterwork, stencilling and gilt are full of gold-rush era pride and optimism. Building began here in 1856 with the two main chambers: the lower house (now the Legislative Assembly) and the upper house (now the Legislative Council). The library was added in 1860 and Queen's Hall in 1879. The original plans for Parliament House included an enormous dome, which was deemed too costly. Plans to 'finish' the building by adding the dome in 2000 were scrapped when it was estimated that it could cost around $4 billion to build. Despite the creative compromise, this structure is one of the city's most impressive public buildings. Australia's first federal parliament sat here from 1901, before moving to Canberra in 1927. Though they've never been used, gun slits are visible just below the roof, and a dungeon is now the cleaners' tearoom.

Free half-hour tours ( ✆ weekday 10am, 11am, 2pm, 3pm, 3.45pm), held when parliament is in recess (bookings required), take you through both houses and the library. Fascinating design features and the symbolism underlying much of the ornamentation are illuminated by the knowledgeable guides. Ask about the mystery of the stolen ceremonial mace that disappeared from the lower house in 1891 – rumour has it that it ended up in a brothel. Another way to see the houses is to visit when parliament is sitting; phone or visit the website to find out when it's in session.

## MELBOURNE TOWN HALL Map pp52–3
☎ 9658 9658; www.melbourne.vic.gov.au; cnr Collins & Swanston Sts
The Melbourne Town Hall has been used as a civic and entertainment venue since 1870. Queen Elizabeth II took tea there in 1954, and the Beatles waved to thousands of screaming fans from the balcony in 1964. In 2001 the town hall's Grand Organ (built in 1929) was given an overhaul; you may want to take the free one-hour tour ( ✆ 11am & 1pm Mon-Fri) to find out exactly what having

the 'largest grand romantic organ in the southern hemisphere' actually means.

## COUNCIL HOUSE 2 Map pp52–3
CH2; ☎ 9658 9658; www.melbourne.vic.gov.au; 218-242 Little Collins St
Melbournians weren't sure what to think about the new council building as it rose from what was a carpark: was this to be yet another grey corporate box? Slowly, all was revealed, and it turned out to be iridescently, award-winningly green.

Officially opened in August 2006, CH2's design is based on 'biomimicry', reflecting the complex ecosystem of the planet. The building uses the sun, water and wind in combination with a slew of sustainable technologies. These include a basement water-mining plant, a façade of richly toned wooden louvres that track the sun (powered by photovoltaic cells), and light and dark air-circulation ducts that either absorb heat or draw in fresh air from the roof. The foyer includes a collection of specially commissioned art works, including an arresting installation by Janet Laurence, evoking the hydrology at work beneath the floor.

CH2 was built in response to meeting the council's own targets for zero carbon emissions by 2020. It's also an elegantly simple example of a building that's healthier for occupants, financially viable for owners and a lot less hungry for finite resources. Tours ( ✆ 2pm Tue & Thu) of the building leave from reception. Bookings required.

## OLD MELBOURNE GAOL Map pp52–3
☎ 8663 7228; www.oldmelbournegaol.com.au; Russell St; adult/child/family $18/9.50/44; ✆ 9.30am-5pm
This forbidding monument to 19th-century justice is now a museum. It was built of bluestone in 1841, and prisoners were locked up here until 1929. The tiny, bleak cells display plaster casts of some of the 130-plus people who were hanged here, a chilling 'byproduct' of the era's obsession with phrenology. The dire social conditions that motivated criminals in 19th-century Melbourne are also highlighted.

The last sound that legendary bushranger Ned Kelly (p24) heard was the clang of the trap here in 1880. His death mask, armour and history are on display.

For extra frisson, take a night tour by candlelight, or even stay overnight. Bookings need to be made through Ticketek (☎ 13 28 49; http://premier.ticketek.com.au; adult/under 15 $30/22.50). Evening events are not recommended for children under 12.

## QUEEN VICTORIA MARKET Map pp52–3

☎ 9320 5822; www.qvm.com.au; 513 Elizabeth St; ☾ 6am-2pm Tue & Thu, 6am-6pm Fri, 6am-3pm Sat, 9am-4pm Sun

With over 600 traders, it's the largest open-air market in the southern hemisphere and attracts thousands of shoppers. The market has been on the site for more than 130 years, prior to which it was a burial ground (see p98).

Melburnians love to shop at the 'Vic'. Fresh produce includes organics and Asian specialties, plus there are deli, meat and fish halls. Saturday mornings are particularly buzzing, with marketgoers breakfasting to the sounds and shows of buskers. Clothing and knick-knack stalls dominate on Sundays; while big on variety, don't come looking for style. If you're in the market for sheepskin moccasins you'll be in luck.

In summer the market is open on Wednesday evenings from 5.30pm to 10pm, when it features hawker-style food stalls, and music and dance performances. It also runs a variety of tours and cooking classes (see p127). Phone for details or visit the website.

## ROYAL ARCADE Map pp52–3

☎ 9670 7777; www.royalarcade.com.au; 335 Bourke St Mall

This Parisian-style arcade was built between 1869 and 1870 and is Melbourne's oldest; the upper walls retain much of the original 19th-century detail. The black-and-white chequered path leads to the mythological figures of giant brothers Gog and Magog, perched with hammers atop the arched exit to Little Collins St. They've been striking the hour here since 1892. The businesses within are a fascinating mix of the classy and the quotidian.

## STATE LIBRARY OF VICTORIA
Map pp52–3

☎ 8664 7000; www.slv.vic.gov.au; 328 Swanston St; ☾ 10am-9pm Mon-Thu, to 6pm Fri-Sun

When the library opened in 1856, people entering were required to sign the visitors' book, be over 14 years old and have clean hands. The only requirements today are

that you leave your bags in the locker room and maintain a bit of shush.

When the octagonal La Trobe Reading Room was completed in 1913, the reinforced-concrete dome was the largest of its kind in the world. Since 1959 the copper sheeting installed over the skylights had kept the room endearingly fusty. The sheeting was removed during the last round of renovations and natural light now illuminates the ornate plasterwork and suitably heavy oak desks and chairs.

The library's vast collections include hundreds of thousands of historical pictures, maps and manuscripts, and almost two million books, newspapers and serials. There are permanent and rotating exhibitions of its rare and unusual treasures, and a beautiful collection of portraits of writers and artists from throughout the 20th century (in the Cowen Gallery's south rotunda). Bookworm-chic café, Mr Tulk (☎ 8660 5700; cnr LaTrobe St & Swanston St) serves coffee, wine, meals and treats every day except Sunday.

## MELBOURNE AQUARIUM Map pp52–3

☎ 1300 882 392; www.melbourneaquarium.com.au; cnr Queenswharf Rd & King St; adult/child/family $25/15/70; ☾ 9.30am-9pm Jan, to 6pm Feb-Dec

Rays, gropers and sharks cruise around a 2.2-million-litre tank, watched closely by visitors from a see-through tunnel that traverses the aquarium floor. You can also get inside the tanks with the aid of scuba equipment, so occasionally you'll see a troupe of brave souls walking by on the other side of the glass. Spread over three levels, the complex also features jellies and coral-atoll displays, as well as a billabong display that rains intermittently. There's a theatre that hosts educational talks, and kids activities run all weekend.

## BOURKE STREET MALL Map pp52–3

btwn Swanston & Elizabeth Sts

West of Swanston St marks the beginning of the Bourke St Mall. This pedestrian mall unusually includes two tram tracks; don't worry, they'll ding if you get in the way. The mall is thick with the sounds of Peruvian bands busking, shop-front spruikers and the general hubbub from shoppers. The expansive entrances of the mall's main department stores, Myer and David Jones, consume waves of eager shoppers, regurgitating them some time later with signature shopping bags.

## QV Map pp52-3

**www.qv.com.au; cnr Lonsdale & Russell Sts**
Taking up a whole city block, this development is on the site of the old Queen Victoria Women's Hospital. It's a medley of apartments, and commercial and retail space designed by three different architects to give the impression that the block was built up over time. It's both parody and homage to the city itself, with artificial laneways and arcades. The complex's retail residents comprise supermarkets, restaurants (including chocolate-maker Max Brenner), a food court and some interesting, edgy stores such as TL Wood, Cactus Jam (p108), Christensen Copenhagen and Aesop.

## GPO Map pp52-3

☎ 9663 0066; www.melbournesgpo.com; cnr Bourke & Elizabeth Sts; 10am-6pm Mon-Thu & Sat, 10am-8pm Fri, 11am-5pm Sun
This was once simply somewhere you went to buy a stamp, but a postfire restoration and subsequent reinvention has made for an airy, atmospheric place to window shop along its gallerias. The top floor houses fashion heavyweights, while the mid- and lower floors have a smattering of interesting Melbourne designers as well as some global chains. There is also a collection of casual eating options in the side alley, and on the top floor, a rather over-the-top bar.

## MELBOURNE CENTRAL Map pp52-3

**www.melbournecentral.com.au; La Trobe St**
This shopping centre complex (with 300 stores, a cinema complex, bars and eateries) subsumed a number of Melbourne's arcades and alleyways when it was built. It also houses a lead shot tower dating from 1889. The old brick chimney props incongruously beneath a great glass pyramid, a staid structure in a fast-moving retail environment. Ironically, the centre's most recent redevelopment re-created the alleyways and arcades over which it was built only a decade or so before. New lanes, made to look old with bluestones, create café and retail precincts. It can be fiendishly noisy, confusing and characterless, but the scores of students who shop, eat and socialise here don't seem to mind.

## CITY LIGHTS Map pp52-3

☎ 9663 0442; www.citylightsproject.com; Centre Place & Hosier Lane

Melbourne's rep for street art is not just a recent thing. The City Lights Project has been shining away for over a decade. Lightboxes are installed in a small alcove off Centre Place (look for the creperie, then down the alley opposite) and along Hosier Lane (also famous for its densely applied stencil work). Local and international artists make use of the illuminated minigalleries; view them 24/7. The project's main man Andrew Mac has also opened a more traditional gallery space, Until Never (2nd fl, 3-5 Hosier Lane, enter from Rutledge Lane; ⏰ noon-6pm Wed-Sat); it highlights underground artists and is an interesting bridge between the two scenes.

## RIALTO TOWERS OBSERVATION DECK Map pp52-3

☎ 9629 8222; www.melbournedeck.com.au; 525 Collins St; adult/child/family $14.50/8/39.50; ⏰ 10am-10pm
The Rialto was once the highest building in the southern hemisphere and, until recently, the city's highest building – pipped in 2006 by the Eureka Tower (which also has an observation floor; see p62). The tower's most distinctive feature is its semi-reflective glass exterior, which changes colour as the sun tracks across the sky. The observation deck is on the 55th floor. There's 1254 steps or 25km/h lifts. The lookout platform provides a spectacular 360-degree view of Melbourne's surrounds – a great way to get your bearings. The entry fee includes a 20-minute video screening.

## CITY MUSEUM AT OLD TREASURY Map pp52-3

☎ 9651 2233; www.citymuseummelbourne.org; Spring St; adult/concession/family $8.50/5/18; ⏰ 9am-5pm Mon-Fri, 10am-4pm Sat & Sun
The fine neo-classical architecture of the Old Treasury, built in 1862, is a telling mix of hubris and functionality. Remarkably, the designer, JJ Clark, was an 19-year-old government draftsman who also designed the City Baths (p175). The huge basement vaults were built to house the millions of pounds worth of loot that came from the Victorian goldfields. Now home to the City Museum, the Treasury features three permanent exhibitions. *Making Melbourne* brings together a collection of objects arranged in a chronological fashion to tell Melbourne's story. *Built on Gold* offers up some rather sketchy interpretive multi-

media in the vaults themselves. *Growing Up in the Old Treasury* is a straightforward but charmingly redolent reconstruction of the 1920s' caretaker's residence. It beautifully reveals what life in Melbourne was like in the early part of last century. Particularly telling is one of the children's recollections that they were forbidden to go into Fitzroy Gardens because it was full of drunks, and that the city was deathly quiet at night and on a Sunday.

The adjacent Treasury Gardens to the south contain the John F Kennedy Memorial. It's a relaxing place for a break from sightseeing.

## IMMIGRATION MUSEUM Map pp52–3

☎ 9927 2700; http://immigration.museum.vic.gov.au; 400 Flinders St; adult/child $6/free; ⏱ 10am-5pm
The Immigration Museum uses personal and community voices, images and memorabilia to tell the many stories of immigration. Symbolically housed in the old Customs House (1858–70), the restored building alone is worth the visit; its most important space, the Long Room, is a magnificent piece of Renaissance revival architecture. The 2nd-floor galleries host a range of excellent temporary exhibitions exploring social and cultural issues, such as various multiethnic rituals surrounding death or preparing food.

## ST PATRICK'S CATHEDRAL Map pp52–3

☎ 9662 2233; www.melbourne.catholic.org.au/cathedral; cnr Gisborne St & Cathedral Pl; ⏱ 8am-6pm, closes at noon on public holidays
One of the world's largest and finest examples of Gothic Revival architecture, St Patrick's Cathedral was designed by William Wardell. It was named after the patron saint of Ireland, reflecting the local Catholic community's main origin. Building began in 1863 and continued until the spires were added in 1939. The imposing bluestone exterior and grounds are but a preview of its contents: inside are several tonnes of bells, an organ with 4500 pipes, ornate stained-glass windows and the remains of former archbishops. It has been visited by two popes, Paul VI in 1970 and John Paul II in 1986.

## ST PAUL'S CATHEDRAL Map pp52–3

☎ 9653 4333; www.stpaulscathedral.org.au; cnr Flinders & Swanston Sts; ⏱ 8am-6pm Sun-Fri, to 5pm Sat
Opposite Federation Square stands the Anglican St Paul's Cathedral. Services were celebrated on this site from the city's first days. Built between 1880 and 1891, the present church is the work of distinguished ecclesiastical architect William Butterfield. It was a case of architecture by proxy, as he did not condescend to visit Melbourne, instead sending drawings from England. It features ornate stained-glass windows (made between 1887 and 1890) and holds excellent music programs. In summer it's open to 6pm daily.

## ST MICHAEL'S UNITING CHURCH

Map pp52–3
☎ 9654 5120; www.stmichaels.org.au; 120 Collins St; ⏱ 10.30am-1.30pm Mon- Sat
St Michael's was designed by Joseph Reed (who also designed the Melbourne Town Hall and the Royal Exhibition Building) in 1866. He chose an unusual Lombardic style, with intricate polychrome brickwork exteriors, open cloisters and sequences of Romanesque arches. The interior is no less striking; it's a theatrelike space with sloping floors and a semicircular gallery. Despite its heritage pedigree, the church's current community is known for its ultraprogressive theology, inclusiveness and positive psychology programs.

On the Russell St side of the church is Mingary ( ⏱ 8am-5pm Mon-Fri, to 1pm Sun), a striking and serene nondenominational 'quiet space' for meditation or contemplation.

## KOORIE HERITAGE TRUST Map pp52–3

☎ 8622 2600; www.koorieheritagetrust.com; 295 King St; entry by gold-coin donation, tours $6; ⏱ 10am-4pm Tue-Sun
This cultural centre is devoted to southeastern Aboriginal culture. There are gallery spaces showing a variety of contemporary and traditional work, a model scar tree at the centre's heart, as well as a permanent chronological display of Victorian Koorie history that is as moving as it is informative.

Behind the scenes, significant objects are carefully preserved; replicas that can be touched by visitors are used in the displays. There's also a shop with books, CDs, crafts and bush-food supplies.

## FLINDERS STREET STATION Map pp52–3

Cnr Flinders & Swanston Sts
Melbourne's first railway station, Flinders Street was built in 1854. Two railway workers won the design tender. This

might explain why the station contained such fabulous facilities for railway workers, now, sadly, in disrepair. In its heyday the building buzzed with a concert hall, a library, a crèche, meeting rooms, even a ballroom.

Stretching along the Yarra for a block, the station is a city landmark. You'd be hard pressed to find a Melburnian who hasn't uttered 'meet me under the clocks' at one time. On any weekday, well over 100,000 people weave through the station's underpasses, escalators, stairs and platforms. The grand old dame's underground tendrils connect the city's north with its south, with art-filled underpasses (such as Campbell Arcade) linked to Southbank via a pedestrian bridge.

### YOUNG & JACKSON'S Map pp52–3

☎ 9650 3884; www.youngandjacksons.com.au; cnr Flinders & Swanston Sts

Across the street from Flinders Street Station you'll find the city's most iconic pub. Apart from the fact that it's been continuously serving beer here since 1861, it's known for the painting that graces the wall upstairs. *Chloe,* painted by Jules Joseph Lefebvre, is an academic-style painting of a naked young woman with luminous skin and dark hair. Her yearning gaze, cast over her shoulder and out of the frame, was a hit at the Paris Salon of 1875. The painting caused an outcry in the pursed-lipped provincial Melbourne, however, and was removed from display at the National Gallery of Victoria. Eventually bought by publican and 'art lover'

Henry Figsby Young in 1909, *Chloe* found an appreciative audience and permanent home at the pub. She was worshipped by the soldiers and sailors who frequented the pub during both world wars. The pub literature poignantly notes that Chloe was often the last (or only) naked woman many saw before meeting death on the battlefield.

### AUSTRALIAN RACING MUSEUM

Map pp48–9

☎ 1300 139 407; www.racingmuseum.com.au; 400 Epsom Rd, Flemington; adult/child/concession $9/free/5; 🕙 10am-6pm

Not November? Never mind; trackgoers can sample some Spring Racing fervour at this museum dedicated to thoroughbred horses, jockeys and trainers. Exhibits cover the history of racing and reverently trumpet the social and cultural importance of the sport in Australia. The line up of Melbourne Cups is a fascinating look at changing tastes.

### NATIONAL DESIGN CENTRE Map pp52–3

NDC; ☎ 9654 6335; www.nationaldesigncentre.com; Federation Sq, cnr Russell & Flinders Sts; 🕙 10am-5pm Mon-Fri, noon-5pm Sat & Sun

The rather ambitiously named NDC (it's actually a privately run affair) comprises a retail shop and the ShowBox gallery space, and showcases excellent work from local and international designers. The centre also hosts workshops and events, including the annual Melbourne Design Festival, held in July.

## WORTH A TRIP: FOOTSCRAY & YARRAVILLE

The city's remaining working docklands divide the western suburbs from the city. Although the distance is not great, the interstitial landscape of containers and their attendant machinery is otherworldly enough to create a strong sense of separateness. The suburbs beyond here have long been proudly working class, though this has changed in the last 10 years, with many young professional families taking advantage of the area's cute cottages and community feel.

The area's 'capital' is the fabulously unfussy Footscray. Over 40% of Footscray's resident population was born outside Australia, the majority in Vietnam, Africa, China, Italy and Greece. The areas around Barkly St bring those in search of Vietnamese and East African cooking and produce. The Footscray Market (Map pp48–9; ☎ 9687 1205; cnr Hopkins & Leeds St; 🕙 7am-4pm Tue, Wed & Sat, to 6pm Thu, to 8pm Fri) is testament to the area's diversity.

Heading south from Footscray, are the newly fashionable residential neighbourhoods of Seddon and Yarraville. Yarraville centres on its train station, with a beautifully well-preserved heritage shopping area around Anderson St; it also boasts some great restaurants, bars and cafés.

For those interested in the west's unique history, head to the Living Museum (Map pp48–9; ☎ 9318 3544; www.livingmuseum.org.au; Pipemakers Park, Van Ness Ave, Maribyrnong; admission free; 🕙 10am-4pm Mon-Fri, 11am-4pm Sun), set in the grounds of Pipemakers Park, featuring a wetlands area and indigenous gardens.

## TASMA TERRACE Map pp52–3
**Parliament Pl**
The three-storey, grey-stuccoed terraces comprising Tasma Terrace were built in 1879 and designed by Charles Webb, who also designed the famous Windsor Hotel (p183). These are one of Melbourne's finest Victorian terrace rows, with exquisite cast-iron verandas and a restrained ecclesiastical air. They are owned by the National Trust ( ☎ 9656 9800; www.nationaltrust.org.au) – an organisation dedicated to preserving historically significant buildings across the state – which has its offices here.

## FLAGSTAFF GARDENS Map pp52–3
**btwn La Trobe, William, Dudley & King Sts**
These small gardens with open lawn are popular with workers taking a lunchtime break. There's a rose garden, children's playground, barbecues and a lawn-bowling green.

First known as Burial Hill, this is where most of the city's early settlers ended up. The hill once provided one of the best views out to the bay, so a signalling station was set up here; when a ship was sighted arriving from Britain, a flag was raised on the flagstaff to notify the settlers (it was also significant for the Wurundjeri for the same useful vista). The gardens contain many trees that are well over 100 years old. These include Moreton Bay fig trees, and a variety of eucalypts, including spotted and sugar gums and at least one river red gum.

## ANNA SCHWARTZ GALLERY
Map pp52–3
☎ 9654 6131; www.annaschwartzgallery.com; 185 Flinders Lane; ◷ noon-6pm Tue-Fri, 1-5pm Sat
Redoubtable Anna Schwartz keeps some of the city's most respected contemporary artists in her stable, as well as representing midcareer names from around the country. The gallery is your standard white cube – the work is often fiercely conceptual.

## GALLERY GABRIELLE PIZZI Map pp52–3
☎ 9654 2944; www.gabriellepizzi.com.au; 3rd fl, 75-77 Flinders Lane; ◷ 10am-5.30pm Tue-Fri, 1-5pm Sat
Gabrielle Pizzi, one of Australia's most respected dealers of indigenous art, ran this Flinders Lane stalwart from the 1980s until her death in 2004. Her daughter has continued her work and shows contemporary city-based artists such as Julie Gough and Leah King-Smith, as well as traditional artists from the communities of Balgo Hills, Papunya, Utopia, Maningrida, Haasts Bluff, and the Tiwi Islands.

## TOLARNO GALLERY Map pp52–3
☎ 9654 6000; www.tolarnogalleries.com; 4th fl, 104 Exhibition St; ◷ 10am-5pm Tue-Fri, 1-5pm Sat
Tolarno was an integral player in Melbourne's most famous midcentury marriage between Georges and Mirka Mora. Once raucously bohemian, now many years and several sites later, it's a serious, cerebral contemporary space with a very diverse and well-regarded stable of artists. The location, on the corner of Flinders Lane, is quite special.

## WESTSPACE Map pp52–3
☎ 9328 8712; www.westspace.org.au; 15-19 Anthony St; admission free; ◷ noon-6pm Wed-Fri, to 5pm Sat
One of Melbourne's oldest artist-run galleries, Westspace has a varied exhibition program. It's on the 1st floor of a 1940s' light-industrial building and features young and emerging artists working in a range of mediums from traditional forms to digital technologies and installation.

# SOUTHBANK & DOCKLANDS

Drinking & Nightlife p152; Eating p133; Shopping p110; Sleeping p188

These riverside locales were once gritty industrial areas but they've now taken up the hard yakka of leisure. Southbank sits directly across the Yarra from Flinders St. Southgate, the first cab off the redevelopment rank, is an airy shopping mall with fabulous views and an eclectic mix of shops, bars and restaurants. Behind here you'll find the city's major arts precinct; the NGV International, Arts Centre and various other arts bodies such as the Australian Ballet. Back down by the river, the promenade stretches to the Crown Casino & Entertainment Complex, a self-proclaimed 'world of entertainment', where the bread and circuses pull in visitors 24/7. To the city's west lies Docklands. The once working wharves of Victoria Harbour have given birth to a new minicity of apartment buildings and smart-offices, restaurant plazas, public art and parkland. It's early days, but its manufactured sameness has yet to be overwritten with the organic cadences and colour of neighbourhood life. But the views are quite something.

## AUSTRALIAN CENTRE FOR CONTEMPORARY ART Map pp64–5

ACCA; ☎ 9697 9999; www.accaonline.org.au; 111 Sturt St; admission free; ☼ 10am-5pm Tue-Fri, 11am-6pm Sat & Sun

The ACCA is one of Australia's most exciting and challenging contemporary galleries. Shows include work specially commissioned for the space. The gallery shows a range of local and international artists. The building is fittingly sculptural, with a deeply rusted exterior evoking the factories that once stood on the site, and a slick, soaring, ever-adapting interior designed to house often massive installations.

## CROWN CASINO & ENTERTAINMENT COMPLEX Map pp64–5

☎ 9292 8888; www.crowncasino.com.au; Southbank

The Crown Entertainment Complex sprawls across two city blocks and includes the enormous luxury Crown Towers (p188), the four-star Crown Promenade (p188) and Crown Casino, with over 300 tables and 2500 gaming machines open 24/7. Time is apparently irrelevant at the casino, which has no clocks and no natural light.

## TRANSPORT

Train Southern Cross Station

Tram Any tram running south across the river from Swanston St will drop you off at Southbank attractions. The 1 to South Melbourne turns right at NGVI and is handy for ACCA and the Malthouse Theatre. The 86 tram down Bourke St runs to Docklands and Telstra Dome.

Thrown in for good measure are waterfalls, fireballs, a giant cinema complex, a bowling alley, a variety of nightclubs and a 900-seat showroom. The complex is also home to a handful of luxury retailers, chain stores and specialty shops, as well as bars, cafés and a food hall. Restaurants here range from the perfunctory to the sublime, with several major culinary players stretched out along the river (see the boxed text, p134).

## EUREKA TOWER & SKYDECK 88 Map pp64–5

☎ 9693 8888; www.eurekaskydeck.com.au; Riverside Quay, Southbank; adult/child/family $16.50/9/39, The Edge extra $12/8/29; ☼ 10am-10pm (last entry 9.30pm)

Eureka Tower, built in 2006, is currently the world's tallest apartment building. The stats? Ninety-two storeys over 300m. Take a wild elevator ride to the top: 88 floors in less than 40 seconds. If you still haven't found what you're looking for, more vertiginous views are to be had. 'The Edge' – not a member of U2, but a slightly sadistic glass cube – propels you out of the building; you've got no choice but to look down.

## POLLY WOODSIDE MARITIME MUSEUM Map pp64–5

☎ 9656 9800; www.pollywoodside.com.au; Lorimer St E, Southbank

At the time of writing, the museum was temporarily closed as part of the refurbishment of the Melbourne Exhibition and Convention Centre precinct. The revamped visitors centre is due to reopen in early 2009. The *Polly Woodside* herself, a restored iron-hulled merchant ship dating from 1885, is still on view from the river and beyond.

Once described as the 'prettiest barque ever built in Belfast', a glimpse of her rigging makes for a tiny reminder of what the Yarra would have looked like in the 19th century, dense with ships at anchor.

## MELBOURNE EXHIBITION CENTRE
Map pp64–5

☎ 9235 8000; www.mecc.com.au; 2 Clarendon St This multipurpose venue hosts conventions, trade shows and public events from bridal shows to Sexpo. Check the calendar on its website for upcoming events. New 5000-seat convention facilities are set to open early in 2009.

## NATIONAL GALLERY OF VICTORIA INTERNATIONAL Map pp64–5

NGVI; ☎ 8620 2222; www.ngv.vic.gov.au; 180 St Kilda Rd; admission free; ◷ 10am-5pm Wed-Mon Beyond the water wall you'll find international art that runs from the ancient to the contemporary. Given Australia's size and isolation, don't expect the collection to rival its European or North American counterparts. But it does have some wonderful pieces and you won't be fighting crowds to see them. Key works include a Rembrandt, a Tiepolo and a Bonnard. You might also bump into a Monet and a Modigliani, a Bacon or a Rubens. The gallery also has an excellent decorative arts collection, with pieces from the late Middle Ages to the present day.

Apart from a range of temporary shows highlighting the collection, this is also the place where visiting international blockbuster shows are hung; crowds for these are huge and the queues long. As well as talks and film screenings, the gallery usually has weekly late-night viewings for these major shows; the mood can be quite festive.

Completed in 1967, the original NGV building – Roy Grounds' 'cranky icon' – was one of Australia's most controversial but ultimately respected Modernist masterpieces. It was designed with a strict geometry and clear circulation patterns, and made extensive use of wood, glass and blue stone. To deal with 30-odd years of wear and tear and the need for more flexible exhibition spaces, interior remodelling was undertaken from 1996 to 2003, overseen by Mario Bellini. The new labyrinthine design does away with the stark simplicity of the

## BUNJIL

As you drive on one of many roads surrounding Docklands, or catch a train to or from Southern Cross Station, you can't miss Eagle. Let's just say this bird has presence. Local sculptor Bruce Armstrong was inspired by the figure of Bunjil, the Wurundjeri creator spirit. The cast aluminium bird contentedly rests on a mammoth jarrah perch, confidently surveying all around with a serene glassy gaze. He's a reminder of the wordless natural world, scaled to provide a gentle parody of the surrounding cityscape's attempted domination. Upon unveiling, a journalist did have the cheek to call him 'a bulked-up budgerigar' but most Melburnians now see him as the city's true mascot.

original but retains key features such as the water wall, Leonard French's stained-glass ceiling of the Great Hall and the austere exterior.

The Australian art collection is on display at the Ian Potter Centre: NGVA (p50) at nearby Federation Square.

## SOUTHGATE Map pp64–5

www.southgate-melbourne.com.au; Southbank Southgate was the first shopping and dining complex built along the south bank of the Yarra, replacing billowing chimney-stacks and saw-toothed factories. The complex joined its illustrious Southbank neighbours (the Arts Centre, Australian Ballet and Opera Australia) in the early '90s. Southgate is well connected to the city via an arched footbridge, and riverside promenades run all the way west to the casino complex (opposite).

You'll find restaurants and cafés among the three levels of dining rooms that all enjoy a stellar outlook over the river and city. (Quality ranges from some of the city's best to those simply after the tourist dollar.) Night transforms the skyline, with spotlights, coloured neons and grids of illuminated office-block windows beyond the inky Yarra; it's a view for hopeless romantics and cityphiles alike. There's an international food hall on the ground floor, as well as boutiques and a collection of specially commissioned sculptures and other artworks. Nearby, check out the the Travellers along the Sandridge Bridge, a series of sculptures depicting the story of arrival that belongs to the many Melburnians of immigrant background.

A number of boat operators are stationed outside Southgate should you want to hail a water taxi (p344) to take you to the sporting precinct or cruise over to Williamstown (p95).

## VICTORIAN ARTS CENTRE Map pp64–5
☎ 9281 8000; www.theartscentre.com.au; 100 St Kilda Rd

The Arts Centre is made up of two separate buildings: the concert hall and the theatres building, linked by a series of landscaped walkways.

Hamer Hall is the circular building closest to the Yarra. It's a favoured performance venue for symphonic concerts, choirs and chamber music. Most of the hall is below ground (resting in Yarra mud so corrosive that a system of electrified

cables is needed to prevent deterioration). The Theatres Building wears the distinctive spire and houses the State Theatre, the Playhouse and the George Fairfax Studio. Both buildings feature works by prominent Australian artists, and in the Theatres Building the George Adams Gallery and St Kilda Road Foyer Gallery are free gallery spaces with changing exhibitions. The Famous Spiegeltent occupies the Theatres Building forecourt each summer. One of the last of the great Belgian mirror tents, the Spiegel comes to town for the International Arts Festival, staging cabaret, live music and afternoon talks.

There are one-hour tours of the complex (adult/concession/family $11/7.50/27.50) at 11am on Monday to Saturday. On Sunday you can visit backstage at 12.15pm

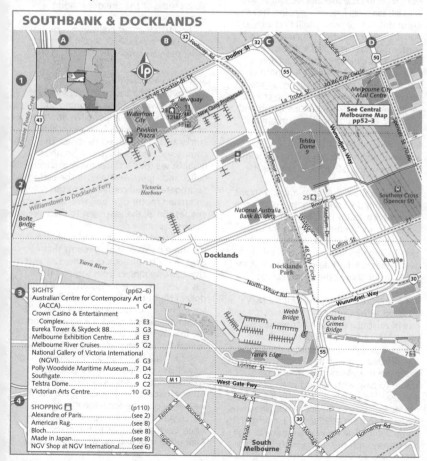

## SOUTHBANK & DOCKLANDS

| SIGHTS | (pp62–6) |
| --- | --- |
| Australian Centre for Contemporary Art (ACCA) | 1 G4 |
| Crown Casino & Entertainment Complex | 2 E3 |
| Eureka Tower & Skydeck 88 | 3 G3 |
| Melbourne Exhibition Centre | 4 E3 |
| Melbourne River Cruises | 5 G2 |
| National Gallery of Victoria International (NGVI) | 6 G3 |
| Polly Woodside Maritime Museum | 7 D4 |
| Southgate | 8 G2 |
| Telstra Dome | 9 C2 |
| Victorian Arts Centre | 10 G3 |

| SHOPPING | (p110) |
| --- | --- |
| Alexandre of Paris | (see 2) |
| American Rag | (see 8) |
| Bloch | (see 8) |
| Made in Japan | (see 8) |
| NGV Shop at NGV International | (see 6) |

($13.50, 1½ hours). Children under 12 years are not allowed in the backstage area.

The Arts Centre undercroft shelters an arts and crafts market every Sunday from 10am to 5pm. Around 150 stalls peddle everything from kaleidoscopes to soaps. Across the way in the Kings Domain is the Sidney Myer Music Bowl, a summer venue with a stage that's been graced by everyone from Dame Kiri to the Asian Dub Foundation.

The small section of park across St Kilda Rd from the Victorian Arts Centre is the rather endearingly retro Queen Victoria Gardens, which contain a memorial statue of the good queen herself, a statue of Edward VII astride his horse, and a huge floral clock.

## DOCKLANDS Map pp64–5

☎ 1300 663 008; www.docklands.vic.gov.au

This waterfront area was the city's main industrial and docking area until the mid-1960s. Demand for larger berths to accommodate modern cargo vessels necessitated a move, leaving the former docklands high and (almost) dry. Its redevelopment as Docklands began in 1996. It's the latest of Melbourne's cities within the city, designed with 'precincts' for certain types of activity. Among them are film and TV studios, a technology-based company hub, and residential, retail and entertainment areas. Of most interest to travellers is the first-born, New Quay, with public art, promenades and a wide variety of cafés and restaurants. Waterfront City also has restaurants, bars, a yacht club and will

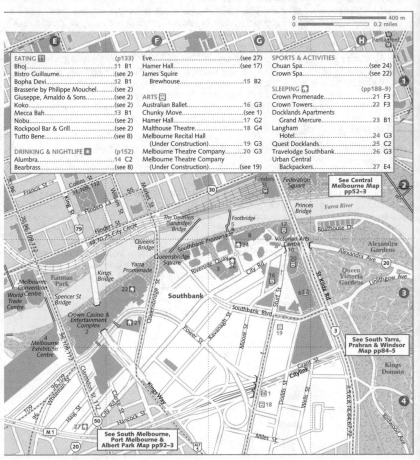

| EATING 🍴 | (p133) |
|---|---|
| Bhoj | 11 B1 |
| Bistro Guillaume | (see 2) |
| Bopha Devi | 12 B1 |
| Brasserie by Philippe Mouchel | (see 2) |
| Giuseppe, Arnaldo & Sons | (see 2) |
| Koko | (see 2) |
| Mecca Bah | 13 B1 |
| Nobu | (see 2) |
| Rockpool Bar & Grill | (see 2) |
| Tutto Bene | (see 8) |

| DRINKING & NIGHTLIFE 🍸 | (p152) |
|---|---|
| Alumbra | 14 C2 |
| Bearbrass | (see 8) |

| Eve | (see 27) |
|---|---|
| Hamer Hall | (see 17) |
| James Squire Brewhouse | 15 B2 |

| ARTS 🎭 | |
|---|---|
| Australian Ballet | 16 G3 |
| Chunky Move | (see 1) |
| Hamer Hall | 17 G2 |
| Malthouse Theatre | 18 G4 |
| Melbourne Recital Hall (Under Construction) | 19 G3 |
| Melbourne Theatre Company | 20 G3 |
| Melbourne Theatre Company (Under Construction) | (see 19) |

| SPORTS & ACTIVITIES | |
|---|---|
| Chuan Spa | (see 24) |
| Crown Spa | (see 22) |

| SLEEPING 🛏 | (pp188–9) |
|---|---|
| Crown Promenade | 21 F3 |
| Crown Towers | 22 F3 |
| Docklands Apartments Grand Mercure | 23 B1 |
| Langham Hotel | 24 G3 |
| Quest Docklands | 25 C2 |
| Travelodge Southbank | 26 G3 |
| Urban Central Backpackers | 27 E4 |

## THE YARRA *Kristin Otto*

Australia's breakfast, Australia's beer, Australia's cars and Australia's art all came from the banks of the Yarra. Weet-bix were made with Yarra catchment hydropower upstream in Warburton, Foster's Lager is brewed at Abbotsford, General Motors Holdens are made at Fishermans Bend, and what's known as the Heidelberg School of painters brilliantly captured Australia's colours. A gold rush ran by the Yarra River in Warrandyte and Warburton. Nineteenth-century water diversions can still be seen; the biggest is the Pound Bend tunnel, in suburban Warrandyte. Some of Melbourne's most famous lunatics and criminals have 'gone round the bend' of it. This phrase refers to someone going mad: Melbourne's mental asylums were around the bend of the river in Kew, and Fairfield. The occasional body and guns have been dumped in it.

The Yarra has given Melbourne some of the best drinking water on the planet, and also the worst, concurrently at times. The locked-up headwater catchments of the city's water supply contained the tallest trees in the world and still produce pristine water. Way downstream in the late 19th century, Marvellous Melbourne was renamed Marvellous Smellbourne. The Yarra was one of the filthiest rivers in the world, receiving the outfall of abattoirs and tanneries, as well as the unsewered city's human waste. Even in the 20th century the public utility responsible for the river saw it as the number-one drain. The changes have been dramatic, with people now living by the river in apartments on what were once such factory sites.

Melbourne was founded exactly where it was because of the Yarra. The Turning Basin, opposite the Casino and Southbank, is an urban design reinstatement of what was once a natural pool or widening of the river below a shallow set of falls. The falls separated the saltwater below from the freshwater above with its constant supply of drinking water. In 1835 the north bank of the pool was an ideal spot to moor and settle. The falls were blown away in the 1880s when Queens Bridge was built, making the saltwater barrier Dights Falls, upstream in Kew/Collingwood.

Once there were billabongs all along the river from the mountains to the sea, with saltwater wetlands below the falls. A billabong is a naturally cut-off bend of the river that fills and empties with the floods and droughts. The largest, where Docklands is now, was as big as the central city grid of Melbourne itself. Most have been filled in, though you can still in high-water times see a few in the suburban area, such as Willsmere, Kew. Particularly important sites were those used by the Wurundjeri, the original inhabitants of Melbourne, for large gatherings. 'Yarra' is derived from the word for 'Flow'. The billabong that became part of the Botanic Gardens ornamental lake was described as a 'veritable Garden of Eden'. The Yarra has been shifted in several locations, such as there. In the early 20th century, several kilometres were rerouted right near Lonely Planet's present offices.

*Extract from* Yarra: a Diverting History of Melbourne's Murky River © *Kristin Otto, 2005. Used by permission of Text Publishing.*

be the site of a London Eye–style observation wheel. Yarra's Edge also has a growing number of retailers and restaurants.

The docks boast world-class marinas, and several boat tours ply the waters around here shuttling up the Yarra to Southbank; check the website for a full listing.

**TELSTRA DOME** Map pp64–5
☎ 8625 7700; Bourke St, Docklands;
www.telstradome.com.au

Upstart Telstra Dome is never going to live up to the MCG in terms of atmosphere or classic design, but it's a well-used, comfortable and easy-to-access sports arena, seating 52,000 for a range of Australian Rules Football games, Melbourne Victory soccer matches and the odd Rugby Union test. Behind-the-scenes tours ( ☎ 8625 7277; adult/child/concession/family $14/7/11/37) of the venue are available Monday to Friday at 11am, 1pm and 3pm, subject to events.

# EAST MELBOURNE & RICHMOND

Drinking & Nightlife p152; Eating p134; Shopping p111; Sleeping p189

Beyond its Wellington St artery, East Melbourne's sedate wide streets are lined with grand double-fronted Victorian terraces, Italianate mansions and Art Deco apartment blocks. Locals here commute to the city by foot, across the Fitzroy Gardens. During the footy season or when a cricket match is played, the roar of the crowd shatters the calm; you're in lobbing distance of the MCG.

Sports fans will become pretty cosy with Yarra Park – Melbourne's main sporting precinct, attracting thousands of adoring fans every year to its many world-class arenas and ovals. A footbridge over the railway line links the granddaddy of 'em all, the MCG, with Melbourne and Olympic Parks.

This area swarms at weekends when people come from far and wide to watch everything from Australian Rules football, cricket, athletics and cycling to marathon dance championships. Various arenas also host weekend-long dance parties and big-name international concerts. That said, the area offers little to a visitor unless you are here for some kind of event.

Across the perpetually clogged arterial of Punt Rd/Hoddle St is the suburb of Richmond, which stretches all the way to the Yarra. It was once a raggle-taggle collection of workers' cottages inhabited by generations of labourers, who toiled in the tanneries, clothing-manufacturing and food-processing industries. It is now rather genteel, although it retains a fair swag of solid, regular pubs and is home to a thriving Vietnamese community along the Victoria St strip. Here you'll find restaurants and grocers, herbalists and karaoke bars. Bridge Rd and Swan St are known for their outlet stores; see the shoppers swarm seven days a week. Richmond's main south–north thoroughfare is Church St, with furniture stores and other associated businesses. Northwards, past the former Bryant & May matchstick factory, and over the railway, it ascends to Richmond Hill, which boasts some of Melbourne's finest Victorian terraces. Swan St is a jumble of food outlets, shops and pubs. Its proximity to the MCG sees thousands trekking along here on match days seeking a postgame ale and a sympathetic ear as the day's play is dissected.

## MELBOURNE & OLYMPIC PARKS
Map pp68–9

☎ 9286 1600; www.mopt.com.au; Batman Ave; 🚇 Jolimont, 🚋 48, 75

Stages at these big-event stadiums morph to accommodate everything from rockgods to cyclists to comedy galas. Melbourne Park comprises Hisense Arena, the multipurpose venue with a retractable roof, and Rod Laver Arena. The Australian Open Tennis takes over the whole complex in January. Daily tours of the Rod Laver Arena (adult/child/family $13/6/30) take you to the dressing rooms, VIP areas and Superboxes.

Olympic Park includes Olympic Stadium, hosting athletics and home to local rugby league team the Melbourne Storm, as well as the Lexus Centre, home to the Collingwood Football Club and Victorian Institute of Sport.

## MELBOURNE CRICKET GROUND
Map pp68–9

MCG; ☎ 9657 8888; www.mcg.org.au; Brunton Ave; 🚇 Jolimont, 🚋 48, 75

It's one of the world's great sporting venues, and for many Australians the 'G' is considered hallowed ground.

In 1858 the first game of Aussie Rules football was played where the MCG and its car parks now stand, and in 1877 it was the venue for the first Test cricket match between Australia and England. The MCG was also the central stadium for the 1956 Melbourne Olympics and the 2006 Commonwealth Games. It recently underwent the biggest building works in its 150-year history, with the William Barak Bridge now linking it to the CBD, as well as creating a new members' stand. MCG membership is a badge of honour for Melburnians of a particular class. It involves having two members propose and second your nomination and a wait of around 20 years.

If you want to make a pilgrimage, tours ( ☎ 9657 8879; adult/child/concession/family $15/8/11/45) take you through the stands, corporate and coaches' areas, the Long Room and (subject to availability) the players change rooms and out onto the ground. They run every half-hour (on non-match days) from 10am to 3pm. Bookings are not essential but recommended. The MCG is now also home to the National Sports Museum (p70), and you can buy tickets that

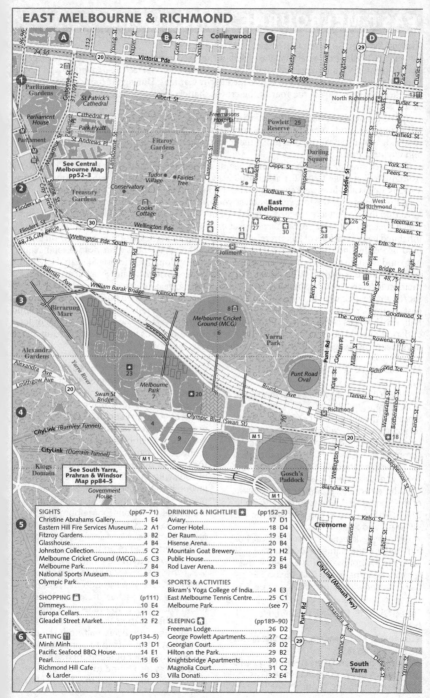

# EAST MELBOURNE & RICHMOND

| SIGHTS | (pp67–71) |
|---|---|
| Christine Abrahams Gallery | 1 E4 |
| Eastern Hill Fire Services Museum | 2 A1 |
| Fitzroy Gardens | 3 B2 |
| Glasshouse | 4 B4 |
| Johnston Collection | 5 C2 |
| Melbourne Cricket Ground (MCG) | 6 C3 |
| Melbourne Park | 7 B4 |
| National Sports Museum | 8 C3 |
| Olympic Park | 9 B4 |

| SHOPPING | (p111) |
|---|---|
| Dimmeys | 10 E4 |
| Europa Cellars | 11 C2 |
| Gleadell Street Market | 12 F2 |

| EATING | (pp134–5) |
|---|---|
| Minh Minh | 13 D1 |
| Pacific Seafood BBQ House | 14 E1 |
| Pearl | 15 E6 |
| Richmond Hill Cafe & Larder | 16 D3 |

| DRINKING & NIGHTLIFE | (pp152–3) |
|---|---|
| Aviary | 17 D1 |
| Corner Hotel | 18 D4 |
| Der Raum | 19 E4 |
| Hisense Arena | 20 B4 |
| Mountain Goat Brewery | 21 H2 |
| Public House | 22 E4 |
| Rod Laver Arena | 23 B4 |

| SPORTS & ACTIVITIES | |
|---|---|
| Bikram's Yoga College of India | 24 E3 |
| East Melbourne Tennis Centre | 25 C1 |
| Melbourne Park | (see 7) |

| SLEEPING | (pp189–90) |
|---|---|
| Freeman Lodge | 26 D2 |
| George Powlett Apartments | 27 C2 |
| Georgian Court | 28 D2 |
| Hilton on the Park | 29 B2 |
| Knightsbridge Apartments | 30 C2 |
| Magnolia Court | 31 C2 |
| Villa Donati | 32 E4 |

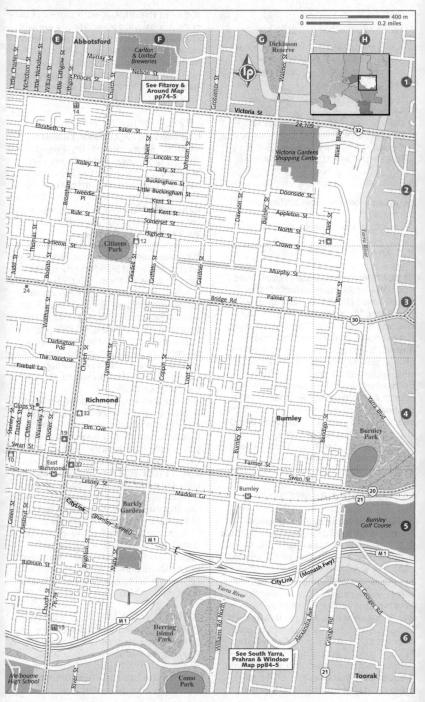

Train Richmond Station is a stop on most southern and eastern suburban routes. For Abbotsford, take either an Epping-line train or a Hurstbridge-line train to Collingwood Station.

Tram The 48 and 75 trams along Flinders St will take you through East Melbourne to Bridge Rd, Richmond. Tram 70, also along Flinders St, will take you along Swan St, Richmond. Swan St intersects Church St, which is serviced by trams 78 and 79. Tram 109 from Collins St heads down to Victoria St, Richmond.

incorporate both the tour and entrance to the museum.

For information on AFL matches, see p168.

## NATIONAL SPORTS MUSEUM
Map pp68–9

☎ 9657 8856; www.nsm.org.au; Olympic Stand, Gate 3, MCG; adult/concession/family $15/11/45, with MCG tour $22/15/50; ☷ 10am-5pm; ☷ Jolimont, ☷ 48, 75

The new National Sports Museum features five permanent exhibitions focusing on Australia's favourite sports and celebrating historic sporting moments. There are some choice sports fetish objects on display: the handwritten notes used to define the rules of Australian Rules Football in 1859; Bradman's baggy green cap; olive branches awarded to Edwin Flack, Australia's first Olympian in 1886; and our Cathy's infamous Sydney Olympics swift suit. There's also an interactive area that gets kids trying out their skills.

## EASTERN HILL FIRE SERVICES MUSEUM Map pp68–9

☎ 9662 2907; http://home.alphalink.com.au /~fsmvic; 39 Gisborne St, East Melbourne; adult/child $5/2; ☷ 9am-3pm Fri, 10am-4pm Sun; ☷ 112

Built on the highest point of the city in 1891, the old fire station's tower provided the necessary vantage point to spot fires across the metropolis. Its ground floor now houses the Eastern Hill Fire Services Museum, which is especially great for kids. Clamber on a fire truck or pour over the collection of historic firefighting equipment, including fire engines, helmets, grand brass-buttoned uniforms, medals and photographs. Guides are often ex-firefighters who are happy to

augment the displays with stories of their craft. Adults will appreciate the elegant engineering of many of the early machines. Facing Albert St is a five-storey mosaic mural designed by Harold Freedman (1915–99), the only person to have been state artist of Victoria, a position he held for 11 years from 1972.

## FITZROY GARDENS Map pp68–9

btwn Wellington Pde, Clarendon, Lansdowne & Albert Sts; ☷ Parliament, ☷ City Circle, 48, 75

The city drops away suddenly just east of Spring St, giving way to Melbourne's beautiful backyard, the Fitzroy Gardens. The stately avenues lined with English elms, flowerbeds, expansive lawns, strange fountains and a creek (both now often empty) are a short stroll from town.

The design of the path system 'accidentally' resembles a Union Jack. While there's no red, white and blue flowerbeds, the gardens do have a pervasive English nostalgia.

Cooks' Cottage ( ☎ 9419 4677; www.cookscottage .com.au; adult/child/family $4/2/11; ☷ 9am-5.30pm) was shipped from Yorkshire in 253 packing cases and reconstructed in 1934 (the cottage actually belonged to the navigator's parents). It's decorated in mid-18th-century style and there is also an exhibition about Cook's eventful, if controversial, voyages to the Southern Ocean.

In the centre of the gardens is a 'model' Tudor village. This well-meaning gift was a way of saying thanks for sending food to Britain during WWII, though we wonder why it's still here. Nearby is writer Ola Cohn's equally kooky carved Fairies' Tree. Efforts to preserve the 300-year-old stump, embellished in 1932 with fairies, pixies, kangaroos, emus and possums, include dissuading true believers from leaving notes to the fairies in the tree's hollows.

In the northwestern corner of the gardens is the People's Path, a circular path paved with 10,000 individually engraved bricks. The delightful 1930s Conservatory ( ☷ 9am-5pm) features a range of different floral displays each year.

## JOHNSTON COLLECTION Map pp68–9

☎ 9416 2515; www.johnstoncollection.org; East Melbourne; adult/concession $20/16.50

The collection of sharp-eyed antique dealer William Johnston is on show in this characteristic East Melbourne mansion. Rooms are decorated in an English country-house style, and also highlight specific interior-decorating fashions from last century – almost as fascinating as the pieces themselves. Visits come with a sense of mystique; for privacy reasons, you need to book a tour and be picked up from the nearby Hilton on the Park (p189) rather than just rocking up to the door. Tours depart three times daily; phone to reserve a place.

## CHRISTINE ABRAHAMS GALLERY
Map pp68–9

☎ 9428 6099; www.christineabrahamsgallery .com.au; 27 Gipps St, Richmond; ⏱ 10.30am-5pm Tue-Fri, 11am-5pm Sat; ⬟ East Richmond, ⬟ 70, 78, 79

This airy commercial gallery shows a mix of well-established, interesting local and national artists. These include iconic photographer Wolfgang Sievers and ceramicist Gwyn Hanssen Pigott, as well as midcareer sculptor Bronwyn Oliver and painter Matthew Johnson. There is a works on paper and ceramics room, and a large stockroom with a rack storage system that allows additional works to be viewed by visitors.

# FITZROY & AROUND

Drinking & Nightlife p153; Eating p135; Shopping p111; Sleeping p190

Fitzroy was Melbourne's first suburb and has a long history of mixed fortune. One thing it's never been is boring. Its streets were once a byword for vice and squalor. Albert Tucker's rendering of Fitzroy nights during WWII are unremitting in their bleakness. A laid-back, rough-around-the-edges feel persists despite rapid gentrification in the 1980s and the ongoing onus of perpetual coolness. Brunswick St, the neighbourhood's main thoroughfare, sports a straggle of cafés, bars, restaurants and shops that veer from the tacky to the genuinely intriguing, and its backstreet pubs have managed to stay one step ahead of the developers. Although most of the artists have moved on in search of cheap studio space, you'll still find a number of galleries and arts-related businesses dotted throughout the suburb.

Gertrude St's rise and rise continues apace; it's flush with decidedly upmarket though passionately individual new shops, bars and restaurants. Spliced among the peddlers of deconstructed Belgian frocks, rare vinyl 12 inches and mandarin-scented hand cream, stalwarts remain: a secondhand fridge shop, the Aboriginal gym that trained boxing great Lionel Rose, habit-clad nuns and residents of rooming houses and tower blocks.

Around the corner, the *jolie-laide* charms of Smith St are also being noticed, particularly by Gen Ys, who come to trawl vintage shops, sip soy lattes or kick back with beers and *gyoza* (Japanese dumplings). It too is far from being a homogenous high street, with Aboriginal groups gathering to drink on prominent corners and a large population of new immigrants busy finding their feet. The stark contrasts of affluence (even in a stealth-wealth guise) and disadvantage can unsettle, but there's a mitigating energy and a genuine community spirit prevails.

The streets behind Smith are home to what were the southern hemisphere's largest industrial complexes. These satanic mills are now packed with million-dollar apartments. Down the hill beyond Smith St is the 'Collingwood flat'. This was once one of the city's most notorious slums. Many houses were cleared in the 1960s to make way for public-housing tower blocks, though many cottages also remain.

Abbotsford, across Hoddle St, is similarly made up of regenerated workers' cottages and converted factories, and its streets stretch down to the river. Here the sacred and the profane face off along the Yarra's banks: the Abbotsford Convent, now a community centre, and the still functioning CUB brewery.

To the north is the leafy residential area of North Fitzroy, which centres around the Edinburgh Gardens. Locals love their park with a fierce devotion. Weekends see it full of picnics, soccer games, children's parties and tennis.

Beyond Merri Creek is Northcote, a sprawling neighbourhood of wooden Federation cottages and big backyards. Its sleepy demeanour shifts once the sun goes down, when High St hums to the sound of a thousand Converse One Stars hitting the pavement in search of fun.

## COLLINGWOOD CHILDREN'S FARM
Map pp74–5

☎ 9417 5806; www.farm.org.au; 1 St Heliers St, Abbotsford; adult/child/family $8/4/16; ☼ 9am-5pm; ⊛ Victoria Park, ⊜ 203

The inner city melts away at this rustic riverside retreat that's not only loved by children. There's a range of frolicking farm animals that children can participate in feeding, as well as rambling gardens and grounds for picnicking on warm days. The farm café is open early and can be visited without entering the farm itself. The monthly **farmers market** (www.mfm.com.au; ☼ 8am-1pm, second Saturday of the month; adult/child $2/free), held right by the river, is a local highlight, with everything from rabbit to roses to organic milk hoisted into baskets.

## CENTRE FOR CONTEMPORARY PHOTOGRAPHY Map pp74–5

CCP; ☎ 9417 1549; www.ccp.org.au; 404 George St, Fitzroy; admission by donation; ☼ 11am-6pm Wed-Sat; ⊛ 86

This not-for-profit centre has a changing schedule of exhibitions across a couple of galleries. Shows traverse traditional technique and the highly conceptual. There's a particular fascination with work involving video projection, including a nightly after-hours screening in a window. It's a nice space and it also sells a range of Lomo cameras and a small selection of books.

## GERTRUDE CONTEMPORARY ART SPACES Map pp74–5

☎ 9419 3406; www.gertrude.org.au; 200 Gertrude St, Fitzroy; ✆ 11am-5.30pm Tue-Fri, 1-5.30pm Sat; ☐ 86

This nonprofit gallery and studio complex has been going strong for over twenty years; many of its alumni are now certified famous artists. The monthly openings are refreshingly come-as-you-are, with crowds often spilling onto the street, two-buck wine in hand. The studio open days, where you get to wander around upstairs and talk to the recipients of the much-sought-after residencies about their work, are worth watching out for.

## ABBOTSFORD CONVENT Map pp74–5

☎ 9415 3600; www.abbotsfordconvent.com.au; 1 St Heliers St, Abbotsford; ✆ 7.30am-10pm; ☐ Victoria Park, ☐ 203

The convent, which dates back to 1861, is spread over nearly seven hectares of riverside land. The nuns are long gone – no-one is going to ask you if you've been to mass lately – and there's now a rambling collection of creative studios and community offices. The Convent Bakery ( ☎ 9419 9426; www .conventbakery.com) supplies impromptu picnic provisions, or the reimagined 'wog bar' Handsome Steve's House of Refreshment (http://house ofrefreshment.com; 1st fl) will mix you up a Campari soda to sip on the balcony while you're overlooking the ecclesiastic architecture and listening to the footy on the radio. There's a Slow Food Market (www.mfm.com.au; ✆ 8am-1pm) every fourth Saturday.

## UTOPIAN SLUMPS Map pp74–5

www.utopianslumps.org; 25 Easey St, Collingwood; ✆ noon-6pm Fri & Sat; ☐ 86

One of the newest nonprofit art spaces, the Slumps has a recherché backstreet location and loads of attitude. Installation is king here, plus the gallery hosts dance parties and other events; check the website for details.

## ALCASTON GALLERY Map pp74–5

☎ 9418 6444; www.alcastongallery.com.au; 11 Brunswick St, Fitzroy; ✆ 10am-6pm Tue-Fri, 11am-5pm Sat; ☐ 112

Set in an imposing boom-style terrace, the Alcaston's focus is on living indigenous artists. The gallery works directly with communities and is particularly attentive

## TRANSPORT

Tram From Collins St, tram 112 runs along Brunswick St, Fitzroy. From Bourke St, tram 86 runs along Gertrude St, Fitzroy and Smith Sts, Collingwood. It continues on through Clifton Hill to High St, Northcote. For North Fitzroy, tram 112 from Collins St runs along Brunswick St and St Georges Rd.

to cultural sensitivities; it shows a wide range of styles from traditional work to contemporary artists. There's also a space dedicated to works on paper.

## SUTTON GALLERY Map pp74–5

☎ 9416 0727; www.suttongallery.com.au; 254 Brunswick St, Fitzroy; ✆ 11am-5pm Tue-Sat; ☐ 112

This gallery is housed in a simple, unassuming warehouse space entered off Greeves St. It's known for championing challenging new work and represents artists such as Nick Mangan, Helga Groves, Gordon Bennett and Lindy Lee.

## CARLTON & UNITED BREWERIES Map pp74–5

☎ 9420 6800; www.carltonbrewhouse.com.au; cnr Nelson & Thompson Sts, Abbotsford; tours adult/child/concession $25/15/20; ☐ 109

Just in case Homer Simpson ever makes it to Melbourne, Foster's beer-brewing empire runs two-hour tours of its Abbotsford operations. Enormous 30m-wide vats of beer and the superfast bottling operation give a whole new meaning to the term 'beer-goggles'. And yes, samples are included in the price. Tours run Monday to Friday; children under 10 and those in open-toed shoes are not admitted. Bookings essential.

## YARRA BEND PARK Map pp74–5

www.parkweb.vic.gov.au

Escape the city without leaving town. About 5km northeast of the city centre, the Yarra River flows through bushland, an area cherished by runners, rowers, cyclists, picnickers and strollers.

Yarra Bend Park has huge tracts of densely treed land (not to mention two golf courses and numerous sports grounds) that are great for walking. Cockatoos screech by the banks and grey-headed flying foxes roost in the trees: it's hard to believe you're 10 minutes from office towers and industry.

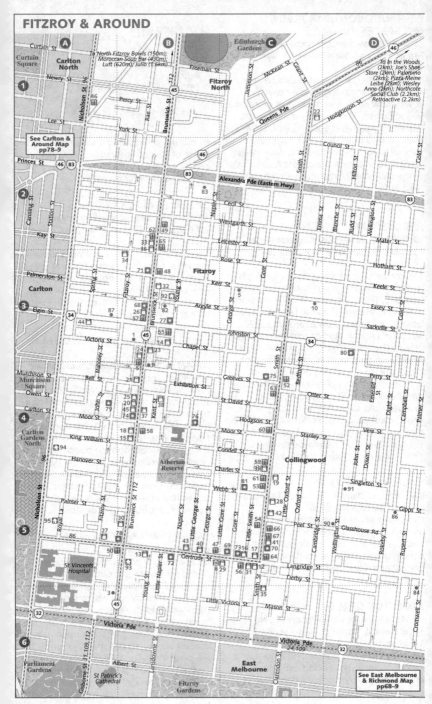

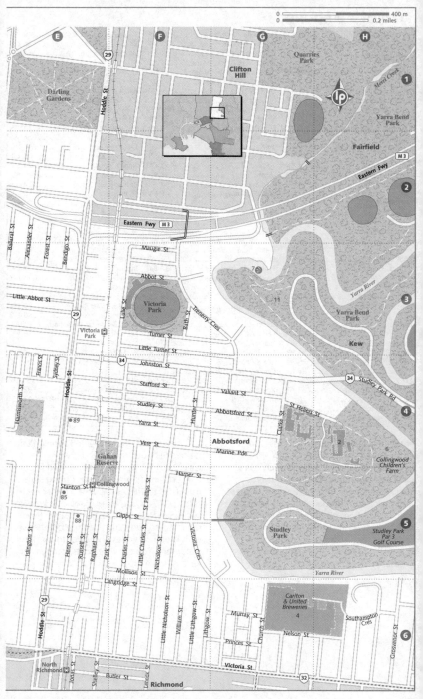

0                        400 m
0                       0.2 miles

**E**    **F**    **G**    **H**

Quarries Park

29

Clifton Hill

Merri Creek

1

Darling Gardens

Yarra Bend Park

Fairfield

Eastern Fwy M3

2

Eastern Fwy M3

Maugie St

Ballarat St
Alexander St
Forest St
Bendigo St

Abbot St

7

11

Yarra River

Little Abbot St

Victoria Park

Yarra Bend Park

3

29

Little St
Bath St
Trenery Cres

Kew

Victoria Park

Turner St

Little Turner St

34

Johnston St

Francis St
Sydney St

Stafford St

34 Studley Park Rd

Hoddie St

Studley St

Valiant St

4

Harmsworth St

89

Yarra St

Abbotsford St

Clarke St
St Heliers St

Vere St

**Abbotsford**

2

6

Hunter St

Marine Pde

Collingwood Children's Farm

Gahan Reserve

Harper St

Stanton St
Collingwood
85

Gipps St

88

Islington St
Henry St
Russell St
Raphael St
Park St
Charles St
Little Charles St
Nicholson St

Victoria Cres

Studley Park

5

Studley Park Par 3 Golf Course

Mollison St

Langridge St

Yarra River

29

Little Nicholson St
William St
Little Lithgow St
Lithgow St

Murray St

Carlton & United Breweries
4

Church St

Southampton Cres

Crosvenor St

6

Nelson St

Princes St

North Richmond

Jonas St
Shelley St
Butler St
Lennox St

Victoria St

32

**Richmond**

75

# FITZROY & AROUND

At the end of Boathouse Rd is the 1860s Studley Park Boathouse (Map pp48–9; ☎ 9853 1972; www.studleyparkboathouse.com.au), which has a kiosk and restaurant, flocks of ducks, and boats and canoes for hire (see p171). Kanes suspension footbridge takes you across the river, from where it's about a 20-minute walk to Dights Falls, at the meeting of the Yarra River and Merri Creek. You can also walk to the falls along the southern riverbank.

Further around the river in Fairfield Park is the site of the Fairfield Amphitheatre (Map pp48–9), a great open-air venue used to stage concerts and film screenings during summer. The Fairfield Park Boathouse & Tea Gardens (Map pp48–9; ☎ 9486 1501; Fairfield Park Dr; h10.30am-5pm Mon-Fri Sept-May, 8.30am-dusk Sat & Sun year-round) is a restored early-20th-century boathouse with broad verandas and an outdoor garden restaurant. You can hire boats, canoes and kayaks (see p171).

# CARLTON & AROUND

Drinking & Nightlife p155; Eating p137; Shopping p115; Sleeping p190

The Carlton Gardens, which house both the Royal Exhibition Buildings and the Melbourne Museum, mark the border between the neighbourhoods of Carlton and Fitzroy to the east and the city to the south.

The sprawling University of Melbourne, and its large residential colleges, takes up Carlton's western edge. Carlton is also the traditional home of Melbourne's Italian community and you'll see the *tricolori* unfurled with characteristic passion come soccer finals and the Grand Prix. The heady mix of intellectual activity, espresso and phenomenal food lured bohemians to the area in the 1950s; by the 1970s it was the centre of the city's bourgeoning counterculture scene and has produced some of the city's most legendary theatre, music and literature. Carlton has now well and truly grown up, and despite its public housing and student population, it is a privileged address. That said, its residents still do tend towards the liberal and literary.

Lygon St starts just north of the city and reaches out through leafy North Carlton to booming Brunswick. Here you'll find a vibrant mix of students, long-established families, renovators and newly arrived migrants. The central Brunswick artery, Sydney Rd, is perpetually clogged with traffic and is packed with Middle Eastern restaurants and grocers. Lygon St, East Brunswick just keeps getting more fashionable; it has a cluster of restaurants, music venues and bars.

Residential North Melbourne lies northwest of Victoria Market. Its wide streets have also recently seen a flurry of new bars and restaurants servicing the area's laid-back locals. In between them all is the expanse of Royal Park and the small collection of pretty residential streets that make up Parkville.

## MELBOURNE MUSEUM Map pp78–9

☎ 13 11 02; http://melbourne.museum.vic.gov.au; 11 Nicholson St, Carlton; adult/concession $6/free; ✸ 10am–5pm; ❡ Parliament, ❡ City Circle, 86, 96, ❒ 250, 251, 402

This confident postmodern exhibition space mixes old-style object displays with themed interactive display areas. The museum's reach is almost too broad to be cohesive but provides a grand sweep of Victoria's natural and cultural histories. Walk through the 1950s, potter in the kitchen from *Neighbours,* or become immersed in the legend of champion racehorse and national hero Phar Lap. Bunjilaka presents indigenous stories and history told through objects and Aboriginal voices. An open-air forest atrium features Victorian plants and animals and there's some traditional (and nonetheless fascinating) displays of pinned insects. There's a hands-on children's area with weekend activities, as well as an Imax cinema (p162) next door.

## ROYAL EXHIBITION BUILDING
Map pp78–9

☎ 9270 5000; www.museum.vic.gov.au/reb; Nicholson St, Carlton; ❡ Parliament, ❡ City Circle, 86, 96, ❒ 250, 251, 402

Built for the International Exhibition in 1880, and winning Unesco World Heritage status in 2004, this beautiful Victorian edifice symbolises the glory days of the Industrial Revolution, Empire and 19th-century Melbourne's economic supremacy. Inside it's equally impressive, with extensive decorative paintwork throughout. Australia's first parliament was held here in 1901; more than a hundred years later everything from trade fairs to designer sales to dance parties take place. It's also the home of the biennale Melbourne Art Fair. Tours ( ☎ bookings 1300 130 152; adult/child $5/3.50) leave from the Melbourne Museum (p77) daily at 2pm.

## UNIVERSITY OF MELBOURNE
Map pp78–9

☎ 8344 4000; www.unimelb.edu.au; Grattan St, Carlton; ❡ 6, 8, 72

The esteemed University of Melbourne was established in 1853 and remains one of Australia's most prestigious universities. Its blend of Victorian Gothic stone buildings, midcentury international-style towers and postmodern showpieces provide a snapshot of changing architectural aspirations. The campus sprawls from Carlton through to the neighbouring suburb of

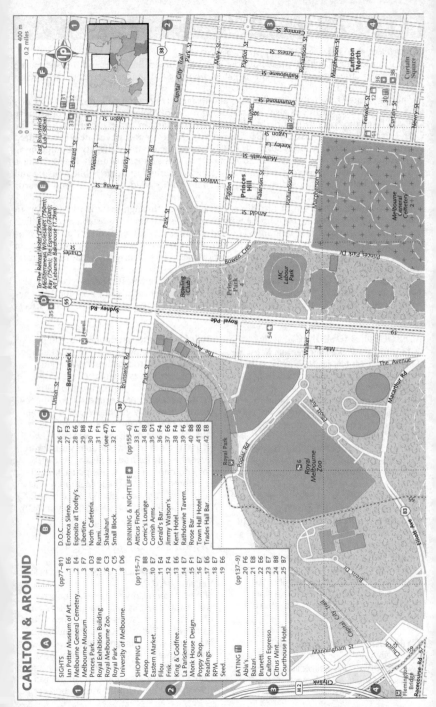

# CARLTON & AROUND

| SIGHTS | (pp77–81) |
|---|---|
| Ian Potter Museum of Art | 1 E6 |
| Melbourne General Cemetery | 2 E4 |
| Melbourne Museum | 3 F7 |
| Princes Park | 4 D3 |
| Royal Exhibition Building | 5 F8 |
| Royal Melbourne Zoo | 6 C3 |
| Royal Park | 7 C5 |
| University of Melbourne | 8 D6 |

| SHOPPING | (pp115–7) |
|---|---|
| Aesop | 9 B8 |
| Eastern Market | 10 E7 |
| Filou | 11 E4 |
| Frisk | 12 F4 |
| King & Godfree | 13 E6 |
| La Parisienne | 14 E7 |
| Monk House Design | 15 F1 |
| Poppy Shop | 16 E7 |
| Readings | 17 E6 |
| RPM | 18 E7 |
| Seed | 19 E6 |

| EATING | (pp137–9) |
|---|---|
| Abla's | 20 F6 |
| Balzari | 21 E8 |
| Brunetti | 22 E6 |
| Carlton Espresso | 23 E7 |
| Citrus Mint | 24 B8 |
| Courthouse Hotel | 25 B7 |

| | |
|---|---|
| D.O.C. | 26 E7 |
| Enoteca Sileno | 27 F3 |
| Esposito at Toofey's | 28 E6 |
| Libertine | 29 B8 |
| North Cafeteria | 30 F4 |
| Rumi | 31 F1 |
| Shakahari | (see 47) |
| Small Block | 32 F1 |

| DRINKING & NIGHTLIFE ★ | (pp155–6) |
|---|---|
| Atticus Finch | 33 F1 |
| Comic's Lounge | 34 B8 |
| Cornish Arms | 35 D1 |
| Gerald's Bar | 36 E7 |
| Jimmy Watson's | 37 E6 |
| Kent Hotel | 38 F4 |
| Rathdowne Tavern | 39 F6 |
| Rrose Bar | 40 B8 |
| Town Hall Hotel | 41 B8 |
| Trades Hall Bar | 42 E8 |

To East Brunswick Club (380m)

To The Retreat Hotel (250m);
Mediterranean Wholesalers (750m);
Ray (750m); Tre Espresso (730m);
A1 Lebanese Bakehouse (1.2km)

78

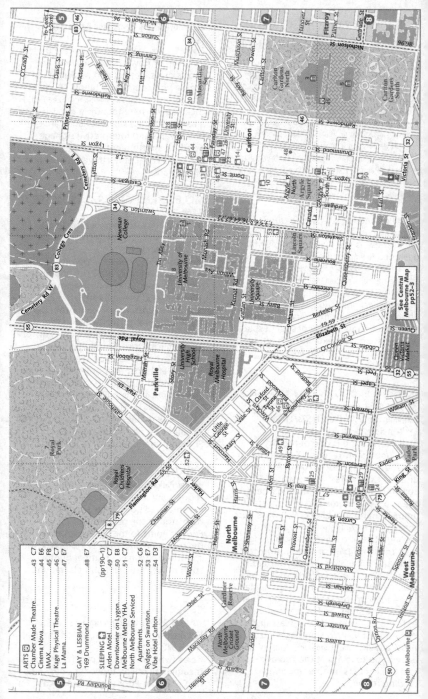

**ARTS** 🎭
Chamber Made Theatre..............43 C7
Cinema Nova...............................44 E6
IMAX.........................................45 F8
Kage Physical Theatre...............46 C7
La Mama....................................47 E7

**GAY & LESBIAN**
169 Drummond..........................48 E7

**SLEEPING** 🛏 (pp190–1)
Arden Motel...............................49 C7
Downtowner on Lygon...............50 E8
Melbourne Metro YHA................51 C7
North Melbourne Serviced
  Apartments.............................52 C6
Rydges on Swanston..................53 E7
Vibe Hotel Carlton......................54 D3

79

Train Upfield-line train to Royal Park or Brunswick Station.

Tram From Swanston St, tram 1 runs to Lygon St, Carlton. Nicholson St, which links Carlton and Fitzroy, is serviced by tram 96 from Bourke St. For North Carlton, take tram 96 from Bourke St, which runs along Nicholson St, or tram 1 from Swanston St along Lygon St. From Elizabeth St, tram 19 runs along Royal Pde through Parkville. This service continues up Sydney Rd, Brunswick. Trams 55 and 68 run from William St through North Melbourne to Parkville.

Parkville, and its extensive grounds house the university colleges. Most notable of these is the Walter Burley Griffin designed Newman College. The Ian Potter Museum of Art ( ☎ 8344 5148; www.art-museum .unimelb.edu.au; admission free; ☼ 10am-5pm Tue-Fri, noon-5pm Sat & Sun) manages the university's extensive art collection, which ranges from antiquities to contemporary Australian work. It's a thoughtfully designed space and always has an exciting exhibition program, plus there's an adjoining Italian café.

### ROYAL MELBOURNE ZOO Map pp78–9
☎ 9285 9300; www.zoo.org.au; Elliott Ave, Parkville; adult/child/family $23/11.50/53; ☼ 9am-5pm; ☒ Royal Park, ☒ 55

Melbourne's zoo is one of the city's most popular attractions. Established in 1861, this is the oldest zoo in Australia and the third oldest in the world. Set in spacious, prettily landscaped gardens, the zoo's enclosures aim to simulate the animals' natural habitats. Walkways pass through the enclosures; you can stroll through the bird aviary, cross a bridge over the lions' park or enter a tropical hothouse full of colourful butterflies. There's also a large collection of native animals in natural bush settings, a platypus aquarium, fur seals, lions and tigers, plenty of reptiles, and a handsome elephant enclosure. Allow at least half a day for your visit. In summer, the zoo hosts a twilight music program. Roar 'n' Snore allows you to camp at the zoo and join the keepers on their morning feeding rounds.

### ROYAL PARK Map pp78–9
btwn Royal Pde & Flemington Rd, Parkville; ☒ 55

Royal Park's vast open spaces are perfect for a run or powerwalk and there are sports ovals, netball and hockey stadiums, a golf course and tennis courts. The ever-popular Royal Melbourne Zoo (left) is tucked away here too. Trin Warren Tam-boore, a recently established wetlands area with boardwalks and interpretive signage, is good for spotting native plants and animals and is in the northwestern section of the park.

### MELBOURNE GENERAL CEMETERY Map pp78–9
☎ 9349 3014; www.necropolis.com.au/old /MGC/MGCindex.htm; College Cres, North Carlton; ☼ 9am-5pm; ☒ 1, 8

Melbourne has been burying its dead in this cemetery since 1852; it's the final resting place of three Australian prime ministers and the ill-fated explorers Burke and Wills. Close to a million other people are interred here, mostly along sectarian lines. Dig up the dirt on the city's history on a White Hat tour ( ☎ 0500 500 655; www .whitehat.com.au; tour $15) on Wednesday and Sunday at 1pm. For spook-seekers, two-hour guided night tours are led by the National Trust of Victoria ( ☎ 9656 9800; www .nationaltrust.org.au; adult/child/concession $24/15/22) twice a year, full-moon tours in April and a Halloween outing on October 31. Bookings are essential.

### PRINCES PARK Map pp78–9
Princes Park Dr, North Carlton; ☒ 19

Joggers and walkers make early morning sorties to pound the 3.2km gravel path around the perimeter of the park. Former home to the Carlton football club, the ground is known as MC Labour Park; the sprawling park has a number of other sporting ovals, a children's playground and barbecues.

### CERES Map pp48–9
☎ 9387 2609; www.ceres.org.au; 8 Lee St, East Brunswick; ☼ 9am-5pm, market 9am-1pm Wed & Sat; ☒ 96

Ceres (which is known soley by its double-meaning acronym, though it does stand for Centre for Education & Research in Environmental Strategies) is a 20-something -year-old community environment project. Stroll around the permaculture and bush-food nursery before refuelling with an organic coffee and cake at the pretty (and extremely popular) café. There are play-grounds and plenty of natural miniworlds to keep children amused. Or better still, come for the community market where you can buy organic and backyard-pro-duced goodies, and have your tarot read while the kids marvel at the chooks and sheep.

# SOUTH YARRA, PRAHRAN & WINDSOR

Drinking & Nightlife p156; Eating p141; Shopping p117; Sleeping p191

This neighbourhood has always been synonymous with glitz and glamour; it might be south but it's commonly referred to as the 'right' side of the river. Access to South Yarra was by boat or punt – hence Punt Rd – before Princes Bridge was built in 1850. Its elevated aspect and large allotments were always considered prestigious. Demand for housing led to many large blocks being subdivided in the 1920s and '30s for the construction of apartments, which are now highly sought after. This predominance of apartment living gives the area a metropolitan feel while parkland is never far away; the Royal Botanical Gardens and Fawkner Park bookmark the suburb's most favoured streets. The Como Centre at the corner of Toorak Rd and Chapel St is a local landmark; it houses upmarket boutiques and shops, offices, cafés, cinemas and the five-star hotel, Como (p191). Chapel St's South Yarra strip still parades itself as a must-do fashion destination, but has seen better days; it's been taken over by chain stores, tacky bars and, come sunset, doof-doof cars.

Chapel St continues south into everyman Prahran, where designer stores mash it up with op shops, cafés, bars and some refreshingly eclectic businesses. Running off Chapel St by Prahran Town Hall, Greville St is a longtime alternative favourite, though it too is gradually losing its edge, but still has some noteworthy clothing shops, a great bookstore, as well as bars, cafés and restaurants. Commercial Rd is Melbourne's pumping pink zone, and has a diverse collection of nightclubs, bars, pubs, bookshops and cafés. It is also home of the Prahran Market, where the locals shop for fruit, veg and upmarket deli delights.

Hawksburn Village, up the Malvern Rd hill, and High St, Armadale make for stylish shopping sorties but, pleasant residential streets and small parks aside, there's little to tempt a visitor. Windsor, along Chapel St's southern strip, is a favourite student haunt, with bars, vintage shopping and a laid-back local vibe.

## ROYAL BOTANIC GARDENS Map pp84–5

☎ 9252 2300; www.rbg.vic.gov.au; admission free;
🕙 7.30am-8.30pm Nov-Mar, to 5.30pm Apr-Oct;
🚍 8

One of the finest botanic gardens in the world, the RBG is one of Melbourne's most glorious attractions. Sprawling beside the Yarra River, the beautifully designed gardens feature a global selection of plantings as well as specific Australian gardens. Mini-ecosystems, such as a cacti and succulents area, herb garden and an indigenous rainforest, are set amid vast lawns. Take a book, picnic or Frisbee; most importantly, take your time.

Along with the abundance of plant species there's a surprising amount of wildlife, including waterfowl, ducks, swans and child-scaring eels in and around the ornamental lake, as well as cockatoos and possums.

The gardens are encircled by the Tan, a 4km-long former horse-exercising track, and now Melbourne's favourite venue for joggers. During the summer months, the gardens play host to the Moonlight Cinema (p163) and theatre performances (see Fridays' EG section of the Age newspaper for details).

You can pick up guide-yourself leaflets at the park entrances; these leaflets change with the seasons and tell you what to look out for at the different times of year.

The visitors centre ( ☎ 9252 2429; 🕙 9am-5pm Mon-Fri, 9.30am-5.30pm Sat & Sun) is at the former centre for stargazers, Observatory Gate, Birdwood Ave. A range of tours departs from here. Choose from a variety of guided walks through assorted horticultural pockets to learn a bit about history, botany and wildlife. Other features include the Observatory for tours of the night sky and the Children's Garden (opposite). Next to the visitors centre, the National Herbarium, established in 1853, contains 1.2 million dried botanical specimens used for identification purposes.

For visitors who can't get enough of gardens, the Royal Botanical Gardens has a recently developed Australian Garden in the outlying suburb of Cranbourne (off map pp48–9). Explore 63 hectares of untouched heathlands, wetlands and woodlands, as well as talk to staff about growing indigenous plants in a domestic setting. The award-winning visitor centre was designed by local architect Kerstin Thompson. See the RBG website for location and opening hours.

## SHRINE OF REMEMBRANCE Map pp84–5

☎ 9654 8415; www.shrine.org.au; Birdwood Ave, South Yarra; ⏰ 10am-5pm; 🚊 5, 6, 8, 16, 64, 67, 72

Beside St Kilda Rd stands the massive Shrine of Remembrance, built as a memorial to Victorians killed in WWI. It was built between 1928 and 1934, much of it with depression-relief or 'susso' labour. Its bombastic classical design is partly based on the Mausoleum of Halicarnassus, one of the seven ancient wonders of the world. Visible from the other end of town, planning regulations continue to restrict any building that would obstruct the view of the shrine from Swanston St as far back as Lonsdale St.

Thousands attend the moving Anzac Day (25 April) dawn service, one of over 120 annual ceremonies hosted at the Shrine. The Remembrance Day service at 11am on the 11th of November commemorates the signing of the Armistice in 1918 marking the formal end to WWI. At this precise moment a shaft of light shines through an opening in the ceiling passing over the Stone of Remembrance and illuminating the word 'love'. The forecourt, with its cenotaph and eternal flame, was built as a memorial to those who died in WWII, and there are several other specific memorials that surround the shrine. The complex is under 24-hour police guard; during opening hours the police are quaintly required to wear uniforms resembling those worn by WWI light-horsemen.

## GOVERNOR LA TROBE'S COTTAGE & GOVERNMENT HOUSE Map pp84–5

Kings Domain; 🚊 48, 75

East of the Shrine of Remembrance (above), near the intersection of Birdwood Ave and Dallas Brooks Dr, is Governor La Trobe's Cottage (www.nationaltrust.org.au), the original government house building that was sent out in prefabricated form from the mother country in 1840. Inside, you can see many of the original furnishings, and the servants' quarters out the back.

This modest cottage sits in stark contrast to the Italianate pile of Government House ( ☎ 9654 4711; Government House Dr; adult/concession $15/10). Built in 1872, it's been the residence of all serving Victorian governors since, and is a replica of Queen Victoria's palace on England's Isle of Wight. As well as being the regal pied-à-terre, the house and gardens

are also used for an array of state functions and celebrations. Book well in advance to take the National Trust tour, which includes both houses. Tours run Monday and Wednesday. There are no tours from mid-December to the end of January.

## IAN POTTER FOUNDATION CHILDREN'S GARDEN Map pp84–5

☎ 9252 2300; www.rbg.vic.gov.au; Observatory Precinct, Royal Botanic Gardens, Birdwood Ave, South Yarra; ⏰ 10am-4pm Wed-Sun, daily during Victorian school holidays; 🚊 8

This whimsical and child-scaled place invites kids and their parents to explore, discover and imagine. The various mini-environments are often directed by the seasons and many plants have been chosen to delight kids with their intrinsic weirdness or strong colours. Programs run in the school holidays; see website for details and book ahead. Note that it is closed for two months each winter.

## COMO HOUSE Map pp84–5

☎ 9827 2500; www.comohouse.com.au; cnr Williams Rd & Lechlade Ave, South Yarra; adult/child/family $12/6.50/30; ⏰ 10am-5pm; 🚊 8

This grand colonial residence overlooking the Yarra was begun in 1840, and underwent renovations up till 1959. The building has been faithfully restored by the National Trust and contains some of the Armytage family's belongings, the last and longest owners. (Of course it's all a matter of taste, but their period-furnishing style can seem more hysterical than stately.) The extensive well-tended grounds are faithful to 19th-century landscaping principles and include a croquet lawn and magnificent flower walks. Tours take around an hour: the first is at 10.30am, and then half-hourly until 3.30pm.

## TRANSPORT

Train On the Sandringham line several stations put you within easy walking distance of Chapel St: South Yarra Station on Toorak Rd, Prahran Station on Greville St, and Windsor Station at the end of Chapel St.

Tram From Swanston St and St Kilda Rd, tram 8 runs down Toorak Rd, tram 72 runs down Commercial Rd (which then becomes Malvern Rd) and tram 6 runs down High St, all crossing Chapel St. From here, trams 78 and 79 run along Chapel St.

# SOUTH YARRA, PRAHRAN & WINDSOR

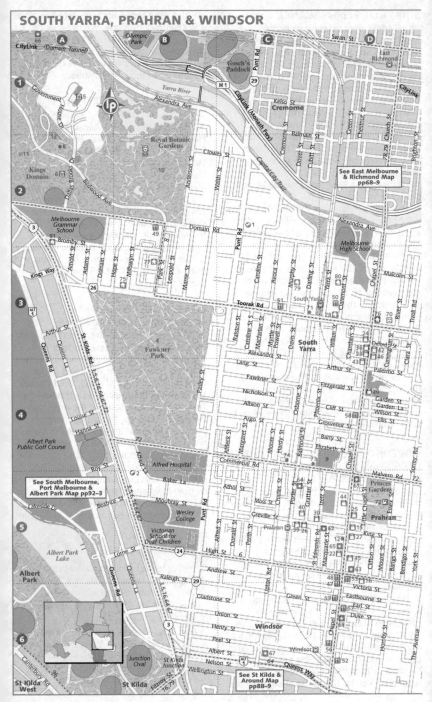

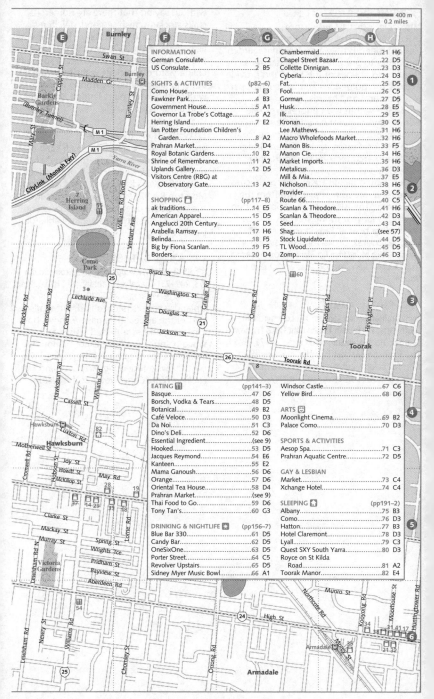

## HERRING ISLAND Map pp84–5
http://home.vicnet.net.au/~herring

Once an unloved dumping ground for silt, Herring Island is now a prelapsarian garden that seeks to preserve the original trees, shrubs and grasses of the Yarra and provide a home for indigenous animals such as parrots, possums and lizards.

Hidden within is an impressive collection of environmental sculpture including work by Brit Andy Goldsworthy and locals Julie Collins, Robert Jacks, Robert Bridgewater and architectural photographer John Gollings.

Designated picnic areas, with barbecues, make for a rare retreat just 3km from the city centre. The island is theoretically open to visitors all year round but can only be reached by boat. A Parks Victoria punt ( ☎ 13 19 63; per person $2; ⏰ noon-5pm Sat & Sun during daylight saving period from Oct-Mar only) operates from Como Landing on Alexandra Ave in South Yarra.

## PRAHRAN MARKET Map pp84–5
www.prahranmarket.com.au; 163 Commercial Rd, South Yarra; ⏰ to 5pm Tue, to 6pm Thu & Fri, dawn-5pm Sat, 10am-3pm Sun; 🚉 Prahran, 🚋 72, 78, 79

The Prahran Market has been an institution for over a century and is one of the finest produce markets in the city. It goes without saying that there are numerous stalls stocking fresh seafood, deli items, meats, fruits and vegetables. The market is also home to the Essential Ingredient ( ☎ 9827 9047; www.theessentialingredient.com.au) a specialty culinary store. Check its website for details of its cooking school, featuring workshops with Melbourne's most lauded chefs and restaurateurs.

## FAWKNER PARK Map pp84–5
btwn Toorak & Commercial Rds, South Yarra; 🚋 72

This huge expanse of green is loved and used by the area's sport folk and lapdogs alike. Walkways lined with elms, oaks and Moreton Bay fig trees provide structure to the otherwise open fields. Barbecues and charming little pavilions are available for public use.

## UPLANDS GALLERY Map pp84–5
☎ 9510 2374; www.uplandsgallery.com; Studio 2/3, 249–251 Chapel St, Prahran; ⏰ 11am-5.30pm Tue-Sat; 🚉 Prahran, 🚋 78, 79

Uplands space is hard to find, but that's part of the appeal. The gallery shows both emerging and established artists, and while being taken increasingly seriously by collectors, loves to push boundaries. With past shows entitled *Big Dirty Love* and *The Fucking Weird Show*, you get the picture.

# ST KILDA & AROUND

Drinking & Nightlife p157; Eating p139; Shopping p119; Sleeping p192

St Kilda, on the bay directly south of the city, was once the city's favoured 19th-century playground. The introduction of public transport brought day-trippers to its dance halls, funpark, ice-skating rink, theatres, sea baths and gardens. The construction of apartments began in the 1930s, with the area's grand old mansions either demolished or divided up. Today St Kilda has the highest number of 25- to 35-year-olds living alone due to the suburb's unusual amount of high-density housing. Postwar migration gave the area an Eastern European Jewish community, which still exists today in the neighbouring suburbs of Balaclava, Caufield and Elsternwick.

By the 1960s and '70s St Kilda had developed a reputation for drugs and prostitution. Its seediness, as well as its low-rent mansions and dilapidated concert halls, was a beacon to students, artists and musicians. Many of Melbourne's acclaimed punk bands, such as the Boys Next Door, fronted by Nick Cave, were based here and played gloriously chaotic gigs at the George Hotel (then known as the Crystal or Seaview Ballroom). Although still affecting the louchness it was known for in the '80s, St Kilda has become something of a spoiled brat. Its real-estate prices are astronomical and development has been piecemeal and often misguided. That's not to say it's entirely lost its appeal. The halcyon days live on via the grand George Hotel and Palais Theatre. Its palm trees, bay vistas, briny breezes and pink-stained sunsets are heartbreakingly beautiful. Come the weekend, the volume is turned up, the traffic crawls and the street-party atmosphere sets in. It's still a neighbourhood of extremes, and often exhilarating contrast: backpacker hostels sit aside fine-dining restaurants, souvlaki bars next to designer shops. Nowhere is this more evident than Fitzroy St, which runs straight from St Kilda Junction to the water's edge. On the western side, the Catani Gardens provide a calm slice of green behind the beach. To the east, it curves into the Esplanade, which runs parallel with the beach and Jacka Blvd. At the time of writing, a large section of the foreshore is being fought over by developers and locals. A large-scale complex of apartments, shops and a hotel is set to be built on the site of the old Palace complex, to the horror of those that treasure the area's original character (others believe that was lost long ago). Acland St runs parallel to the Esplanade, from Fitzroy St's Prince Hotel. Its western strip is pleasantly leafy and nostalgically residential. Beyond Carlisle St, crowds jostle for footpath space at weekends and on summer evenings; restaurants, bars and the strip's famous cake shops are the draw. Many longtime locals have found respite from the relentless pace in Carlisle St's eastern reach, traditionally a devout Jewish neighbourhood but now known for its wine bars, all-day breakfast cafés and quirky shops as much as its kosher butchers and bagel stores. Southeast along the bay is the mainly residential area of Elwood. It too provides a respite from the St Kilda crowds, though on a hot summers day its beach can be as packed as Acland St.

## JEWISH MUSEUM OF AUSTRALIA
Map pp88–9

☎ 9534 0083; www.jewishmuseum.com.au; 26 Alma Rd, St Kilda; adult/child/family $10/5/20; ⏰ 10am-4pm Tue-Thu, 11am-5pm Sun; 🚊 Balaclava

Interactive displays tell the history of Australia's Jewish community from the earliest days of European settlement, while permanent exhibitions celebrate Judaism's rich cycle of festivals and holy days. The museum also has a good curatorial reputation for its contemporary art exhibitions.

## LINDEN ARTS CENTRE & GALLERY
Map pp88–9

☎ 9209 6794; www.lindenarts.org; 26 Acland St, St Kilda; ⏰ 1-6pm Tue-Sun; 🚊 16, 96

Housed in a wrought-iron clad 1870s mansion, Linden champions the work of emerging artists. There's a diverting children's sculpture garden and a peaceful front lawn for postshow lolling. The annual postcard show, which coincides with the St Kilda festival in February/March is a highlight.

## LUNA PARK Map pp88–9

☎ 9525 5033; www.lunapark.com.au; Lower Esplanade, St Kilda; adult/child 1-ride ticket $7/5.50, unlimited-ride ticket $36/26; ⏰ check website for seasonal opening hours; 🚊 16, 96

It opened in 1912 and still retains the feel of an old-style amusement park with creepy Mr Moon's gaping mouth swallowing you up whole on entering. There's a heritage-listed scenic railway and a beautifully baroque carousel with hand-painted horses, swans and chariots. There is also the full complement of gut-churning

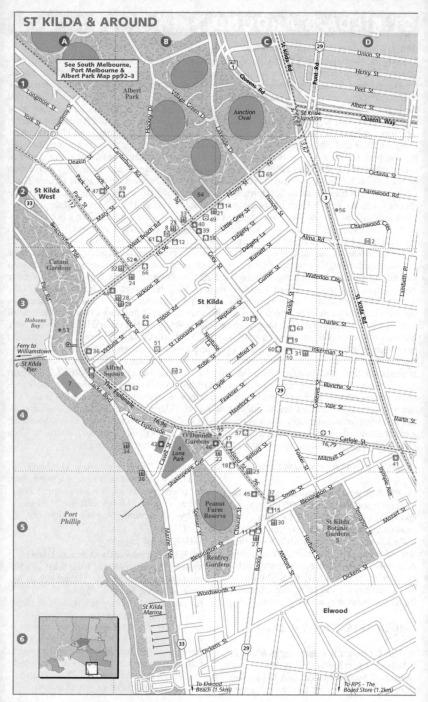

# ST KILDA & AROUND

See South Melbourne,
Port Melbourne &
Albert Park Map pp92–3

Albert Park

Junction Oval

St Kilda West

Catani Gardens

Hobsons Bay

Ferry to Williamstown

St Kilda Pier

Alfred Square

Port Phillip

Luna Park

Peanut Farm Reserve

Renfrey Gardens

St Kilda Marina

St Kilda Botanic Gardens

Elwood

O'Donnell Gardens

St Kilda Junction

St Kilda

To Elwood Beach (1.5km)

To RPS - The Board Store (1.2km)

88

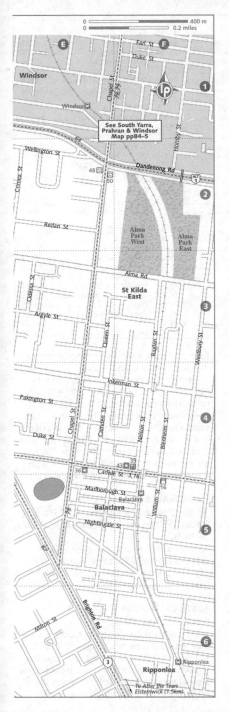

modern rides. For grown-ups, the noise and lack of greenery or shade can pall all too fast.

### ST KILDA BOTANIC GARDENS
Map pp88–9

☎ 9209 6777; www.portphillip.vic.gov.au/stkilda botanic.html; cnr Blessington & Tennyson Sts, St Kilda; ☼ sunrise-sunset; ☒ 96

Only a few blocks from Acland St, the Botanic Gardens are an unexpected haven from the St Kilda hustle. Wide gravel paths invite a leisurely stroll, and there are plenty of shady spots to sprawl on the open lawns. There are local indigenous plants and a subtropical rainforest conservatory to ponder, as well as the springtime splendour of the Alister Clarke Rose Garden. The duck pond is a favourite for children.

### ST KILDA FORESHORE Map pp88–9
Jacka Blvd, St Kilda; ☒ 16, 96

There are palm-fringed promenades, a parkland strand and a long stretch of sand. Still, don't expect Bondi or Noosa. St Kilda's seaside appeal is more Brighton, England than *Baywatch,* despite 20-odd years of glitzy development. And that's the way Melburnians like it; a certain depth of character and an all-weather charm, with wild days on the bay providing for spectacular cloudscapes and terse little waves, as well as the more predictable sparkling blue of summer. Two popular St Kilda restaurants are superbly located in historic foreshore buildings: the stylish Donovans (p140), once a bathing pavilion, and the Stokehouse (p140), originally an Edwardian teahouse.

The kiosk at the end of St Kilda Pier (an exact replica of the original, which burnt down in 2003, a year short of its centenary) is as much about the journey as the destination. Piers have always made good fodder for music videos (Elton John, Elvis Costello et al) and this one is no different. The clip for Paul Kelly's melancholic '80s hit 'From St Kilda to Kings Cross' was shot here. You can book a ferry ( ☎ 9682 9555; www.williamstownferries.com.au) to make the voyage across the bay to Williamstown but regular scheduled passenger services no longer run.

The breakwater near the pier was built in the '50s as a safe harbour for boats competing in the Olympic Games. It's

# ST KILDA & AROUND

now home to a colony of little penguins that have, incredibly, chosen the city's most crowded suburb in which to reside. Penguin Waters ( ☎ 9386 8488; www.penguinwaters.com.au; Berth 1; adult/child $55/30) offers a two-hour scenic tour, which passes the penguins. Tours depart every evening from Southbank and include a barbecue and beverage. During summer, the Port Phillip Eco Centre (www.eco centre.com) also runs family tours of the St Kilda coastal environment, which end up at the penguin colony. They can't guarantee a sighting but will do their best, and all

tour proceeds go towards keeping the local penguin outpost flourishing.

On the foreshore south of the pier, the Moorish-style St Kilda Sea Baths ( ☎ 9525 3011; www. stkildaseabaths.com.au; 10-18 Jacka Blvd) is a spectacular public folly. The complex contains a health club, shops and food outlets, but is markedly lacking in atmosphere and visitors, a hard call in this location. There's an indoor saltwater pool, but at $11 a dip, it's really only attractive on frosty days.

### ÜBER GALLERY Map pp88–9

☎ 8598 9915; www.ubergallery.com; 52 Fitzroy St, St Kilda; 10am-6pm Tue-Fri, noon-6pm Sat & Sun; 16, 96
This commercial contemporary gallery exhibits work in a variety of mediums. A cerebral pit stop on the hedonist's highway that is Fitzroy St.

### ELWOOD BEACH off Map pp48–9
**Ormond Esplanade, Elwood**
A short drive or concerted foreshore walk will take you to this swimming beach. It tends to be less windswept, though often no less crowded, than St Kilda and is surrounded by leafy Elwood Park and Point Ormond Reserve. There are playgrounds and kiosks.

## TRANSPORT

**Train** The Sandringham line has stations at Balaclava, handy for Carlisle St, and Elsternwick, which is close to some parts of Elwood.

**Tram** The 16 tram runs down St Kilda Rd from the city to Fitzroy and Acland Sts. Tram 96 also goes to Fitzroy and Acland Sts but from Bourke St via a light-rail track from South Melbourne. Alternatively, take the slower but more scenic tram 112 from Collins St, which terminates at Park and Fitzroy Sts. Tram 67 runs down St Kilda Rd and will take you to St Kilda Junction or to Carlisle St, a little further on.

# SOUTH MELBOURNE, PORT MELBOURNE & ALBERT PARK

Drinking & Nightlife p159; Eating p143; Shopping p121; Sleeping p194

Bordered by the sweep of Port Phillip Bay, each of these residential neighbourhoods has its own personality. Streets are quiet and densely packed with single-fronted Victorian and Federation houses. When you do make your way out into the open, it's to a sweeping waterfront broken by a number of weatherworn piers. South Melbourne's humble beginnings as a shantytown of canvas and bark huts belie its current status as a suburb for moneyed professionals. The area was originally called Emerald Hill, after the grassy knoll of high ground that rose above the muddy flatlands. Its Victorian-era town hall still stands on this vantage point. The suburb's pretty residential streets are also home to ad agencies and film-related companies, as well as a small number of public-housing towers. Its main thoroughfare, Clarendon St, is dissected by laid-back but upmarket shopping streets Coventry and Park.

West from South Melbourne, Albert Park is a villagelike suburb that you can miss if you limit your strolling to the waterfront. Albert Park's Bridport St runs into Victoria, or 'Vic', Ave. Lined with cute cafés, restaurants and shops, there's a casual weekend bustle. Like its neighbour, many residents are well-to-do, fashionable young families, and its gracious streets are full of cottages and terrace houses renovated to within an inch of their lives.

The waterfront continues northwest to Port Melbourne and Station Pier, the passenger terminal for the ferry service between Melbourne and Tasmania (see p344). Port Melbourne's regeneration has come more slowly than its leafy neighbours but its cottages and converted factories are now populated with professionals too. Beacon Cove, the area directly inland from Station Pier, is a surreal but sublimely comfortable new housing estate (referred to by longtime locals as Legoland), mixing town houses with view-seeking apartment buildings. This end of the bay's Garden City, modelled on workers' garden housing in Britain, still faintly hints at what was once a rollicking, working-class port.

The common thread to these neighbourhoods is Canterbury Rd. It's permanent peak hour on the beachfront footpath here as joggers, dog-walkers, Rollerbladers and cyclists take in the sea air.

## ALBERT PARK LAKE Map pp92–3
**btwn Queens Rd, Fitzroy St, Aughtie Dr & Albert Rd, Albert Park; ☒ 96, 112**
Elegant black swans give their inimitable bottoms-up salute as you circumnavigate the 5km perimeter of this man-made lake. Jogging, cycling, walking or clamouring over play equipment is the appropriate human equivalent. Lakeside Dr was used as an international motor-racing circuit in the 1950s, and since 1996 the revamped track has been the venue for the Australian Formula One Grand Prix (p14) each March. Also on the periphery is the Melbourne Sports & Aquatic Centre (p175), with an Olympic-size pool and child-munching wave machine.

## SEE YUP TEMPLE Map pp92–3
**☎ 9699 7388; 76-80 Raglan St, South Melbourne; entrance by gold coin donation; ☒ 9am-4pm; ☒ 112**
Prayers have floated heavenward here since 1866 and it's still a working place of worship. The high-Victorian architecture is infused with many traditional Chinese elements and the space is embellished with exquisite hand-carved artefacts from Guangzhou. Three memorial halls off the main temple space hold the only existing records of the lives of around 13,000 early Chinese immigrants who died in Australia.

## SOUTH MELBOURNE MARKET
Map pp92–3
**☎ 9209 6295; cnr Coventry & Cecil Sts, South Melbourne; ☒ 8am-4pm Wed, to 6pm Fri, to 4pm Sat & Sun; ☒ 96**
The market's labyrinthine interior is packed to overflowing with an eccentric collection of stalls selling everything from carpets to

### TRANSPORT

Tram There's tram 1, which trundles along St Kilda Rd to South Melbourne and Albert Park. Alternatively, take tram 112 from Collins St, which then goes down Clarendon St.

# SOUTH MELBOURNE, PORT MELBOURNE & ALBERT PARK

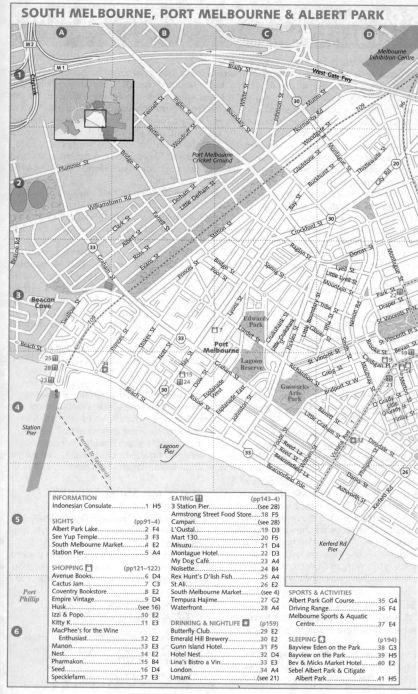

## INFORMATION
Indonesian Consulate.................1 H5

## SIGHTS (pp91–4)
Albert Park Lake........................2 F4
See Yup Temple.........................3 F3
South Melbourne Market...........4 E2
Station Pier...............................5 A4

## SHOPPING (pp121–122)
Avenue Books...........................6 D4
Cactus Jam...............................7 C3
Coventry Bookstore...................8 E2
Empire Vintage.........................9 D4
Husk....................................(see 16)
Izzi & Popo.............................10 E2
Kitty K....................................11 E3
MacPhee's for the Wine
  Enthusiast............................12 E2
Manon...................................13 E3
Nest.......................................14 E2
Pharmakon.............................15 B4
Seed......................................16 D4
Specklefarm............................17 E3

## EATING (pp143–4)
3 Station Pier.......................(see 28)
Armstrong Street Food Store....18 F5
Campari.............................(see 28)
L'Oustal.................................19 D3
Mart 130...............................20 F5
Misuzu...................................21 D4
Montague Hotel......................22 D3
My Dog Café..........................23 A4
Noïsette.................................24 B4
Rex Hunt's D'lish Fish..............25 A4
St Ali.....................................26 E2
South Melbourne Market......(see 4)
Tempura Hajime......................27 G2
Waterfront.............................28 A4

## DRINKING & NIGHTLIFE (p159)
Butterfly Club.........................29 E2
Emerald Hill Brewery...............30 E2
Gunn Island Hotel...................31 F5
Hotel Nest..............................32 D4
Lina's Bistro a Vin....................33 E3
London..................................34 A4
Umami.............................(see 21)

## SPORTS & ACTIVITIES
Albert Park Golf Course............35 G4
Driving Range.........................36 F4
Melbourne Sports & Aquatic
  Centre.................................37 E4

## SLEEPING (p194)
Bayview Eden on the Park........38 G3
Bayview on the Park................39 H5
Bev & Micks Market Hotel........40 E2
Sebel Albert Park & Citigate
  Albert Park...........................41 H5

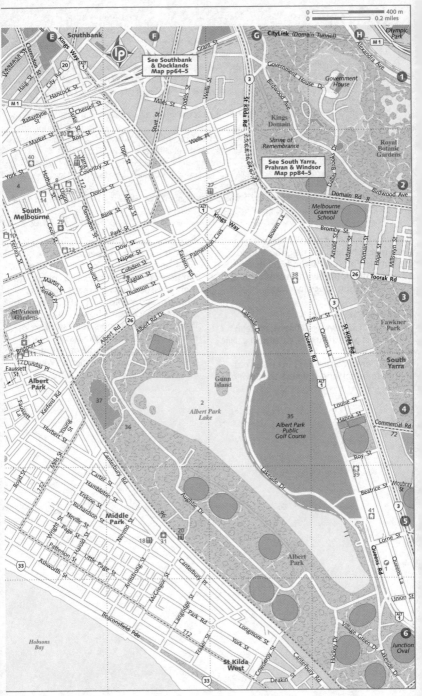

## FREE FOR ALL

- Throw a Frisbee, read a book, sprawl on the lawn or smell the flowers at one of Melbourne's parks and gardens. Try the Royal Botanic Gardens (p82), St Kilda Botanic Gardens (p89) and Birrarung Marr (p51).
- Catch a free ride on the City Circle tram. The wine-coloured tram, with recorded commentary, loops along Flinders St, Harbour Esplanade (Docklands), La Trobe and Spring Sts before heading back along Flinders St. It runs every 10 minutes or so between 10am and 6pm (to 9pm Thursday to Saturday during summer), and you can jump on and off at any of the frequent stops.
- Jump on and off the free Tourist Shuttle (see p344) at key sights: from the Melbourne Museum (p77) to the Shrine of Remembrance (p83).
- Gallery hop: start with some conceptual art at the Australian Centre for Contemporary Art (ACCA; p62), Australian art at the Ian Potter Centre: NGVA (p50) and the permanent collection of the NGVI (p63).
- Browse around the Queen Victoria Market (p57) and soak up the atmosphere.
- Read to your heart's content at the State Library of Victoria (p57), play chess in the Chessroom (especially good for a rainy day), or attend one of their fascinating talks.
- Wander into an AFL game at the MCG (p67) at three-quarter time; you'll see the best part of the action and get to sing the winner's theme song at the end.

bok choy (Chinese greens). It's been on this site since 1864 and is a neighbourhood institution. The surrounding streets are conveniently dotted with decent cafés and other interesting specialty shops.

### STATION PIER Map pp92–3
☎ 1300 85 7662; www.portofmelbourne.com;
⏱ 6am-9pm pedestrians only, closed during some ship visits; 🚊 109
Station Pier is Melbourne's main sea passenger terminal, and is where the *Spirit of Tasmania*, cruise ships and navy vessels dock. It has been in operation since 1854, and the first major railway in Australia ran from here to the city. It has great sentimental associations for many migrants who arrived by ship in the 1950s and '60s, and for servicemen who used it during WWII. There has been significant development of the area over the last 10 years and there is now a gaggle of restaurants built on and around the pier, as well as a marina.

# WILLIAMSTOWN

Eating p144; Sleeping p194

Williamstown is a historic seafaring town that can turn on the seaside charm or wrap you in windswept melancholy depending on the day and the season.

Back in 1837, two townships were laid out simultaneously at the top of Port Phillip Bay: Melbourne, the main settlement, and Williamstown, the seaport. With the advantage of the natural harbour of Hobsons Bay, Williamstown thrived and government services such as customs and immigration were based here. Many early buildings were built from locally quarried bluestone.

When the Yarra River was deepened and the Port of Melbourne developed in the 1880s, Williamstown's role became less important. Tucked away in a corner of the bay, it was bypassed and forgotten for years. Its rediscovery was inevitable and it's become a very desirable Melbourne address. Weekends see crowds of day-trippers promenade along the Esplanade. 'Willy' also has a quaint little beach on the other side of Gellibrand Point.

Nelson Pl is Williamstown's main waterfront street. It's lined with gracious historic buildings blessed with exceptional views of the city, many of which are now restaurants and cafés. Between Nelson Pl and the bay are Commonwealth Reserve and Gem Pier, the main departure point for ferries. Past the café strip, Nelson Pl changes name to Battery Rd, which was made from bluestone that was extracted by convict labour; it's believed that Ned Kelly (p24) contributed to building the retaining wall in 1873. Battery Rd leads to the historic Point Gellibrand Coastal Heritage Park, and turns into the Esplanade and the Williamstown Botanic Gardens and Williamstown Beach. Beyond the touristy waterfront is Ferguson St, Williamstown's local shopping precinct and well worth a wander for its cafés, restaurants and shops.

The Williamstown Information Centre ( ☎ 9399 8641; www.williamstowninfo.com.au; Commonwealth Reserve; ☉ 9am-5pm) is between Nelson Pl and the waterfront. A series of self-guided heritage-walk brochures are available covering the waterfront and seaside areas. Commonwealth Reserve is also the site of the craft market ( ☉ 10am-4pm), held on the third Sunday of every month.

## GEM PIER Map p96
### Syme St

Gem Pier is where passenger ferries dock to drop off and collect those who visit Williamstown by boat. It's a fitting way to arrive, given the area's maritime ambience. Williamstown Ferries ( ☎ 9517 9444; www.williamstown ferries.com.au) plies Hobsons Bay daily, stopping at Southgate and visiting a number of sites along the way, including Scienceworks (p96) and Docklands (p65). Melbourne River Cruises ( ☎ 9629 7233; www.melbcruises.com.au) also docks

at Gem Pier, travelling up the Yarra River to Southgate. Ticket prices vary according to your destination. Pick up a timetable from the visitors centre in Williamstown or at Federation Square, or contact the companies directly; bookings are advised.

Also on Gem Pier, visit the lovingly refurbished WWII minesweeper HMAS Castlemaine ( ☎ 9397 2363; www.hmascastlemaine.com; adult/child/family $5/2.50/12.50; ☉ noon-5pm Sat & Sun) for an interesting look at life at sea. The bridge is complete with wheel, compasses and radar screen.

## TRANSPORT

Melbourne Water Taxis ( ☎ 9686 0914; www .melbournewatertaxis.com.au) pick up from most destinations along the Yarra and Maribyrnong Rivers, from Richmond to Williamstown. You can book the ferry ( ☎ 9682 9555; www.williamstownferries .com.au; adult/child return $12/6) from St Kilda Pier across the bay to Williamstown, but regular scheduled passenger services no longer run.

Train Williamstown-line train to Williamstown Station.

## POINT GELLIBRAND COASTAL HERITAGE PARK Map p96

☎ 13 19 63; ☉ dawn-dusk; ☒ Williamstown

Along the waterfront of this expansive stretch of parkland, the roadway has intermittent information panels. These explain the area's significance as the first disembarkation point for early Victorian settlers. Historic buildings also dot the area, such as the convict-built Timeball Tower, once used to calibrate ships' gauges, and the remains of Fort Gellibrand, which staged many a mock battle. Access to the park is via Nelson Pl.

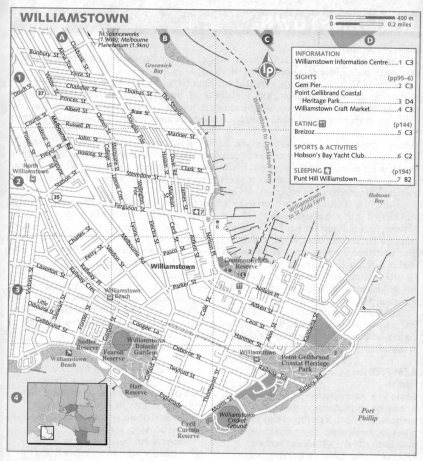

| | | 0 | 400 m |
| | | 0 | 0.2 miles |

**INFORMATION**
Williamstown Information Centre......1 C3

**SIGHTS** (pp95–6)
Gem Pier.................................................2 C3
Point Gellibrand Coastal
Heritage Park...................................3 D4
Williamstown Craft Market................4 C3

**EATING** (p144)
Breizoz..................................................5 C3

**SPORTS & ACTIVITIES**
Hobson's Bay Yacht Club..................6 C2

**SLEEPING** (p194)
Punt Hill Williamstown.....................7 B2

## SCIENCEWORKS & MELBOURNE PLANETARIUM Map pp48–9

☎ 9392 4800; http://scienceworks.museum.vic
.gov.au; 2 Booker St, Spotswood; Scienceworks
adult/child $6/free, Planetarium adult/child/
concession $5/3.50/4; ⏰ 10am-4.30pm
Scienceworks wants you to push buttons, lift flaps and pull levers. Built on the site of the Spotswood pumping station, Melbourne's first sewerage works, Scienceworks' range of permanent interactive displays includes the science of sport, household items and the human body.

Additional temporary exhibitions are usually scheduled for the school holidays. Scienceworks is *very* popular with school groups; the quietest times are weekday afternoons during school terms and Saturday morning. The museum is a 10-minute signposted walk from Spotswood train station.

The Melbourne Planetarium re-creates the night sky on a 16m-domed ceiling using a hi-tech computer and projection system. Several shows suitable for children of all ages also screen.

# WALKING TOURS

Exploring Melbourne on foot isn't at all taxing. The city's central grid of straight intersecting streets makes it easy to navigate, and its inclines are gentle. It's also almost entirely encircled by parks and gardens, rivers and the bay, which means you're never far from a pleasant place to rest. If you want to speed things up a bit, jump on a tram for a couple of stops.

## NEW MELBOURNE David Burnett

This walk traverses several kilometres of Melbourne's old docks and waterfront, much of which is now flanked by striking buildings constructed in the last couple of decades – symbols of the latest of the city's periodic great booms.

**1 Waterfront City** One of the newer developments on the north side of Victoria Harbour in the expanding Docklands precinct. Waterfront City (2005, development ongoing; p65) has restaurants, bars and a yacht club.

**2 New Quay** Catch a Docklands-bound ferry or water-taxi from anywhere along the city-fringe stretch of the Yarra to New Quay (2002; p65). Pass the excellent eateries lining the northern edge of Victoria Harbour until you reach Harbour Esplanade.

**3 Central Pier** Head south along the waterfront to Central Pier (redeveloped 2007), where the peeling woodwork of old goods sheds whistle and creak. To the left towers the giant retractable roof of Docklands Stadium, aka Telstra Dome (2000; p66). Across the harbour is the distant Bolte Bridge (1999).

**4 Docklands Park** Continue south past the award-winning National Australia Bank building (2004) to Docklands Park. This park is home to some of the precinct's excellent public art, including the contemplative *Reed Vessel* and whimsical *Blowhole* sculptures, next to a terrific children's playground.

**5 Webb Bridge** (2004) Sinuous Webb Bridge includes the architectural motif of an Aboriginal eel trap in its design.

**6 Spencer St** First is Southern Cross Station (2006), where trains clatter and hoot beneath the spectacular wavelike roof. Walk down the hill past a contrasting landmark of the 1880s railway network, the former Victorian Railways headquarters (1888), now the Grand Hotel (p184). Then walk beneath the railway overpasses and past the brutalist (current/former) Melbourne Convention Centre (1990).

**7 Melbourne Exhibition Centre** Across the river is the aerodynamic Melbourne Exhibition Centre (1996; p63) and its emerging companion convention centre (due to open in 2009).

**8 Crown Casino & Entertainment Complex** Traverse the river frontage of the controversial Crown Casino & Entertainment Complex

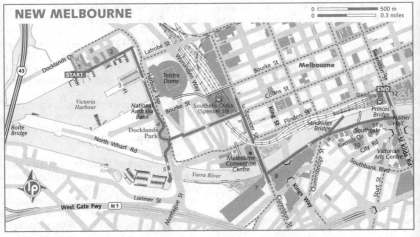

97

(1994; p62), described by the planning minister who approved it as something Mussolini might have built. Briefly the world's largest casino, it's so enormous that a major arterial bridge must tunnel through the heart of the building. Only 20 years ago most of this riverbank was taken up with derelict industrial buildings and car yards.

**9 Queensbridge Square** Beyond the casino is Queensbridge Square (2005), a public square with a bold red amphitheatre. Angling across the river is the historic Sandridge Bridge (1888), once part of Melbourne's first railway line and now reborn as a pedestrian bridge over which the kinetic sculpture *The Travellers* marches, a tribute to Melbourne's immigrant history.

**10 Eureka Tower** One hundred metres east and a block back from the river is Australia's tallest building, Eureka Tower (2006; p62). Its eclectic façade of blue-and-white panels, shimmering crown and splash of red evokes the flag, gold and spilled blood of the Eureka Stockade (p23), one of the country's few citizens' rebellions.

**11 Southbank** In Eureka Tower's shadow is Southgate (1992; p63), the first (and best) Southbank project, with a range of restaurants bustling with crowds fresh from a performance at the adjacent Victorian Arts Centre (1984; p64). Climb to the podium of Hamer Hall (1982; p64) to reach the magnificent boulevard of St Kilda Rd.

**12 Federation Square** Cross the river via stately Princes Bridge (1888) to finish the walk at the stone-and-glass riot of Federation Square (2002; p50), increasingly embraced as the dynamic heart of 'New Melbourne'.

# RADICAL MELBOURNE *Jeff Sparrow*
There are two sides to Melbourne. Traditionally seen as stuffy and respectable, the city also has a long-standing radical tradition. This walk gives you a glimpse into Melbourne's unruly past.

**1 Flagstaff Gardens** The gardens (p50) played a dual role in early Melbourne: the flagpole served to communicate with Williamstown as ships arrived, and the lower area was Melbourne's earliest cemetery. Interred here is settler Charles Franks, whose death in 1836

was thought to have been at the hands of indigenous Australians. The leaders of the colony killed perhaps 10 Aboriginal people in a reprisal raid.

**2 Queen Victoria Market** Now Melbourne's largest open-air market (p57), this was the city's biggest cemetery from 1838–1920. Commercial demands saw the area ceded to local traders. Identifiable graves were disinterred but some 9000 corpses remain buried under what is now the carpark. They include the bodies of the first people executed in the city, Aboriginal resistance fighters Robert Smallboy and Jack Napoleon Tunninerpareway. Most of the cemetery wall remains intact – a brown and cream arched brick wall running through the middle of the market.

**3 Australian Federal Police** Head to 383 La Trobe St – the headquarters of the Australian Federal Police. In the late '80s Melbourne was the centre of a thriving computer-hacker scene. When a computer worm originating from Melbourne disrupted a controversial plutonium-powered NASA (National Aeronautics & Space Administration) launch in 1989, police established one of the world's first computer-crime teams in this building.

**4 Duke of Kent Hotel** At 293 La Trobe St, you'll find the Duke of Kent Hotel . The room that is now a beer garden was in 1937 the home of the New Theatre, a left-wing drama society affiliated to the Communist Party. It established its own theatre after the government banned its antifascist plays on the grounds that they might be offensive to a friendly government – that is, Nazi Germany.

**5 Socialist Hall** The Aussie Disposals store at 283 Elizabeth St used to be the office of the Victorian Socialist Party (VSP). Founded in 1906 by famous English agitator Tom Mann, the VSP ran political meetings, a socialist Sunday school and a choir, and campaigned for free speech and against unemployment. Some of its members went on to found the Communist Party of Australia.

**6 State Library of Victoria** During the 19th century the strict enforcement of the Presbyterian Sabbath meant the library (p57) was closed on Sunday, the only day working people could use its facilities. Anarchists, socialists and sundry other agitators ran a long-running cam-

# RADICAL MELBOURNE

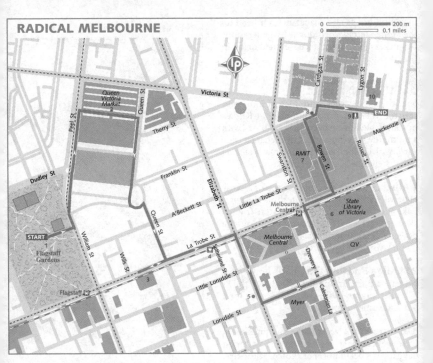

paign against Sunday closing, and rallies saw a number of activists imprisoned on charges of 'insulting behaviour', 'loitering' and 'taking part in a procession'. The library eventually relented in 1904.

**7 RMIT University** Among the postmodern architecture at RMIT University, you'll see the columns of a much older building, now called Storey Hall. In 1916 it was Guild Hall, and provided the base for the Women's Political Association (WPA), founded by Vida Goldstein, the first woman in the British Empire to stand for parliament. WPA campaigned for equal pay and divorce rights, and international female suffrage. During WWI it agitated against conscription and militarism, and supported the Russian Revolution.

**8 Public execution site** In 1842 a 6000-strong crowd stood on this site to witness the hangings of Jack Napoleon Tunninerpareway and Robert Smallboy, who had led a guerrilla campaign against settlers near Bass River. The sentencing judge stated that the punishment was to 'deter similar transgressions'. The same year, an Aboriginal man was hanged for killing a white man in western Victoria, possibly

in reprisal for the molestation of Aboriginal women. Three white bushrangers were also executed here.

**9 Eight Hour Day monument.** Unveiled by the veteran socialist Tom Mann, the statue's (1803) three '8s' represent the slogans of working-class agitation of the 1850s – eight hours' work, eight hours' rest and eight hours' recreation. In 1856 stonemasons working at Melbourne University led a march through the city and Victorian workers became some of the first in the world to enjoy the eight-hour day.

**10 Trades Hall** One of the oldest purpose-built union buildings still in use, unionists raised a substantial amount of money to construct this 'working-class parliament'. The building functioned as an educational centre for workers, providing classes on everything from mathematics to landscape painting, and the tower at the top once housed a radio station in an attempt to provide a union response to right-wing electronic media. The building today houses community and activist groups, union meetings and alternative theatre. Check out the New International Bookshop, specialising in radical books and magazines. Or head up the stone stairs (worn down by generations of workers' boots) for a well-earned drink in the Trades Hall bar (p155).

# ST KILDA STROLL

Sea air, palm trees and picturesque pier scream 'relax' like nothing else. St Kilda's nostalgic pleasure palace feel combines with a thumping very-now scene to enchant a wide variety of visitors. Fun park, lively watering holes, stellar restaurants? Check.

**1 Albert Park Lake** From the top of Fitzroy St head down towards the waterfront. Just past Lakeside Dr to your right is the palm-fringed Albert Park Lake (p91). Take a detour and join the powerwalkers around its 5km circumference if you're in your trainers.

**2 St Kilda Bowling Club** Lawn bowls have become a popular Sunday activity for the St Kilda set; pop in to this bowling club (p172) for a pot and some petanque.

**3 George Hotel** Many of the buildings along Fitzroy St recall its heady past as the Victorian daytripper's destination of choice. The George, built in 1857, was known as the Seaview; it has seen St Kilda's status rise and fall, and rise again. As with most of the buildings along here, the George now houses a restaurant, the Melbourne Wine Room, and several bars, including the George Public Bar (p157).

**4 Esplanade** If it's a Sunday, when you reach the waterfront take the Esplanade and browse at the Esplanade Sunday Market (p120). Also on the Esplanade is the Esplanade Hotel (Espy; p158). This rock-and-roll institution has managed to survive the developers and still serves up loud and live music seven days a week.

**5 St Kilda Beach** No matter what day it is, take a stroll along the beach; it's enthralling for its sparkle in summer and its deep wintery hues in the colder months.

**6 Palais Theatre** On Cavell St you'll soon come to the gracious Palais (p147). Built in 1927, it was one of the largest and best picture palaces in the country; it seats over 3000 and is still used as a venue for live music.

**7 Luna Park** To the right of the Palais, the scenic railway rises and dips above the fence

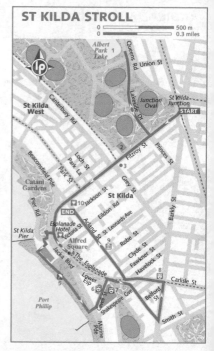

line of Luna Park (p87), which was opened in 1912 by the founder of Warner Bros Pictures.

**8 National Theatre** Turn right and take a turn down frenetic Acland St. Take a left at Barkly St, past its collection of shops, then on to the National Theatre on the corner of Barkly and Carlisle Sts.

**9 Linden Arts Centre & Gallery** From the theatre, turn left at Carlisle St, which will lead you back to Acland St. Take a right and stroll up the leafy, residential section of Acland St, flanked with apartment buildings from the 1920s and 30s. Stop in at the gallery (p87) at No 26, set in one of St Kilda's remaining grand terraces, before popping back out at Fitzroy St.

**10 Coffee** Grab a coffee at Il Fornaio (p140) or a Moscow mule at Mink (in the Prince; p157) if you've worked up a thirst. Trams 16 and 96 run along here and into the city.

# WHITE CUBE FEVER

Melbourne's art world revolves around innovation and experimentation and collections reflect both the youth and isolation of the city. The National Gallery Victoria Australia (NGVA) is strong on indigenous art and Australian impressionism, as well as championing contemporary work by a broad range of artist and designers. But to really feel the creative pulse, get ready for some white cube fever at the city's best commercial and artist-run spaces. The following galleries are generally open from 11am to 5.30pm Tuesday to Friday and between 1pm and 5pm Saturday.

## 1 Australian Centre for Contemporary Art
Start at ACCA (p62), then walk up Grant St past the *Vault* sculpture, sadly once known as the *Yellow Peril*, now finally given the respect it deserves.

## 2 National Gallery of Victoria International
Along St Kilda Rd is the National Gallery of Victoria International (p63) From here, cross the Yarra River at Princes Bridge, then make your way over to Federation Square.

## 3 Federation Square
Here you'll find two iconic venues: the Australian Centre for the Moving Image (ACMI; p51) and the Ian Potter Centre: National Gallery of Victoria Australia (p50).

## 4 Flinders Lane
Duck into Flinders Lane, home to a number of commercial galleries. Don't miss Anna Schwartz Gallery (p61), Gallery Gabrielle Pizzi (p61) for indigenous art, Tolarno (p61) and Fortyfivedownstairs ( ☎ 9662 9233; www.fortyfivedownstairs.com; 45 Flinders Lane). For design and craft, visit Craft Victoria ( ☎ 9650 7775; www.craftvic.asn.au; 31 Flinders Lane).

## 5 Self Preservation
Turn left up Spring St, then left down Bourke St for around 200m to Self Preservation (p109), which will provide refreshments while not taking you too far off-topic. There's a small gallery at the back and the cabinets in the store itself house both estate jewellery and the work of local artisans.

## 6 Alcaston
With renewed energy, turn right at the top end of Little Bourke St and navigate your way to Alcaston (p73) to explore its shows of contemporary Aboriginal art (they have one gallery devoted to small works on paper if you're looking to buy but aren't up for shipping a canvas home).

## 7 Gertrude St
This stretch is an artist's delight, lined with galleries and art suppliers. Start at Dianne Tanzer Gallery ( ☎ 416 3956; www.diannetanzergallery.net.au; 108 Gertrude St). Her small side space has some particularly interesting shows from emerging artists. Next up is Intrude ( ☎ 9417 6033; www.intrudegallery.com.au; 122 Gertrude St). Seventh ( ☎ 0407 112 482; 155 Gertrude St), across the road, is an artist-run space with a new, and often very good, show every two weeks. Cross back to the seminal Gertrude Contemporary Art Spaces (p73). Australian Print Workshop ( ☎ 9419 5466; www.australianprintworkshop.com; 210 Gertrude St) is the longest-running public-access print workshop in Victoria, and presents individually editioned prints by local artists.

## 8 Smith St
Turn right at Smith St to the artist-run 69 Smith ( ☎ 9432 0795; www.vicnet.net.au/~smith69; 69 Smith St). Across the road is Australian Galleries: Works on Paper ( ☎ 9417 0800; 50 Smith St), representing established artists including

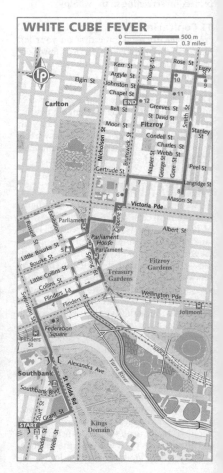

### WHITE CUBE FEVER

luminaries such as Lloyd Rees. A little further along is the exquisite St Luke Artist Colourmen (p111), an artist's supply shop stocking the finest of materials. Talk pigment and glaze then head back down Smith St.

**9 Utopian Slumps** Keeping walking all the way up Smith St, cross Johnston St and turn right into Easey St. Not many artists get to live on easy street, but some get to show here; about half a block down on your right is Utopian Slumps (p73).

**10 Centre for Contemporary Photography** Head back up to Smith St and cross the road over into Kerr St. On the corner of George St you'll find the CCP (p72), where exhibitions include a nightly after-hours video projection screening in the window.

**11 Conical Inc** Walk up to Johnston St and cross over, then take the first on your left for artist-run Conical Inc ( ☎ 9415 6958; www.conical .org.au; 3 Rochester St), which exhibits a range of disciplines.

**12 Sutton Gallery** Head up to Brunswick St and take a left for some challenging new art at the Sutton Gallery (p73). Time to celebrate your cerebral stamina; beer and coffee flow freely round these parts; otherwise take tram 96 or 112 back into the city where you started.

## LANEWAY LABYRINTH

Between Melbourne's grid of wide, dignified main streets lies an enticing network of lanes, passageways and arcades. These laneways and 'little' streets were a happy accident. Not part of city designer John Hoddle's grand vision, they came into being as service lanes. The hunger for real estate then saw them fronted with shops, warehouses and residences and the tale of two cities began. Although they've always bustled with commerce (and in some cases, vice), it's been within the last twenty years that the laneways have taken on a life of their own. Join the constant eddy of crowds who come to shop, sup, sip and stroll.

**1 Flinders Lane** Start at the top of Flinders Lane, temporarily farewelling nature as you turn your back on Treasury Gardens. This is one of Melbourne's busiest laneways, and has always been so. It was once the centre of the city's '*schmate* business', the Jewish rag

trade. The former warehouses, now occupied with galleries, shops and apartments, give it a Soho-like feel.

**2 Duckboard Place** There's not much to see by day, but do a lap of Duckboard Place. This street boasted the city's famous Honkytonks club, now the bar 3rd Class ( ☎ 9662 4555; Level 2, 96 Flinders St), nothing but an unmarked back door but once the scene of the some of city's most talked-of nightlife. Swing by the basement bar Cherry (p148)on AC/DC Lane; this street was renamed in honour of some of Melbourne's most famous rock-and-roll sons.

**3 Hosier Lane** Head down Oliver Lane for a stencil and graffiti preview, then briefly onto Flinders St before turning right into Hosier Lane. This is street-art central, and its cobbled length draws camera-wielding crowds. You'll also find MoVida (p131) and City Lights (p58) projections here.

**4 Nicholas Building** Turn left on Flinders Lane and head over Swanston St to the Nicholson Building (37 Swanston St), an example of Beaux Arts–style architecture and home to an eclectic array of shops and creative studios. You can take a detour up the Port Phillip Arcade or stop for lunch at Journal Canteen (p131), hidden up a short flight of stairs in the CAE building foyer.

**5 Degraves St and Centre Place** Wander down Degraves St to Platform (http://platformartists group.blogspot.com/), a small gallery in the bowels of the railway underpass (the entry is beside the waffle stand). Go back across Flinders Lane to Centre Place, taking in the shops and making note of where you might eat later. City Lights (p58) also displays artwork at the northern end.

**6 Block Arcade** Cross Collins St and take a stately stroll through the Block Arcade. You might want to grab a chocolate frog from Haighs ( ☎ 9654 7673; www.haighschocolates.com.au) while you're there.

**7 Royal Arcade** Wander through the oddly workaday but very Parisian Royal Arcade (p57), stopping to see the Gaunt's Clock and the fearsome Gog and Magog, who do their thing on the hour. Emerging into Bourke St mall, you'll be in a big open space – don't panic, just duck into the restaurant-stuffed laneway that runs beside the GPO (p58).

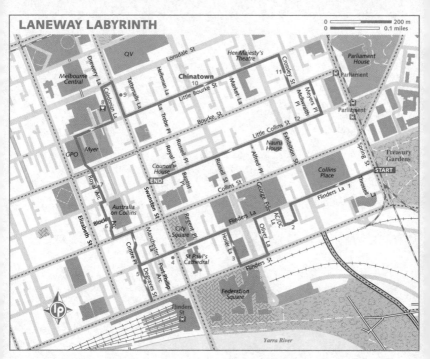

# LANEWAY LABYRINTH

0 ——— 200 m
0 ——— 0.1 miles

**8 Caledonian Lane** Past the dumpsters you'll find plenty of street art as well as the legendary St Jerome's (p150), where you can grab a good, super cheap coffee if you're not intimidated by people whose main form of communication is Myspace.

**9 Curtin House** One of the city's new breed of 'vertical villages'. Browse in the shops or head to the roof for a Manhattan-esque view.

**10 Chinatown** Go off-map and try your luck in as many Chinatown (p55) lanes as you can handle. Some are dead-ends; others secrete bars, live venues, conceptual art, the city's best Chinese restaurant, and maybe someone taking a quick leak.

**11 Crossley St** If a sense of exploration evades you, continue up through Chinatown to Crossley St, which boasts a wonderful selection of shops and restaurants. Say *ciao bello* to the barista as you pass the city's most enduring café, Pellegrini's (p132).

**12 Little Collins St** On your way here pay your respects at Meyers Place (p149), one of the city's first bars-in-laneways. You'll see the Naval & Military Club ( ☎ 9650 4741; 27 Little Collins St) to your left and the walls of the garden belonging to the proud establishment Melbourne Club. End your tour here with a glass of wine at Bar Lourinhã (p131), or head back down Little Collins for some more shopping and a tour of the eco-licious Council House 2 (p56).

# SHOPPING

## top picks

# SHOPPING

Melbourne's reputation as a shopping mecca is, we are pleased to announce, utterly justifiable. It's a city of passionate, dedicated retailers catering to a broad range of tastes, whims and lifestyles. City laneways and suburban Victorian shopping streets make for eclectic, often reasonably priced, rental spaces that encourage creativity rather than conformity in shop owners; their often brave vision contributes much to the city's identity and atmosphere. Yes, the chains and big global designers are all well represented, and there's shopping malls aplenty (including Chadstone, one of the largest in the southern hemisphere; www.chadstoneshopping.com.au), but the city and its inner suburbs boast a host of alternatives. In this chapter we've highlighted a few of the unique, the useful, the absolutely fashionable and the downright weird.

## OPENING HOURS

Most shops open between 9am and 10am and close between 5pm and 6pm Monday to Thursday and Saturday. Melbourne's late-night shopping night is Friday, with many shops closing between 7pm and 9pm. Department stores are open late on both Thursday (to 7pm) and Friday (to 9pm). On Sunday, stores open between 11am and noon and close from around 4pm to 5pm. Some book shops will keep later hours most nights of the week. In the following listings, we've quoted opening hours only if they vary greatly from these general times; if you are making a special trip it is always worth a call to check.

## CENTRAL MELBOURNE

Melbourne's CBD lets you experience big-city department-store bustle as well as the thrill of finding intriguing individual shops tucked down alleys and hidden up flights of stairs. The city's main department stores, Myer and David Jones, are both on the Bourke St Mall. DJ's has stores on either side, as well as a small homewares and bedding department on Little Bourke. Myer reaches over Little Bourke with a walkway. You'll also find the requisite big chain stores on Bourke St Mall too. There's a new breed of 'minimalls' that have the convenience of lots of shops under one roof, while still retaining varying amounts of character. These include the GPO (p58), QV (p58), Melbourne Central (p58) and Southgate (p62). The huge outlet mall DFO (Map pp52–3) can be found at Southern Cross Station on Spencer St. There are also a couple of specialist retail zones worth noting. Little Collins St, from Swanston to Russell Sts is, with a few exceptions, a dedicated menswear strip. Little Bourke St, from Elizabeth to Queen Sts, hosts the city's camping, trekking and adventure-travel retailers. Collins St, north from Queen St, but particularly up the hill from Swanston St, is where you will find the city's complement of luxury brands. All the lanes and Little streets boast clusters of interesting shops. Don't miss Crossley St, at the Spring St end of town, as well as the vertical villages of Curtin House (252 Swanston St) and the Nicholas Building (37 Swanston St). Walking, with a quick tram

## CLOTHING SIZES

### Women's clothing

| Aus/UK | 8 | 10 | 12 | 14 | 16 | 18 |
|---|---|---|---|---|---|---|
| Europe | 36 | 38 | 40 | 42 | 44 | 46 |
| Japan | 5 | 7 | 9 | 11 | 13 | 15 |
| USA | 6 | 8 | 10 | 12 | 14 | 16 |

### Women's shoes

| Aus/USA | 5 | 6 | 7 | 8 | 9 | 10 |
|---|---|---|---|---|---|---|
| Europe | 35 | 36 | 37 | 38 | 39 | 40 |
| France only | 35 | 36 | 38 | 39 | 40 | 42 |
| Japan | 22 | 23 | 24 | 25 | 26 | 27 |
| UK | 3½ | 4½ | 5½ | 6½ | 7½ | 8½ |

### Men's clothing

| Aus | 92 | 96 | 100 | 104 | 108 | 112 |
|---|---|---|---|---|---|---|
| Europe | 46 | 48 | 50 | 52 | 54 | 56 |
| Japan | S | | M | M | | L |
| UK/USA | 35 | 36 | 37 | 38 | 39 | 40 |

### Men's shirts (collar sizes)

| Aus/Japan | 38 | 39 | 40 | 41 | 42 | 43 |
|---|---|---|---|---|---|---|
| Europe | 38 | 39 | 40 | 41 | 42 | 43 |
| UK/USA | 15 | 15½ | 16 | 16½ | 17 | 17½ |

### Men's shoes

| Aus/UK | 7 | 8 | 9 | 10 | 11 | 12 |
|---|---|---|---|---|---|---|
| Europe | 41 | 42 | 43 | 44½ | 46 | 47 |
| Japan | 26 | 27 | 27½ | 28 | 29 | 30 |
| USA | 7½ | 8½ | 9½ | 10½ | 11½ | 12½ |

Measurements approximate only, try before you buy

boost if your spoils are weighing you down, is the best mode of transport.

## CITY HATTERS Map pp52–3 — Accessories
☎ 9614 3294; 211 Flinders St
Beside the main entrance to Flinders St Station, this is the most convenient place to purchase an iconic Akubra hat. Or better yet, a unique creation that doesn't scream 'tourist' or hark back to times gone by.

## WUNDERKAMMER Map pp52–3 — Antiques
☎ 9642 4694; www.wunderkammer.com.au; 439 Lonsdale St; ⊗ closed Sun & Mon
Surprises abound in this, the strangest of shops: taxidermy, bugs in jars, antique scientific tools, surgical equipment and carnivorous plants to name a few.

## ARCHITEXT Map pp52–3 — Books
☎ 9650 3474; www.architext.com.au; 41 Exhibition St
Architext's stock covers the gamut of design and architecture-related titles, including environmental architecture, urban design, photography, theory, journals and magazines. It also stocks the best range of Melbourne-specific books: look for titles by author Philip Goad or the work of local photographer John Gollings.

## PAPERBACK BOOKS Map pp52–3 — Books
☎ 9662 1396; www.paperbackbooks.com.au; 60 Bourke St
A small space jam-packed with carefully selected titles; great when you need a novel fast.

## COLLECTED WORKS BOOKSHOP
Map pp52–3 — Books
☎ 9654 8873; www.collectedworks.com.au; Level 1, Nicholas Bldg, 37 Swanston St
Melbourne's only dedicated poetry bookshop is hidden away in the suitably bookish Nicholas Building. It specialises in the work of Australian poets but also has a large stock of international writers and poetry in translation. Staff will happily order in the most obscure of titles for you too.

## HILL OF CONTENT Map pp52–3 — Books
☎ 9662 9472; www.hillofcontentbookshop.com; 6 Bourke St
Old-fashioned bookshop with a wide range of general books as well as an ex-

# top picks

## BOOKSHOPS

- Metropolis (below)
- Readings (p116)
- Brunswick St BookStore (p112)
- Reader's Feast (below)
- Books for Cooks (p112)
- Avenue Books (p121)
- Paperback Books (left)

tensive stock of arts, classics and poetry. It showcases covetable visual-arts titles from publisher Thames & Hudson.

## KAY CRADDOCK ANTIQUARIAN BOOKSELLER Map pp52–3 — Books
☎ 9654 8506; www.kaycraddock.com; 156 Collins St; ⊗ closed Sun
In the basement of a neogothic building, Kay Craddock has an impressive collection of antiquarian and secondhand books, from the 15th to the 21st centuries. There's a hoard of local curiosities as well intriguing books about books and book-collecting.

## METROPOLIS Map pp52–3 — Books
☎ 9663 2015; www.metropolisbookshop.com.au; Level 3, Curtin House, 252 Swanston St
Lovely bookish eyrie with a particular focus on art, architecture, fashion and film. It also has some very special kids books and a desert-island discs selection.

## READER'S FEAST Map pp52–3 — Books
☎ 9662 4699; www.readersfeast.com.au; Midtown Plaza, cnr Bourke & Swanston Sts
Extensive range of titles across all genres, with friendly service and an author reading program.

## BUTTONMANIA Map pp52–3 — Craft
☎ 9650 3627; 2nd fl, 37 Swanston St; ⊗ closed Sun
OK, a cache of buttons isn't on every traveller's must-have list. Still, Cathy Boulton's fastener-filled drawers are famous among Melbourne's creative types. She stocks rare and antique buttons that you won't find elsewhere; they are a delight to behold. This small shop is not easy to find, but that's part of the appeal.

## HANDMADE MELBOURNE *George Dunford*

The Paris of the South has always had a reputation as being artsy, but lately it's been getting crafty. Melburnians will be knitting in pubs long after it's fashionable and almost every second waiter designs their own jewellery or wants to start up a handbag-making business. Boutiques such as Genki (opposite) and Alice Euphemia (p112) will get you into the Nicholas Building, but then explore upstairs to find Buttonmania (p107) among the warren of artists studios. Don't go barging in on the geniuses at work though; head to Counter (below) to sample the state's best. You can find other great little shops selling local jewellery, clothing and bags along Gertrude and Brunswick Sts (see p111). Or make for the Rose Street Artists' Market (p114; www.rosestmarket.com.au/) where emerging performers and designers strut their stuff.

If you're after a little tram reading, head underground to Sticky (Map pp52–3; ☎ 9654 8559; Shop 10, Campbell Arcade, City; www.stickyinstitute.com; ⏰ noon-6pm Mon-Fri, to 5pm Sat), where local zinesters staple and photocopy together their latest minibooks about local indie music, crap temp jobs or bleeding-edge comics. If you're looking for a few tips, head for Meet Me At Mike's (p112) where they have an inspiration window, or check their blog (http://meetmeatmikes .blogspot.com), which shows off the bread they made this morning or latest dress pattern they're working on. You might even end up buying crocheting needles or a toy-making kit that you'll never use. Procrastination is also *very* Melbourne.

*At last count George Dunford had over a hundred unfinished craft projects.*

### COUNTER Map pp52–3 — Craft, Design
☎ 9650 7775; www.craftvic.asn.au; 31 Flinders Lane; ⏰ 10am-5pm Tue-Sat
The retail arm of Craft Victoria, Counter showcases the handmade. Its range of jewellery, textiles, accessories, glass and ceramics bridges the art/craft divide and makes for some wonderful mementos of Melbourne.

### ANNA THOMAS Map pp52–3 — Fashion
☎ 9639 5562; www.annathomas.com.au; 146 Little Collins St
Max Mara–alum Anna Thomas is known for her tailoring, perfect patterns and luxurious knits. Grown-up with just a hint of girly charm, her designs can go from a boardroom brunch to a picnic in the park.

### ASSIN Map pp52–3 — Fashion
☎ 9654 0158; www.assin.com.au; 138 Little Collins St
Big basement of challenging artwear from international, mostly Belgian, designers. Menswear is particularly strong, though they do clothoing for women too. Prices might give you a fright but you can scurry up the stairs and think no more of that distressed-seam jacket.

### CACTUS JAM Map pp52–3 — Fashion
☎ 9654 0798; www.cactusjam.com.au; QVB, 12-14 Albert Coates Lane
Tucked away in one of QVB's pseudo-lanes, this reliably up-to-the-minute shop is split along us/them lines. Global giants Cloë, Cacherel and some interesting names like Duro Olowu live to the left; locals like Yeojin Bae and Ginger & Smart, as well as a wide assortment of denim, are on the right. There's also a branch at Port Melbourne (Map pp92–3; ☎ 9646 2685; 200 Bay St, Port Melbourne).

### CHRISTINE Map pp52–3 — Fashion, Accessories
☎ 9654 2011; 181 Flinders Lane; ⏰ closed Sun
The toile and tartan entrance of Christine Barro's basement hints at the bold style within. Art doyennes and architects, Toorak types and club kids meet at this legendary shrine to precious wearables. Join them for the inspired mix of stalwarts (Sonia Rykiel, Etro, Longchamp) and locals such as Dhini and jeweller Adrian Lewis. Although the focus is on accessories, there's also a select range of separates.

### CLAUDE MAUS Map pp52–3 — Fashion
☎ 9654 9844; www.claudemaus.com; 19 Manchester Lane
Subtly gothic, darkly urban local label by lapsed artist Rob Maniscalco. You'll find great jeans and lovely leather for men and women in a heritage-listed shop with soaring pressed-metal ceilings and the textured remains of '70s leopard-print wallpaper. The pieces have a cross-seasonal appeal too.

### DON'T COME Map pp52–3 — Fashion
☎ 9639 2227; dontcome.com.au; Level 2, Royal Arcade, 314 Little Collins St; ⏰ noon-6pm Mon-Sat
Yes, do. The shop's parent label Schwipe is known for its highly provocative, sharply graphic, street-savvy T-shirts. Kanye West and the LCD Soundsystem popped in and seemed to like them that way. (If you're lost, look for the pink Marais sign.)

### GENKI Map pp52–3 Fashion, Accessories
☎ 9650 6366; www.genki.com.au; Shop 5, Cathedral Arcade, 37 Swanston St; ⊘ closed Sun
Cute-peddling Genki can deck out the whole family in signature I-heart T-shirts: declare your passion for everything from kissing to reading to vodka. Also stocks street-y labels such as Lover and Rittenhouse, plus ever-so kooky homewares, stationery and Japanese magazines.

### LE LOUVRE Map pp52–3 Fashion
☎ 9654 7641; 74 Collins St; ⊘ closed Sat & Sun
Society lady Lillian Wightman founded this treasure in 1935; it's now run by her daughter, the formidably fashionable Georgina Weir. This is not somewhere you come to rifle through the racks on a whim. Service is personal: sit on the sofa and frocks will be brought to you (much of the stock is imported with specific clients in mind). It may appear from another time, but the clothes themselves are often cutting edge.

### METALICUS Map pp52–3 Fashion
☎ 9639 3545; www.metalicus.com; Midlevel, GPO, cnr Bourke & Elizabeth Sts
Metalicus makes a wide range of endlessly versatile pieces to layer, from leggings to tunics to cardigans. Scrunch-proof, they are perfect for filling the gaps in a travel wardrobe. Basic black is always available, plus a host of seasonal brights. Also in South Yarra (Map pp84–5; ☎ 826 0096; 565 Chapel St, South Yarra).

### NUDIE Map pp52–3 Fashion
☎ 9650 0373; 190 Little Collins St
Cult Swedish jeans are cut from top-quality denim and keep on keeping on (especially if you follow its rock-and-roll dictate to spare them the washing machine for at least a month). It also does a range of T-shirts and underwear and staff are helpful. Although it's firmly in a menswear zone, Nudies can be worn by both sexes.

### ORDER & PROGRESS Map pp52–3 Fashion
☎ 9654 1329; www.orderandprogress.com.au; Level 6, Curtin House, 252 Swanston St
Brazilian cool of the dressed-up rather than kit-off kind. Latin labels such as Alexandre Herchcovitch and Maria Bonita Extra are joined by Eley Kishimoto, Katherine Hamnet and cult Scots, Folk. Girls with a nostalgia for jelly-sandals will find them here too.

# top picks
## MADE IN MELBOURNE
- Aesop (p116)
- SpaceCraft (p114)
- Third Drawer Down (p120)
- Vixen (p113)

### SARTI Map pp52–3 Fashion
☎ 9639 7811; www.sarti.com.au; 144 Little Collins St
Bespoke suits and shirts can be made by local tailors or whipped up by hand in Italy ('su misura'). There's also a range of snappy ready-to-wear pieces for both men and women that can be individually altered.

### BISON Map pp52–3 Homewares
☎ 9650 1938; www.bisonhome.com; Shop 9, Howey Pl, 273-277 Little Collins St
David Tunks creates beautifully tonal and tactile stoneware, which begs everyday use. The shop stocks the full range, including his signature milk bottles, plus some textiles and wooden kitchen and table implements.

### GALLERY FREYA
Map pp52–3 Jewellery, Accessories
☎ 96544657; www.galleryfreya.com; Level 1, GPO, cnr Bourke & Elizabeth Sts
This tiny shop hidden on the GPO's top floor has some amazing pieces, from vintage Georg Jensen to African beads and Parisian bangles. It's run by a talented collector with a wonderful eye for delicious detail. And she's more than happy to take you through the finer points of Jensen's work.

### GLITZERN Map pp52–3 Jewellery, Accessories
☎ 9663 7921; 1a Crossley St; ⊘ closed Sun
Moi Rogers' horde of vintage accessories and jewellery fills this former storage-cupboard space. Pieces run from high-'70s camp to exquisite Deco Australiana. Roger's own bold work also features.

### SELF PRESERVATION
Map pp52–3 Jewellery, Accessories
☎ 9650 0523; www.selfpreservation.com.au; 70 Bourke St; ⊘ 7.30am-10pm Wed-Fri, 7.30am-6pm Mon & Tue, 9.30am-6pm Sat & Sun
Iron cases hold a range of jewels from local artisans and from long ago, some lovely

leather bags, plus there's a small gallery space out back. Not only can you shop for silver and gold, you can sit down for a coffee or a glass of wine while you decide. Multitasking never was nicer.

### SMITTEN KITTEN Map pp52–3 Lingerie
☎ 9654 2073; http://smittenkitten.com.au; 6 Degraves St
Beneath all those luxurious Melbourne layers, there's something just as considered. Miss Kitten stocks the nicest smalls, from sequined hot-pants to Italian lace camis. Labels include Pleasure State, Chantal Thomass, Willow and Roberta Glass.

### BASEMENT DISCS Map pp52–3 Music
☎ 9654 1110; www.basementdiscs.com.au; 24 Block Pl
Apart from a broad range of CD titles across all genres, Basement Discs has regular in-store performances by big-name touring and local acts. Descend the long, narrow staircase to the basement for a browse; you never know who you might find playing.

### BERNARD'S MAGIC SHOP
Map pp52–3 Tricks & Novelty Items
☎ 9670 9270; www.bernardsmagic.com.au; 211 Elizabeth St; ☽ closed Sun
Australia's oldest magic shop, open since 1937, Bernard's sure knows a good whoopee cushion, fake vomit or fly-in-the-ice-cube when it sees one. Practical jokes aside, there are also items for the budding magician such as rope and card tricks and instructional videos.

# SOUTHBANK & DOCKLANDS

Both Southgate (the development along the south bank of the Yarra) and the Crown Casino complexes house shops within. Southgate's shops are eclectic though somewhat insubstantial, while the casino offers up a range of solid midrange chain stores, tourist-oriented places and the expected luxury giants that go hand-in-hand with high rolling. Docklands' shops are few, and tend to provide services for residents rather than be a destination in themselves.

### ALEXANDRE OF PARIS
Map pp64–5 Accessories
☎ 9682 1388; Crown Casino Complex; ☽ 11am-7pm Sun-Thu, to 8pm Fri & Sat
Alas, the great Alexandre – the original hairdresser to the stars – is no longer with us, having departed for hair-coiffing heaven early in 2008. But his top-quality range of French-made barrettes, headbands, clips and fascinators live on in this bijou shop. They range from the whimsical to the practical, from affordable to otherwise.

### AMERICAN RAG Map pp64–5 Fashion, Vintage
9699 2978; Midlevel, Southgate, Southbank
American Rag has been dressing Melbournians in vintage threads long before the fashion magazines got hold of the notion. It is particularly strong on '50s and '70s pieces; most tend towards rock and roll rather than couture.

### BLOCH Map pp64–5 Fashion
☎ 9645 7999; www.blochworld.com; Midlevel, Southgate, Southbank
Dancewear for professional dancers and for those who don't know a plié from a *pas de chat* but just like the ballet flat and wraparound cardie look. Bloch's collection of dance-themed bits and bobs will please little ballerinas too.

### NGV SHOP AT NGV INTERNATIONAL
Map pp64–5 Gallery Store
☎ 8620 2243; www.ngv.vic.gov.au; 180 St Kilda Rd; ☽ 10am–5pm Wed–Mon
Although not of the same calibre as the great museum shops of the world (OK, London's V&A or New York's Met), this stylish retail space offers some well-designed and thoughtful show-based merchandise, specially mixed CDs, an obligatory but beautifully produced range of posters, as well as an erudite collection of books. Also at Ian Potter Centre: NGVA (p50).

### MADE IN JAPAN Map pp64–5 Homewares
☎ 9690 9261; www.mij.com.au; Upper Level, Southgate, Southbank
This small shopfront of a national Japanese homewares importer has a few pieces of furniture but specialises in smaller pieces. *Kokeshi* dolls, kitchenware and vintage kimonos make perfect gifts.

# EAST MELBOURNE & RICHMOND

Bridge Rd, Richmond, is renowned for off-the-rack bargains, and is lined with clearance outlets and seconds stores. If you're after wardrobe staples from reliable big-name labels, then prepare for an overweight-luggage surcharge at the airport after a stint along here. Swan St is a mishmash of retail shops and supermarkets. Victoria St's Asian marts have aisles dedicated to imported goods, joss sticks, incense and kitchenware. Church St is where fashionable Melbourne comes to shop for big-name designer furniture, imported tiles and the latest in taps and showerheads.

## EUROPA CELLARS Map pp68–9        Wine
☎ 9417 7220; www.europacellars.com.au; 150 Wellington Pde, East Melbourne; 🚆 Jolimont, 🚊 48, 75
The boys know their stuff here – they run a weekly schedule of tastings with proselytising zeal – and you can often score a bargain on one of the European drops that are gracing the smartest wine lists 'round town.

## DIMMEYS Map pp68–9        Outlet
☎ 9427 0442; www.dimmeys.com.au; 140 Swan St, Richmond; 🚊 70
According to the tower clock-face, it's always Dimmey's time, and this 153-year-old discount store is indeed bizarrely addictive. You'll regret the purchase of salmon-pink handtowels and an op-art patterned Calvin Klein G-string the minute you leave, but you'll have experienced a Melbourne institution and not broken the bank.

## GLEADELL STREET MARKET
Map pp68–9        Market
Gleadell St, Richmond; 🕙 7am-1pm Sat; 🚊 48, 75, 78, 79
Buy a bag of nuts and shuffle past the fish caravan, the spruiking stallholders and hundreds of locals laden with a week's worth of fruit and veg. This little open-air market is a genuine community experience, and a terrific start to any Saturday.

# FITZROY & AROUND

Though it remains a mostly chain-free zone, Brunswick St's rapidly multiplying streetwear and cheap shoe shops seemed set to erode its

# top picks

## MELBOURNE DESIGNERS

- Gorman (p113)
- TL Wood (p118)
- Signet Bureau (p113)
- Alphaville (p112)
- Anna Thomas (p108)

edgy charm. Luckily, the number of interesting, individual retailers has held firm too. Gertrude St has transformed into one of the city's most stylish shopping strips. Smith St is undeniably everyday but has its own blend of secondhand (ahem, sorry, vintage) stores, discount barns and young designer shops among the Vietnamese bakers and pharmacies. Its northern end, beyond Johnston St, is jam-packed with clearance stores, including a massive Converse outlet. Both North Fitzroy's St Georges Rd and Northcote's High St have interesting collections of homewares, vintage and young designer shops too. All these neighbourhoods are also excellent for midcentury-design hunters.

## ST LUKE ARTIST COLOURMEN
Map pp74–5        Art Supplies, Craft
☎ 9486 9992; http://stlukeart.com; 32 Smith St, Collingwood; 🕙 closed Sun; 🚊 86
An inspiring artist's supply shop for both professionals and Sunday painters, St Luke stocks journals, kits and all manner of materials. Some of its beautifully packaged materials are objects in themselves.

## CRUMPLER Map pp74–5        Accessories
☎ 9417 5338; www.crumpler.com.au; cnr Gertrude & Smith Sts, Fitzroy; 🚊 86
Crumpler's bike-courier bags started it all. Its durable, practical designs can now be found around the world, and it makes bags for cameras, laptops and iPods as well as its original messenger style. The full range is available or hop next door to the custom Store ( ☎ 9417 5776), where you can have a bespoke bag whipped up in your choice of colours.

## ARTISAN BOOKS Map pp74–5        Books
☎ 9416 4805; www.artisan.com.au; 159 Gertrude St, Fitzroy; 🕙 closed Sun; 🚊 86
This moody-looking shop keeps a wonderful range of books, periodicals and exhibition

catalogues on art, craft, design and material culture. It also hosts exhibitions of local craftwork from beanies to baskets to ceramics. Staff are knowledgeable too.

### BOOKS FOR COOKS Map pp74–5 Books
☎ 8415 1415; www.booksforcooks.com.au; 233-235 Gertrude St, Fitzroy; 🚋 86
The breadth of this shop's new and second-hand collection is astounding, ranging from obscure gastronomic histories to Ferran Adrià's recipes in *español* to the latest celeb chef how-to. With the books arranged by region, you're in for some delightful, if hunger-inducing, browsing; a comfy chair awaits if you want to settle in for a few hours.

### BRUNSWICK STREET BOOKSTORE
Map pp74–5 Books
☎ 9416 1030; 305 Brunswick St, Fitzroy; 🕑 10am-11pm; 🚋 112
Fiction titles and a nice little theory section are supplemented by an upstairs room stocked with hardcover art monographs.

### POLYESTER BOOKS Map pp74–5 Books
☎ 9510 3012; 330 Brunswick St, Fitzroy; 🚋 112
Take kinky and subversive and then go several steps beyond. This unapologetic store specialises in literature, magazines and audiovisual materials on topics from satanic cult sex to underground comics, and everything in between. Across the road, Polyester Records (Map pp74–5; ☎ 9510 3012; 387 Brunswick St, Fitzroy) sells independent music from around the world.

### LITTLE SALON Map pp74–5 Craft, Fashion
☎ 9419 7123; 71 Gertrude St, Fitzroy; 🚋 86
Part art gallery and part retail outlet, this little store is hipster heaven. Wearable art pieces, including bags woven from seat belts, knitted corsages and button bracelets, share space here with decorative items for your wall or shelf. Everything in the store is locally made and extremely well priced.

### MEET ME AT MIKE'S
Map pp74–5 Craft, Children's Wear
☎ 9416 3713; http://meetmeatmikes.bigcartel. com/; 63 Brunswick St, Fitzroy; 🚋 112
Mixed assortments of '70s greeting cards are sold alongside quilts and children's

# top picks

## MARKETS

- Rose St Artists' Market (p114)
- St Kilda Esplanade Sunday Market (p120)
- Shirts and Skirts Markets (opposite)
- Queen Victoria Market (p57)

clothes lovingly crafted from '50s fabric. There's also a range of kits and beautiful materials that will go down well with the Etsy generation.

### ALICE EUPHEMIA
Map pp74–5 Fashion, Jewellery
☎ 9417 4300; www.aliceeuphemia.com; 114 Gertrude St, Fitzroy; 🕑 noon-5pm Tue-Fri, 11am-6pm Sat; 🚋 86
Art-school cheek abounds in labels like Romance was Born, Maus cat berlin and Antipodium. Jewellery similarly sways between the shocking and exquisitely pretty. Check also for regular exhibitions by artists, designers and illustrators. There's also a branch on Swanston St (Map pp52–3; Shop 6, Cathedral Arcade, 37 Swanston St, Melbourne; ☎ 9650 4300).

### ALPHAVILLE Map pp74–5 Fashion
☎ 9416 4296; www.alpha60.com.au; 179 Brunswick St, Fitzroy; 🚋 112
Alphaville keeps the cool kids of both genders happy with Alpha 60's sharp clothes. Look out for tilts to Jean-Luc Godard and other filmic favourites (we loved the body-bagged Laura Palmer pillow slips). It also stocks Cheap Monday jeans.

### DOUGLAS & HOPE Map pp74–5 Fashion, Craft
☎ 9417 0662; www.douglasandhope.com.au; 181 Brunswick St, Fitzroy; 🚋 112
The window displays are sigh-inducing; the husband-and-wife owner's singular style bursts brightly from this quintessentially Melbourne store. Cathy Hope creates vintage fabric quilts and other home accessories with a modern sensibility; Paul Douglas will see you right with a Princess Tina tee or a Ginger & Smart frock. There's also a branch on Collins St (Map pp52–3; Block Arcade, 282 Collins St, Melbourne; ☎ 9650 0585).

### GORMAN  Map pp74–5      Fashion, Accessories

☎ 9419 5999; www.gorman.ws; 285 Brunswick St, Fitzroy; ☒ 112

Lisa Gorman makes everyday clothes that are far from ordinary: boyish but sexy shapes are cut from exquisite fabrics, pretty cardies are coupled with relaxed, organic tees. Jeans, jewellery and clogs will complete the look. The store is a modern fairytale in itself, part Scando forest, part secret attic filled with velvet butterflies and antique furniture. Also in the city centre (Map pp52–3; ☎ 9654 8488; GPO, 250 Bourke St, Melbourne) and Prahran (Map pp84–5; ☎ 9510 1151; 248 Chapel St, Prahran).

### LEFT  Map pp74–5      Fashion, Jewellery

☎ 9419 9292; 161 Gertrude St, Fitzroy; ☒ 86

LEFT champions the looks that only a few can pull off: there's the *arte povera* chic of Carpe Diem, arts-admin darling Yohji Yamamoto and talented gender-bender Anne Valérie Hash. But browsing is a treat; it even has a small stock of genuine Byzantine jewellery.

### TOOLZ  Map pp74–5      Fashion, Craft

☎ 9419 1645; www.toolz.com.au; 120 Smith St, Collingwood; ☒ 86

A unique collection of clothes made in the softest cottons, sourced from Japan and South Korea. Equal parts Marni global sophisticate, Vermont bake-sale ingénue and ascetic Japanese, the artsy, textured aesthetic that emerges is very Smith St.

### SHIRTS & SKIRTS MARKETS
Map pp74–5      Fashion, Craft

☎ 0408-660 646; www.shirtandskirtmarkets.com.au; Abbotsford Convent, 1 St Heliers St, Abbotsford; ☒ 10am-4pm 3rd Sun of the month; ☒ Victoria Park

Buy limited-run clothes and accessories from emerging designers, for both adults and kids. The Convent makes for leisurely outdoor browsing. Check the website for the regular stallholder details.

### SHWESHWE  Map pp74–5      Fashion, Craft

☎ 8415 1666; www.shweshwe.com; 210 Brunswick St, Fitzroy; ☒ 112

Named for the ubiquitous waxed cloth of Africa, this enticing shop evokes the rhythm and pace of its owner's birthplace. Look for contemporary fashion from Cape Town, as well as exclusive ranges from

Brazilian and Swedish designers. Homewares are handcrafted and ethically sourced and include luxurious wool blankets, eye-catching toys, felt cushions that resemble smooth pebbles and Madagascan recycled-plastic screens.

### SIGNET BUREAU  Map pp74–5      Fashion, Shoes

☎ 9415 7470; 165 Gertrude St, Fitzroy; ☒ closed Sun; ☒ 86

This creative *ménage a trois* between cobblers Preston Zly, and designers Ess Laboratory and Munk, makes for thoroughly thoughtful fashion. The three labels show their entire (and usually monochromatic) collections here. Ess.Hoshika, a collaborative effort between fashion designer Hoshika Oshimie and her sound artist husband, Tatsuyoshi Kawabata, is one of Melbourne's most exciting.

### SOMEBUDDY LOVES YOU
Map pp74–5      Fashion, Accessories

☎ 9415 7066; 193 Smith St, Collingwood; ☒ 86

Announced by the sneaker-draped power lines on neighbouring Charles St, Buddy does local variations on the global hipster theme: ironic T-shirts, cult-brand jeans, scenester-in-training babywear and kidult toys. Their stock always has some pleasant surprises.

### VIXEN  Map pp74–5      Fashion, Homewares

☎ 9419 2511; www.vixenaustralia.com; 163 Gertrude St, Fitzroy; ☒ 86

Georgina Chapman's hand-printed silks, velvets and knits are beloved by Melbourne women for their grown-up glamour and sensuous, figure-enhancing cuts. Her cushions are as covetable as her sarongs.

### SIMON JOHNSON  Map pp74–5      Food

☎ 9486 9456; www.simonjohnson.com; 12-14 Saint David St, Fitzroy; ☒ 112

National gourmet retailer Simon Johnson sure knows how to make your tummy rumble (and your credit card quake). This is his Melbourne headquarters, set in a backstreet warehouse that makes browsing a treat. Staff are up for a chat and will make you a complimentary coffee or Mariage Fréres tea while you poke around the Welsh salt, Puy lentils and Moroccan pottery.

## IN THE WOODS
Map pp48–9         Homewares, Design
☎ 9486 3311; www.inthewoods.com.au; 246 High St, Northcote; 🚋 86
A bright blond-wood interior houses homewares and other witty or well-designed objects from around the world.

## LUFT Map pp48–9      Homewares, Accessories
☎ 9489 0891; 212 St Georges Rd, North Fitzroy; 🚋 112
A neighbourhood favourite for big-name design stars like iittala, Hackman and Marimekko; it knows its lighting. Look for local Mark Pascal's curvy woven shades that can be made to order in a range of colours and shapes.

## ZAKKAYA Map pp74–5      Homewares, Craft
☎ 9419 1882; www.zakkaya.com.au; 52 Johnston St, Fitzroy; 🕐 noon-5.30pm Tue-Fri, 11am-5pm Sat; 🚋 112
Cute without the kitsch, these Japanese homewares, accessories and small range of fashion pieces have a touch of '70s nostalgia and a slather of Gen-Y joyfulness. Rare craft magazines will get your stitching juices flowing, even in kanji.

## SPACECRAFT Map pp74–5    Homewares, Fashion
☎ 9486 0010; www.spacecraftaustralia.com; 255 Gertrude St, Fitzroy
An excellent place to find a made-in-Melbourne souvenir that won't end up at the back of the cupboard. Textile artist Stewart Russell's botanical and architectural designs adorn everything from stools to socks to single-bed doonas. For a more substantial investment, his stretched printer's backcloths are sought after as wittily deconstructionist artworks.

## LOST & FOUND MARKET
Map pp74–5         Market, Vintage
☎ 0438-599 701; www.lostandfoundmarket.com.au; 132a Smith St, Collingwood; 🕐 noon-6pm Mon-Fri, 11am-6pm Sat & Sun; 🚋 86
Housed in the shabby but definitely not chic remains of a legendary live venue, this market has a nice variety of vintage traders. You'll find everything here from Penguin classics to Finnish enamelware to frill-front shirts that last saw the light of day at Shazza and Bazza's wedding c 1973. On the last Friday of each month, the doors stay open until 10pm with a live soul DJ spinning discs.

## ROSE STREET ARTISTS' MARKET
Map pp74–5                 Market
☎ 9419 5529; www.rosestmarket.com.au; 60 Rose St, Fitzroy; 🕐 11am-5pm; 🚋 112
One of Melbourne's best and most popular art-and-craft markets, just a short stroll from Brunswick St. Firmly of the new-gen variety (no dolly toilet roll covers to be had for love or money), here you'll find up to 70 stalls selling jewellery, clothing, furniture, paintings, screen prints and ugly-cute toys.

## KLEIN'S Map pp74–5      Perfume, Skincare
☎ 9416 1221; 313 Brunswick St, Fitzroy; 🚋 112
Just what you need in a neighbourhood apothecary: candles, rare scents and unguents from far and wide. Stock ranges from the utterly indulgent (L'Artisan Perfumes) to the totally practical (Weleda lip balm). Staff will recommend the perfect gift (and are especially knowledgeable about perfume) and wrap even the most modest purchase with style.

## NORTHSIDE Map pp74–5         Records
☎ 9417 7557; www.northsiderecords.com.au; 236 Gertrude St, Fitzroy; 🕐 11am-6pm Mon-Thu, to 7pm Fri, to 5pm Sat; 🚋 86
Northside's stock is DJ mashup eclectic, from Curtis to NY hard salsa to hip-hop; from straight-up funk to Bollywood soundtrack, much of it on vinyl. Despite appearances to the contrary, staff are never too cool for school, and are happy to track down rare albums on request.

## TITLE Map pp74–5         Records, DVDs
☎ 9417 4477; www.titlespace.com; 183 Gertrude St, Fitzroy; 🚋 86
This cleverly designed corner store mixes things up with rare release CDs, including the complete Trojan catalogue, new local indie releases as well as a good collection of less-than-predictable world music artists. Its classic DVDs come in way-too-tempting box sets and there's a small range of music books perfect for gifts. In-store music events happen upstairs from time to time too.

## KAMI Map pp74–5        Stationery, Craft
☎ 9419 5735; www.paperandbookarts.com.au; 217 Brunswick St, Fitzroy; 🚋 112
This shop does bookbinding as well as selling a large range of traditional high-quality

paper from Japan and other countries by the roll. There are journals, photo frames, pencil holders and other household objects too, all made in the company's Byron Bay studio. The riot of patterns that decks the walls is paradoxically soothing, as are the gracious staff.

### ZETTA FLORENCE
Map pp74–5                              Stationery, Craft
☎ 9416 2236; www.zettaflorence.com.au; 197 Brunswick St, Fitzroy; 🚋 112
Zetta Florence is both a professional preservation-supplies retailer (with a clientele of photographers, artists and archivists) and a superstore for stationery tragics. Binders, folios and archive boxes are joined by covetable leather-bound notebooks, quality papers and envelopes, and tin boxes of postcards. You'll find international brands like Cavallini, as well as local letterpress cards and kits.

### JASPER JUNIOR
Map pp74–5                          Toys, Children's Wear
☎ 9417 4139; 269 Brunswick St, Fitzroy; 🚋 112
You don't need a wicked witch bearing lollies to lure in the little ones here; this stuffed-to-the-rafters toy emporium offers sweet sustenance for babes and big kids, from well-crafted wood to the odd bit of plastic, but undeniably cute, tat. Local babywear labels Pure Baby and Blink make lovely gifts. There's also a branch on Bourke St (Map pp52–3; Royal Arcade, Bourke St, Melbourne; ☎ 9650 6003).

### HERCYNIA SILVA
Map pp74–5                          Vintage, Homewares
☎ 9482 5770; 656 Smith St, Clifton Hill; www.hercyniasilva.com.au; 🕑 closed Mon & Tue; 🚋 86
Artist and carpenter Michael Conole and partner Viveka de Costa's exquisite shop is a little remote, but worth the time if you're after a unique and beautiful object. There's a mix of antique and custom-made wooden pieces ranging from the functional to the exquisitely decorative. Mike is often at work in the sunshine out the front of the shop.

### MAX WATTS INDUSTRIA
Map pp74–5                          Vintage, Homewares
☎ 9417 1117; 202 Gertrude St, Fitzroy; 🕑 Wed-Sun; 🚋 86
Maps of the world, industrial furniture, wooden letterpress forms, doctor's cabinets, scientific equipment, vintage kid's

wear and secondhand designer clothes: it's all here. This is a favourite locals haunt and a great Ikea antidote.

### TONGUE & GROOVE
Map pp74–5                          Vintage, Homewares
☎ 9416 0349; www.tongueandgroove.com.au; 84 Smith St, Collingwood; 🚋 86
The store has an interesting mix of classic midcentury furniture, much of it Australian, as well as contemporary Scandinavian homewares from Flensted mobiles to Höganäs ceramic tea sets. The owners know their stuff and are hands-on – the smell of woodworking permeates from the workshop beyond.

### RETROACTIVE
Map pp48–9                          Vintage, Homewares
☎ 9489 4566; www.retroactive.net.au; 307 High St, Northcote; 🚋 86
This modest-looking store yields some fabulous finds. It specialises in Australian modernist furniture, along the lines of Fred Lowan's Fler and Tessa, Parker and Danish Deluxe. As well as a good stock of decorative pottery (including German and Italian ceramics) it also has an assortment of vintage goods from dresses to magazines to old-school hi-fi sets.

# CARLTON & AROUND

Lygon St in Carlton has a range of practical shops servicing locals and the university population. Fashion here is split between the chains (Country Road, Witchery, FCUK, Sportsgirl) and elegant shops that would not be out of place in Rome. There's also the fabulous range of delis and food stores you'd expect in a proudly Italian neighbourhood. The seemingly endless strip of Sydney Rd, Brunswick has a host of Middle Eastern grocers as well as shops catering for its rapidly growing hip-kid population.

## READINGS Map pp78–9 Books
☎ 9347 6633; 309 Lygon St, Carlton; www.readings .com.au; ☺ 9am-11pm Mon-Sat, 10am-11pm Sun; 🚊 16

A potter around this defiantly prospering indie bookshop can occupy an entire afternoon if you're so inclined. There's a dangerously loaded (and good-value) specials table, switched-on staff and everyone from Lacan to *Charlie & Lola* on the shelves.

## SEED Map pp78–9 Children's Wear, Toys
☎ 9347 3955; www.seedchild.com.au; 208 Faraday St, Carlton; 🚊 16

Seed's range lets small people in on current trends but with a sweet restraint and with beautiful fabrics and finishes. It dresses newborns to 10 year olds. Toys, bedding and books are also well chosen and make pretty presents. There's also branches at South Yarra (Map pp84–5; ☎ 9824 0283; 541 Chapel St, South Yarra) and Albert Park (Map pp92–3; ☎ 9690 3145; 121 Dundas Pl, Albert Park).

## EASTERN MARKET Map pp78–9 Fashion
☎ 9348 0890; www.easternmarket.com.au; 107 Grattan St, Carlton; 🚊 16

Fashion maven territory with a deconstructed Euro-Tokyo edge. The space is itself an attraction; it's a 19th-century chapel with the owner's inimitable additions.

## EPISODE Map pp48–9 Fashion, Accessories
☎ 9380 1777; 175-179 Sydney Rd, Brunswick; 🚊 19

The place to go when you need an Pucci-looking evening dress in a hurry and only have $35 left on your credit card. This barn does it all: dirndls, cowboy boots, sunglasses, bowling shirts, PS 44 basketball T-shirts as well as small range of own-brand new stuff. There's also a branch in Collingwood (Map pp74–5; 172 Smith St, Collingwood; ☎ 9486 0226)

## FRISK Map pp78–9 Fashion
☎ 9348 1499; 721 Rathdowne St, North Carlton; 🚊 1, 8

A local's one-stop shop when they need something smart but interesting. Well-chosen Australian designers like Alice

McCall, Josh Goot and Obus. It's run by a mother and daughter and the stock also crosses the generational divide.

## MONK HOUSE DESIGN Map pp78–9 Fashion
☎ 9381 1191; www.myspace.com/monkhouse design; 102 Lygon St, East Brunswick; 🚊 1, 8

There's a whole lot of indie design talent to be found at this design hothouse, including Skin and Threads, Ammo, Queen and Sunday Morning. In summer the Brazilian jelly shoes walk out the door, in winter it's the house-brand coats.

## RPM Map pp78–9 Fashion
☎ 9347 3648; 332 Lygon St, Carlton; ☺ closed Sun; 🚊 16

Carlton girls don't mind being the smartest in the room, and RPM stocks the labels that aren't going to call anyone's IQ into question. There's elegant, edgy Zambesi, Kirrily Johnston and Marnie Skillings, as well as great jeans and cult T-shirts from Jac&Jack.

## KING & GODFREE Map pp78–9 Food, Wine
☎ 9347 1619; www.kingandgodfree.com.au; 293-297 Lygon St, Carlton; ☺ 9am-9pm Mon-Sat, 11am-7pm Sun; 🚊 16

This cheerful wine shop and deli has been keeping Carlton cellars well stocked for years. It has a particularly good range of Victorian wines and also some stellar Italian drops. Staff are always happy to help.

## LA PARISIENNE Map pp78–9 Food
☎ 9349 1852; 290 Lygon St, Carlton; 🚊 16

A French interloper in this most Italian of streets, Parisienne specialises in small goods and take-home dishes that are authentically Gallic. *Boudin blanc* and *noir*, duck *confit* and its famous pâtés and terrines will not disappoint. It also does a nice range of bread and little pies that are perfect for picnic provisions, and keeps a range of evocatively packaged pantry items.

## AESOP Map pp78–9 Perfume, Skincare
☎ 9329 3850; www.aesop.net.au; 2 Errol St, North Melbourne; 🚊 57

Home-grown skincare company that eschews the industry's usual marketing ploys, instead showcasing products made from simple ingredients in simple packaging. The range is wide and based on botanical extracts. Shops are a haven of good sense

# top picks

## KIDS

- Jasper Junior (p115)
- Poppy Shop (p117)
- Big by Fiona Scanlan (below)
- Bernard's Magic Shop (p110)
- ak Traditions (below)

and calm sensuality. See p173 for the details of its day spa. There are also branches in the city centre (Map pp52–3; ☎ 9639 2436; 35 Albert Coates Lane, Melbourne), St Kilda (Map pp88–9; ☎ 9534 9433; 2 Acland St, St Kilda) and Fitzroy (Map pp74–5; ☎ 9419 8356; 242 Gertrude St, Fitzroy).

## POPPY SHOP  Map pp78–9                    Toys
☎ 9347 6302; 283 Lygon St, Carlton; 🚊 16
A Carlton stalwart, tiny Poppy is a riot of intriguing toys, decorative objects and other happy-making paraphernalia. From beautiful handcrafted German dolls for a very special dolls house to Marx brothers masks for a few dollars, there's plenty to keep whole families entertained (if you can all fit at one time).

# SOUTH YARRA, PRAHRAN & WINDSOR

Chapel St's South Yarra strip these days has lost its fashion lustre, with a large percentage of chains setting up shop. But the designers are still here and there's a definite buzz on Friday afternoons and the weekend. Over Commercial Rd and into Prahran and Windsor, there's a far more eclectic mix. Cute Greville St runs off Chapel, and has a good smattering of shopping opportunities too. Prahran is also known for its midcentury design delights. Hawksburn Village in East Prahran and High St, Armadale have always drawn stylish locals, but are currently enjoying a particular moment in the sun.

## BIG BY FIONA SCANLAN
Map pp84–5                          Children's Wear
☎ 9827 8002; www.bigbyfiona.com; 617 Malvern Rd, Toorak; 🚊 72
The clothes in legendary designer Fiona Scanlan's bright, bold kids' shop manage to be bang on-trend while retaining

the whimsy that is the under-eight's due. Parents will wish they still inhabited a world where a tutu teamed with a chunky knit cardie was perfectly acceptable daywear.

## MILL & MIA  Map pp84–5        Children's Wear
☎ 9510 5275; www.millandmia.com; 582 Malvern Rd, Prahran; 🚊 72
Melbourne's Mill & Mia dresses babes to six-year-olds in sweet cotton frocks, denim and stripy tees, chunky but soft knits. Its stylish bed linen is a world away from evil teds and TV characters: instead a delicate floral here, a woodsy motif there.

## CHAPEL STREET BAZAAR
Map pp84–5                              Collectables
☎ 9529 1727; 217-223 Chapel St, Prahran; 🚊 Prahran, 🚊 78, 79
Calling this a 'permanent undercover collection of market stalls' won't give you any clue to what's tucked away here. This old arcade is a retro-obsessive riot. It doesn't matter if Italian art glass or Noddy egg cups are your thing, you'll find it here. Be prepared to lose an afternoon.

## AK TRADITIONS
Map pp84–5                   Craft, Children's Wear
☎ 9533 7576; www.aktraditions.com; 524 Malvern Rd, Prahan; 🚊 72
ak's stock of exquisitely soulful dolls, toys and quilts are made in Kyrgyz using handmade wool felt and yarn-dyed cotton. It also stocks a range of luxurious organic knits for babies, and for the crafty there's inspiring DIY kits and materials. Dinara, its signature doll, can be dressed off the peg, or you can buy knitting patterns to make her clothes yourself.

## KRONAN  Map pp84–5                     Cycling
☎ 0415-304 117; www.kronancycles.com.au; 4/155 Greville St, Prahran; 🚊 Prahran, 🚊 78, 79
Scando-style town-cycling fans delight, Kronan is here. Test drive one in your chosen colour or just marvel at the beautiful function-dictated design. Great for a bike-chat too.

## AMERICAN APPAREL  Map pp84–5        Fashion
☎ 9529 6852; www.americanapparel.net; 262 Chapel St, Prahran; 🚊 Prahran, 🚊 78, 79
Dov Charney's multihued basics have their first Australian home. If you're the

kind of person that likes the same old same old (be it hoody, T-shirt or leggings) but want it in teal, asphalt, cranberry and possibly silver lurex, this is the place to go *crazy*.

## COLLETTE DINNIGAN Map pp84–5 · Fashion
☎ 9827 2111; www.collettedinnigan.com.au; 553 Chapel St, South Yarra; 🚇 South Yarra; 🚊 78, 79
Need a special-occasion frock? New Zealand-born, Australian-claimed and internationally renowned Collette Dinnigan dresses celebrities every other day for premieres and parties. Signature delicate lace gowns and underwear, as well as shimmering satin pieces and the softest cashmere knits are something to celebrate all on their own.

## CYBERIA Map pp84–5          Fashion, Accessories
☎ 9824 1339; 579 Chapel St, South Yarra; 🚇 South Yarra, 🚊 78, 79
Cyberia ups the designer anti. Basics – jeans, jumpers and tees – are anything but average and share the racks with edgy, glamorous frocks. There's sunglasses and jewellery, and the odd pair of screen-printed undies. Not for shrinking violets.

## FAT Map pp84–5               Fashion, Accessories
☎ 9510 2311; www.fat4.com; 272 Chapel St, Prahran; 🚇 Prahran, 🚊 78, 79
The Fat girls' empire has changed the way Melbourne dresses, catapulting a fresh generation of designers into the city's consciousness. There's an antifashion edge here, with labels that are more darkly interesting, witty and irreverent than glam. It also has a great range of kid's wear and some of the best boy's tees in town. There are also branches in the city centre (Map pp52–3; ☎ 9662 3332; GPO, 250 Bourke St, Melbourne) and Fitzroy (Map pp74–5; ☎ 9486 0391; 209 Brunswick St, Fitzroy).

## FOOL Map pp84–5                       Fashion
☎ 9521 4909;118 Greville St, Prahran; 🚇 Prahran, 🚊 78, 79
Long-time Greville St resident Rowena Doolan designs practical (though never boring) wearables in compelling rainbow colours. Her winter collections of cable knits and warming wide scarves are particularly strong and well suited to Melbourne's chilly days.

## HUSK Map pp84–5            Fashion, Homewares
☎ 9827 2700; www.husk.com.au; 557 Malvern Rd, Toorak; 🚊 72
Long-time love of the local bobo (bourgeois bohemian) tribe. The clothes on the hangers here are as eclectic and earthy as the surrounds and take in the best Australian and New Zealand designers. There's a selection of own-brand teas and homewares, as well as a peaceful café serving healthy dishes and morish, slightly Moorish cakes. There are also branches in the city centre (Map pp52–3; ☎ 9663 0655; 176 Collins St, Melbourne) and Albert Park (Map pp92–3; ☎ 9690 6994; 123 Dundas Pl, Albert Park)

## SCANLAN & THEODORE
Map pp84–5                    Fashion, Accessories
☎ 9824 1800; 66 Chapel St, South Yarra; 🚇 South Yarra, 🚊 78, 79
S&T helped define the Melbourne look back in the 1980s and are still going strong with superfeminine, beautifully tailored everyday and special-occasion wear. Although now considered a mature, mainstream label, its clothes always manage to make a statement. Cleverly sourced accessories and luxurious knits are very hard to pass up. There are also branches in the city centre (Map pp52–3; ☎ 9650 6195; 285 Little Collins St, Melbourne) and Armadale (Map pp84–5; ☎ 9824 6444; 1061 High St, Armadale).

## STOCK LIQUIDATOR
Map pp84–5                    Fashion, Homewares
☎ 9521 4655; 287 Chapel St, Prahran; 🚇 Prahran, 🚊 78, 79
Come to this discount barn – usually known by its snappy acronym TSL (for 'The' Stock Liquidator) – to stock up on basics. You'll find a huge range of Australia's cherished cotton-knit label Bonds, including, of course, the iconic Chesty singlet, in sizes 000 to XXL, plus new-fangled basics like yoga pants and bandeau bikinis.

## TL WOOD Map pp84–5                    Fashion
☎ 9510 6700; www.tlwoodaustralia.com; 216 Chapel St, Prahran; 🚇 Prahran, 🚊 78, 79
Teresa Liano has styled Melbourne's best dressed behind the scenes for years. Her luscious label gives women what they really want: the loveliest silks and wools, and cuts that both flatter the female form and subtly demand attention. One of her soft knit scarves will keep you warm for years.

The shop, which feels more like a very stylish front room, also has a wonderful range of jewellery by local artisans. There's also a branch in the city centre (Map pp52–3; ☎ 9671 4792; 1 Albert Coates Lane, QV, Melbourne).

## MANON BIS  Map pp84–5  Homewares

☎ 9521 1866; 568 Malvern Rd, Hawksburn; 🚃 72

Homewares that come with loads of French flair. The range takes in both traditional and contemporary tastes. It also stocks cult canvas plimsoles by Bensimon.

## PROVIDER  Map pp84–5  Shoes, Fashion

☎ 9529 2629; www.provider.com.au; 114 Greville St, Prahran; 🚉 Prahran, 🚃 78, 79

If the term 'Air Max' flips your burger, you'll love this trainer temple that stocks Nike to New Balance and what's known as street apparel. There's also a branch in the city centre (Map pp52–3; ☎ 9654 4055; 11 Manchester Lane, Melbourne)

## ZOMP  Map pp84–5  Shoes

☎ 9827 1933; 546 Chapel St, South Yarra; 🚉 South Yarra, 🚃 78, 79

At sale time or on a Saturday afternoon there's a thinly veiled air of hysteria in here; shoes can do it to the best of us. The range is the main draw: you can get anything from a pair of superb Italian boots that will cost most of a week's wage to a pair of knock-off ballet flats or flip-flops for well under $100. There are also branches on Little Collins St (Map pp52–3; ☎ 9639 6728; 271 Little Collins St, Melbourne) and Flinders Lane (Map pp52–3; ☎ 9650 4431; 277 Flinders Lane, Melbourne).

## ANGELUCCI 20TH CENTURY

Map pp84–5  Vintage, Homewares

☎ 9525 1271; www.angelucci.net.au; 192 High St, Windsor; 🚃 6

Specialising in furniture from the '50s and '60s, Dean Angelucci's store is well known for its treasures. There are smaller pieces such as lighting and ceramics as well as the best-of-the-bunch sofas and sideboards.

## ROUTE 66  Map pp84–5  Vintage, Fashion

☎ 9529 4659; www.route66.com.au; 2 Grattan St Prahran; 🚉 Prahran

Route 66 has been dressing Melbourne cowboys and girls in American vintage for years. Find top-quality bowling shirts, va-va-voom pencil skirts, seamed stockings and baseball jackets, as well as its own range of custom clothing. The Garage also has in-store gigs; check the website for details. There's also a branch on Swanston St (Map pp52–3; ☎ 9639 5669; Shop 7, Cathedral Arcade, 37 Swanston St, Melbourne).

## SHAG  Map pp84–5  Vintage, Fashion

☎ 9510 8817; 130 Chapel St, Windsor; 🚉 Windsor, 🚃 78, 79

This shop is jam-packed with super stylist-ordained vintage pieces, including shoes, furs and bags (and often jam-packed with the girls that love them). Those in the know also snap up the well-priced collection of frighteningly fashion-forward new dresses, jackets and tops shipped from Hong Kong. There are also branches in the city centre (Map pp52–3; ☎ 9663 8166; Shop 20, Centre Way Arcade, Collins St, Melbourne) and Fitzroy (Map pp74–5; ☎ 9417 3348; 377 Brunswick St, Fitzroy).

# ST KILDA & AROUND

As you'd expect from a suburb so dedicated to leisure, St Kilda has a slew of interesting boutiques and homewares stores. Things are spread out, and Grey, Blessington and Barkly Sts shouldn't be overlooked. The suburb's east, Carlisle St (over Brighton Rd), is more local, but no less urbane and has a couple of fashion stores that are worth a stroll.

## CHRONICLES BOOKSHOP

Map pp88–9  Books

☎ 9537 2677; 91 Fitzroy St, St Kilda; 🕙 10am-10pm; 🚃 16, 96

Contemporary fiction – particularly Australian literature and crime – is the thing in this petit space. Nonfiction specialities include travel and cooking. Savvy staff at this compact store can help you find your perfect read.

## CHALK N CHEESE

Map pp88–9  Children's Wear

☎ 9534 4939; www.chalkncheeseclothing.com.au; 27 Blessington St, St Kilda; 🚃 96

Chalk N Cheese offers a limited range of beautifully made kids clothes (for babes and up to six) with a gently nostalgic style and luxurious (though practical) fabrics. The vintage aesthetic carries through to the colours, which are a rich departure from the usual pastels.

## HIGH STREET, ARMADALE

Once the place to shop for a Chesterfield or bid at Sotheby's, picturesque High St's core demographic has recently got a whole lot hipper. Designers such as Arabella Ramsay (Map pp84–5; ☎ 9824 4490; http://arabellaramsay.com; 1073 High St), Nicholson (Map pp84–5; ☎ 9824 4311; 1037 High St), Lee Matthews (Map pp84–5; ☎ 9822 8174; www .leematthews.com.au; 1059 High St) and Scanlan & Theodore (Map pp84–5; ☎ 9824 6444; 1061 High St) have flagship shops here and are joined by other inspired retailers such as Chambermaid (Map pp84–5; ☎ 9576 0529; 1052 High St) and Manon Cie (Map pp84–5; ☎ 9821 0760; 1011 High St). Macro WholeFoods Market (Map pp84–5; ☎ 9947 1111; www.macrowholefoods.com.au; 1068 High St) has set up shop in an old pub to keep the fashionistas in fuel (yes, green *is* the new black). The back streets near the grand Victorian train station also boast a maze of shops. Don't miss Market Imports (Map pp84–5; ☎ 9500 0764; 19 Morey St), which lovingly sources its ceramics, textiles, toys and other assorted wares from artisans in Mexico and Italy.

### THIRD DRAWER DOWN
Map pp88–9                     Craft, Homewares
☎ 9534 4088; www.thirddrawerdown.com; 52 Robe St, St Kilda; ⊗ 1-6pm Thu-Fri, 11am-4pm Sat; ⊕ 96
Abigail Crompton designs and commissions witty rethinks of everyday objects. Illustrative, hand-printed tea towels were the beginning, now there's 'artkerchiefs', 'bubkins' and 'artprons'. Both shop and gallery, it's equally good for grabbing gifts or leisurely browsing.

### 8 INKERMAN Map pp88–9     Fashion, Accessories
☎ 9534 1123; www.8inkerman.com; 8 Inkerman St, St Kilda; ⊗ closed Sun; ⊕ 96
While 'beach' and 'cashmere' won't score points in a word association test, it all makes sense on a wild and woolly St Kilda day. Simple styles and basic shades in the yarn of the moment, plus odd little accessories like rosettes and long-armed mittens.

### DOT & HERBEY
Map pp88–9                     Fashion, Accessories
☎ 9593 6309; www.dotandherbey.com; 229 Barkly St, St Kilda
Grandma Dot and Grandpa Herb smile down upon this tiny corner boutique from a mural-sized photo, right at home among the vintage floral fabrics and retro style. This is definitely not somewhere to go if you're looking for chain-store same-same; its also a colourful departure from the Melbourne black dictate.

### HOSS Map pp88–9           Fashion, Accessories
☎ 9537 0933; Shop 3, 135 Fitzroy St, St Kilda; ⊕ 16, 96
Hoss has saved many a St Kilda-ite from I-need-a-new-outfit-by-6pm meltdown.

There's a great range of jeans, shirts, knitwear and, yes, party dresses, as well as menswear. It stocks locals but keeps the St Kilda–Bondi bonding going with an emphasis on Sydney labels. There's another branch on Barkly St (Map pp88–9; ☎ 9537 1750; 210 Barkly St, St Kilda) so you're never far from a fashion fix.

### HUDSON Map pp88–9        Fashion, Accessories
☎ 9525 8066; 229 Carlisle St, Balaclava; ⊕ Balaclava
Local artists regularly take over the front window – this cute shop doesn't know how to do boring. From kid's wear to streetwear, the pieces are all individually sourced from Japan, Europe and the US.

### MONARCH CAKE SHOP Map pp88–9     Food
☎ 9534 2972; 103 Acland St, St Kilda; ⊗ 7am-10pm; ⊕ 96
St Kilda's Eastern European cake shops have long drawn crowds that come to peer at the sweetly stocked windows. This is a favourite; its *kugelhof*, plum cake and poppy-seed cheesecake can't be beaten.

### ST KILDA ESPLANADE SUNDAY MARKET Map pp88–9     Market
www.esplanademarket.com; Upper Esplanade, btwn Cavell & Fitzroy Sts, St Kilda; ⊗ 10am-5pm Sun; ⊕ 96
Fancy shopping with a seaside backdrop? A kilometre of trestle tables joined end-to-end carry individually crafted products from toys to organic soaps to large metal sculptures of fishy creatures. Souvenir alert: longtime stallholder Matt Irwin sells photographic images of Melbourne at its moody best, from postcards to framed prints.

## BITCH IS BACK

Map pp88–9      Vintage, Homewares

☎ 9534 8025; 100a Barkly St, St Kilda;
☼ closed Mon

Great stock of retro furniture from the fun to the obsessively collectible. Among the flokati rugs and Danish sofas there's plenty of pieces of bright Italian pottery that won't make too much of a dint in your luggage space.

## HUNTER GATHERER

Map pp88–9      Vintage, Fashion

☎ 9593 8168; www.huntergatherer.com.au; 82a Acland St, St Kilda; 🚋 96

Run by the welfare organisation Brotherhood of St Laurence, Hunter Gatherer filters through its 26-odd op shops to bring you the cream of secondhand gear. It also stocks its own vintage-inspired label, designed by recent fashion graduates and guaranteed to be made without sweat-shop labour. All profits go to programs to assist low-income families, the elderly and the unemployed. There's also a branch in Fitzroy (Map pp74–5; ☎ 9415 7371; 274 Brunswick St, Fitzroy).

# SOUTH MELBOURNE, PORT MELBOURNE & ALBERT PARK

While you might not necessarily cross town for the shopping alone, this area's seaside location makes for a relaxed (though none the less considered) retail environment. Head for Dundas Pl in Albert Park; a wander in either direction affords some leisurely window shopping. In and around the South Melbourne Market (p91) there is a vibrant scene: don't miss the quietly stylish Coventry St. Port Melbourne's Bay St, once most noted for its supermarket facilities, is now giving its bayside sisters a run for their pin money.

## AVENUE BOOKS Map pp92–3    Books

☎ 9690 2227; www.avenuebookstore.com.au; 127 Dundas Pl, Albert Park; ☼ 9am-7pm; 🚋 1

Everyone needs a neighbourhood bookshop like this one, full of nooks and crannies to perch with literary fiction, cooking, gardening, art and children's books. Cluey staff make spot-on recommendations too.

## COVENTRY BOOKSTORE

Map pp92–3           Books

☎ 9686 8200; www.coventrybookstore.com.au; 265 Coventry St, South Melbourne; 🚋 112

A fab independent bookstore with a good travel section as well as titles that appeal to the designers, architects and ad-land creatives that work around here. It's warm and woody and there's also a special children's area.

## SPECKLEFARM

Map pp92–3      Craft, Stationery

☎ 9696 2477; www.specklefarm.com.au; 111 Bridport St, Albert Park; 🚋 1

Striped grosgrain ribbon and sweetly patterned stationery will appeal to both big and little girls (and some boys too). Craft-envy doesn't hit so hard here, as it's all made to look easy and the staff are superhelpful.

## MANON Map pp92–3      Homewares

☎ 9686 1530; 294 Park St, South Melbourne; 🚋 112

French homewares specialist Manon features pieces with a provincial earthiness and a contemporary twist. You'll find lots of products you've not seen anywhere else before, as well as stylish staples such as Diptyque candles. The store is a little bit of a hike from the action, but all the more special in its wide corner Victorian shopfront. Also in Hawksburn (p119) and Armadale (opposite).

## NEST Map pp92–3      Homewares

☎ 9699 8277; 291 Coventry St, South Melbourne; 🚋 112

This light, bright homewares store stocks Spacecraft screen-printed textiles as well as Aesop skincare. It does its own range of cotton knit 'comfort wear' that's way too nice to hide at home in.

## KITTY K Map pp92–3      Lingerie

☎ 9699 4100; 113 Bridport St, Albert Park; 🚋 1

This splendidly girly-girl shop is the place to go for special-occasion lingerie designed by the likes of Kirrily Johnston. Unlike the rest of the stock, Zoe Elizabeth's Liberty Print bikinis can be worn in public without causing too much of a commotion. The rest will need to be kept under wraps.

## PHARMAKON Map pp92–3 · Perfume, Skincare

☎ 9646 8188; 86 Bay St, Port Melbourne; 🚊 109
Underneath the chandeliers there's a huge
collection of the world's most intriguing
perfumes, candles and skincare. Carthusia,
10 Corso Como and more will please the
pickiest of noses. Up the back, there's a
compounding pharmacy hard at work.

## EMPIRE VINTAGE

Map pp92–3 · Vintage, Homewares

☎ 9682 6677; 63 Cardigan Pl, Albert Park; 🚊 1
Lyn Gardener's style is evident in every
last piece of stock in this bounteous space.
Vintage dresses, aprons, bedspreads, fabrics
and jewellery share the shelves with some
wonderfully strange industrial paraphernalia. All pieces are sourced from far and wide
or lovingly handcrafted from
beautiful materials.

## IZZI & POPO Map pp92–3 · Vintage, Homewares

☎ 9696 1771; www.izziandpopo.com.au; 258
Ferrars St, South Melbourne; 🕙 closed Tue; 🚊 96
This charming superstuffed antiques store
sources much of its stock from Belgium. You
could possibly ship an antique zinc bath
home, but if you're looking for something
more suitcase sized there's plenty of kooky
gems from asparagus dishes to lithographs.

## MACPHEE'S FOR THE WINE
## ENTHUSIAST Map pp92–3 · Wine

9696 2300; www.macphees.com; 249 Coventry St,
South Melbourne; 🚊 112
This shop is the retail arm of one of Melbourne's largest private cellaring outfits. It
stocks a huge range of top-quality stemware,
decanters and other vinous accessories such
as corkscrews. There's also a good selection
of reference books for wine buffs.

# top picks

- Vue de Monde (p128)
- Circa at the Prince (p139)
- Press Club (p129)
- Tempura Hajime (p143)
- Bar Lourinhã (p131)
- Seamstress (p130)
- Cumulus Inc (p130)
- St Jude's Cellar (p135)
- Journal Canteen (p131)
- Gill's Diner (p130)

# EATING

Melbourne is one of the world's great food cities. While it doesn't have the deeply ingrained traditions and profound self-confidence of, say, Paris, Rome, Bangkok or Tokyo, it has an open, genuine exuberance about food and cooking and a talent for innovation and adaptation. It's a thrilling city for anyone who lives to eat. It shares with Sydney the Modern Australian cooking style (Mod Oz to its mates), a loose term that describes a mix of European and Asian or Middle Eastern techniques and ingredients, with a seasonal, produce-driven philosophy similar to Californian cuisine. It can also be used to describe a more straightforward adoption of dishes or ingredients from various cultures that have appeared on menus and in home kitchens; toasted pide, avocado and vegemite, anyone? This hybrid way of eating has gathered its influences from the migrants that make up the city's population. Melbourne's version of Mod Oz, and the city's culinary offerings in general, tend slightly more towards European and Mediterranean traditions, rather than Sydney's firmly Pacific Rim take. This is both a product of the city's very untropical climate, with four distinct seasons, and also perhaps due to the stronger impact Melbourne's Italian, Greek and Middle Eastern communities made on the city during the 1960s and 70s. That's not to say that you won't find wonderful Asian cooking and a host of varied Asian influences here. There's a particularly vibrant Vietnamese restaurant scene and an increasing breadth of Chinese cuisines available too.

Chefs in Melbourne aren't *exactly* celebs in the Ramsey/Roubouchon/Batali mould, with multiple franchises and massive marketing budgets, but they do enjoy a very high profile. Melburnians gobble up the *Age*'s food supplement 'Epicure' every Tuesday to keep up with who's doing what in which restaurant kitchen. They watched with an air of polite distain as the Crown Casino (p62) imported several stellar Sydney chefs (and one international franchise, Nobu; see p134) but in the name of a good feed, have embraced these as well.

The Melbourne Food & Wine Festival (see p13) in March is a highlight for gourmets and greedy amateurs alike; the city's best restaurants offer fixed-price lunches for a steal. As well as 'Epicure', the *Age* newspaper publishes the annual *Good Food Guide* and its companion *Cheap Eats*. Many of the restaurant reviews can be found on the newspaper's website (www.theage.com.au); its coverage reaches further into the suburbs than this chapter can.

## HISTORY & CULTURE

The site of Melbourne was seen as a very special place to live long before John Batman set eyes on the natural falls of the Yarra. The Wurunjeri thrived because of the area's incredible bounty; the wetlands that spread south of the Yarra were teeming with life, and the Yarra itself brimmed with fish, eels and shellfish. Depending on the season, indigenous 'Melburnians' would have eaten roast kangaroo, waterfowl, fish and eel, as well as greens, grubs, yam daisies and sweet cordial concocted from banksia blossoms. The first Europeans didn't stop to notice the prelapsarian supermarket they had stumbled upon, instead rather quickly going about planting European crops and tending large flocks of sheep. Although many new arrivals were astounded by the ready supply of fresh food (especially the Irish, who were escaping the famine of the 1840s), the early settlers dined mainly on mutton, bread and butter, tea, beer

and rum. But it's hard to imagine that a few of them familiar with the gentle art of poaching didn't dine on ducks and geese. A recent archaeological dig in Little Lonsdale St area of the city revealed bones, seeds and shells that suggest, by the later part of the 19th century at least, Melburnians diets were, in fact, pretty diverse. Fine cuts of meat, fresh fruits and vegetables graced their tables. Seafood was also a staple, and oysters were not considered a luxury.

Melbourne has always been a multicultural city, but apart from the long-standing influence of the Chinese community, food tastes didn't really begin to shift from the Anglo-Celtic basics until the 1950s, when there was a large influx of Eastern European and southern Mediterranean migrants. As well as importing the goods they couldn't do without, such as olives, they set to producing cheeses, sauces and small goods that gradually found their way from specialist delis into mainstream supermarkets.

As far as restaurant culture goes, the dominance of the pub and the local 'Chinese' also began to be challenged it the 1950s. The 1956 Olympics organisers imported European chefs to help with catering, many of whom chose to stay on long after the athletes had gone home. Immigrants Georges and Mirka Mora opened their seminal restaurant at this time too. The Vietnamese, Lebanese and Turkish migrants that came to Melbourne in the 1970s have also had a lasting impact on the city's food culture. These days, rice-paper rolls, falafel and flat breads are more common on school 'tuckshop' menus than meat pies.

The last 10 years have seen an increasing interest in organic produce and provenance. Many Melburnians often shop at markets for locally grown or produced specialties, and at ethnic grocers and markets for imported spices and other ingredients. The Slow Food movement has a strong presence state-wide and there's a monthly Slow Food Market (p73), which joins a host of other farmers markets in Melbourne and around the state. Famed chef and writer Stephanie Alexander has developed a kitchen garden and cooking curriculum at an inner-city school that aims to instil a love of fresh produce and the culinary arts in a new generation. The program is set to be rolled out to other schools. What might be considered 'gourmet' in many other places, is just keeping it real in Melbourne.

# HOW MELBOURNE EATS

Many Melburnians have grown up with at least one other culinary culture besides the rather grim Anglo-Australian fare of the mid-20th century; they are also inveterate travellers. This makes for a city of adventurous, if often highly critical, palates. Melbourne's food scene is one of almost limitless choice; there is a constant flow of new ideas, new places and reinvention.

At the top end of the food chain, fine diners thrive. You'll find menus rove across regions rather than slavishly following the posh Anglo-French model. There are those that closely follow a contemporary French direction, such as Vue du Monde (p128) but you're more likely to see a thoughtful pan-Mediterranean menu, like that of the Botanical (p141). Others incorporate Asian ideas and flavours in what is often termed Mod Oz: Andrew McConnell at his legendary Carlton restaurant Three, One, Two (at time of writing relocating to Gertrude St, Fitzroy with a name change) and at Circa at the Prince (p139), Fed Square's Taxi (p129), Ezard at Adelphi (p128) and Richmond's Pearl (p134) to name a few. Upmarket Italian is done well: old school at Grossi Florentino Grill (p129) or casual at Becco (p129). Eastern Mediterranean is done with five-star flair at Greg Malouf's Momo (due to open in late 2008; see www.momorestaurant.com.au) or Maha (p130). The Press Club (p129) and Mini (p129) champion Mod Greek dining. While many Melbourne chefs experiment widely, mixing and matching technique and ingredient, you'll rarely find chefs doing fusion for fusion sake. There's too much respect for providence and context.

Given that there's so much to try, Melburnians love to eat out often. The city really shines when it comes to a more informal, grazing style of dining and you'll find that quality produce and attention to detail don't flag. Small and large plates override the standard three course chronology, flavours sing and everyone digs in. Bar food is no longer seen as a mere consort to booze, nowadays it's an equal marriage of tastes and experiences. It's something that locals love to do, but it's also a great way for visitors to taste some of the city's best cooking without the credit-card king-hit of a fine dining dinner. Pub grub is also popular, and ranges from what constitutes full-blown restaurants in a pub environment to a basic counter-meal service with heartily nostalgic dishes such as bangers and mash, steaks, roasts and the ubiquitous multicultural chimera, the chicken parma (a flattened chicken breast served in loose appropriation of the Sicilian *parmiggiana* style).

There's also no shortage of *really* casual food that's done with the love and attention and is great value for money. A steaming bowl of pho, a square of spanakopita, a teriyaki salmon inari or a provolone and prosciutto piadina will probably leave you change from a tenner, but not leave you in any doubt of Melbourne's status as a food city. And while some Melburnians lunch on wan sandwiches at their desks, there's also plenty who are slurping noodles or hoeing into a slice of very good pizza.

Cafés are an integral part of life, with many Melburnians up early so they can catch up with colleagues (or just the newspaper) over a coffee and a slice of sourdough toast before the work day begins. Coffee quality is hotly debated; everyone has a favourite roaster and

## MELBOURNE CHEFS TO TAKE AWAY

### MoVida; Spanish Culinary Adventures (Frank Camorra & Richard Cornish)

The recipe for Camorra's divinely light flaky *empanada* pastry is worth the sticker-price alone. The bright pages provide a wealth of tapas recipes as well as capturing the verve of this evergreen laneway bar.

### The Press Club (George Calombaris)

Beautifully photographed and laid out, George Calombaris' inspired take on Greek cooking at the Press Club (p129), jumps from the pages of this lovely book. His recipes cover all aspects of the cuisine, and the book includes a chapter on ouzo.

### Arabesque (Greg & Lucy Malouf)

The force behind Melbourne's happening Modern Middle Eastern scene, Greg Malouf co-wrote this exquisite book with his ex, Lucy. It's now been in print for several years, bringing the exciting flavours, techniques and culinary traditions of his Lebanese heritage to a new audience.

### My French Vue: Bistro Cooking at Home (Shannon Bennett)

Shannon Bennett's degustation dining belongs strictly to the don't-try-this-at-home camp of cooking, but this book concentrates on bistro staples. The recipes have his signature creative twist but are explained thoughtfully and with a nod to solid traditions.

### Lotus Asian Flavours (Teague Ezard)

Learn all the tricks to conjure up great hawker dishes, curries and fragrant salads. Ezard has a wonderful take on Southeast Asian flavours, which is on show at his casual restaurant Gingerboy (p129), and in this book shows a knack for demystifying techniques for a non-Asian audience.

### Cook's Companion (Stephanie Alexander)

Although she no longer graces the city's stoves on a regular basis, Alexander's work continues via her writing, community programs and lasting influence on a whole generation of chefs. This is one of Australia's most well-thumbed cookbooks.

### Cooking from Memory: A Journey Through Jewish food (Hayley Smorgon, Gaye Weeden & Natalie King)

Not exactly a chef's book, but a collection of culinary journeys collected from 21 cooks. It's filled with recipes and stories that reflect the breadth and complexity of Australia's Jewish community, and show the lasting influence they have had on Melbourne's culinary landscape.

barista. Melbourne (and indeed most of Australia) wipes the floor with the coffee you'll get in London or Los Angeles – you'll need to hotfoot it to Milan to do better. And while the big chains like Starbucks have sprung up, they are shunned by locals who can't imagine why you need a cookie-cutter multinational to tell you how it's done when we've been getting the crème correct for well over 20 years. Soy coffee is polarising; some purist cafés refuse to offer it, along with skim or 'skinny' milk, while it forms a large part of many other's trade. Within the soy camp, there's two schools: Bonsoy and Vitasoy. These different brands of soy milk produce widely different tastes so it's worth noting which is used and deciding which (if either) you prefer.

Produce-wise, Queen Victoria Market (p57) and its suburban counterparts in South Melbourne (p91) and Prahran (p86), are beloved by locals for their fresh fruit and vegetables, meat and fish, as well as their groaning deli counters. There is also a weekly rota of Farmers Markets (www.mfm.com.au), which bring local suppliers and fresh produce to town. They make for a pleasant Saturday morning coffee and food-related stroll.

# VEGETARIANS & VEGANS

While Melbourne doesn't have the shout-out vegan culture of Los Angeles or New York, vegetarians and vegans will have no trouble finding at least a few dishes on most menus that will please and no one will look askance at special requests. A few fine dining restaurants offer vegetarian degustation options, including Ezard at Adelphi (p128) and Jacques Reymond (p141), and while both of these are not vegan, with advance warning they can can be made dairy-free. Carlton's legendary Shakahari (p138) is one of the city's longest-running vegetarian places and it's both fancy enough for a night out but casual enough if you're just looking for a quick but lovingly prepared bite.

Most Asian restaurants will have large meat-free menus, but you'll need to be clear that you don't want oyster or fish sauce used, as these are common additions in Chinese, Vietnamese and Thai cooking. Japanese places, especially the more casual ones (see Alt-Japanese, p135) also have many vegetarian options, though again you'll need to ask if they can prepare your dish with *dashi*, or stock, that hasn't been made with bonito. Lunch in the Fo Guang Yuan Tea House ( ☎ 9642 2388; 141 Queen St, City) is guaranteed vegan; they also have a wonderful range of healing tea. Inner neighbourhoods also have their fair share of exclusively vego restaurants. In Fitzroy look for the big bustling Vegie Bar (Map pp74–5; ☎ 9417 6935; www.vegiebar.com.au; 380 Brunswick St, Fitzroy), Bala's (Map pp74–5; ☎ 9416 4077; 406 Brunswick St), Soul Food (Map pp74–5; ☎ 9419 2949; www.soulfoodcafe.com.au; 273 Smith St, Fitzroy) and the Moroccan Soup Bar (p136). In St Kilda try Soulmama (p140), Bala's (Map pp88–9; ☎ 95346116; 1C Shakespeare Grove, St Kilda) and Lentil as Anything (p141).

# COOKING COURSES & TOURS

Queen Victoria Market has its own cooking school (Map pp52–3; ☎ 9326 5048; www.qvm.com.au/cooking_school.php; 69 Victoria St, City) with short demonstration classes featuring local chefs and cookery writers. The range is wide and provides a great snapshot of the city's current culinary obsessions.

Prahran Market's Essential Ingredient (Map pp84–5; ☎ 9827 9047; www.theessentialingredient.com.au; Elizabeth St, South Yarra) has a well-regarded cooking school featuring Melbourne chefs with classes ranging from demonstrations to weekend workshops ($65 to $275) and will suit happy amateurs to kitchen pros.

Tony Tan's (off Map pp84–5 ☎ 9827 7347; www.tonytan.com.au; 28A Lansell Rd, Toorak) cooking school has classes that cover everything from Nonya secrets and effortless Cantonese to Mod Med, spice therapy and the something entitled 'sexy healthy'. His knowledge of Asian cuisines is consummate; he also has guest chefs from both Melbourne and around the country.

Learn how to make the perfect coffee with Lavazza Coffee Training ( ☎ 1300 307 171; www.coffeeclass.com). Courses run for three hours and are geared for either for the home user ($95) or the professional ($125). Are you experienced? Then do a postgrad in froth ($75) or grind ($125).

For tours, look to Alan Campion ( ☎ 0408-555 679; www.melbournefoodtours.com), author of the *Foodies' Guide to Melbourne*, who shares his knowledge of the city's food culture either by foot or bus. Suzie Wharton ( ☎ 9686 4655; www.chocoholictours.com.au) organises a range of popular chocolate tours. Chef and food writer Meera Freeman ( ☎ 9348 2221; www.meerafreeman.com.au) will take you on a three-hour tour of Richmond's Vietnamese precinct if you can organise a group of six to 12 ($75 per person). Learn about ingredients such as tiger lily buds and fish maw, and finish with a lunch of authentic specialties. If you are a long-term visitor, she also holds Italian, Thai, Vietnamese and North African cooking classes that run over four weeks in her fabulously stylish studio.

# PRACTICALITIES
## HOURS

Cafés and restaurants often open seven days a week, although some are closed on Sundays and/or Mondays. It's unusual for restaurants to open for lunch on a Saturday.

Cafés serve food all day and can open as early as 6.30am, especially in the city. Unless they also function as a bar or restaurant, they will start packing up at around 4pm. Restaurants serve lunch from noon to around 3pm and dinner from 6pm to around 10pm. It's always worth checking what time the kitchen closes if you are eating late. Many places will also offer an all-day bar meal that fills the midafternoon gap, as well as a supper menu. Only hours that deviate substantially from these will be mentioned in the reviews.

## PRICE GUIDE

The price ranges for food in this book use the $ symbol to indicate the cost of a two-course meal for one person, excluding drinks.

| $ | under $20 |
| $$ | $20-50 |
| $$$ | over $50 |

## BOOKING A TABLE

Most restaurants take reservations for both lunch and dinner. For the best restaurants, try to book at least a week ahead (more for weekends), but it's not unheard of to sneak in with a few hours' notice. Some, such as Vue du Monde and the Flower Drum, often require a booking at least a month in advance. It's increasingly popular for restaurants *not* to take bookings, which is handy if you want to eat early or are happy to wait at the bar.

## TIPPING

Hospitality staff in Australia have the 'luxury' of a minimum wage, so tipping is not compulsory and is usually based on the level of service you receive. That said, they often rely on tips to supplement what can be a pretty paltry living, depending on the establishment. If service is okay, leave around 10%; if it's exceptional, a little more. Cafés do not generally expect tips but will sometimes have a jar on the counter for you to show your love with loose change.

## CENTRAL MELBOURNE

Cafés spring into life at dawn during the week, and there's many places catering to the lunch needs of the city's workers and shoppers. Swanston St, north of Bourke St, is popular with students. Restaurants rarely rely on views (Taxi is a notable exception) and are spread throughout the city, with many hidden down alleys, in arcades or off the 'Little' streets.

### VUE DE MONDE

Map pp52–3                    French, Modern Australian $$$

☎ 9691 3888; www.vuedemonde.com.au; 430 Little Collins St; lunch/dinner menu gourmand from $100/150; ☺ lunch & dinner Tue-Fri, dinner Sat

# top picks

- Ladro (p136)
- Pizza e Birra (p140)
- DOC (p138)
- I Carusi II (p140)

Melbourne's favoured spot for occasion dining isn't stuffy; although set in a 19th-century barrister's chamber, the space is starkly luxe. This is degustation dining with a capital D: you choose how much gastronomic immersion you're up for and courses will be tailored accordingly. Two course lunch specials are available too ($55). Book ahead. If you're after something a little less rigorous, Bistro Vue ( ☎ 9691 3838) does brilliant French staples (goose-fat *frites* anyone?) in a riotous rendition of haute-bourgeois décor. The shopfront Café Vue ( ☎ 9691 3899) is open Mon-Fri from 7am and does astonishingly good-value breakfasts, brunches and lunch boxes (not to mention perfect Illy coffee and amazing pastries).

### EZARD AT ADELPHI

Map pp52–3                    Modern Australian $$$

☎ 9639 6811; www.ezard.com.au; 187 Flinders Lane; mains $45; ☺ lunch & dinner Mon-Fri, dinner Sat

Teague Ezard runs one of the city's enduring fine dining rooms. The space, a lanky basement beneath the Adelphi Hotel, is elegant but not as desperately fashion-forward as some. The food has an emphasis on Chinese and Thai flavours, though not exclusively so. Ezard's plating is bold, his

### ETHNIC EATS

Melbourne's ethnic cuisines were once tightly zoned, and although now spread widely over the city, there are still dedicated clusters. Richmond's Victoria St is packed with Vietnamese restaurants and providores; the western suburb of Footscray also draws those looking for the most authentic Vietnamese – as well as great African – food. Lygon St, Carlton has long been home to simple red-sauce Italian cooking, with a few notable innovators, and the coffee and delis are great. Chinatown is home to one of Australia's most renowned restaurants of any culinary persuasion, the Flower Drum (opposite). You'll find regional gems such as Dainty Sichuan (p131) as well as Japanese, Malaysian and Korean here too. One street up, Lonsdale St has a handful of Greek tavernas and bars. The northern suburb of Brunswick has a number of wonderful Middle Eastern bakers and grocers, as well as cafés. What's off the boil? Thai food often lacks the zing of that's found in Sydney, there's not a lot of upmarket Indian to be had, and (at the time of writing) nothing in the way of Modern Scando. But it's only a matter of time.

pairings inspired. An eight-course tasting menu ($135; $115 for the vegetarian option) is available as well as à la carte.

### TAXI Map pp52–3     Modern Australian $$$

☎ 9654 8808; www.transporthotel.com.au; Level 1, Transport Hotel, Federation Sq; mains $40-45; ☯ lunch & dinner

It takes a space this big to accommodate the reputation of head chef Michael Lambie. He creates audacious Asian-inspired dishes that have earned him a loyal following. The sushi menu is one of the city's finest. All glass, steel and concrete, the hangar-sized dining room looks over the river and Flinders Street Station. It's stagy, or as some Melburnians might mumble, a little bit 'Sydney'. After dinner, sip a *digestif* at Transit and watch the lights sparkle.

### FLOWER DRUM Map pp52–3     Chinese $$$

☎ 9662 3655; 17 Market Lane; mains $35-55; ☯ lunch Mon-Sat, dinner daily

The Flower Drum continues to be Melbourne's most celebrated Chinese restaurant. The finest, freshest produce prepared with absolute attention to detail keeps this Chinatown institution booked out for weeks in advance. The sumptuous but ostensibly simple Cantonese food is delivered with the slick service you'd expect in such elegant surrounds.

### PRESS CLUB Map pp52–3     Modern Greek $$$

☎ 9677 9677; 72 Flinders St; mains $35-45; ☯ lunch Sun-Fri, dinner daily

Melbourne's Mod-Greek scene is thriving, and George Calombaris' grand city space gives it the glamour it deserves. There's no fusion fussing, but rather a respect for the basics and a creative, playful sensibility. Think dolmades stuffed with roast quail, salmon cooked slowly in tzatziki and served with almond skordalia, or the 'Santorini breakfast' dessert (honey sorbet, yoghurt jelly and walnut biscuit). The separate bar area has a wonderful snacks menu that gives you a sense of the food without blowing the budget. Bookings required.

### GROSSI FLORENTINO GRILL

Map pp52–3     Italian $$

☎ 9662 1811; www.grossiflorentino.com; 80 Bourke St; mains $35; ☯ lunch & dinner Mon-Fri, dinner Sat

The Grill won't wow you with culinary curiosity, but it does offer an authentic regional

Italian menu with metropolitan flair and great produce. The Cellar Bar next door is brooding, intimate and affordable: a great place to have a quick bowl of pasta and a glass of pinot grigio. Service is snappy and professional. If you're into grand statements (with mains hitting the $50 mark), upstairs is an opulent fine dining stalwart.

### GINGERBOY Map pp52–3     Modern Hawker $$

☎ 9662 4200; www.gingerboy.com.au; 27-29 Crossley St; small dishes $12-14, large dishes $30-35; ☯ lunch & dinner Mon-Fri, dinner Sat

Brave the aggressively trendy surrounds and weekend party scene, as talented Teague Ezard does a fine turn in flash hawker cooking. Flavours pop in dishes such as scallops with green chilli jam or coconut kingfish with peanut and tamarind dressing. There are two dinner sittings, and bookings are required. Otherwise nab a seat at the bar and get eating. Don't overlook the sublime desserts: coconut tapioca topped with paw paw and lime salad or five spice ice cream will make for fond food memories.

### MINI Map pp52–3     Modern Greek $$

☎ 9650 8830; 141 Flinders Lane; mains $29-35; ☯ lunch & dinner Mon-Fri, dinner Sat

This warm, contemporary basement space does earthy, authentic Greek food that goes way beyond the dips and spit roast clichés. Seafood, pastries and interesting vegetable sides are all fresh and delicious, and the Greek wine list surprises too.

### SARTI RESTAURANT BAR

Map pp52–3     Italian $$$

☎ 9639 7822; 6 Russell Pl; mains $29-35; ☯ lunch & dinner Mon-Fri, dinner Sat

There's a lot of *ciao bella* schmooze going on, but the menu doesn't just flirt – it delivers. A joyful mix of the knowingly modern and rustically nostalgic: wild harvested venison is prettily parsed with pickled beetroot, celeriac puree and crispy beets or a perfect pistachio panna cotta is embellished with salted popcorn. Or a plate of pasta ($24) on the terrace makes for a soothing city lunch.

### BECCO Map pp52–3     Modern Italian $$$

☎ 9663 3000; www.becco.com.au; 11-25 Crossley St; mains $28-39; ☯ lunch & dinner Mon-Sat

Airy, bright Becco is a long-established favourite with a top end of town clientele.

EATING CENTRAL MELBOURNE

Staff are attentive and the menu is faultless, straight-up-and-down Italian. The laneway locale with wide window frontage ups the see-and-be-seen factor.

## COMME KITCHEN

Map pp52–3      Modern Australian $$$

☎ 9631 4000; www.comme.com.au; 7 Alfred Place; small plates $16-23, large plates $28-35; ⏰ lunch & dinner Mon-Fri, dinner Sat

Comme does great produce-driven European dishes that eschew prissiness in favour of robust flavours. The space is grand but not stuffy. It's unashamedly chic, filled with statement contemporary furniture and black-clad locals lounging on the broad banquettes.

## TRUNK Map pp52–3      Italian $$

☎ 9663 7994; www.trunktown.com.au; 275 Exhibition St; mains $28-35; ⏰ lunch & dinner Mon-Fri, dinner Sat

Trunk turns into a prime CBD watering hole on Friday nights, but don't let Bryan from the marketing department put you off. The building is over a hundred years old and was once a synagogue. It's had a thoughtful, witty fit-out and the seasonal pan-Italian menu is very now, while retaining an endearingly rustic edge. Bar snacks such as salt cod and green chilli fritters are great too.

## LONGRAIN Map pp52–3      Thai $$$

☎ 9671 3151; www.longrain.com; 44 Little Bourke St; mains $25-40; ⏰ lunch & dinner Mon-Fri, dinner Sat

The Wegner chairs and raw décor are fabulous, but like its Sydney sibling, the off-hand service, big-night-outers and woo-woo ear candy can make a chore out of getting your fill of the best Thai food in town. It's best at lunch, when you can book a table or bolt a few trout-topped betal leaves and gin slings at the bar.

## GILL'S DINER Map pp52–3      Modern European $$

☎ 9670 7214; rear, 360 Little Collins St; mains around $25; ⏰ lunch Mon, lunch & dinner Tue-Fri, dinner Sat

Tucked up the back of the Commercial Bakery, Gill's postindustrial pastiche is an immediate charmer. Add old vinyl and freshly baked bread to the mix and it makes for an archetypal Melbourne moment. Lunch can be as simple as smoked

salmon and *prosecco*; dinners are hearty, simple European fare – squid ink pasta, cotechino duck – done with effervescent flair. Details are attended to: the *clafouti* (custard) is individually baked to order and made with the most deliciously sour cherries.

## SEAMSTRESS Map pp52–3      Modern Chinese $$

☎ 9663 6363; www.seamstress.com.au; 113 Lonsdale St; mains $24-35; ⏰ lunch & dinner Mon-Fri, dinner Sat

Start off with a cocktail under a canopy of tiny *qipao* on the top floor, then make your way downstairs to the dining room for some contemporary Chinese cooking. The food – coconut and roe rice balls, curly-fried snapper or Onkaparinga venison with Szechuan pepper and a Chinese wine reduction – is as delicious as it sounds. The 19th-century warehouse, complete with rickety wooden stairs, is fabulously atmospheric. Their basement bar Sweatshop could be on the cards when you're done.

## CUMULUS INC

Map pp52–3      Modern Australian $$

www.cumulusinc.com.au; 45 Flinders Lane; mains $21-32; ⏰ breakfast, lunch & dinner Mon-Sat

Pascale Gomes-McNabb, Andrew McConnell and new partner Jayden Ong have created a casual, ever-changing city space to really settle into. The focus is on beautiful produce and simple but artful cooking: from breakfasts of sardines and smoked tomato on toast at the marble bar to suppers of freshly shucked clair de lune oysters tucked away on the leather banquettes.

## MAHA Map pp52–3      Middle Eastern $$

☎ 9629 5900; www.mahabg.com.au; 21 Bond St; small dishes $8-10, large dishes $20-26; ⏰ lunch & dinner Mon-Fri, dinner Sat

This is a sexy subterranean space that's great for lunch or dinner but even better for a late-night supper (the kitchen stays open until 3am Thursday to Saturday). It pays homage to the richness and complexity of Middle Eastern and Eastern Mediterranean cooking, but is done with a light, modern touch. Chef Shane Delia's Maltese heritage gets a look in too – rabbit is seldom off the menu.

## JOURNAL CANTEEN Map pp52-3    Italian $$

☎ 9650 4399; mezzanine, 253 Flinders Lane; mains $18; ☾ lunch Mon-Fri

Journal Canteen, tucked away up an obscure flight of stairs off the CAE building foyer, is no secret. It's packed to the rafters each lunchtime with diners lapping up Rosa Mitchell's sensational Sicilian-style antipasto plates, pastas, roasts and *ragus*. Be spared the agony of choice: Rosa bases her few offerings on what is fresh and seasonal on any given day. There's a $30 degustation deal, which comes with a complimentary *caffitere*-brewed coffee.

## COOKIE Map pp52-3    Thai $$

☎ 9663 7660; 1st fl, 252 Swanston St; mains $15-30; ☾ lunch & dinner

The Thai menu isn't the only surprise at this noisy, crowd-pleasing beer hall. The wine list is huge and features interesting by-the-glass drops from around the world, as well as a menu of spritzers that aren't just for mature ladies. Grab an Udinese (pinot grigio, soda and a twist) to go with prawns and lemongrass-scented coconut custard and then a wine flight to see you through your snapper curry. Bar side, you can't go past the DIY 'bliss bombs' – betel leaves to wrap around some very tasty morsels.

## HAKO JAPANESE Map pp52-3    Japanese $$

☎ 9620 1881; 310 Flinders Lane; mains $15-30; ☾ lunch & dinner Mon-Fri, dinner Sat

This Japanese restaurant, housed in a laneway warehouse space, is more downtown Tokyo than Kyoto tea ceremony. Lunch is a simple affair, with city workers opting for the fresh and tasty lunch set. Dinner sees Masahiro Horie pushing the menu beyond the basics; go for his specials to get the full measure of his talent.

## SUPPER INN Map pp52-3    Chinese $$

☎ 9663 4759; 15 Celestial Ave; mains $15-30; ☾ dinner

No-one minds queuing on the stairs to wait for a high-turnover table in the unglamorous upstairs dining room (especially as downstairs is cramped and clamorous). Bored waiters dressed in black and white, and dated décor don't detract: you're here for the top-quality Cantonese food. Open until 2.30am, Supper Inn is also a favoured after-drinks stop.

## SUNGS KITCHEN Map pp52-3    Chinese $$

☎ 9329 2636; www.sungskitchen.com.au; 118 Franklin St; mains $15-23; ☾ lunch & dinner

This bright and bustling pan-Chinese restaurant offers a beyond standard selection of authentic food, including a whole range of duck dishes (tea-smoked is a favourite) and some interesting vegetarian offerings. They do yum cha and have an extensive tea menu including those with pretty floating flowers.

## DAINTY SICHUAN Map pp52-3    Chinese $$

☎ 9663 8861; 26 Corrs Lane; mains $12-25; ☾ lunch Mon-Fri, dinner Sat & Sun

This hidden restaurant has a cult-like following and might just claim you too, if you like it hot. Chilli oil, dried chillies, ground chilli seeds, Sichuan peppercorns and well, chillies, join other less than dainty flavourings such as peanuts and vinegar to give you a range of pork, chicken and beef dishes that will rock your world. Bookings advised.

## MOVIDA Map pp52-3    Spanish $$

☎ 9663 3038; www.movida.com.au; 1 Hosier Lane; tapas $4-6, raciones $10-17; ☾ lunch & dinner

Movida is nestled in a cobbled laneway emblazoned with one of the world's densest collections of street art; it doesn't get much more Melbourne than this. Line up along the bar, cluster around little window tables or, if you've booked, take a table in the dining area. Tapas' tired reputation will be dispelled by one look at Frank Camorra's menu. It highlights regional styles and surprises with little treats such as *piquillo* peppers filled with crab and potato or mackerel served with pine-nut gazpacho sorbet.

## BAR LOURINHÃ Map pp52-3    Tapas $$

☎ 9663 7890; www.barlourinha.com.au; 37 Little Collins St; tapas $9-15 ☾ lunch & dinner Mon-Fri, Sat dinner

Matt McConnell's wonderful northern Spanish-Portuguese specialties have the swagger and honesty of an Iberian shepherd, but with a cluey, metropolitan touch. Start light with the melting, zingy kingfish pancetta and finish with the hearty house-made chorizo or baked *morcilla* (blood sausage). There's an intriguing wine list sourced from the region too. Come Friday night, the sardines are not just on the plate; but a lone spoonful of the Arabesque *crema* (custard) is worth the squeeze and the service is always accommodating.

### YU-U Map pp52-3      Japanese $$

☎ 9639 7073; 137 Flinders Lane; small dishes $8-15; ☽ lunch & dinner Mon-Fri

The sign is the size of a postage stamp and the doorway nondescript, so it's easy to miss. This sparsely elegant basement restaurant does smart Japanese fare, artfully presented and assuredly delivered. Go for the set-lunch menu ($15) of *bento* boxes, soup and noodles. Dinner is a progression of small dishes that can challenge and delight.

### ITALIAN WAITERS CLUB
Map pp52-3      Italian $

☎ 9650 1508; 1st fl, 20 Meyers Pl; mains $15-18; ☽ lunch & dinner

Down a laneway and up some stairs, once inside the Italian Waiters Club you'll feel like you stepped into another era. Opened in 1947, it still bears '50s drapes, wood panelling and Laminex tables. Once only for Italian and Spanish waiters to unwind after work over a game of *scopa* (a card game) and a glass of wine, now everyone from suits to students is allowed in for hearty plates of red-sauce pasta and the regularly changing roster of specials.

### PELLEGRINI'S ESPRESSO BAR
Map pp52-3      Italian, Café $

☎ 9662 1885; 66 Bourke St; mains $12-16; ☽ breakfast, lunch & dinner

The iconic Italian equivalent of a classic '50s diner, Pellegrini's has remained genuinely unchanged for decades. A gleaming coffee machine (often trumpeted as the first in Melbourne) churns out the good stuff. Pick and mix from the variety of pastas and sauces; from the table out the back you can watch it all thrown together from enormous ever-simmering pots. In summer, finish with a ladle of watermelon granita.

### KENZAN@GPO Map pp52-3      Japanese $

☎ 9663 7767; 350 Bourke St; mains $10-25; ☽ lunch Mon-Sat, dinner Thu & Fri

The casual kid sister of posh Kenzan ( ☎ 9654 8933; 56 Flinders Lane) makes the best sushi rolls in Melbourne. Yes, there's spicy tuna, but they also up the ante with soft-shell crab,

intriguing sesame-coated inside-outies, and a large range of *inari*. All come prewrapped for lasting crunch. There's sashimi, ramen, lunch sets and tea as well.

### LAKSA ME Map pp52-3      Malaysian $

☎ 9639 9885; www.laksame.com; Shop 1, 16 Liverpool St; mains $10-14; ☽ lunch & dinner Mon-Fri, dinner Sat & Sun

One of the city's more eccentric (and, we suspect, ironic) interiors is home to some great Malaysian grub. Laksa is king here (they even do a 'skinny' version), but there are also some out-of-the-ordinary entrée options like Chinese pastry triangles of diakon, yam bean and chive. There's a nice little beer list; wine drinkers will need to BYO.

### SUSHI TEN Map pp52-3      Japanese $

9639 6296; Port Phillip Arcade, 228 Flinders St; mains $8-15; ☽ Mon-Fri noon-4pm

This cheap and cheerful Japanese canteen pulls the lunchtime crowds that know the sushi is fresh. They also do a range of simple but authentic soups and rice dishes.

### PIADINA SLOWFOOD Map pp52-3      Café $

☎ 9662 2277; rear, 57 Lonsdale St; piadinas $8-12; ☽ breakfast & lunch Mon-Fri

Piadina fever took hold in Melbourne a few years back and still simmers away at this small, stealthily sited café. They make their own version of the Romagnan flat bread in house and fold them up with all manner of cleverly concocted combinations. A provolone and roast tomato one beats a regular breakfast toastie hands down (note that they open at 6am); at lunch, the meatball filling is a treat. They also do stews, curries and hearty bakes. Service doesn't take its cue from the titles: it's swift but the atmosphere cruises. There's often Studio One or Fat Freddy tunes in the air and the clientele tends towards the creative.

### CAMY SHANGHAI DUMPLING
### RESTAURANT Map pp52-3      Chinese $

☎ 9663 8555; 23-25 Tattersalls Lane; dishes $6.50; ☽ lunch & dinner

The best fast food in the CBD – wait a few minutes for a table, help yourself to plastic cups of overboiled tea and order a variety of dumplings – in broth, fried or steamed (don't go past the chilli oil

## COFFEE

Melburnians get anxious when there isn't a Gaggia hissing away every 20m, so you'll never be short of options. Here are our city favourites, just in case:

Brother Baba Budan (Map pp52–3; ☎ 9606 0449; 359 Little Bourke St) Cute city outpost of indie roasters St. Ali (p143). There's coffee, of course, and only the odd ruglach or biscuit to distract you. They also sell beans and a good range of coffee-related equipment.

Café Vue (Map pp52–3; ☎ 9691 3899; 430 Little Collins St) Excellent Illy coffee and a wondrous range of cakes, pastries and sandwiches. Join the cult that's sprung up around the pistachio cupcakes.

Commerical Bakery (Map pp52–3; ☎ 9670 7214; rear, 360 Little Collins St) Sweet things fresh from the oven sing a siren song: don't come here if a little sweet thing is out of the question.

Degraves (Map pp52–3; ☎ 9654 1245; Degraves St) Long-time latte champs keep it calm during the rush; chase a short black with a Bloody Mary if it's one of those mornings/early afternoons. The muffins are magnificent too.

Federal Coffee Palace (Map pp52–3; ☎ 9662 2224; GPO, Elizabeth St) Atmosphere plus, with tables beneath the colonnades of the GPO and the fashion retailer fave. Space heaters keep you toasty when the city turns chilly.

Journal Canteen (Map pp52–3; ☎ 9650 4399; Level 1, 253 Flinders Lane) Sweetly redolent of a library from days gone by, this is great place for wasting time. Coffee, of course, but also wine and good value meals.

Pellegrini's Espresso Bar (Map pp52–3; opposite) The coffee-in-a-tumbler fascination began here for most Melburnians over 40, and they're still serving it strong and with love. Granitas are great too.

Pushka (Map pp52–3; 20 Pesgrave Pl, off Howey Pl) Relaxed hipster hideaway with home-away-from-home charm, excellent coffee and Portuguese custard tarts. Just keep on going up that alley.

Superfino (Map pp52–3; ☎ 0407-773 754; 275 Flinders Lane) Hole in the wall deli-café that's stuffed to the rafters with provisions to fuel up hungry office workers.

Switchboard (Map pp52–3; Manchester Unity Arcade, 220 Collins St) Beneath the Man-U mosaics, there's Nana-style wallpaper, cupcakes and a coffee machine in a cupboard.

variety) – and some greens. This is one of the last places in town you can fill up for under $10.

### DON DON Map pp52–3 Japanese $
☎ 9670 3377; 321 Swanston St; mains $6-8; ☺ lunch Mon-Fri
Students, retailers and city kids storm the door come lunch at this uptown Japanese outlet. From the counter, order good quality *bento* boxes and bowls of curry and noodles; vegetarian options are also available, then keep up the pace and woof it down.

# SOUTHBANK & DOCKLANDS

If you're looking for flash, sparkle and a water view, you're in the right place. Many of the places you'll find in these areas are more about investment dollars than creative obsession, but Southbank, Docklands and even Crown do have some fabulous and surprisingly good-value dining options. New Quay's offerings are also delightfully diverse.

### ROCKPOOL BAR & GRILL
Map pp64–5 Steak, Modern Australian $$$
☎ 8648 1900; www.rockpoolmelbourne.com; Crown Complex, Whiteman St, Southbank; mains $20-150; ☺ lunch Sun-Fri, dinner daily
The Melbourne outpost of Perry's empire offers his signature seafood raw bar, but it's really all about beef, from grass-fed to full-blood wagyu. This darkly masculine space is simple and stylish, as is the menu. Even a side of humble mac'n'cheese is done with startlingly fab ingredients. The bar provides a respite from the formality of the dining room, but offers the same level of food service.

### GIUSEPPE, ARNALDO AND SONS
Map pp64–5 Italian $$
☎ 9694 7400; Crown Complex, Whiteman St, Southbank; mains $28-33; ☺ noon-midnight
Prodigal (and preternaturally talented) Maurizio Terzini sold Melbourne's *café e cucina* concept to Sydney and now he's brought North Bondi Italian back south. It's a splendid space – with the drama of a marble bar hung with small goods

## CROWN HEIGHTS

As well as Giuseppe, Arnaldo and Sons (p133) and Rockpool Bar & Grill (p133), the Crown Casino complex also boasts the following eating options:

Bistro Guillaume (Map pp64–5; ☎ 9693 3888; www.bistroguillaume.com.au; mains $25-120; ☿ lunch & dinner) Sydney's famed Frenchman does bistro food with fine-dining flair, star local recruit Philippa Sibley is the pudding queen.

Nobu (Map pp64–5; ☎ 9696 6566; www.noburestaurants.com; mains $20-200; ☿ lunch & dinner) We're still not sure if Melbourne really needed a Nobu in the first place, but it's a seductive space for those out to impress.

Brasserie by Philippe Mouchel (Map pp64–5; mains $29-100; ☎ 9292 7808; www.thebrasserieatcrown.com.au; ☿ lunch & dinner) Local chef's French comfort food is probably just what you'll need when the roulette table has got the better of you.

Koko (Map pp64–5; ☎ 9292 6886; www.kokoatcrown.com.au; mains $34-200; ☿ lunch & dinner) Very traditional Japanese dining with ultra-fresh fish, teppanyaki and a sake bar.

and a spot-lit bread station – and but be prepared for some noise and bustle. Food is enticing, stunningly fresh and exciting, while retaining a produce-driven simplicity. The menu is flexible and great for sharing.

### TUTTO BENE Map pp64–5 Italian $$
☎ 9696 3334; www.tuttobene.com.au; Midlevel, Southgate; mains $18-36; ☿ lunch & dinner
There's other *primi piatti* on offer but the main event here is risotto. They range from a simple Venetian *risi e bisi* (rice and peas) to some fabulously luxe options involving truffles or roast quail or aged balsamic. Fine house-made gelato is the requisite desert; you can drop in anytime just for a *coppa* scooped from an outside servery.

### MECCA BAH Map pp64–5 Middle Eastern $$
☎ 9642 1300; www.meccabah.com; 55a New Quay Promenade; mains $17-20; ☿ lunch & dinner
This opulent hexagon-shaped restaurant serves Turkish pizza and a selection of mezze all day. Their mains – mostly tagines and grills – are hearty and spicy (welcome when the wind is whipping up the bay outside), as are the open Bedouin-style fireplaces.

### BOPHA DEVI Map pp64–5 Cambodian $$
☎ 9600 1887; www.bophadevi.com; 27 Rakaia Way, Docklands; mains $15-25; ☿ lunch & dinner
The modern Cambodian food here is a delightful mix of novel and familiar Southeast Asian flavours and textures. Herb-strewn salads, noodles and soups manage to be both fresh and filling.

### BHOJ Map pp64–5 Indian $$
☎ 9600 0884; www.bhoj.com.au; 54 New Quay Promenade; mains $10-25; ☿ lunch & dinner
Dockland locals are lucky: they're sitting on Melbourne's best Indian. Posh surroundings don't dim the authentic flavours. Order up big: the Konkan fish curry is great, as are the standard dhals, naans and tandoori dishes. The lunch menu is a steal. Service is charming but can be slow.

# EAST MELBOURNE & RICHMOND

Richmond's main draw is restaurant-packed Victoria St. Most places here offer a similar menu with a long list of Vietnamese and Chinese favourites, and there are also a number of *pho* shops.

### PEARL Map pp68–9 Modern Australian $$$
☎ 9421 4599; www.pearlrestaurant.com.au; 631-633 Church St, Richmond; mains $35-48; ☿ lunch & dinner daily; ☒ South Yarra, ☒ 69
Owner-chef Geoff Lindsay proclaims himself 'a fifth-generation Aussie boy who is seduced by ginger, chilli and palm sugar, Turkish delight, chocolate and pomegranate'. We're seduced too: his exquisitely rendered food really does epitomise Modern Australian cooking. The space is slick but comfortable, service is smart, and the bar, which stays open till midnight, jumps with the fashion crowd from across the river.

## PACIFIC SEAFOOD BBQ HOUSE
Map pp68–9                                          Chinese $$

☎ 9427 8225; 240 Victoria St, Richmond; mains $15-25; 🕑 lunch & dinner daily; 🚇 North Richmond, 🚊 24, 109

Seafood in tanks and script-only menus on coloured craft paper make for an authentic, fast and fabulous dining experience. Tank-fresh fish is done simply, perhaps steamed with ginger and greens, and washed down with Chinese beer. Book, or be ready to queue.

## RICHMOND HILL CAFE & LARDER
Map pp68–9                                       Mediterranean $$

☎ 9421 2808; www.rhcl.com.au; 48-50 Bridge Rd, Richmond; brunch $12-30; 🕑 breakfast & lunch; 🚇 West Richmond, 🚊 48, 75

A weekend brunch here is worth the queues, not only because you can browse the produce store and rifle the cheese room while you wait. The food is simple, comforting, often surprising and always made with the best seasonal ingredients.

## MIHN MIHN
Map pp68–9                                    Vietnamese, Laotian $$

☎ 9427 7891; 94 Victoria St, Richmond; mains $10-18; 🕑 lunch Wed-Sun, dinner Tue-Sun; 🚇 North Richmond, 🚊 109

Mihn Mihn specialises in fiery Laotian dishes – the herby green and chilli red beef salad is a favourite – but does all the Vietnamese staples too. Service is swift and it's always packed with families, hip kids, students and boys fuelling up for a night out at the Laird Hotel (p178).

# FITZROY & AROUND

Brunswick St's reputation as a place to eat might seem unfounded if you encounter another same old variation on the same old café theme. But there are some gems among the dross. Likewise, Gertrude St has some very in-teresting food options, all in a low-key setting, while Smith St offers at least one of everything from pork rolls to *moules frites*.

## OLD KINGDOM Map pp74–5                    Chinese $$
☎ 9417 2438; 197 Smith St, Fitzroy; around $50 per duck; 🕑 lunch Tue-Fri, dinner Tue-Sun; 🚊 86

The queues are here for three things: duck soup, Peking duck, and duck and bean shoots. The owner's one-man show is a bonus, as is the classic no-style décor. You'll need to preorder for Peking duck.

## ST JUDE'S CELLAR
Map pp74–5                                Modern Australian $$

☎ 9419 7411; www.stjudescellars.com.au; 389-391 Brunswick St, Fitzroy; mains around $30; 🕑 lunch & dinner Tue-Sun, breakfast Sat & Sun; 🚊 112

A cavernous warehouse space has been given a clever, cool and humanising fit-out while not losing its airy industrial feel. The restaurant stretches out from behind the shopfront cellar, affording respite from the Brunswick St hustle. The food is a departure from usual restaurant fancy; it could be described as home cooking, though only if you were lucky enough to be shacked up with Elizabeth David. Mains (lentil and rabbit shepherds pie, venison with orange and ginger compote, fish wrapped in vine leaves) are designed to share; accompany them with at least a few of the hearty, inventive vegetable sides.

## PANAMA DINING ROOM Map pp74–5
Modern European $$

☎ 9417 7663; 3rd fl, 231 Smith St, Fitzroy; mains $18-25; 🕑 dinner Wed-Sun; 🚊 86

The Franco-Fitzroy pub grub on offer here is great value and just right over a bottle or two while gawping at the ersatz Manhattan views. The large space also does double duty as a bar, so come early or be prepared for some happy hubbub with your *frites* and *rillettes*.

## ALT-JAPANESE

We're not sure if it constitutes a trend, but the casual Japanese cafés on the south end of Smith St, Collingwood, just keep multiplying. Funky Wabi Sabi Salon (Map pp74–5; ☎ 9417 6119; 94 Smith St, Collingwood) and sweet Peko Peko (Map pp74–5; ☎ 9415 9609; 199 Smith St, Fitzroy) started it all; they've been joined by slick Wood Spoon Kitchen (Map pp74–5; ☎ 9416 0588; 88 Smith St, Collingwood) and the elegant Cocoro (Map pp74–5; ☎ 9419 5216; 117 Smith St, Fitzroy), as well as the trad Tokushima (Map pp74–5; ☎ 9486 9933; 70 Smith St, Collingwood). In the same vein, but serving up bold Korean, is Goshen (Map pp74–5; ☎ 9419-6750; 189 Smith St, Fitzroy).

## MARIOS Map pp74–5 Café $
☎ 9417 3343; 303 Brunswick St, Fitzroy; mains around $18 ☺ breakfast, lunch & dinner; ⓡ 112
Mooching at Marios is part of the Melbourne 101 curriculum. Breakfasts are big and served all day, the service is swift and the coffee is old-school strong.

## MOROCCAN SOUP BAR
Map pp48–9 North African, Vegetarian $
☎ 9482 4240; 183 St Georges Rd, North Fitzroy; banquet $16; ☺ dinner Tue-Sun; ⓡ 112
The menu is delivered verbally; dishes consist of authentic recipes served up in Maghrebi surrounds, festooned with cloth and drums. Pay attention (the owner, Hana, can be very stern) and pick your order from three soups and nine mains, which might be vegetables and quince on couscous, a *tagine* or chickpea bake. Local Arab women run the kitchen and it's an alcohol-free zone.

## AUX BATIFOLLES Map pp74–5 French $$
☎ 9481 5015; 400 Nicholson St, North Fitzroy; mains $15-26; ☺ lunch Tue-Sun, dinner daily; ⓡ 96
This French bistro does the trick for both big occasions or simple weeknight dinners. All the standards are here: duck *confit*, *moules frites* and steak tartare. Desserts too: *crème brûlée* and *tarte Tartin* just the way *maman* used to make. While you won't be wowed by culinary innovation, you'll love the delightful service, careful presentation, hearty serves and very modest prices. Bookings advised.

## COCONUT PALMS Map pp74–5 Vietnamese $
☎ 9419 6429; 183 Smith St, Fitzroy; mains $12-18; ☺ lunch Mon-Fri, dinner daily; ⓡ 86
The specials board may never change, but the above-par Vietnamese standards keep plenty of backsides on the no-frills seats. Famous for their flavour-packed veggie rice-paper rolls, fat silken tofu hotpot, prawn and pork coleslaw, and beef in vine leaves, as well as ever-obliging service.

## LADRO Map pp74–5 Pizza, Italian $$
☎ 9415 7575; 224a Gertrude St, Fitzroy; mains$11-30; ☺ dinner Wed-Sun; ⓡ 86
Breathtakingly simple, just-right pizza, pasta and roasts pack in a diverse, if polished, crowd every night. Book ahead:

believe us, the Lazio, smeared with an artichoke and anchovy paste and strewn with *fior di latte*, is worth getting organised for.

## CAVALLERO Map pp74–5 Modern Australian $$
☎ 9417 1377; 300 Smith St, Collingwood; mains $10-28; ☺ breakfast, lunch & dinner Tue-Sat, brunch Sun; ⓡ 86
A supersmart, subtle fit-out lets the charm of this grand Victorian shopfront shine. Morning coffee and house-made bikkies make way for piadina and pinot gris. Come teatime, there's pan-Med comfort food, and later still, cocktails, draught beer and dub tunes on the turntable. Sunday brunch goes off.

## PIZZA MEINE LIEBE off Map pp48–9 Pizza $
☎ 9482 7001; 231 High St, Northcote; pizza $10-18; ☺ dinner Tue-Sun; ⓡ 86
While Meine Liebe falls squarely into the 'new pizza' camp, with a wonderful range of simple toppings, it still feels reassuringly old-school, with a central gas oven, simple shopfront space and lots of bustle. Salads and gelato keep the menu suitably simple. For those about to rock (ie if you're seeing an act at the Northcote Social Club), we salute you, but also suggest booking for a preshow pizza.

## COMMONER
Map pp74–5 Modern Mediterranean $$
☎ 9415 6876; www.thecommoner.com.au; 122 Johnston St, Fitzroy; mains $9-24; ☺ breakfast, lunch & dinner Sat & Sun, dinner Wed-Fri; ⓡ 112
If you need to be convinced of this off-strip restaurant's serious intent, the house-roasted goat they offer up come Sunday lunch should do it. There's a nice, neat wine list and posh beer to complement the Eastern-Med-inflected dishes. Breakfast dishes too, are out of the ordinary.

## AÑADA Map pp74–5 Tapas $$
☎ 9415 6101; www.anada.com.au; 197 Gertrude St, Fitzroy; tapas $3-5, *raciones* $8-17; ☺ dinner; ⓡ 86
Dishes such as mackerel with orange-blossom and pistachio or veal meatballs and braised cuttlefish are alive with hearty Spanish and Muslim Mediterranean flavours. It's unpretentious, passionate cooking and the place fills up most nights. There's the usual arrangement of big and little plates plus a good selection of Iberian wines. Book ahead or try to nab a table at the bar or outside.

## BABKA BAKERY CAFE

Map pp74–5                           Bakery, Café $

☎ 9416 0091; 358 Brunswick St, Fitzroy; mains $8-16; ☺ breakfast & lunch Tue-Sun; ☒ 112

Russian flavours infuse the lovingly prepared breakfast and lunch dishes, and the heady aroma of cinnamon and freshly baked bread makes even just a coffee worth queuing for. Cakes are notable and can be taken away whole.

### JULIO Map pp48–9                       Café $

☎ 9489 7814; 171 Miller St, North Fitzroy; mains $7-12; ☺ breakfast & lunch; ☒ 112

This cute corner café, down by the schoolyard, is off the beaten track but always busy with locals. It keeps them content with fresh sardines on toast, baked eggs and tortilla. Their custard-filled doughnuts are legendary.

## BRUNSWICK STREET ALIMENTARI

Map pp74–5                                  Café $

☎ 94162001; 251 Brunswick St, Fitzroy; mains $6-10; ☺ breakfast & lunch; ☒ 112

Part deli, part fuss-free canteen, Alimentari stocks artisan bread, smallgoods and cheeses. The kitchen serves up delicious Lebanese pies (some love the lamb but we say the silverbeet can't be beat) with *labne*, as well salads, bruschettas, meatball wraps and homemade cakes.

### PALOMINO Map pp48–9                   Café $

☎ 9481 0699; 236 High St, Northcote; mains $5.50-8; ☺ breakfast & lunch; ☒ 86

Airy café that keeps locals coming back for sourdough toast, coco pops, cupcakes and absolutely zero attitude. Eggs here come baked or boiled in the shell ready for dunking with sourdough soldiers. Loppers face off with spoon crackers: underneath we're all the same. The coffee is the best you'll get north of Merri Creek.

### ROSAMOND Map pp74–5                   Café $

☎ 9419 2270; rear, 191 Smith St, Fitzroy; dishes $5-10; ☺ breakfast & lunch; ☒ 86

Rosamond's tiny interior is a warm haven for the local freelance creative crew, who like their daily rations simple but well considered. And that they are: free-range eggs only come scrambled, but with first-rate toast and fresh sides, and there's soup, toasties, baguettes, salads and cupcakes.

### NEWTOWN SC Map pp74–5               Café $

☎ 9415 7337; 180 Brunswick St, Fitzroy; all dishes $5-8; ☺ breakfast & lunch Mon-Sat; ☒ 112

Kate and the gang never tire of making perfect coffee – nabbing the window seat at Newtown isn't always easy. Weekday morns take on a family breakfast feel with avocado on toast the order of the day.

# CARLTON & AROUND

Visitors come to Carlton looking for some *dolce vita*, but instead they often just find spruikers and some very spurious cooking. Fortunately, north of Grattan St there's a more local vibe and far more reliable food. North Melbourne has a nice collection of interesting places as well as a strip of cheap Asian restaurants catering to students along Victoria St. Brunswick is Melbourne's Middle Eastern hub, and its busy A1 Lebanese Bakehouse (off Map pp48–9; ☎ 9386 0440; www.a1bakery.com.au; 643-645 Sydney Rd, Brunswick) and Mediterranean Wholesalers (Map pp48–9; ☎ 9380 4777; www.leosimports.com.au; 482-492 Sydney Rd, Brunswick) are worth a trip in themselves. Both Sydney Rd and Lygon St, East Brunswick offer a wide range of other cuisines too.

## ESPOSITO AT TOOFEY'S

Map pp78–9                        Seafood, Italian $$$

☎ 9347 9838; www.toofeys.com.au; 162 Elgin St, Carlton; mains $34-38; ☺ lunch Mon-Fri, dinner Mon-Sat; ☒ 1, 8, 96, ☒ 205

There are no ocean views, modish manners or maritime decoration here – just the freshest seafood done with simple Italian style. There's beef and fowl if you're not in the mood for fish, and the desserts, like the rest of the menu, are both clever and seasonal.

## COURTHOUSE HOTEL

Map pp78–9                            Pub food $$

☎ 9329 5394; www.thecourthouse.net.au; 86 Errol St, North Melbourne; mains $30-40; ☺ lunch & dinner Mon-Sat; ☒ 57

This corner pub has managed to retain the comfort and familiarity of a local while taking food, both in its public bar and its more formal dining spaces, very seriously. The European-style dishes are both refined and hearty. Lunch deals, including a glass of wine, are great value, and there is a tasting menu ($90) at dinner.

## ENOTECA SILENO Map pp78–9 Italian $$
☎ 9389 7070; www.enoteca.com.au; 920 Lygon St, Carlton North; mains around $30; ☽ breakfast, lunch & dinner Tue-Sat; breakfast & lunch Sun; 🚊 1, 8
This groaning enoteca imports some of the city's best quality Italian provisions; you'll see them employed in the small but smart menu of regional standards. The Italian wines are also exemplary; pick up a bottle and a jar of *carciuga* (artichoke anchovy spread) to take home.

## LIBERTINE Map pp78–9 French $$$
☎ 9329 5228; www.libertinedining.com.au; 500 Victoria St, North Melbourne; mains $28-33; ☽ lunch Tue-Fri, dinner Tue-Sat; 🚊 57
Locals love this small, traditionally decked-out shopfront for its real French country cooking and va-va-voom interiors. The menu includes whole suckling pigs (though you'll need to bring nine of your friends to help out with that order) and is requisitely strong on its game and cheeses.

## BALZARI Map pp78–9 Mediterranean $$
☎ 9639 9383; www.balzari.com.au; 130 Lygon St, Carlton; mains $25-32; ☽ lunch & dinner; 🚊 1, 8, 96
A nice respite right in the heart of the Lygon St mayhem. This place reaches out to embrace Greek cooking as well as Italian and a few other Mediterranean influences. The space is simple but elegant, and dishes – either entrees or soupy mains – are great to share.

## ABLA'S Map pp78–9 Lebanese $$
☎ 9347 0006; www.ablas.com.au; 109 Elgin St, Carlton; mains $25; ☽ lunch Thu & Fri, dinner Mon-Sat; 🚊 1, 8, 96, 🚌 205
The kitchen here is steered by Abla Amad, whose authentic, flavour-packed food has inspired a whole generation of local Lebanese chefs. Bring a bottle of your favourite plonk and settle in for the compulsory banquet on Friday and Saturday night.

## RUMI Map pp78–9 Modern Middle Eastern $$
9388 8255; 132 Lygon St, Brunswick East; mains $17-22; ☽ dinner Tue-Sat; 🚊 1, 8
A fabulously well-considered place that serves up a mix of traditional Lebanese cooking and contemporary interpretations of old Persian dishes. The *sigara boregi*

(cheese and pine-nut pastries) are a local institution and tasty mains like meatballs are balanced with a large and interesting selection of vegetable dishes (the near-caramelised cauliflower and the broad beans are standouts). Cool décor and excellent Victorian wines are a bonus.

## SHAKAHARI Map pp78–9 Vegetarian $$
☎ 9347 3848; www.shakahari.com.au; 201 Faraday St, Carlton; mains $15-18; ☽ lunch Mon-Sat, dinner daily; 🚊 1, 8, 96, 🚌 205
Shakahari's limited seasonal menu reflects both Asian and European influences, with dishes made from great produce. Established over 20 years ago, and bedecked with a wonderful collection of Asian antiques, Shakahari takes its mission seriously. If the weather is in your favour, ask to be seated in the palm-fringed courtyard. The curries, *tagines* (spicy Moroccan stews) and noodle dishes are delicious, whatever the setting.

## CITRUS MINT Map pp78–9 Thai $$
9329 5568; www.citrusmint.com.au; mains around $15; 357 Victoria St, North Melbourne; 🚊 57
This neat little place has a menu of Thai standards a notch above the ordinary. Ingredients are fresh and the spicing never muddied. They do a very good-value lunch deal that gives you a choice of a few mains, with rice, a spring roll and a glass of wine, beer or soft drink thrown in.

## DOC Map pp78–9 Pizza $$
☎ 9347 2998; 295 Drummond St, Carlton; pizzas around $13-18; ☽ dinner daily, lunch & dinner Sun; 🚊 1, 8, 96, 🚌 205
DOC has jumped on the Milanese-led mozzarella bar trend and serves up the milky white balls – your choice of local cow or imported *buffala* – as entrees, in salads or atop fabulous pizzas. Toppings include creamy broccoli puree and prosciutto, bittersweet *cicoria* (chicory) and lemon, and the litmus-test *margherita* gets rave reviews. The buffalo milk gelato is a delight or they do dessert pizzas if you're up for double dough.

## CARLTON ESPRESSO
Map pp78–9 Italian, Café $
☎ 9347 8482; 326 Lygon St, Carlton; piadinas $10; ☽ breakfast & lunch Mon-Sat; 🚊 1, 8, 96, 🚌 205
Piadinas and panini are stuffed with a wonderful array of fillings and the little tarts and biscotti are homemade. This place

brims with contemporary Italian brio – a nice change from the drab nostalgia found elsewhere.

### TRE ESPRESSO Map pp48–9  Café $
☎ 9381 0209; 459-475 Sydney Rd, Brunswick; mains $8-15; ❤ breakfast & lunch; 🚋 Brunswick, 🚌 19
Part of the new Sparta Place development, which promises much in terms of bars, shops and general Brunswick bonhomie, this café keeps to a simple formula of Italian staples. Paninis, cakes and coffee are supplemented by comforting dishes such as lasagne and risotto if you're in for more than a quick bite. At time of writing they were planning to open for wine evenings; they know their *vino* so it's worth a call.

### RAY Map pp48–9  Café $
☎ 9380 8593; 332 Victoria St, Brunswick; meals $8-12; ❤ breakfast & lunch; 🚋 Brunswick, 🚌 19
Ray mashes up the flavour legacy of the neighbourhood with the tastes of the vanguard residents. The big communal table is the place to try *labna* (yoghurt cheese) and rose jam on toasted pide, tomato and *bocconcini* bread and really good coffee.

### SMALL BLOCK Map pp78–9  Café $
☎ 9381 2244; 130 Lygon St, Carlton North; mains $8-12; ❤ breakfast & lunch; 🚌 1, 8
With salvaged service-station signage and concrete floors, plus warm and efficient service, Small Block acts as a community centre with a neighbourly drop-in and stay-awhile vibe. Big, beautiful breakfasts (eggs and otherwise) are worth writing home about.

### BRUNETTI Map pp78–9  Café, Pasticceria $
☎ 9347 2801; www.brunetti.com.au; 194-204 Faraday St, Carlton; panini around $8; ❤ breakfast, lunch & dinner; 🚌 1, 8, 96, 🚍 205
Bustling from dawn to midnight, Brunetti is a mini-Roman empire. It's famous for its coffee, granitas and authentic *pasticceria* (pastries). *Bain-marie* meals can be on the stodgy side (and sometimes that's just what the locals want) but the toasted *tremezzini* always please.

### NORTH CAFETERIA Map pp78–9  Café
☎ 9348 1276; 717 Rathdowne St, Carlton North; breakfasts $6-15; ❤ breakfast & lunch; 🚌 1, 8
Great neighbourhood café that breaks from the north-side mould with a light white interior and wow-factor chairs (Eero Saarinen, if you must know). Breakfast is the thing here and they have really interesting ways with eggs as well as fabulous French toast.

# ST KILDA & AROUND

Fitzroy St is one of the city's most popular eating strips, and you'll find the good, the very good and the downright ugly along its in-your-face length. Acland St also hums with dining options, as well as its famed cake shops. Low-key Carlisle St has more than its fair share of cute cafés and a couple of restaurants that keep the locals happy.

### CAFE DI STASIO Map pp88–9  Italian $$$
☎ 9525 3999; 31a Fitzroy St, St Kilda; mains $32-41; ❤ lunch & dinner daily; 🚋 16, 96, 112
Capricious white-jacketed waiters, a tenebrous Bill Henson photograph and a jazz soundtrack set the mood. The Italian menu has the appropriate drama and grace. Weekly fixed-price lunch menus (two courses and a glass of wine) are great value.

### CIRCA AT THE PRINCE
Map pp88–9  Modern Australian $$$
☎ 9536 1122; www.circa.com.au; mains $32-40; Prince of Wales, 2 Acland St, St Kilda; mains around $40; ❤ breakfast & dinner daily, lunch Sun-Fri; 🚋 16, 96, 112
This dining room has a persistent, all-pervading glamour and produces some of the city's finest food. Exec Chef Andrew McConnell no longer mans the stoves nightly (at time of writing he was busy relocating his famed Carlton restaurant Three One Two to Gertrude St, Fitzroy) but his stamp is all over the menu in its precise, intense tastes and eclectic influences. Bookings required.

### MIRKA'S AT TOLARNO
Map pp88–9  International, Italian $$$
☎ 9525 3088; www.mirkatolarno.com; Tolarno Hotel, 42 Fitzroy St, St Kilda; mains $32-36; ❤ breakfast, lunch & dinner daily; 🚋 16, 96, 112
The dark dining room has a history (it's been delighting diners since the early '60s) and Guy Grossi's carefully tweaked, knowingly retro food – truffle poached eggs, steak tartare, duck à l'orange – adds to the sense of occasion. But you don't get gravitas with your Chateaubriand. Beloved St Kilda painter Mirka Mora's murals grace the wall infusing all with a rare joy de vivre.

## DONOVANS
Map pp88–9      Modern Mediterranean $$$

☎ 9534 8221; www.donovanshouse.com.au;
40 Jacka Blvd, St Kilda; mains $28-45; ⏰ lunch &
dinner; 🚋 16, 96

Donovans has a big reputation and a
marquee location to match. Overlooking
the beach, the interior conjures up a com-
forting Long Island bolthole. The food is far
from fussy; rather it's solid on flavour and
technique, and broad enough to please all
comers. Book well ahead.

## STOKEHOUSE
Map pp88–9      Modern Australian $$$

☎ 9525 5555; www.stokehouse.com.au; 30 Jacka
Blvd, St Kilda; mains upstairs $28-32, downstairs
$10-20; ⏰ lunch & dinner; 🚋 16, 96

Two-faced Stokehouse makes the most of
its beachfront position, cleverly catering to
families and drop-ins downstairs, and turning on its best upstairs for finer diners. It's a
fixture on the Melbourne dining scene and
known for its seafood, service and the bay
views on offer. Book for upstairs.

## PIZZA E BIRRA Map pp88–9      Italian $$

☎ 9537 3465; 60 Fitzroy St, St Kilda; mains $22-28;
⏰ dinner Tue-Thu, lunch & dinner Fri-Sun;
🚋 16, 96, 112

The old train station's great bones and the
sharp, graphic fit-out make for a lovely
night out. Sit under black-and-white photos
straight from the *Cinecittà* archives and eat
hand-stretched, wood-fired pizzas (both
*tradizionali*, with tomato *sugo*, and *bianche*,
without) or venture on through their mains
of pastas, grills and tasty salads.

## CICCIOLINA
Map pp88–9      Modern Mediterranean $$

☎ 9525 3333; www.cicciolina.com.au; 130 Acland St,
St Kilda; mains $19-36; ⏰ lunch & dinner; 🚋 16, 96

This warm room of dark wood, subdued
lighting and pencil-sketches is a St Kilda
institution. The inspired Mod-Med menu is
smart and generous, and the service warm.
They don't take bookings; eat early or while
away your wait in the moody little back bar.

## MR WOLF Map pp88–9      Pizza $$

☎ 9534-0255; www.mrwolf.com.au;
9-15 Inkerman St, St Kilda East; pizza $18-20;
⏰ lunch Tue-Fri & Sun, dinner Tue-Sun; 🚋 16

Local celeb chef Karen Martini's casual but
stylish space is out of the action but always

packed to the gills. The pizzas here are renowned (crisp with top quality ingredients)
but there's also a great menu of antipasti
and pastas that display her flair for matching ingredients. Don't let the groove factor
put you off taking the kids; they have a
couple of special *bambini* pizzas and lots
of kid-friendly desserts. If there are no little
ones in tow, the next-door bar is open late.

## LAU'S FAMILY KITCHEN
Map pp88–9      Chinese $$

☎ 8598 9880; www.lauskitchen.com.au; 4 Acland St,
St Kilda; mains $16-32; ⏰ dinner daily, lunch Sun-
Fri; 🚋 16, 96

The owner's family comes with absolutely
flawless pedigree (father Gilbert Lau is the
former owner of famed Flower Drum) and
the restaurant is in a lovely leafy location.
The mainly Cantonese menu is simple, and
dishes are beautifully done if not particu-
larly exciting, with a few surprises thrown
in for more adventurous diners. Super-
attentive staff and the moody dark interior
make for a great night out.

## SOULMAMA Map pp88–9      Vegetarian $$

☎ 9525 3338; www.soulmama.com.au; St Kilda
Sea Baths, Shop 10, 10 Jacka Blvd, St Kilda; mains
$15-18; ⏰ lunch & dinner; 🚋 16,96

Despite the stylish organic fittings and
large windows with gob-smacking views
over Port Phillip Bay, this ethical diner
can feel a bit like a campus canteen with
its *bain-maries* and quiet posturing. Still,
there's a nice flexibility to portion sizes
and choice (a standard bowl lets you try
four dishes, which tend towards Indian and
Asian flavours), a large selection and some
very tempting desserts.

## IL FORNAIO Map pp88–9      Bakery/Café

☎ 9534 2922; www.ilfornaio.net.au; mains $14-26;
2 Acland St, St Kilda; 🚋 96, 16

Famous for its bread, croque monsieurs
and cakes, Il Fornaio also does simple Italian pastas, risottos and wine at night. The
street tables are a St Kilda summer must, or
cosy up inside when the wind blows.

## I CARUSI II Map pp88–9      Pizza $$

☎ 9593-6033; 231 Barkly St, St Kilda; pizza $14-18;
⏰ dinner; 🚋 16, 96

Beautifully located beyond the Acland St
chaos in this nostalgic corner shop, I Carusi
II was opened (though no longer owned

by) one of the people who started the real pizza revolution in Melbourne. I Carusi pizzas have a particularly tasty dough and follow the less-is-more tenet, with top-quality mozza, pecorino and small range of other toppings. Bookings advised.

### WALL TWO 80 Map pp88–9     Café $
☎ 9593 8280; www.wallcoffee.com.au; rear, 280 Carlisle St, Balaclava; dishes $8-11; ☼ breakfast & lunch; ☒ 3, 69
With a look that was so Melbourne, Sydney had to have one too. Wall Two 80's coffee is some of the best, as are the toasted *pide* and pastries. Prop with other loners at the communal table, nestle in a nook with a mate or line up outside along the eponymous wall.

### PELICAN Map pp88–9     Tapas $$
☎ 9525 5847; cnr Fitzroy & Park Sts, St Kilda; mains $7-20; ☼ breakfast, lunch & dinner; ☒ 16, 96, 112
This modern space evokes beach shacks of days gone by, and makes for a lovely spot to watch the Fitzroy St circus in full swing. Tapas here is not aiming for Iberian authenticity, just good-tasting accompaniments to the extensive drinks menu.

### BAKER D CHIRICO
Map pp88–9     Bakery, Café $
☎ 9534 3777; 149 Fitzroy St, St Kilda; light meals $5-9; ☼ breakfast & lunch Tue-Sun; ☒ 16, 96, 112
The Baker's sourdough is some of the city's finest. Stock up on house-baked granola, or stop for a coffee, rhubarb danish or a *calzone*. Beautifully designed packaging (look for the boxed nougat) spreads the good taste around, and their footpath seating is some of the neighbourhood's most popular.

### CACAO Map pp88–9     Bakery, Café $
☎ 8598 9555; www.cacao.com.au; 52 Fitzroy St, St Kilda; light meals $4.50-11; ☼ 7am-7pm; ☒ 16, 96, 112
Set among the trees, Cacao creates award-winning chocolates with the best *couverture*. They also do a full French patisserie range, with all the standards you'd expect.

### LENTIL AS ANYTHING
Map pp88–9     Vegetarian $
☎ 9534 5833; www.lentilasanything.com; 41 Blessington St, St Kilda; prices at customers' discretion; ☼ lunch & dinner; ☒ 16, 96
Choosing from the always-organic, no-meat menu is easy. Deciding what to pay can be

hard. This unique not-for-profit operation provides training and educational opportunities for marginalised people, as well as tasty, if not particularly notable, vegetarian food for everyone else. Whatever you do end up paying for your meal goes to a range of services that help new migrants, refugees, people with disabilities and the long-term unemployed. They also have a branch at the Abbotsford Convent (Map pp74–5; ☎ 9534 5833; 1 St Heliers St, Abbotsford).

# SOUTH YARRA, PRAHRAN & WINDSOR
It's perpetual peak hour at Chapel St's many cafés. You'll also find a few excellent dining options in Prahran, including on Greville St. The southern Windsor strip just keeps getting hotter, with a great new clutch of recent openings.

### JACQUES REYMOND
Map pp84–5     Modern Australian $$$
☎ 9525 2178; www.jacquesreymond.com.au; 78 Williams Rd, Prahran; degustation menu from $98; ☼ lunch & dinner Tue-Sat; ☒ 6
Housed in a Victorian terrace of ample proportions, Reymond was a local pioneer of degustation dining and still encourages you to eat this way (there's a much-lauded vegetarian version). Expect a French-influenced, Asian-accented menu with lovely details including house-churned butter. Mod Oz at its best; fine dining at its most calm and grown up.

### BOTANICAL Map pp84–5   Modern Australian $$$
☎ 9820 7888; www.thebotanical.com.au; 169 Domain Rd, South Yarra; mains around $40; ☼ breakfast, lunch & dinner; ☒ 3, 5, 6, 8, 55, 112
With its languid location opposite the Botanic Gardens, a bold menu and seductive décor, this is one of Melbourne's favourite fine-dining options. Prime produce is partnered cleverly with an emphasis on Mediterranean flavours. There's impeccable service and a serious wine list, of course. Bookings advised.

### DA NOI Map pp84–5     Italian $$$
☎ 9866 5975; 95 Toorak Rd, South Yarra; mains $25-32; ☼ lunch Fri-Sun, dinner daily; ☒ 8
Da Noi serves beautiful Sardinian dishes chosen for the season. The spontaneous

kitchen might reinterpret the chef's special three times a night. Just go with it; it's a unique experience and harks back to a different way of dining. The five-course chef's selection is worth making room for. Bookings advised.

## MAMA GANOUSH
Map pp84–5     Modern Middle Eastern $$
☎ 9521 4141; www.mamaganoush.com; mains around $25; 56 Chapel St, Windsor; ☾ dinner Mon-Sat; ☒ Windsor

This is Middle Eastern food that remains true to its roots while being modern and new. The space is full of delicate arabesque screens; the kibbes, tagines and puddings are full of thought, passion and flavour. It's run by the brother of renowned chef and writer Greg Malouf, Geoff, and he also knows a thing or two about Levantine flavours.

## DINO'S DELI
Map pp84–5     Modern Mediterranean $$
☎ 9521 3466; 34 Chapel St, Windsor; mains $22-32; ☾ breakfast, lunch & dinner; ☒ Windsor

At the time of writing, the deli half of Dino's was yet to open, but the clubby café-bistro is in full swing. The Pan-Med menu is especially strong on Spanish flavours and the space beguilingly eclectic. And it's busy, busy, busy.

## BORSCH, VODKA & TEARS
Map pp84–5     Polish $$
☎ 9530 2694; www.borschvodkaandtears.com; mains $19-25; 173 Chapel St, Windsor; ☾ breakfast, lunch & dinner; ☒ Prahran, ☒ 6

We'd consider this one for the name alone, but it's also the business for spruced-up Polish food and an impressive variety of everyone's favourite white spirit, vodka. Przekazki spreads let you sample; the dumplings, herrings and blintzes are top-notch, and the borsch is suitably authentic. There are more vegetarian options on the menu than you'd expect too.

## ORANGE
Map pp84–5     Café/Bar $$
☎ 9529 1644; 126 Chapel St, Windsor; mains $16-26; ☾ breakfast & lunch daily, dinner Wed-Sun; ☒ Windsor

Orange straddles the café-bar label with ease, its well-worn vinyl banquettes cushioning fashionable backsides for early breakfasts (from 7am) and late-night beverages (open until 2am Thursday to Sunday). Serving good coffee during the day, Orange slows its grinders at night, replaces teaspoons with bar coasters, and chooses Screamin' Jay Hawkins over Nina Simone LPs.

## HOOKED
Map pp84–5     Fish & Chips $
☎ 9529 1075; www.hooked.net.au; 172 Chapel St, Windsor; mains $9-15; ☾ lunch & dinner; ☒ Prahran, ☒ 72

Great fish and chippery with décor that will make you change your mind on the takeway and eat in at the communal table. Old-school chips are made on site and fish is either done traditionally or with light Asian accents.

## THAI FOOD TO GO
Map pp84–5     Thai $
☎ 9510 2112; 141 Chapel St, Windsor; mains $8-18; ☾ lunch & dinner; ☒ Windsor

The happy hipster nonchalance of the staff and décor, plus a nicely buzzing local crew of diners, make up for fairly standard, if fresh and tasty, Thai food. The menu is also fabulously flexible and the salads are a steal. Plus they deliver.

## CAFÉ VELOCE
Map pp84–5     Italian $
☎ 8080 9995; 9-11 Claremont St, South Yarra; dishes $8-15; ☾ breakfast & lunch; ☒ South Yarra, ☒ 8

Tucked at the back of Dutton's, this Fender Katsalidis shrine to auto design (and car lust in general) turns out perfect house-baked pasticceria, eggs and interesting breakfast dishes like baked ricotta served with fresh berries. Lunches (reminiscent of classic Café e Cucina fare) are more than good enough to assuage the sight of baby boomers getting gooey over classic Porsches.

## ORIENTAL TEA HOUSE
Map pp84–5     Chinese/Yum Cha $$
☎ 9824 0128; www.orientalteahouse.com.au; 455 Chapel St, South Yarra; mains $5-17; ☾ lunch & dinner; ☒ Prahran, ☒ 72

They've ditched the trolley ritual, but David Zhou's intriguing Shanghainese offerings are just as good à la carte as off the cart. (And they still do the kid-pleasing lurid jellies for dessert.) The bright refit of an old pub is a departure from the norm too. The excellent teashop is worth a concerted postprandial browse.

### KANTEEN Map pp84–5
Café/Bar $

☎ 9827 0488; 150 Alexandra Ave, South Yarra; mains $5-14; ⊗ breakfast & lunch

This rare alfresco riverside café morphed from an old ablutions block into a firm neighbourhood favourite (it's also handy for Herring Island). It supplements its toasted pide selection with interesting breakfast options such as sticky rice with coconut, and lunch specials such as a Japanese-inspired noodle and duck salad. Fab as the location is, the service can be off-puttingly slow; loud commercial chill-out tunes don't make the wait any easier.

### BASQUE Map pp84–5
Spanish $$

☎ 9533 7044; 159 Chapel St, Windsor; tapas $3-11; ⊗ breakfast, lunch & dinner; ⊛ Windsor

Locals come en masse to sit and slurp, nibble and chat in this cute corner joint. The tapas is straightforward, authentic and made with love, with a drinks list to match.

# SOUTH MELBOURNE, PORT MELBOURNE & ALBERT PARK

These neighbourhoods are perfect for casual footpath dining on a sunny weekend and offer some solidly epicurean options too. While the superscaled restaurants along the bay have stunning views, some also have fairly non-descript food.

### TEMPURA HAJIME Map pp92–3
Japanese $$$

☎ 9696 0051; 60 Park St, South Melbourne; set meal $72; ⊛ 112

Completely unmarked door, tiny and almost impossible to get a booking? Check. Cult status is assured, and in this case, warranted. Hajime takes you on an edible journey with a set menu of beautifully pondered on and prepared small dishes made with seasonal produce.

### L'OUSTAL Map pp92–3
French $$

☎ 9699 8969; www.montaguehotel.com.au; 166 Bridport St, Albert Park; mains $30-35; ⊗ lunch Wed-Sat, dinner Tue-Sat; ⊛ 96

No cookie-cutter Francophilia here. This cute neighbourhood bistro is breezy and informal (more Carla Bruni than Edith Piaf) and does French standards with good pro-

duce and the odd contemporary twist. The winter menu is when the chef really comes into their own.

### MONTAGUE HOTEL
Map pp92–3
French, Modern Australian $$

☎ 9690 9044; www.montaguehotel.com.au; 355 Park St, South Melbourne; mains around $28; ⊗ lunch Thu-Fri, dinner Wed-Sun; ⊛ 96

No architect's wit at work here, just a smart, comfortable and essentially old-fashioned space. The mainly French food, with some Northern Asian ideas as well, is cooked with precision and care; it's definitely not just an adjunct to a bottle or two.

### MISUZU Map pp92–3
Japanese $$

☎ 9699 9022; 3-7 Victoria Ave, Albert Park; mains $13-33; ⊗ lunch & dinner; ⊛ 1

The ground floor is a popular café, with a more formal restaurant upstairs. Misuzu's menu includes whopping noodle, rice and curry dishes, tempuras and takeaway options from the neatly displayed sushi bar. Sit outside under lantern-hung trees, or inside surrounded by murals and dark wood. Pop next door to Umami for a drink and sample sake from a vast selection.

### ARMSTRONG STREET FOOD STORE
Map pp92–3
Café $

☎ 9690 4784; 30 Armstrong St, Middle Park; mains from $10; ⊗ breakfast & lunch; ⊛ 96, 112

Take in the slower pace of Armstrong St from the outside tables at this local's favourite. Well-priced café mains are made with care, or pop in for some pastries to take to the beach. Staff are friendly too.

### REX HUNT'S D'LISH FISH
Map pp92–3
Fish & Chips $

☎ 9646 0660; 105 Beach St, Port Melbourne; basic fish & chips $9; ⊗ lunch & dinner; ⊛ 109

The self-titled fish-and-chipper of the fish-kissing celebrity angler draws the crowds, selling two tonnes of chips on a summer Sunday. It might not be gourmet, but it's perfect for taking down to the beach or watching the Spirit of Tassie sail into the sunset.

### ST ALI Map pp92–3
Café $

www.stali.com.au; 12-18 Yarra Pl, South Melbourne; mains $8-13; ⊗ breakfast & lunch; ⊛ 112

This hide-away warehouse space is a lovely jumble of communal tables, nooks

## PORT VIEWS

Station Pier holds many memories for generations of Victorian immigrants and it's still a working passenger port today. There's a clutch of swish mega-restaurants on the pier itself – including Waterfront, Campari and 3 Station Pier (see Map pp92–3) – serving up bay vistas and variable food to large numbers of visitors. The best view, however, definitely belongs to the diminutive My Dog Café (Map pp92–3; www.mydog.com.au; 🕑 breakfast & lunch Wed-Sun), which has a human food menu as well as a selection of canine treats. And yes, pooches can, and do, eat from the table.

and balconies to accommodate any mood. The food is simple, fresh Modern Middle Eastern. Coffee is carefully sourced, roasted and bagged on site, and guaranteed to be good. It's particularly perfect to wash down the chocolate-swirled pound cake.

### MART 130 Map pp92–3 Café $

☎ 9690 8831; 107a Canterbury Rd, Middle Park; dishes $6-10; 🕑 breakfast & lunch; 🚊 96
Where the light-rail trams now run was once a fully fledged railway line with a string of Federation-style stations. Mart 130 has painted the walls and floors a smart black and white, and serves up corncakes, granola and eggs with decks overlooking the park. Weekend waits can be long.

### NOÎSETTE Map pp92–3 Café, Bakery $

☎ 9646 9555; www.noisette.com.au; 84 Bay St, Port Melbourne; breads & pastries from $3; 🕑 6.30am-6pm; 🚊 109
Good bread gets Melburnians going and the fifth-generation French baker at work here turns out some excellent Gallic-style loaves. There's also a wide range of authentic pastries – come January they even do a galette des rois for Epiphany.

# WILLIAMSTOWN

Not somewhere you'd go just to eat, but there's hordes of fish-and-chip shops, produce stores and pubs that cater to the day trippers (plus a few cafés that locals don't let on about).

### BREIZOZ Map p96 Creperie

☎ 9397 2300; www.breizoz.com.au; cnr. 139 Nelson Pde; crepes $6-12 🕑 breakfast Sun, lunch Wed-Sub, dinner Tue-Sun; 🚊 Williamstown
An authentic, if idiosyncratic, charmer with buckwheat crepes and cloudy farm-fresh Breton cider. There's no concession to bistro tastes; it is what it is, and that's a creperie. Fillings include boudin blanc, ratatouille, onion soubise (a jammy jumble of onion) or 'the brick', which piles on egg, ham, cheese, mushrooms and tomato. On Sundays, brioche and croissants are baked and Francophiles take their coffee in a bowl. The house meringues, jam and ice cream can, and should, be taken home. Also in Fitzroy (Map pp74–5; ☎ 9415 7588; cnr Gertrude & Brunswick Sts).

# DRINKING & NIGHTLIFE

## top picks

# DRINKING & NIGHTLIFE

Melbourne's thriving bar scene is one of its biggest attractions. Since the days of early settlement, when teetotal founder John Fawkner set up a public house on the banks of the Yarra, Melbourne has always used the demon drink as a social lubricant. For many years this revolved around pubs, but when liquor licensing laws were liberalised in the late 1980s, bars began to spring up anywhere that rents were cheap and space was atmospheric. Although there's currently much talk about the perils of binge drinking and alcohol-fuelled violence in the city, for the most part Melbournians have a sophisticated, if dedicated, relationship with the bottle.

Many of the first wave of new bars were opened by artists, architects or young hospitality workers and fitted out with creative verve in lieu of spending huge wads of cash. Today that spirit of invention persists, even if the stakes are higher. No one is sure just how many bars the city can sustain, but the scene shows no sign of letting up any time soon.

The liquour licensing laws also made it easy for cafés and restaurants to serve alcohol, an idea common enough throughout Europe, but one that other Australian capitals have only just cottoned on to. This has meant that bars and pubs are often family-friendly and that the boundaries between what constitutes a restaurant, bar or café are gloriously blurred. The place you take your morning short black could quite easily be, come 1am, where you find yourself dancing to Cut Copy. Neighbourhoods such as St Kilda, Prahran, Fitzroy and Collingwood all have their own versions of the city bar, and shopfront fit-outs fan out into the suburbs following the hip kids to Brunswick, Northcote and Yarraville.

Wine bars continue to spring up; these function as upmarket bottle shops where you can buy a bottle to take away or pay a modest corkage and drink at the bar. They often have a daunting range of wines from around the world, and food that won't let the side down.

The bar revolution ironically has done nothing to dim the appeal of the neighbourhood pub, though it has meant that most have had to do some rethinking and some judicious refurbishing. And while Melburnians still profess to love a good old-fashioned boozer, they're often secretly pleased when their local offers a flirty little *anéis* by the glass and keeps a few different vodkas chilled in the fridge.

With many bars concealed up an anonymous flight of stairs or down an alley off a back street, how does a visitor keep up? Melburnians are normally more proud than proprietorial about their favourites, so it's always worth asking a barman or fellow drinker at somewhere you've already discovered. Bar reviews can be found on the website of the Age (www.theage.com .au) newspaper, while Three Thousand (www.threethousand.com.au) keeps a pretty close eye on the latest places to pop up.

## LIVE MUSIC & DJS

Melbourne's thriving band scene loses venues every year as inner-city development gains pace and the residents of new apartment buildings make noise complaints. It's also often more profitable for publicans to open dining rooms than band rooms. Still, there are several pubs that keep the flag flying, showcasing local bands every night of the week. Touring acts play at a handful of venues in the city, St Kilda, Fitzroy, Northcote and Richmond, as well as at city theatres such as the Forum, and the Palais in St Kilda. Gigs are listed in the *Entertainment Guide (EG)* section of the *Age* on Fridays. Pick up free street papers *Beat* and *Inpress* for reviews, interviews and a comprehensive weekly gig guide. They're available from pubs, cafés and entertainment venues. Also see Tickets & Reservations (p357) for major booking agencies, or check the individual venues for booking details.

Dance music is altogether a more elusive beast. The city boasts an amazingly diverse and happening scene but it's not always easy to find or keep up with. Most clubs are concentrated in the city, though other inner-city neighbourhoods are not entirely without options. Big parties, especially during the summer months, are also an integral part of the calendar.

Gay clubs can be found in Commercial Rd, Prahran and in Collingwood (p178-9); the scene covers everything from the ultra-commercial (hello Kylie!) to 'queer and alternative'. Three Thousand (www.threethousand.com.au) lists

## HEADLINE ACTS

When the rock gods (or more commonly pop, R&B and hip-hop stars) roll into town and are too big for Melbourne's beloved medium-sized venues, such as the Corner Hotel (p153) or the Prince Bandroom (p158), they are likely to play at one of the following venues (book tickets through one of the agencies listed on p357):

Forum Theatre (Map pp52–3; www.marrinertheatres.com.au; 150-152 Flinders St) One of the city's most atmospheric live music venues, it does double duty as a cinema during the Melbourne Film Festival. The Arabic-inspired exterior houses an equally interesting interior, with the southern sky rendered on the domed ceiling.

Hamer Hall (Melbourne Concert Hall; Map pp64–5; www.theartscentre.net.au; Victorian Arts Centre, 100 St Kilda Rd) The concert hall is well known for its excellent acoustics, with a décor inspired by Australia's mineral and gemstone deposits.

Palais Theatre (Map pp88–9; ☎ 9537 2444; Lower Esplanade, St Kilda) Standing gracefully next to Luna Park, the Palais is a St Kilda icon. Not only is it a beautiful old space, but it also stages some pretty special performances. It's pegged for major development, which has St Kilda holding its collective breath.

Rod Laver Arena (Map pp68–9; www.mopt.com.au; Batman Ave) A giant, versatile space used for headline concerts and the Australian Open tennis (p12), with a huge sunroof. Not the most atmospheric of venues, but then it's all about the spectacle. Ditto for the nearby Hisense Arena (p67).

Sidney Myer Music Bowl (Map pp84–5; www.theartscentre.net.au; Kings Domain) This beautiful amphitheatre in the park is used for a variety of outdoor events, from the Tropfest (www.tropfest.com.au) film festival to Opera in the Bowl to the New Year's Day rave Summerdayze.

touring djs and special events, and In the Mix (www.inthemix.com.au), a national dance-devoted site, has a comprehensive Melbourne section that caters for those that know what they are looking for.

## COMEDY & CABARET

Melbourne prides itself on being the home of Australian comedy and isn't remotely reticent about turning the joke on itself. The annual International Comedy Festival (p14) sees the entire city become a sprawling comedy venue. Local comedians join forces with international performers from the festival circuit to take the stage in pubs, clubs, theatres and on city streets.

Melbourne has a few regular comedy venues and nightspots where stand-up comics stand or fall. Weekly gigs are listed in the 'EG' section of the *Age*.

## WHEN TO GO OUT

Most bars and pubs stay open until at least midnight or 1am, but it's always worth checking ahead for opening hours if you're planning a late one. Inner-city bars with djs and most clubs will open until 3am on weekend nights, some much, much later (or should we say earlier, as it's often past dawn). Again, it's best to check with the venue beforehand. At the time of writing the government has introduced trial 'lockout' legislation banning people from entering, or re-entering, bars or clubs after 2am (although venues can stay open past that, hence the term 'lockout'), hoping to curb late-night violence. How this affects the city's nightlife is yet to be seen; many fear it will dampen a vibrant scene and also lead to *increased* violence at the new communal pumpkin hour.

## WHAT TO WEAR

What *not* to wear might be more of an apt question. And really, it depends on the destination. Melburnians might affect a casual air, but that doesn't mean that most city bars won't be full of people that have put in some effort, even if it's about graphic hoodies, jeans and trainers. Pubs, especially those in neighbourhood back streets, can be a lot more laidback, but can also deliver the odd sartorial surprise. Bayside venues can go a variety of ways: flip-flops and shorts, rock and roll, or ultra glam.

### SMOKE GETS IN YOUR EYES

Smoking is banned in all bars and pubs, though there will often be a balcony or courtyard provided. In lieu of this, many smokers congregate on the footpath outside.

## WHAT TO DRINK

Beer is taken seriously in Melbourne and most places serve a variety of local, boutique and imported beers on tap, as well as a wider range by the bottle. Beer is ordered by the pot (285ml) or pint (600ml). The big commercial brews are Carlton Draught and Victoria Bitter (VB). Boutique brands include Mountain Goat, Little Creatures and the vegan's friend, Coopers. Wine is served by the glass and the bottle and liquors. It's now common to find wines from France, Italy, Spain and New Zealand among the well-loved Yarra Valley and Mornington Peninsula labels. Cocktails are increasingly made with skill and premium ingredients, with prices to match. At most bars you'll also find a range of good-quality spirits and European aperitifs and liquors. Pubs are increasingly following this lead, but still often use acrid house spirits unless you specify otherwise.

# CENTRAL MELBOURNE

The city has a diverse range of bars, many of which are the iconic up-an-alley places Melbourne is known for. The suits take over during cocktail hour, especially come Friday night, but there's enough variety if that's not your scene. Things can be pretty quiet early in the week, apart from live music gigs. The city doesn't slow down for the Sabbath – having a big night on a Sunday isn't usually a problem. Despite the constant talk of small hidden bars, there are also plenty of larger pubs and clubs spread throughout the city too. King St was once the nightlife hub of Melbourne. Today it's a rather tawdry strip of 'gentlemen's clubs' and is notorious for its late-night violence.

### BLUE DIAMOND Map pp52–3      Bar/Club
☎ 8601 2720; 15th fl, 123 Queen St; ☷ 5pm-late Thu-Fri & Sun, 7pm-late Sat
This 'social salon and cabaret' is ostensibly a private club, but nonmembers do make it in, especially on Thursday and Sunday nights. It's a dark, dramatic space but the main attraction is the view; it's as good as it gets this side of the Rainbow Room. There's live entertainment from 10.30pm Friday to Sunday, with live soul and funk acts taking the stage.

### CARLTON HOTEL Map pp52–3      Bar
☎ 9663 3246; 193 Bourke St; ☷ 4pm-late
Once upon a time, you went to the Carlton because there was nowhere else to go.

These days, you can still prop up the bar but you'll be drinking a Peninsula pinot gris. OTT Melbourne rococo gets another workout here and never fails to raise a smile. Check the rooftop Palmz if you're looking for some Miami-flavoured vice or just a great view.

### CHERRY Map pp52–3      Bar
☎ 9639 8122; 103 Flinders Lane; ☷ 5pm-late Tue-Fri, 9pm-late Sat
This rock'n'roll refuge is still going strong. There's often a queue, but once inside a relaxed, slightly anarchic spirit prevails. Music is rarely live but never electronic.

### COLLINS QUARTER Map pp52–3    Bar/Pub
☎ 9650 8500; www.collinsquarter.com; 86a Collins St; ☷ 7am-late Mon-Fri, 11am-late Sat
This collection of bars is like a hotel without the rooms upstairs and without the bellhop palaver or aggressive pricing. It's a grown-up space with few rough edges but has a timeless appeal. There's a variety of different areas and moods. A magnolia tree sprouts from the courtyard and inside there's a wood fire burning.

### CROFT INSTITUTE Map pp52–3      Bar
☎ 9671 4399; www.thecroftinstitute.com.au; 21-25 Croft Alley; ☷ 5pm-late Mon-Fri, 8pm-late Sat
Located in a laneway off a laneway, the lab-themed Croft is a test of drinkers' determination. Prescribe yourself a beaker of house-distilled vodka in the downstairs laboratory and venture up the rickety stairs to inspect the Departments of Male and Female Hygiene (aka the toilets, complete with hospital beds).

### DOUBLE HAPPINESS Map pp52–3      Bar
☎ 9650 4488; http://doubledouble.com.au; 21 Liverpool St; ☷ 5pm-late Mon-Fri, 6pm-late Sat & Sun
This stylish hole in the wall doesn't just do Chinese-themed décor, it also offers Chinese beers. Try a Tsingtao beer or a cardamom- or ginger-flavoured cocktail.

### GIN PALACE Map pp52–3      Bar
☎ 9654 0533; 190 Little Collins St; ☷ 4pm-late
With a drinks list to make your liver quiver, Gin Palace is the perfect place to grab a soft couch or secluded alcove, sip, and take it slow. Martinis here are legendary and it's open superlate most nights.

## LONG ROOM Map pp52–3     Bar

☎ 9663 7226; www.thelongroom.com.au; Georges Bldg, 162-168 Collins St, 4pm-late Tue-Fri, 5pm-late Sat

This decadent space runs the length of a city block, and is bedecked with animal heads, clusters of low-lying tables, a sushi bar and private tatami rooms. The loud after-work crowd recognise the top-40 tunes and loiter till late.

## LOOP Map pp52–3     Bar

☎ 9654 0500; www.looponline.com.au; 23 Meyers Pl; ◷ 3pm-late

Loop has large double screen and scattered projectors; find yourself a dark seat or a spot at the bar and watch the 'Video Jockeys' display their wares. Not as wanky as it sounds.

## MADAME BRUSSELS Map pp52–3     Bar

☎ 9662 2775; www.madamebrussels.com; Level 3, 59-63 Bourke St; ◷ noon-11pm Sun-Wed, noon-1am Thu-Sat

Head here if you've had it with Melbourne moody and all that dark wood. Although named for a famous 19th-century madam, it feels as though you've fallen into a camp '60s rabbit hole, with much Astroturfery and staff dressed à la the country club. And just like in a Richard Yates novel, they certainly know their booze. The décor might veer towards the hysterical, but it's just the tonic on a chilly winter's day; they even provide lap rugs for the terrace.

## MELBOURNE SUPPER CLUB

Map pp52–3     Bar

☎ 9654 6300; 1st fl, 161 Spring St; 8pm-4am Sun & Mon, 5pm-4am Tue-Thu, 5pm-6am Fri, 8pm-6am Sat

Melbourne's own Betty Ford's (the place you go when there's nowhere left to go), the Supper Club is open very late and is a favoured after-work spot for performers and hospitality types. Leave your coat at the door and cosy into a Chesterfield. Browse the encyclopaedic wine menu and relax; the sommeliers will cater to any liquid desire. Upstairs the Fuller Bar has wonderful views and is open to the elements for the cigar smokers.

## MEYERS PLACE Map pp52–3     Bar

☎ 9650 8609; 20 Meyers Pl; ◷ 4pm-2am Mon-Thu, 4pm-4am Fri & Sat

Local rock-star architects Six Degrees made their mark with this little place, the Ur-laneway bar. Much copy has been devoted to its recycled materials and interesting demarcation of space over the last 14 years, but for most Melburnians, it's now just a great place to drink.

## MISTY Map pp52–3     Bar

☎ 9663 9202; 3-5 Hosier Lane; ◷ to late Tue-Sat

Misty's white walls, '70s curves and glowing lights has been packing them in for almost a decade. Its location is archetypal; Hosier Lane's colour is right out the window.

## MOO Map pp52–3     Bar

Money Order Office; ☎ 9639 3020; Driver Lane; ◷ 5pm-late Mon, noon-late Tue-Fri, 6pm-late Sat

This sumptuous hideaway has the air of an exclusive gentlemen's club. Overstuffed leather couches, private booths lining the walls and excellent service complete the picture. It's the perfect place to work your way through a wine list. Its street-level little sister Penny Blue is more of the same décor wise, but with big street-side windows and outdoor seating that suits afternoon imbibing. They spin some great tunes from the dj cage, but the staff can be a little offhand.

## NEW GOLD MOUNTAIN

Map pp52–3     Bar

☎ 9650 8859; www.newgoldmountain.org; Level 1, 21 Liverpool St; ◷ 5pm-late Mon-Fri, 8pm-late Sat & Sun

Unsignposted, New Gold Mountain's intense Chinoiserie interior comes as a shock. Two upstairs floors are filled with tiny screen-shielded corners, with decoration so delightfully relentless you feel as if you're trapped in an arthouse dream sequence. Sours are the thing, though they do great things with vodka too. Harbin heaven.

## ORDER OF MELBOURNE Map pp52–3     Bar

☎ 9663 6707; www.theorder.com.au; Level 2, 401 Swanston St; ◷ noon-11pm Wed-Sun, noon-1am Thu & Fri, 3pm-3am Sat

This warehouse space is loved by RMIT students but also has a nicely mixed crowd of after-work drinkers. There are lots of nooks and crannies, a gleefully eclectic aesthetic and reasonably priced wines. The rooftop space is the place to be in summer.

### PHOENIX Map pp52–3 Bar/Pub

☎ 9650 4976; http://phoenixbar.com.au; 82 Flinders St; ☼ noon-late Mon-Fri, 5pm-late Sat
Phoenix's retro-safari theme and split-level surprises are popular with after-workers on the prowl. Late closing on weekends ensures that most Melburnians have ended up here at some stage. A regularly updated *meze* (hors d'oeuvre) menu is also available.

### RECORDED MUSIC SALON
Map pp52–3 Bar

☎ 9650 3821; www.recordedmusicsalon.com.au; Level 1, 11 Collins St; ☼ 7am-late Mon-Fri, 6pm-late Sat
All that's left of the original analogue retailer is the name and signage, but the wooden interior has the warmth of an old LP. This unpretentious drinking hole has a long cocktail list, good wine, a day/night menu and window seats with views of the Paris end of Collins St.

### RIVERLAND Map pp52–3 Bar

☎ 9662 1771; www.riverlandbar.com; Vaults 1-9, Federation Wharf (below Princes Bridge); ☼ 7am-late
This bluestone beauty, another by architects Six Degrees, keeps things simple with good wine, beer on tap and bar snacks that hit the mark: charcuterie, cheese and BBQ. A rare riverside drinking hole that doesn't give off the scent of corporate investors. Outside tables are a treat when the weather is kind.

### ROBOT Map pp52–3 Bar

☎ 9620 3646; www.robotsushi.com; 12 Bligh Pl; ☼ 5pm-late Mon-Fri, 8pm-late Sat
If neo-Tokyo is your thing or you just have a sudden urge for a sushi hand roll washed down with an Asahi, check out Robot. It has an all-welcome door policy, big windows that open to the laneway, a cute mezzanine level and attracts a laid-back young crowd. There's even anime every Tuesday night.

### SECTION 8 Map pp52–3 Bar

☎ 0408-971 044; www.section8.com.au; 27-29 Tattersalls Lane; ☼ 8am-late Mon-Fri, noon-late Sat & Sun
The latest in shipping container habitats, come and sink a Little Creatures brew with the after-work crowd, who make do with packing cases and Chinese lanterns for décor.

### SISTER BELLA Map pp52–3 Bar

Sniders Lane; ☼ 10am-1am Mon-Sat
The St Jerome's crew colonised this dilapidated laneway warehouse and it's definitely staked its claim as the older sibling. Still, the ramshackle is only knocked back by degrees and they keep the formula similar: cheap beer and wine, cheap food and kids running the place that know they're cooler than you but won't let that ruin the friendship.

### ST JEROME'S & SHIT TOWN
Map pp52–3 Bar/Club

7 Caledonian Lane; ☼ 8am-late Mon-Fri, noon-late Sat & Sun
Tiny St Jerome's does great coffee and toasties all day for the students that flock here. Come sundown, its time for longnecks and beats in the cloistered back alley. It's also time for Shit Town, its twisted next-door sister, to open the door (actually a hole in the wall). Here the 80s crack-house aesthetic is fully realised and the music is loud and left-field.

### TRANSPORT Map pp52–3 Bar/Pub

☎ 9658 8808; www.transporthotel.com.au; Federation Sq; ☼ 11am-late
A people-watcher's paradise from any angle, this pub looks ultramodern but is unrepentant in its pubiness. It's big, brassy and busy, serving every drink imaginable, plus utilitarian pub food and entertainment: djs, bands and beer-tasting nights (from the 150 varieties available). Also good for an afternoon drop, with views of the Yarra River, Flinders Street Station and Fed Sq.

### BROWN ALLEY Map pp52–3 Club

☎ 9670 8599; www.brownalley.com; cnr King & Lonsdale Sts; ☼ Mon-Fri 11.30am-late, Sat & Sun 6pm-late
This historical pub hides away a fully fledged nightclub with a 24-hour licence. It's enormous, with distinct rooms that can fit up to 1000 people. Their sound equipment is the business and the rota of djs includes breakbeat, psy-trance and deep house.

### FFOUR Map pp52–3 Club/Bar

☎ 9650 4494; www.ffour.com.au; 2nd fl, 322 Little Collins St; entry $10-12; ☼ till late Thu-Sun
This stark all-nighter is also popular earlier with Friday after-work drinkers, when

entry is free and drinks specials drown out the week that was. It's your basic garden-variety club; each night brings a different crowd-pleasing flavour, from R&B through to Asian cocktail night to commercial house. Join gangs of girlfriends and student types on a big night out.

## LA DI DA Map pp52-3 — Club
☎ 9670 7680; www.ladidapeople.com; 577 Little Bourke St; ☾ 9am-late Mon-Fri, 3pm-late Sat & Sun
This large multileveled space attempts to bring back the glam to the seedy old King St area. The Chesterfield-strewn public house feeds and waters an after-work crowd; downstairs the club hosts a selection of djs who spin commercial house or something much more interesting depending on the night.

## LOUNGE Map pp52-3 — Club/Lounge
☎ 9663 2916; www.lounge.com.au; 1st fl, 243 Swanston St; ☾ 11am-late
The Lounge has seen a lot of years and a lot of extremely big nights. It still feels like a share house from the early '90s, and that's the way the crowd likes it. From Wednesday to Sunday there's usually something on, with all-night djs Friday and Saturday (door charge $10). Lounge's big balcony, where you can shovel down some reasonably priced food, is a treat in summer.

## 3RD CLASS Map pp52-3 — Club
☎ 9662 4555; www.myspace.com/3rdclassclub; Duckboard Pl; ☾ to late Wed-Sun
Legendary 'if your name is not on the list, you're not coming in' club Honkytonks imploded a few years back and was reborn as this perversely dingy club that draws a very young, very up-for-it crowd. The anti-aesthetic can be both shocking and appealing, depending on the time of night.

## LAST LAUGH COMEDY CLUB
Map pp52-3 — Live Comedy Venue
☎ 9650 6668; www.comedyclub.com.au; Athenaeum Theatre, 188 Collins St, Melbourne
The Last Laugh is open Friday and Saturday year-round, with additional nights in summer. This is professional stand-up, featuring local and international artists. Dinner/show packages are available – bookings recommended. The club is also a venue for acts during the Comedy Festival.

## BENNETTS LANE Map pp52-3 — Live Music/Bar
☎ 9663 2856; www.bennettslane.com; 25 Bennetts Lane; tickets from $12; ☾ 8.30pm-late
Bennetts Lane has long been the boiler room of Melbourne jazz. It attracts the cream of local and international talent and an audience that knows when it's time to applaud a solo. Beyond the cosy front bar, there's another space reserved for big gigs.

## DING DONG LOUNGE
Map pp52-3 — Live Music/Club
☎ 9662 1020; www.dingdonglounge.com.au; 18 Market Lane, Melbourne; ☾ 7pm-late Wed-Sat
Ding Dong walks the rock-and-roll walk and is a great place to see a smaller touring act or catch local bands. The monthly Weekender night hosted by radio RRR dj Steve Wide pulls in the crowds to dance to indie, retro and electro.

## MISS LIBERTINE Map pp52-3 — Live Music/Club
☎ 9663 6855; www.misslibertine.com.au; 34 Franklin St; ☾ 8am-late Mon-Fri, noon-late Sat, 9pm-late Sun
This rambling old pub mixes its crowd and keeps its musical outlook Catholic. The front bar goes off, but the main draw is their diverse line-up of local and touring acts, both live and on the turntables.

## PONY Map pp52-3 — Live Music/Club
☎ 9662 1026; www.pony.net.au; 68 Little Collins St, Melbourne
Bands thump away upstairs (from Wednesday to Saturday), above the low ceilings and din of downstairs. You can also saddle up for the long haul, with Pony open downstairs until 7am Friday and Saturday night.

## ROXANNE PARLOUR
Map pp52-3 — Live Music/Club
☎ 9663 4600; www.roxanneparlour.com.au; Level 3, 2 Coverlid Pl
Music venue from central casting: up some stairs 'tween porn shop and pool hall. You'll find two rooms of happy indie kids and a varied line up from rock and roll to electro avant-pop to trance/psy djs.

## TOFF IN TOWN Map pp52-3 — Live Music/Bar
☎ 9639 8770; www.thetoffintown.com; Level 2, Curtin House, 252 Swanston St; ☾ 5pm-late Sun-Thu, noon-late Fri
An atmospheric venue well suited to cabaret but also works for intimate gigs

by rock gods, avant-folksters or dancehall queens. The moody bar next door serves postset drinks of the French wine and cocktail variety.

### CITY WINE SHOP Map pp52–3    Wine Bar

☎ 9654 6657; 159 Spring St; ⏲ 7am-late
Take home or sample the *de jour* drops by the glass from the wall of local and international wines. You can also buy by the bottle, which adds a corkage charge to the marked price. Counter meals such as crab cakes or goat's cheese omelette (the bar shares a kitchen with the European restaurant next door) demand you make a night of it. Its prime footpath tables are a delight in summer.

# SOUTHBANK & DOCKLANDS

As befits areas that sprang seemingly fully formed from postindustrial wasteland in little over a decade, the bars and entertainment options around here don't tend to the earthy or authentic. What you do get with your boutique ale is views and some provocative interior design.

### BEARBRASS Map pp64–5    Bar

☎ 9682 3799; www.bearbrass.com.au; River level, Southgate, Southbank; ⏲ 8am-late Mon-Fri, 9am-late Sat & Sun
This happy, mainstream bar has a lot to offer: big breakfasts, interesting bar snacks and a wonderful riverside location. And that's all before you notice there's a breakfast cocktail menu with Mexican and Japanese interpretations of the bloody mary and the delightfully entitled 'crack of dawn', a posh play on the mimosa with vodka, verjuice, fresh orange juice and a bit of fizz.

### JAMES SQUIRES BREWHOUSE
Map pp64–5    Bar/Pub

☎ 9600 0700; www.jamessquirebrewhouse.net; 439 Docklands Dr, Docklands; ⏲ noon-late
Big, brassy and boozy – a good place to work off a waterview-aquired thirst or if you've just dropped anchor. The pilsner and IPA are good for a sweltering day or there's some darker drops for when the weather comes in.

### ALUMBRA Map pp64–5    Club

☎ 8623 966; www.alumbra.com.au; Shed 9, Central Pier, 161 Harbour Esplanade, Docklands; ⏲ 4pm-late Wed-Fri, 2pm-late Sat & Sun
Beware the meat-market antics on weekends; during the week it's rather more subdued and the great music, bar staff and stunning location will impress – even if the Bali-meets-Morocco follies of the decorator don't. If you're going to do one megaclub in Melbourne (and like the idea of a glass dance floor), this is going to be your best bet.

### EVE Map pp64–5    Club

☎ 96967388; www.evebar.com.au; 334 City Rd, South Melbourne; ⏲ 8pm-5am Thu-Sun
Florence Broadhurst wallpapers, a black granite bar and Louis chairs set the tone, which gets rapidly lower as the night progresses. Footballers, glamour girls and the odd lost soul come for cocktails and commercial house. Expect to queue after 9pm.

# EAST MELBOURNE & RICHMOND

Richmond's factory-fodder roots are evident in its plethora of corner pubs. This is where you'll find the Corner Hotel, one of the city's best live music venues. East Melbourne isn't on anyone's big night out list, so you'll have to look further east to Richmond or west to town for a drink.

### AVIARY Map pp68–9    Bar

☎ 9428 7727; www.theaviary.com.au; 271 Victoria St, Richmond; ⏲ closed Mon; 🚋 24, 109
If you want a nightcap after your rice-paper rolls and beef in betel leaf dinner, this is a nice, laid-back inner-city bar in an area that's never been too flush with them.

# top picks

## TOP ROOFTOPS

- Madame Brussels (p149)
- Order of Melbourne (p149)
- Supper Club's Fuller Bar (p149)
- Shit Town (p150)
- Palmz at the Carlton Hotel (p148)

There's a good range of beers and wines (including sangria), plus enough vodkas to keep a serious drinker happy. It's also great if you fancy a dessert but are thinking chocolate mousse rather than bean-thread jelly; the menu is interesting to warrant a second visit.

### DER RAUM Map pp68–9        Bar
☎ 9428 0055; www.derraum.com.au; 438 Church St, Richmond; ✆ 6pm-late Tue-Sat; 🚊 East Richmond, 🚋 70

The name conjures up images of a dark Fritz Lang flick and there's definitely something noir-ish about the space and their extreme devotion to hard liquor. Cocktails are not cheap but are muddled and mixed with fresh juices, premium spirits and an encyclopaedic knowledge of the craft.

### PUBLIC HOUSE Map pp68–9       Bar
☎ 9421 0187; www.publichouse.com.au; 433-435 Church St, Richmond; ✆ noon-late; 🚊 East Richmond, 🚋 70

Not in any way resembling a public house from any period of history, this great Six Degrees fit-out features their signature blend of found glass and earthy raw and recycled materials. There's imported beer on tap and a short but sweet wine list.

### MOUNTAIN GOAT BREWERY
Map pp68–9        Brewery
☎ 9428 1180; www.goatbeer.com.au; cnr North & Clark St, Richmond; ✆ from 5pm Fri only

This local microbrewery's varieties of bottled beer (two premium, two seasonal) are available in lots of bars about town, but there's no better place to really get your Goat than from the brewers themselves. Drop in on a Friday when Cam and Dave answer questions about beer, the universe and everything, cook pizzas and put on a tasting.

### CORNER HOTEL Map pp68–9    Live Music/Pub
☎ 9427 9198; www.cornerhotel.com; 57 Swan St, Richmond; 🚊 Richmond, 🚋 70

The band room here is one of Melbourne's most popular midsized venues and has seen plenty of loud and live action over the years. If your ears need a break, there's a friendly front bar. The rooftop has stunning city views, but gets superpacked, and often with a different crowd from the music fans below.

# FITZROY & AROUND

Possessing the highest density of pubs of any suburb, Fitzroy has a big drinking scene. Neighbouring Collingwood is getting in on the act too, and distant Northcote sees a lot of action along its High St strip.

### BAR OPEN Map pp74–5        Bar
☎ 9415 9601; www.baropen.com.au; 317 Brunswick St, Fitzroy; ✆ 3pm-late; 🚋 112

This 10-year-old veteran, as the name suggests, is often open when everyone else is closed. The bar attracts a relaxed young local crowd ready to kick on. Bands play upstairs and are almost always free.

### CAZ REITOP'S DIRTY SECRET
Map pp74–5        Bar
☎ 9415 8876; www.crds.com.au; 80 Smith St, Collingwood; ✆ 5pm-late Wed-Sat; 🚋 86

Speakeasy chic with a couple of snugs for contriving your own cocktail-fuelled dirty secrets. Down the tiny stairs, there's a cosy (or claustrophobic) bluestone basement. If there's not a private party going on here, you might find djs, acoustic acts or comedy. The drinks menu is broad and they have an excellent range of spirits.

### JOE'S SHOE STORE Map pp48–9     Bar
☎ 9482 7666; 233 High St, Northcote; ✆ 4pm-late Tue-Thu, 2pm-late Fri-Sun; 🚋 86

Someone called Joe will no longer sell you lace-up brogues but you'll be pleased with the wine list, featuring around 20 both Australian and 'Continental' wines by the bottle or the glass. It's packed with Northcote cool kids who order pizza from Meine Liebe (p136) or just stick to drinks.

### KENT ST Map pp74–5        Bar
☎ 9419 6346; 201 Smith St, Fitzroy; ✆ 10am-late; 🚋 86

If you like a beer for brunch and your bars dishevelled, Kent St keeps it coming morning, noon and night. Join the gearless bike set on the footpath or explore the nooks and crannies within. Coffee and all-day snacks too.

### LABOUR IN VAIN Map pp74–5     Bar/Pub
☎ 9417 5955; www.labourinvain.com.au; 197a Brunswick St, Fitzroy; ✆ 3pm-late Mon-Wed, 1pm-late Thu-Sun; 🚋 112

Boy's own beer barn with a pool table and lots of Marvellous Melbourne–era charm.

Upstairs there's a deck perfect for lazy afternoons doing a spot of Brunswick St perving and imagining the horrors of 6pm closing.

**LAMBSGO BAR** Map pp74–5      Bar
☎ 8415 0511; www.lambsgobar.com.au; 136 Greeves St, Fitzroy; 5pm-late Mon-Wed, 4pm-late Thu-Sat, 4-11pm Sun; 86
This little temple to beer has been quietly going about its business for quite a few years. They stock an astounding range of the amber fluid: the bar rivals the UN for representation. There's a pool table and a few hidey-hole spaces beyond the front bar.

**EVELYN HOTEL** Map pp74–5    Live Music/Pub
☎ 9419 5500; www.evelynhotel.com; 351 Brunswick St, Fitzroy; 112
Playing mostly local acts, the Evelyn also pulls some biggish-name international performers. The Ev doesn't discriminate by genre: if it's quality it gets a look-in here. Both one-off gigs and band residencies feature from Tuesday to Sunday (free to $30).

**GERTRUDE HOTEL**
Map pp74–5    Live Music/Pub
☎ 9419 2823; www.thegertrudehotel.com.au; 148 Gertrude St, Fitzroy; noon to late daily; 86
This was until recently the last regular pub on Gertrude St, and some of the old-timers brave the new scene. With its yes-this-is-Fitzroy screaming band posters and a very young crowd, it's a jarring mix. But the counter meals have remained refreshingly unambitious (they do parmas) and the bar staff are fast and friendly.

**NIGHT CAT** Map pp74–5    Live Music/Pub
☎ 9417 0090; www.thenightcat.com.au; 141 Johnston St, Fitzroy; 9pm-late Thu-Sun; 112
The Night Cat is a barn-sized space that saw the birth of the upside-down lampshade aesthetic in the mid-90s. There are two bars, a stage and a black-and-white checked dance floor that sees lots of action. Music is generally in the Latin jazz or funk vein. There's a door charge Friday and Saturday.

**NORTHCOTE SOCIAL CLUB**
Map pp48–9    Live Music/Pub
☎ 9489 3917; www.northcotesocialclub.com; 301 High St, Northcote; 86
This is one of Melbourne's best Live Musics with a stage that's seen the likes of Jose

Gonzalez, Deerhoof and Spoon one album out from star status. Their home-grown line-up is also notable. If you're just after a drink, the front bar buzzes every night of the week, or there's a large deck out the back for lazy afternoons. A perfect, and well-loved, local.

**ROB ROY** Map pp74–5    Live Music/Pub
☎ 9419 7180; 51 Brunswick St, Fitzroy; 112
The Rob Roy is does live and local music, usually of the guitar variety. Its small back band room is watched over by a determined Johnny Cash, and its front bar is a kitschy collection of furniture. Entry fees are extremely affordable and sometimes free. (By the by, staff have reported spooky sightings and things that go bump in the night.)

**TOTE** Map pp74–5    Live Music/Pub
☎ 9419 5320; www.thetotehotel.com; cnr Johnston & Wellington Sts, Fitzroy; 4pm-late; 86, 203
This noisy relic of Melbourne's '80s punk/postpunk scene will steal the heart of anyone who loves sticky carpets and sweaty, guitar-driven tunes. Both local and international acts feature. And there's always the promise of an extant rock god sighting in the resolutely grungy front bar.

**WESLEY ANNE** Map pp48–9    Live Music/Bar
☎ 9482 1333; www.wesleyanne.com.au; 250 High St, Northcote; 4pm-late Mon-Fri, 2pm-late Sat & Sun; 86
This atmospheric pub set up shop in a church mission's house of assembly. What else can you expect when the demon drink wins out against the forces of temperance? Booze, yes, but also interesting food, live music, a big beer garden with space heaters and a cruisy crowd who often bring their kids along in daylight hours.

**BUILDERS ARMS HOTEL**
Map pp74–5    Pub/Restaurant
☎ 9419 0818; 211 Gertrude St, Fitzroy; 3pm-late Mon-Thu, noon-late Fri-Sun; 86
A completely re-imagined bad old boozer that's retained its charm despite theatrical new threads. Come for a pot by all means, but there's also decent wine by the glass, a blackboard cocktail list and big Middle-Eastern flavours at the bar or

in the dining room. Picnic style tables on the footpath outside are perfect for taking in Gertrude St.

### NAPIER HOTEL Map pp74–5      Pub
☎ 9419 4240; 210 Napier St, Fitzroy; ⏰ 3-11pm Mon-Thu, 1pm-1am Fri & Sat, 1-11pm Sun; 🚊 112, 86

The Napier has stood on this corner for over a century; many pots have been pulled as the face of the neighbourhood changed. The nostalgic should note the memorabilia of the sadly departed Fitzroy footy team still adorning the walls. Worm your way around the central bar to the boisterous back dining room or to the skinny passage that serves as a beer garden. Outside tables aren't flash but look out over the grand Fitzroy Town Hall.

### STANDARD Map pp74–5      Pub
☎ 9419 4793; 293 Fitzroy St, Fitzroy; 🚊 96, 112

The snug front bar is an old haunt of local barflies. Behind lies a larger drinking space and a sprawling beer garden. It's a favourite with students. Summer Sundays are particularly sweet.

### UNION CLUB HOTEL Map pp74–5      Pub
☎ 9417 2926; www.unionclubhotel.com.au; 164 Gore St, Fitzroy; ⏰ 3pm-late Mon-Thu, noon-late Fri-Sun; 🚊 86

Every inch a local's local, the Union comes into its own in winter with the fire roaring and the footy on. The dining room serves generous pub favourites and there's a rambling courtyard and footpath tables.

### GERTRUDE ST ENOTECA
Map pp74–5      Wine Bar
☎ 9415 8262; www.gertrudestreetenoteca.com; 229 Gertrude St, Fitzroy; ⏰ 8am-late Mon-Fri, 9am-late Sat; 🚊 86

The Fitzroyalty regulars don't mind sharing the banquette space and there are a few more tables out the back among the wine. The 'list' at this svelte wine bar/bottle shop changes regularly and favours European grapes with erudite advice on same. Bar snacks are sourced from Victoria's top suppliers; you can easily make a meal of a couple of plates. While cake doesn't normally score a mention in bar reviews, the Enoteca's are made fresh each day and are wonderful. Order a sticky if you need an excuse.

# CARLTON & AROUND

There's plenty of pubs to be found throughout Carlton and you'll quickly become aware of the area's large student population in many of them. There are also some grown-up gems. Both Brunswick and North Melbourne have a thriving drinking scene which is branching beyond pubs to the odd interesting little bar.

### ATTICUS FINCH Map pp78–9      Bar
⏰ 9387 0188; 129 Lygon St, East Brunswick; ⏰ 5-11pm Wed-Thu, 5pm-1am Fri, 2pm-1am Sat, 2-10pm Sun; 🚊 1, 8

There's a judicious wine list and back-in-fashion cider at this Brunswick haunt named for everyone's favourite lawyer from literature. The space is smartly and simply done with a slight brooding quality (though perhaps we're overidentifying with the novel). A nice alternative to the bigger pubs in these parts, it still sports the requisite beer garden.

### RROSE BAR Map pp78–9      Bar
☎ 9328 1550; 7 Errol St, North Melbourne; ⏰ 2pm-late; 🚊 57

This small bar does both stylish and homey in equal measures (something that's harder to pull off than it looks). A wooden bar that could double as a family dining table, bentwood stools and terrazzo floors add to the eclectic appeal. Not to be overlooked for an afternoon coffee either.

### TRADES HALL BAR Map pp78–9      Bar
☎ 9650 5699; www.tradeshallarts.com.au; cnr Lygon & Victoria Sts, Carlton; ⏰ 4-7pm Fri; 🚊 1, 8

The ballroom in this fascinating old building runs a weekly bar with 'socialist chardonnays, proletariat reds, beer by the belly full'. Prices are cheap, the chat is not purely political and the high-ceilinged dishabille space is truly unique.

### COMIC'S LOUNGE
Map pp78–9      Live Comedy Venue
☎ 9348 9488; www.thecomicslounge.com.au; 26 Errol St, North Melbourne; 🚊 57

There is stand-up every night of the week here. Admission prices vary, but are usually between $8 and $12. Monday night features local comedians and has recently featured notorious funny man Mark 'Chopper' Read. Tuesday is kind of an open-mic night, where aspiring comics have their eight minutes of fame (or shame).

### CORNISH ARMS Map pp78–9 — Live Music/Pub

☎ 9380 8383; www.cornisharms.com.au; 163a Sydney Rd, Brunswick; ⏱3pm-3am Mon-Sat, 3-11pm Sun; 🚉Jewell, 🚃19

The Cornish Arms is a big, friendly venue hosting performances by local talents, some of them firmly from the '80s, but nonetheless interesting. There's some form of entertainment nightly, be it music, comedy or cabaret. Sunday-afternoon sessions are popular with young families.

### EAST BRUNSWICK CLUB
Map pp48–9 — Live Music/Pub

☎ 9388 2777; www.eastbrunswickclub.com; 280 Lygon St, East Brunswick; 🚃1, 8

One of the newer live venues in town with a very cheering line up of local and international acts. Their front bar also has a friendly local scene with ten-buck specials on a Monday night: jugs, burgers, parmas and pasta are all $10 each. Vegos and vegans can often miss out on pub grub but they do meatless and dairy-free versions of all the above too.

### RETREAT Map pp48–9 — Live Music/Pub

☎ 9380 4090; 280 Sydney Rd, Brunswick; 🚉Brunswick, 🚃19

This pub is so big as to be a tad overwhelming. Find your habitat – garden backyard, grungy band room or intimate front bar – and relax. There's blues, roots and acoustic during the week, and djs on the weekends. Sundays are very popular with locals who like to laze in the grass.

### KENT HOTEL Map pp78–9 — Pub/Restaurant

☎ 9347 5672; www.kenthotel.com.au; 370 Rathdowne St, Carlton North; ⏱noon-late; 🚃1,8

This is the quietly upmarket Rathdowne Village's local and its position opposite leafy Curtin Square and footpath tables make it very popular. There's no shortage of good wines as well as beer on tap, and the restaurant has had a respectable reputation for many years.

### RATHDOWNE TAVERN
Map pp78–9 — Pub/Restaurant

☎ 9348 1133; 184 Rathdowne St, Carlton; ⏱noon-late; 🚃96

This grand old hotel has had the decorators in and the smart open room seamlessly segues from the more formal dining space to a nice place to pull up a chair and order a glass of wine (there's a huge range of by the glass options) and some olives. Bar snacks are a treat.

### TOWN HALL HOTEL Map pp78–9 — Pub

☎ 9328 1983; 33 Errol St, North Melbourne; 🚃57

The Town Hall is an unfussy local. Live music is staged free in the front room from Thursday to Saturday, otherwise they'll be spinning some classic vinyl. There's a beer garden and pub meals are also available.

### GERALD'S BAR Map pp78–9 — Wine Bar

☎ 9349 4748; 386 Rathdowne St, Carlton North; ⏱5-11pm Mon-Sat; 🚃1, 8, 🚌253

Wine by the glass is democratically selected at Gerald's and they spin some fine vintage vinyl from behind the curved wooden bar. Gerald himself is out the back preparing to feed you whatever he feels like on the day: goat curry, seared calamari, meatballs, trifle. Whatever it is, it's good.

### JIMMY WATSON'S Map pp78–9 — Wine Bar

☎ 9347 3985; 333 Lygon St, Carlton; ⏱Mon 10.30am-6pm, Tue-Sat 11am-late; 🚃1, 8

Keep it tidy at Watson's wine bar with something nice by the glass, or go a bottle of dry and dry (vermouth and ginger ale) and settle in for the afternoon and evening. If Roy Ground's stunning midcentury building had ears, there'd be a few generations of writers, students and academics in trouble.

# SOUTH YARRA, PRAHRAN & WINDSOR

South Yarra and Windsor may be in walking distance of each other but are a world away in terms of their bar scene. Windsor has a number of artfully grungy, loungey locals; South Yarra is all about shouting over the music while clutching a lurid-coloured drink. Not so precious Prahran is somewhere in the middle.

### BLUE BAR 330 Map pp84–5 — Bar

☎ 9529 6499; www.bluebar.com.au; 330 Chapel St, Prahran; 🚉Prahran, 🚃72

A narrow and dimly lit sanctum away from the bustle of Chapel St, Blue Bar's linear architecture and street-smart clientele contrast with the sprawl of couches within.

And Blue Bar blessedly debunks the theory that you have to look like a model to drink in Chapel St.

### CANDY BAR Map pp84–5 — Bar/Club
☎ 9529 6566; www.candybar.com.au;162 Greville St, Prahran; ☸ 10am-late; 🚊 Prahran, 🚌 72
Harking back to Greville St's clubland heyday, it's a café by day and the djs move in after dark. Check website to find a night that suits: current picks are Monday's drag-queen bingo, or Friday for Sandwich Machine.

### YELLOW BIRD Map pp84–5 — Bar
☎ 9533 8983; 122 Chapel St, Windsor; ☸ 7am-late; 🚊 Windsor, 🚌 6
Keeps Windsor's cool kids happy with all-day drinks (including an evil coffee, sugar and beer shot) and wi-fi access. Owned by the drummer from local band Something for Kate, the rock'n'roll ambience is genuine.

### ONESIXONE Map pp84–5 — Club
☎ 9533 8433; www.onesixone.com.au; 161 High St, Prahran; ☸ till late Wed-Sat; 🚊 Prahran, 🚌 6
Front up to the peephole and if you pass muster, snaffle a couch or a pouf. A wiggle on the small dance floor is obligatory. Friday is house till 9am before the recovery takes over, running all the way through to 11am Sunday.

### REVOLVER UPSTAIRS
Map pp84–5 — Live Music/Club
☎ 9521 5985; www.revolverupstairs.com.au; 229 Chapel St, Prahran; ☸ noon-4am Mon-Thu, 24hr Fri-Sun; 🚊 Prahran, 🚌 6
Rowdy Revolver can feel like an enormous version of your own lounge room, but with 54 hours of nonstop music come the weekend, you're probably glad it's not. Live music, interesting djs and film screenings keep the mixed crowd wide awake.

### WINDSOR CASTLE Map pp84–5 — Pub
☎ 9525 0239; 89 Albert St, Windsor; 🚊 Windsor
Cosy nooks, sunken pits, fireplaces and flocked wallpaper make the Windsor Castle extremely attractive – if on a winter's night this way you stumble. The Castle gets chaotic on sunny Sundays when the grass umbrellas and, later, tea lights make for an entirely different mood out the back.

# ST KILDA & AROUND

We could fill an entire guide with all the options for a tipple in St Kilda. Most can be found in Fitzroy, Grey and Acland Sts, so (beyond those below) you'll not have much trouble sorting yourself out for a casual beer or a couple of caipiroskas. Carlisle St has a surprisingly lively scene too, though it's more indoors.

### AFTER THE TEARS ELSTERNWICK
Map pp48–9 — Bar
☎ 9523 0969; 9B Gordon St, Elsternwick; ☸ 11am-11pm; 🚊 Elsternwick, 🚌 67
This offshoot of long-time Prahran hangout Borsch, Vodka & Tears (p142) is next to the Classic Cinema. It serves an astonishing range of vodkas and its Polish feel is authentic; many of its regulars are Eastern Europeans who settled in the area quite a few decades ago. If you're daunted by shots, ask for a wonderfully warming sharlotka zubrówka (Bison vodka and cloudy apple juice).

### GEORGE LANE BAR Map pp88–9 — Bar
☎ 9593 8884; www.georgelanebar.com.au; 1 George Lane (off Grey St), St Kilda; ☸ 6pm-1am Tue-Sat; 🚌 96, 16
Hidden behind the hulk of the George Hotel, this little bar is a good rabbit hole to dive into and its pleasantly ad-hoc décor a relief from the inch-of-its-life design aesthetic elsewhere. There's beer on tap and djs (and queues) on the weekends.

### GEORGE PUBLIC BAR Map pp88–9 — Bar
☎ 9534 8822; Basement, 127 Fitzroy St, St Kilda; 🚌 96, 16
Upstairs/downstairs divisions live on, even in egalitarian St Kilda. Behind the crumbling paint and Edwardian arched windows of the George Hotel, there's the Melbourne Wine Room and a large front bar that keeps the after-work crowd happy. In the bowels of the building is the George Public Bar, often referred to as the Snakepit. It's often rough, rowdy and the perfect spot to nurse a pot and play some pool.

### MINK Map pp88–9 — Bar
☎ 9536 1199; 2b Acland St, St Kilda; 🚌 96, 16, 112
In this dimly lit Trans-Siberian–styled bar there's no shortage of vodka and glam

good times. Get there early to nab the much sought-after private 'sleeper' and start working your way through the extensive list.

### PAUSE BAR Map pp88–9 Bar

☎ 9537 0511; www.pausebar.com.au; 268 Carlisle St, St Kilda; ☯ 4pm-1am Mon-Fri, noon-1am Sat & Sun; ▣ Balaclava, ▣ 3, 16, 79

Pause draws a mixed local crowd for cocktails and mezes who like to settle into the dim North African–inspired interior for the night. Staff are laid-back.

### VELUDO Map pp88–9 Bar

☎ 9534 4456; www.veludo.com.au; 175 Acland St, St Kilda; ▣ 96

It's big, it's brassy and it's got a balcony. Over two levels, Veludo's relatively late closing means that most St Kilda-ites have ducked in here after everything else has closed.

### VINEYARD Map pp88–9 Bar

☎ 9525 4527; 71a Acland St, St Kilda; ▣ 96, 16

The perfect corner position and a courtyard barbie attracts crowds of backpackers and scantily clad young locals who enjoy themselves so much as to drown out the neighbouring scenic railway.

### GREYHOUND HOTEL

Map pp88–9 Live Music/Pub

☎ 9534 4189; cnr Carlisle St & Brighton Rd, St Kilda; ▣ 16, 67, 79

This is one of the few Melbourne pubs that *hasn't* been refurbished, and is an original all right – it does drag on Saturday night, karaoke on Sunday and bands from Thursday to Saturday. It's dark, grungy and welcomes everyone from bikies to transvestites to bands like the Cosmic Psychos. Just don't ask the barmaid for a Frangelico and lime.

### ESPLANADE HOTEL

Map pp88–9 Live Music/Pub

☎ 9534 0211; http://espy.com.au; 11 The Esplanade, St Kilda; ☯ noon-1am Sun-Wed, Thu-Sat noon-3am; ▣ 96, 16

Rock-pigs rejoice. The Espy remains gloriously shabby and welcoming to all. Bands play most nights and there's a spruced-up kitchen out the back. And for the price of a pot you get front row seats for the pink-stained St Kilda sunset.

### PRINCE BANDROOM

Map pp88–9 Live Music

☎ 9536 1168; www.princebandroom.com.au; 29 Fitzroy St, St Kilda; ▣ 96, 16, 112

This venue is an institution with everyone from Tricky to Fat Freddy's Drop to Lee Scratch Perry having graced its stage. Its leafy balcony and raucous downstairs bar are added attractions. Dance acts are a feature, but there's also a good mix of indie, electropop, soul and blues.

### BARKLY HOTEL Map pp88–9 Pub

☎ 9525 3354; www.hotelbarkly.com; 109 Barkly St, St Kilda; ▣ 16, 67, 79

The street-level public bar is the place to go if you're up for sinking a few pints, wiggling to whatever comes on the jukebox and snogging a stranger before last drinks are called. The rooftop bar feigns a bit of class, but things get messy up there too. The look (Gold Coast penthouse, perhaps?) and the music might be just your thing or set your teeth on edge; either way it's worth braving for the abso-bloody-lutely spectacular sunset view across the rooftops to the Palais Theatre and bay beyond.

### DOULTON BAR Map pp88–9 Pub

☎ 9534 2200; 202 Barkly St, St Kilda; ▣ 96

Keep your eyes on the prize: a spot at the curved front window with gold-tinted views down the length of Acland St. Weighty wooden furniture and wood-panelled walls merge with a modern split-level floor plan, in keeping with the original building and mindful of its casual late-20s crowd.

### ST KILDA BOWLING CLUB

Map pp88–9 Sports Club/Bar

☎ 9537 0370; http://home.vicnet.net.au/~sksc; 66 Fitzroy St, St Kilda; ▣ 96, 16, 112

This fabulously intact old clubhouse is tucked behind a neatly trimmed hedge and a splendid bowling green. The long bar serves drinks at 'club prices' (ie cheap) and you'll be joined by St Kilda's hippest and hottest on Sunday afternoons. Francophiles take note: the petanque club convenes every Friday afternoon.

### WEST ST KILDA RSL

Map pp88–9 Sports Club/Bar

☎ 9534 2485; 23 Loch St, St Kilda; ▣ 112

As far removed from the beer barn RSLs of the northern states as you can get, this club is housed in a beautiful Victorian villa tucked away in a leafy residential street. Come here for a nostalgically cheap beer and a game of pool.

### CARLISLE WINE BAR Map pp88–9 Wine Bar
☎ 9531 3222; 137 Carlisle St, Balaclava; ⏱ brunch Sat & Sun, dinner daily; ⊕ Balaclava, 🚊 3, 16
Locals love this often rowdy, wine-worshiping former butcher's shop. The staff will treat you like a regular and find you a glass of something special, or effortlessly throw together a cocktail amid the weekend rush. The rustic Euro food is good too.

# SOUTH MELBOURNE, PORT MELBOURNE & ALBERT PARK

These neighbourhood's pubs are probably the most gussied up in the city. It's a lively scene, with the area's ad land and media types joining locals at the bar.

### EMERALD HILL BREWERY
Map pp92–3 Brewery
☎ 9696 5491; www.emeraldhillbrewery.com.au; 20 Ross St, South Melbourne; ⏱ 5pm-midnight Fri only; 🚊 112
This bastion of bloke is only open once a week; the rest of the time they're busy brewing their natural pale, wheat and stout beers. At beer o'clock, up comes the roller door and you're welcome for a pint among the vats.

### GUNN ISLAND HOTEL Map pp92–3 Pub
☎ 9690 1958; 102 Canterbury Rd, Middle Park; 🚊 112
Friendly regular pub with 16 beers on tap and popular counter meals, including par-

mas the size of your head. It's park-side and really pleasant for a Sunday afternoon, but it gets very crowded on weekend nights.

### HOTEL NEST Map pp92–3 Pub
☎ 9699 9744; www.hotelnest.com.au; 111 Victoria Ave, Albert Park; ⏱ closed Mon; 🚊 1
The Nest's super slick and airy makeover is deeply Vic Ave. As befits the surroundings, the food is pub-plus (ie wagyu burgers), the wine list is long, and the beers obscure or imported.

### LONDON Map pp92–3 Pub
☎ 9646 4644; thelondon.com.au; 92 Beach St, Port Melbourne; 🚊 109
This was often a sailor's first (and only) point of call, but today this portside pub is as well known for its food as the coldness of its beer. It's ideal for watching the sunset or the *Spirit of Tasmania* depart.

### BUTTERFLY CLUB Map pp92–3 Live Music
☎ 9690 2000; www.thebutterflyclub.com; 204 Bank St, South Melbourne; ⏱ 5pm-late Wed-Sun; 🚊 96, 112
This eccentric little place remains largely undiscovered; expect acts that aren't really theatre, aren't quite straight comedy and that might just throw in a song. The teeny rooms display an extraordinary collection of kitsch, which adds to the feeling that you're never quite sure what you're in for.

### LINA'S BISTRO A VIN
Map pp92–3 Wine Bar
☎ 9645-5515; 114 Bridport St, Albert Park; ⏱ 4pm-late Mon-Fri, 3pm-late Sat & Sun; 🚊 1, 96
Although serving up admirable bistro fare, this Parisian-styled wine bar is loved by locals as a drinking spot, especially the cheery back courtyard. The *vin* selection is comprehensive.

160

# top picks

- Rooftop Cinema at Curtin House (p163)
- MSO Metropolis concert (p16)
- Chunky Move (p164)
- Opera in the Bowl (p163)
- A classic musical at the Princess Theatre (p165)
- A new Australian play at the Malthouse (p164)

# ARTS

Melbourne's landscape belongs to the arts. Its architecturally designed buildings plot the city's social and political history. The CBD is a fertile ground for the arts, with art growing out of most surfaces: in the underground walkways at Flinders Street Station, sprouting out of the sides of buildings in laneways across town, stencilled on walls and thriving on city pavements. It's mostly watered with public funds, and breathes stimulating life into the city. The city's Arts Centre stretches along St Kilda Rd between the National Gallery of Victoria and the concert venue, Hamer Hall, with Federation Square across the road commanding the Flinders St corner.

The arts in Melbourne are highly accessible, both for the sheer number of art spaces and their appeal to a broad audience. For most Melburnians, seeing a film or exhibition is part of an average week. Do some digging, though, and you'll discover there's also a keen enterprising side to Melbourne's arts scene that's less visible but no less important.

## CINEMA

Cinema multiplexes are spread throughout Melbourne city and the suburbs and belong either to the Hoyts (hoyts.ninemsn.com.au), Dendy (www.dendy.com.au), Village (villagecinemas.com.au) or Greater Union (www.greaterunion.com.au) chains. Tickets cost around $15 and screening times are published in the daily newspapers. The Australian cinema-goer's ritual embraces the standards of postmix soft drinks and popcorn, but includes the unique choc-top – an ice-cream cone covered in hard (and often oddly tasteless) chocolate. Village and Hoyts offer a 'premium' cinema experience with cushy seating and three-course meals and alcohol available in their Gold Class and Director's Suites respectively. See the websites for details.

Melbourne's truly independent cinemas are few and far between, but for arthouse, foreign-language and otherwise interesting films, check out the following:

### ASTOR Map pp88–9

☎ 9510 1414; www.astor-theatre.com; cnr Chapel St & Dandenong Rd, St Kilda; 🚋 Windsor; 🚌 64
This rep cinema screens all the classics in stunning Art Deco surrounds. The Astor is magic: the candy-bar staff appear to have stepped out of a film noir set, and the Astor cat makes celebrity appearances. Double features screen most nights.

### AUSTRALIAN CENTRE FOR THE MOVING IMAGE Map pp52–3

ACMI; ☎ 9663 2583; www.acmi.net.au; Federation Sq, Melbourne
ACMI's cinemas screen an incredibly diverse range of films. It programs regular events and festivals for film genres and audiences, as well as screening one-offs. Check the website for information on what's coming up.

### CINEMA NOVA Map pp78–9

☎ 9347 5331; www.cinemanova.com.au; 380 Lygon St, Carlton; 🚌 1, 8
Nova has the latest in art-house, documentary and foreign films, and has cheap Monday screenings: sessions before 4pm cost $6 and after 4pm $8 (except public holidays). Special events include Script Alive – readings of unproduced screenplays – and cry-baby sessions for parents with young children.

### CLASSIC CINEMA Map pp48–9

☎ 9524 7900; www.classictheatre.com.au; 9 Gordon St, Elsternwick; 🚋 Elsternwick, 🚌 67
Arthouse classics screen in what is Melbourne's longest-running cinema (it housed a Yiddish theatre troop in 1950s). They also host an annual festival of Jewish cinema.

### DENDY KINO Map pp52–3

☎ 9650 2100; www.kinodendy.com.au; Collins Pl, 45 Collins St
The Kino screens art-house films in its comfy licensed cinemas. Monday is cheap (all tickets $7) and there's a seniors' special ($6.50 for the first session from Tuesday to Friday). Kino also participates in special events such as festivals and 'Reel Mums' screenings for parents and carers of small children.

### IMAX Map pp78–9

☎ 9663 5454; www.imaxmelbourne.com.au; Melbourne Museum, Carlton Gardens; 🚌 86, 96
Who'd have predicted that 3-D films would be relegated to kid-friendly genres?

Animal and adventure films in 3-D screen on a grand scale here, with movies specially made for these giant screens.

### PALACE COMO Map pp84–5
☎ 9827 7533; www.palacecinemas.com.au; cnr Toorak Rd & Chapel St, South Yarra; 🚈 South Yarra, 🚋 8
Arthouse and foreign language favourites are shown across four new luxury cinemas with a plush foyer and bar and café. One of the hosts of the annual Italian and Greek film festivals.

### PALACE GEORGE Map pp88–9
☎ 9534 6922; www.palace.net.au; 135 Fitzroy St, St Kilda; 🚋 16, 96
The George is small but is a well-loved part of St Kilda life. Apart from screening arty-type major releases, it's a venue for the St Kilda and Short Film Festivals and VCA film and TV graduate screenings. It's also fully licensed.

Outdoor cinemas are popular in the summer; check the websites for seasonal opening dates and their program details. These include:

Moonlight Cinema (Map pp84–5; www.moonlight.com.au; Gate D, Royal Botanic Gardens Melbourne, Birdwood Ave, South Yarra; 🚋 8)

Rooftop Cinema (Map pp52–3; www.rooftopcinema.com.au; Level 6, Curtin House, 252 Swanston St, City)

St Kilda Open Air Cinema (Map pp88–9; www.stkildaopenair.com.au; St Kilda Sea Baths, 10-18 Jacka Blvd, St Kilda; 🚋 16, 96)

## CLASSICAL
Following are a few of the city's main players. These groups play at various venues across town. Check their websites or the local press for venues and concert dates. Melbourne also has a number of small, independent and often very innovative classical groups. Check the *Age* for listings.

### MELBOURNE SYMPHONY ORCHESTRA
MSO; www.mso.com.au
Averaging 130 performances a year, the MSO has a loyal following. Their reach is broad: while not afraid to be populist (they've done sell-out performances with Burt Bacharach, Neil Sedaka and the

Whitlams), they can also do edgy. The Metropolis series premieres new Australian composition and challenging works from international contemporary composers. The well-regarded Melbourne Chorale has joined forces with the orchestra and is now known as the Melbourne Symphony Orchestra Chorus. The MSO performs regularly at Hamer Hall (see the boxed text, p147), but also at other venues around the city, including the Malthouse (p164) and St Paul's Cathedral (p59).

### MUSICA VIVA
http://musicaviva.com.au
National group Musica Viva stages ensemble music and performances around once a month at Hamer Hall (see boxed text, p147) and includes preshow talks. Its Ménage chamber concert series, where pioneering new music is performed in informal venues, is specifically aimed at 18- to 35-year-olds. They also hold midweek morning 'coffee' concerts at the Collins St Baptist Church.

## OPERA
Melbourne has nurtured internationally acclaimed opera singers and continues to stage world-class productions. People do dress up for a night at the opera, especially opening and weekend nights of Opera Australia, but no one will blink an eyelid if you don't.

### CHAMBER MADE THEATRE Map pp78–9
☎ 9329 7422; www.chambermade.org.au; Arts House, Meat Market, 1 Blackwood St, North Melbourne; 🚋 55, 59
Founded in 1988, Chamber Made productions showcase contemporary music and music-based performance art. Performances aren't usually more frequent than quarterly, though they supplement productions with work in progress presentations.

### MELBOURNE OPERA
☎ 9614 4188; www.melbourneopera.com; 401 Collins St
A not-for-profit company that performs a classic repertoire in the stunning Athenaeum Theatre (p357). Prices are reasonable.

### OPERA AUSTRALIA
www.opera-australia.org.au
The national opera company performs with some regularity at Melbourne's

Victorian Arts Centre (p64). The company also performs a springtime Opera in the Bowl concert at the Sidney Myer Music Bowl, which is worth looking out for if you're in town; it's free and unticketed. OzOpera, the company's education and access arm, tours schools and regional centres. Check the website for upcoming performances, as well as tips and recommendations for first timers.

### VICTORIAN OPERA

www.victorianopera.com.au

This relatively new company is dedicated to innovation and to accessibility, with B reserve tickets under $60 and a subscriber's 'balcony club' that has seats for $25. Their program pleasingly doesn't always play it safe. They also tour to regional cities.

## DANCE

Melbourne's dance scene has companies specialising in both traditional ballet performances and genre-busting modern pieces; see also p35.

### AUSTRALIAN BALLET Map pp64–5

☎ 1300 369 741, 9669 2700; www.australian ballet.com.au; 2 Kavanagh St, Southbank

Based in Melbourne and now more than 40 years old, the Australian Ballet performs traditional and new works at the State Theatre at the Victorian Arts Centre. See p35, or visit the website for an extensive history as well as pending performances. The Southbank centre also includes a school. You can take an hour-long tour that includes a visit to the production and wardrobe departments as well as the studios of both the company and the school. It's $10 per person and bookings are essential.

### CHUNKY MOVE Map pp64–5

☎ 9645 5188; www.chunkymove.com; 111 Sturt St, Southbank

The state's contemporary dance company performs at its sexy venue behind the Australian Centre for Contemporary Art. Chunky Move's pop-inspired pieces are internationally acclaimed. The company also runs a variety of dance (contemporary, ballet, funk, breakdance), yoga and pilates classes; see the website for details.

### KAGE PHYSICAL THEATRE Map pp78–9

☎ 9328 2474; www.kagephysicaltheatre.com; Meat Market, 8/5 Blackwood St, North Melbourne; 🚊 19, 59

This modern dance company works between theatre and dance. This is witty and innovative stuff, well worth a look if you're not after a straight narratives. Check the website for performance details.

## THEATRE

There is no distinct theatre district in Melbourne: individual companies and theatres are spread across town. Tickets start at about $20 for independent productions, and $30 upwards for mainstream theatre. See p35 for more on Melbourne's theatre scene.

### LA MAMA Map pp78–9

☎ 9347 6948; www.lamama.com.au; 205 Faraday St, Carlton; 🚊 19

La Mama is historically significant to Melbourne's theatre scene. This tiny, intimate forum produces new Australian works and experimental theatre, and has a reputation for developing emerging playwrights. For a profile of La Mama see boxed text, p36.

### MALTHOUSE THEATRE Map pp64–5

☎ 9685 5111; www.malthousetheatre.com.au; 113 Sturt St, South Melbourne; 🚊 1

The Malthouse Theatre Company often produces the most exciting theatre in Melbourne. Dedicated to promoting Australian works, the Malthouse tours nationally and to Asia. Housed in the atmospheric Malthouse Theatre since 1990, it includes a number of theatre spaces of varying sizes and includes the Tower Theatre.

### New Theatres

At time of going to press the rhythmic sounds of construction were the only music to be heard taking place on the corner of Sturt St and Southbank Blvd, the site of the new Melbourne Recital Hall and the Melbourne Theatre Company's eventual Southbank home. That is set to change when they open in 2009. The 1000-seat recital hall will bear the name of arts philanthropist Dame Elisabeth Murdoch and will be a world-class venue for chamber music. The MTC's 500-seat space promises to break the 'brass and carpet' theatre aesthetic and will embrace new technologies with gusto.

## CURTAINS UP

Blockbuster musicals have the good fortune of playing in Melbourne's graceful old theatres, including the following. Book tickets through one of the agencies listed on p357.

Athenaeum (Map pp52–3; ☎ 9650 1500; www.ticketmaster.com.au; 188 Collins St) The old dame dates back to the 1830s and the theatre now hosts Melbourne Opera and the International Comedy Festival

Comedy Theatre (Map pp52–3; ☎ 9299 9800; www.marrinertheatres.com.au; 240 Exhibition St) This midsize 1920s Spanish–style venue is dedicated to comedy theatre and musicals.

Her Majesty's (Map pp52–3; ☎ 8643 3300; www.hmt.com.au; 219 Exhibition St) On the outside Her Maj is red-brick Second Empire; on the inside it's 1930s Moderne. It's been the home of musical comedy since 1880 and is still going strong.

Princess Theatre (Map pp52–3; ☎ 9299 9800; www.marrinertheatres.com.au; 163 Spring St) This gilded Second-Empire beauty has a long and colourful history. It's reputed to have a resident ghost – that of singer Federici, who died as he descended through the stage trap in 1888 after playing Mephistopheles in the opera *Faust*.

Regent Theatre (Map pp52–3; ☎ 9299 9500; www.marrinertheatres.com.au; 191 Collins St) The Regent, a Rococo picture palace from the 1920s, is used less as a venue than the Princess, but when it hosts musicals and live acts, it's a fabulous opportunity to experience its elegant grandeur.

### MELBOURNE THEATRE COMPANY
Map pp64–5

MTC; ☎ 9684 4500; www.mtc.com.au; Victorian Arts Centre, 100 St Kilda Rd
Melbourne's major theatrical company performs at the Victorian Arts Centre. The MTC stages around 15 productions each year, ranging from contemporary and modern (including many new Australian works) to Shakespearean and other classics.

### RED STITCH ACTORS THEATRE
Map pp88–9

☎ 9533 8082; www.redstitch.net; rear, 2 Chapel St, St Kilda

This independent company of actors stages new international works that are often premieres in Australia. The tiny black-box theatre, opposite the Astor (p162) and down the end of the driveway, is a cosy, intimate space.

### THEATREWORKS Map pp88–9

☎ 9534 3388; www.theatreworks.org.au; 14 Acland St, St Kilda; 🚊 64
Theatreworks is a community theatre dedicated to supporting a range of arts practitioners, housed in a parish hall that looks like it's straight out of *The Vicar of Dibley*. The company has been around for 25-odd years.

# SPORTS & ACTIVITIES

## top picks

- **Australian Rules Football** (p168)
  See the big men fly at the MCG during the AFL season
- **Cricket** (p169)
  Join the capacity crowd at the Boxing Day Cricket Test
- **Jogging** (p174)
  Do the Tan: run, jog or walk
- **Lawn Bowls** (p172)
  Barefoot bowl with a pot in hand
- **Football** (p169)
  Be part of the Melbourne Victory cheer squad for a night

What's your recommendation? www.lonelyplanet.com/melbourne

# SPORTS & ACTIVITIES

Cynics snicker that sport is the sum of Melbourne's culture, although they're hard to hear above all that cheering, air punching and applause. Sport is undeniably the most dominant expression of common beliefs, practices and social behaviour. Melbourne is the birthplace of Australian Rules football and hosts a disproportionate number of international events, including the Australian Open, Australian Formula One Grand Prix and Melbourne Cup. The city's arenas, tracks, grounds and courts are regarded as the world's best-developed and well-situated cluster of facilities.

Sport is promoted and followed with such fervour in this city that the attendant surge of humanity is a spectacle in itself. And that's exactly why people love it: sporting attendance brings Melbourne's disparate communities together for the single resounding purpose of following their team. Sport acts as a social glue that binds communities.

Australians are frequently perceived as 'armchair experts', and experts they invariably are. And while spectating may be perceived as an entirely passive pastime, think about the intense concentration and outpouring of emotion expended. There may not be too many muscles moving but a good game is sure to raise a heart rate, and the brain will be working overtime to scrutinise every nuance, decision, kick, call and turn.

Media attention fuels the culture of celebrity surrounding Melbourne's sporting heroes. There's an incessant hunger for snippets of players' private lives, and sportspeople are often used to endorse commercial products. Sporting heroes have sung the praises of products ranging from milk and watches to hair-replacement therapy and toilet paper.

There's some spectacle in the city's sporting calendar whatever month or week you're in Melbourne. Getting along to some sport is an often exhilarating way to witness Melbourne culture.

Exhilarating in a different way, activities including canoeing, cycling and sailing are super options for seeing the city and its surrounds. Melbourne's landscape is flat as a tack, so cycling can be as leisurely as you like. Traversing the city's waterways offers a unique perspective on equally unique surrounds.

Personal fitness can range from a weekly walk in one of Melbourne's many parks to a boot camp–style regime at a nearby gym. If you insist on exercising while on holiday, there are plenty of ways to work out. Of course, not all healthy activities involve exertion; see Day Spas (p173) for some suggestions for healthy indulgence.

## SPECTATOR SPORT

Underneath the cultured chat and designer threads of your typical Melbournian, you'll find a heart that truly belongs to one thing: sport. The city takes the shared spectacle and tribal drama of the playing field very seriously; at the same time, it's also seen as an excuse to get together with some mates. Sport is promoted and followed with such fervour in this city that the crowds are often entertainment in themselves.

### AUSTRALIAN RULES FOOTBALL

Understanding the basics of Australian Rules Football (AFL, or just 'the footy') is definitely a way to get a local engaged in conversation, especially between March and September, when the game is played. Melbourne is the national centre for the sport, and the Melbourne-based Australian Football League (AFL; www.afl.com.au) administers the national competition.

During the footy season, the vast majority of Victorians become obsessed: entering tipping competitions at work, discussing groin injuries and suspensions over the water cooler, and devouring huge chunks of the daily newspapers devoted to mighty victories, devastating losses and the latest bad-boy behaviour (on and off the field) of the sport's biggest stars. Monday night disciplinary tribunals allocate demerit points for every bit of blood and biffo, and players can then be banned from playing. Fans follow these proceedings with almost as much attention as the games themselves. One thing is certain: footy fans always know better than the umpires, who have been a longstanding target for hecklers. Once disparagingly referred to as 'white maggots' because of their lily white uniforms, they're now decked out in bright-coloured livery so players can spot them in the thick of the game. Now fans just call them 'maggot' for short.

The MCG, affectionately referred to as the 'G', has been the home of football since 1859 and its atmosphere can't be replicated. The AFL now has teams in every mainland state but nine of its 16 clubs are still based in Melbourne (as well as the regional team Geelong). Since the demise of the local grounds, all of these teams will play their home games at either the MCG or Telstra Dome; the current MCG tenant clubs are Melbourne, Richmond, Collingwood and Hawthorn, the rest, besides Geelong, reside at the Dome. Games are held on Friday or Saturday nights, as well as Saturday or Sunday afternoons. Those between two Melbourne teams ensure a loud, parochial crowd. Tickets are reasonably priced, with reserved seats from $33 a pop, and unreserved admission even less. For sustenance, there are meat pies and hot chips at half-time. Thirsts are quenched with beer sipped from plastic cups at quarter time and three-quarter time. (A BYO thermos of tea and a sandwich is a perfectly acceptable substitute, particularly if you're of a certain age.) Barracking has its own lexicon and is often a one-sided 'conversation' with the umpire. When the siren blows, and after the winning club theme song is played (usually several times over), it's off to the pub. Supporters of opposing teams often celebrate and commiserate together. Despite the deep tribal feelings, and passionate expression of belonging that AFL engenders, violence is almost unheard of pre-, post-, or during games.

For game fixtures, see the AFL website or check the *Age* newspaper. Reserved ticketing for the MCG, Telstra Dome and Skilled Stadium in Geelong can be purchased from Ticketmaster (1300 136 122; www.ticketmaster.com.au).

## AUSTRALIAN TENNIS OPEN

The last two weeks of January is tennis time in Melbourne, when the city hosts the Australian Open (www.australianopen.com) tennis championships. The world's top players come to compete at Melbourne Park (p67) in the year's first of the big four Grand Slam tournaments. With daily attendance figures breaking world records (well over half a million people come through the turnstiles over the two weeks) a carnival atmosphere prevails around the grounds. While there are picnics and musical diversions in the sunshine, there's a hushed respect during key matches. National tensions between fans have been met with heavy-handed policing in the past, but the most disruptive element is usually the elements themselves. The chance of at least one 40°C scorcher is high. Tickets are available through Ticketek (premier.ticketek.com.au) and range from about $25 for ground passes to well over $100 for finals.

## CRICKET

For any cricket fan, seeing a game at the Melbourne Cricket Ground (p67) is a must-do-before-you-die rite of devotion. International test matches, one-day internationals and the Pura Cup (formerly the Sheffield Shield, the national cricket competition) are all played here. Warm days, cricket's leisurely pace and gangs of supporters who've travelled from far and wide often make for some spectator theatrics (the good, the bad and the ugly). The cricket season in Australia is from October to March. General admission to international matches starts at around $30 and reserved seats start going from $45 to upwards of $100, with finals costing more and usually requiring a booking. The cricket event of the year is the traditional Boxing Day Test (held on 26 December, and for many bigger than Christmas). It sells out fast. Tickets can be purchased from from Ticketmaster (1300 136 122; www.ticketmaster.com.au).

## FOOTBALL

With so many other codes to compete with, the original game of football is most often referred to as soccer in Australia, despite the Football Federation of Australia's official assertion of the football tag. Despite all the competition, the game's rise in Melbourne has been spectacular. A new A League national competition was formed in 2005 and with it came a large supporter base and a higher profile for the game. Australia's solid performance in the 2006 FIFA World Cup also contributed to its new-found popularity, as does its status as the 'world game'. There are eight teams in the national competition (including a team from honorary 'state' New Zealand). After winning the FFA Grand Final in 2007, Melbourne Victory did not fare so well in 2008. The team has amazingly vocal supporters (including a British-style cheer squad); with the Dome's cauldronlike acoustics it makes for some atmospheric play. Melbourne Victory plays its home games at Telstra Dome (p66) and the season runs from October to May. Go to Melbourne Victory's website (www.melbournevictory .com.au) for more details.

## RUGBY LEAGUE

Northern import rugby league attracts a moderate following, with around 11,000 fans showing up to cheer on the National Rugby League's (NFL) only Melbourne team, the Melbourne Storm (www.melbournestorm.com.au), although crowds rise to between 20,000 and 30,000 for key clashes. The team had an incredibly successful year in 2007, losing only three games and going on to comprehensively defeat favourites Manly in the 2007 NFL Grand Final. The Storm also played in the 2008 World Club Challenge, losing to the Leeds Rhinos. Rugby league is an acquired taste (one which we admit to), and its proud supporter base tends to be drawn from the northern states and from across the Tasman. The Storm's home ground is Olympic Park (p67) and the season runs from April to September.

## RUGBY UNION

Rugby union does not have a professional league in Melbourne, but draws surprisingly large, often sell-out, crowds to international matches at the Telstra Dome. The stadium recorded its highest sporting attendance (56,605) during a Wallabies tour. But it's a long time between drinks for Melbourne union fans, with only one or two nights out per year. Visit www.rugby.com.au for more details.

## HORSE RACING

They're racing every Saturday at either Flemington, Caulfield, Moonee Valley or Sandown. Every Friday the *Age* and *Herald Sun* newspapers publish what's happening around the fields. For a long-term calendar, visit the website of Racing Victoria (www.racingvictoria.com.au).

The Melbourne Cup, watched by 700 million people in over 170 countries, is the feature event of Melbourne's Spring Racing Carnival, which runs through October and culminates with the Cup in early November. The whole city's a-jitter, and milliners, fashion retailers, beauty therapists and caterers hit pay dirt during this time. The carnival's major races are the Cox Plate, the Caulfield Cup, the Dalgety, the Mackinnon Stakes and the Holy Grail itself, the Melbourne Cup. Apart from these

races, the ultrasocial Derby Day and Oaks Day feature prominently on the spring racing calendar.

The 2-mile (3.2km) Melbourne Cup, always run on the first Tuesday of November at Flemington Racecourse, was first staged in 1861. The Cup brings the whole of Australia to a standstill for the three-or-so minutes during which the race is run. Serious punters and fashion-conscious racegoers (who spend an estimated $54.5 million on clothes and accessories) pack the grandstand and lawns of the racecourse. The city's once-a-year gamblers each make their choice or organise Cup syndicates with friends, and the race is watched or listened to on TVs and radios in pubs, clubs, TAB betting shops and houses across the land.

### FLEMINGTON RACECOURSE Map pp48–9
☎ 1300 727 575; www.vrc.net.au; 400 Epsom Rd, Flemington; ⛐ Flemington Racecourse

Home of the Victoria Racing Club and the Melbourne Cup, Flemington has regular race meets. During the Spring Racing Carnival, Flemington's roses bloom, the lawns are manicured and the bars are groomed for the thousands who visit at this time of the year.

## MOTOR SPORTS

The Australian Formula One Grand Prix ( ☎ 9258 7100; www.grandprix.com.au/cars), held in March, has the kind of figures that make petrolheads swoon: 300km/h, 950bhp and 19,000rpm. The 5.3km street circuit around normally tranquil Albert Park Lake is known for its smooth, fast surface. The buzz, both on the streets and in your ears, takes over Melbourne for four fully sick days. The fortunes of Australia's own F1 hero Mark Webber have been mixed of late, but his presence generates a lot of local interest. If the F1 and F3 cars aren't enough, October brings their two-wheeled counterparts to town, with the Motorcycle Grand Prix (www.grandprix.com.au/bikes) on Phillip Island.

## BASKETBALL

The National Basketball League (www.nbl.com.au) follows the American model, with cheerleaders and odd music grabs. Melbourne's Tigers (www.tigers.com.au) has been around for 70-odd years. Its biggest asset was Andrew Gaze; now retired from the game (though now a lively commentator), he's played the most NBL games (611) of any player and played in the Australian Olympics team five times.

The Melbourne Tigers claimed the 2007/08 National Basketball League (NBL) championship, beating the Sydney Kings. The season runs from October to March and the Tigers play at the State Netball and Hockey Centre in Royal Park (p80), Melbourne.

# ACTIVITIES

## CANOEING & KAYAKING

Yarra Bend Park (p73) stretches 12km north of Richmond. It's within easy cycling distance of Southbank along the Main Yarra Trail. Studley Park Boathouse (Map pp48–9; ☎ 9853 1972; www.studleyparkboathouse.com.au) hires two-person canoes for $28 for the first hour. Further out, try Fairfield Boathouse (Map pp48–9; ☎ 9486 1501; www.fairfieldboathouse.com), which rents a variety of leisure craft, including canoes and replicas of the Thames craft used in the 19th century – poetry and parasols are optional. Prices per hour range from $15 to $30. Both boathouses have cafés, open for breakfast and lunch.

Sea-kayaking is popular along Victoria's beaches and bays, with lots of opportunities to spot sea lions, gannets, penguins and dolphins. Close to town try East Coast Kayaking ( ☎ 9597 0549; www.eastcoastkayaking.com). Apollo Bay offers some beautiful scenery and the chance to see fur seals. Contact Apollo Bay Surf & Kayak for details ( ☎ 5237 1189; www.apollobaysurfkayak.com.au).

## CYCLING

You're cycling beside the river through a grove of trees, bellbirds are singing, and rosellas are swooping low over the path. You're miles from anywhere, right? No, you're on the Main Yarra Trail, one of Melbourne's many inner-city bike paths along the riverside green belts. Melbourne's bike lane network is a great way to actively appreciate the city. Disused railway lines have also been turned over to cyclists, with a number of rail trails in greater Melbourne providing excellent touring possibilities.

Maps are available from the Visitor Information Centre at Federation Sq (Map pp52–3) and Bicycle Victoria ( ☎ 8636 8888; www.bv.com.au). The urban series includes the Main Yarra Trail (35km), off which run the Merri Creek Trail (19km), the Outer Circle Trail (34km), the Maribyrnong River Trail (22km) and the western beaches. At least 20 other long urban cycle paths exist, all marked in the Melway Greater Melbourne Street Directory. In addition, VicRoads (www.vicroads.vic.gov.au) has print-

able maps of Melbourne's cycle paths on its website. You'll not be alone on the roads either. There is a large club scene, with the less hard-core as into the postride café breakfasts as much as the ride itself. Spoke(n), a cult St Kilda bike shop, lists events and clubs on its website (www.spoken.com.au/events/).

Wearing a helmet while cycling is compulsory in Melbourne (as it is in the rest of Australia).

## DIVING

Diving the reefs and wrecks along Vic's coast reveals a wealth of underwater critters including weedy and leafy sea dragons. Port Phillip Bay has the richness of a tropical reef due to nutrient-rich waters. The sponge communities at the heads of the bay rival their coral counterparts in colour, shape and endless variation. Popular diving sites are located off Portsea (p208) on the Mornington Peninsula and Queenscliff on the Bellarine Peninsula (p220). Both have dive centres that operate dive boats and courses for those wishing to learn or add another level of qualification to their dive belts.

## GOLF

Melbourne's golf courses are rated among the best in the world. The illustrious Sandbelt refers to 10 courses stretching along the bay; they're built on a sand base, creating perfect conditions year-round. Among them are Royal Melbourne (www.royalmelbournegc.com), Australia's best and rated No 6 in the world, Huntingdale (www.huntingdalegolf.com.au), home of the Australian Masters tournament, and Kingston Heath (www.kingstonheath.com.au), ranked No 2 in Australia and host to high-profile tournaments. Unfortunately, many are private courses: you'll need a letter of introduction from your own club, and often a verifiable handicap, to get a hit.

For public courses, it's best to book ahead. Green fees cost around $25 for 18 holes during the week, and all courses have clubs and buggies for hire. You'll find a summary of the state's courses at www.ausgolf.com.au. Some good public courses close to town include the following.

### ALBERT PARK GOLF COURSE
Map pp92–3

☎ 9510 5588; www.golfvictoria.com.au; Queens Rd, Albert Park; ☽ dawn-dusk; 🚊 3, 5, 6, 16, 64, 6 This 18-hole championship golf course is set on the fringes of Albert Park Lake (p91), just 2km from the city. Located alongside the Australian Formula One Grand Prix racing circuit, a separate driving range (Map pp92–3; ☎ 9696 4653; Aughtie Dr; ☼ 7am-10pm) allows golfers to hit off from 65 two-tier all-weather bays.

### BRIGHTON GOLF COURSE
Off Map pp48–9
☎ 9592 1388; www.brightongolfclub.com.au; 232 Dendy St, Brighton; ☼ dawn-dusk
One of the adored Sandbelt courses for which Melbourne is known, this 18-hole course keeps golfers on their toes with water hazards and deep bunkers. It's about 10km southeast of the CBD.

### YARRA BEND GOLF COURSE
Map pp48–9
☎ 9481 3729; www.parkweb.vic.gov.au; Yarra Bend Rd, Fairfield; ☼ dawn-dusk
Yarra Bend is just 4km from the city, and affords views of the Yarra River. It's an 18-hole course that also offers instruction, and a Japanese-speaking staff member is on hand.

## INDOOR ROCK CLIMBING
### HARDROCK@VERVE Map pp52–3
☎ 9631 5300; www.hardrock.com.au; 501 Swanston St; ☼ noon-10pm Mon-Fri, 11am-7pm Sat & Sun
Not the bar franchise but an indoor climbing centre with naturalistic surfaces to 16m and city views. With a few storeys of glass frontage, the city gets to view you too.

## IN-LINE SKATING
The best skating paths are those around Port Phillip Bay, particularly the stretch from Port Melbourne south through St Kilda to Brighton. Rock'n Skate Shop (Map pp88–9; ☎ 9525 3434; Suite 3, 22 Fitzroy St, St Kilda; ☼ 10am-7pm Mon-Fri, 9am-7pm Sat & Sun summer, 11am-6pm daily winter) hires skates and padding for $10 for the first hour, $5 for every hour after that. Overnight hire, with pick up after 5pm and return before noon, costs $15, while 24-hour hire is $25. You'll need an Australian drivers license, a passport or a credit card as ID.

## LAWN BOWLS
Formerly the domain of senior citizens wearing starched white uniforms, bowling clubs have recently been inundated by younger

types: barefoot, with a beer in one hand and a bowl in the other. With a game costing between $5 and $10 (including bowls' hire), and cheap beer on tap, bowls makes for a leisurely afternoon with mates.

### NORTH FITZROY BOWLS Map pp48–9
☎ 9481 3137; www.fvbowls.com.au; 578 Brunswick St, North Fitzroy; 🚊 112
Officially known as the Fitzroy Victoria Bowling & Sports Club, this centre comes equipped with lights for night bowls, barbecues and a beer garden. The dress code is neat-casual, with slippers or thongs acceptable. Phone to make a booking and for opening times, which vary from day to day.

### ST KILDA BOWLING CLUB Map pp88–9
☎ 9537 0370; 66 Fitzroy St, St Kilda; ☼ noon-sunset Tue-Sun; 🚊 16, 96
The only dress code at this popular bowling club is shoes off. So join the many others who de-shoe to enjoy a beer and a bowl in the great outdoors. This club provides bowls and a bit of friendly instruction for first timers; Francophiles can opt for boules.

## SAILING
With about 20 yacht clubs around the shores of Port Phillip, yachting is one of Melbourne's most popular passions. Races and regattas are held on most weekends, and the bay is a memorable sight when it's sprinkled with hundreds of colourful sails. Conditions can change radically and without warning, making sailing on the bay a challenging, and sometimes dangerous, pursuit. Other popular boating areas around the state include the sprawling Gippsland Lakes system, the watersports playground of Lake Eildon (p311) and the low-key cruisey Mallacoota Inlet (p295) near the border.

If you want to feel the wind in your hair, Hobsons Bay Yacht Club (Map p96; ☎ 9397 6393; www.hbyc .asn.au; 268 Nelson Pl, Williamstown) welcomes volunteers on Wednesday nights (arrive by 5.30pm). In summer you can stow away with the Royal Melbourne Yacht Squadron (Map pp48–9; ☎ 9534 0227; www.rmys.com.au; Pier Rd, St Kilda) on Wednesday nights ($15); arrive by 4.30pm. Be sure to wear nonmarking shoes and take along waterproof gear if you have it.

Melbourne's two main ocean races are the Melbourne to Devonport and Melbourne to Hobart events, held annually between Christmas and New Year. The Melbourne to Hobart race goes around Tasmania's wild western coast; the more famous Sydney to Hobart event runs down the eastern coast.

## SURFING

One of the few places you'll feel at home wearing a skin-tight black rubber suit is among the waves that crash along the Victorian coast. The closest surf beaches to Melbourne are those on the Mornington (p204) and Bellarine Peninsulas (p220), both about an hour's drive from the city. The best stretches are further out along the Great Ocean Rd (p224) and Phillip Island (p200). Boards and wetsuits are available to hire from seaside shops, as are lessons on how to carve up the swell. The Rip Curl Pro (www.ripcurl.com/?proHome_en) is held at legendary Bells Beach (or wherever the surf is pumping nearby) each Easter. Visit the website of Surfing Australia (www.surfingaustralia.com.au) for a list of competitions and surf schools, as well as the ever-important rules of local etiquette.

## TENNIS

It's not just as spectators that Melbournians really dig tennis. You'll find enthusiastic clubs and beautifully sited courts scattered throughout the inner city. The East Melbourne Tennis Centre (Map pp68–9; ☎ 9417 6511; cnr Simpson & Albert Sts, East Melbourne) charges between $20 and $30 for court hire depending on the time of day and week, including rackets, for the hour. Melbourne Park (Map pp68–9; ☎ 9286 1244; www.mopt.com.au; Batman Ave), venue of the Australian Open, has 23 outdoor and five indoor courts; prices are per hour and vary depending on the time of day and week. Indoor court hire ranges from $34 to $40 and outdoor courts cost between $26 and $34, plus racquet hire.

## WINDSURFING & KITE-SURFING

Elwood, just south of St Kilda, is a popular sailboarding area. RPS – the Board Store (Map pp48–9; ☎ 9525 6475; www.rpstheboardstore.com; 87 Ormond Rd, Elwood) hires gear and offers tuition. A 1½-hour group introductory lesson in kitesurfing costs $70. A three-hour introductory course in windsurfing costs $130. All gear is included; courses are weather-dependent and mainly limited to the summer months. Book at least a week ahead.

# HEALTH & FITNESS
## DAY SPAS

Melbourne has some luxuriously indulgent day spas that offer the usual range of 'treatments' that go way beyond the basic massage/mani/pedi formula. The trend is definitely to the organic and the spiritual, though there is nothing aesthetic about any of the following places.

For day spas in the Daylesford & Hepburn Springs area, see the boxed text, p261. Or you could try a spa in Koonwarra (see p278), Lakes Entrance (see p288), Mt Buller (see p300), Mt Hotham (see p302), Falls Creek (see p304) or Mildura (see p325).

### AESOP SPA Map pp84–5
☎ 9866 5250; www.aesop.net.au; 153 Toorak Rd, South Yarra; ☉ appointments 10am-2pm Mon-Fri; ☒ South Yarra, ☒ 8
The intensely pleasurable facials offered by this local skincare guru raise the bar. Choose from five basic treatments (as well as your preferred musical accompaniment); your lactate surge or detox overhaul will be further customised to your skin while you're wrapped up in a mohair blanket on a cotton futon.

### AURORA SPA RETREAT Map pp88–9
☎ 9536 1130; www.aurorasparetreat.com; Prince Hotel, 2 Acland St; ☒ 96, 16, 112
There's an enormous and creative menu of wellness treatments that range from water-based massage and full-body wraps, all within a beautiful setting. But the staff's hard sell on product can rattle after you've just reached a max relaxation mode.

### CHUAN SPA Map pp64–5
☎ 8696 8111; www.chuanspa.com; Langham Hotel, 1 Southgate Ave, Southbank; ☉ 10am-8pm Mon-Sat, to 6pm Sun
This is a spin-off from the Hong Kong spa of the same name. Its Chinese garden–themed ambience is designed to 'liberate your reflective *Yin* side from its more active *Yang* counterpart'. It offers a full range of treatments, including water-based ones, and has a steam room and swimming pool.

### CROWN SPA Map pp64–5
☎ 9292 6182; www.crowntowers.com.au; Crown Towers, Southbank
Miles of marble and plenty of pamper at this traditional hotel spa. You can't go past

the luxuriously large (25m) indoor pool and two Rebound Ace tennis courts; your serve might be off but the views are breathtaking.

### HEPBURN SPA AT ADELPHI Map pp52–3

☎ 8080 8888; www.hepburnspa.com.au; 187 Flinders Lane, Melbourne; ☽ 10am-10pm)
This new spa is run by spa-country old-timers. Treatments, using the Australian botanical range LI'TYA, are relaxation-oriented and usually an hour plus, so not an on-the-run option. It offers Turkish-style *rasul* (mud treatments) too.

### JAPANESE BATH HOUSE Map pp74–5

☎ 9419 0268; www.japanesebathhouse.com; 59 Cromwell St, Collingwood; bath $26, shiatsu from $44; ☽ 11am-10pm Tue-Fri, to 8pm Sat & Sun, ☒ 109
Urban as the setting may be, it's as serene as can be inside this authentic *sentō* (bathhouse). Perfect for some communal skin-ship, a shiatsu and a postsoak sake in the *tatami* lounge.

### RETREAT ON SPRING Map pp52–3

☎ 9948 8331; www.retreatonspring.com.au; 49 Spring St, Melbourne; ☽ 10am-6pm Mon & Tue, 10am-8pm Wed & Thu, 10am-7pm Fri, 9.30am-6pm Sat, 10am-5pm Sun
Retreat on Spring is an Aveda outfit, so toes a gently new-age line. The relaxing lounge area looks over Treasury Gardens and the treatment rooms are simple and luxurious. If you don't want a full treatment it also offers waxing services and has a nail bar.

## YOGA & PILATES

Both yoga and Pilates are popular in Melbourne and you'll find studios offering either one or both spread through the city and suburbs. Yoga studios will usually have at least some casual classes on their timetables. There are both general studios as well as specialist Iyengar, Ashtanga and Bikram studios. Well-regarded studios include the St Kilda Iyengar Yoga School (Map pp88–9; ☎ 9537 1015; www.skys.com.au; 11/82 Acland St); Bikram's Yoga College of India (Map pp68–9; ☎ 9429 2112; www .bikramyogamelbourne.com.au; lvl1, 179 Bridge Rd, Richmond), and the Ashtanga Yoga Centre of Melbourne (Map pp74–5; ☎ 9419 1598; www.ash tangamelbourne.com.au; Level 1, 110-112 Argyle St, Fitzroy). Check the Find Yoga website

(www.findyoga.com.au) for a comprehensive listing.

Some Pilates studios will allow visitors to do casual mat classes, although you will often need to have some experience. Aligned for Life (Map pp52–3; ☎ 9642 4500; www.alignedforlife.com.au; 1/99 Queen St, Melbourne), which has fully qualified, professional staff, does offer small group mat classes; book ahead. See the Find Pilates website (www.findpilates.com.au) for a listing of more studios around town.

## GYMS

Most gyms are open only to members, but sometimes offer casual fitness classes as well as yoga and Pilates to the general public. A casual gym visit at the charismatic Melbourne City Baths (Map pp52–3; ☎ 9663 5888; 420 Swanston St; gym visit $18) includes a swim, sauna, spa and locker.

## JOGGING

Favourite locations for a run include the Tan track around the Royal Botanic Gardens (4km; p82), the path around Albert Park Lake (5km; p91) and the sweeping paths of Fitzroy Gardens. The bicycle tracks beside the Yarra River and along the bay are also good choices; see Cycling, p171.

The Melbourne Marathon (www.melbournemarathon .com.au) is held in October. For those wanting something gentler, the popular Run Melbourne (www.theageruntotheg.com.au), better known as the Run to the G, offers a 5km run/walk, 7.5km walk, 10km run or a half-marathon in June. Or there's the national charity event, the Mother's Day Classic (www.mothersdayclassic.org), held in May with 8km, 4km and walking events.

## SWIMMING

In summer do as most Melburnians do, and hit the sand at one of the city's metropolitan beaches. St Kilda, Middle Park and Port Melbourne are popular patches, with suburban beaches at Brighton and Sandringham. Public pools are also well loved.

### FITZROY SWIMMING POOL Map pp74–5

☎ 9417 6493; Alexandra Pde, Fitzroy; adult/child $4.20/1.80; ☒ 112
Between laps, locals love catching a few rays up in the bleachers or on the lawn; there's also a toddlers' pool. The pool's Italian 'Aqua Profonda' sign was painted

in 1953 – an initiative of the pool's manager who frequently had to rescue migrant children who couldn't read the English signs. The sign is heritage-listed (misspelled and all – it should be 'Acqua').

### HAROLD HOLT SWIM CENTRE
Map pp48–9

☎ 8290 1678; 9 High St, Glen Iris; adult/child $4.90/3.80; 🚊 72

There's an indoor pool and a 50m heated outdoor pool open daily. The pool has lovely shaded grassy areas. The swimming centre is oddly named in honour of Harold Holt, the Australian prime minister who went missing at Portsea surf beach – presumed drowned.

### MELBOURNE CITY BATHS Map pp52–3

☎ 9663 5888; www.melbournecitybaths.com.au; 420 Swanston St, Melbourne; casual swim adult/child/family $4.90/2.25/11, gym $18; 🕑 6am-10pm Mon-Thu, 6am-8.30pm Fri, 8am-6pm Sat & Sun

The City Baths were literally public baths when they first opened in 1860 and were intended to stop people bathing in and drinking the seriously polluted Yarra River.

They now boast the CBD's largest pool (it's 30m), plus you get to do your laps in a 1903 heritage-listed building. There is also a public spa, the full complement of gym facilities and squash courts.

### MELBOURNE SPORTS & AQUATIC CENTRE Map pp92–3

☎ 9926 1555; www.msac.com.au; Albert Rd, Albert Park; adult/child $5.90/4.40; 🚊 96, 112

In the parklands of Albert Park the Aquatic Centre features everything you could want in a pool. A 50m outdoor pool was added for the 2006 Commonwealth Games, plus there's a 25m lap pool, wave pool and water slide.

### PRAHRAN AQUATIC CENTRE
Map pp84–5

☎ 8290 7140; 41 Essex St, Prahran; adult/child $4/3.20; 🕑 Oct-Apr; 🚊 72, 78, 79

This glam 50m heated outdoor pool is surrounded by a stretch of lawn. Families love the toddlers' pool, inflatable crocodile and teeny water slide. The on-site café is a must for the locals that can't do without their latte, seminaked or not.

# GAY & LESBIAN MELBOURNE

# GAY & LESBIAN MELBOURNE *Richard Watts*

Melbourne's gay and lesbian community is well integrated into the general populace; spread throughout the densely populated inner-city suburbs that encircle the CBD, rather than clustered into a single gay ghetto.

The majority of clubs and bars are found in two distinct locations on the north and south sides of the Yarra River – a distance easily traversed by a 15-minute taxi ride come nightfall.

South of the river, the area known colloquially as 'Southside', takes in the fashionable suburbs of St Kilda, South Yarra and Prahran. Commercial Rd, which separates the latter two suburbs, is home to numerous gay clubs and cafés. Glamour and style reign supreme on the Southside, with the locals described as debonair sophisticates or shallow devotees of the body beautiful, depending on who you speak to.

North of the Yarra, more commonly known as 'Northside', you'll find the lesbian enclave of Northcote with its strip of funky High St bars and shops, and a cluster of gay venues in the inner-city suburbs of Abbotsford, Collingwood and Fitzroy. Northside residents are reputedly more down to earth than their cousins across the river; as well as a little more bohemian, a little less pretentious and (again, depending who you speak to) slightly more feral.

Still in its infancy, another gay village is developing in the inner west, around the narrow streets of Yarraville.

## SHOPPING

### DUNGEON WAREHOUSE
Map pp74–5                          Fashion, Accessories
☎ 9416 4800; www.dungeonwarehouse.com.au; 130 Hoddle St, Abbotsford; ⊛ Collingwood
A retail outlet specialising in leather and fetish clothing for men.

### HARES & HYENAS BOOKSHOP
Map pp74–5                                       Books
☎ 9495 6589; www.hares-hyenas.com.au; 63 Johnston St, Fitzroy; ⊛ 96, 86
A well-resourced and welcoming gay and lesbian bookshop, which regularly features readings by visiting authors.

### OUTVIDEO Map pp88–9                  DVD/Video
☎ 9525 3669; www.out.com.au; 108 St Kilda Rd, St Kilda; ⊛ 11am-10pm; ⊛ 67
This video/DVD store specialises in GLBT films to rent or buy.

## DRINKING & NIGHTLIFE

### MARKET Map pp84–5                            Club
☎ 9826 0933; www.markethotel.com.au; 143 Commercial Rd South Yarra; ⊛ 10pm-8am Fri-Sat; ⊛ Prahran, ⊛ 72
The queen of clubs is undoubtedly Melbourne's largest gay venue and popular with experienced clubbers who love house music and late-night drag shows. International djs and guests appear regularly.

### XCHANGE HOTEL Map pp84–5            Pub
☎ 9867 5144; www.xchange.com.au; 119 Commercial Rd, South Yarra; ⊛ 4pm-1am Mon-Thu, 2pm-3am Fri-Sun; ⊛ Prahran, ⊛ 72
Features drag shows most nights of the week as well as djs playing Top 40 and commercial dance tunes. Attracts a young, stylish clientele.

### PRINCE OF WALES HOTEL
Map pp88–9                                        Pub
☎ 9536 1111; www.princebars.com.au; 29 Fitzroy St, St Kilda; ⊛ noon-2am Mon-Thu, noon-3am Fri-Sat; ⊛ 16, 96, 122
This landmark in bayside St Kilda is home to the iconic monthly night Girlbar (www.girlbar.com.au). Downstairs, on street level, the back bar attracts a predominantly gay and lesbian crowd seven days a week.

### LAIRD HOTEL Map pp74–5            Pub/Club
☎ 9417 2832; www.lairdhotel.com; 149 Gipps St Collingwood; ⊛ 5pm-late; ⊛ Collingwood
A men-only venue that attracts an older, denim and leather crowd.

### OPIUM DEN Map pp74–5                      Bar
☎ 9417 2696; www.opiumden.com.au; 176 Hoddle St, Abbotsford; ⊛ 7pm-1am Wed-Thu, 7pm-3am Fri-Sat, 5pm-1am Sun; ⊛ Collingwood
Home of Melbourne's gay and lesbian Asian community, the Laird features drag shows and live entertainment.

### GLASSHOUSE HOTEL Map pp74–5 Pub
☎ 9419 4748; www.glass-house.com.au; 51-55 Gipps St, Collingwood; ⏲ 11am-1am Wed-Thu, 11am-5am Fri, noon-5am Sat, noon-midnight Sun; 🚊 16, 96, 12
Caters for a mostly lesbian crowd with entertainment including live bands, drag kings and djs.

### PEEL HOTEL Map pp74–5 Club
☎ 94194762; www.thepeel.com.au; cnr Peel & Wellington Sts, Collingwood; ⏲ 9pm-dawn Thu-Sun; 🚊 86
Features a mostly male crowd dancing to house music, retro and commercial dance.

### COMMERCIAL HOTEL Map pp48–9 Pub
☎ 9687 9578, 238 Whitehall St, Yarraville; 🚉 Yarraville
A friendly, low-key pub in Melbourne's inner west that presents drag shows every Thursday and Saturday night.

## SLEEPING

### OPIUM DEN Map pp74–5 Hotel $
☎ 9417 2696; www.opiumden.com.au; 176 Hoddle St, Abbotsford; ⏲ 7pm-1am Wed-Thu, 7pm-3am Fri-Sat, 5pm-1am Sun; d $77; 🚊 Collingwood
As well as being a popular gay bar, Opium Den is also a residential hotel, and popular with gay and lesbian visitors from regional Victoria.

### 169 DRUMMOND
Map pp78–9 Guesthouse $$
☎ 9663 3081; www.169drummond.com.au; 169 Drummond St, Carlton; d $135-145; 🚊 1, 8
A privately owned guesthouse in a renovated, 19th-century terrace in the inner north, one block from vibrant Lygon St.

## FESTIVALS
Held each year over late January-early February is the Midsumma Festival (www.midsumma.org

.au), with a diverse program of cultural, community and sporting events, including the popular Midsumma Carnival, Pride March and much more.

Australia's largest GLBT film festival, the Melbourne Queer Film Festival (www.melbournequeerfilm .com.au) screens 140 films from around the world each March. Opening night at the Art Deco Astor Theatre (Map pp88–9; ☎ 9510-1414, cnr Dandenong Rd & Chapel St, St Kilda) is one of the social events of the year, with the majority of sessions held at the Australian Centre for the Moving Image (Map pp52-3; ☎ 8663 2200; Federation Square).

Less than two hours' drive from Melbourne is the ChillOut Festival (www.chilloutfestival .com.au), held each Labour Day long weekend in March in the gay-friendly country town of Daylesford (p259).

## RESOURCES
Two free weekly newspapers, each published on Thursdays, service Melbourne's gay and lesbian community and are excellent sources of up-to-the-minute information and resources for visitors: MCV (www.mcv.net.au) and Bnews (www.bnews.net.au).

The gay and lesbian community radio station JOY 94.9 FM (www.joy.org.au) is another important resource for visitors and locals alike, and provides regular updates about key community events.

The Gay and Lesbian Switchboard ( ☎ 9510 5488; ⏲ 6-10pm Mon, Tue & Thur, 2-10pm Wed, 6-9pm Fri-Sun) operates a telephone counselling service.

The Victorian AIDS Council/Gay Men's Health Centre ( ☎ 9865 6700; www.vicaids.asn.au; 6 Claremont St, South Yarra; ⏲ 9am-9pm Mon-Thu, 9am-5pm Fri) is a community health centre providing medical and counselling services for the gay, lesbian, bisexual and transgender communities, and people living with HIV/AIDS.

*Richard Watts is the editor of Melbourne's weekly gay and lesbian newspaper MCV and presents a weekly arts program on radio station 3RRR*

**lonely planet** Hotels & Hostels

Want more Sleeping recommendations than we could ever pack into this little ol' book? Craving more detail – including extended reviews and photographs? Want to read reviews by other travellers and be able to post your own? Just make your way over to **lonelyplanet.com/hotels** and check out our thorough list of independent reviews, then reserve your room simply and securely.

# SLEEPING

# top picks

- Sofitel (p183)
- Adelphi Hotel (p183)
- Jasper Hotel (p185)
- Urban (p193)
- Pensione Hotel (p187)
- Villa Donati (p189)

# SLEEPING

While you'll have no trouble finding a place to stay that suits your taste and budget, for a city that's big on style Melbourne has surprisingly few truly inspirational boltholes and only a handful of atmospheric, individual small hotels. Still, prices are rarely stratospheric and quality is generally high.

For a standard double room in a deluxe hotel, expect to pay upwards of $350. For a top-end room you'll pay between $250 and $300, midrange around $150 and for budget double around $80 to $100. Prices peak during the Australian Open in January, Grand Prix weekend in March, AFL finals in September and the Spring Racing Carnival in November. Midrange to deluxe hotels publish 'rack rates', but always ask for current specials and for inclusions such as breakfast or parking. All accommodation has a 10% goods and services tax (GST) included in the price.

Apartment-style accommodation is easy to find in Melbourne – there are several local as well as national chains – and suits those that want a smart, functional space to relax and stow their shopping, but who don't need full hotel accoutrements. There are also plenty of budget hostels, pubs and B&Bs. Many big hostels offer private rooms alongside basic dorms and Melbourne has an increasing number of 'flashpacker' hostels that provide a raft of comforts while retaining the social hostel vibe.

## AIRPORT ACCOMODATION

Melbourne Airport is 25km from the city with no direct public transport links, so odd-hour flights require taxis or a sleepover. There are three main airport hotels, ranging from bells, whistles and direct 'air bridge' access at the Hilton Melbourne Airport ( ☎ 8336 2000; www1.hilton.com; Arrival Drive; from $225) and the smart but slightly further away Holiday Inn Melbourne Airport ( ☎ 1300 724 944; www.holidayinn.com.au; 10-14 Centre Rd; from $135) to the Hotel Formule 1 ( ☎ 8336 1811; www.formule1.com. au; 12 Caldwell Drive; from $89), which has basic rooms with bunks and is just over 500m away.

## CENTRAL MELBOURNE

The city will please everyone. If you like to take a morning stroll in something resembling nature, choose somewhere towards Spring St for easy access to Fitzroy Gardens, or close to Flinders St for a riverside run. There's a lot of places across all price ranges that will put you in the heart of the action, whether you've come to town and want to shop, party, catch a match or take in some culture. Spencer St has a lot of hotels, historically sited to catch country train passengers; while they're only a

few tram stops away from the city centre (and in spitting distance of Telstra Dome), it's not as atmospheric as staying in Flinders Lane or Little Collins St.

### PARK HYATT Map pp52–3 · · · · · · · · Hotel $$$
☎ 9224 1234; www.melbourne.park.hyatt.com; 1 Parliament Sq; r from $355
Resembling a Californian shopping mall from the outside, the interior understands luxury to be about wood panelling, shiny surfaces and miles of marble. Rooms are elegantly subdued, and most come complete with supersized baths, clever layouts that maximise your chance of seeing natural light and lovely treetop-level views. There's a lavish indoor pool, plus a great tennis court and whiz-bang business facilities. Perfect if you want to be superclose to the city but also have some park-fuelled peace and quiet too.

### WESTIN Map pp52–3 · · · · · · · · · · · · · Hotel $$$
☎ 9635 2222; www.westin.com.au; 205 Collins St; r from $335
An odd mix of ocean liner meets Haussmann-era apartment building design from the outside, inside the Westin gets timeless luxury hotel style right. The any-city lobby, with its high ceilings and sweeping central staircase, is humanised with work by artists such as Bill Henson. Standard rooms feature Country Road furniture and signature (and trademarked) 'heavenly beds'. Not

## WORTH A TRIP

Just 20 minutes down the Princes Hwy from the spectacular hump of the Westgate Bridge, among market gardens, abandoned factories and new housing estates, is one of Melbourne's most surprising sleeping options. The Sofitel Mansion and Spa ( ☎ 97314000; www.mansionhotel.com.au) manages to be both stylish and modern and has a leisurely country house ambience. Rooms are small – this was a former seminary – but smartly configured and furnished, but there's plenty of space to enjoy. Relax among the clever collection of contemporary art in the lounge, library or billiards room. Or do laps of the large indoor pool and collapse in the adjoining spa. A short, bucolic stumble away is Shadowfax Winery ( ☎ 9731 4420; www.shadowfax.com.au). Tastings and wood-fired pizzas are available in the stunning Wood Marsh–designed space, or pull up an outside table overlooking the plantings of Shiraz. The Werribee Mansion ( ☎ 9741 6879; www.parkweb.vic.gov.au; K Rd, Werribee), a stolid 1870s edifice brimming with colonial arriviste ambition, is also just next door. The mansion's gracious grounds host the often-controversial Helen Lempriere Sculpture Prize (p13) each March.

all rooms have spire or treetop views; ask when booking.

### MEDINA EXECUTIVE FLINDERS ST
Map pp52–3  Serviced Apartments $$$
☎ 8663 0000; www.medina.com.au; 88 Flinders St; apt from $320
These cool monochromatic apartments are extra-large and luxurious. Ask for one at the front for amazing parkland views; many have balconies too. There's no room service but the full kitchens are supplemented by a restaurant delivery service.

### HOTEL LINDRUM Map pp52–3  Hotel $$$
☎ 9668 1111; www.hotellindrum.com.au; 26 Flinders St; r from $310-425
This attractive hotel was once the pool hall of the legendary and literally unbeatable Walter Lindrum. Expect rich tones, subtle lighting and tactile fabrics. Spring for a deluxe room and you'll snare either arch or bay windows and marvellous Melbourne views. Nice as they are, some of the standard rooms feel like corners have been cut. But it's still easily one of the city's finest boutique hotels. And yes, there's a pool table.

### SOFITEL Map pp52–3  Hotel $$$
☎ 9653 0000; www.sofitelmelbourne.com.au; 25 Collins St; r from $270
Guestrooms at the Sofitel start on the 36th floor, so you're guaranteed views that will make you giddy. Corner rooms get you double the panorama. The rooms are high international style, opulent rather than minimal, and much more up-to-date than that of many of its five-star friends. The hotel entrance, despite the superb IM Pei–designed ceiling, is relentlessly workaday, but you'll soon be a world (or at least 36 floors) away.

### WINDSOR Map pp52–3  Hotel $$$
☎ 9633 6000; www.thewindsor.com.au; 103 Spring St; r from $265
One of Australia's most famous and self-consciously grand hotels, this five-star example of Marvellous Melbourne–era opulence exudes old-fashioned luxury. Beware those whose Victorian tat meter is set to high; if you don't mind a plump, swagged pelmet or two, you'll love the walk-in robes, large marble bathrooms and the old wing's original high ceilings. Service is exemplary while being refreshingly down to earth.

### GRAND HYATT MELBOURNE
Map pp52–3  Hotel $$$
☎ 9657 1234; http://melbourne.grand.hyatt.com; 123 Collins St; r from $260
There's change afoot in this famous Collins St five star. At time of writing the extensive public areas were being completely renovated, with the Club Floor bar and lounge being made available for all guests as way of compensation. Despite excellent views and standard luxury comforts, rooms are currently looking a bit tired and will get their turn in 2009.

### ADELPHI HOTEL Map pp52–3  Hotel $$$
☎ 9650 7555; www.adelphi.com.au; 187 Flinders Lane; r from $245
This discreet Flinders Lane property, designed by Denton Korker Marshall in the early '90s, was one of Australia's first boutique hotels. It helped establish Melbourne's reputation as a design-conscious town, as well as sparking the laneway revolution. Rooms have a warehouse

quality, despite spatial limitations. Its fabulous cantilevered rooftop pool juts out above the street and the rooftop club bar has wonderful river views. Its rigid aesthetic can be polarising. The new Hepburn Spa wellness retreat, on the other hand, will please all. Teague Ezard's basement restaurant (p128) is not your average hotel diner either. It's worth looking to online room resellers for far better rates than the hotel's own.

### GRAND HOTEL MELBOURNE
Map pp52–3　　　　Hotel $$$
☎ 9611 4567; www.grandhotelsofitel.com.au; 33 Spencer St; r $235-355
This grand Italianate building housed the Victorian Railways administration back in the day when rail ruled the world. Its self-catering rooms were originally offices, and have high ceilings with loft-style mezzanines. All vary in size and layout and are subtly furnished without succumbing to high-heritage frump. Spencer St is not the best locale for shopping and bars, but you're only a short tram ride away from the action.

### NAVAL AND MILITARY CLUB
Map pp52–3　　　　Hotel $$$
☎ 9650 4741; www.nmclub.com.au; 27 Little Collins St; r incl breakfast from $220
You once had to be an officer *and* a gentleman to get past the door here, but in these more democratic times you just need a little cash (and be able to find the place). There are only 18 rooms in this fabulously located modernist bunker of a building and they all are light, crisp and well equipped. Rooms with balconies have treetop and city views. You also get access to club facilities: a business centre, health club and a formally landscaped rooftop garden. A hidden gem.

# top picks

## SHOPPING & BAR HOPPING

- Hotel Causeway (opposite)
- Pensione (p187)
- Jasper Hotel (opposite)
- The Naval & Military Club (above)

### SEBEL MELBOURNE Map pp52–3　Hotel $$$
☎ 9211 6600, 1800 500 778; www.mirvachotels.com.au; 394 Collins St; r from $220
The Sebel is a low-key alternative in the grand Bank of Australasia building, right in the heart of the business district. The clean, minimalist rooms have self-catering facilities and washing machines, and the airy split-level loft suites are spacious. Ask for a room on a higher floor to avoid dim back-alley views.

### MANHATTAN
Map pp52–3　　Serviced Apartments $$$
☎ 9631 1111; www.manhattan.punthill.com.au; 57 Flinders Lane; apt from $205
While not quite avoiding the serviced-apartment furnishing clichés, these loft spaces are set in a former warehouse and have original industrial-age details. Large marble bathrooms, granite-benched full kitchens, a stylish muted palette and prime laneway location make this a good option. There's also a functional lap pool and gym; ask for a room at the back for an outlook.

### MAJORCA APARTMENT 401
Map pp52–3　　Serviced Apartments $$$
9428 8104; www.apartment401.com.au; 258 Flinders Lane; apt from $200
This is the ultimate in like-a-local living. The Majorca, a single apartment, is one of the city's loveliest Art Deco buildings and watches over a bustling vortex of laneways. It's stylishly furnished, has timber floorboards and the windows are huge. Who needs a concierge when you're right in the centre of things already? There's a two-night minimum and sliding scale according to length of stay; the owners can arrange transfers and provisions if you so desire.

### MEDINA GRAND MELBOURNE
Map pp52–3　　Serviced Apartments $$$
☎ 9934 0000; www.medina.com.au; 189 Queen St; apt from $199
Set up the hill in leafy lawyer-land, the Medina Grand's suites have large windows and are slickly furnished. Legendary Vue de Monde is your local and you're also superclose to shopping and bars. There's an indoor lap pool and gym, with judiciously grand views.

# top picks

- Sofitel (p183)
- Crown Promenade Hotel (p188)
- Adelphi Hotel (p183)
- Hotel Lindrum (p183)

VIBE SAVOY HOTEL Map pp52–3    Hotel $$$
☎ 9622 8888; www.vibehotels.com.au;
630 Little Collins St; r from $195
This lovely heritage building at Collins St's
western end has been given a bold makeo-
ver, though its grand proportions aren't
so in evidence in its somewhat truncated
rooms. But they do offer a concoction of
traditional hotel comforts, bright colours
and contemporary furnishings.

## JASPER HOTEL Map pp52–3    Hotel $$$
☎ 8327 2777; www.jasperhotel.com.au;
489 Elizabeth St; r from $190
A refurb has done what the Village People
did for the YWCA's male equivalent: sexed it
up. The old Hotel Y has had a makeover by
Jackson Clements Burrows and now sports
moody down-lighting, a veritable Pantone
swatch-book of colours, louvered bathrooms
and some lovely graphic soft furnishing.
There's a range of light-filled rooms from
standard up to two-bedroom suites, with
LCD TVs and wi-fi. Guests have complimentary use of the sporting facilities at the nearby
Melbourne City Baths. All profits still go to
the YWCA's community and welfare services.

## PUNT HILL LITTLE BOURKE
Map pp52–3    Serviced Apartments $$$
☎ 9631 1111; www.littlebourke.punthill.com.au;
11-17 Cohen Place; apt from $185
Neat and modern apartments have bright
colours, balconies and stainless steel kitch-
ens. Lots of light, an indoor lap pool and a
cute Chinatown laneway location lift this
little place above the ordinary.

## QUEST HERO
Map pp52–3    Serviced Apartments $$$
☎ 8664 8500; www.questhero.com.au;
140 Little Collins St; apt from $185
These spacious and well-equipped apartments have fabulous urban views. Housed

in an architecturally interesting residential
building, you're sitting on top of some
amazing retailers as well as the cute Postal
Hall Café, which bustles away on the ground
floor facing Russell St. Lofts make for good
long-term stays and the larger apartments
are a great option for families.

## CROSSLEY Map pp52–3    Hotel $$
☎ 9639 1639; www.accorhotels.com.au;
51 Little Bourke St; r from $179
The hotel's 80-odd rooms are housed in a
'30s building with Deco details, although
rooms are decked out rather blandly. That
said, it's simple and neat and perfectly
positioned a stone's throw from many of
Melbourne's best restaurants, great shopping and theatres.

## HOTEL CAUSEWAY Map pp52–3    Hotel $$$
☎ 9660 8888; www.causeway.com.au;
275 Little Collins St; r $165-330
This Art Deco gem, with a discreet entrance
in covered arcade Howey Place, will appeal to those who've come to Melbourne
to shop and barhop. It's intimate in scale,
so don't expect the facilities of a big hotel.
Instead you get crisp white linen, light-filled
rooms and dark, modern styling. There's a
roof garden, smart and helpful staff, and
lots of little touches (slippers, robes, apples)
that are a rare treat at these prices.

## BATMAN'S HILL Map pp52–3    Hotel $$
☎ 9614 6344; www.batmanshill.com.au;
66-70 Spencer St; r from $165
Recently renovated, this hotel is fresh and
comfortable. There are two standards of
accommodation to choose from: standard
rooms are reasonable, if a little boxy and
without views; the family option can sleep
up to five, with some offering separate
bedrooms. The Club rooms and apartments
are in the new wing and feature terrific
vistas and new furniture and fittings, not to
mention more space.

## ALTO HOTEL ON BOURKE
Map pp52–3    Hotel $$
☎ 9606 0585; www.altohotel.com.au;
636 Bourke St; r from 135, apt from $160
With its conservative appearance, you'd
never guess this new kid on the block is
promoting itself as a 'green' hotel. The
building is fitted with water-saving show-
ers, energy-efficient light globes and

Book your stay at lonelyplanet.com/hotels

SLEEPING CENTRAL MELBOURNE

double-glazed windows that open. In-room recycling is promoted. Rooms are also well equipped, light and neutrally decorated. Apartments (but not studios) have full kitchens and multiple LCDs, and some have spas (presumably more than one telly and a big bubbling bath is for extra-special treats only).

## RENDEZVOUS HOTEL Map pp52–3 Hotel $$
☎ 9250 1888; www.rendezvoushotels.com; 328 Finders St; r from $159
Built in 1913 and heritage-listed, this well-located hotel features a stunning circular interior balcony, sweeping staircases and an understated charm. Contemporary rooms are smart, while heritage rooms have high ceilings and Edwardian flourishes.

## STAMFORD PLAZA
Map pp52–3 Suite Hotel $$$
☎ 9659 1000; www.stamford.com.au; 111 Little Collins St; r from $155
The Stamford offers big rooms and suites and loads of facilities at reasonable rates. There's an indoor and outdoor pool plus two 'mini' gyms. Space and professional staff are the draws here (and the location is sweet too). Décor can be a little on the fussy side but slick enough to avoid the granny tag.

## MANTRA 100 EXHIBITION
Map pp52–3 Serviced Apartments $$
☎ 9631 4444; http://cityhotels.mantraresorts .com.au; 100 Exhibition St; apt from $155
Great midcity location and streamlined apartment facilities. Big windows and the use of blond wood, white and the odd splash of intense colour are a surprise at this price. Nice location between the bustle of Bourke and the calm of Collins.

## SOMERSET GORDON PLACE
Map pp52–3 Serviced Apartments $$
☎ 9663 2888; www.somersetgordonplace.com; 24 Little Bourke St; apt from $155
The Somerset's smart, pint-sized apartments are concealed inside a prim heritage building at the top end of town. There's a range from small studios to two-bedroom, all with kitchenettes. A sunny courtyard with outdoor pool is an unexpected bonus in this midcity location.

## ATLANTIS HOTEL Map pp52–3 Hotel $$
☎ 9600 2900; www.atlantishotel.com.au; 300 Spencer St; r from $150
Across from Docklands and Southern Cross Station, this place offers two-bedroom suites perfect for families for not much more than the standard room charge. The low-slung rooms are soothingly neutral if not superstylish. A highlight is the proportionally huge bathrooms, which include a shower area with fold-down bench seating, as well as some great Bolte Bridge views from the upper rooms.

## MERCURE Map pp52–3 Hotel $$
☎ 9205 9999; www.accorhotels.com.au; 13 Spring St; r from $149
The Mercure squats among lofty office towers facing lush gardens. At the sedate end of town, but within stumbling distance of many good bars and restaurants, this link in an international chain offers high-quality, dependable rooms and service.

## CAUSEWAY INN ON THE MALL
Map pp52–3 Hotel $$$
☎ 9650 0688; www.causeway.com.au; 327 Bourke St Mall; r $140-225
Dowdy as the décor is, the Causeway Inn is always busy and often full. It's a pretty simple set-up: small rooms and shower only, but with helpful staff and a lcoation bang in the middle of the city. Note the hotel entrance is actually in the Causeway, a lane running between Bourke St Mall and Little Collins St.

## CITY LIMITS
Map pp52–3 Serviced Apartments $$
☎ 9662 2544; www.citylimits.com.au; 20-22 Little Bourke St; r incl breakfast $130
If you can ignore the schizophrenic mix of décor styles, and the self-proclaimed four stars, the staff are welcoming and you're in an ideal Chinatown location. The rooms have small but decently stocked kitchenettes.

## ROBINSONS IN THE CITY
Map pp52–3 Hotel $$
☎ 9329 2552; www.robinsonsinthecity.com.au; 405 Spencer St; r from $135
Robinsons really is an intimate hotel (there's only six bedrooms), though the comfortable rooms are anything but small.

The building is a former bakery, dating from 1850, but the owners have gone for a modern, eclectic – if not particularly edgy – look. Its location puts you midway between the city and Docklands, and the stroll to the city is a pleasant one. Service is warm and personal; repeat visits are common.

### HOTEL ENTERPRIZE Map pp52–3 Hotel $$
☎ 9629 6991; www.hotelenterprize.com.au; 44 Spencer St; r $100-140
Hotel Enterprize has two distinct personalities and three different sets of clothes. Confusing? Not really. Well-kept but essentially plain budget rooms are set around a central courtyard decked out with pot plants and ferns. Business rooms are either woody or 'boutique'-style contemporary. It's not cutting edge but it's comfortable.

### VICTORIA HOTEL Map pp52–3 Hotel $$
☎ 9653 0441; www.victoriahotel.com.au; 215 Little Collins St; r with shared bathroom $85-95, with private bathroom $95-$180
The original Vic opened its doors in 1880 but don't worry: they've updated the plumbing since then. This city institution offers a flexible range of comfortable, if not exactly stylish, accommodation in an unbeatable location: the heart of the city's designer-fashion and arts precinct. Contemporary Bellerive rooms are a little more soothing. Facilities include an indoor pool.

### CITY CENTRE HOTEL Map pp52–3 Hotel $
☎ 9654 5401; www.citycentrebudgethotel.com.au; 22 Little Collins St; r from $90
Intimate, independent and inconspicuous, this 38-room budget hotel is a find. It's located at the city's prettier end, down a 'Little' street, up some stairs, inside an unassuming building. All rooms share bathroom facilities but the fresh rooms are light-filled with working windows; there's also free wi-fi and a laundry. On the roof there's a fabulous patch of domesticity – swing seats and banana lounges – amid a sea of midcity slick. The service is genuine and genial, and everyone is accommodated, from solo travellers to families.

### CITY SQUARE MOTEL Map pp52–3 Hotel $
☎ 9654 7011; www.citysquaremotel.com.au; 67 Swanston St; r from $90
Want to feel special? Then look elsewhere. Want to stay in the living, breathing heart

of Melbourne, but spend your hard-earned cash on food, drink and fun (and don't mind a vintage en suite)? Rooms are basic but comfortable and serviced daily; some have deep, old-style baths.

### PENSIONE HOTEL Map pp52–3 Hotel $
☎ 9621 3333; www.pensione.com.au; 16 Spencer St; r from $90
The Pensione isn't being cute christening some rooms 'petit double'. It's a rare thing for hotels not to be opaque on their room's relative squeeziness. They've got reasons to be honest. What you don't get in size is more than made up for in spot-on style, room extras and superreasonable rates. This recent refurb and rebranding is a welcome jolt to the Melbourne hotel scene.

### HOTEL FORMULE 1 MELBOURNE CBD
Map pp52–3 Hotel $
☎ 9642 0064; www.formule1.com.au; 97-103 Elizabeth St; r from $79
Offers a backpacker level of comfort though all rooms are en suite. Rooms utilise the latest in bunk-bed technology to maximise space. The location is perfect for those that want to be in the thick of it.

### GREENHOUSE BACKPACKER
Map pp52–3 Hostel $
☎ 9639 6400; www.friendlygroup.com.au; 6/228 Flinders Lane; dm/s/d incl breakfast $30/65/80
Greenhouse has a low-key, relaxed vibe and is extremely well run – they know what keeps backpackers content. This includes freebies: daily half-hour internet access, pancakes on Sunday, rooftop BBQs, luggage storage and activities. There's also chatty, helpful staff and spic-and-span facilities. There's double bed bunks for couples in the mixed dorms; solo travellers can opt for single-sex dorms. The location could hardly be better, smack in the middle of one of Melbourne's most bustling laneways.

### HOTEL DISCOVERY Map pp52–3 Hostel $
☎ 9642 4464; www.hoteldiscovery.com.au; 167 Franklin St; dm $25-28, d from $85
Housed in a rather grand old building, Discovery offers standard hostel rooms with lots of extras such as a rooftop garden, 'cinema' and a great location just near Victoria Market. There's also lounging areas,

pool tables, a bar and café, which make for a very social atmosphere. Family rooms and en suite doubles are available too.

## MELBOURNE CONNECTION TRAVELLERS HOSTEL Map pp52–3    Hostel $

☎ 9329 7525; www.melbourneconnection.com; 205 King St; dm $22-28, d $67-80

This 79-bed little charmer follows the small-is-better principle. It offers simple, clean and uncluttered budget accommodation with modern facilities, well-organised staff and basement lounge area.

# SOUTHBANK & DOCKLANDS

Southbank boasts some of the city's higher-end options, which take advantage of the city views to be had while being just a short stroll across a bridge back into town. Accommodation has sprung up all around Docklands, servicing a business clientele and those who want an apartment with great, if industrial, views of Victoria Harbour and the city. It has its own swag of dining options, and is convenient to the Telstra Dome, but it can be a pain to make your way back to the midcity action, especially at night.

## CROWN TOWERS Map pp64–5    Hotel $$$

☎ 9292 6666, 1800 811 653; www.crowntowers.com.au; 8 Whiteman St, Southbank; r from $355

Conspicuous consumption and even more conspicuous everything else combine to create one the country's most lavish places to sleep. Rooms pull out all the stops with views, gadgetry, original artworks and contemporary-styled opulence. This being a casino hotel should be a hint to anyone looking for a subdued atmosphere to reconsider. On weekends, most of the guests are here to party.

## LANGHAM HOTEL Map pp64–5    Hotel $$$

☎ 8696 8888; www.langhamhotels.com; 1 Southgate Ave, Southbank; r from $320

The Langham lobby screams luxury, but its restaurants can feel a little mall-like and the rooms, while perfectly equipped, are past their prime in the style stakes. Still, if you want river views, and can opt for something above the smallish 'King classic', it's going to be a pleasant five-star stay. The Chuan Spa is well regarded.

## CROWN PROMENADE

Map pp64–5    Hotel $$$

☎ 9292 6688; www.crownpromenade.com.au; 8 Whiteman St, Southbank; r from $245

This is Crown's 'diffusion line' hotel and linked to the mother ship by an air bridge. It is much more laid-back than the Towers and offers large, modern and gently masculine rooms with luxurious bathrooms, big windows, flat screens and Sony Playstations. Views vary but many are as breathtaking as the Towers.

## DOCKLANDS APARTMENTS GRAND MECURE Map pp64–5    Serviced Apartments $$$

☎ 9606 0561; www.docklandsservicedapartments.com.au; 23 Saint Mangos Lane, New Quay, Docklands; apt from $230, min 2-night stay

Spectacular floor-to-ceiling windows make the most of the water and city views. Apartments have balconies, full kitchens with stainless steel appliances and are furnished with pleasing contemporary style. New Quay has lots of good eating options as well as shops to procure provisions.

## QUEST DOCKLANDS

Map pp64–5    Serviced Apartments $$$

☎ 9630 1000; www.questdocklands.com.au; 750 Bourke St, Victoria Point, Docklands; apt from $195

Join the new breed of Melburnians on the Docklands frontier. These apartments are serviced daily and all have a fully kitted kitchen. The interiors' crisp lines are cushioned with subtle, earthy-toned furniture and fixtures, and most have a balcony. Literally on the doorstep of Telstra Dome, so perfect for big-game visits.

## TRAVELODGE SOUTHBANK

Map pp64–5    Hotel $$$

☎ 8696 9600; www.travelodge.com.au; 9 Riverside Quay, Southbank; r from $154

You won't be able to forget that this is a Travelodge, but if you can get past the queasy tones of the bedspreads and wall colours, comfort levels are high, and the service and riverside location are quite special. Some rooms also have views that you'll pay a lot more for elsewhere.

## URBAN CENTRAL BACKPACKERS

Map pp64–5    Hostel $$$

☎ 1800 631 288, 9639 3700; www.urbancentral.com.au; 334 City Rd, South Melbourne; dm/d/f from $23/90/120

This just-south-of-the-river hostel is pretty much the perfect package. It's neat, new and trendy, and houses bright, white dorms. There's a great bar downstairs (with dangerously cheap happy hours) and the staff are friendly and helpful. You'll need to contend with several floors of fellow guests, but that might be just what you're looking for. Private rooms are offered, and all dorms have individual lockers with internal charge points for your laptop, camera or iPod.

# EAST MELBOURNE & RICHMOND

East Melbourne takes you out of the action and has few attractions of its own apart from the splendid expanses of Fitzroy Gardens, peace and quiet and ready access to the MCG. Richmond's ideal if you also want a local feel only a 20-minute walk or short taxi trip from the city.

## HILTON ON THE PARK
Map pp68–9      Hotel $$$

☎ 9419 2000; www.hilton.com; 192 Wellington Pde, East Melbourne; r from $200; ☒ Jolimont, ☒ 48, 75
The brown-brick Hilton building, on the verge of stunning gardens, is a monument to '70s functionalism. Sadly, most guest rooms have some '90s rococo thing going on, but a progressive refurbishment augers well. The freshly done 'relaxation suites' are furnished simply, stylishly and in a way that suits the building's boxy dimensions. The location is superb for sports fans and for those who like to team city life with a walk in the park.

## VILLA DONATI Map pp68–9    B&B $$$

☎ 9428 8104; www.villadonati.com; 377 Church St, Richmond; s/d $170/185; ☒ 70
An impeccably maintained Italianate villa, Donati is great value. The rooms are individually decorated and all have en suites. Villa Donati doesn't give into the heritage cliché that this type of architecture might encourage; instead it's got personality and an endearingly eclectic, haute-bourgeois style.

## KNIGHTSBRIDGE APARTMENTS
Map pp68–9    Serviced Apartments $$

☎ 9470 9100; www.knightsbridgeapartments.com.au; 101 George St, East Melbourne; apt from $125; ☒ Jolimont, ☒ 48, 75

Rejuvenated studio apartments over three floors each feature a well-equipped kitchen plus furniture and accessories that suggest a higher price bracket. From the chirpy welcome to the free guest laundry, the overall impression is one of 'nothing's too much trouble'. If you don't score an apartment with a teensy private courtyard (rooms 7, 8 and 9), opt for the upper floors for a better outlook and light (note there's no lift).

## GEORGIAN COURT Map pp68–9   B&B $$

☎ 9419 6353; www.georgiancourt.com.au; 21 George St, East Melbourne; r from$119; ☒ West Richmond, ☒ 48, 75
This gently crumbling mansion has an old-school, relaxed appeal that's proven popular with families for many years. Rooms are diminutive and slightly overwrought but come with shiny bathrooms (shared or private). The breakfast area is reminiscent of prewar Britain, with period furniture, high ceilings, lead-light windows and seemingly bottomless pots of tea.

## MAGNOLIA COURT Map pp68–9   Hotel $$

☎ 9419 4222; www.magnolia-court.com.au; 101 Powlett St, East Melbourne; r from $99; ☒ Jolimont, ☒ 48, 75
It may be a little fussy for some but they've recently done a gentle refurbishing of facilities here and there's plenty of heritage charm and high ceilings in a peaceful location. There's a large variety of room types, from singles to a self-contained Victorian cottage. Staff are sweetly accommodating.

## GEORGE POWLETT APARTMENTS
Map pp68–9    Self-Contained $$

☎ 9419 9488; www.georgepowlett.com.au; cnr George & Powlett Sts, East Melbourne; studio apt from $95; ☒ Jolimont, ☒ 48, 75
These older-style (read frumpy) rooms have kitchenettes and are a 10-minute walk from town through the fabulous Fitzroy Gardens. The low-rise complex, located in the shadows of the MCG light towers, has 45 compact rooms, some with balconies.

## FREEMAN LODGE Map pp68–9   Hostel $

☎ 9421 8038; www.freemanlodge.com.au; 151-153 Hoddle St, Richmond; dm/d $26/64; ☒ West Richmond, ☒ 48, 75
This kooky little guesthouse (with just 15 rooms) is on the city's notoriously clogged Hoddle St, so light sleepers and asthmatics

take note. But across the road are the MCG and some glorious parkland. And Freeman is around the corner from retail-littered Bridge Rd and Vietnamese Victoria St. Small rooms (from four-bunk dorm to triple) are supplemented by homey communal areas, including a small kitchen.

# FITZROY & AROUND

Although Fitzroy hums with attractions day and night, and is seductively close to the city, it sadly comes up short for interesting sleeping options.

## METROPOLE HOTEL APARTMENTS

Map pp74–5         Self-Contained $$$

☎ 9411 8100; 44 Brunswick St, Fitzroy; apt $205-285; 🚇 86, 112

If you can forgive the mid-'90s façade that blights this heritage strip at the top of Brunswick St, the Metropole is worth considering for its city skip-and-jump location and small outdoor pool. The rooms are large and well equipped, though the beyond-bland interiors will also require quite some forgiveness.

## ROYAL GARDENS APARTMENTS

Map pp74–5         Serviced $$ Apartments

☎ 9419 9888; www.questroyalgardens.com.au; 8 Royal Lane, Fitzroy; apt from $158; 🚇 86, 96

This rather dauntingly monumental complex of apartments is softened by hidden gardens, and has recently been updated with new furniture and full kitchens. Situated in a quiet nook of this happening suburb, it's so relaxed you'll feel like a local.

## NUNNERY  Map pp74–5         Hostel $

☎ 9419 8637; www.nunnery.com.au; 116 Nicholson St, Fitzroy; dm incl breakfast $28-32, s $70-80, d $95-115; 🚇 96

The Nunnery oozes atmosphere, with sweeping staircases and many original features; the walls are dripping with

religious works of art and ornate stained-glass windows. You'll be giving thanks for the big comfortable lounges and communal areas. Apart from the main building there's also the Nunnery Guesthouse, which has larger rooms in a private setting. It's perennially popular, so try to book ahead.

## HOME ON ARGYLE  Map pp74–5      Hostel $

☎ 9419 1119; http://homeonargyle.alphalink.com .au; 109 Argyle St, Fitzroy; prices on application; 🚇 112

This hostel resembles a bright, happily chaotic share house more than a backpackers, and the owners want their guests to feel part of the family. Long-term stays of two to six months are preferred. Not everyone's cup of tea, but they are happy to let you stay a night to see if you like it before committing to a longer-term arrangement.

# CARLTON & AROUND

Carlton has quite a few midrange places aimed at the university and hospital crowd, but like Fitzroy it disappoints when it comes to interesting hotel options. North Melbourne has a few budget options, some of them more attractive than others.

## RYDGES ON SWANSTON

Map pp78–9         Hotel $$

☎ 9347 7811; www.rydges.com; 701 Swanston St, Carlton; r from $159; 🚇 1, 8

Rydges is a neat little hotel close to the University of Melbourne with neutral styling and a no-nonsense approach. Even standard rooms sleep three and have good facilities and fresh bathrooms. Parkview rooms have just that, as well as more space and, usually, a better layout. A highlight of the hotel is the heated rooftop pool, which includes a large area for lazing around as well as a spa-sauna room.

## VIBE HOTEL CARLTON

Map pp78–9         Hotel $$

☎ 9380 9222; www.vibehotels.com.au; 441 Royal Pde, Carlton; r from $150; 🚇 19

This early 1960s motel was once noted for its glamorous, high-Californian style. One wonders how fabulous it could have been in the hands of an individual owner with an interest in its history. Small chain Vibe doesn't live up to the promise, but apart from overexuberance in the public areas,

## top picks

### HOSTELS

- Nunnery (above)
- Urban Central Backpackers (p188)

some period charm does shine through. Rooms have floor-to-ceiling windows and clean lines. There's also a signature '60s central pool. Its Parkville location is pretty (and close to the zoo and golf courses); the city is a short tram ride away and Brunswick or Carlton North cafés aren't too far by foot.

### DOWNTOWNER ON LYGON

Map pp78–9      Hotel $$

☎ 9663 5555; www.downtowner.com.au; 66 Lygon St, Carlton; r from $145; ⊠ 1, 8

The Downtowner is a friendly, popular, perpetually busy hotel at the start of Little Italy. This place has an easy manner and innocuous design. There are a variety of rooms, including secure adjoining rooms for families.

### NORTH MELBOURNE SERVICED APARTMENTS

Map pp78–9      Serviced Apartments $$

☎ 9329 3977; www.northmelbourneapartments .com.au; 113 Flemington Rd, North Melbourne; apt from $135; ⊠ 55, 59

These light-filled, neat and nondescript apartments come in studio to two-bedroom configurations, and share a communal laundry. The proximity to Royal Park and the zoo make them a good choice for families, and long-term rates are attractive.

### MELBOURNE METRO YHA

Map pp78–9      Hostel $$

☎ 9329 8599; www.yha.com.au; 78 Howard St, North Melbourne; dm/d from $26/80, apt from $110; ⊠ 55

The defining feature of this place is 'space': from the rooms to the common area it avoids the claustrophobic, cattle-pen feel of many hostels. The rooftop area has seriously breathtaking panoramic views of Melbourne's CBD. Everything's clean and spotless, plus there's a pool table, friendly staff and a travel agency. Unlike most Melbourne accommodation options, prices here aren't hiked for major events.

### ARDEN MOTEL Map pp78–9    Motel $

☎ 9329 7211; www.lygonst.com/ardenmotel; 15 Arden St, North Melbourne; r from $86; ⊠ 55, 57

Sometimes you just need a bed. A bastion of budget accommodation, the Arden is emphatically unfashionable and a tad

weary (though the chaise longues that resemble a 3-D modelled virus are strangely compelling). It's friendly though. Some rooms come with a kitchen, and there's a share laundry.

# SOUTH YARRA, PRAHRAN & WINDSOR

South of the river, South Yarra has a number of boutique and upmarket places set in pretty tree-lined residential streets. You'll be close to shopping, parkland, bars and cafés.

### COMO Map pp84–5      Hotel $$$

☎ 9825 2222; www.mirvachotels.com.au; 630 Chapel St, South Yarra; r from $295; ⊠ South Yarra, ⊠ 8

Located at the junction of the city's most hyped fashion streets, Como is requisitely stylish and long beloved by local celebs. The rooms use an ever-reliable burnt umber palette – flattering in any light. The 105 studios and penthouses come in 25 different shapes and sizes: you're bound to find one to fit. The rooftop pool is a treat.

### LYALL Map pp84–5      Hotel $$$

☎ 9868 8222; www.thelyall.com; 14 Murphy St, South Yarra; r from $290; ⊠ South Yarra, ⊠ 8

The Lyall is tucked away in a leafy residential street. The spacious rooms are beautifully appointed, with little luxuries including gourmet cheese in the minibar, laundry facilities, and televisions in the bathrooms. Furnishings are woody but sleek. The Lyall boasts a well-regarded spa, a gym, a swish champagne bar, and a bistro. It's all done to perfection. Plus there's 24-hour room service, including a 'spa menu'.

### ROYCE ON ST KILDA ROAD

Map pp84–5      Boutique Hotel $$$

☎ 9677 9900; www.roycehotels.com.au; 379 St Kilda Rd; r from $245; ⊠ 3, 16, 64, 67, 72

Housed in an ornate 1920s hacienda-style building, the Royce's successful mix of period details and stylish modern fit-out extends from bathroom to bed. Room types are not just a matter of scales of space – they also differ in mood from the softly minimal deluxes to the subtly decorative executive suites.

# top picks

## LEAFY BOUTIQUE HOTELS

- Hatton (below)
- Lyall (p191)
- Villa Donati (p189)
- Albany (below)

### HATTON Map pp84–5      Hotel $$$
☎ 9868 4800; www.hatton.com.au; 65 Park St, South Yarra; incl breakfast r from $195; 🚇 8
This Victorian terrace is enjoying a luxurious reincarnation as a boutique hotel. Each room is uniquely styled: waxed floorboards and wooden mantels are matched with stainless steel, while antiques and contemporary local furniture are thrown effortlessly together. The Eastern Balcony suite is particularly opulent with Asian decorative pieces and exclusive use of the 1st-floor balcony.

### QUEST SXY SOUTH YARRA
Map pp84–5      Serviced Apartments $$
8825 3700; www.questsxysouthyarra.com.au; 27-29 Claremont St, South Yarra; apt from $160; 🚇 South Yarra, 🚇 8
A great position just off the Toorak Rd strip, though it's a 'South Yarra at work' street rather than leafy and leisurely. Apartments have the full range of facilities and sport simple contemporary décor. The Yarra's not far if you fancy joining the locals for a morning jog. You're also steps away from great *pasticceria* at Café Veloce; takeaway on your balcony will beat a wan continental breakfast any day.

### TOORAK MANOR Map pp84–5      Hotel $$
☎ 9827 2689; www.toorakmanor.net; 220 Williams Rd, Toorak; r from $155; 🚇 Hawksburn, 🚇 72
This graceful old mansion sports frills and flowing chiffon in its 18 period-style rooms. Some of the décor is looking a bit tired but you're in a top spot near happening Hawksburn Village, and its only about 10 minutes into the city from the quaint train station.

### ALBANY Map pp84–5      Hotel $$
☎ 9866 4485; www.thealbany.com.au; cnr Toorak Rd & Millswyn St, South Yarra; r from $125; 🚇 8
We're not sure what to make of this eccentric hotel, though it's certainly not

bland. The front is an 1890s mansion with high-ceilinged rooms and a penthouse that recalls late-'60s swinging London. At the back is a motel-like wing with music-vid-style moody corridors and small, basic rooms that have been hit with the Ikea stick and boast excellent beds with lovely linen. The executive rooms are the pick: still not much wiggle room, but they face pretty Millswyn St and have smart new open-plan bathrooms.

### HOTEL CLAREMONT
Map pp84–5      Guesthouse $
☎ 9826 8000, 1300 301 630; www.hotelclaremont.com; 189 Toorak Rd, South Yarra; dm/s/d $39/76/86; 🚇 South Yarra, 🚇 8
In a large heritage building dating from 1868, the Claremont is good value, with comfortable rooms, high ceilings and a fair spread of facilities. Don't expect fancy décor: it's simply a clean, welcoming cheapie. Plus it's in a terrific location for shopping, eating or rambling along the Yarra.

# ST KILDA & AROUND

St Kilda is a hotel hub boasting both one of the city's most famed boutique hotels and a budget traveller enclave. Although bay views can be found, don't count on them – but the beach is usually only a short walk away.

### PRINCE Map pp88–9      Hotel $$$
☎ 9536 1111; www.theprince.com.au; 2 Acland St, St Kilda; r from $260; 🚇 16, 79, 96, 112
The Prince is Melbourne's best-known 'design' hotel. The small lobby is suitably dramatic and the rooms are an interesting mix of the original pub's proportions, natural materials and a pared-back aesthetic. Larger rooms and suites feature some key pieces of vintage modernist furniture. Onsite 'facilities' take in some of the city's most mentioned: Circa restaurant (p139), the Aurora day spa (p173), bars, band rooms (p158) and even a fabulous wine shop downstairs. Unless you're in party mode yourself, be prepared for the seepage of nightclub noise if you're staying the weekend.

### NOVOTEL ST KILDA Map pp88–9      Hotel $$$
☎ 9525 5522; www.novotel.com; 14-16 The Esplanade, St Kilda; r from $210; 🚇 3, 67
OK, it's a sprawling, generic chain hotel, but the location, a flip-flop's throw from St Kilda

beach, and the accompanying views are appealing. And while there are serene bay vistas to contemplate, you're also equidistant from the area's twin action-packed streets.

### URBAN Map pp88–9        Hotel $$$

☎ 8530 8888; www.urbanstkilda.com.au; 35-37 Fitzroy St, St Kilda; r from $185; ⊠ 16, 79, 96, 112
Rooms at the Urban (formerly the Marque) use a lot of blond wood and white to maximise space, and are simple, light and calming. Some rooms have freestanding in-room spas and are Faraway Tree–shaped (ie circular). Staff are helpful, but despite boutique aspirations, the public areas can feel a tad soulless.

### FOUNTAIN TERRACE Map pp88–9     B&B $$

☎ 9593 8123; www.fountainterrace.com.au; 28 Mary St, St Kilda; r from $155/185; ⊠ 96, 112
The seven rooms here are lovingly appointed in honour of famous Australians such as Henry Lawson and Melba (the vintage of which will give you a clue to the style and ambience at work here). All are impeccably presented, with brocades, silks and all manner of frills. The Melba Suite is the most lavish, with access to the front veranda. Our pick is the Edna Walling suite; landscape pioneer Walling's taste for black-and-white photography has inspired a nicely restrained room.

### HOTEL TOLARNO Map pp88–9       Hotel $$

☎ 9537 0200; www.hoteltolarno.com.au; 42 Fitzroy St, St Kilda; r from $145; ⊠ 16, 79, 96, 112
Tolarno was once the site of Georges Mora's seminal gallery Tolarno. The fine-dining restaurant downstairs (p139) now bears the name of his artist wife Mirka, as well as her original paintings. Rooms upstairs aren't quite so chic but are brightly coloured and eclectically furnished, with good beds and crisp white linen. Those at the front of the building might get a bit noisy for some, but have balconies, floorboards and enormous windows.

### QUEST ST KILDA BAYSIDE
Map pp88–9       Serviced Apartments $$

☎ 9593 9500; www.questapartments.com.au; 1 Eildon Rd, St Kilda; apt from $140; ⊠ 16, 79, 96, 112
A link in the very extensive chain of Quest apartments. As usual these come fully fitted with kitchens, bathrooms and living areas. This block is older than some, so if you're a

regular Quest guest don't expect the contemporary style that characterises many of their accommodations. These are, however, in a particularly charming St Kilda street.

### HOTEL BARKLY Map pp88–9       Hotel $$

☎ 9525 3354; www.stkildabeachhouse.com;109 Barkly St, St Kilda; dm/d from $18/110; ⊠ 3, 67
Hotel Barkly is the party; you're just the guest list. Or, actually, the guest. Bright dorms are on the 1st floor; moody, though not luxurious, private rooms, some with balconies and views, are on the 2nd and 3rd. Below is a heaving pub, above is a happy house-cranking bar. Noisy? You bet. But if you're up for it, there's definitely fun to be had. Though perhaps not a lot of sleep.

### OLEMBIA GUESTHOUSE
Map pp88–9       Hostel $

☎ 9537 1412; www.olembia.com.au; 96 Barkly St, St Kilda; dm/s/d $30/80/100; ⊠ 3, 67
Olembia offers impeccably presented, if slightly fusty, rooms at backpacker prices. The small, elegant old house also has a cosy lounge and a spacious leafy courtyard out front. Bookings are advised, especially for the upstairs family room. Helpful staff can provide recommendations and tips galore.

### BASE Map pp88–9       Hostel $

☎ 9536 6109; www.basebackpackers.com; 17 Carlisle St, St Kilda; dm from $30, r from $99; ⊠ 16, 79, 96
Accor spinoff Base does away with random backpacker challenges like dirty sheets, clashing bedspreads and wet clothes in the communal bathroom. There's streamlined dorms, each with en suite, or slick doubles. There's a 'sanctuary' floor for female travellers. A bar and a full range of leisure options, including a pool table, complete the package. A good-time party atmosphere prevails.

### COFFEE PALACE Map pp88–9       Hostel $

☎ 9534 5283; www.coffeepalacebackpackers.com .au; 24 Grey St, St Kilda; dm/d from $20/60; ⊠ 16, 79, 96, 112
This rambling old-school backpackers has lots of rooms, lots of activities and lots of years behind it. It has a travel desk, communal kitchen, bar, pool tables, lounge and TV room, plus a rooftop terrace with bay views. Dorms sleep from four to 10, with some for women only. There are also private rooms with shared bathrooms.

**RITZ** Map pp88–9                                     Hostel $

☎ 9525 3501; www.ritzbackpackers.com; 169
Fitzroy St, St Kilda; dm from $19, d from $50;
🚇 16, 79

Above a corner pub renowned for hosting
the riotously popular *Neighbours* nights
(served with a healthy dose of irony; see
boxed text, p35), the Ritz has an excellent
location, opposite an inner-city lake and
park, and is only a five-minute walk from
St Kilda's heart. Women can retreat to their
own dorm, which includes a male-free
kitchen and bathroom.

# SOUTH MELBOURNE, PORT MELBOURNE & ALBERT PARK

The majority of accommodation here is
geared towards business travellers who want
to be near the offices of St Kilda Rd (and the
golf course in Albert Park we suspect). It's also
convenient to public transport and both the
city and the bay, but doesn't offer too much
in the way of nightlife.

### SEBEL ALBERT PARK & CITIGATE ALBERT PARK Map pp92–3        Hotel $$$

☎ 9529 4300; www.mirvachotels.com.au;
65 Queens Rd, Albert Park; Citigate r from $175,
Sebel r from $189; 🚇 3, 5, 6, 16, 64, 67

An odd pairing of not particularly dissimilar
choices here with a couple of stablemate
chain properties occupying the same address. The Citigates 3½-star rooms are new,
neat and inoffensive. The Sebel's 4½-star
rooms, which were getting the once-over at
the time of writing, are bigger and promise
to be a little more vibrant. Both sport some
rooms with views. Depending on your time
of travel, prices can be surprisingly similar.

### BAYVIEW EDEN ON THE PARK

Map pp92–3                                              Hotel $$

☎ 9250 2222; www.bayviewhotels.com/eden; 6
Queens Rd, Albert Park; r from $175; 🚇 3, 5, 6, 16,
64, 67, 72

The Bayview Eden is indeed on the park,
or just across the road, but is not to be
confused with Bayview On The Park, a little
further down Queens Rd. The Eden fronts
Albert Park's golf course and is the closest

# top picks

### BAYSIDE DIGS

- Prince (p192)
- Hotel Tolarno (p193)

to town of this Queen's Rd strip of hotels.
Some of its simple, straightforward and
comfortable rooms have superb views.
There's a 17m indoor pool too.

### BAYVIEW ON THE PARK

Map pp92–3                                              Hotel $$

☎ 9243 9999; www.bayviewonthepark.com.au;
52 Queens Rd, Albert Park; r from $125; 🚇 3, 5, 6,
16, 64, 67

The Bayview is one of many large, facility-
toting hotels lining Queens Rd, competing
for the corporate dollar. The rooms are
clean and comfortable, though the pastel
colour scheme is dated. Premier rooms and
suites do, however, have excellent Albert
Park Lake views, and they offer substantial
discounts on weekend rates.

### BEV & MICKS MARKET HOTEL

Map pp92–3                                             Hostel $

☎ 9690 2220; 115 Cecil St, South Melbourne;
dm/d $15/40; 🚇 96, 112

In a converted pub, still with a working bar,
this hostel is right near the bustling produce market. It's a personable place, thanks
to its modest size, though it still boasts a
small kitchen and communal area.

# WILLIAMSTOWN

Not a usual base for travellers but perfect for
an atmospheric seaside break.

### PUNT HILL WILLIAMSTOWN

Map p96                          Serviced Apartments $$$

☎ 9631 1111; www.williamstown.punthill.com.au;
4-18 Ferguson St, Williamstown; apt from $180;

Bright and streamlined, this is a fashionable
little bolthole in a suburb more known for
maritime nostalgia. There are views of the
bay from the breezy rooftop spa and BBQ
area (though not the rooms) and a variety
of one- to three-bedroom apartments, all
fully equipped.

**REGIONAL VICTORIA**

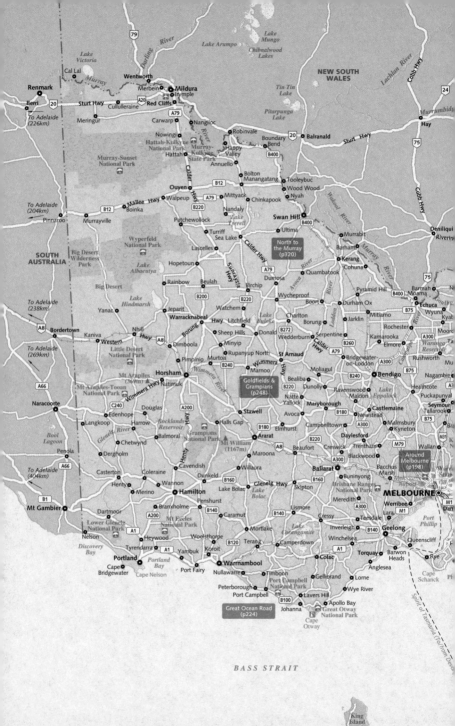

# AROUND MELBOURNE

Melbourne sits at the northern end of Port Phillip Bay, which, at nearly 2000 sq km, is a vast (and relatively shallow) body of water. The bay's heads – the famous Rip – are just 3.5km apart, making Port Phillip Bay almost an inland sea. With more than 3.2 million people living around its shoreline it's the country's most densely populated area. Port Phillip Bay and her little sister Westernport Bay (to the east), their peninsulas and islands, and the mountains and valleys of the hinterlands are all rich with natural beauty and opportunities for activities and adventures, and culinary and cultural pursuits. Indeed, within an hour or two of Melbourne you can experience mountains, rivers, beaches, bush and wildlife, and lovely little historic towns that you'll never want to leave. While there are many superb national parks, countless wineries and brilliant restaurants that are all accessible as day trips, there are also some great B&Bs and guesthouses where you can unpack a toothbrush and fresh set of smalls for the morning.

Walkers and cyclists can explore the many trails that criss-cross the region's national parks, from the cool mountain air and birdsongs of the Dandenongs and Yarra Valley to the briny sea winds of Point Nepean National Park. Gourmands and wine buffs can overindulge at the outstanding restaurants and wineries in the Yarra Valley and the Bellarine and Mornington Peninsulas. Surfers can zip up their steamers, strap on their leg ropes and ride some of the best waves in Australia at Phillip Island, the ocean breaks between Flinders and Portsea, and Point Lonsdale to Barwon Heads.

Best of all, Melbourne, one of the world's largest cities in area and within the top 90 most-populated cities, sits amid a region of sparsely peopled, broad open spaces and native bushland that teem with local flora and fauna. The Melbourne environs are ideal for short-stay escapes as well as longer sojourns. Don't come to Australia's greatest city without getting out of it for a while.

## NATIONAL PARKS & WILDLIFE

The area around Melbourne offers excellent opportunities to commune with nature and see Australian wildlife. Some of the easily accessible national parks include Dandenong Ranges National Park (p211), with fantastic day walks among the towering mountain ash trees and bellbird songs; the Mornington Peninsula National Park (p209) that covers swathes of coastal dunes between Point Nepean and Cape Schanck; pretty Kinglake National Park (p214) on the Great Dividing Range; Yarra Ranges National Park (p215), home to Mt Donna Buang; and Cape Woolamai State Faunal Reserve, where you'll find a good surf beach (p201) on Phillip Island.

Wildlife-spotters should head to Phillip Island for the Penguin Parade (p200) and the Phillip Island Wildlife Park (p202), or go to Healesville Sanctuary (p213) to cluck over the koalas and hand-feed kangaroos. There's also an interesting wildlife reserve at the Briars (p206) on the Mornington Peninsula. Those that want to get up close and personal can try swimming with dolphins off Sorrento (p207) and Queenscliff (p220).

## QUAFF!

Victoria is endowed with some of the best wine-growing regions in Australia (nay, the world!). While northern and central Victoria are famous for fat shiraz and cabernet sauvignon vintages, wine-producers nearer Melbourne tend to produce cool-climate drops like chardonnay, pinot gris and pinot noir. The Mornington Peninsula (p204), Yarra Valley (p213), the Geelong (p216) region and Bellarine Peninsula (p220) are peppered with vineyards – mostly small boutique operations. Most have cellar-door tastings and many have fine restaurants. Phillip Island (p203) also has a couple of great wineries. Some wineries charge between $2 and $5 for tastings, although this is redeemable against the purchase price of a bottle. Tourist offices issue wine-touring guides with maps and stacks of information, including how to get to more off-the-beaten-track wineries. See the Lush & the Liquid Lunch boxed text (p207) for our recommendations.

## JUST FOR KIDS

The kids are in the car dripping ice cream on the upholstery, and Dad looks over his shoulder and says, 'Whatcha wanna do?' The region

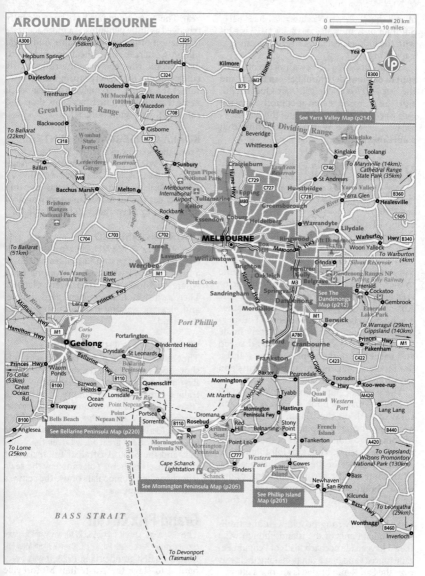

around Melbourne has some great things for kids. Go to Phillip Island and watch the Penguin Parade (p200), do a tour of the Grand Prix Circuit (p200) and go to Amaze'n Things (p201).

In the Dandenongs, ride on Puffing Billy (p211), check out the Emerald Lake Model Railway (p211) and SkyHigh Mount Dandenong (p213) for amazing views over Melbourne.

At Mornington you can hire a boat at Schnapper Point Boat Hire (p204) and catch a fish. Enjoy

amazing views from the summit at Arthurs Seat (p206) and lose the kids at the Enchanted Maze Garden (p206). Put your togs on and take the kids for a swim at the delightful bay beaches at Portsea (p208) on your way out to see the fascinating old battlements at Point Nepean (p209). Take a tour of Cape Schanck Lightstation (p210) and walk down the boardwalks for outstanding views.

In the Yarra Valley visit Healesville Sanctuary (p213) and tickle a koala, or ride your bikes along the Lilydale to Warburton Rail Trail (p214). Summer or winter, Mt Donna Buang (p215) is a hit with the kids, especially if the tobogganing is happening.

Check out Geelong (p216), with stacks of kiddie stuff to do along delightful Eastern Beach, and the Ford Discovery Centre (p218). At Queenscliff, ride the restored steam locomotive on the Bellarine Peninsula Railway (p220) and the Queenscliff–Sorrento Ferry (p222). Watch for dolphins that sometimes swim alongside.

# PHILLIP ISLAND & THE PENGUIN PARADE

### pop 7500

Phillip Island – about 100 sq km – sits at the entrance to Western Port Bay, 140km southeast of Melbourne, connected to the mainland by a bridge across the Narrows from San Remo to Newhaven. The island is home to the world-famous Penguin Parade, Victoria's biggest tourist attraction, as well as the Australian Motorcycle Grand Prix – rather a schizoid visitor demographic. The permanent islander population is largely made up of sheep and cattle farmers (and sheep and cattle), surfers, hippies, retirees and a few retailers flogging penguin souvenirs and petrol-head paraphernalia.

The summer population swells to 40,000 as holiday-makers book out every bed and caravan park on the island. Excellent surf beaches bring day-tripping boardriders from Melbourne to ride the swells of the southern oceanside beaches, while kids loll about in the calmer shallows of the north-side beaches. With some terrific accommodation options and a vibrant café and restaurant scene, Phillip Island has plenty to keep you busy for a few days.

The Boonerwrung people were the traditional inhabitants of the island, though what they'd have made of coach loads of Penguin Parade tourists and biker gangs making their way over the San Remo bridge is anyone's guess.

The island's main town is Cowes, on the north coast. On the east coast is Rhyll, with the island's main boat ramp.

## Phillip Island Nature Park

### PENGUIN PARADE

The Penguin Parade ( ☎ 5951 2800; www.penguins.org.au; Summerland Beach; adult/child/family $20/10/50; ☉ 10am-nightfall) attracts more than 500,000 visitors a year. The 'fairy penguins' have been recently rebadged as 'little penguins' – a more accurate translation of the scientific name *Eudyptula minor*. Concrete amphitheatres hold up to 3800 people who coo over the ridiculously cute penguins that emerge from the sea after sunset and waddle resolutely up to their beach nests. The visitors centre has a gift shop and café (try the penguin burger!).

### KOALA CONSERVATION CENTRE

From the boardwalks at the Koala Conservation Centre ( ☎ 5952 1307; www.phillipislandguide.com/koala; Phillip Island Rd; admission adult/child/family $10/5/25; ☉ 10am-5pm) you can watch koalas chewing on tasty eucalyptus leaves (or more probably dozing – they sleep about 20 hours a day!).

### CHURCHILL ISLAND

Churchill Island ( ☎ 5956 7214; off Phillip Island Rd; adult/child/family $10/5/25; ☉ 10am-4.30pm), connected by a bridge near Newhaven, is a working farm where Victoria's first crops were planted. There's a historic homestead and gardens here, and pleasant walking tracks looping round the island.

### SEAL ROCKS & THE NOBBIES

The Nobbies are a couple of large craggy offshore rocks at the island's southwestern tip. Beyond them are Seal Rocks, inhabited by Australia's largest fur-seal colony. The Nobbies Centre ( ☎ 5951 2816; www.penguins.org.au/nobbies index.asp; Ventnor Rd; admission free, tours adult/child $10/5; ☉ 10am-8pm Dec-Feb, to 5pm Mar-May, to 4pm Jun-Aug, to 6pm Sep-Nov) offers great views over the Nobbies and the 6000 Australian fur seals that sun themselves there. You can view the seals from boardwalk binoculars or use the centre's underwater cameras.

## Grand Prix Circuit

The Grand Prix Circuit ( ☎ 5952 2710; www.phillipisland circuit.com.au; Back Beach Rd; ☉ 8.30am-5.30pm Mon-Fri) hosted it's first grand prix in 1928. It was overhauled to stage the Australian Motorcycle Grand Prix in 1989. The visitors centre ( ☎ 5952 9400; ☉ 9am-5pm) runs one-hour walking tours (adult/child/family $18/9/42) of the track, and you can have your photo taken on the winner's podium.

The History of Motor Sport Museum (adult/child/family $14/7/30) is here too, where you can strap yourself into a V8 Supercar for three Hot Laps (1/2/3 people $199/299/349) of the track.

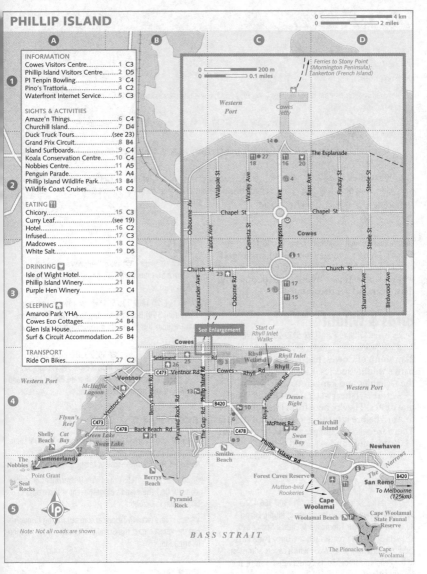

**INFORMATION**
Cowes Visitors Centre.................1 C3
Phillip Island Visitors Centre........2 D5
PI Tenpin Bowling.......................3 C4
Pino's Trattoria...........................4 C2
Waterfront Internet Service...........5 C3

**SIGHTS & ACTIVITIES**
Amaze'n Things..........................6 C4
Churchill Island..........................7 D4
Duck Truck Tours..................(see 23)
Grand Prix Circuit.......................8 B4
Island Surfboards........................9 C4
Koala Conservation Centre.........10 C4
Nobbies Centre.........................11 A5
Penguin Parade.........................12 A4
Phillip Island Wildlife Park...........13 B4
Wildlife Coast Cruises.................14 C2

**EATING** 🍴
Chicory....................................15 C3
Curry Leaf...........................(see 19)
Hotel.......................................16 C2
Infused....................................17 C3
Madcowes................................18 C2
White Salt................................19 D5

**DRINKING** 🍷
Isle of Wight Hotel....................20 C2
Phillip Island Winery..................21 B4
Purple Hen Winery....................22 C4

**SLEEPING** 🛏
Amaroo Park YHA.....................23 C3
Cowes Eco Cottages..................24 B4
Glen Isla House.........................25 B4
Surf & Circuit Accommodation...26 B4

**TRANSPORT**
Ride On Bikes...........................27 C2

# Surf Beaches

Some of the island's south-side ocean surf
beaches, including Woolamai, have rips and
currents, and are only suitable for experienced surfers. Beginners and families can go
to Smiths Beach, which is often teeming with
surf-school groups. Both beaches are patrolled in summer. Around the Nobbies, Cat Bay
and Flynns Reef will often work when the wind

is blowing onshore at the Woolamai and
Smiths areas.

Island Surfboards ( ☎ 5952 3443; www.islandsurfboards
.com.au; 65 Smiths Beach & 147 Thompson Ave, Cowes; lessons
$50) gives surfing lessons and hires gear.

# Amaze'n Things

The kids will bug you to take them to Amaze'n
Things ( ☎ 5952 2283; www.amazenthings.com.au; 1805

## TRANSPORT: PHILLIP ISLAND

Distance from Melbourne Cowes 143km

Direction Southeast

Travel time 1½ hours

Bicycle Hire bicycles from Ride On Bikes ( ☎ 5952 2533; www.rideonbikes.com.au; 2-17 The Esplanade, Cowes; half-/full-day $25/35).

Bus V/Line ( ☎ 13 61 96; www.vline.com.au) buses ($10, 3¼ hours, one daily) depart Melbourne's Southern Cross station at 3.50pm Monday to Friday.

Car From Melbourne take the Monash Fwy (M1); take the Phillip Island exit onto South Gippsland Hwy (M420) near Cranbourne.

Ferry Inter Island Ferries ( ☎ 9585 5730; www.interislandferries.com.au; return adult/child/bike $20/10/8; ☾ every 30min 8.30am-5pm daily, plus 7pm Friday) run between Stony Point and Cowes via French Island.

Taxi Cowes/San Remo Taxis ( ☎ 5952 2200).

Phillip Island Rd; adult/child/family from $13/10/44; ☾ 9am-6.30pm). There's a maze (naturally), 'maxi golf' course and a building full of 'illusions' rooms where water flows uphill and people fly, disappear and get decapitated.

## Birds & Wildlife

Phillip Island Wildlife Park ( ☎ 5952 2038; Phillip Island Rd; adult/child/family $15/8/40; ☾ 10am-5pm), about 2km south of Cowes, has over 100 Australian native wildlife species. Kids love handfeeding the wallabies and kangaroos.

Mutton birds (shearwaters) nest in the Woolamai dunes. They're here from late September to April before returning to Japan and Alaska. There are pelicans (that are fed at Newhaven at 11.30am daily), and swans and ibises at Rhyll Inlet. Rhyll Wetland has a boardwalk and lookout.

## INFORMATION

Phillip Island visitors centres ( ☎ 1300 366 422, 5956 7447; www.phillipisland.net.au; Phillip Island Rd, Newhaven & cnr Thompson & Church Sts, Cowes; ☾ 9am-5pm) Both centres sell the Three Parks Pass (adult/child/family $34/17/85) which covers admission to the Penguin Parade, Koala Conservation Centre and Churchill Island.

PI Tenpin Bowling ( ☎ 5952 3977; 91 Settlement Rd, Cowes; ☾ noon-late Mon-Fri, 10am-late Sat, 10am-6pm Sun) Internet access $8 per hour.

Pino's Trattoria ( ☎ 5852 2808; Thompson St, Cowes; ☾ breakfast, lunch & dinner) Free wi-fi for customers.

Waterfront Internet Service ( ☎ 5952 3312; Shop 1/30 Thompson Ave, Cowes; ☾ 9am-5pm Mon-Fri) Internet access $8 per hour.

## TOURS

Duck Truck Tours ( ☎ 5952 2548; www.yha.com.au; 97 Church St; tours from $70) Based at Amaroo Park YHA (opposite).

Go West ( ☎ 1300 736 551; www.gowest.com.au; 1-day tour $99) Does a one-day tour from Melbourne that includes lunch and iPod commentary in several languages.

Wildlife Coast Cruises ( ☎ 5952 3501; www.baycon nections.com.au; Rotunda Bldg, Cowes Jetty; tours $22-181; ☾ Nov-May) Runs a cruise around Phillip Island and Seal Rocks, and trips to French Island.

## FESTIVALS & EVENTS

Pyramid Rock Festival (www.thepyramidrockfestival.com; New Year) This huge event coincides with New Year's festivities and features some of the best Aussie bands.

Australian Motorcycle Grand Prix (http://bikes.grandprix .com.au; Oct) The island's biggest event – three days of bike action in October.

V8 Supercars (www.v8supercar.com.au) Racing through-out the year. Contact the Grand Prix Circuit (p200) for more information.

## EATING

Infused ( ☎ 5952 2655; 115 Thompson Ave, Cowes; mains $22-32; ☾ lunch & dinner) Infused's groovy mix of timber, stone and lime-green décor makes a relaxed place to enjoy a stunningly presented lunch or dinner, or a late-night cocktail. It's at once a café, restaurant and bar, and the eclectic menu moves from entrée portions of sashimi through to rib-eye steak and salmon croquettes.

Chicory ( ☎ 5952 2665; 115 Thompson Ave, Cowes; mains $25-35; ۞ lunch & dinner) One of the few fine-dining places on the island, Chicory serves contemporary dishes like New Zealand trevalla (blue eye) soused in a passionfruit and peppercorn glaze. There's a select wine list and less expensive lunchtime fare, but dinner is what people talk about.

White Salt ( ☎ 5956 6336; 7 Vista Pl, Woolamai; meals from $10; ۞ lunch & dinner Thu-Mon) White Salt serves gourmet fish and chips – selected fish fillets and hand-cut chips, tempura prawns and marinated BBQ octopus salad with corn, pesto and lemon. The bench seats out front are usually packed, but you can make off for the beach with a parcel under your arm.

Hotel ( ☎ 5952 2060; 11-13 The Esplanade, Cowes; mains $14-26; ۞ lunch & dinner) Formerly the Hotel Phillip Island, this corner pub has had a snazzy makeover and features a lovely light-filled main dining room that looks out over the pier. The straightforward pub-grub menu is tricked up with kangaroo kebabs and Moroccan chickpea curry. The nightclub upstairs is lively and popular on weekends.

Curry Leaf ( ☎ 5956 6772; 9 Vista Pl, Woolamai; mains $12-18; ۞ lunch & dinner) This cheery Indian restaurant and takeaway is popular for its piquant meat, seafood and vegetarian curries and aromatic biryani dishes.

Madcowes ( ☎ 5952 2560; 17 The Esplanade, Cowes; mains $6-15; ۞ breakfast & lunch) A stylish, breezy café-foodstore cooking big, hearty breakfasts and quality lunches. Try the ricotta hotcakes with caramelised banana, yoghurt and maple syrup. At lunch wash down a roast beef and brie sandwich with some Victorian wine – all by the glass.

## DRINKING

Isle of Wight Hotel ( ☎ 5952 2301; The Esplanade, Cowes; mains $16-24; ۞ lunch & dinner) This Cowes icon is a classic rambling pub and a great place for a beer or simple pub meal. The hotel has planning approval for a huge redevelopment that will replace the existing building with a five-star hotel and convention centre. Drink a toast to the old girl before they 'doze her!

Phillip Island Winery ( ☎ 5956 8465; www.phillip islandwines.com.au; Berrys Beach Rd; platters $14-17; ۞ 11am-5pm Apr-Oct) Here you can sample excellent wines made by renowned Diamond Valley wine-makers and share platters of cheese, terrine, smoked salmon, trout fillets and pâté.

Purple Hen Winery ( ☎ 5956 9244; www.purplehen wines.com.au; 96 McPhees Rd, Rhyll; ۞ 10am-5.30pm Mon-Fri) Try the signature pinot at the cellar door of this pretty winery off the main tourist route, with views over Westernport Bay. It's a light, pale red with almost a rosé-style palate – not too overcooked like many Australian pinots.

## SLEEPING

During big motor-racing events, Christmas, Easter and school holidays, rates are sky-high and you'll need to book your bed way in advance. There's a dozen caravan parks, mostly around Cowes – pick up a *Caravan Parks on Phillip Island* flyer from the visitors centres.

Glen Isla House ( ☎ 5952 1882; www.glenisla.com; 230 Church St, Cowes; d $265-395; ❀ ▫ ) This brilliant boutique hotel is probably the best address on the island. Ensconced in a renovated 1870 homestead and outbuildings, Glen Isla is all about understated old-world luxury and all rooms have private access, huge plasma TVs, bathrooms, refrigerators and complimentary wi-fi. Children under 12 are not welcome.

Cowes Eco Cottages ( ☎ 5952 6466; www.coweseco cottages.com.au; cnr Justice & Ventnor Rds, Ventnor; d $175-250) These comfortable, roomy cottages are set on 2½ acres of rural land near Cowes. There are two two-bedroom cottages that sleep four, and one one-bedroom cottage with a spa-bathroom. They're purpose-built with kitchens and comfortable lounges with TV/DVD.

Amaroo Park YHA ( ☎ 5952 2548; www.yha.com.au; 97 Church St, Cowes; unpowered sites $30, dm/s/d/f from $30/60/90/145; ▫ ☎ ) In a shady bush setting, the Amaroo Park YHA has a range of well-maintained accommodation options, a communal kitchen and BBQ areas, bar, lounge and TV room. It also organises surfing lessons and tours through Duck Truck Tours (opposite).

Surf & Circuit Accommodation ( ☎ 5952 1300; www .surfandcircuit.com; 113 Justice Rd, Cowes; r $220-315; ❀ ) This is ideal for families or groups. Eight large, comfortable units accommodate up to six and ten people, and have kitchens and lounges with plasma TVs and patios, and some have spas. Tariffs are levied on a per-unit basis regardless of the number of occupants – terrific value. Outside there are barbecue areas, a tennis court and a playground.

# MORNINGTON PENINSULA

Holiday-makers from Melbourne have been visiting the Mornington Peninsula since the 1870s, when paddle-steamers ran down to Portsea. Thirty years ago the Mornington Peninsula was a rural region of cattle farming and fruit orchards without a grape in sight. Today, the farmers are gone and their lands have been subdivided for low-density suburban-style housing and vineyards that now number nearly 100. The peninsula still retains lovely stands of native bushland, rugged ocean beaches and national parks, and you can enjoy wine tastings, pick your own fruit in orchards and berry farms, bushwalk and swim, or surf some of Victoria's best breaks.

The calm 'front beaches' are on the Port Phillip side. The rugged ocean 'back beaches' face Bass Strait, and there are stunning walks along this coastal strip, part of Mornington Peninsula National Park.

Foodies love the peninsula, where a winery lunch is a definite highlight. Several property agents manage private holiday rentals, including Sandy Ridge Retreat ( ☎ 5988 6641; www.srr.com.au).

## MORNINGTON

**pop 21,000**

Originally part of the lands of the Boonerwrung people, pretty Mornington began life as a European township in 1854. The town thrived and by 1890 there were steamers and a daily train service from Melbourne (now sadly defunct). Many of Mornington's original buildings survive, and historic Schnapper Point Pier and the colourful Mills Beach bathing boxes make it a nice place to visit. Melbourne's relentless suburban sprawl has all but engulfed the little town, stopping (for now) just 10km away in Frankston.

There are several grand old buildings around Main St, including the 1892 Grand Hotel. The Old Court House on the corner of Main St and the Esplanade was built in 1860, and the Police Lock-Up behind it was built in 1862. On the adjacent corner is the 1863 Old Post Office Museum ( ☎ 5976 3203; cnr Main St & The Esplanade; ☯ 1.30pm-4.30 Sun & public holidays). On the other corner of this intersection is a monument to the 15 members of Mornington's football team who lost their lives in 1892 when their boat, *Process*, sank returning from a game against Mordialloc.

For views over the harbour, take a walk along the 1850s pier and around the Schnapper Point foreshore past the Matthew Flinders monument that commemorates his 1802 landing. Mothers Beach is the main swimming beach, while at Fossil Beach limestone was mined in the 1860s and there are remains of a lime-burning kiln. Fossils found here date back 25 million years! You can hire a boat with Schnapper Point Boat Hire ( ☎ 5975 5479; www.fishingmornington.com; Boatshed 7, Scout Beach).

The first three Sundays of each month the Mornington Railway ( ☎ 1300 767 274; www.mornington railway.org.au; Mornington train station; return adult/child/family $12/6/34) runs steam locomotives between Mornington and Moorooduc.

## Information

IT-Tech ( ☎ 5977 1116; 12 Mornington Village Shopping Centre) Internet access $8 per hour.

Mornington Library ( ☎ 5950 1820; Vancouver St; ☯ 9am-2pm Mon & Sat, to 8pm Tue & Thu, to 6pm Wed & Fri) Free internet access.

Mornington visitors centre ( ☎ 5975 1644; www.visit morningtonpeninsula.org; 320 Main St; ☯ 9am-5pm) Has useful regional information and a Mornington walking-tour map.

## Eating

Kazu ( ☎ 5976 1323; 37d Main St; mains $15-22; ☯ dinner Mon-Sat) Tucked away behind some other shops, little Kazu is the real deal in Japanese cuisine. Wonderfully light tempura and lovely teriyaki dishes, but we baulked at the eel…

Afghan Marco Polo ( ☎ 5975 5154; 9-11 Main St; mains $17-21; ☯ dinner) Marco Polo is an atmospheric place with Persian rugs and brass hookahs, and serves traditional Afghan cuisine. Kebabs, kormas, *boranis* – a Central Asian mash up!

Brass Razu ( ☎ 5975 0108; 13 Main St; tapas $7-16; ☯ noon-late Tue-Sun) This convivial bar serves drinks and tapas to trendy Morningtonians until the wee hours.

## Sleeping

Morning Star Estate ( ☎ 9788 6611; www.morningstarestate .com.au; 1 Sunnyside Rd, Mt Eliza; d $150-300; ☒ ☐ ☒ ) Morning Star is a huge 1867 Victorian mansion on 38 acres that operates as winery, restaurant and boutique hotel. Once owned by the Catholic Church, it was a home for delinquent boys. The many outbuildings, rose gardens and sweeping bay vistas make it a lovely place to wander around.

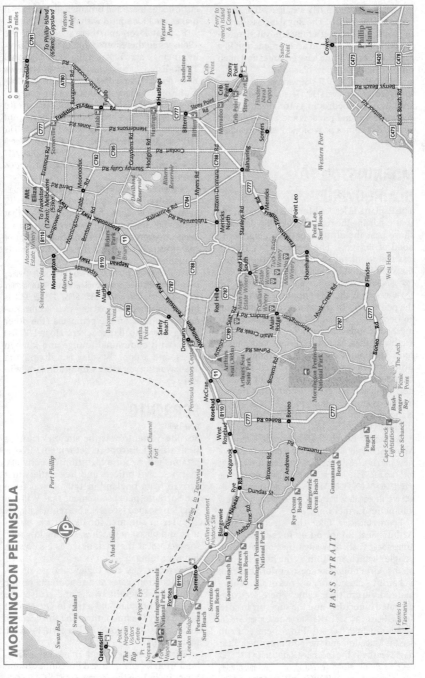

# MORNINGTON PENINSULA

Royal Hotel ( ☎ 5975 9115; www.theroyal.com.au; 770 Esplanade; d $90-145; 🐾 ) The Royal is classified by the National Trust. It's fully renovated, offering authentic old-world accommodation in a range of rooms. Some have en suites and open onto brilliant sea-view balconies.

Apsley Cottage ( ☎ 9787 3166; www.apsleycottage.com; 19 King Georges Ave; d from $150) Decorated in period style, this two-bedroom 1910 self-contained cottage has open fireplaces and a large garden. The larder comes provisioned with breakfast goodies.

## MORNINGTON TO BLAIRGOWRIE

The Esplanade leaves Mornington and heads south, skirting the rocky Port Phillip Bay foreshore past the affluent bayside neighbourhood of Mt Martha. The Nepean Hwy takes a less scenic inland route and again becomes the Mornington Peninsula Freeway. The Briars ( ☎ 5974 3686; 450 Nepean Hwy, Mt Martha; adult/child $5/4; ☺ 10am-4pm) is the 1840 homestead of one of the peninsula's first pastoral runs. Sitting on 96 hectares, it includes original farm buildings, parklands and a wildlife reserve. There are bird hides, koalas, echidnas and kangaroos. The homestead houses the Dame Mabel Brookes collection of Napoleon relics, which includes locks of the emperor's hair and his death mask. Her great-grandfather owned the lands on the island of St Helena where Napoleon was exiled by the British for the final six years of his life.

At Safety Beach the Esplanade becomes Marine Dr and goes *under* the entry to a huge new marina-residential Martha Cove (www.martha cove.com.au). The Mornington Peninsula visitors centre ( ☎ 1800 804 009, 5987 3078; www.visitmorningtonpenin sula.org; Nepean Hwy, Dromana; ☺ 9am-5pm) is a few kilometres further on.

From Dromana take the steep hair-pin Arthurs Seat Rd inland up to the lookout at Arthurs Seat (called Wonga by Boonerwrung people), which, at 314m, is the highest point on the Port Phillip Bay coast. Forlorn chairs of a chairlift – closed after a series of accidents – hang idly from their cable. There are coin-operated binoculars and the superbly located Arthurs Hotel ( ☎ 5981 4444; Arthurs Seat; mains $16-28; ☺ breakfast, lunch & dinner). From here you can see Mt Macedon and the You Yangs on a clear day. Nearby is the Enchanted Maze Garden ( ☎ 5981 8449; www.enchantedmaze.com.au; 55 Purves Rd, Arthurs Seat; adult/child/family $15/9/45; ☺ 10am-6pm), a fan-

tastic hedge maze and ornamental garden that makes the kids squeal with delight.

Back at Dromana there's a relic of the 1960s when there were more than 330 drive-in cinemas across Australia. The National Trust–listed Dromana Drive-In ( ☎ 5987 2492; www .drivein.net.au; 113 Nepean Hwy; adult/child/family $14/7/40) is one of just a handful that remain. The eateries along this stretch of Point Nepean Rd towards Sorrento are all fairly generic, but exceptions include Fed-Up Fish Café ( ☎ 5986 4716; 1571 Point Nepean Rd, Rosebud; mains $15-28; ☺ lunch Fri-Sun, dinner daily) and Bamboo ( ☎ 5989 7700; 2257 Nepean Hwy, Rye; mains $19-31; ☺ breakfast, lunch & dinner).

Peninsula Hot Springs ( ☎ 5950 8777; www.peninsula hotsprings.com; Springs La, Rye; adult/child Tue-Thu $24/15, Fri-Mon $30/20) is a large, luxurious complex that utilises hot, mineral-rich waters pumped from deep underground. There's a huge menu of spa, private bathing and massage treatments available.

At Blairgowrie, further down the road, Bayplay Lodge ( ☎ 5988 0188; www.bayplay.com.au; 46 Canterbury Jetty Rd, Blairgowrie; dm/d/f $35/75/95; 🐾 🖥 🐾 ) is one of only two backpacker-style accommodation options on the peninsula (the other being Sorrento Backpackers Hostel YHA; p208), with communal lounge and kitchen areas, and a pool. Bayplay is a diving and sea-kayaking operator with headquarters in Portsea.

## SORRENTO
### pop 1500

Seaside Sorrento was the site of Victoria's first official European settlement. It was established by an expedition of convicts, marines, civil officers and free settlers that arrived from England in 1803. It was from the Sorrento penal settlement that William Buckley escaped (see p208). Sorrento is hugely popular in summer for its historic buildings and pleasant beaches. During low tide, the rock pool at the back beach is a safe spot for swimming.

Sorrento has the biggest range of accommodation, cafés and restaurants on the peninsula. Dolphin swims and cruises are incredibly popular, and a trip to Queenscliff on the ferry is a fun outing. The small Sorrento visitors centre ( ☎ 5984 5678; 2 St Aubins Way) is on the main drag.

There are some grand 19th-century buildings built from locally quarried limestone around town, including the Sorrento Hotel (1871), Conti-

## LUSH & THE LIQUID LUNCH

Victoria has more than 500 wineries, many of them a day trip from Melbourne. The state's southern region is particularly suited to producing cold-climate chardonnay and pinot varieties. Cellar doors aren't the bargains they once were, but boutique wineries often sell exclusively to restaurant sommeliers, so cellar-door sales can turn up some excellent, interesting and unusual wines, even if they're not bargains.

Many wineries have superb restaurants, and there are few experiences as pleasurable as a long lunch with great wine, bucolic surrounds and panoramic vistas (ease up if you're seeing double). Look out for *The Penguin Good Australian Wine Guide*, and James Halliday's *Wine Companion*, published each year.

Here are some of our favourite wineries around Melbourne (this list could've been *much* longer). Opening hours vary so call ahead:

**TarraWarra Estate** ( ☎ 5957 3510; www.tarrawarra.com.au; 311 Healesville-Yarra Glen Rd, Yarra Glen) Convivial bistro and art gallery come together in a striking building (see also p214).

**Coldstream Hills** ( ☎ 5964 9410; www.coldstreamhills.com.au; 31 Maddens Lane, Coldstream) The chardonnay, pinot noir and merlot are the star picks here.

**Rochford** ( ☎ 5962 2119; www.rochfordwines.com; cnr Maroondah Hwy & Hill Rd, Coldstream) Reason enough alone to head into the Yarra Valley.

**Yering Station** ( ☎ 9730 0100; www.yering.com; 38 Melba Hwy, Yering) A modern complex with a fine restaurant, gourmet provedore and bar, it's home to the heady shiraz-viognier blend. The Yarra Valley Farmers' Market is held here on the third Sunday of every month.

**Pettavel Winery** ( ☎ 5266 1120; www.pettavel.com; 65 Pettavel Rd, Waurn Ponds) The Geelong region's premier winery, with a fabulous restaurant.

**Kilgour Estate** ( ☎ 5251 2223; www.kilgourestate.com.au; 85 McAdams Lane, Bellarine) Outstanding Port Phillip Bay views and a restaurant that features famous Portarlington mussels. Known for its oaked chardonnay.

**Montalto** ( ☎ 5989 8412; www.montalto.com.au; 33 Shoreham Rd, Red Hill South) One of the Mornington Peninsula's best winery restaurants. Montalto pinot noir and chardonnay are terrific (see also p211).

**T'Gallant** ( ☎ 5989 6565; www.tgallant.com.au; 1385 Mornington-Flinders Rd, Main Ridge) Pioneered luscious pinot gris in Australia and produces the country's best. There's fine dining at La Baracca Trattoria.

**Red Hill Estate** ( ☎ 5931 0177; www.redhillestate.com.au; 53 Red Hill Rd, Red Hill South) Max's Restaurant at Red Hill Estate is one of the best restaurants on the Mornington Peninsula, while the winery's signature pinot is outstanding (see also p211).

**Morning Star Estate** ( ☎ 9788 6611; www.morningstarestate.com.au; 1 Sunnyside Rd, Mt Eliza) Best known for its chardonnay, pinot noir and merlot cabernet wines, this is a delightful place for a long lunch (see also p204).

---

nental Hotel (1875) and Koonya (1878). Interestingly, there was once a steam tram service (built in 1876) that ran until 1921 from Sorrento pier to the back beach.

There are plenty of swimming and walking opportunities along Sorrento's wide, sandy beaches and bluffs. At low tide, the rock pool at the back beach is a safe spot for adults and children to swim and snorkel. The 10-minute climb up to Coppins Lookout is worthwhile.

Apart from four graves that are believed to hold the remains of 30 original settlers, there's little evidence of Sorrento's original abandoned settlement. The Collins Settlement Historic Site (Leggett Way), midway between Sorrento and Blairgowrie, marks the settlement site at Sullivan Bay, and a display centre tells its story.

Several operators offer sightseeing and dolphin-swimming cruises that depart from Sorrento Pier, including the following:

**Moonraker Charters** ( ☎ 5984 4211; www.moonraker charters.com.au; adult/child sightseeing $44/33, dolphin swimming $90/88)

**Polperro Dolphin Swims** ( ☎ 5988 8437; www.polperro.com.au; adult/child observers $50/30, all swimmers $110)

## Eating

**Acquolina Ristorante** ( ☎ 5984 0811; 26 Ocean Beach Rd; mains $20-30; ☽ lunch Sun, dinner Thu-Mon, closed Jun-Sep) Acquolina upped the ante when it opened in Sorrento with its authentic northern Italian fare. This is hearty simple food – handmade

## BUCKLEY'S CHANCE

In October 1803 William Buckley (1780–1856), a strapping 6ft 7in bricklayer, was transported to Victoria's first settlement (now Sorrento) as a convict for receiving stolen goods.

Buckley and three others escaped in December, though one was shot dead during the escape. The remaining three set off around the bay, thinking they were heading to Sydney, but two turned back and died from lack of food and water.

Buckley wandered for weeks, surviving on shellfish and berries. He was on his last legs when two Wathaurong women found him, and Buckley spent the next 32 years living with the nomadic clan on the Bellarine Peninsula, learning their customs and language.

In 1835 Buckley surrendered to a party from a survey ship. He was almost unable to speak English, and the startled white settlers dubbed him the 'Wild White Man.' Buckley was subsequently pardoned, and acted as an interpreter and mediator between white settlers and the Wathaurong people. John Morgan's 1852 book *The Life & Adventures of William Buckley* provides an insight into Aboriginal life before white settlement.

The Australian colloquialism 'Buckley's chance' (or 'You've got Buckley's' – meaning a very slim or no chance) is said to be based on William Buckley's story, but there's dispute about this. Some claim the expression gained currency later in the late 1800s and derived from the name of the Melbourne department store Buckley's & Nunn ('You've got two chances – Buckley's and none'). 'Buckley's chance' first appeared in print in the *Bulletin* magazine in 1898, but the etymology of the phrase remains a mystery…and we've got Buckley's chance of ever knowing the truth.

pasta dishes matched with imported Italian wines. The owners winter in Italy.

Baths ( ☎ 5984 1500; 3278 Point Nepean Rd; mains $17-30; ☽ breakfast, lunch & dinner) Formerly the sea baths, this place does excellent breakfast cookups served on its fantastic waterfront decking. Lunch and dinner get more sophisticated.

Continental Cafe ( ☎ 5984 2201; 1 Ocean Beach Rd; mains $17-26; ☽ breakfast, lunch & dinner) The Continental Hotel does gourmet fish and chips and stylish Mod Oz grub. Eat outside at weathered picnic tables overlooking the bay or in the funky and cosy café. Tuesday is pizza-and-pasta night, and Thursday is 300g steak night – both $15 flat rate.

Stringer's ( ☎ 5984 2010; 2 Ocean Beach Rd; light meals $4-8; ☽ breakfast & lunch) Stringer's is a Sorrento institution, with house-made meals and Mornington wines for sale in the attached grocery shop.

## Sleeping

Carmel of Sorrento ( ☎ 5984 3512; www.carmelofsorrento .com.au; 142 Ocean Beach Rd; s $160, d $185-210, self-contained units from $220; ☒ ) This lovely old limestone house in central Sorrento has been tastefully restored in period style. There are four Edwardian-style B&B guestrooms with bathrooms and two self-contained units.

Oceanic Whitehall Guesthouse ( ☎ 5984 4166; www .oceanicgroup.com.au; 231 Ocean Beach Rd; r $125-220, apt $170-220; ☒ ) The timber veranda of this limestone, two-storey guesthouse near the back beach has lovely views. The simple rooms have shared bathrooms but better ones have en suites.

Hotel Sorrento ( ☎ 5984 2206; www.hotelsorrento .au; 5-15 Hotham Rd; motel r $195-280, apt $220-320; ☒ ▯ ) The legendary Hotel Sorrento trades on its famous name and has a swag of accommodation. 'Sorrento on the Park' offers standard and overpriced motel rooms, but the lovely 'On the Hill' double and family apartments have airy living spaces, spacious bathrooms and private balconies.

Sorrento Backpackers Hostel YHA ( ☎ 5984 4323; www .yha.com.au; 3 Miranda St; dm/d $35/90; ▯ ) This purpose-built hostel maintains high standards and the staff can organise horse riding, snorkelling and diving trips. To get here, take bus 788 to stop 18.

## PORTSEA
### pop 650

Portsea is where many of Melbourne's wealthiest families have built seaside mansions. Head to the back beach to see London Bridge, an impressive natural rock formation, and hang-gliders launching off the cliff face. This ocean beach has wild, dangerous surf – swim between the flags. The front beaches offer more sheltered swimming spots.

Bayplay ( ☎ 5988 0188; www.bayplay.com.au; 3755 Point Nepean Rd; ☽ 8.30am-5.30pm) offers aquatic activities (diving, snorkelling, swimming with dolphins, sea kayaking and surfing) and land pursuits like horse riding. Accommodation is available at Bayplay Lodge in Blairgowrie (p206).

Dive Victoria ( ☎ 5984 3155; www.divevictoria.com.au; 3752 Point Nepean Rd; snorkelling with gear $65, 1/2 dives without gear $50/100) runs diving and snorkelling trips and hires out equipment.

## HAROLD HOLT

On a hot day in December 1967, Harold Holt (1908–67) disappeared in wild surf off Cheviot Beach, aged 59, while serving as Australia's prime minister . Despite a three-week air and land search – the biggest in Australia's history – his body was never recovered. This, and the fact that it was the height of the Cold War, led to a raft of conspiracy theories.

It was suggested that the CIA had Holt murdered because he wanted to withdraw Australian troops from Vietnam. It was also alleged that the Rockefeller family/Mobil Oil company/CIA had him bumped off because, with the covert activities of the Atomic Energy Commission (AEC) at Lucas Heights in Sydney, Australia was secretly emerging as a major nuclear energy supplier. Some said that Holt suicided because he was depressed and there was a leadership challenge emerging within the Liberal Party. The most colourful theory was that Holt was a Chinese spy, and that he climbed aboard a Chinese submarine waiting off Cheviot Beach and died in the mid-1980s after living out his days with a lover in France.

The lack of a body meant that an inquest was never held, but in 1985 the Victorian Coroner's Act was amended so that 'suspected deaths' had to be investigated. The inevitable 2005 coroner's inquest found he died by accidental drowning.

But we reckon he was taken by a UFO…

The iconic, faux-Tudor Portsea Hotel ( ☎ 5984 2213; www.portseahotel.com.au; 3746 Point Nepean Rd; s $65-250, d $110-250, mains $17-30; ☺ breakfast, lunch & dinner) is most of what there is to Portsea township. The Mod Oz menu in the restaurant is very good, and clean rooms provide comfortable accommodation.

## MORNINGTON PENINSULA NATIONAL PARK

The peninsula's tip is marked by the stunning Point Nepean section of the Mornington Peninsula National Park ( ☎ 13 19 63; www.parkweb.vic.gov.au; Point Nepean Rd, Portsea; ☺ 9am-5pm, to dusk Jan), originally a quarantine station and army base and off-limits to the public. Quarantine is a legendary surf break at the Rip, and is still only accessible by boat.

### Point Nepean

Point Nepean visitors centre ( ☎ 5984 4276; www.park web.vic.gov.au; Point Nepean; pedestrian or bicycle admission adult/child/family $7/4/20, incl return transport $16/10/42, bike hire per 3hr $17; ☺ 9am-6pm Jan, to 5pm Feb-Apr & Oct-Dec, 10am-5pm May-Sep) has stacks of information. You can walk or cycle to the point (12km return), or take the Point Explorer, a hop-on, hop-off bus service. There are walking trails throughout the park.

Observatory Point is a sheltered picnic spot with wheelchair access from Gunners car park – en route, take a look at the graves of Victoria's first settlers and shipwreck victims.

Cheviot Beach is where prime minister Harold Holt drowned in 1967 (see boxed text, above). On the end of the point is Fort Nepean, which played an important role in Australian defence from the 1880s to 1945. On the parade ground are two historic gun barrels that fired the first Allied shots in WWI and WWII.

This is also home to the annual Point Nepean Music Festival ( ☎ 1300 788 161; www.pointnepeanmusic .com; 2-day ticket adult/child $195/20) held over the Easter weekend.

## Ocean Beaches

The southwestern coastline of the peninsula faces Bass Strait. Along here are the beautiful and rugged beaches of Portsea, Sorrento, Blairgowrie, Rye, St Andrews, Gunnamatta and Cape Schanck. This is spectacular coastal scenery, most familiar to the birdlife, surfers and fisherfolk who all have their secret spots. There are also lovely tidal rock pools where kids like to poke at sea anemones and crab holes. Swimming and surfing is dangerous at these beaches: the undertow and rips can be severe, and drownings continue to occur. Swim only between the flags at Gunnamatta and Portsea during summer.

Parks Victoria staff collect a $4.30 car park fee along this stretch during summer, but the one ticket allows you to come and go and enter any of the beach car parks. One exception is postcard-perfect Koonya Beach at the end of Hughes Rd, where there's no fee. Here there are march flies as big as budgerigars – lather up with repellent!

Occasionally these ocean beaches are used by surf schools (but mostly they operate at Point Leo in Westernport Bay). If you want to learn to surf contact East Coast Surf School ( ☎ 0417-526 465; www.east coastsurfschool.net.au) or Mornington Peninsula Surf School ( ☎ 0417-338 079; www.greenroomsurf.com.au).

You can ride along wild Gunnamatta beach with Gunnamatta Trail Rides ( ☎ 5988 6755; www.gunna matta.com.au; cnr Truemans & Sandy Rds, Rye; 1-/2-hour rides $39/77).

## TRANSPORT: MORNINGTON PENINSULA

Distance from Melbourne Mornington 65km, Flinders 109km, Sorrento 112km

Direction Southeast

Travel time Mornington one hour, Flinders 1½ hours, Sorrento two hours

Bus From Frankston train station (on Melbourne's suburban network), Portsea Passenger Service ( ☎ 5986 5666; www.grenda.com.au) bus 788 runs to Portsea ($5, 1½ hours, half-hourly Monday to Saturday, two-hourly Sunday) via Mornington, Dromana and Sorrento.

Peninsula Bus Lines ( ☎ 9786 7088; www.grenda.com.au) buses 782 and 783 run from Frankston train station to Flinders ($5.50, 1½ hours, hourly Monday to Friday, two-hourly Saturday and Sunday) via Hastings.

Car Moorooduc Hwy and Point Nepean Rd both siphon into the Mornington Peninsula Fwy, the main peninsula access. Alternately, exit the freeway at Mornington and take the coast road around Port Phillip Bay. Access to the back beaches between Rye and Flinders is via a tangle of roads best approached with a map.

Ferry Inter Island Ferries ( ☎ 9585 5730; www.interislandferries.com.au; return adult/child/bike $20/10/8; ☺ every 30min 8.30am-5pm daily, plus 7pm Friday) runs between Stony Point and Cowes via French Island.

Queenscliff–Sorrento Car & Passenger Ferries ( ☎ 5258 3244; www.searoad.com.au; one-way foot passenger adult/ child $9/7, 2 adults & car standard/peak $58/64; ☺ hourly) runs between Sorrento and Queenscliff.

## Cape Schanck

Built in 1859, Cape Schanck Lightstation ( ☎ 5988 6184, 0500-527 891; museum only adult/child/family $10/8/30, museum & lighthouse $14/11/38, parking $4; ☺ 10.30am-4pm) is an operational lighthouse, with a kiosk, museum and visitors centre. You can stay at Cape Schanck B&B ( ☎ 5988 6184; www.austpacinns.com.au; d $165) in the limestone Keeper's Cottage.

From the lightstation, descend the steps of the boardwalk that lead to the craggy cape for outstanding views. Longer walks include tracks to Bushrangers Bay, which can be approached from Cape Schanck or the Bushrangers Bay car park on Boneo Rd – about 40 minutes each way. Wild Fingal Beach is a one-hour return walk, 2km north of the cape.

## FLINDERS
### pop 750
Where development has irreparably changed many small coastal communities, little Flinders, where the thrashing ocean beaches give way to Westernport Bay, has been largely spared. It's a delightful little town, originally known as Black Head, and is home to a busy fishing fleet. Surfers have been coming to Flinders for decades, drawn by oceanside breaks like Gunnery, Big Left and Cyril's, and golfers know the clifftop Flinders course as the most scenic and wind-blown in Victoria. Hang-gliders launch off the oceanside cliffs.

European settlement started here around 1850, and Chinese prospectors on their way to the Western District goldfields landed at Flinders to avoid the £10 immigration tax that Melbourne and Geelong ports exacted. The Navy still maintains the West Head Gunnery Range and lets a few big'uns off into Bass Strait now and then – BOOM!

Flinders Bakehouse Café ( ☎ 5989 0091; 60 Cook St; mains $6-18; ☺ breakfast & lunch daily, dinner Wed) This is the original home of Flinders Bread (now owned by a conglomerate and made in Dandenong!), but the folks who operate this licensed bakery-café-food store still bake great bread in a wood oven, and serve up pasta, pies and fresh sandwiches.

Flinders Hotel ( ☎ 5989 0201; www.flindershotel.com .au; cnr Cook & Wood Sts; d $110-130; mains $17-28; ☺ lunch & dinner; ☒ ) The historic Flinders Hotel has been a beacon on this sleepy street corner longer than anyone can remember. Out back is a modern accommodation wing with recently refurbished en suite units that are comfortable with tasteful décor. The real joy is in the award-winning pub dining room where pub grub goes gastronomic – nothing too fussy, just staple dishes done really well.

Flinders Caravan Park ( ☎ 5989 0458; www.flinderscara vanpark.com.au; 1- 7 The Avenue; powered sites $40, d cabins $95-135) Just a short walk to the bay beach, this is a shady park with good amenities. Ask proprietor Judy about midweek discounts and deals for longer stays.

Papillon B&B ( ☎ 5989 1071; www.papillonbb.com.au; 21 King St; d $150-180; ⊠ ) This purpose-built mud-brick place has two self-contained units in a delightful 1-acre garden. The units are large and comfortable, and 'homely' in their decorative style.

## RED HILL
### pop 480

Red Hill is the centre of the Mornington Peninsula's viticulture and wine-making industries, and is famed for its pinot noir. It's a lovely region of trees and tumbling hills. Online, check out the Mornington Peninsula Vignerons website: www.mpva.com.au.

The popular Red Hill Market (www.craftmarkets.com.au/redhill.asp; ⊗ 8am-1pm) is held the first Saturday of each month.

Among the stand-out wineries here are Montalto ( ☎ 5989 8412; www.montalto.com.au; 33 Shoreham Rd; ⊗ 11am-5pm) and Tuck's Ridge ( ☎ 5989 8660; www.tucksridge.com.au; 37 Shoreham Rd; ⊗ 11am-5pm), both of which produce top-shelf wines and have excellent restaurants.

The Red Hill Brewery ( ☎ 5989 2959; www.redhillbrewery.com.au; 88 Shoreham Rd; ⊗ 11am-5pm Thu-Sun), one of the state's best microbreweries, is a great spot for a German/Belgian-inspired lunch.

La Pétanque ( ☎ 5931 0155; 1208 Mornington-Flinders Rd; set menu $65; ⊗ lunch Wed-Sun, dinner Fri-Sat) and Max's Restaurant ( ☎ 5989 2204; 53 Shoreham Rd; set menu from $70; ⊗ lunch daily, dinner Fri & Sat) are two of the best restaurants in the region. If all this booziness is too much, pick your own strawberries at Sunny Ridge Strawberry Farm ( ☎ 5989 4500; www.sunnyridge.com.au; cnr Shands & Mornington-Flinders Rds; ⊗ 9am-5pm).

## THE DANDENONGS

The verdant Dandenong Ranges, just 35km from Melbourne, make a lovely day trip. You can see the ranges from Melbourne on a clear day. Hardly the Himalayas, Mt Dandenong (633m) is the tallest peak, but the hills do occasionally get a winter sprinkling of snow. The area was intensively logged and most of the majestic mountain ash had been cleared by the end of the 19th century. European settlers planted deciduous oaks, elms and poplars, and now the landscape is a patchwork of exotic and native flora with a lush understorey of tree ferns.

The consumption of tea and scones with lashings of jam and cream is *de rigueur* in the hills, or you can stop for lunch in lovely towns like Olinda, Sassafras and Emerald.

Perennially popular Puffing Billy ( ☎ 9754 6800; www.puffingbilly.com.au; Old Monbulk Rd, Belgrave; Belgrave-Gembrook return adult/child/family $49/25/99) is a restored steam train that toots its way through the Dandenongs' picturesque hills. Kids dangle their feet out the windows and passengers pick flakes of coal dust out of their hair when they alight. There are six departures on holidays, three or four on other days, so you can hop-on/hop-off and enjoy a picnic or walk. Puffing Billy train station is a short walk from Belgrave train station on Melbourne's suburban network.

Emerald Lake Park ( ☎ 1300 131 683; www.emeraldlakepark.com.au; Emerald Lake Rd, Emerald; admission free, full-day parking $6) has picnic areas, a waterslide and swimming pool, paddle boats and Emerald Lake Model Railway ( ☎ 5968 3455; adult/child/family $5.50/3.50/14.50; ⊗ 11am-4pm Tue-Sun). It's the largest HO scale model (1:87) railway in the southern hemisphere, with over 2km of tracks, miniature hills, tunnels, towns and little people.

Dandenong Ranges National Park ( ☎ 13 19 63; www.parkweb.vic.gov.au) is made up of the four largest areas of remaining forest in the Dandenongs. The Ferntree Gully Area has several short walks, including the popular 1000 Steps Track up to One Tree Hill picnic ground (two hours return), part of the Kokoda Memorial Track, which commemorates Australian WWII servicemen who served in New Guinea.

William Ricketts Sanctuary ( ☎ 13 19 63; www.parkweb.vic.gov.au; Mt Dandenong Tourist Rd, Mt Dandenong; adult/child/family $7/3/17; ⊗ 10am-4.30pm) features Ricketts'

---

### TRANSPORT: THE DANDENONGS

**Distance from Melbourne** Upper Ferntree Gully 37km, Olinda 45km, Belgrave 42km

**Direction** East

**Travel time** Upper Ferntree Gully 45 minutes, Olinda one hour, Belgrave one hour

**Bus** Companies operating services within the Dandenong Ranges include Martyrs ( ☎ 5966 2035; www.martyrs.com.au) and US Bus Lines ( ☎ 9752 1444; www.usbus.com.au).

**Car** The Dandenong Ranges are easily accessed from Melbourne via the Burwood Hwy B26 or down the South Eastern Fwy M1 and exiting at Ferntree Gully Rd B22.

**Train** Melbourne's Metlink ( ☎ 13 16 38; www.metlinkmelbourne.com.au) suburban trains run to Belgrave train station.

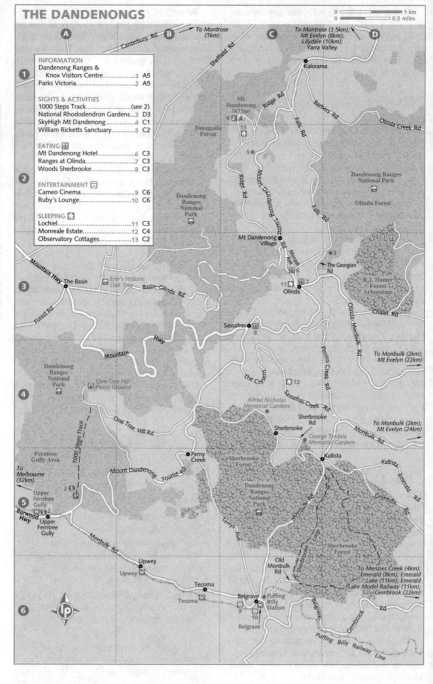

# THE DANDENONGS

0 — 1 km
0 — 0.5 miles

**INFORMATION**
Dandenong Ranges &
  Knox Visitors Centre............1 A5
Parks Victoria.........................2 A5

**SIGHTS & ACTIVITIES**
1000 Steps Track...................(see 2)
National Rhododendron Gardens....3 D3
SkyHigh Mt Dandenong............4 C1
William Ricketts Sanctuary........5 C2

**EATING**
Mt Dandenong Hotel...............6 C3
Ranges at Olinda.....................7 C3
Woods Sherbrooke...................8 C3

**ENTERTAINMENT**
Cameo Cinema........................9 C6
Ruby's Lounge.......................10 C6

**SLEEPING**
Lochiel...................................11 C3
Monreale Estate.....................12 C4
Observatory Cottages..............13 C2

212

sculptures of Aboriginal people, inspired by years spent living among them. We find his renderings, however well intentioned, rather twee, paternalistic and unsettling – Aborigines as angelic bush fairies rather than real people. The sanctuary is set in damp fern gardens with trickling waterfalls.

Giant eucalypts tower over shady lawns and brilliant flowerbeds at the National Rhododendron Gardens ( ☎ 9751 1980; www.parkweb.vic.gov.au; Georgian Rd, Olinda; adult/child/family $8.50/3/19.50; ☘ 10am-5pm) that feature over 15,000 rhododendrons and 12,000 azaleas.

It's worth driving up to SkyHigh Mt Dandenong ( ☎ 9751 0443; www.skyhighmtdandenong.com.au; Observatory Rd, Mt Dandenong; vehicle entry $4; ☘ 10am-10pm Mon-Thu, 8am-10.30pm Fri-Sun) for amazing views over Melbourne from the highest point in the Dandenongs. There's a café-restaurant, garden and picnic areas, and a maze (adult/child/family $6/4/16) here too.

## INFORMATION

Dandenong Ranges & Knox visitors centre ( ☎ 9758 7522; www.dandenongrangestourism.com.au; 1211 Burwood Hwy, Upper Ferntree Gully; ☘ 9am-5pm) Outside the Upper Ferntree Gully train station.

Parks Victoria ( ☎ 13 19 63; www.parkweb.vic.gov.au; Ferntree Gully Picnic Ground, Mt Dandenong Tourist Rd; ☘ 8am-4.30pm Mon-Fri)

## EATING & ENTERTAINMENT

Ranges at Olinda ( ☎ 9751 2133; 5 Olinda-Monbulk Rd, Olinda; lunch $12-20, dinner $22-29; ☘ breakfast & lunch daily, dinner Tue-Sat) This stylish place features Mod Oz food. Breakfasts (available until noon) are hearty and excellent. Pasta and risotto dishes, and pita wraps filled with tandoori chicken or Mexican beef, are among the lunchtime offerings. You can eat alfresco on the deck overlooking the nursery.

Mt Dandenong Hotel ( ☎ 9751 1202; 1451 Mt Dandenong Tourist Rd, Olinda; mains $18-26; ☘ lunch & dinner) Award-winning chef Jake Ward dishes up great gourmet pub food in a relaxed and convivial setting. There's live music on weekends, trivia on Thursday and a $12 'Parma Night' on Wednesday.

Woods Sherbrooke ( ☎ 9755 2131; 21 Sherbrooke Rd, Sherbrooke; mains $18-26; ☘ breakfast & lunch Thu-Sun, dinner Thu-Sat) Hidden in the hills, this is another great café by day, serious mod-Asian restaurant by night. You can dine outdoors in a pleasant garden.

Ruby's Lounge ( ☎ 9754 7445; www.rubyslounge.com.au; 1648 Burwood Hwy, Belgrave; ☘ Tue-Sun) Head to Ruby's for a night out in the Dandenongs. Ruby's is a café-restaurant by day, and at night it morphs into a funky 330-capacity music venue with live gigs Thursday to Sunday.

Cameo Cinema ( ☎ 9754 7844; www.cameocinemas.com.au; 1628 Burwood Hwy, Belgrave; tickets adult/child $15/11) The Cameo is a beautifully restored cinema that has kept its old-fashioned grace. See arthouse, new-release and golden oldie flicks on one of its six screens. It also screens films outdoors in its garden.

## SLEEPING

Observatory Cottages ( ☎ 9751 2436; www.observatorycottages.com.au; 10 Observatory Rd, Mt Dandenong; r $220-300; 🛇 🖳 ) Near the peak of Mt Dandenong, these sumptuous cottages are beautifully decorated in heritage style and furnished with antiques. The grounds are lovely, with formal hedges and flowers.

Monreale Estate ( ☎ 9755 1773; www.monreale-estate.com.au; 81 The Crescent, Sassafras; cottages $200-380; 🛇 ) This beautifully restored 1920s country house has four luxurious cottages in its grounds. The fireside spa is an inspired innovation.

Lochiel ( ☎ 9751 2300; www.lochielaccommodation.com; 1590 Mt Dandenong Tourist Rd, Olinda, d $250-350; 🛇 🖳 ) Nothing quaint or old-world about this place – modern design and décor with every luxury taken care of. Choose one of the three-level cottages or stay in the superb Lochiel house: open fires, timber floors, modern kitchens, tree-top decks, huge plasma TVs and spas, all in a rainforest setting.

# YARRA VALLEY

An hour from Melbourne, the Yarra Valley is brimming with boutique vineyards. Ballooning is popular here, and there are cycling and walking trails. While the Yarra Valley is a popular day trip from Melbourne, the region boasts some fantastic B&Bs and cottages, and there's more to do than you can manage in a day. Healesville has the ever-popular wildlife sanctuary, and is a good base for exploring the Lower Yarra Valley region. Warburton is the centre of the Upper Yarra Valley.

One of Australia's best places to see native fauna is Healesville Sanctuary ( ☎ 5957 2800; www.zoo.org.au; Badger Creek Rd, Healesville; adult/child/family $23/11.50/52.50; ☘ 9am-5pm), a wildlife park that's a huge hit with international visitors who come

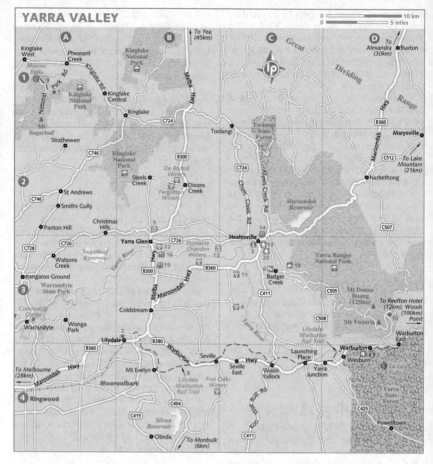

# YARRA VALLEY

to see kangaroos, dingoes, lyrebirds, Tasmanian devils, bats, koalas, eagles, snakes and lizards. The Platypus House displays these shy underwater creatures that you'll never see in the wild, and the exciting Birds of Prey presentation (noon and 2pm daily) features huge wedge-tailed eagles and owls soaring through the air.

The superb TarraWarra Museum of Art ( ☎ 5957 3100; www.twma.com.au; 311 Healesville-Yarra Glen Rd, Healesville; admission $5; ☼ 11am-5pm Tue-Sun) has a permanent collection of modern Australian art dating from the 1950s. Contemporary exhibitions change regularly.

Just north of Yarra Glen is Gulf Station ( ☎ 9730 1286; www.gulfstation.com.au; 1029 Melba Hwy; adult/child $10/free; ☼ 10am-4pm Wed-Sun), a National Trust–classified farm dating back to the 1850s, with

an old slab-timber farmhouse, barns, stables and a slaughterhouse.

Kinglake National Park ( ☎ 13 19 63; www.parkweb .vic.gov.au) is the largest national park near Melbourne, a huge eucalypt forest on the slopes of the Great Dividing Range. In the centre of the park is Kinglake, a small township with a pub and a few shops (but no lake!). Toolangi, 18km east, was the home of CJ Dennis, who wrote the *Sentimental Bloke*. Near the Parks Victoria ( ☎ 5786 5351; www.parkweb.vic.gov.au; National Park Rd, Pheasant Creek; ☼ 8.30am-5pm Mon-Fri, later Dec-Feb) office is the popular Masons Falls Track, an easy 15-minute walk to a waterfall.

Following a 1901 railway line, the 38km Lilydale to Warburton Rail Trail ( ☎ 1300 368 333; www .railtrails.org.au) is a lovely cycling trail. The whole route takes about three hours one way, but it's relatively flat and can be done in sections. The trail starts about 1km from the Lilydale train station. You can hire bikes next door from Lilydale Cycles ( ☎ 9735 5077; 6-8 William St E).

Towering above Warburton is the ruggedly beautiful Yarra Ranges National Park ( ☎ 13 19 63; www.parkweb.vic.gov.au). Mt Donna Buang (1250m) is the highlight of the park, snow-topped in winter. Toboggans can be rented at the toboggan run. Before the summit, the Rainforest Gallery ( ☎ 5966 5996; admission free; Acheron Way), also known as the Mt Donna Buang Skywalk, is a fantastic tree-top walk along a 40m observation platform through the rainforest canopy. Check at visitors centres for brochures on other walks in the region's national and state parks, including Warrandyte State Park.

Ballooning over the Yarra Valley is a peaceful way to view the hills and vineyards. Flights with the following operators average about $290 (some offer cheaper midweek rates):

Balloon Sunrise ( ☎ 1800 992 105; www.hotairballooning.com.au)

Global Ballooning ( ☎ 9428 5703; www.globalballooning.com.au)

Go Wild Ballooning ( ☎ 9739 0772; www.gowildballooning.com.au)

## INFORMATION

Warburton Water Wheel visitors centre ( ☎ 5966 9600; www.yarravalleytourism.asn.au; 3400 Warburton Hwy,

Warburton; 🕒 11am-3pm Mon-Fri, 10am-5pm Sat, Sun & holidays) Information on the Upper Yarra Valley.

Yarra Valley visitors centres ( ☎ 5962 2600; www.yarravalleytourism.asn.au; Harker St, Healesville; 🕒 9am to 5pm) The main info centre for the Lower Yarra Valley.

Yarra Valley Wine (www.yarravalleywine.com) The latest on the local wine scene.

## TOURS

Adventure Canoeing ( ☎ 9844 3323; www.adventurecanoeing.com.au; self-guided tour 2hr/full-day per person $45/60, guided tour $120) Hires out canoes and runs Yarra River tours around Warrandyte State Park.

Eco Adventure Tours ( ☎ 5962 5115; www.ecoadventuretours.com.au) Offers nocturnal wildlife-spotting walks in the Healesville and Marysville area.

Yarra Valley Winery Tours ( ☎ 5962 3870; www.yarravalleywinerytours.com.au; tours from $85)

## EATING & SLEEPING

Bodhi Tree Café ( ☎ 5962 4407; 317 Maroondah Hwy, Healesville; mains $9-16; 🕒 dinner Wed-Fri, lunch & dinner Sat & Sun) Friendly eco vibes and chillin' karma flow from the earth-conscious hippies milling about the salvaged-wood furniture and pot-belly stove here. There are vego options aplenty, a kiddie-friendly menu, shifting art exhibitions and mellow live music on Friday and Saturday.

Yarra Valley Dairy ( ☎ 9739 0023; www.yvd.com.au; McMeikans Rd, Yering; mains/degustation platters from $18/20; 🕒 lunch) These renowned cheesemakers sell cheese, produce and wine from their picturesque farm gate. Eat cheese platters in the dairy's refurbished milking shed, while feasting on the valley views.

Reefton Hotel ( ☎ 5966 8555; 1600 Woods Point Rd, McMahons Creek; meals $7-15; 🕒 lunch & dinner) A bona fide slice of colonial Australiana, the Reefton is authentic. Eat your fish and chips or burger out back near the kiln or in the fancier restaurant. The beautiful winding drive to get out here is popular with motorcyclists who discuss conrods on the veranda. Follow Warburton's Main Rd east.

Badger Creek Holiday Park ( ☎ 5962 4328; www.badgercreekholidays.com.au; 419 Don Rd, Badger Creek; powered sites $35, d cabins $80-160; 🐕 🏊 ) This riverside park has an adventure playground, games rooms, camp kitchen, pool and tennis courts. The many accommodation options include a house that sleeps 10.

## TRANSPORT: YARRA VALLEY

**Distance from Melbourne** Healesville 65km, Warburton 113km

**Direction** Northeast

**Travel time** Healesville one hour, Warburton 1½ hours

**Bus** McKenzie's Bus Lines ( ☎ 5962 5088; www.mckenzies.com.au) runs from Lilydale train station to Healesville ($2.70, 1½ hours) and Yarra Glen ($2.70, 30 minutes) at least hourly from 6am to 9pm.

Martyrs ( ☎ 5966 2035; www.martyrs.com.au) buses run from Lilydale train station to Yarra Junction ($2.70, 35 minutes) and Warburton ($2.70, 50 minutes) at least hourly between 6am and 9pm.

**Car** Maroondah Hwy (B360) runs east from Melbourne to Lilydale, continuing northeast through Coldstream and Healesville. The Warburton Hwy (B380) runs east from Lilydale to Warburton. The Melba Hwy (B300) branches off the Maroondah Hwy at Coldstream running north to Yarra Glen and Kinglake.

**Train** Melbourne's Metlink ( ☎ 13 16 38; www.metlinkmelbourne.com.au) suburban trains run to Lilydale train station.

**Healesville Hotel** ( ☎ 5962 4002; www.healesvillehotel.com.au; 256 Maroondah Hwy, Healesville; d Sun-Thu $100, Fri $130, Sat incl dinner $315) An iconic Healesville landmark, this restored 1910 hotel offers classic upstairs pub rooms with TV and shared bathrooms. The Saturday night accommodation-and-dinner package books out months in advance. Downstairs there's a café (mains $8 to $16) and a formal dining room (mains $29 to $39) that's one of the area's culinary showstoppers.

**Tuck Inn** ( ☎ 5962 3600; www.tuckinn.com.au; 2 Church St, Healesville; d incl breakfast $145-175) This former Masonic Lodge has been refitted in contemporary style – a beautiful and stylish guesthouse with friendly hosts. Five immaculate en suite rooms – three queen and two king – have plush mattresses with quality linen and luxury woollen quilts.

**Alpine Retreat Hotel** ( ☎ 5966 2411; www.alpineretreat.com.au; 12 Main St, Warburton; budget s/d from $60/85, standard s/d/f $105/145/165) The sprawling, 33-room, faux-Tudor Alpine Retreat has budget, upmarket and family rooms with and without en suites, views, TVs and ghosts in the cupboards. There's good eating here (mains $16 to $30, open for breakfast, lunch and dinner) in wonderful Art Deco surrounds.

# GEELONG

**pop 161,000**

Geelong has long been regarded as Melbourne's ugly little sister. Melburnians tend to laugh derisively when you mention the place, but ask them when they last visited and it'll be years ago. Perhaps because of this, people from Geelong are fiercely parochial – their Geelong Cats football team won the 2007 AFL Grand Final (after a 44-year drought), and the city,

home to the Ford Motor Company, has long been a lynchpin of Victorian manufacturing.

The Wathaurong people – the original inhabitants of Geelong – called the area Jillong. Today's Geelong has had a stunning waterfront makeover, replete with beaches, restaurants and bars, on the shores of Corio Bay. Add to that the thriving student scene and a recent population boom, and you'll find an edgy and bohemian enclave at Geelong's heart. The city continues to suffer a weird, architectural identity crisis, with superb historic buildings and even Bauhaus-style industrial buildings sitting next to tragic '70s-era prefab-slab shopping malls. But those historic buildings are superb indeed, and there are many likeable aspects to this town. Most people blow through Geelong along the Princess Hwy, past railyards, factories and fast-food chains, and from there it does look unremarkable. But get off the highway and into Geelong's historic heart and brilliant waterfront and be prepared for a surprise!

Wander Geelong's glittering, revamped waterfront, where you can swim, picnic at a foreshore reserve or just gaze at yachts bobbing on Corio Bay. Walking trails extend from Rippleside Park (Bell Pde) – which has a playground, rock pool, jetty, BBQs and picnic tables – right up the hill to Limeburners Point.

Pick up a *Bay-Walk Bollards* brochure from the information kiosk at Cunningham Pier so you can more formally acquaint yourself with Jan Mitchell's 104 famous painted bollards that give the waterfront its unique character. For a different perspective on town, cruise the bay with Freedom Bay Cruises ( ☎ 0418-522 328; cruises adult/child $12/6) or spend five minutes aloft on a 'fun fly' with Geelong Helicopters ( ☎ 0422-515 151; www

# GEELONG

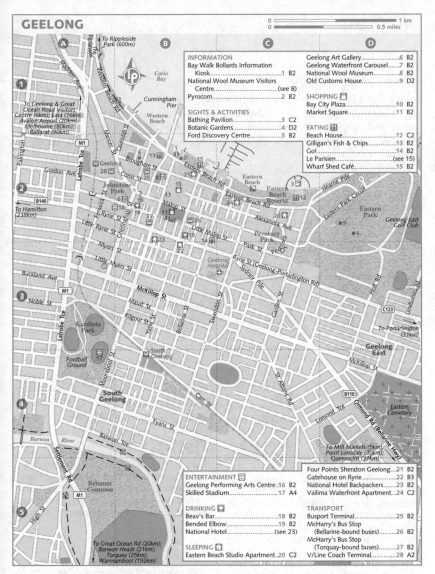

```
0                    1 km
0              0.5 miles
```

**INFORMATION**
Bay Walk Bollards Information
  Kiosk...................................1 B2
National Wool Museum Visitors
  Centre............................(see 8)
Pyrocom..............................2 B2

**SIGHTS & ACTIVITIES**
Bathing Pavilion...................3 C2
Botanic Gardens..................4 D2
Ford Discovery Centre.........5 B2

Geelong Art Gallery..............6 B2
Geelong Waterfront Carousel.....7 B2
National Wool Museum.........8 B2
Old Customs House...............9 D2

**SHOPPING**
Bay City Plaza......................10 B2
Market Square......................11 B2

**EATING**
Beach House.........................12 C2
Gilligan's Fish & Chips..........13 B2
Go!........................................14 B2
Le Parisien......................(see 15)
Wharf Shed Café..................15 B2

**ENTERTAINMENT**
Geelong Performing Arts Centre..16 B2
Skilled Stadium....................17 A4

**DRINKING**
Beav's Bar............................18 B2
Bended Elbow......................19 B2
National Hotel.................(see 23)

**SLEEPING**
Eastern Beach Studio Apartment..20 C2

Four Points Sheraton Geelong...21 B2
Gatehouse on Ryrie..............22 B3
National Hotel Backpackers......23 B2
Vailima Waterfront Apartment...24 C2

**TRANSPORT**
Busport Terminal..................25 B2
McHarry's Bus Stop
  (Bellarine-bound buses).......26 B2
McHarry's Bus Stop
  (Torquay-bound buses).........27 B2
V/Line Coach Terminal..........28 A2

.geelonghelicopters.com.au; flights adult/child $45/35). Both operate on-demand from the waterfront.

Those with kids can ride the ornate hand-carved Geelong Waterfront Carousel ( ☎ 5224 1547; adult/child $3.50/3; ⏰ 10.30am-5pm Mon-Fri, to 8pm Sat, to 6pm Sun), a refurbished 1898 steam-driven carousel built in New York.

At Eastern Beach, stop for a splash about at the Art Deco bathing pavilion, opposite the promenade.

The 1851 Botanic Gardens (in Eastern Park) are a peaceful place for a stroll or picnic. Old Customs House, also in Eastern Park, is Victoria's oldest timber building, built in Sydney in 1838 and transported here in sections. Eastern Park surrounds the gardens and is Geelong's largest foreshore reserve, with many trees planted as early as 1859.

Geelong Art Gallery ( ☎ 5229 3645; www.geelonggallery .org.au; Little Malop St; admission free; ⏰ 10am-5pm Mon-Fri,

## TRANSPORT: GEELONG

Distance from Melbourne **74km**

Direction **South**

Travel time **One hour**

**Air** For Jetstar ( ☎ 13 15 38; www.jetstar.com.au) services to/from Avalon Airport, see p344.

**Bus** Avalon Airport Shuttle ( ☎ 5278 8788; www.avalonairportshuttle.com.au) meets all flights at Avalon Airport and goes to Geelong ($18, 35 minutes) and along the Great Ocean Road to Lorne ($70, 1¾ hours).

Gull Airport Service ( ☎ 5222 4966; www.gull.com.au; 45 McKillop St) has 14 services a day between Geelong and Melbourne Airport ($25, 1¼ hours).

McHarry's Buslines ( ☎ 5223 2111; www.mcharrys.com.au) runs frequent buses to Torquay and the Bellarine Peninsula.

V/Line ( ☎ 13 61 96; www.vline.com.au) buses run from Geelong to Apollo Bay ($13, 2½ hours, two to four daily) via Torquay ($2.50, 30 minutes) and Lorne ($8.50, 1½ hours). On Monday, Wednesday and Friday a bus continues to Port Campbell ($13, four hours) and Warrnambool ($19.40, 5¼ hours). V/Line also runs to Ballarat ($7.50, 1½ hours, three or four daily).

**Car** Princes Hwy (M1) is the main entry and exit point. For Geelong's waterfront, take Bell Pde and follow the Esplanade along the bay.

**Taxi** Geelong Radio Cabs ( ☎ 1800 636 088, 13 10 08).

**Train** V/Line ( ☎ 13 61 96; www.vline.com.au) runs from Geelong train station ( ☎ 5226 6525; Gordon Ave) to Melbourne's Southern Cross station ($9, one hour, frequently). Trains also continue to Warrnambool ($18, 2½ hours, three daily).

1-5pm Sat & Sun) houses over 4000 works in one of the city's most impressive buildings. The Australian collection is strong and includes Frederick McCubbin's 1890 *A Bush Burial*, the gallery's most celebrated painting.

The National Wool Museum ( ☎ 5227 0701; www .nwm.vic.gov.au; 26 Moorabool St; adult/child/family $7.50/4/20; ☻ 9.30am-5pm), in a lovely 1872 bluestone building, showcases the history, politics and heritage of wool growing. There's a sock-making machine and a massive 1910 Axminster carpet loom that still works.

The Ford Discovery Centre ( ☎ 5227 8700; www .forddiscovery.com.au; cnr Gheringhap & Brougham Sts; adult/ child/family $7/3/18; ☻ 10am-5pm Wed-Mon) takes a then-and-now look at Ford (still Geelong's biggest employer). See the 'Cars of the Future' display and the Bathurst-winning Falcons, as well as heritage exhibits. You can buy combined Wool Museum/Ford Discovery Centre tickets for $11.50/5.50/30 per adult/ child/family.

## INFORMATION

Geelong & Great Ocean Road visitors centre ( ☎ 5275 5797; www.greatoceanroad.org; Stead Park, Princes Hwy, Corio; ☻ 9am-5pm) A huge and well-resourced tourist

office by the highway in Geelong, 72km from Melbourne, sharing a prominent roadside spot with McDonalds and KFC.

National Wool Museum visitors centre ( ☎ 5222 2900; www.nwm.vic.gov.au; 26 Moorabool St; ☻ 9.30am-5pm)

Pyrocom ( ☎ 5229 0288; 28 Malop St; ☻ 10.30am-10pm Mon-Sat) Internet access $4 per hour.

## FESTIVALS & EVENTS

Skandia Geelong Week ( ☎ 5229 1418; www.geelong week.com.au; 22-27 Jan) Held on the Eastern Beach foreshore, Skandia is Australia's largest keel-boat regatta and is a sister event to Skandia Cowes Week in the UK. Around 400 yachts compete, and there's a heap of entertainment.

## SHOPPING

The Little Malop St precinct has the boutique speciality shops and designer clothing, or try the following big-scale shopping extravaganzas:

Bay City Plaza ( ☎ 5224 2384; http://westfield.com /geelong; Malop St)

Market Square ( ☎ 5221 2411; www.marketsquare geelong.com.au; cnr Malop & Moorabool Sts)

Mill Markets ( ☎ 5248 2390; http://themillmarkets.com .au; 114 Bellarine Hwy, Newcomb; ☻ 10am-6pm) For collectibles and curios.

# EATING

**Gilligan's Fish & Chips** ( ☎ 5222 3200; 100 Western Beach Rd; mains $10-17; ☽ lunch daily, dinner Thu-Sun) Gilligan's has been frying chips and flippin' flake for eons. It's a colourful, licensed place with jaunty sea creatures painted on the walls and a slightly deranged shark out front.

**Go!** ( ☎ 5229 4752; 37 Bellarine St; mains from $8; ☽ breakfast & lunch Mon-Sat, dinner Mon-Fri) Go! is a fun café that serves great food in a riot of colour and amusement, though you may need an interpreter to make sense of the humorous menu.

**Wharf Shed Café** ( ☎ 5221 6645; 15 Eastern Beach Rd; pizzas $13-17, mains $12-22; ☽ lunch Mon-Sun, breakfast Sat & Sun) Below Le Parisien, this spacious waterfront café serves good Mod Oz meals like chicken souvlaki, gourmet pizzas, beef burgers and filo parcels. But really, it's all about the view. Sit outside and they'll hold onto your credit card lest you do a runner!

**Le Parisien** ( ☎ 5229 3110; 15 Eastern Beach Rd; mains $30-45; ☽ lunch Sat & Sun, dinner Thu-Mon) You can feast on classic French cuisine *à l'Australienne* (try the kangaroo fillet with bush-tomato chutney) right on the water. All the favourites on the meat-heavy menu are done extremely well.

**Beach House** ( ☎ 5221 8322; Eastern Beach Reserve; mains $28-35; ☽ dinner Wed-Sat) In a town blessed with fantastic waterfront restaurants, this might be the best. The modern international menu includes a seafood paella, eye fillet and char-grilled pork over braised cabbage. A sure bet for starters is the pan-seared Lakes Entrance scallops. The café downstairs is more casual.

# DRINKING & ENTERTAINMENT

**Bended Elbow** ( ☎ 5229 4477; www.thebendedelbow.com.au; 69 Yarra St; meals $8-24) This Brit boozer with English brews on tap has live bands Friday and Sunday nights and snug booths where you can curl up with a jar or two. Upstairs, Level 1 is a club space that plays dance pop.

**National Hotel** ( ☎ 5229 1211; www.nationalhotel.com.au; 191 Moorabool St) Live bands play regularly at Geelong's rockingest pub, which has a young clientele and upstairs backpacker accommodation (see right). Feast on the cheap, generous wok-tossed noodles and Asian soups at the Noodle Bar (mains $8 to $11; lunch Tuesday to Friday, dinner Tuesday to Sunday).

**Beav's Bar** ( ☎ 5222 3366; www.beavsbar.com.au; 77 Little Malop St; ☽ 4pm-late Wed-Sat) Chilled out with lounge chairs, soft lighting and eclectic décor. On Tuesday nights the space hosts screenings for the Red Rum Film Society (http://redrumfilmsociety.googlepages.com).

**Geelong Performing Arts Centre** (GPAC; ☎ 5225 1200; www.gpac.org.au; 50 Little Malop St) Geelong's major arts venue has two theatres – an 800-seater and a 300-seater. Local amateur productions are performed here, as well as touring professional dance, musicals and theatre shows.

**Skilled Stadium** ( ☎ 5225 2300; Kardinia Park; Moorabool St; tickets through www.ticketmaster.com.au from $23.90) This is the home of the mighty Cats, and on weekends in winter you can join the one-eyed crowd to watch Gary Ablett Jnr (son of God), Jimmy Bartel (2007 Brownlow Medal winner) and Lingie 'run around the park'. Cricket is played here over summer.

# SLEEPING

**Gatehouse on Ryrie** ( ☎ 0417-545 196; www.bol.com.au/gatehouse/g.html; 83 Yarra St; s $80, d incl breakfast $95-120; ☐ ) This central guesthouse (built in 1897) has good-value rooms with double-glazed windows that are warm in winter and quiet year-round. There's a communal kitchen and lounge area.

**Eastern Beach Studio Apartment** ( ☎ 0431-301 642; kaninaglen@dodo.com.au; 2 Pevensey St; d from $140) In a great location above the bathing pavilion, this modern, compact, two-bedroom apartment can sleep four.

**Vailima Waterfront Apartment** ( ☎ 5229 8818; www.vailima.com.au; 26 Eastern Beach Rd; d from $250; ☒ ) The apartment in this 1908 Edwardian home is tastefully decorated with modern kitchen and laundry, large lounge and brilliant Corio Bay views from the sun deck.

**National Hotel Backpackers** ( ☎ 5229 1211; www.nationalhotel.com.au; 191 Moorabool St; dm $22) 'The Nash' (see also left) is a friendly place and Geelong's only backpacker accommodation. The dorms are old, tired and squishy, but there are free lockers, tea and coffee, and linen is supplied. Downstairs there's one of Geelong's favourite watering holes, with live bands and DJs to keep you going all night – a mixed blessing.

**Four Points Sheraton Geelong** ( ☎ 5223 1377; www.fourpoints.com/geelong; 10-14 Eastern Beach Rd; r from $200; ☒ ☐ ☒ ) The Four Points is the top digs in town. It's a true international hotel in a great waterfront location with everything that opens and shuts, and efficient uniformed staff to attend to your every whim (almost). The beach-facing balcony rooms come at a premium, but rooms without views are often available as packages.

# BELLARINE PENINSULA

The Bellarine Peninsula forms the northwestern side of the entrance to Port Phillip Bay. The bay itself is huge but the heads between Point Nepean on the Mornington Peninsula and the Bellarine's Point Lonsdale are just 3.5km apart. Bellarine beach communities are affluent areas, and the region has surf beaches, mellow seaside towns, cafés and restaurants, making it a nice region to explore. The peninsula also has accessible diving and snorkelling sites.

Accommodation prices soar from Christmas to the end of January, when even some caravan parks have minimum-stay requirements. Many places also charge more at weekends, even in the depths of winter.

## QUEENSCLIFF

**pop 3900**

Historic Queenscliff is a lovely spot, popular with day-tripping and overnighting Melburnians who come for fine food and wine, boutique and antique shopping and leisurely walks along the splendid beach. The views across the Port Phillip Heads and Bass Strait are glorious.

Queenscliff was established for the pilots who to this day steer all ships through the treacherous Port Phillip Heads. Known as 'the Rip', this is one of the most dangerous seaways in the world. In the 1850s Queenscliff was a favoured settlement for diggers who'd struck it rich on the goldfields, and wealthy Melburnians and the Western District's squattocracy flocked to the town. Extravagant hotels

and guesthouses built then are operational today, giving Queenscliff a historic charm and grandness.

Impressive historic buildings line Gellibrand St. Check out the old Ozone Hotel (being refurbished as apartments), Lathamstowe (44 Gellibrand St), Queenscliff Hotel (16 Gellibrand St), and a row of old pilots' cottages (66 & 68 Gellibrand St) dating back to 1853. The main drag, Hesse St, runs parallel to Gellibrand St. King St takes you to Point Lonsdale, and the ferry terminal is on Larkin Pde.

The visitors centre (see Information) runs the 45-minute guided Queenscliff Heritage Walk ($12 incl afternoon tea) at 2pm each Saturday or by appointment.

Fort Queenscliff ( ☎ 5258 1488; cnr Gellibrand & King Sts; adult/child/family $10/5/20; ⏲ tours 1pm & 3pm Sat & Sun) was built in 1882 to protect Melbourne from a feared Russian invasion, although some of the buildings within the grounds date from the 1860s. The 30-minute guided tours take in the military museum, magazine, cells and Black Lighthouse.

The Bellarine Peninsula Railway ( ☎ 5258 2069; www.bpr.org.au; Queenscliff train station; return adult/child/family $18/10/48; ⏲ trips 11.15am & 2.30pm Sun year-round, Tue & Thu school holidays, daily late Dec-early Jan, Tue-Thu, Sat & Sun mid-late Jan) is run by a group of cheerful volunteer steam-train tragics, and has some beautiful steam-hauled trains that ply the 1¾-hour return journey to Drysdale.

Popular with cyclists, joggers and walkers, the adjacent Bellarine Rail Trail runs 34km between the Geelong Showgrounds and Queenscliff.

Queenscliff Maritime Museum ( ☎ 5258 3440; 1 Weeroona Pde; adult/child $6/3; ⏲ 10.30am-4.30pm Mon-Fri, 1.30-4.30pm Sat & Sun) is home of the last lifeboat to serve the Rip, and out back there's a quaint boat shed lined with paintings. They also run 30-minute tours of the working Point Lonsdale Lighthouse.

Sea-All Dolphin Swims ( ☎ 5258 3889; www.dolphinswims.com.au; Larkin Pde; sightseeing adult/child $60/50, 4hr swim $115/100; ⏲ 8am & 1pm Sep-May) offers sightseeing tours and swims with seals and dolphins in Port Phillip Bay.

Queenscliff Dive Centre ( ☎ 5258 1188; www.divequeenscliff.com.au; 37 Learmonth St; per dive with/without gear $110/55) can get you out exploring the wrecks of the area.

## Information

Queenscliff visitors centre ( ☎ 5258 4843; www.queenscliffe.vic.gov.au; 55 Hesse St; ⏲ 9am-5pm; 🖵 ) Internet access $6 per hour (also available next door at the library).

**BELLARINE PENINSULA**

0 _____ 10 km
0 _____ 5 miles

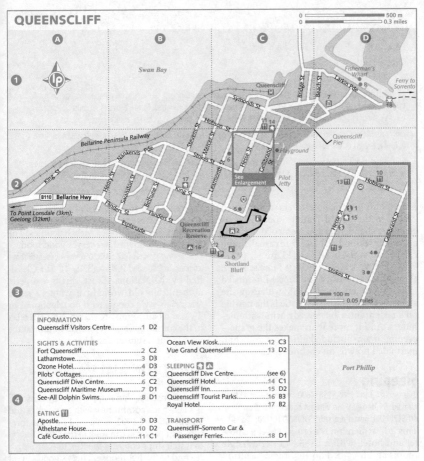

**INFORMATION**
Queenscliff Visitors Centre................1 D2

**SIGHTS & ACTIVITIES**
Fort Queenscliff..................................2 C2
Lathamstowe.....................................3 D3
Ozone Hotel.......................................4 D3
Pilots' Cottages..................................5 C2
Queenscliff Dive Centre.....................6 C2
Queenscliff Maritime Museum............7 D1
See-All Dolphin Swims.......................8 D1

**EATING**
Apostle..............................................9 D3
Athelstane House.............................10 D2
Café Gusto.......................................11 C1

Ocean View Kiosk.............................12 C3
Vue Grand Queenscliff......................13 D2

**SLEEPING**
Queenscliff Dive Centre................(see 6)
Queenscliff Hotel.............................14 C1
Queenscliff Inn................................15 D2
Queenscliff Tourist Parks.................16 B3
Royal Hotel......................................17 B2

**TRANSPORT**
Queenscliff–Sorrento Car &
 Passenger Ferries...........................18 D1

## Festivals & Events

Queenscliff Music Festival ( ☎ 5258 4816; www.qmf.net
.au; last weekend Nov) Features Australian musos with a
folksy, bluesy bent.

Blues Train (www.thebluestrain.com.au) Get your foot
tapping with irregular train trips that feature rootsy music
and meals; check the website for dates and artists.

## Eating

Ocean View Kiosk ( ☎ 5258 4488; 140 Hesse St; lunch $6-10;
☺ breakfast & lunch Thu-Mon, daily Jan) Vicki and Ben
run this takeaway kiosk serving up whopping
burgers, tasty falafels, good coffee and shakes
overlooking the beach. This is the best takeaway
eatery in Queenscliff and the locals know it!

Athelstane House ( ☎ 5258 1024; www.athelstane.com
.au; 4 Hobson St; lunch $12-25, dinner $39-49; ☺ lunch &
dinner) OK, you'll have to rob the Queenscliff
ferryman to pay for it, but the food and wine
at multi-award-winning Athelstane are simply
outstanding. Feast on a ploughman's lunch in
the all-day café or take your cheesecake to the
courtyard or deck. At dinner it gets serious
with a menu of superb Mod Oz mains, like
the oven-roasted barramundi fillet. Stylish
accommodation is also available.

Café Gusto ( ☎ 5258 3604; 25 Hesse St; breakfast $7-12,
lunch $14-16; ☺ breakfast & lunch daily, dinner Fri & Sat) An-
other favourite Queenscliff eatery, great for
breakfast with a spacious garden out the back.
Even basics like sausages become gourmet
snags in sourdough with onion and homemade
tomato relish. On summer Saturday nights
Gusto runs film screenings in its courtyard.

Vue Grand Queenscliff ( ☎ 5258 1544; 46 Hesse St; café
mains $17-28, restaurant mains $32-39; ☺ breakfast, lunch

221

## TRANSPORT: BELLARINE PENINSULA

Distance from Melbourne Queenscliff 105km

Direction South

Travel time Queenscliff 1½ hours

Bus McHarry's Buslines ( ☎ 5223 2111; www.mcharrys.com.au) connects Geelong with most peninsula towns. A two-hour adult ticket costs $3.50, taking you to Barwon Heads (30 minutes), Ocean Grove (45 minutes), Portarlington (45 minutes), Queenscliff (one hour) and Point Lonsdale (55 minutes). Full-day adult ticket $6.50.

Car From Melbourne the Bellarine Peninsula is easily accessible via the Princess Fwy (M1) to Geelong. Form there follow the signs to the Bellarine Hwy (route 91).

Ferry Queenscliff-Sorrento Car & Passenger Ferries ( ☎ 5258 3244; www.searoad.com.au; one-way foot passenger adult/child $9/7, 2 adults & car standard/peak $58/64; �) 7am-6pm) runs between Queenscliff and Sorrento.

& dinner) This historic hotel offers sophisticated dining in the Grand Dining Room with its elaborate chandeliers and menu of dory fillets and other seafood dishes. More casual dining can be had at the hotel's Café Lure.

Apostle ( ☎ 5258 3097; 79 Hesse St; mains $20-32; ☉ breakfast & lunch daily, dinner Thu-Sun) Ensconced in a lofty former church (1888) with exquisite stained-glass windows, Apostle is the newbie on a restaurant scene already brim with big-hitters. And it more than makes the grade – evening mains include kaffir lime and chilli marinated prawns on coconut rice.

## Sleeping

Queenscliff Inn ( ☎ 5258 4600; www.queensclliffinn.com.au; 59 Hesse St; inn without bathroom incl breakfast d/f $120/188, hostel dm/s/d/f $30/80/110/120; ☒ ☐ ) This Edwardian inn is a cross between a hostel and hotel, with a choice of period-style rooms and four-bed dorms, and a beautiful common area.

Queenscliff Dive Centre ( ☎ 5258 1188; www.divequeenscliff.com.au; 37 Learmonth St; dm/d $33/95; ☒ ) This diving operator has recently opened up some excellent hostel-style accommodation at their Learmonth St headquarters. The terrific shared kitchen and lounge facilities are bright and airy in a central atrium. There's a pool to share with aqualunged diving students.

Queenscliff Tourist Parks ( ☎ 5258 1765; www.queensclifftouristparks.com.au; 134 Hesse St; unpowered sites/cabins $33/120) This simple, council-run camping ground on Queenscliff's recreation reserve is the closest camping ground to town and right on the beach. Shady sites are scarce.

Royal Hotel ( ☎ 5258 1669; www.queenscliff.com.au; 34 King St; d from $95) At the time of writing, the Royal was in the throes of renovations. This remarkable old building (1853) has an amaz-

ing cellar and turret, both of which you can access. The large rooms are nicely refurbished, and some open onto sea-view balconies. The friendly pub downstairs serves good food.

Queenscliff Hotel ( ☎ 5258 1066; www.queensclliffhotel.com.au; 16 Gellibrand St; d from $215; ☒ ☐ ) Classified by the National Trust, this is a superb, authentically old-world luxury hotel – small Victorian-style rooms with no telephones or TVs, and bathrooms are shared. You can relax in the comfortable guest lounges or dine at the wonderful restaurant and bar.

## POINT LONSDALE
### pop 2500

Point Lonsdale, 5km southwest of Queenscliff, is a laid-back community with a few cafés and an operational 1902 lighthouse. From the foreshore car park you can walk to the Rip View lookout to watch ships entering the Rip, to Point Lonsdale Pier and to the lighthouse. There's good surf off the rocky beach below the car park.

Below the lighthouse is Buckley's Cave, where William Buckley lived with Aborigines for 32 years after he escaped from the Sorrento convict settlement (see p208).

Kelp ( ☎ 5258 4797; 67 Point Lonsdale Rd; mains $18-29; ☉ breakfast, lunch & dinner) is a funky, modern café-restaurant. The locals come for all-day breakfasts, lunchtime pita-bread wraps, and Asian and Middle Eastern–inspired evening meals.

Grow Naturally ( ☎ 5258 2508; 59 Point Lonsdale Rd; mains $10-15; ☉ breakfast & lunch) is the new kid on the block – a gourmet café that turns out fine fare for mums with bubs and salty surfers.

Point Lonsdale Guest House ( ☎ 5258 1142; www.pointlonsdaleguesthouse.com.au; 31 Point Lonsdale Rd; r $90-220; ☒ ) has a range of rooms in the former Terminus House (1884), from basic motel rooms to lavish B&B affairs. Lighthouse views come at a premium. There's a communal kitchen, tennis court, games room and BBQ facilities.

Check with the Queenscliff visitors centre (p220) for holiday-house rentals for groups.

## OCEAN GROVE
**pop 11,300**

Ocean Grove, 3km northeast of Barwon Heads and 12km west of Queenscliff, is the big smoke of the Bellarine Peninsula, where folks come for their supermarket and department-store shopping. There are some good surfing breaks around here, and some good scuba diving and snorkelling spots beyond the rocky ledges of the bluff.

Groovy 7th Wave ( ☎ 5255 1521; 64b The Terrace; mains $18-33; ✆ breakfast, lunch & dinner) is one of a clutch of cafés along the Terrace that caters to casual café diners by day and scrubbed-up dinner guests by night. The Bellarine Seafood Sizzle, a sample plate of the day's seafood catch, is the house special.

Ti-Tree Village ( ☎ 5255 4433; www.ti-treevillage.com.au; 34 Orton St; cottages $160-230; ✖ ) is like a glamorous retirement home, with cosy, self-contained garden and spa cottages. The playground and communal barbecue areas make it a popular spot with families grilling their day's catch. There's a weekend two-night minimum stay.

Terrace Lofts ( ☎ 5255 4167; www.terracelofts.com.au; 92 The Terrace; d from $175; ✖ ▣ ) is a terrific spot: four luxurious, self-contained, split-level apartments where the bedrooms overlook cosy, open-plan living areas from huge mezzanines. A short walk to the beach and town, these apartments have wood combustion fires, TVs with DVD and relaxed, modern décor.

## BARWON HEADS
**pop 3000**

At the mouth of the broad Barwon River, Barwon Heads is a haven of sheltered beaches, tidal river flats and chilled-out holiday-makers. Feisty Thirteenth Beach, 2km west, is beacon for surfers. Just 3km west of Ocean Grove, Barwon Heads was made famous as the setting for *Seachange* – a popular TV series – and a decade on still trades on the kudos.

There are short walks around the headland and the Bluff with panoramic sea vistas, and there are scuba-diving spots under the rocky ledges below.

Follow the signs 2km from the town centre to Jirrahlinga Koala & Wildlife Sanctuary ( ☎ 5254 2484; www.jirrahlinga.com.au; Taits Rd; adult/child $14/8), an animal park with pelicans, koalas and a few other Australian natives.

## Eating

Barwon Orange ( ☎ 5254 1090; 60 Hitchcock Ave; mains $18-20; ✆ breakfast, lunch & dinner) Big Bertha – the orange wood-fired oven that cooks up Barwon Orange's crazily topped pizzas – helps the mood along. Innovative menus and quality food earn this café-restaurant a high distinction; breakfast is served until a civilised 3pm.

Starfish Bakery ( ☎ 5254 2772; 78 Hitchcock St; meals $5-9; ✆ breakfast & lunch) This relaxed, colourful bakery-café has views from its windows. Come here for strong coffee, fresh sourdough bread, chunky muffins and toasties, or grab a sandwich. Breakfasts here are fantastic.

At the Heads ( ☎ 5254 1277; Jetty Rd; meals $17-32; ✆ lunch & dinner daily, breakfast Sat & Sun) Built on stilts over the mouth of the river, this light, airy café-restaurant has huge breakfasts, Italian fare and the most amazing views. Its bustling family ambience makes it a fun daytime locale. After dark try the seafood bouillabaisse.

Barwon Heads Hotel ( ☎ 5254 2201; 1 Bridge Rd; mains $18-24; ✆ lunch & dinner) Serving slap-up counter meals from its massive bistro, this is where to come for serious drinking and a few bets on the greyhounds. Accommodation is available, but it's noisy on the weekends.

## Sleeping

Barwon Heads Caravan Park ( ☎ 5254 1115; www.barwoncoast.com.au; Ewing Blyth Dr; unpowered/powered sites $36/45, d/f cabins $123/190, f beach house $235) Right on the Barwon River, this park has tea-tree-shaded sites, tennis courts and playgrounds.

Seahaven Village ( ☎ 5254 1066; www.seahavenvillage.com.au; 3 Geelong Rd; d $170-270; ✖ ) Seahaven, opposite Village Park, is a cluster of self-contained studios and cottages with electric blankets, open fires, full kitchens and entertainment systems.

Moonah Beach House ( ☎ 5254 3145; www.moonahbeachhouse.com.au; 9 Reid St; d from $250) This lovely place, two blocks behind the main drag (Hitchcock Ave), is a fully equipped three-bedroom house that can sleep eight. Tariffs vary depending on the time and length of stay and the numbers of stayers.

A lot of private holiday accommodation is managed by agents, including the following:

Barwon Grove Holiday Rentals ( ☎ 5254 3263; www.bgholidayrentals.com.au)

Beds By the Beach ( ☎ 5254 2419; www.bedsbythebeach.com.au)

# GREAT OCEAN ROAD

The Great Ocean Rd (B100) is one of Australia's most famous road-touring routes, where the Otway Ranges and the sheer limestone cliffs of Port Campbell and Peterborough collapse into the crashing surf of the Southern Ocean. Beyond Apollo Bay, the treacherous Shipwreck Coast – from Cape Otway to Port Fairy – is littered with wrecked vessels. This is some of the planet's most beautiful coastal scenery, a point not lost on the hordes of international tourists in rental Winnebagos making their languorous way past the road's hills and hair-pin turns. The road weaves its way along classic surf beaches before sliding into the Otway Ranges just after Apollo Bay.

The lush Otway Ranges, stretching from Aireys Inlet to Cape Otway, offer revitalising landscapes for bushwalking and camping – most of the coastal section is part of the Great Otway National Park.

Too many visitors drive straight through the open stretches of road, pit-stopping only at the towns and major sights – Lorne, Apollo Bay, the Twelve Apostles – but it's the isolated beaches in between the towns and the thick eucalypt forests in the Otway hinterlands where you can really escape the crowds and truly commune with nature. To miss this is to experience only part of what the region offers. Spend a few weeks scratching below the surface here – this is God's own country.

As we make our way along the Great Ocean Rd we pay our respects to the indigenous peoples of this region – from east to west they include the Gulidjan, Gadubanud, Giraiwurung and the Gunditjmara people.

The first sections of the Great Ocean Rd were constructed by hand – picks, shovels and crowbars – by returned WWI soldiers. Work began in September 1919 and the road between Anglesea and Apollo Bay was completed in 1932.

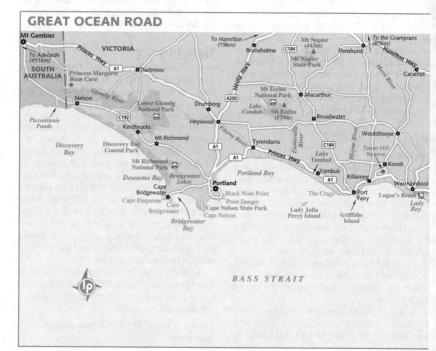

GREAT OCEAN ROAD

## LIGHTHOUSES & SHIPWRECKS

In the era of sailing ships, Victoria's beautiful and rugged southwest coastline was one of the most treacherous on Earth. Between the 1830s and 1930s, more than 200 ships were torn asunder along the so-called Shipwreck Coast between Cape Otway and Port Fairy. From the early 1850s to late 1880s, Victoria's gold rush and subsequent economic boom brought countless ships of prospectors and hopefuls from Europe, North America and China. After spending months at sea many vessels (and lives) were lost on the final 'home straight'. The lighthouses along this coast – at Aireys Inlet (p229), Cape Otway (p237) and Port Fairy (p244) – are still operating. The Cape Otway Lighthouse was also involved in the first telegraph cable laid between Tasmania and the Australian mainland in 1859. The spectacular coast around Port Campbell (p238) is where the *Loch Ard* famously sank, and the town is littered with material salvaged from this and many other shipwrecks. At Wreck Beach (p238) you can see the anchors of the *Marie Gabrielle* which sank in 1869, and the *Fiji*, driven aground in 1891.

## WALKING

The Victorian west coast attracts walkers of all ages and fitness levels who come to enjoy the wide coastal vistas and sea air. The are many coastal walks, along beachfronts and over headlands, that can be done in stages as leisurely strolls or as multiday treks. Visitors centres issue maps of town walking tours that take in historic landmarks and points of interest. The gentle 30km Surf Coast Walk (p227) leaves Torquay and goes to Moggs Creek; the Great Ocean Walk (p234) starts at Apollo Bay and runs all the way to the to the Twelve Apostles; but the biggie is the Great South West Walk (p246), a 250km epic.

## SURFING

The Great Ocean Rd offers fantastic opportunities for surfers with great year-round Southern Ocean swells lashing every beach and point. Wannabes can have lessons in beachside towns between Torquay to the South Australian border. Bells Beach (p227) is one of the most famous surfing spots on the planet, and there's a legendary (read: suicidal) break at Johanna Beach (p237), but every stretch of this coast offers a mix of breaks for beginners and surf-nazis

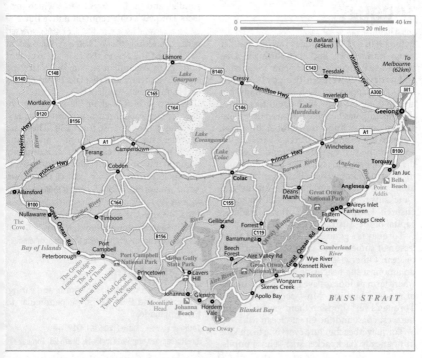

## TRANSPORT: GREAT OCEAN ROAD

Direction from Melbourne Southwest

Travel time Melbourne to Torquay 1¼ hours

Air Fly to Avalon Airport (22km from Geelong) with Jetstar ( ☎ 13 15 38; www.jetstar.com.au). Avalon Airport Shuttle ( ☎ 5278 8788; www.avalonairportshuttle.com.au) runs door-to-door along the Great Ocean Rd as far as Lorne.

Bus McHarry's Bus Lines ( ☎ 5223 2111; www.mcharrys.com.au) runs frequently from Geelong to Torquay, Anglesea and Lorne.

Car M1 Melbourne to Geelong; B100 along the Great Ocean Rd.

Organized tours Go West Tours ( ☎ 1300 736 551; www.gowest.com.au); Ride Tours ( ☎ 1800 605 120; www .ridetours.com.au); Autopia Tours ( ☎ 1800 000 507; www.autopiatours.com.au); Goin South ( ☎ 1800 009 858; www.goinsouth.com.au); Otway Discovery ( ☎ 9654 5432; www.otwaydiscovery.com.au); Wayward Bus ( ☎ 1300 653 510; www.waywardbus.com.au)

Train V/Line ( ☎ 13 61 96; www.vline.com.au) from Melbourne's Southern Cross station to Geelong, connecting with V/ Line buses to Apollo Bay via Torquay, Anglesea and Lorne (continuing to Port Campbell and Warrnambool thrice-weekly). V/Line train/train-bus services also connect Melbourne to Warrnambool, Port Fairy and Portland via the inland A1.

alike. While there are surf shops with hire gear seemingly every 100m along the Great Ocean Rd, it's hard to go past the big-name retail outlets at Surf City Plaza (right) in Torquay, where you can fit yourself out with surf gear, apparel and all possible surfer-guy/chick accoutrements.

# TORQUAY

**pop 6700**

In the 1960s and '70s Torquay was just another sleepy seaside town. Back then surfing in Australia was a decidedly counter-cultural pursuit, and its devotees were crusty hippy drop-outs living in clapped-out Kombis, smoking pot and making off with your daughters. Since then surfing has become unabashedly mainstream and a huge transglobal business. Torquay's rise and rise directly parallels the boom of the surfing industry (and especially the surf-apparel industry). The town's proximity to world-famous Bells Beach and status as home of two iconic surf brands – Ripcurl and Quicksilver, both initially wetsuit makers – ensured Torquay's place as the undisputed capital of the Australian surf industry.

Torquay is a good spot if you're after a surf lesson or some serious shopping for surfwear or gear. Otherwise there's not too much to do amongst the beachside suburban sprawl, where farm paddocks have given way to blocks of modern housing. Most people drop into Torquay's surf shops on their way to or from the west coast and the Great Ocean Rd.

Torquay's beaches lure everyone from kids in floaties to backpacker surf-school pupils.

Fisherman's Beach, protected from ocean swells, is the family favourite. Ringed by shady pines and sloping lawns, the Front Beach beckons lazy bums, while surf life-savers patrol the frothing Back Beach during summer.

There are several good walking trails including the Foreshore Trail, which features a giant sundial, and the Deep Creek Reserve, which protects Torquay's only remnant native flora.

The Surfworld Museum ( ☎ 5261 4606; www.surf world.org.au; adult/child/family $9/6/20; ☼ 9am-5pm), at the rear of the Surf City Plaza, is an excellent homage to Australian surfing, with shifting exhibits, a theatre and displays of old photos and monster balsa mals.

Have a professional surf lesson at one of the gentle beach breaks around Torquay. Two-hour lessons cost from $50. There are countless surf shops in Torquay and along the coast where you can hire boards and buy secondhand equipment. Surf lesson operators include Go Ride A Wave ( ☎ 1300 132 441; www .gorideawave.com.au; 1/15 Bell St, Torquay; 143b Great Ocean Rd, Anglesea; ☼ 9am-5pm summer), Torquay Surfing Academy ( ☎ 5261 2022; www.torquaysurf.com.au; 2/32 Bell St, Torquay; ☼ 9am-5pm summer) and Westcoast Surf School ( ☎ 5261 2241; www.westcoastsurfschool.com; ☼ 9am-5pm summer).

## INFORMATION

The two main streets for shopping and eating, Gilbert St and Bell St, run perpendicular to the Esplanade.

Torquay visitors centre ( ☎ 5261 4219; www .greatoceanroad.org; Surf City Plaza, Beach Rd) Torquay has a well-resourced tourist office in the same building as the Surfworld Museum.

## EATING

**Imperial Rhino** ( ☎ 5261 6780; 3 Bell St; mains $15-25; ☯ breakfast, lunch & dinner) Oodles of noodles – vermicelli, Hokkien, ramen, udon, Singapore, rice stick or just plain flat – with wok-tossed Asian veggies, tofu or Thai red curry. The relaxed atmosphere is 'mod-Zen', with long wooden tables and loads of natural light – a great place for a late lazy breakfast.

**Growlers** ( ☎ 5264 8455; 23 The Esplanade; mains $15-26; ☯ breakfast, lunch & dinner) From the shaded veranda or dark-wood interior you can sneak peeks of the beach through the pines. The menu is inventive; order the coconut-and-banana pancake with mango marmalade.

**Nocturnal Donkey Café** ( ☎ 5261 9575; 6/13 Bell St; mains $17-28; ☯ breakfast, lunch & dinner) This place features seafood in its pastas and risottos, and a non sequitur for a name.

**Scorched** ( ☎ 5261 6142; 17 The Esplanade; mains $27-36; ☯ breakfast, lunch & dinner) This might be the swankiest restaurant in Torquay, overlooking the waterfront, with classy understated décor and windows that open right up to let the sea breeze in. Innovative dishes include a prawn baklava with cardamom-infused cream.

## SLEEPING

**Bells Beach Lodge** ( ☎ 5261 7070; www.bellsbeachlodge.com.au; 51-53 Surfcoast Hwy; dm/d $25/65; ☐ ) This neat budget option is on the highway with good shared facilities, large garden and surfboard

### TRANSPORT: TORQUAY

Distance from Melbourne 98km

Direction Southwest

Travel time Melbourne to Torquay 1¼ hours

Bus McHarry's Buslines ( ☎ 5223 2111; www.mcharrys.com.au) runs buses at least hourly from Geelong to Torquay ($3.50, 30 minutes), arriving/departing Torquay from the corner of Pearl and Boston Sts (behind the Gilbert St shopping centre). V/Line ( ☎ 13 61 96; www.vline.com.au) buses run four times daily Monday to Friday (two on weekends) from Geelong to Torquay ($2.50; 30 mins).

Car Torquay is 30 minutes south of Geelong on the B100.

and bike hire. The dorm rooms are a little 'cosy' but the doubles are good value.

**Woolshed B&B** ( ☎ 5261 2228; www.woolshed.info; 75 Aquarius Way; d $165; ☒ ☒ ) This restored woolshed is 110 years old and has been fitted out with two comfortable suites (with en suites) that share a large lounge area. There's a 25m pool and a tennis court.

**Wattle Court Retreat** ( ☎ 5261 9354; www.wattlecourt.experiencetorquay.com.au; 12 Wattle Ct, Jan Juc; d $200; ☒ ) In suburban Jan Juc, this bright, two-storey timber apartment has a wonderful bush-garden decking and two generous bedrooms. The view from your king-size bed will make you feel nestled amongst the tree tops.

**Torquay Foreshore Caravan Park** ( ☎ 5261 2496; www.gorcc.com.au; unpowered sites from $27, d cabins $70-125) Just behind Back Beach, this is the largest camping ground on the Surf Coast. It has good facilities.

## TORQUAY TO ANGLESEA

The Great Ocean Rd between Torquay and Anglesea heads slightly inland, with a turn-off about 7km from Torquay to Bells Beach. The powerful point break at Bells is part of international surfing folklore (it's here, in name only, that Keanu Reeves and Patrick Swayze had their ultimate showdown in the film *Point Break*). It's notoriously inconsistent, but when the long right-hander is working it's one of the longest rides in the country. Since 1973, Bells has hosted the Rip Curl Pro (www.aspworldtour.com) every Easter – *the* glamour event on the world-championship ASP World Tour. The event draws thousands to watch the world's best surfers carve up the big autumn swells – where waves have reached 5m during the contest! The Rip Curl Pro regularly decamps to Johanna, two hours west, when fickle Bells isn't working. Contact Surfing Victoria ( ☎ 5261 2907; www.surfingaustralia.com) for more details.

Nine kilometres southwest of Torquay is the turn-off to spectacular Point Addis, 3km down this road. It's a vast sweep of pristine 'clothing optional' beach that attracts surfers, hang-gliders and swimmers. There's a signposted Koorie Cultural Walk, a 1km circuit trail to the beach through the Ironbark Basin nature reserve.

The Surf Coast Walk (www.surfcoast.vic.gov.au/walking tracks.htm) follows the coastline from Torquay to Moggs Creek south of Aireys Inlet, and can be done in stages – the full route takes 11 hours. It's marked on the *Surf Coast Touring Map*, available from tourist offices.

## GREAT OCEAN ROAD TRAVEL DISTANCES

| | |
|---|---|
| Melbourne to Geelong | 76km |
| Geelong to Torquay | 22km |
| Torquay to Anglesea | 17km |
| Anglesea to Aireys Inlet | 10km |
| Aireys Inlet to Lorne | 19km |
| Lorne to Apollo Bay | 43km |
| Apollo Bay to Cape Otway | 31km |
| Cape Otway to Port Campbell | 86km |
| Port Campbell to Warrnambool | 67km |
| Warrnambool to Port Fairy | 39km |
| Port Fairy to Portland | 72km |

# ANGLESEA
### pop 2300

Kids in neon-coloured togs and swimming rings with zinc cream striped across their noses, eating ice creams and squinting in the sunlight – it's a classic scene from an overexposed family photograph, and mums and dads have been taking this picture in Anglesea for decades. The town is all about the family seaside getaway, with terrific beaches and good camping. Downtown Anglesea is just a strip of shops on the Great Ocean Rd next to the gum-green Anglesea River, but you can get some good grub here and a decent coffee. The accommodation makes the most of tranquil bush settings. Online, check out www.anglesea.org.au.

Anglesea Golf Club ( ☎ 5263 1582; www.angleseagolf club.com.au; Noble St; 9 holes $25) has a resident kangaroo population that grazes on the fairways as golfers drive and chip balls around them, particularly at early morning and dusk.

Main Beach has some gentle beach-break beginner's surf, while sheltered Point Roadknight Beach is good for kiddies. Hire surf or beach-play equipment from the Anglesea Surf Centre ( ☎ 5263 1530; www.secondhandsurfboards.com.au; 111 Great Ocean Rd; 9am-6pm), which also stocks a huge range of secondhand boards. Go Ride A Wave ( ☎ 1300 132 441; www.gorideawave.com.au; 143b Great Ocean Rd; 9am-6pm), also hires out gear and runs surfing lessons from $55 for two hours.

Eco Logic Education & Environment Services ( ☎ 5263 1133; www.ecologic.net.au) guides kid-oriented 'marine rock-pool rambles', night-time 'possum prowls' and tours of Split Point Lighthouse at Aireys Inlet.

Anglesea Paddleboats ( ☎ 0408-599 942; www.anglesea paddleandcanoe.com), by the river, hires canoes and paddleboats, or you could saddle up at Spring Creek Horse Rides ( ☎ 5266 1541; www.springcreekhorserides .com.au; 245 Portheath Rd, Bellbrae; per hr adult/child $35/28).

## INFORMATION

Offshore Café ( ☎ 5264 5110; 16/87 Great Ocean Rd; breakfast & lunch) Located in the mini mall; has internet access.

## EATING

Angahook Café ( ☎ 5263 1420; 119 Great Ocean Rd; mains $9-$15; breakfast & lunch) This café-cum–gourmet food store is always busy and does excellent coffee, slices and smoothies, good focaccias and freshly made sandwiches.

Pete's Place ( ☎ 5263 2500; 113 Great Ocean Rd; mains $20-29; breakfast, lunch & dinner Tue-Sun) Café by day; classy Mod-Oz seafood restaurant by night. The tables on the front deck make for fine evening alfresco dining and you can choose from a select list of regional wines.

38 Degrees South ( ☎ 5263 1010; 12/87-89 Great Ocean Rd; mains $18-24; breakfast, lunch & dinner) The groovy local café-bar has changed hands (and names) a few times in recent years, but it's still a good spot for some simple food and a drink. This place hosts some of the best live musicians touring the Surf Coast.

## SLEEPING

Anglesea Backpackers ( ☎ 5263 2664; http://home.iprimus.com .au/angleseabackpacker; 40 Noble St; dm/d $35/95) Brightly coloured but basic, daggy but fun, this bunkhouse offers surfboard hire from $25 per day.

Rivergums B&B ( ☎ 5263 3066; 10 Bingley Pde; d $100-160; ) Tucked by the river with tranquil views, these two spacious, tastefully furnished

### TRANSPORT: ANGLESEA

Distance from Melbourne 115km

Direction Southwest

Travel time Melbourne to Anglesea 1½ hours

Bus V/Line ( ☎ 13 61 96; www.vline.com.au) buses link Anglesea with Geelong four times daily Monday to Friday and twice daily on weekends ($4.50, one hour) and Apollo Bay ($8.50, 2½ hours).

Car Anglesea is 15 minutes west of Torquay on the B100.

rooms (a self-contained bungalow and a room attached to the house) are excellent value and 10 minutes' walk to the shops.

Fruit Tree Cottage ( ☎ 5263 2725; 60b Fifth Ave; d from $130; 🐾 ) About 1km from the Point Road-knight beaches, this three-bedroom cottage sleeps six. It has a full kitchen with dishwasher and laundry. Fruit Tree is dog-friendly.

Berean B&B ( ☎ 5263 3633; bereanbb@bigpond.com; 50 Eighth Ave; d $220; 🐾 ) Just 100m from the beach, Berean B&B is stylish, modern and well fitted out with kitchenette and luxurious black-tiled spa bathroom, complete with candles and pebble decorations for canoodling couples. *Très romantique!*

Anglesea Beachfront Family Caravan Park ( ☎ 5263 1583; www.angleseafcp.com.au; 35 Cameron Rd; unpowered sites $30, d cabins from $100; 🖳 🕿 ) With good river and beach access, pool, wireless internet, camp kitchen and the latest camping-park fad: the jumping pillow.

# AIREYS INLET

**pop 760**

The Great Ocean Rd finally meets the coast south of Anglesea and starts its spectacular coastal run. Aireys Inlet is midway between Anglesea and Lorne, and next door to some of the southwest's prettiest beaches. It was originally established as a terminus for the Cobb & Co coach service from Geelong.

There are some great beaches in Aireys, backed by tall, volcanic cliffs, with tidal rock pools along the foreshore just below the lighthouse. A few kilometres towards Lorne, you'll find two particularly glorious stretches at Fairhaven and Moggs Creek. A Surf Life Saving Club patrols the beach at Fairhaven during summer, and at Moggs Creek, hang-gliders launch themselves from the clifftops to land on the sands below.

The 34m-high Split Point Lighthouse and its keepers' cottages were built in 1891. The lighthouse (now fully automated) is still operational and visible 30km out to sea. There are great views from the walking tracks and lookout, and tours are conducted by Eco Logic Education & Environment Services ( ☎ 5263 1133; www .ecologic.net.au) in Anglesea.

Signposted off the main road is a replica of an 1852 settler's hut, made from bark, which was destroyed by the devastating 1983 Ash Wednesday bushfires.

The lovely 3.5km Aireys Inlet Cliff Walk begins at Painkalac Creek, rounds Split Point and makes its way to Sunnymead Beach. The Surf Coast Walk

**TRANSPORT: AIREYS INLET**

Distance from Melbourne 125km

Direction Southwest

Travel time Melbourne to Aireys Inlet 1¾ hours

Bus V/Line ( ☎ 13 61 96; www.vline.com.au) buses link Aireys Inlet with Geelong ($6.50, 1¼ hours) and Apollo Bay ($6.50, 1½ hours) four times daily.

Car Aireys Inlet is 15 minutes west of Anglesea on the B100.

continues along the coast here – pick up a copy of *Walks of Lorne & Aireys Inlet* from visitors centres. Aireys Inlet Caravan Park has a free guide to local walks – signposted trails start from Distillery Creek picnic ground, 2.5km north of Aireys, and the Moggs Creek picnic ground, 3km west of Aireys Inlet.

Blazing Saddles ( ☎ 5289 7322; Lot 1 Bimbadeen Dr; 1¼/2¼hr rides $40/60), about 2km inland, runs horse rides in the bush and along the beach.

# INFORMATION

There's no visitors centre here but you can get good visitor information at www.aireysinlet. org.au. You can access the internet at Aireys Inlet Caravan Park.

# EATING

A La Grecque ( ☎ 5289 6922; 60 Great Ocean Rd; mains $17-30; 🕓 breakfast, lunch & dinner) This modern Greek taverna is outstanding, serving up Greek staples with a contemporary twist and a strong leaning towards local fish and seafood. Kosta, the host, ran famous Kosta's in Lorne for 27 years before decamping to Aireys. This is a great stop for lunch while motoring along the coast road or, better, make a reservation for dinner.

Truffles Café Deli ( ☎ 5289 7402; 34 Great Ocean Rd; mains $15-25; 🕓 breakfast, lunch & dinner) Truffles does the lot – eat in or takeaway, pizza, pasta, curries, good vegetarian choices, licensed and BYO, coffee, homemade cakes, cheerful efficient service and a happy ambience. Big tick.

# SLEEPING

Cimarron B&B ( ☎ 5289 7044; www.cimarron.com.au; 105 Gilbert St; d $180) This house was built in 1979 from local timbers using only wooden pegs and shiplap joins, and is an idyllic getaway with views over Point Roadknight. Rustic yet sophisticated, the large lounge area has book-lined walls and a cosy fireplace, while upstairs there are two unique, loft-style doubles with vaulted timber ceilings, or there's a den-like apartment. Out back, it's all state park and wildlife. Gay friendly but no kids.

Ocean Inlet at Fairhaven ( ☎ 5289 7313; www.ocean inlet.com; 34 Wybellenna Dr, Fairhaven; d $90) This cute gazebo-style bedsit with sofa bed and floor-to-ceiling windows overlooking native gardens has a teensy cabin next door containing a kitchenette (with breakfast bar) and bathroom. Well-heeled couples can swing cats in the sleek Coral Cove or Shorehouse apartments for $250 and $275 respectively.

Surf Coast Cabins ( ☎ 5289 6066; www.surfcoastcabins .com.au; 42 Hopkins St; d from $120) These large, self-contained cabins in a bush setting come in one-, two- and three-bedroom configurations and are ideal for couples or families. They're well fitted out with kitchens and BBQ facilities and are tastefully furnished.

Pole House ( ☎ 5220 0200; 60 Banool Rd, Fairhaven; www.greatoceanroadholidays.com.au; per 2 nights from $780) The Pole House, in nearby Fairhaven, is an iconic Great Ocean Rd landmark, sitting, as the name suggests, atop a pole, with extraordinary views. It was built in the late '70s and retains its authentic kitsch décor, and was one of the few buildings in the area to survive the 1983 Ash Wednesday bushfires. Sleeps four; two-night minimum.

Aireys Inlet Caravan Park ( ☎ 5289 6230; www.aicp .com.au; 19-25 Great Ocean Rd; unpowered/powered sites from $28/30, d en suite cabins from $80; 🖳 🖳 ) This neat little park lacks shade but it's close to the township's few stores.

# LORNE

**pop 1000**

Lorne is packed – 'Full!' say the locals. During summer weekends and holidays it's hard to find a car park let alone a bed for the night, and making your way down the main street can be a challenge, with all the café tables on the footpath, window-shoppers and folks ambling along in holiday-mode. Thanks to its natural beauty, great restaurants, boutique shopping and proximity to the big smoke, Lorne is extremely popular for weekending Melburnians – it's like an outpost of South Yarra chic. It's come a long way since the days of Rudyard Kipling's 1891 visit, whence he penned the poem *Flowers*: 'Gathered where the Erskine leaps, Down the road to Lorne…'

Out of season there's a little more breathing space, but thronged with tourists or not, Lorne is a lovely place built around the Erskine River and the shores of Loutit Bay. Log on to www.visitlorne.org.

Apart from the obvious beachy-themed activities, kids will love the foreshore trampolines, swimming pool and skate park. You can rent paddleboats from Lorne Paddleboat Hire ( ☎ 0408-895 022; www.lorneswingbridgecafe.com; 20min $10; 🕑 8am-sunset) on the Erskine River. The visitors centre has information on the self-guided Lorne Historical Walk and the Shipwreck Plaque Walk. Art-lovers can take in the excellent Qdos Art Gallery ( ☎ 5289 1989; www.qdos.com; 35 Allenvale Rd; 9am-5.30pm Thu-Mon) in the hills about 500m behind town.

There are more than 50km of walking tracks through the Otway Ranges around Lorne. Eco Logic Education and Environment Services ( ☎ 5263 1133; www.ecologic.net.au; walks from $10), based in Anglesea, organises guided walks.

Teddy's Lookout makes for a scenic drive, and heading inland onto picturesque Erskine Falls Rd, there's good walking. At Erskine Falls it's an easy walk to the viewing platform or 250 steps down to the base of the waterfall. Lorne Surf Shop ( ☎ 5289 1673; 130 Mountjoy Pde; 🕑 9am-5.30pm) hires boards and wetsuits, while Southern Exposure ( ☎ 5261 2170; www.southernexposure.com.au; 2hr lessons $55) offers surfing lessons.

## INFORMATION

Lorne visitors centre ( ☎ 1300 891 152, 5289 1152; www.visitsurfcoast.com; 15 Mountjoy Pde; 🕑 9am-5pm) Stacks of information, helpful staff and an accommodation booking service.

Parks Victoria ( ☎ 5289 4100; www.parkweb.vic.gov.au; 86 Polwarth Rd; 🕑 8am-4.30pm Mon-Fri) If you're interested in camping, come here for more details.

## FESTIVALS & EVENTS

Falls Festival (www.fallsfestival.com; tickets $100) A two-day knees-up over New Year's on a farm not too far from town. A top line-up of rock groups; tickets include camping.

Pier to Pub Swim (www.lornesurfclub.com.au) This popular event in January inspires up to 4500 swimmers to splash their way 1.2km across Loutit Bay to the Lorne Hotel; a photo opportunity for local politicians and celebrities.

## EATING

Lorne is the Great Ocean Rd's gourmet capital, and Mountjoy Pde is bumper-to-bumper with great cafés and restaurants. Most are open day and night during summer, but have shorter winter hours. There's a well-provisioned Foodworks Supermarket ( ☎ 5289 1645; 1-3 Great Ocean Rd) at the northern end of town, and for the state's freshest fish and seafood supplies head to Lorne Fisheries ( ☎ 5289 1453; Lorne Pier; ☽ 10am-6pm).

Grandma Shield's Bakery ( ☎ 5289 2639; 152 Mountjoy Pde; sandwiches from $7; ☽ 8am-4pm) No hoity-toity *pain au chocolat* or *ciabatta* here – this old-fashioned hot-bread shop has good pies, pasties and freshly made sandwiches.

Salty Dog Fish & Chippery ( ☎ 5289 1300; Shop 1 Cumberland Resort; ☽ lunch & dinner) Consistently good fish and chips. You can feed yourself and a flock of seagulls for about $8 to $10.

Kafe Kaos ( ☎ 5289 2639; 52 Mountjoy Pde; lunch $8-15; ☽ breakfast & lunch) Bright and perky, Kafe Kaos typifies Lorne's relaxed foodie philosophy – barefoot patrons in boardies or bikinis tucking into first-class *paninis*, bruschettas, burgers and chips. With great veggie options, all-day breakfasts, and coffee, cocktails, beer and wine to wash the sand out of your hair.

Pizza Pizza ( ☎ 5289 1007; 2b Mountjoy Pde; pizzas $12-14; ☽ noon-10.30pm) This tiny shopfront is only big enough for the kitchen – diners takeaway or eat on the footpath tables – but it's been a huge hit, offering pizzas like Punkrock, Alfonz and Spinner.

B Bar & Grill ( ☎ 5289 2882; 81 Mountjoy Pde; mains $18-30; ☽ breakfast, lunch & dinner) This new Greek taverna, right on the sandy beachfront, doles up simple grilled meat and seafood dishes. The location is the best in Lorne. Opens summer only.

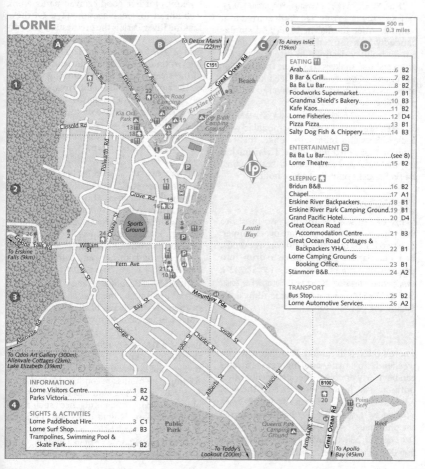

**LORNE**

0 — 500 m
0 — 0.3 miles

EATING 🍴
Arab...................................................6 B2
B Bar & Grill.....................................7 B2
Ba Ba Lu Bar....................................8 B2
Foodworks Supermarket....................9 B1
Grandma Shield's Bakery.................10 B3
Kafe Kaos.......................................11 B2
Lorne Fisheries...............................12 D4
Pizza Pizza.....................................13 B1
Salty Dog Fish & Chippery...............14 B3

ENTERTAINMENT 🎭
Ba Ba Lu Bar..............................(see 8)
Lorne Theatre................................15 B2

SLEEPING 🛏
Bridun B&B....................................16 B2
Chapel...........................................17 A1
Erskine River Backpackers...............18 B1
Erskine River Park Camping Ground..19 B1
Grand Pacific Hotel.........................20 D4
Great Ocean Road
   Accommodation Centre................21 B3
Great Ocean Road Cottages &
   Backpackers YHA.........................22 B1
Lorne Camping Grounds
   Booking Office............................23 B1
Stanmorr B&B.................................24 A2

TRANSPORT
Bus Stop........................................25 B2
Lorne Automotive Services...............26 A2

To Deans Marsh (22km)
To Aireys Inlet (19km)
Beach
C151
Great Ocean Rd
Richardson Blvd
Waverley Ave
Erskine Ave
Ocean Road Camping Ground
Erskine River
Kia Ora Park
Log Bank Camping Ground
Clissold Rd
Polwarth Rd
Grove Rd
Otway St
Sports Ground
Loutit Bay
Erskine Falls Rd
To Erskine Falls (9km)
William St
Fern Ave
Cay St
Bay St
George St
John St
Charles St
Smith St
Mountjoy Pde
Albert St
Francis St
Allenvale Rd
To Qdos Art Gallery (300m);
Allenvale Cottages (2km);
Lake Elizabeth (39km)
Armitage St
Great Ocean Rd
B100
Point Grey
Reef
Public Park
Queens Park Camping Ground
To Teddy's Lookout (200m)
To Apollo Bay (45km)

INFORMATION
Lorne Visitors Centre.........................1 B2
Parks Victoria..................................2 A2

SIGHTS & ACTIVITIES
Lorne Paddleboat Hire.......................3 C1
Lorne Surf Shop...............................4 B3
Trampolines, Swimming Pool &
   Skate Park...................................5 B2

Arab ( ☎ 5289 1435; 94 Mountjoy Pde; mains $20-24; ☺ breakfast, lunch & dinner; ▣ ) Arab started as a beatnik coffee lounge in 1956, and single-handedly transformed Lorne from a daggy family holiday destination into a place for groovers and shakers. It's been trading ever since, and is *the* spot for coffee and all-day breakfasts. Motorcyclists converge on this place like seagulls to a hot chip.

Ba Ba Lu Bar ( ☎ 5289 1808; 6a Mountjoy Pde; mains $18-28; ☺ breakfast, lunch & dinner) Ever-popular with backpackers and billionaires alike, this is a good spot for a predinner tipple. The menu has inspired tapas and some seafood-based mains. Ba Ba Lu kicks on into the wee hours.

## ENTERTAINMENT

Many of Lorne's restaurants add music to their menus and open until late over summer. The two hotels offer live bands on weekends. Ba Ba Lu Bar is a popular place to drink into the morning hours. Lorne Theatre ( ☎ 5289 1272; www.greatoceanroadcinemas.com.au; 78 Mountjoy Pde; adult/child $12.50/9.50) shows new-release films daily during the peak season.

## SLEEPING

There's often a minimum two-night stay on weekends in Lorne, and high-season rates can be nearly double winter prices. For other options, ask the visitors centre or the Great Ocean Road Accommodation Centre ( ☎ 5289 1800; www.gorac.com.au; 136 Mountjoy Pde; ☺ 9am-5.30pm), next to the pharmacy. Lorne Camping Grounds Booking Office ( ☎ 5289 1382; 2 Great Ocean Rd; unpowered/powered sites from $20/25, onsite vans $60, d cabins from $100) manages

bookings for five good caravan parks. Book well ahead for peak-season stays. Of these Erskine River Park is the prettiest; on the left-hand side as you enter Lorne, just before the bridge. The four others are Top Bank Camping Ground, nestled along the southern bank of the river; Ocean Road Camping Ground, on the right-hand side of the Great Ocean Rd as you enter Lorne, opposite Erskine River Park; Kia Ora Park, also on the right, tucked beside the bridge; and hillside Queens Park Camping Ground, 2½ kilometres further at the southern end of town.

Great Ocean Road Cottages & Backpackers YHA ( ☎ 5289 1070; www.yha.com.au; 10 Erskine Ave; tents $20, dm $20-24, d $55-62, cottages $170) Tucked away in the bush among the cockatoos and koalas, this two-storey timber lodge has spacious dorms, bargain tents with beds already set up, and top-value doubles. Unisex bathrooms take some getting used to. The A-frame cottages sleep four (six at a squeeze), with kitchens and bathrooms.

Erskine River Backpackers ( ☎ 5289 1496; 6 Mountjoy Pde; dm/d $25/70) Beautiful verandas line this classic old building by the river at the north end of town. It's a relaxed place with four-bunk dorms and great communal spaces.

Stanmorr B&B ( ☎ 5289 1530; www.stanmorr.com; 64 Otway St; d $140, ste $250) Sheltering in the hills, this B&B is a Lorne institution, with helpful owners and kookaburras that come for hand-feeding. The rooms are comfortable and some have bay views. The suite has the best aspect, along with romantic indulgences such as the gas fire, spa and languorous 11am checkout.

Bridun B&B ( ☎ 5289 1666; www.bridun.com.au; 1 Grove Rd; d $190) One of Lorne's original buildings, this 1920s weatherboard place, just off the main street, has timber floors and many authentic period furnishings. A hearty breakfast is thrown in, but it's the location that's the clincher – 25m to the main drag and 100m to the beach.

**Allenvale Cottages** ( ☎ 5289 1450; www.allenvale.com.au; 150 Allenvale Rd; d from $195) We keep coming back here – four self-contained early-1900s timber cottages that each sleep four (or more) that have been luxuriously restored. They're 2km northwest of Lorne, arrayed among shady trees and green lawns, complete with bridge and babbling brook. There are walking and cycling trails and it's ideal for families.

**Chapel** ( ☎ 5289 2622; thechapellorne@bigpond.com; 45 Richardson Blvd; d $200; ☒ ) Outstanding – this contemporary two-level bungalow has been lifted from the pages of a glossy magazine, with tasteful Asian furnishings, splashes of colour and bay windows that open into the forest. It's secluded and romantic, with double shower and complimentary robes.

**Grand Pacific Hotel** ( ☎ 5289 1609; www.grandpacific.com.au; 268 Mountjoy Pde; d from $180) This iconic Lorne landmark, harking back to 1875, has been restored with a sleek modern décor that retains some classic period features. The best rooms have balconies and stunning sea views, though plainer rooms are still luxurious. It's a popular weekend wedding venue.

# CUMBERLAND RIVER TO SKENES CREEK

Just 7km southwest of Lorne is Cumberland River. There's nothing here – no shops or houses – other than the wonderful Cumberland River Holiday Park ( ☎ 5289 1790; www.cumberlandriver.com.au; Great Ocean Rd; unpowered sites $28, en suite cabins from $105). This splendidly located bushy camping ground is next to a lovely river and high craggy cliffs that rise on the far side. The ocean beach offers surfing and swimming, and there are many walks upriver and over the hills. We've been coming here since we were kids.

The Great Ocean Rd snakes spectacularly around the cliff-side for another few kilometres until it levels out at the mouth of Wye River (pop 140). Nestled discreetly in the pretty (steep!) hillsides are some modest holiday houses and a few grander steel-and-glass pole-frame structures built on the 'challenging' housing sites. A large part of town is taken up by the 25-acre Wye River Valley Tourist Park ( ☎ 5289 0241; www.wyerivervalleypark.com.au; 25 Great Ocean Rd; unpowered/powered sites $30/38, d en suite cabins

$120), which has all the facilities of a modern 'holiday park' including the essential jumping pillow. The pretty Wye River babbles through the park and there's a beach across the road. From December through April the Wye River Foreshore Camping Reserve ( ☎ 5289 0412) offers powered beachside camp sites.

Also here is the Wye Beach Hotel ( ☎ 5289 0240; www.wyebeachhotel.com.au; 19 Great Ocean Rd; d $140-170, mains $18-30; ☽ lunch & dinner; ☐ ), where people come for excellent pub food. It's in a fantastic location on the hillside with rugged ocean views. There are comfortable motel-style double rooms, all with great views. This hotel is a favourite stop along the Great Ocean Rd, if only for a soft drink and a bowl of chips.

Several private holiday houses in Wye River are managed by Holiday Great Ocean Road ( ☎ 5237 4201; www.holidaygor.com.au).

Another 5km along is Kennett River, which has the best koala spotting on the southwest coast. Behind the caravan park, walk 200m up Grey River Rd and you'll see bundles of sleepy koalas clinging to the branches. *Ooh aah!* There are glow worms that shine at night up the same stretch of Grey River Rd (take a torch).

The Kennett River Caravan Park ( ☎ 1300 664 417, 5289 0272; www.kennettriver.com; unpowered/powered sites $25/29, d cabins from $110; ☐ ) has free wireless internet throughout the park and coin-operated electric BBQs for multitaskers. Be camera-ready for stunning Cape Patton lookout, about 4km beyond Kennett River. From here to Skenes Creek, the land rolls and folds dramatically in camel-hump hills. Wongarra, 8km south of Cape Patton, has an appealing moody, windswept quality.

# APOLLO BAY

**pop 1400**
Apollo Bay is a lovely place, one of the Great Ocean Rd's major attractions. While this former fishing town is more relaxed and less trendy than Lorne, property moguls seem to be using her big sister to the northeast as a template for Apollo Bay's impending rampant overdevelopment. When every shop is a surf-boutique or coffee shop there'll be nowhere to buy an onion. Locals – fisherfolk, artists, musicians and sea-changers – seem to be resigned to this, and while they lament the loss of the old pre-yuppie days, their house values have doubled while you've been reading this.

Majestic rolling hills provide a postcard backdrop to the town, while broad, white-sand beaches dominate the foreground. It's

## DETOUR: APOLLO BAY–LAVERS HILL–BEECH FOREST

A great day-drive is from Apollo Bay to Beech Forest via Lavers Hill and Melba Gully State Park. It becomes a loop if you take Aire Valley Road (which becomes Binns Track) from Beech Forest back to Apollo Bay, but be warned: this narrow, logging-truck route is not advised for conventional vehicles. It is badly corrugated, mushy clay, arduous driving and certainly no short cut! In winter, it's out of bounds to everyone.

Lavers Hill is 48km from Apollo Bay. This often mist-shrouded hilltop was once a thriving timber town but today it's a favourite feed-stop with two excellent cafés. International folk love the Fauna Australia Wildlife Retreat ( ☎ 5237 3234; www.faunaaustralia.com.au; 5040 Colac-Lavers Hill Rd, Lavers Hill; d $220) where almost-tame native animals (bred on the property) snoop about at night.

Seven kilometres southwest of Lavers Hill is tiny Melba Gully State Park. The marked Madsen's Track rainforest nature walk goes under a canopy of blackwoods and myrtle beeches and the fat, 300-year-old 'Big Tree', a messmate eucalypt. After dark, glow worms glimmer in the park. You won't escape the well-signposted Otway Fly (p238), 5km from Beech Forest.

Triplet Falls, further along the same road as the Fly (Phillips Track), is also worth the hike. The 900m walk passes an historic timber site. The Beauchamp and Hopetoun Falls are just past Beech Forest, down the Aire Valley Rd.

For a real slice of Otways' life, meet the locals by staying overnight in Beech Forest. Amid rolling mists, the Beechy Pub ( ☎ 5235 9220; Beech Forest; d $95; ☽ lunch & dinner Wed-Sun) is a welcoming shelter. Mains cost $15 to $18.

also an ideal base for exploring magical Cape Otway and Otway National Park. Online, check out www.visitapollobay.com and www.visitotways.com.

There's stacks to do in and around Apollo Bay. The local Saturday community market (www.apollobay.com/market_place; ☽ 8.30am-4.30pm), along the main strip, is good for homemade jams and weird table lamps made from tree stumps. Signposted Marriners Lookout is 1.5km from town back towards Cape Patton – from the car park the lookout is a rewarding 20-minute return walk.

Otway Shipwreck Tours ( ☎ 0417-983 985; msbrack@bigpond.com; 3hr tours adult/child $50/15) are run by Mark Brack, son of the Cape Otway Lighthouse keeper, who knows this stretch of coast, its history and ghosts better than anyone around. His tours are small, personal and very informative. Minimum two people.

The Old Cable Station Museum ( ☎ 5237 7441; 6250 Great Ocean Rd; admission $2.50; ☽ 2-5pm Sat & Sun) has a huge collection of photographs and local artefacts relating to the 1859 laying of submarine telegraph cable from Cape Otway to Tasmania.

Highly recommended are the seal colony visits at the Marengo Marine Sanctuary with Apollo Bay Sea Kayaking ( ☎ 0405-495 909; www.apollobaysurfkayak.com.au; 2hr tours $55), which are safe and suitable for children over 12. They depart from Marengo Beach at 10.30am and 2pm most days. This outfit also runs the Apollo Bay Surf School (1½hr lessons $45) and rents boards, bikes, sports gear and camping equipment.

Reel in the big' uns with Apollo Bay Fishing & Adventure Tours ( ☎ 5237 7888, www.apollobayfishing.com.au; 4hr trips adult/child $85/75) or go mountain-bike riding with Otway Expeditions ( ☎ 5237 6341; http://otwayexpeditions.tripod.com; rides from $60) through the Otways. Amphibious all-terrain 8x8 'argo buggies' are also available.

Tandem hang-glide or paraglide from Marriners Lookout with Wingsports Flight Academy ( ☎ 0419-378 616; www.wingsports.com.au; 9 Evans Crt; flights from $150), or strap yourself into a Cessna 206 flight over the Twelve Apostles with Apollo Bay Aviation ( ☎ 0407-306 065; www.apollobayaviation.com.au; 3 Telford St; flights $95). Minimum two people.

The superb multiday Great Ocean Walk (www.greatoceanwalk.com.au) starts at Apollo Bay and runs all the way to the Twelve Apostles. You can do shorter walks or the whole trek over six days; see the website for details.

## TRANSPORT: APOLLO BAY

Distance from Melbourne 187km

Direction Southwest

Travel time Melbourne to Apollo Bay three hours

Bus V/Line ( ☎ 13 61 96; www.vline.com.au) buses connect with Melbourne trains in Geelong and travel onto Apollo Bay three times Monday to Friday (twice on both Saturday and Sunday; $19.50 including train fare, $13 bus only to/from Geelong, 2½ hours from Geelong). Buses stop at the Apollo Bay visitors centre; one bus continues on to Warrnambool via Port Campbell on Monday, Wednesday and Friday ($15, 3½ hours).

Car Apollo Bay is 45 minutes west of Lorne on the B100.

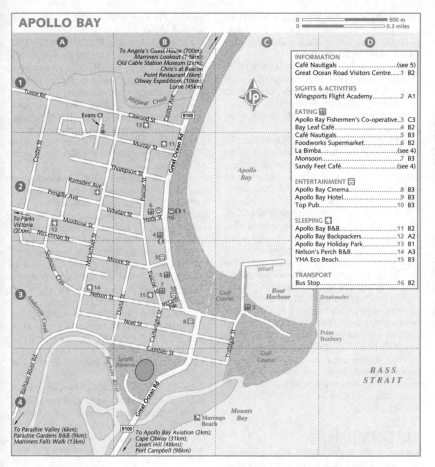

## APOLLO BAY

To Angela's Guest House (700m);
Marriners Lookout (1.5km);
Old Cable Station Museum (2km);
Chris's at Beacon
Point Restaurant (6km);
Otway Expeditions (10km);
Lorne (45km)

**INFORMATION**
Café Nautigals ....................................(see 5)
Great Ocean Road Visitors Centre......1  B2

**SIGHTS & ACTIVITIES**
Wingsports Flight Academy..............2  A1

**EATING** 🍴
Apollo Bay Fishermen's Co-operative..3  C3
Bay Leaf Café....................................4  B2
Café Nautigals..................................5  B3
Foodworks Supermarket....................6  B2
La Bimba.......................................(see 4)
Monsoon..........................................7  B3
Sandy Feet Café.............................(see 4)

**ENTERTAINMENT** 🎭
Apollo Bay Cinema............................8  B3
Apollo Bay Hotel...............................9  B3
Top Pub..........................................10  B3

**SLEEPING** 🛏
Apollo Bay B&B..............................11  B2
Apollo Bay Backpackers...................12  A2
Apollo Bay Holiday Park..................13  B1
Nelson's Perch B&B.........................14  A3
YHA Eco Beach................................15  B3

**TRANSPORT**
Bus Stop.........................................16  B2

To Parks
Victoria
(200m)

To Paradise Valley (6km);
Paradise Gardens B&B (9km);
Marriners Falls Walk (13km)

To Apollo Bay Aviation (2km);
Cape Otway (31km);
Lavers Hill (48km);
Port Campbell (98km)

# INFORMATION

**Café Nautigals** ( ☎ 0402-825 590; 57 Great Ocean Rd;
🕑 8.30am-11pm) Internet access.

**Great Ocean Road visitors centre** ( ☎ 5237 6529;
100 Great Ocean Rd; 🕑 9am-5pm) In the same building, there's an impressive 'eco-centre' with displays on
Aboriginal history, rainforests, shipwrecks and the building
of the Great Ocean Rd.

**Parks Victoria** ( ☎ 5237 2500; www.parkweb.vic.gov.au;
cnr Oak Ave & Montrose St; 🕑 8am-4.30pm Mon-Fri)

# FESTIVALS & EVENTS

**Apollo Bay Music Festival** ( ☎ 5237 6761; www.apollo
baymusicfestival.com; weekend pass adult/youth/under 13
$130/70/free) Held over a weekend in late April; features
classical, folk, blues, jazz, rock and some edgy contemporary

sounds too. It's an outstanding event, but accommodation
is scarce and expensive – book well ahead.

# EATING

There's good eating at the two pubs on the
main drag, and the Apollo Bay Fishermen's Co-operative
( ☎ 5237 6591; Nelson St; 🕑 9.30am-4.30pm) sells fresh
fish and seafood. The Foodworks Supermarket
( ☎ 5237 7355; 4 Hardy St) is just behind the post
office.

Sandy Feet Café ( ☎ 5237 6995; 139 Great Ocean Rd;
mains $6-12; 🕑 breakfast & lunch) Tofu, tempeh,
wholefoods and good karma.

Café Nautigals ( ☎ 0402-825 590; 57 Great Ocean Rd; mains
$14-16; 🕑 breakfast, lunch & dinner; 🖥 ) With an eclec-
tic menu of Asian noodle, rice and curry dishes,
tofu plates for vegetarians, chicken-mayo

wraps and great coffee, Nautigals is a favourite with backpackers and hip locals. The backpackers' menu includes a free drink and internet access with your meal.

**Monsoon** ( ☎ 5237 6776; 1/8 Pascoe St, mains $15-26; ☺ lunch & dinner) This Thai restaurant-bar is a newbie on the culinary scene, cooking up traditional piquant curries and satay skewers with some funky modern inflections. Fully licensed; takeaway available.

**Bay Leaf Café** ( ☎ 5237 6470; 131 Great Ocean Rd; mains $10-16; ☺ breakfast & lunch daily, dinner Tue-Sat) Morning pancake stacks and evening chicken-and-leek pie – great! A local favourite for its innovative menu, good coffee, friendly atmosphere and fair prices.

**La Bimba** ( ☎ 5237 7411; 125 Great Ocean Rd; mains $25-45; ☺ breakfast, lunch & dinner Thu-Mon) This upstairs Mod Oz restaurant is outstanding – definitely worth the splurge. It's a warm, relaxed smart-casual place with views, great service and a good wine list. Try the Portuguese bouillabaisse-style seafood broth with prawns, clams, potato, chorizo, baby spinach and a half-crab. It comes with an array of surgeon's tools and a dainty finger bowl – very messy! We'll be back.

**Chris's at Beacon Point Restaurant** ( ☎ 5237 6411; Skenes Creek Rd; mains $30-48; ☺ lunch & dinner) A hilltop fine-dining sanctuary with breathtaking views over Bass Strait and Apollo Bay, 6km away. It's a beautifully designed restaurant with stone feature walls, sandstone floors and vaulted ceilings.

## ENTERTAINMENT

Lots of Apollo Bay's restaurants have evening bar services, and **Apollo Bay Hotel** ( ☎ 5237 6250; 95 Great Ocean Rd) and **Top Pub** (Great Ocean Hotel; ☎ 5237 6240; 29 Great Ocean Rd) have live bands on weekends.

During holidays, the **Apollo Bay Cinema** ( ☎ 5289 1272; www.greatoceanroadcinemas.com.au; cnr Great Ocean Rd & Nelson St; adult/child $12.50/9.50) operates from the local hall.

## SLEEPING

**YHA Eco Beach** ( ☎ 5237 7899; 5 Pascoe St; dm $27-37, d $75-89, f $95-109; ✿ ▯ ) Even if you're not on a budget this new three-million-dollar, architect-designed hostel is an outstanding place to stay. Its eco-credentials are too many to list here, but it's a wonderful piece of architecture with great lounge areas, kitchens, TV rooms, internet lounge and rooftop terraces. The location, just a block behind the beach in the guts of

town, is the icing on the cake. It's often full, so book ahead.

**Apollo Bay Backpackers** ( ☎ 1800 113 045, 5237 7360; www.apollobaybackpackers.com.au; 47 Montrose St; dm/d from $20/50; ▯ ) This friendly, blue-fibro hippie digs is kinda daggy, but has all the facilities and complimentary breakfast.

**Angela's Guest House** ( ☎ 5237 7085; www.angelas guesthouse.com.au; 7 Campbell Ct; d from $130) This large family home has spotless double and family rooms with bright, cheerful décor. Some share a bathroom, most have balconies, and they're all excellent value.

**Apollo Bay Holiday Park** ( ☎ 5237 7111; www.kooringal -park.com.au; 27 Cawood St; unpowered sites $25, d cabins from $110) Formerly Kooringal Holiday Park, this place looks prefab-suburban, complete with speed humps, car parks and kit homes. It's in a good location on the northern end of town.

**Nelson's Perch B&B** ( ☎ 5237 7176; www.nelsonsperch .com; 54 Nelson St; d $160; ✿ ▯ ) Nelson's looks fresher than some of the town's weary B&Bs. There are three rooms, each with courtyard, and free wireless internet throughout.

**Apollo Bay B&B** ( ☎ 5237 7153; www.apollobaybandb .com.au; 4 Murray St; s/d $160/190; ✿ ) A great mix of creature comforts (king-size beds), amenities, location and value, not to mention the breakfast. Stroll over the main road and you're on the beach.

**Paradise Gardens B&B** ( ☎ 5237 6939; www.paradise gardens.net.au; 715 Barham River Rd; d B&B from $160, self-contained cottages $220; ✿ ) Drive up the beautiful Barham Valley, 9km from Apollo Bay, to this genteel minimanor beside a lovely lake with green lawns, weeping willows and wild ducks. The cottage is large and well appointed, though rockstars may find the décor a little twee and feminine.

## AROUND APOLLO BAY

Head 6km southwest of Apollo Bay along the Great Ocean Rd to the signposted Shelley Beach turn-off. It's an unsealed road. There are toilets and wood BBQs in the reserve, a track down to the beach and the 4km Elliot River Walk.

The narrow Barham River Road Scenic Drive from Apollo Bay runs a delightful 12km past tumbling grassy hills, sheep and stands of colossal eucalypts. Before returning walk the Marriners Falls Walk, which follows the babbling Barham River, and pull into the aptly named Paradise Valley picnic area. Seventeen kilometres past Apollo Bay is Maits Rest Rainforest Boardwalk, an easy 20-minute rainforest-gully walk.

## Detour: Skenes Creek to Forrest

An alternative return route from Apollo Bay to Geelong is via the C119 through Forrest. The road leaves the coast at Skenes Creek and dips and weaves through beautiful Otways hills to Forrest 32km away. The sleepy town is tiny but Parks Victoria and the Department of Sustainability & Environment (DSE) have recently opened more than 50km of mountain bike trails (ranging from beginner to suicidal) nearby. There are trail maps in town. The park hosts the Otway Odyssey Mountain Bike Marathon (www.rapidascent.com.au/otwayodyssey) in late February.

Accommodation options include the very swish Forest River Valley B&B ( ☎ 5236 6322; www.forrestrivervalley .com.au; 135 Yaugher Rd; d $240; 🐕 ) outside town, and Otways Forrest Retreat ( ☎ 0428-689 297; www.otways forrestretreat.com.au; 6 Station St; d from $120).

# CAPE OTWAY

Cape Otway is the second most southerly point of mainland Australia (after Wilsons Promontory) and one of the wettest parts of the state. This coastline is particularly beautiful, rugged and dangerous. More than 200 ships came to grief between Cape Otway and Port Fairy between the 1830s and 1930s, which led to the 'Shipwreck Coast' moniker.

The turn-off for Lighthouse Rd, which leads 12km down to the lighthouse, is 21km from Apollo Bay. About 8km down Lighthouse Rd is a signposted unsealed road to spectacular Blanket Bay, Parker Hill, Point Franklin and Crayfish Beach. Camping is allowed here; it's free but you need to book through Parks Victoria ( ☎ 13 19 63; www.parkweb.vic.gov.au) in Apollo Bay.

You can climb to the top of Cape Otway Lighthouse ( ☎ 5237 9240; www.lightstation.com; adult/child/ family $14/8/36; 🕙 9am-5pm) for amazing views. This lighthouse was built in 1848 by more than 40 stonemasons without mortar or cement. The Telegraph Station has fascinating displays on the 250km undersea telegraph cable link with Tasmania laid in 1859. A mammoth logistical exercise, the first cable failed after six months.

As many as 16 people can be accommodated at the windswept Lighthouse Keeper's Residence (d from $185), though there's a two-night minimum stay on weekends.

You won't be the only guests at Great Ocean Eco Lodge ( ☎ 5237 9297; www.capeotwaycentre.com; 635 Lighthouse Rd, s/d from $250/300), just off the Great Ocean Rd, as the attached Cape Otway Centre for Conservation Ecology also serves as an animal hospital for a menagerie of local fauna. The luxurious en suite rooms in the post-and-beam, solar-powered, mud-brick homestead have bush-view decks and the centre offers guided walking tours and eco activities.

# CAPE OTWAY TO PORT CAMPBELL NATIONAL PARK

After Cape Otway, the Great Ocean Rd levels out and enters the fertile Horden Vale flats, returning briefly to the coast at tiny Glenaire. Then the road returns inland and begins the climb up to Lavers Hill (see p234). On overcast or rainy days the hills here can be seriously fog-bound, and the twists and turns can be challenging when you can't see the end of your car bonnet.

Six kilometres north of Glenaire, a 5km detour goes down Red Johanna Rd winding through rolling hills and grazing cows to the wild thrashing surf of Johanna Beach (forget swimming). The world-famous Rip Curl Pro surfing competition (p227) relocates here when Bells Beach isn't working.

There's a lovely camping ground at Johanna on a protected grassy area between the dunes and the rolling hills. It's maintained by Parks Victoria ( ☎ 13 19 63; www.parkweb.vic.gov.au) but there are no fees due or permits required. There's an ablutions facility, but fires are banned and you'll need to bring in your own drinking water.

There are several places to stay tucked down the Red Johanna and Blue Johanna Rds (which together make a loop back to the Great Ocean Rd), some managed by Holiday Great Ocean Road ( ☎ 5237 4201; www.holidaygor.com.au). Boomerangs ( ☎ 5237 4213; www.theboomerangs.com; cnr Great Ocean Rd & Red Johanna Rd; d $340) is great for well-heeled folks with a penchant for plush, boomerang-shaped cabins: vaulted ceilings, jarrah floorboards, leadlighting, spas and commanding views of the Johanna Valley.

About 16km from the former timber town of Lavers Hill is the turn-off to Moonlight Head, a lumpy 5km unsealed road that forks near the coast: to the left is the cemetery and a walking track along the clifftops; to the right is a car park with a track to Wreck Beach and the anchors of the *Marie Gabrielle*, which sank off here in 1869, and the *Fiji*, driven aground in a storm in 1891.

Twenty kilometres inland from Lavers Hill on the Colac Rd (C155) is the Otway Fly ( ☎ 5235 9200; Phillips Track; www.otwayfly.com; adult/child/family $20/9/50; ☉ 9am-5pm), 5km from Beech Forest. It's an elevated steel walkway in the forest canopy with a lookout tower, affording great views for the up-to-2000 people pumped through here each day. Arrive early.

# PORT CAMPBELL NATIONAL PARK

The road levels out after leaving the Otways and enters narrow, relatively flat scrubby escarpment lands that fall away to sheer, 70m cliffs along the coast between Princetown to Peterborough – a distinct change of scene. This is Port Campbell National Park – home to the Twelve Apostles – the most famous and most photographed stretch of the Great Ocean Rd. For eons, waves and tides have crashed against the soft limestone rock, eroding, undercutting and carving out a fascinating series of rock stacks, gorges, arches and blowholes.

The Gibson Steps, hacked by hand into the cliffs in the 19th century by local landowner Hugh Gibson (and more recently replaced by concrete steps), lead down to feral Gibson Beach, an essential stop. This beach, and others along this stretch of coast, are not suitable for swimming because of strong currents and undertows – you can walk along the beach, but be careful not to be stranded by high tides or nasty waves. This is the only place along this stretch of coast where you can ac-

cess the open beach, and it's possible to walk around the first headland to the west if the tide is low.

Opposite Gibson Steps is Hugh Gibson's original 1869 Glenample Homestead, where the survivors of the famed *Loch Ard* shipwreck recovered (see opposite).

The lonely Twelve Apostles are rocky stacks that have been abandoned to the ocean by retreating headland. Today, only seven apostles can be seen from the viewing platforms (see below). The understated roadside display centre (Great Ocean Rd; ☉ 9am-5pm) at the Twelve Apostles, 6km past Princetown, has public toilets and informative displays. There's pedestrian access to the viewing platforms from the car park via a tunnel beneath the Great Ocean Rd. Timber boardwalks run around the clifftops. Amid howls of protest from locals, Parks Victoria ( ☎ 13 96 63; www.parkweb.vic.gov.au), which manages this facility, intends to 'commercialise' this site constructing a café and takeaway food outlet. Golden arches? Nobody knows… It seems a shame, but why stop there? Put up a nightclub and shopping mall too!

There are several outfits that offer helicopter tours over the Twelve Apostles, including the Edge Helicopters ( ☎ 5598 8283; www.theedgehelicopters .com.au) just behind the car park at the display centre, and 12 Apostles Helicopters ( ☎ 5598 6161; www .12apostleshelicopters.com.au), 5km past the display centre. Both offer a range of tours from $90 per person for an eight-minute flight.

Nearby Loch Ard Gorge is where the Shipwreck Coast's most famous and haunting tale unfolded when two young survivors of the wrecked iron clipper *Loch Ard* made it to shore (see opposite).

---

## How Many Apostles?

The Twelve Apostles are not 12 in number. From the viewing platform you can clearly count seven Apostles, but maybe some obscure others? We consulted widely with Parks Victoria officers, tourist office staff and even the cleaner at the car park display centre, but obfuscation is the better part of valour around these parts, and locals like to say, 'It depends' or, 'Do you want the short answer or the long answer?'

The Apostles are called 'stacks' in geologic lingo, and the rock formations were originally called the 'Sow and Piglets'. Someone in the '60s (nobody can recall who) thought they might attract some tourists with a more venerable name, so they were renamed 'the Apostles.' Since apostles tend to come by the dozen, the number 12 was added sometime later. The two stacks on the eastern (Otway) side of the viewing platform are not technically Apostles – they're Gog and Magog (picking up on the religious nomenclature yet?). But if they help you to count to 12, then that's OK too.

So there aren't 12 stacks – there are more or less, depending which ones you want to count and how far along the coastline you include. The soft limestone cliffs are dynamic and changeable, constantly eroded by the unceasing waves – one 70m-high stack collapsed into the sea in July 2005. If you look carefully at how the waves lick around the pointy part of the cliff base, you can see a new Apostle being born. The labour lasts many thousands of years.

## The Wreck of the Loch Ard

The Victorian coastline between Cape Otway and Port Fairy was a notoriously treacherous stretch of water in the days of sailing ships, due to hidden reefs and frequent heavy fog. More than 80 vessels came to grief on this 120km stretch in just 40 years.

The most famous wreck was that of the iron-hulled clipper *Loch Ard*, which foundered off Mutton Bird Island at 4am on the final night of its long voyage from England in 1878. Of 37 crew and 19 passengers on board, only two survived. Eva Carmichael, a nonswimmer, clung to wreckage and was washed into a gorge, where apprentice officer Tom Pearce rescued her. Tom heroically climbed the sheer cliff the next day and raised the alarm at a local farmhouse, but no other survivors were found. Eva and Tom were both 19 years old, leading to speculation in the press about a romance, but nothing actually happened – they never saw each other again and Eva soon moved to Ireland.

# PORT CAMPBELL

**pop 260**

This small, windswept town is poised on a dramatic, natural bay, eroded from the surrounding limestone cliffs, and almost perfectly rectangular in shape. It was named after Scottish Captain Alexander Campbell, a whaler who took refuge here on trading voyages between Tasmania and Port Fairy. The tiny bay has a lovely sandy beach, the only safe place for swimming along this tempestuous coast.

After the throngs of people, bars and cafés of Lorne and Apollo Bay, sleepy Port Campbell is a nice small-town antidote. There's still the souvenir trash and everything's 'Twelve Apostles this' and 'Loch Ard that' but there are no pretensions here – it's got a bit of a hokum back-country feel and remains an authentic seaside town.

The 4.7km Discovery Walk, with signage, gives an introduction to the area's natural and historical features. It's just out of town on the way to Warrnambool.

There is stunning diving in the kelp forests, canyons and tunnels of the Arches Marine Sanctuary and to the *Loch Ard* wreck, as well as boat tours to the Twelve Apostles; inquire at Port Campbell Marine Services ( ☎ 5598 6411; 32 Lord St) at the Mobil Service Station.

Port Campbell Touring Company ( ☎ 5598 6424; www.portcampbelltouring.com.au; 129 Currells Rd; half-day tours $38) runs tours, fishing trips and the like.

## INFORMATION

Parks Victoria ( ☎ 5558 6233; www.parkweb.vic.gov.au; 6 Lord St; ⏰ 8am-4.30pm Mon-Fri)

Port Campbell visitor centre ( ☎ 5598 6089; www.visit12apostles.com; 26 Morris St; ⏰ 9am-5pm) Stacks of regional and accommodation information and interesting historic displays – the anchor from the *Loch Ard* is out the front, salvaged in 1978.

## EATING

12 Rocks Café ( ☎ 5598 6123; 19 Lord St; mains $8-15; ⏰ breakfast, lunch & dinner) This busy place, with the best beachfront views, does a roaring daytime trade of coffee and light meals, plus reasonable pasta and seafood mains.

Waves ( ☎ 5598 6111; 29 Lord St; mains $20-26; ⏰ breakfast, lunch & dinner) Waves, the only flash eatery in town, does good morning coffee and breakfast. At night the menu is strong on local seafood, or you can pop in for a drink.

## SLEEPING

Port Campbell Hostel ( ☎ 5598 6305; www.portcampbellhostel.com.au; 18 Tregea St; dm $25) This rustic-looking hostel has good dorms and communal facilities, and it's in the throes of building some comfy double rooms.

Ocean House Backpackers ( ☎ 5598 6492; www.portcampbell.nu/oceanhouse; Cairns St; dm $27) Occupying the best real estate in town overlooking the main beach, this hot-pink, pine-panelled house has a cosy guest lounge with an open fireplace. Bookings through Port Campbell Caravan Park office (below).

Port Campbell Caravan Park ( ☎ 5598 6492; www.portcampbell.nu/camping; Morris St; unpowered/powered sites $27/30, en suite cabins $125; 🖥 ) Neat, small, and a two-minute walk to the beach and town.

Port Bayou ( ☎ 5598 6009; www.portbayou.portcampbell.nu; 52 Lord St; d B&B $120, cottage $145; ✖ ) Choose from the cosy in-house B&B or a rustic self-contained cottage fitted with exposed ceiling beams and corrugated-tin walls.

Daysy Hill Country Cottages ( ☎ 5598 6226; www.greatoceanroad.nu/daysyhill; 7353 Timboon-Port Campbell Rd; d from $145; ✖ ) These hillside cedar-and-sandstone cottages are few minutes from town and are decorated in a modern colonial style. The newer deluxe cabins have the best views and include spas.

# PORT CAMPBELL TO WARRNAMBOOL

The Great Ocean Rd continues west of Port Campbell passing more rock stacks. The next one is the Arch, offshore from Point Hesse.

Nearby is London Bridge…fallen down! Now sometimes called London Arch, it was once a double-arched rock platform linked to the mainland. Visitors could walk out across a narrow natural bridge to the huge rock formation. In January 1990, the bridge collapsed leaving two terrified tourists marooned on the world's newest island – they were eventually rescued by helicopter. Nearby are the Grotto and the Crown of Thorns.

The Bay of Islands is 8km west of tiny Peterborough, where a two-hour coastal walk from the car park takes you to magnificent lookout points.

The Great Ocean Rd then heads inland through to Warrnambool. About 16km inland from Peterborough, Timboon Farmhouse Cheese ( ☎ 5598 3387; cnr Ford & Fells Rd; ⏱ 10.30am-4pm daily Oct-Apr, Wed-Sun May-Sep) has free tastings of its award-winning, biodynamic cheeses – a worthy detour.

Not to be out-cheesed, Cheese World ( ☎ 5563 2130; www.cheeseworld.com.au; Great Ocean Rd, Allansford; ⏱ 8.30am-5pm Mon-Fri, 9am-4pm Sat, 10am-4pm Sun) is 12km before Warrnambool, with a museum, restaurant, cheese cellar and free tastings.

The Great Ocean Rd ends near here where it meets the Princess Hwy, which continues through the traditional lands of the Gunditjmara people into South Australia.

# WARRNAMBOOL

## pop 30,400

Warrnambool was originally a whaling and sealing station – now it's booming as a major regional commercial centre. Its historic buildings, waterways and tree-lined streets are attractive, and there's a large student population who attend the Warrnambool campus of Deakin University. The major housing and commercial development around the fringes of the city look much like city suburbs anywhere in Australia, but the regions around the waterfront have largely retained their considerable historic charm.

Warrnambool's major tourist attraction is the impressive Flagstaff Hill Maritime Village ( ☎ 1800 556 111; www.flagstaffhill.com; Merri St; adult/child/family $16/7/39; ⏱ 9am-5pm), modelled on an early Australian coastal port. See the cannon and fortifications, built in 1887 to withstand the perceived threat of Russian invasion, and Shipwrecked (adult/child/family $26/14/65), a lame evening sound-and-laser show of the Loch Ard's plunge. Grab a meal at Pippies by the Bay (see Eating) while you're here.

Warrnambool has excellent beaches such as sheltered Lady Bay, the main swimming beach, which has fortifications at the breakwater at its western end. Logan's Beach has the best surf, and there are breaks at Levy's Beach and Second Bay. Hang five with Easyrider Surf School ( ☎ 5521 7646; www.easyridersurfschool.com.au; 2hr lessons $45) or saddle up with Rundell's Mahogany Trail Rides ( ☎ 0408-589 546; www.rundellshr.com.au; 2hr beach rides $50).

Southern right whales come to mate and nurse their bubs in the waters off Logan's Beach from July to September, breaching and fluking off Logan's Beach Whale Watching Platform. It's a major tourist drawcard, but you'll need 20/20 eyesight or a pair of binoculars. Dive Inn Charters ( ☎ 0419-349 058; www.diveinncharters.com.au) and Shipwreck Coast Diving ( ☎ 5561 6108; www.shipwreckcoastdiving.com.au) are among several operators offering whale-watching boat tours and diving and fishing charters.

Walking trails in and around Warrnambool include the 3km Heritage Trail. The short Thunder Point stroll shows off the best coastal scenery in the area; it's also the starting point for the 22km coastal Mahogany Walking Trail.

The Warrnambool Art Gallery ( ☎ 5564 7832; www.warrnambool.vic.gov.au; 165 Timor St; admission free; ⏱ 10am-5pm Mon-Fri, noon-5pm Sat & Sun) is well worth a visit. The permanent Australian collection includes such notable painters as Tom Roberts, James Gleeson and Arthur Boyd.

TRANSPORT: PORT CAMPBELL

Distance from Melbourne 304km

Direction Southwest

Travel time Melbourne to Port Campbell 4½ hours

Bus V/Line ( ☎ 13 61 96; www.vline.com.au) buses run from Geelong to Port Campbell ($23, 5¼ hours, three weekly). Wayward Bus ( ☎ 1300 653 510; www.waywardbus.com.au) stops here on its Melbourne-to-Adelaide trip.

Car Port Campbell is 1½ hours west of Apollo Bay on the B100.

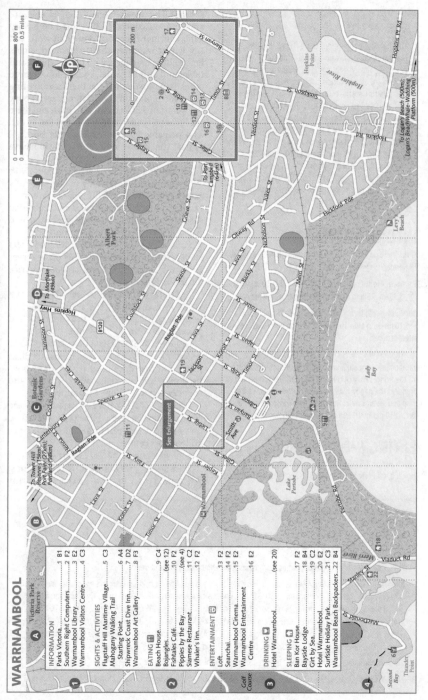

## WARRNAMBOOL

| INFORMATION | |
|---|---|
| Parks Victoria | 1 B1 |
| Southern Right Computers | 2 F2 |
| Warrnambool Library | 3 E2 |
| Warrnambool Visitors Centre | 4 C3 |

| SIGHTS & ACTIVITIES | |
|---|---|
| Flagstaff Hill Maritime Village | 5 C3 |
| Mahogany Walking Trail | |
|   Starting Point | 6 A4 |
| Shipwreck Coast Dive Inn | 7 D2 |
| Warrnambool Art Gallery | 8 F3 |

| EATING 🍴 | |
|---|---|
| Beach House | 9 C4 |
| Bojangles | (see 12) |
| Fishtales Café | 10 F2 |
| Pippies by the Bay | (see 4) |
| Siamese Restaurant | 11 C2 |
| Whaler's Inn | 12 F2 |

| ENTERTAINMENT 🎭 | |
|---|---|
| Loft | 13 F2 |
| Seanchai | 14 F2 |
| Warrnambool Cinema | 15 E2 |
| Warrnambool Entertainment | |
|   Centre | 16 E2 |

| DRINKING 🍷 | |
|---|---|
| Hotel Warrnambool | (see 20) |

| SLEEPING 🛏 | |
|---|---|
| Ban Kor House | 17 F2 |
| Bayside Lodge | 18 B4 |
| Girt by Sea | 19 C2 |
| Hotel Warrnambool | 20 E2 |
| Surfside Holiday Park | 21 C3 |
| Warrnambool Beach Backpackers | 22 B4 |

## THE MAHOGANY SHIP

The *Mahogany Ship* is said to be a Portuguese vessel that ran aground off Warrnambool in the 1500s – there have been alleged sightings of the elusive wreck sitting high in the dunes dating back to 1846. Portuguese naval charts from the 16th century known as the *Dieppe Maps* are said to depict parts of Australia's southern coastline, including Armstrong Bay 6km west of Warrnambool, and this has further fuelled the *Mahogany Ship* legend. Alternative theories claim that the *Mahogany Ship* was an even earlier Chinese junk. For 150 years people have been trying to find the remains of the *Mahogany Ship* – some say it's buried deep in the dunes or was swallowed by the sea. However, there's no direct evidence that the ship ever existed.

## INFORMATION

Parks Victoria ( ☎ 5561 9920; www.parkweb.vic.gov.au; 78 Henna St; ⏰ 8am-4.30pm Mon-Fri)

Southern Right Computers ( ☎ 5561 7762; 105a Liebig St; ⏰ 8.30am-5.30pm Mon-Fri) Internet access $6 per hour.

Warrnambool Library ( ☎ 5562 2258; 25 Liebig St; ⏰ 10am-5pm Mon-Thu, to 8pm Fri, to noon Sat) Free internet access.

Warrnambool visitors centre ( ☎ 5559 4620; www.warrnamboolinfo.com.au; Merri St; ⏰ 9am-5pm) Signposted off the Princes Hwy (A1) in the Flagstaff Hill complex, it produces the handy *Warrnambool Visitors Guide*, a bike map and several walking maps. There's also internet access here ($10 per hour) and bicycle hire ($30 per day).

## EATING & DRINKING

Beach House ( ☎ 5562 2223; Warrnambool Surf Life Saving Club, off Pertobe Rd; mains $12-22; ⏰ breakfast, lunch & dinner) The views from Beach House are amazing, ensconced in the Surf Life Saving Club's former function room – sip your cab sav whilst watching the surfers and yachts below. It's a bit daggy, with plastic chairs and tables and grubby carpet, and the food's more good than outstanding, yet there's something really nice going on here. If things aren't busy the wait staff will sit down for a chat, and there are highchairs and crayons for the kids, as well as a palpable good vibe. Gourmet burgers, pastas, Thai red seafood curry, occasional live music and no haughty pretensions.

Fishtales Café ( ☎ 5561 2957; 63 Liebig St; mains $10-18; ⏰ breakfast, lunch & dinner) This upbeat, friendly eatery-takeaway has well-prepared fare from excellent burgers, fish and chips and vegetarian specials to slightly less impressive seafood and Asian dishes. There's a cheery courtyard.

Siamese Restaurant ( ☎ 5561 3596; 108 Lava St; mains $10-18; ⏰ lunch & dinner Tue-Sat) This place serves authentic Thai food – noodles, soups and rice dishes. Eat in or takeaway.

Whaler's Inn ( ☎ 5562 8391; cnr Liebig & Timor Sts; mains $12-22; ⏰ lunch & dinner) It's a family-friendly setup here. Meals are tasty and generous, and prices include an all-you-can-eat salad bar.

Bojangles ( ☎ 5562 8751; 61 Liebig St; mains $15-22; ⏰ lunch & dinner) Bojangles is an upmarket pizza restaurant that does great pastas and wood-fired pizzas. It has an excellent wine list and friendly service. Highly recommended.

Pippies by the Bay ( ☎ 5561 2188; Flagstaff Hill Maritime Village, Merri St; mains $26-30; ⏰ lunch & dinner daily, breakfast Sat & Sun) A fine restaurant in the Flagstaff Hill visitors centre.

Hotel Warrnambool ( ☎ 5562 2377; cnr Koroit & Kepler Sts; mains $14-28; ⏰ lunch & dinner) This is the most welcoming place in town – a cheerful, earthy

## TRANSPORT: WARRNAMBOOL

Distance from Melbourne 371km

Direction Southwest

Travel time Melbourne to Warrnambool 5¼ hours (three hours via A1 inland route)

Bus V/Line ( ☎ 13 61 96; www.vline.com.au) has three buses on weekdays (two on Saturday and one on Sunday) to Port Fairy ($3.50, 30 minutes) and Portland ($9, 1½ hours), one bus each weekday to Hamilton ($4.50, 1½ hours) and Ballarat ($13, 3 hours), and one on Monday, Wednesday and Friday to Apollo Bay ($15, 3½ hours). Wayward Bus ( ☎ 1300 653 510; www.waywardbus.com.au) services Warrnambool on its Melbourne-to-Adelaide route. Viclink ( ☎ 13 61 38; www.viclink.com.au) connects Warrnambool with Port Fairy ($3.50, 45 minutes, three weekly), continuing to Hamilton ($14, two hours), Dunkeld ($18.50, 2½ hours), Halls Gap ($27.50, 3¼ hours) and Ararat ($32, four hours).

Car Warrnambool is 45 minutes west of Port Campbell on the B100.

Train V/Line ( ☎ 13 61 96; www.vline.com.au; Merri St) trains run to Melbourne ($25, 3¼ hours, three or four daily).

and cavernous place with exposed mud bricks and railway sleepers, slouchy lounges, pool table and weekend live music. Eleven beers on tap and excellent pub food.

## ENTERTAINMENT

**Loft** ( ☎ 5561 0995; 58 Liebig St; ✆ 5.30pm-1am Wed, Fri & Sat, daily Dec-Feb) Perhaps the pick of the local nightclubs, Loft is relaxed with live music on weekends.

**Seanchai** ( ☎ 5561 7900; 62 Liebig St; ✆ 2pm-1am Wed-Sun) Seanchai (pronounced 'Shannakee', which is Gaelic for storyteller) has live music and traditional Irish jigs on Sunday.

**Warrnambool Entertainment Centre** ( ☎ 5564 7885; www.entertainmentcentre.com.au; cnr Liebig & Timor Sts) This is a major venue for live theatre, ballet and music.

**Warrnambool Cinema** ( ☎ 5562 2709; 54 Kepler St; adult/child/student $13.50/9.50/11.50) Mainstream movies. All tickets for sessions starting before 11am are $9.

## SLEEPING

**Warrnambool Beach Backpackers** ( ☎ 5562 4874; www.beachbackpackers.com.au; 17 Stanley St; dm/d $23/65; 🖸 🖳 ) Close to the sea, this former museum has a huge living area with a bar, internet access, kitchen and free pick-up. It has self-contained family rooms and fills up quickly with seasonal workers who pick vegetables at nearby farms. It's a good place to seek casual employment.

**Surfside Holiday Park** ( ☎ 5559 4700; www.surfsidepark.com.au; Pertobe Rd; unpowered/powered sites $35/40, cabins from $111) Surfside is one of several Warrnambool caravan parks, and offers good self-contained cabins as well as tent and caravan sites. It's perfectly situated between the town and the beach.

**Hotel Warrnambool** ( ☎ 5562 2377; fax 5561 7248; ozone1@hotkey.net.au; cnr Koroit & Kepler Sts; d with/without en suite $140/100; 🖸 🖳 ) Recent renovations upstairs in this historic 1894 pub have done wonders with the rooms, which have plasma TVs and access to a kitchenette and lounge. Some have bathrooms and balconies. Downstairs is one of the friendliest pub-eateries in town.

**Bayside Lodge** ( ☎ 5562 7323; baysidelodge@dodo.com.au; 30 Pertobe Rd; q $100-150; 🖸 🖳 ) With free wireless internet throughout, these large self-contained two-bedroom apartments are great value for a group or family. Stuck in a '70s time warp, but literally spittin' distance from the beach.

**Girt by Sea** ( ☎ 0418-261 969; www.girtbyseabandb.com.au; 52 Banyan St; d/ste from $145/200; 🖳 ) This re-stored 1856 sandstone home has been tastefully refurbished. Large bathrooms boast antique vanities and Baltic pine floors. There are various suites with huge brass beds, private garden decks, plasma TVs and massage chairs. There's a large, bright guest lounge and great breakfasts. Free wireless internet throughout.

**Ban Kor House** ( ☎ 5562 9461; www.bankorhouse.com.au; cnr Banyan & Koroit Sts; d from $180; 🖸 ) This is a nice refit of an old sandstone cottage, retaining many original features. The rooms have been decorated with an eclectic mix of period features and modern styles. One block from town, two from the beach.

## TOWER HILL RESERVE

Tower Hill, 15km west of Warrnambool, is a vast caldera born in a volcanic eruption 30,000 years ago. Aboriginal artefacts unearthed in the volcanic ash show that indigenous people lived in the area at the time. It's jointly administered by the Worn Gundidj Aboriginal Cooperative, which operates the **visitors centre** ( ☎ 5561 5315; www.worngundidj.org.au; ✆ 9am-5pm Mon-Fri, 10am-4pm Sat, Sun & public holidays) with Parks Victoria. There are excellent day walks, including the steep 30-minute Peak Climb with spectacular 360-degree views. There's a fascinating painting in the Warrnambool Art Gallery (p240) by Eugene von Guérard of Tower Hill painted in 1855. After a century of deforestation and environmental degradation, this incredibly detailed painting was used to identify species used in a replanting program begun in 1961 when Tower Hill became a state game reserve. Since then over 300,000 trees have been replanted.

## PORT FAIRY
### pop 2600

This seaside township at the mouth of the Moyne River was settled in 1835, and the first arrivals were whalers and sealers. Port Fairy still has a large fishing fleet and a relaxed, salty feel, with its old bluestone and sandstone buildings, whitewashed cottages, colourful fishing boats and tree-lined streets. The tiny town centre is along and around Sackville St, and the many historic buildings (some falling down!) remain authentic to Port Fairy's bygone era. The town has been reborn as a tourist destination and is home to art galleries, antique shops and boutiques.

Port Fairy has a rich and sometimes gloomy heritage that enraptures local history buffs. The visitors centre has brochures and maps that show the popular Shipwreck Walk and History Walk signposted around town. Also from the visitors centre is a guide to the many local art galleries.

The Port Fairy History Centre (http://historicalsociety.port-fairy.com; 30 Gipps St; admission adult/child $3/50c; ⌚ 2-5pm Wed, Sat & Sun), housed in the old bluestone courthouse (complete with dusty mannequins acting out a courtroom scene), has shipping relics, old photos and costumes, and a prisoner's cell.

On Battery Hill there's a lookout point, and cannons and fortifications positioned here in the 1860s. Down below there's a lovely walk around Griffiths Island where the Moyne River empties into the sea. The island is connected to the mainland by a footbridge, and is home to a protected mutton bird colony and a modest lighthouse.

Mulloka Cruises ( ☎ 0408-514 382; cruises adult/child $10/free) runs half-hour cruises of the port, bay and Griffiths Island. Or you can learn to surf with the Port Fairy Surf School ( ☎ 5568 2800; www.daktarisport.com.au; 33 Bank St), run out of the Port Fairy Surf Shop.

## INFORMATION

Port Fairy Community House ( ☎ 5568 2681; Railway Pl; ⌚ 9am-3.30pm Mon-Fri; 💻 ) Internet access $4 per hour.

Port Fairy visitors centre ( ☎ 5568 2682; www.port-fairy.com/vic; Bank St) Ocean end of Bank St.

Ramella's Café ( ☎ 5568 3322; 19 Bank St; ⌚ 9.30am-late) Internet access $6 per hour; good coffee and food too.

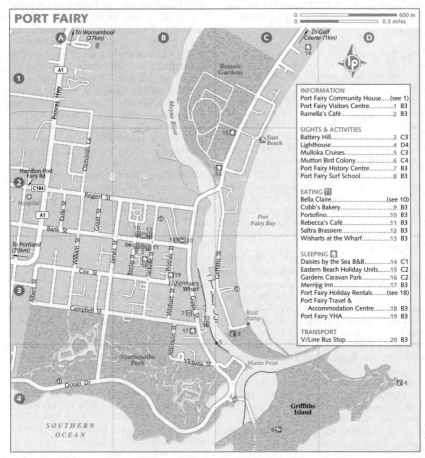

**PORT FAIRY**

0 — 600 m
0 — 0.3 miles

INFORMATION
Port Fairy Community House......(see 1)
Port Fairy Visitors Centre..............1 B3
Ramella's Café................................2 B3

SIGHTS & ACTIVITIES
Battery Hill....................................3 C3
Lighthouse.....................................4 D4
Mulloka Cruises.............................5 C3
Mutton Bird Colony........................6 C4
Port Fairy History Centre................7 B3
Port Fairy Surf School.....................8 B3

EATING 🍴
Bella Claire..............................(see 10)
Cobb's Bakery................................9 B3
Portofino.....................................10 B3
Rebecca's Café.............................11 B3
Saltra Brassiere............................12 B3
Wisharts at the Wharf....................13 B3

SLEEPING 🛏
Daisies by the Sea B&B.................14 C1
Eastern Beach Holiday Units.........15 C2
Gardens Caravan Park...................16 C2
Merrijig Inn..................................17 B3
Port Fairy Holiday Rentals........(see 18)
Port Fairy Travel &
    Accommodation Centre............18 B3
Port Fairy YHA.............................19 B3

TRANSPORT
V/Line Bus Stop...........................20 B3

## TRANSPORT: PORT FAIRY

**Distance from Melbourne** 410km

**Direction** Southwest

**Travel time** Melbourne to Port Fairy 5¾ hours (3½ hours via A1 inland route)

**Bus** V/Line ( ☎ 13 61 96; www.vline.com.au) buses run three times daily on weekdays (twice on Saturday and once on Sunday) to Portland ($6.50, one hour) and Warrnambool ($3.50, 35 min). Viclink ( ☎ 13 61 38; www.viclink.com .au) services connect Port Fairy with Hamilton ($10, 1¼ hours, three weekly), continuing to Halls Gap ($23.50, 2½ hours) and Ararat ($30, 3¼ hours).

**Car** Port Fairy is 45 minutes west of Warrnambool on the A1.

# FESTIVALS & EVENTS

Port Fairy Folk Festival (www.portfairyfolkfestival.com) Australia's premier folk-music festival, held on the Labour Day long weekend in early March. Accommodation for the festival is routinely booked a year in advance.

# EATING

Cobb's Bakery ( ☎ 5568 1713; 25 Bank St) This is where the locals come for sandwiches, pies, pasties, burgers and (naturally) fresh bread. Delicious fresh sandwiches cost from $7.

Bella Claire ( ☎ 5568 1610; 28 Bank St; mains $6-14; ☺ breakfast & lunch) This new café and gourmet provedore does outstanding coffee, ice cream and lunches. Just try to get away without buying some chutney or mustard or olive oil or cheese…

Rebecca's Café ( ☎ 5568 2533; 72 Sackville St; mains $5-12; ☺ breakfast & lunch) Excellent for breakfast and light lunches, Rebecca's serves up cakes, muffins, slices, scones and biscuits as well as homemade ice cream until 6pm.

Wisharts at the Wharf ( ☎ 5568 1884; 29 Gipps St; mains $17-23; ☺ lunch & dinner) Wharfside dining doesn't come prettier than this. Plump, fresh fish and chips are always assured here. Adventurous presentation and flavours in very relaxed surrounds.

Saltra Brassiere ( ☎ 5568 3058; 20 Bank St; mains $18-38; ☺ lunch-late Tue-Sun) Saltra, a Mod Oz restaurant that becomes a late-night lounge bar, is new on the Port Fairy scene and has made quite a splash. With a funky modern interior and courtyard, superb food and live music at weekends, it's getting people out of the house.

Portofino ( ☎ 5568 2251; 26 Bank St; mains $28-42; ☺ dinner Mon-Sat) Portofino does high-end Mod Oz-cum-Mediterranean food with style – one of the best restaurants in western Victoria. Roast duck over couscous with a dried fig and radish salad, or venison with Moorish spinach and potatoes Catalan style – sounds OK huh? Portofino offers splendid vegetarian dishes too, and local seafood is a feature.

# SLEEPING

Much of Port Fairy's holiday accommodation is managed by agents, including Port Fairy Travel & Accommodation Centre ( ☎ 5568 3150; www.hearns .com.au; 2/54 Sackville St) and Port Fairy Holiday Rentals ( ☎ 5568 1066; www.lockettrealestate.com.au; 62 Sackville St). The visitors centre also offers a booking service for $2, or check out My Port Fairy (www .portfairy.com.au) for more.

Port Fairy YHA ( ☎ 5568 2468; www.portfairyhostel.com .au; 8 Cox St; dm $22-26, d/f/2-bed apt from $60/85/150; ▣ ) In the rambling 1844 home of merchant William Rutledge, this friendly and well-run hostel has a large kitchen, pool table, free cable TV and peaceful gardens. There's a huge newly opened self-contained apartment with its own lounge that can sleep six.

Gardens Caravan Park ( ☎ 5568 1608; www.portfairy caravanparks.com; 111 Griffiths St; unpowered/powered sites $28/33, cabins from $95) One of several local caravan parks, this park is next to the botanical gardens, 200m from the beach and a short walk to the town centre.

Eastern Beach Holiday Units ( ☎ 5568 1117; www.port -fairy.com/easternbeach; 121 Griffiths St; d $95) What these units lack in old-world style they more than make up for in price and amenities – large, comfortable self-contained units with separate bedrooms, lounges and kitchens. Excellent value just near the beach.

Daisies by the Sea B&B ( ☎ 5568 2355; www.port-fairy .com/daisiesbythesea; 222 Griffiths St; d from $140) Bright, airy and contemporary, Daisies is the perfect antidote to Port Fairy's claustrophobic old-world charm. Nod off to the sound of the crashing waves just 50m from your door in these two cosy beachfront suites, 1.5km from town. Daisies is a modest, snug and appealing getaway for couples.

Merrijig Inn ( ☎ 5568 2324; www.merrijiginn.com; cnr Campbell & Gipps Sts; d incl breakfast from $150) This is Victoria's oldest inn, and the tiny attic doubles are about as authentic as you can get. The queen suites are roomier and the restaurant downstairs is splendid.

# PORTLAND

## pop 9800

Portland, Victoria's first European settlement, was a whaling and sealing base from the early 1800s. The Henty family came here from Van Diemen's Land in 1834 and were the first permanent settlers. Blessed Mary MacKillop, Australia's first saint, arrived here from Melbourne in 1862 and founded Australia's first religious order. Portland is the only deep-water port between Melbourne and Adelaide, and home to the massive Portland Aluminium Smelter. The huge industrial wharf is an eyesore on an otherwise attractive colonial-era township.

The restored 1886 Portland Cable Tram ( ☎ 5523 2831; www.portlandcabletrams.com.au; rides adult/child/family $12/10/30; ☉ 10am-4pm) does five trips a day plying an 8km circular route linking the vintage-car museum, botanic gardens, Maritime Discovery Centre and WWII memorial water tower. You can hop on and off as you please.

The Powerhouse Motor & Car Museum ( ☎ 5523 5795; www.portlandnow.net.au/powerhouse; cnr Glenelg & Percy Sts; adult/child/family $6/2/12) has 30 vintage Australian and American vehicles and motorbikes dating from 1920.

The grand old Burswood Homestead ( ☎ 5523 4686; burswood@ansonic.com.au; 15 Cape Nelson Rd; admission adult/

## GREAT SOUTH WEST WALK

This 250km signposted loop begins and ends at Portland, and takes in some of the southwest's most stunning natural scenery, from the remote, blustery coast, through the river system of the Lower Glenelg National Park and back through the hinterland to Portland. Brilliantly conceived to connect some of the region's best camping grounds, comfortable accommodation and dining options can also be included. The whole loop would take at least 10 days, but it can be done in sections, and parts can be done as day-walks. Maps are available from the Portland visitors centre (right) and the Parks Victoria and visitors centre in Nelson (opposite). All information, FAQs and registration details are available online at www.greatsouthwestwalk.com.

(right)
(opposite)

## TRANSPORT: PORTLAND

Distance from Melbourne 482km

Direction Southwest

Travel time Melbourne to Portland 6½ hours (4¼ hours via A1 inland route)

Bus V/Line ( ☎ 13 61 96; www.vline.com.au) buses connect Portland with Port Fairy three times daily and once on Sunday ($6.50, 55 minutes) and Warrnambool ($9, 1½ hours). Buses depart from Henty St.

Car Portland is 45 minutes west of Port Fairy on the A1.

child $3/free; ☉ 10am-5pm) was built for Edward Henty in 1850, with 5.5 hectares of gardens.

## INFORMATION

Parks Victoria ( ☎ 5522 3454; www.parkweb.vic.gov.au; 8-12 Julia St; ☉ 8am-4.30pm Mon-Fri)

Portland visitors centre ( ☎ 5523 2671; www.great oceanroad.org; Lee Breakwater Rd; ☉ 9am-5pm) In the impressive-looking Maritime Discovery Centre.

## EATING

Sullys Café & Wine Bar ( ☎ 5523 5355; 55 Bentinck St; mains $15-18; ☉ breakfast, lunch & dinner) 'Safe, sustainable cuisine' is the ethos at Sullys, a narrow and pleasant nook across from the waterfront.

Sandilands ( ☎ 5523 3319; 33 Percy St; mains $16-24; ☉ dinner Mon & Wed-Sat) This elegant manor's imposing façade suggests scary sophistication, but reception-centre chairs tone it down a notch. There are some good vegetarian options with stir-fry, pasta and risotto dishes.

## SLEEPING

Burswood Homestead ( ☎ 5523 4686; burswood@ansonic .com.au; 15 Cape Nelson Rd; s/d incl breakfast from $105/150) Set in beautiful gardens, this rather regal place is an indulgent, antique-laden minimansion. Spacious master rooms have bathrooms, and Devonshire tea is served on arrival.

Clifftop Accommodation ( ☎ 5523 1126; www.portland accommodation.com.au; 13 Clifton Ct; s/d from $115/135; ☒ ) The panoramic ocean views from the balconies here are incredible. These two self-contained rooms are huge, with big brass beds, telescopes and a modern maritime feel.

Victoria House ( ☎ 5521 7577; www.babs.com.au/vic house; 5 Tyers St; s/d incl breakfast from $130/145) This excellent two-storey Georgian bluestone dwelling right in the town centre was built in 1853 and is National Trust classified. It's been stylishly renovated with nine heritage-style guestrooms with bathrooms, a comfy lounge, open fires and a garden.

Henty Bay Van & Cabin Park ( ☎ 5523 1904; www.henty bay.com.au; 342 Dutton Way; unpowered/powered sites from $20/25, cabins from $80; 🖳 ) This park, 5km from town, has wireless internet and cybercafé, ATM, kitchen, laundry, covered BBQs, boat ramps, TV lounge and disabled access.

# PORTLAND TO SOUTH AUSTRALIA

From Portland you can go north to Heywood and rejoin the Princes Hwy to SA, or head northwest along the slower, beautiful coastal route known as the Portland-Nelson Rd. This road runs inland from the coast, but along the way there are turn-offs leading to beaches and national parks.

## NELSON
pop 230

Tiny Nelson is the last vestige of civilisation before the South Australian border – just a general store, pub and a handful of accommodation places. It's a popular holiday and fishing spot at the mouth of the Glenelg River, which flows through Lower Glenelg National Park. Note that Nelson uses South Australia's 08 telephone area code. Why? We dunno!

The Parks Victoria & Nelson visitors centre ( ☎ 08-8738 4051; nelsonvic@hotkey.net.au; 🕑 9am-5pm; 🖳 ) is just before the Glenelg River bridge.

Nelson Boat & Canoe Hire ( ☎ 08-8738 4048; www .nelsonboatandcanoehire.com.au) can rig you up for serious river-camping expeditions – canoe hire costs from $40 a day.

Book a leisurely 3½-hour cruise with Glenelg River Cruises ( ☎ 08-8738 4191; www.glenelgrivercruises .com.au; cruises adult/child $25/10). The cruise stops at the Princess Margaret Rose Cave ( ☎ 08-8738 4171; www .princessmargaretrosecave.com; admission adult/child/family $12/7/28), but tickets for the cave tour cost extra. Cruises depart daily in summer at 1pm, but don't operate Monday and Friday during the rest of the year. If you travel to the cave on your own, it's about 17km from Nelson, towards the border.

Nelson Cottage ( ☎ 08-8738 4161; www.nelsoncottage .bigpondhosting.com; cnr Kellett & Sturt Sts; d $80) has old-fashioned rooms with clean shared amenities.

The 1848 Nelson Hotel ( ☎ 08-8738 4011; www .nelsonhotel.com.au; Kellett St; d/apt from $60/135; mains $14-18; 🕑 lunch & dinner) has a dusty stuffed pelican above the bar and a few vegetarian meals on the fishy menu. The quarters are plain but adequate with shared facilities, and the apartments are large and self-contained.

Wrens on Glenelg ( ☎ 08-8738 4198; www.wrenson glenelg.com.au; 5 Acacia St; d incl breakfast $160) is a swish, modern B&B done in designer corrugated iron in a nice bush setting, with a private landing on the Glenelg River.

The Kywong Caravan Park ( ☎ 08-8738 4174; www .kywongcp.com; North Nelson Rd; unpowered/powered sites $15/20, d cabins from $50) is next to the national park and Glenelg River.

There are nine camp sites between Nelson and Dartmoor along the Glenelg River that are popular with canoeists but accessible by road, with rain-fed water tanks, toilets and fireplaces (BYO firewood). Camping permits are issued by Parks Victoria in Nelson. Forest Camp South is the nicest of these, right on the river, rich in bird life and easily accessible from the Portland-Nelson Rd.

---

## DETOUR: CAPE BRIDGEWATER

Cape Bridgewater is an essential 21km detour off the Portland-Nelson Rd. The stunning 4km arc of Bridgewater Bay is perhaps one of Australia's finest stretches of white-sand surf beach, backed by pristine dunes. The road continues on to Cape Duquesne where walking tracks lead to a Blowhole and the Petrified Forest on the clifftop. A longer two-hour return walk takes you to a seal colony where you can see dozens of fur seals sunning themselves on the rocks.

There's plenty of accommodation available at Cape Bridgewater (inquire at Portland visitors centre, opposite), but standouts include Sea View Lodge B&B ( ☎ 5526 7276; fax 5526 7125; Bridgewater Rd; d from $140), Abalone Beach House ( ☎ 0408-808 346; www.abalonehouse.com.au; Bridgewater Rd; house sleeping 4 from $230) and Cape Bridge-water Bay House ( ☎ 9439 2966; www.capebridgewater.com.au; Bridgewater Rd; up to 4 people $190, extra person $25), an outstanding original bluestone house, refurbished with recycled timber and designer flare, which can sleep eight. For those with more meagre means there's Cape Bridgewater Holiday Camp ( ☎ 5526 7267; darrjen@hotkey .net.au; Blowhole Rd; unpowered sites/dm/cabins $20/15/80).

Gold, gold, gold. Over a third of the world's gold has come out of Victoria. So how come all the locals aren't rich? Share a little of the rewards by heading to one of the state's most interesting areas, the goldfields region. Gold fever informed the area's history, and everywhere you go are reminders of the rich heritage of the gold rush days: grand, classic Victorian buildings; boulevards wide enough to turn a bullock team in; imposing banks with bushranger-proof vaults and fortified yards alongside for the wagons; old mining sites; fascinating museums and cemeteries. Fabulous attractions are linked to the era. Sovereign Hill, in Ballarat, is one of Australia's most popular tourist spots; Bendigo has the famous Chinese dragons, Old Loong and Sun Loong; Castlemaine is surrounded by charming, historic hamlets. Up around Moliagul it's called the 'Golden Triangle' because so many nuggets were found, big ones too, including the Welcome Stranger, the largest alluvial nugget ever found in the world.

Daylesford and Hepburn Springs, in the scenic central highlands, are famous for their mineral spas. Along with the healing waters are masseurs and naturopaths, gardens and craft shops, restored guesthouses and cottages, and great eateries.

This blend of quaint townships and grand regional centres sprawls across dramatically contrasting landscapes, from pretty countryside and green forests to red earth and granite country. The Grampians, an adventurer's paradise, stand majestically over the idyllic Wartook Valley and cute, touristy Dunkeld. Further north amidst the expanses of wheat and sheep properties are the wide open spaces of the Little Desert.

Go exploring, go bike touring, horse riding, prospecting. Bush-walkers will find trails everywhere and never too far from a musty old pub, rose garden café, olive farm or winery. Whatever you want is what you'll find.

## PROSPECTING

The old diggers dug up most of the gold, but even today significant nuggets are unearthed. This adds a whole new dimension to walking in the bush! First check out all the major gold-rush centres – there's a well-signposted Goldfields Tourist Route; get a route map from any visitors centre. Join other prospectors on the alluvial goldfields of Maryborough (p266). Buy a gold-panning kit at Castlemaine visitors centre and go splash around at nearby Forest Creek Historic Gold Diggings (p258). Carmen's Tunnel, out of Maldon (p265), never produced much gold, so that may be a good place to start. Or get some help, on a tour with one of the adventure companies that guarantees you will find gold. If all else fails, try to pick up a little gold dust at Sovereign Hill (opposite) in Ballarat and experience the Eureka spirit of the times when the miners struggled against injustice. Then see goldmining 500m underground at Central Deborah Goldmine in Bendigo (p255).

## LUXURIATING

This area is rich in produce and services to keep your senses glowing with gratitude. Daylesford and Hepburn Springs (p259) have been famous for their spa baths and body treatments since the 1800s, when wealthy city slickers came up from Melbourne to relax. Nowadays there are also olive farms, wineries, trout farms, lavender farms, produce stores with bottles of healthy goodies, and chocolate outlets where you can watch the production of the little nuggets. Then, when you've been totally massaged and eaten sufficient lavender ice cream, take a stroll through one of the magnificent botanic gardens, like Baron Ferdinand von Mueller's work of art in Kyneton (p262), or the very old Botanic Gardens (p264) in Castlemaine, which has National Trust–registered trees.

## ADVENTURE SPORTS

The Grampians are renowned for spectacular scenery and kilometres of walks throughout, but the rock climbing and abseiling in the area are thrilling. You'll find adventure companies (p266) ready to give you a wild and wonderful time. While you're enjoying the great outdoors, head north to the Little Desert National Park (p271) for a totally grounding holiday. Then hop on a horse for a ride through bush and desert, along creeks and past lagoons at any horse riding centre from Wartook Valley (p271) to Daylesford and up to Bendigo.

# GENEALOGY

Many aspects of Australia's history are brought alive in the region's historic towns, museums and sites, but the goldfields provide another rich resource for anyone tracing a family history. Each weekend, there's an exodus of people from Melbourne to the area's cemeteries (p264) and associated historic societies. The Goldfields Historical Chinese Cemetery in Bendigo is a moving place to visit, even if you're not looking for ancestors. The Pennyweight Children's Cemetery in Castlemaine will leave a memory of the sad and impossibly difficult years the pioneers struggled through. The mausoleum at Maryborough gives further insights into the past, as do the gravestones in the cemetery at Maldon, where ghosts still linger.

# BALLARAT

**pop 78,300**

The area around here was known to the local Koories as 'Ballaarat', meaning 'resting place'. When gold was discovered in August 1851, thousands of diggers flooded in, forming a shanty town of tents and huts. Ballarat's alluvial goldfields were the tip of the golden iceberg, and when deep shaft mines were sunk they struck incredibly rich quartz reefs. About 28 percent of Victoria's gold came from Ballarat.

The original town of canvas and bark was replaced with a wealth of gracious Victorian-era buildings. The main drag, impressive Sturt St, had to be three chains wide (60m) to allow for the turning circle of bullock wagons. Lydiard St is a historic precinct with some of the finest examples of Victorian architecture, reminding us of how prosperous the town was, and

still is. The Camp St arts precinct buzzes with student activity and includes a public open space for the performing arts. The jewel in this historic and architecturally intriguing precinct is Ballarat Fine Art Gallery ( ☎ 5320 5858; www .balgal.com; 40 Lydiard St Nth; adult/child $5/free; ☺ 9am-5pm) which houses a wonderful collection of early colonial paintings, works from noted Australian artists (including Tom Roberts, Sir Sidney Nolan, Russell Drysdale and Fred Williams) and contemporary works. A section is devoted to the Lindsay family who lived in nearby Creswick.

Allow at least half a day to visit Sovereign Hill ( ☎ 5331 1944; www.sovereignhill.com.au; Magpie St; adult/child/family $35/16/90; ☺ 10am-5pm), a fascinating re-creation of an 1860s gold-mining township. The site was mined in the gold-rush era and much of the equipment is original, as is the mine shaft. There are above-ground and underground diggings. You can pan for gold in the stream – maybe you'll find a speck or two – and watch an hourly gold pour. The main street is a living history museum with people performing their chores dressed in costumes of the time. Several places offer food, from pies at the Hope Bakery to a three-course lunch at the United States Hotel. Sovereign Hill opens again at night for the impressive sound-and-light show Blood on the Southern Cross ( ☎ 5333 5777; ticket combined with Sovereign Hill admission adult/child/family $74/36/196; ☺ summer 9.15 & 10.30pm, winter 6.45 & 8pm), a simulation of the Eureka Stockade battle. Bookings are essential (and check the show times).

Your ticket also gets you into the nearby Gold Museum ( ☎ 5331 1944; Magpie St; adult/child $9/4.50; ☺ 9.30am-5.20pm) which sits on a mullock heap from an old mine. There's imaginative displays and samples from all the old mining

## TRANSPORT: BALLARAT

Distance from Melbourne 116km

Direction Northwest

Travel time 1½ hours

Bus Greyhound Australia ( ☎ 13 14 99; www.greyhound.com.au) has Adelaide-to-Melbourne buses that stop at Ballarat (departs Adelaide 8pm; adult/child $72/51, 8½ hours) if you ask the driver. Airport Shuttlebus ( ☎ 5333 4181; www.airportshuttlebus.com.au) goes direct from Melbourne Airport to Ballarat train station (return $45, 1½ hours, seven times daily).

Car Ballarat is a smooth drive up the Western Hwy from Melbourne.

Train V/Line ( ☎ 13 61 96; www.vline.com.au) runs between Melbourne (Southern Cross station) and Ballarat (return $20, 1½ hours, 21 daily).

# GOLDFIELDS & THE GRAMPIANS

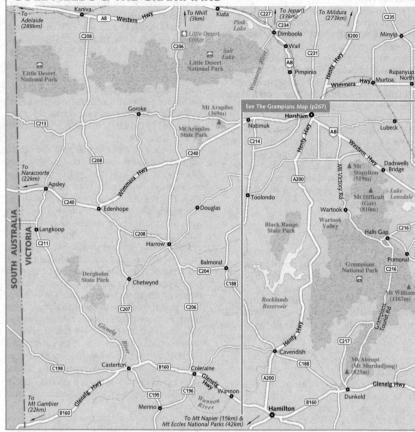

areas, as well as gold nuggets, coins and a display on the Eureka Rebellion.

On the site of the rebellion is the Eureka Centre ( ☎ 5333 1854; www.eurekaballarat.com; cnr Eureka & Rodier Sts; adult/child/family $8/4/22; ☺ 9am-5pm) – look out for the huge Eureka sail. Connect with Australia's fighting spirit through multimedia galleries simulating the battle, then move into the 'contemplation space' to be soothed by the sound of running water.

Beautiful and serene, Ballarat's Botanic Gardens ( ☎ 5320 5135; www.ballarat.com/botanicgardens; Wendouree Pde; admission free; ☺ sunrise-sunset) were first planted in 1858. Stroll through the 40 hectares of immaculately maintained rose gardens, wide lawns and colourful conservatory. Visit the cottage of poet Adam Lindsay Gordon or walk along the Prime Ministers' Avenue, a collection

of bronze portraits. A Tourist Tramway ( ☎ 5334 1580; www.btm.org.au; rides adult/child $3/1.50; ☺ noon-5pm Sat & Sun) operates around the gardens, departing from the Tram Museum. Across Wendouree Pde is a fantastic, wooden Adventure Playground. Drive slowly: the swans step gracefully over the road at unexpected moments.

Don't miss the attractive Ballarat Wildlife Park ( ☎ 5333 5933; www.wildlifepark.com.au; cnr York & Fussell Sts; adult/child/family $20/13/60; ☺ 9am-5.30pm, tour 11am) where you walk among sweet little King Island wallabies in a tranquil park. Happily, the crocodiles are in a compound. Other native species include Tasmanian devils, emus, quokkas, snakes, eagles and a giant tortoise. Weekend programs include a koala show, wombat show and crocodile-feeding. If you like them with feathers, go to Ballarat Bird World

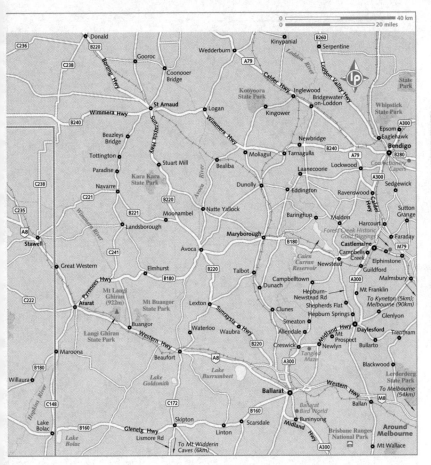

( ☎ 5341 3843; www.ballaratbirdworld.com.au; 408 Eddy Ave; adult/child/family $10/6/30; ☼ 10am-5pm), where 40 different types of birds hang out in peaceful gardens with ponds and waterfalls.

Equally peaceful is the charming space of Kirrit Barreet ( ☎ 5332 2755; www.aboriginalballarat.com.au; 403 Main Rd; admission free, tours $5; ☼ 9am-5pm Mon-Fri, 10am-4pm Sat & Sun, tours 11am & 3pm), a place of creation where you'll find work by distinguished artists who also conduct workshops.

Despite its notoriously hardy climate, Ballarat has four large outdoor pools. The heated Eureka Swimming Centre ( ☎ 5331 2820; cnr Stawell & Eureka Sts; ☼ 1-7pm Mon-Fri, 11am-7pm Sat & Sun) has a giant water slide and minigolf. The indoor Ballarat Aquatic Centre ( ☎ 5334 2499; Gillies St Nth; adult/child/family $5/3/12; ☼ 6am-9pm Mon-Fri, 8am-6pm Sat & Sun) has several pools and a gym.

Lake Wendouree, a large artificial lake, is a focal point for the town. Old timber boatsheds spread along the shore, and when there's water in the lake you'll often see rowing boats being stroked across. The jogging track around the lake is also popular. In early 2008, the lake was scarily dry; hopefully the drought will have broken by the time you read this.

So you think minigolf is kid's stuff? Not at this place. Gold Rush Mini Golf ( ☎ 5334 8150; www .goldrushgolf.com.au; Western Hwy, Warrenheip; 1/2 rounds adult $12/16, child $7/11, family $32/48; ☼ 10am-8pm, to 10pm Fri & Sat) has two 18-hole courses with cute themes (in case your game's too bad to watch). There's arcade games, a barbecue and café as well.

Pick up the brochures Eureka Trails and Tracks & Trails from the visitors centre. They walk you through interesting parts of Ballarat,

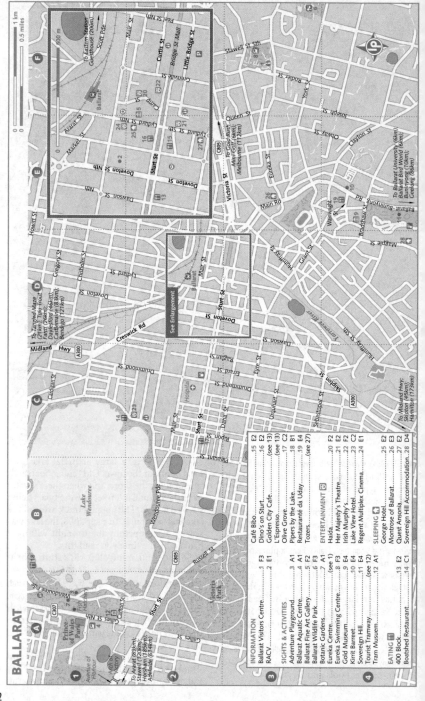

# BALLARAT

0 ———————— 1 km
0 ———————— 0.5 miles

**INFORMATION**

| | |
|---|---|
| Ballarat Visitors Centre | 1 F3 |
| RACV | 2 E1 |

**SIGHTS & ACTIVITIES**

| | |
|---|---|
| Adventure Playground | 3 A1 |
| Ballarat Aquatic Centre | 4 A1 |
| Ballarat Fine Art Gallery | 5 F2 |
| Ballarat Wildlife Park | 6 F3 |
| Botanic Gardens | 7 A1 |
| Eureka Centre | (see 1) |
| Eureka Swimming Centre | 8 F3 |
| Gold Museum | 9 E4 |
| Kirrit Barreet | 10 E4 |
| Sovereign Hill | 11 E4 |
| Tourist Tramway | (see 12) |
| Tram Museum | 12 A1 |

**EATING**

| | |
|---|---|
| 400 Block | 13 E2 |
| Boatshed Restaurant | 14 C1 |
| Café Bibo | 15 E2 |
| Dino's on Sturt | 16 E2 |
| Golden City Cafe | (see 13) |
| L'Espresso | 17 C2 |
| Olive Grove | 18 B1 |
| Pipers by the Lake | 19 E4 |
| Restauranté da Uday | (see 27) |
| Tozers | |

**ENTERTAINMENT** 

| | |
|---|---|
| Haida | 20 F2 |
| Her Majesty's Theatre | 21 E2 |
| Irish Murphy's | 22 F2 |
| Lake View Hotel | 23 C2 |
| Regent Multiplex Cinema | 24 E1 |

**SLEEPING**

| | |
|---|---|
| George Hotel | 25 E2 |
| Montrose of Ballarat | 26 E3 |
| Quest Ansonia | 27 E2 |
| Sovereign Hill Accommodation | 28 D4 |

following historical, nature, cultural, literary, sculpture and many other themed trails. Another brochure, *Parks & Gardens*, gives you info on all local gardens and which ones have barbecue facilities and playgrounds. Or be collected for a 90-minute Heritage & History Sight Seeing Tour ( ☎ 1800 626 666; www.Go2000.com.au; tours $20) in a small bus.

## INFORMATION

Ballarat visitors centre ( ☎ 1800 446 633, 5320 5741; www.visitballarat.com.au; Eureka Centre, cnr Eureka & Rodier Sts; ☯ 9am-5pm) Stacks of info about sights and activities, right beside absorbing Eureka displays and galleries. Ask here about all your accommodation options, or browse www.ballarat.com.

Royal Automobile Club of Victoria (RACV; ☎ 5332 1946; www.racv.com.au; 20 Doveton St Nth) Has an information section and accommodation-booking service.

## FESTIVALS & EVENTS

Open Road Cycling (www.visitballarat.com.au) Five days of time trials and road races over a 10.2km circuit; held in early January.

Organs of the Ballarat Goldfields (www.ballarat.com /organs) A week of recitals and musical celebrations held outdoors or in grand cathedrals and churches; occurs in mid-January.

Arts in the Park (www.ballarat.vic.gov.au) Free music on the foreshore of Lake Wendouree every Sunday from early January to late February.

Begonia Festival (www.ballaratbegoniafestival.com) This 100-year-old festival, held in early March, includes sensational floral displays, a street parade, fireworks, art shows and music.

Heritage Weekend (www.ballaratheritageweekend.com) Free entry to heritage sites in mid-May.

Ballarat Antique Fair (www.ballaratantiquefair.com .au) Three days in mid-March, 95 exhibitors and antiques, buyers and sellers from all over Australia.

Australian Cycling Grand Prix (www.ballarat.vic.gov.au/ calendar/events_ballarat.asp) Time trials and road race events for the national championships; held in August.

Royal South St Eisteddfod (www.visitballarat.com.au) If you learnt music as a child, you were probably dragged off to Australia's oldest eisteddfod; held September or October .

## EATING

There are interesting eating options in the city. The cafés along the 400 Block (Sturt St) from L'Espresso

( ☎ 5333 1789; 417 Sturt St; mains $11-18.50; ☯ 7am-6pm, to 11pm Fri & Sat) up to Golden City Cafe ( ☎ 5331 6211; 427 Sturt St; mains $16-28; ☯ 8am-11pm) spill their tables out all day, along with the aroma of coffee.

Café Bibo ( ☎ 5331 1255; 205 Sturt St; mains $11-27; ☯ breakfast & lunch) Bibo is a retro café lined with copies of 1960s *Women's Weekly* and shelves holding regulars' coffee cups.

Dino's on Sturt ( ☎ 5332 9711; 212 Sturt St; mains $14-28; ☯ breakfast, lunch & dinner) Across the road from Bibo, Dino's is welcoming, child-friendly and sophisticated, with a menu that you'll love.

Tozers ( ☎ 5338 8908; 32 Lydiard St Sth; mains $27-33; ☯ breakfast daily, lunch Tue-Fri, dinner Mon-Sat) For fine dining, Tozers has fabulous food. Since it moved into Quest Ansonia, it opens for breakfast as well. What a way to start the day!

Restauranté day Uday ( ☎ 5331 6655; 7 Wainwright St; mains $21-31; ☯ breakfast, lunch & dinner) Come to this pretty converted cottage and enjoy the intoxicating aromas, or collect takeaway – Indian, Thai or Italian.

Olive Grove ( ☎ 5331 4455; 1303 Sturt St; pies $9; ☯ 8.30am-7pm) Up towards the lake is this fantastic deli, full of gourmet delights, including pies, focaccias, cakes and cheeses.

Boatshed Restaurant ( ☎ 5333 5533; Lake Wendouree; mains $18-27; ☯ breakfast, lunch & dinner) Sit on the deck over the lake or stay inside with the open fire and armchairs. Either way there's a busy atmosphere, excellent coffee and an exciting menu.

Pipers by the Lake ( ☎ 5334 1811; Lake Wendouree; mains $18-25; ☯ breakfast & lunch) This 1890 Lakeside Lodge was designed by WH Piper. Huge windows look out over the lake where swans and ducks stick their bottoms up and look for water. The $15 lunch-with-a-drink deal is good value.

## ENTERTAINMENT

With its large student population, Ballarat has a lively nightlife. You can club till 5am, but you cannot enter a venue after 3am.

Irish Murphy's ( ☎ 5331 4091; 36 Sturt St; ☯ to 3am Wed-Sun) An atmospheric place; the live music draws people of all ages and there's plenty of Guinness on tap.

Haida ( ☎ 5331 5346; www.haida.com.au; 12 Camp St; ☯ 5pm-late Wed-Sun) Around the corner from Irish Murphy's, Haida is a fresh new space with day beds, fireplaces, a barbecue and totally cocky cocktails.

Lake View Hotel ( ☎ 5331 4592; www.thelakeview .com.au; 22 Wendouree Pde; ☯ 7am-midnight) With its modern spaces in a truly gorgeous old pub, this venue has a buzzy atmosphere and great views over the lake.

**Her Majesty's Theatre** ( ☎ 5333 5800; www.hermaj.com; 17 Lydiard St Sth) Ballarat's main venue for the performing arts is a wonderful building. Ring to find out what's on while you're in town.

**Regent Multiplex Cinema** ( ☎ 5331 1399; www.regentmultiplex.com.au/ballarat; 49 Lydiard St Nth; ☾ 9.30am-9.30pm) Ballarat's main cinema complex.

## SLEEPING

Ballarat's grand old pubs, B&Bs and cottages all offer gracious accommodation, and there are many motels and holiday resorts, all with budget through to luxury units. Accommodation is scarce in September/October, when the Royal South St Eisteddfod takes place.

**Eastern Station Guesthouse** ( ☎ 5338 8722; www.ballarat.com/easternstation.htm; 81 Humffray St Nth; s/d/f $35/60/80) Built in 1862, this guest house opens as a corner pub on weekends. In the meantime, there's fresh and spacious rooms, a grand kitchen opening onto a deck and two large games and TV rooms.

**George Hotel** ( ☎ 5333 4866; www.georgehotelballarat.com.au; 27 Lydiard St Nth; ✖ ) This gorgeous pub in historic Lydiard St was rebuilt in 1902 with towering ceilings and sweeping walnut staircases. It was due to reopen late 2008, so check the 'newly renovated' rates as they're bound to be reasonable.

**Montrose of Ballarat** ( ☎ 0429-439 448; www.montroseofballarat.com.au; 111 Eureka St; cottages from $190; ✖ ▣ ) For a 'golden era' experience this bluestone cottage is classified by the National Trust, but offers total luxury as well.

**Quest Ansonia** ( ☎ 5332 4678; www.ballarat.com/ansonia.htm; 32 Lydiard St Sth; d from $149; ✖ ) An upmarket retreat, this place exudes calm with its minimalist design, polished cement floors and light-filled atrium. Rooms range from studio apartments for two to family suites.

**Sovereign Hill Accommodation** ( ☎ 5337 1159; www.sovereignhill.com.au; Magpie St) You can choose from several spots, inside and outside Sovereign Hill. There's the little **YHA Cottage** (dm/s/tw $22/34/60) set in the pine forest – it's quietly fantastic. Up the hill, the **Lodge B&B** (s/d/f $115/135/165) has gorgeous heritage rooms around a cosy guest lounge with fireplace and bar, along with some dorm rooms for large groups ($22 per person). There are also **motel rooms** (s/d/f $115/135/165) out the back, or go over the fence and stay in the 1850s township at **Steinfeld's**.

The rates are all the same as above; facilities are good (and often fully booked) and there are often packages and specials.

# BENDIGO
**pop 76,000**

Beautiful, glorious Bendigo – centre of the fantastically rich Bendigo Diggings, which covered more than 360 sq km. It looks solid, imposing and extravagant, the impressive Victorian architecture a testimony to gold. When the precious blobs were discovered at Ravenswood in 1851, diggers converged on the area. When they ran out of surface gold they turned their pans and cradles to Bendigo Creek. It is said the maids at the Shamrock Hotel mopped the floor every night to collect the gold dust brought in on the drinkers' boots. Yep, this is gold territory.

The arrival of thousands of Chinese miners in 1854 had a lasting effect on the town, despite the racial tensions that surfaced. Reminders of the Chinese diggers can be seen everywhere.

In the 1860s the scene changed again as independent miners were outclassed by the powerful mining companies, with their heavy machinery. The companies poured money into the town and some 35 quartz reefs were found. The ground underneath Bendigo is still honeycombed with mine shafts. Work was halted in the mid-1950s but Bendigo Mining is about to recommence extracting the high-grade mineralisation.

Bendigo is still prosperous, and you'll find an interesting collection of mines, museums and historic buildings, one of the best regional

---

## TRANSPORT: BENDIGO

**Distance from Melbourne 148km**

**Direction Northwest**

**Travel time 1½ hours**

**Bus** Bendigo Airport Service ( ☎ 5439 4044; www.bendigoairportservice.com.au) runs direct to Melbourne Airport (return $65, two hours, three daily). Bookings essential.

**Train** V/Line ( ☎ 13 61 96; www.vline.com.au) runs between Melbourne (Southern Cross station) and Bendigo (return $30, two hours, 16 daily).

**Car** Bendigo is a pleasant drive up the Calder Hwy from Melbourne.

# BENDIGO

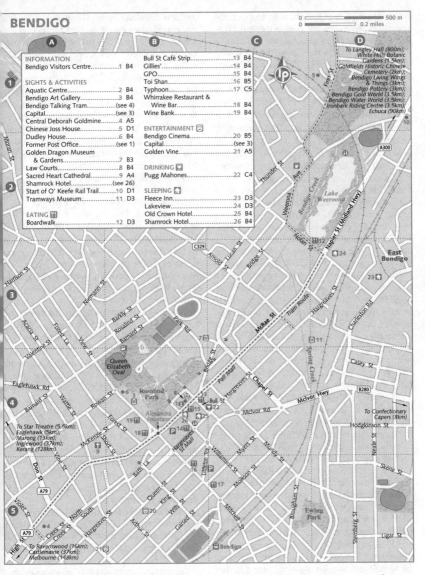

| INFORMATION | |
|---|---|
| Bendigo Visitors Centre................1 | B4 |

| SIGHTS & ACTIVITIES | |
|---|---|
| Aquatic Centre.............................2 | B4 |
| Bendigo Art Gallery.....................3 | B4 |
| Bendigo Talking Tram............(see 4) | |
| Capital..................................(see 3) | |
| Central Deborah Goldmine..........4 | A5 |
| Chinese Joss House......................5 | D1 |
| Dudley House..............................6 | B4 |
| Former Post Office..................(see 1) | |
| Golden Dragon Museum | |
| & Gardens................................7 | B3 |
| Law Courts.................................8 | B4 |
| Sacred Heart Cathedral...............9 | A4 |
| Shamrock Hotel.....................(see 26) | |
| Start of O' Keefe Rail Trail........10 | D1 |
| Tramways Museum....................11 | D3 |

| EATING 🍴 | |
|---|---|
| Boardwalk................................12 | D3 |

| | |
|---|---|
| Bull St Café Strip.......................13 | B4 |
| Gillies'......................................14 | B4 |
| GPO.........................................15 | B4 |
| Toi Shan...................................16 | B5 |
| Typhoon...................................17 | C5 |
| Whirrakee Restaurant & | |
| Wine Bar................................18 | B4 |
| Wine Bank................................19 | B4 |

| ENTERTAINMENT 🎭 | |
|---|---|
| Bendigo Cinema........................20 | B5 |
| Capital...................................(see 3) | |
| Golden Vine..............................21 | A5 |

| DRINKING 🍸 | |
|---|---|
| Pugg Mahones...........................22 | C4 |

| SLEEPING 🛏 | |
|---|---|
| Fleece Inn................................23 | D3 |
| Lakeview..................................24 | D3 |
| Old Crown Hotel.......................25 | B4 |
| Shamrock Hotel.........................26 | B4 |

art galleries in Australia, plus some great wineries in the surrounding district.

The city's impressive buildings are first seen in Pall Mall as a splendid trio: the Shamrock Hotel, Law Courts and former Post Office, which is now the visitors centre, with a permanent exhibition commemorating the city and its role in Federation. Wander inside all three – the interiors are just as elaborate as the exteriors.

View St is a historic streetscape with some fine buildings, including the Capital, which houses the Bendigo Art Gallery, and Dudley House, classified by the National Trust.

For a very deep experience, go down the 500m-deep Central Deborah Goldmine ( ☎ 5443 8322; www.central-deborah.com; 76 Violet St; adult/child/family $19/10/49; ☿ 9.30am-5pm) with a geologist. Worked on 17 levels, about 1000kg of gold has been removed. After donning hard hats and lights, you're taken down the shaft to inspect the operations, complete with drilling demonstrations. Other packages are available, including a very fast drop in a mining cage (for the young of heart). If you pay $29/16/75 per adult/child/family, you get the mine tour plus a ride on the Bendigo Talking Tram ( ☎ 5443 8322; www.bendigotramways.com; 76 Violet St; adult/child/family $13/8/37; ☼ 9.30am-3.30pm) from the mine, through the city, out to the Tramways Museum ( ☎ 5442 2821; 1 Tramways Rd; admission free with tram ticket; ☼ 10am-5pm).

You can get off at the Chinese Joss House ( ☎ 5442 1685; Finn St; North Bendigo; adult/child $3/1; ☼ 11am-4pm Wed, Sat & Sun) and catch a later tram back; this is a practising joss house (a temple where idols are worshipped). Painted red, the traditional colour for strength, its entrance is guarded by a pair of *kylin* – mythical guardian beasts. Exhibits include figures representing the Chinese solar cycle, commemorative tablets to the deceased, paintings and Chinese lanterns.

Construction of the massive Sacred Heart Cathedral (www.sand.catholic.org.au/cathedral; cnr Wattle & High Sts; ☼ 7.30am-3.30pm) began in the 19th century and was completed in 2001 with the installation of bells from Italy in the belfry. Inside, there's a magnificently carved bishop's chair, some beautiful stained-glass windows and wooden angels jutting out of the ceiling arches. The pews are made from Australian blackwood and the marble is Italian.

The Bendigo Art Gallery ( ☎ 5443 4991; www.bendigoartgallery.com.au; 42 View St; admission by donation; ☼ 10am-5pm, tours 2pm) is a most special place. Its permanent collection includes outstanding colonial and contemporary Australian art, such as work by Charles Blackman, Fred Williams, Rupert Bunny and Lloyd Rees; the annual temporary exhibitions are cutting edge.

Walk through a huge wooden door into an awesome chamber filled with dragons. It's the Golden Dragon Museum & Gardens ( ☎ 5441 5044; www.goldendragonmuseum.org; Bridge St; adult/child/family $8/4/20; ☼ 9.30am-5pm), and its glorious dragons include the Imperial Dragons Old Loong (the oldest in the world) and Sun Loong (the longest in the world – it just keeps on going). Old Loong arrived in 1892 to feature in the Easter Procession. Sun Loong took over in 1970 when Old Loong retired. The museum also displays amazing Chinese heritage items and costumes. Outside, the classical Chinese gardens have bridges, water features and ornamental shrubs. The tearoom serves simple, Chinese-style dishes.

Rosalind Park (north of Pall Mall) is a lovely, spacious place, with lawns, big old trees, fernery and the fabulous Cascades Fountain, which was excavated after being buried for 120 years. Climb to the top of the lookout tower for sensational 360-degree views, or if you love roses, wander through the Conservatory Gardens.

The White Hills Botanic Gardens (Midland Hwy, White Hills; ☼ 7.30am-sunset), 2km north of town, features many exotic and rare plant species, a small fauna park, aviary, and barbecue facilities.

It's fun, fun, fun at Confectionery Capers ( ☎ 5449 3111, 0429-409 773; www.confectionerycapers.com; 1028 McIvor Hwy, Junortoun; adult/child/family $6/4/16; ☼ 10am-5pm). No lollies here (8km southeast of town), just an amazing display of whirls, whizzes and word plays: Barbie dolls in a line? A tree in a toilet? You have to go there for it all to make sense…

Bendigo has four big blue outdoor swimming pools – the Aquatic Centre ( ☎ 5443 6151; 191 Barnard St; adult/child $4/3; ☼ 6am-7pm Mon-Fri, 10am-7pm Sat & Sun, closed Jun-Aug) is the closest to the centre of town. There are also ice-skating rinks, an outdoor skating park, an indoor go-kart track, rock climbing and golf courses – ask at the visitors centre for details.

About 4km north of the town centre is the Ironbark Complex (Watson St), with three major activities: Ironbark Riding Centre ( ☎ 5448 3344; www.bwc.com.au/ironbark; rides 1/2hr $35/65; ☼ 8.30am-5pm Mon-Sat) organises various horse rides including the Great Australian Pub Ride to Allies Hotel in Myers Flat (with lunch $75); Bendigo Gold World ( ☎ 5448 4140; www.bendigogold.com.au; half-day $170; ☼ 8.30am-5pm Mon-Sat) has fossicking and detecting tours into the bush with metal detectors, or gold panning at the Mobile Gold-panning Centre (per hr $12); and Bendigo Water World ( ☎ 5448 4140; www.bendigowaterworld.com.au; admission $3, with slides $8, family day pass $65; ☼ 4-7pm Mon-Wed, 4-9pm Thu-Fri, 10.30am-9pm Sat, 10.30am-7pm Sun) where a giant slide zaps you into a pool.

The O'Keefe Rail Trail, a hike-or-bike trail along a disused railway line, starts near the corner of Midland Hwy and Baden St. Pant and push through bushland for 19km to Axedale – allow three/5½ hours to ride/walk one way.

Bendigo Pottery ( ☎ 5448 4404; www.bendigopottery.com.au; Midland Hwy, Epsom; admission free; ☼ 9am-5pm) is the oldest pottery works in Australia. It was founded in 1857 and is classified by the National Trust. The historic kilns are still used; watch potters at work or throw a pot yourself. Also on site is Bendigo Living Wings & Things ( ☎ 5448 3051; adult/child/family $7/4.50/18), where you walk among butterflies, native birds, dingoes and wallabies, or look at reptiles behind glass.

# INFORMATION

Bendigo visitors centre ( ☎ 1800 813 153, 5444 4445; www.bendigotourism.com; 51 Pall Mall; ☼ 9am-5pm) In the historic former post office, offering an accommodation booking service. Ask for the *Daily fun tours!* brochure. For themed city tours see www.snapshotsofbendigo.com.au.

# FESTIVALS & EVENTS

Easter Festival (www.bendigoeasterfestival.org.au) Bendigo's major festival, held in March or April, attracts thousands with its carnival atmosphere and colourful and noisy procession of Chinese dragons.

Bendigo Cup (www.racingvictoria.net.au/vcrc/bendigo) Part of the Spring Racing Carnival; held in November.

Swap Meet (www.bendigoswap.com.au) For enthusiasts in search of that elusive vintage-car spare part. It's so popular that accommodation is at a premium. Held in November.

# EATING

You'll find an interesting range of cafés, pubs and restaurants here. There's the Bull St café strip, or try out the charming spots along View St.

Gillies' ( ☎ 5443 4965; Hargreaves St Mall; pies $3.50; ☼ 8am-6pm Mon-Fri, 9am-4pm Sat & Sun) A Bendigo institution, you queue at the little window, order one of their pies, then sit in the mall to eat it.

Toi Shan ( ☎ 5443 5811; 67 Mitchell St; mains $12-18; ☼ lunch & dinner) Toi Shan had been owned and operated by the same family since 1892. Fortunately the new owners are carrying on the traditional cooking methods and everyone approves.

Whirrakee Restaurant & Wine Bar ( ☎ 5441 5557; 17 View Point; mains $13-28; ☼ dinner Tue-Sat) In the 1908 Royal Bank, there's live music in the gold-weighing room on Friday night. Upstairs, the surroundings and the food are exquisite.

Wine Bank ( ☎ 5444 4655; 45 View St; mains $14-20, ☼ lunch & dinner) Musicians pop in to play any time, the aged bottles soar up the walls and the eating areas are intimate.

Typhoon ( ☎ 5443 3111; cnr Myers & Mitchell Sts; mains $14-16; ☼ dinner) You'll be straight back for more from this metal-and-glass contemporary place serving food with Southeast Asian influences.

GPO ( ☎ 5443 9777; Pall Mall; mains $14-28; ☼ breakfast, lunch & dinner) A splendid, spacious renovation of an old post office, with a courtyard, water feature, big couches for people-watching and a top menu.

Boardwalk ( ☎ 5443 9855; Nolan St; mains $18-29; ☼ breakfast, lunch & dinner) On the shores of Lake Weeroona; watch the moorhens on the lake as you sip your coffee. At night the city lights flicker gold off the water.

Bendigo ninesevensix ( ☎ 5443 8255; www.bendigonine sevensix.com.au; set meal $89; ☼ dinner Sat) On Saturday night a 1952 Melbourne W-class tram becomes a restaurant, but first there's a 6.30pm pre-dinner drink at the Wine Bank (see above).

# ENTERTAINMENT

Pugg Mahones ( ☎ 5443 4916; 224 Hargreaves St; ☼ 10.30am-late Mon-Sat) With Guinness (and many other beers) on tap, Puggs has a thickly welcoming atmosphere, a beer garden and live music every Thursday, Friday and Saturday night till 3am.

Golden Vine ( ☎ 5443 6063; 135 King St; ☼ noon-1am, noon-11pm Sun) One of the best venues, the Vine has popular jam sessions on Tuesday and top bands playing on Wednesday, Friday and Saturday.

Capital ( ☎ 5441 5344; www.bendigo.vic.gov.au; 50 View St) In the beautifully restored Capital Theatre, this is the main venue for the performing arts, with hundreds of performances and exhibitions each year.

Bendigo Cinema ( ☎ 5442 1666; www.bendigocinemas .com.au; 107 Queen St; adult/child $13/10) This cinema shows mainstream Hollywood films in lovely surroundings several times a day.

Star Theatre ( ☎ 5446 2025; www.starcinema.org.au; Eaglehawk Town Hall; adult/child $13/7; ☼ from 1.30pm) Watch a flick with a drink in decadent armchair comfort.

# SLEEPING

Fleece Inn ( ☎ 5443 3086; www.thefleeceinn.com.au; 139 Charleston Rd; B&B dm/s/d $33/44/74; ✸ ) It's looking good! A 145-year-old pub turned accommodation only and sparkling. There's a new breakfast room, spacious bathrooms, wide balcony and a back courtyard with barbecues and games room. Swish up the original timber staircase to the smart upstairs bedrooms and lounges.

Old Crown Hotel ( ☎ 5441 6888, 0408-899 560; 238 Hargreaves St; s/d $40/70) This place is great because it's right in the middle of everything. It has little old pub rooms with shared bathrooms and a TV lounge.

Shamrock Hotel ( ☎ 5443 0333; www.shamrockbendigo .com.au; cnr Pall Mall & Williamson St; r/ste from $110/195; ✸ ) No matter which of the rooms and suites you choose here, you'll feel pampered. Sit out on the grand balcony and lord it over the street, or swan about like one of the famous guests who've been here before you.

**Langley Hall** ( ☎ 5443 3693; www.innhouse.com.au /langleyhall.html; 484 Napier St; B&B s/d from $120/185; 🐾 ) Built in 1904 for the first bishop of Bendigo, Langley Hall offers unfussy opulence: magnificent suites, expansive verandas, parlour, drawing room and billiard room. Or wander across the lawns to the fountain.

**Lakeview** ( ☎ 5445 5300; www.lakeviewresort.com.au; 286 Napier St; B&B d/f/spa room from $130/160/175; 🐾 🏊 ) You've got Lake Weeroona across the road, spacious units around the central courtyard, shaded pool, piazza, and Quills, a fine-dining restaurant with a fab reputation.

Two new services offer stunning maisonettes, suites and apartments in the heart of the city (maisonette/ste/house from $100/160/180):

**Allawah Bendigo** ( ☎ 5444 4655; www.allawahbendigo .com)

**Bendigo Holiday Accommodation** ( ☎ 5439 3588; www .bendigoholidayaccommodation.com)

# GOLDFIELDS TOWNS

Ballarat and Bendigo are big and splendid, but the rest of central Victoria is dotted with former gold-mining communities with enchanting relics of the past and surprisingly modern wine and food. The world's largest alluvial nugget, the 72kg Welcome Stranger, was found in Moliagul in 1869 by John Deason and Richard Oates, who hid it for two days before concealing it in a wagon and taking it to Dunolly, where it was cut into pieces because it was too big to fit on the scales! See a replica of Welcome Stranger and the anvil it was cut up

on at Dunolly's Goldfields Historical Museum ( ☎ 5468 1405; admission free; Broadway; 🕑 1.30-4.30pm Sat & Sun).

**Chewton** (www.chewton.net) is a charming and historic township, with some interesting antique and bric-a-brac shops and a very sweet town hall. Towards Castlemaine is Forest Creek Historic Gold Diggings ( ☎ 5470 6200, 5471 1795; info@ parks.vic.gov.au; Pyrenees Hwy), a section of an 1850s diggings. Take a self-guided tour and pan in the old sluicing dam (just in case you think the old-timers left anything behind). It might be a good idea to first check out how to do it at www.finders.com.au/gold-pages, or contact Golden Triangle Tours ( ☎ 0429-024834; www.goldentriangle tours.com.au), who guarantee you'll find gold.

**Creswick**, just minutes from Ballarat and another old gold-mining town, hosts the fun Forestry Fiesta (www.creswickforestryfiesta.com) in late October. Lose yourself amidst climbing plants and delightful perfumed pathways at the botanical Tangled Maze ( ☎ 5345 2847; www.ballarat.com /tangledmaze.htm; cnr Midland Hwy & Smokeytown Rd, Creswick; adult/child/family $8.50/7.50/30; 🕑 10am-5.30pm). There's 18 holes of minigolf in its landscaped setting between the café, bocce green, nursery and mystery maze puzzles. Alternatively, head north to Smeaton and the Tuki Trout Fishing Complex ( ☎ 5345 6233; www.tuki.com.au; Stoney Rises, Smeaton; adult/child $8/4, rod $5, family with rods $30; 🕑 11am-6pm), catch a fish, and have it barbecued and served in the shearing-shed restaurant.

Arrive in quaint, quiet Talbot at night and visit the Talbot Observatory ( ☎ 5463 2029; www.talbot tourism.org; 9 Camp St; adult/child $5/2.50; 🕑 dusk Fri-Sun). You'll not only see the rings of Saturn and learn about Brown Dwarfs, but you can also join in a 'star-b-que'. Ring to inquire or to arrange your own times.

---

## VICTORIA'S GOLD RUSH

When gold was discovered in New South Wales in May 1851, a reward was offered to anyone who could find gold within 300km of Melbourne. By June, a significant discovery was made at Clunes, a charming little town 32km north of Ballarat, and prospectors headed to Central Victoria.

Over the next few months, fresh gold finds were made almost weekly around Victoria. Then in September 1851 the greatest gold discovery ever known was made at Moliagul, followed by others at Ballarat, Bendigo, Mt Alexander and many more.

By the end of 1851 hopeful miners were coming from England, Ireland, Europe, China and the failing goldfields of California across the Pacific. During 1852 about 1800 people a week arrived in Melbourne ready to head north.

While the gold rush had its tragic side (including epidemics that swept through the camps, plus its share of rogues (including bushrangers who attacked the gold shipments), it ushered in a fantastic era of growth and prosperity for Victoria. Within 12 years, the population had increased from 77,000 to 540,000. Mining companies invested heavily in the region, the development of roads and railways accelerated, and huge shanty towns were replaced by Victoria's modern provincial cities, most notably Ballarat, Bendigo and Castlemaine, which reached the height of their splendour in the 1880s.

## TRANSPORT: GOLDFIELDS TOWNS

**Distance from Melbourne** Castlemaine 120km, Maryborough 165km, Kyneton 80km

**Direction** North-northwest

**Travel times** Castlemaine 1½ hours, Maryborough two hours, Kyneton one hour

**Bus & Train** V/Line (☎ 13 61 96; www.vline.com.au) trains run between Melbourne (Southern Cross station) and Castlemaine (return $22, 1½ hours, 15 daily) and Kyneton (return $17, 1¼ hours, 16 daily). V/Line train/bus services run from Melbourne to Maryborough ($32, three hours, seven daily) via Geelong, Ballarat or Castlemaine; and Daylesford ($18, two hours, four daily) via Woodend or Ballarat. A free shuttle bus runs from Daylesford visitors centre to Hepburn Springs (four daily on weekdays). Castlemaine Bus Lines (☎ 5472 1455; www.castlemainebuslines.com.au) runs to/from Maldon ($6, 20 minutes, weekdays only). Bendigo Airport Service (☎ 5439 4044; www.bendigo airportservice.com.au) runs direct from Melbourne Airport to Castlemaine (return $65, 1½ hours, three daily) and Kyneton (return $55, one hour); bookings essential.

**Car** Maryborough is an easy drive up the Western Hwy from Melbourne, turning off to Creswick and on to Maryborough. Kyneton is on the Calder Hwy a little further north; Castlemaine is just off the Calder Hwy.

Mt Franklin, 10km north of Daylesford, is an extinct volcanic crater. Walking trails take you through lush vegetation, a beautiful picnic area and a lookout. But wait, forget the walk because (oh joy!) the Chocolate Mill (☎ 5476 4208; www.chocmill .com.au; 5451 Midland Hwy, Mt Franklin; ☿ 10am-4.45pm Tue-Sun; talks 11am & 2pm) lets you see the little dollops being made, lets you buy as many as you want and serves the ultimate hot chocolate.

Just north of Hepburn Springs at Shepherds Flat are two interesting spots. Cricket Willow (☎ 5476 4277; www.cricketwillow.com.au; 355 Hepburn-Newstead Rd; ☿ 10.30am-5.30pm Sat-Sun) was where the Oz cricket bat was developed. Tour the workshop, willow tree nursery and museum, or improve your bowling. Across the road, Lavandula (☎ 5476 4393; www.lavandula.com.au; 350 Hepburn-Newstead Rd; adult/child $3.50/1; ☿ 10.30am-5.30pm Sep–mid-Jul) is a Swiss-Italian farm and stone cottage where you can meet the farm animals, check out the gardens and produce, wander between lavender bushes and enjoy lunch in the Ticinese grotto.

# DAYLESFORD & HEPBURN SPRINGS

### pop 3600

Set among the scenic hills, lakes and forests of the Central Highlands, delightful Daylesford and Hepburn Springs together form the 'spa centre of Victoria'. The health-giving properties of the area's mineral springs were first claimed back in the 1870s, attracting droves of fashionable Melburnians, the spas and relaxed scenic environment rejuvenating even the most stressed-out 19th-century city-dweller. The well-preserved and restored buildings show the prosperity of these towns, as well as the lasting influence of the many Swiss-Italian miners who came to work the tunnel mines in the surrounding hills.

These days both towns are popular centres that boast everything you need to promote health and well-being, including fabulous foodie places. The local population is an interesting blend of alternative-lifestylers and old-timers; there's also a thriving gay and lesbian scene here.

Daylesford sits above pretty Lake Daylesford, a popular fishing and picnicking area; boats and kayaks are available for hire. Or hire canoes at Jubilee Lake, about 3km southeast of town, another pretty picnic spot.

Back in town, Vincent St is the major café strip. It turns into Hepburn Rd, which goes straight to the original spa resort. Daylesford's popular attraction, the Convent Gallery (☎ 5348 3211; www.conventgallery.com.au; cnr Hill & Daly Sts; admission $4.50; ☿ 10am-6pm), is a massive 19th-century convent brilliantly converted into a craft and art gallery with soaring ceilings, grand archways, winding staircases and magnificent gardens. The gallery is on Wombat Hill and has an elegant café at the entrance. Also up on the hill is Wombat Hill Botanic Gardens (Central Springs Rd, Daylesford), with a picnic area and lookout tower from where you can get fine views of the countryside. Then take off into those hills on an old railway trolley or restored train: Daylesford Spa Country Tourist Railway (☎ 5348 1759; www.dscr.com.au; Daylesford train station; rides adult/child/family $8/6/20; ☿ 10am-2.45pm Sun) operates one-hour rides up to Bullarto. It's a buzz, but for extra sparkle go on the first Saturday of the month when the Silver Streak Champagne Train Journey (☎ 5348 3622; adult $22; ☿ 5.30pm) indulges

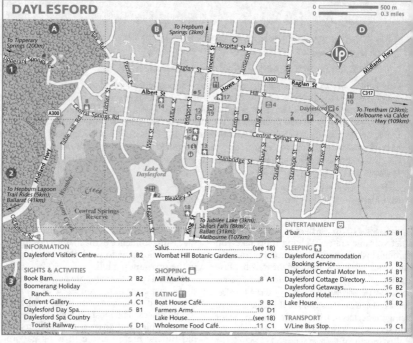

## DAYLESFORD

| 0 | 500 m |
| --- | --- |
| 0 | 0.3 miles |

you with champagne and finger food served on board.

Daylesford and Hepburn Springs are all about health, relaxation and the inner-self (see boxed text, opposite). You'll find traditional massage, reiki, shiatsu, spiritual healing, tarot readings and all sorts of other services. Or treat yourself on long or short walking trails to and from places like Sailors Falls, Tipperary Springs and the Central Springs Reserve; the visitors centre has maps and walking guides.

Horse-lovers will find interesting trails signposted throughout the region, including the Major Mitchell Trail. Or head to the Boomerang Holiday Ranch ( ☎ 5348 2525; http://users.netcon nect.com.au/~b_ranch/intro.htm; Ranch Rd, Daylesford; 1hr rides adult/child $35/30), which runs leisurely trail rides in the state forest. Ten minutes from town, between a picturesque lagoon and the Wombat Forest, is Hepburn Lagoon Trail Rides ( ☎ 5345 7267; www.hepburnlagoonrides.com.au; 60 Telegraph Rd, Mount Prospect; 2hr lagoon/3hr wombat/5hr historic pub lunch rides $80/100/150). Forget your sore bottom and enjoy the gourmet treat you'll be given on your return.

Book lovers must check out Book Barn ( ☎ 5348 3048; notlob@netconnect.com.au; cnr Leggatt & Bleakley Sts,

Daylesford; 11am-5.30pm), which has an unbelievable range of quality secondhand books.

If you feel like dancing, d'bar ( ☎ 5348 2982, 0417-544 035; 1st fl, 74 Vincent St, Daylesford; 8pm-1am Fri, 10pm-1am Sat), a lounge, club and bar, is a local favourite. The DJ plays dance music and R&B on Saturday, while the dinner crowd can listen to live jazz on Friday. For an old Aussie pub experience go out to the Old Hepburn Hotel ( ☎ 5348 2207; 236 Main Rd, Hepburn Springs). There's live music on Saturday from 9pm and Sunday from 4pm. For true suffering, there's karaoke on Friday.

The Palais ( ☎ 5348 4849; www.thepalais.com.au; 111 Main Rd, Hepburn Springs; mains $15-25; dinner Thu-Sun), an atmospheric 1920s theatre, is now a restaurant, café and cocktail bar with lush lounge chairs and a pool table. Performance nights include well-known bands, or there are locals' nights when meals are $10.

For a grand night, catch a movie at the Grande ( ☎ 5348 8500; www.thegrande.com.au; 1-3 Church Ave, Hepburn Springs; movie with snack/meal $15/29; Wed & Sun). Classic, art-house or modern, it doesn't matter: it'll be a special experience in this 1920s cinema.

For shopaholics, the Mill Markets ( ☎ 5348 4332; www.millmarkets.com.au; 105 Central Springs Rd, Daylesford;

○ 10am-6pm) is a playground of antiques and collectables.

# Information

Daylesford visitors centre ( ☎ 5321 6123; www.visit daylesford.com; 98 Vincent St, Daylesford; ○ 9am-5pm) A cheery place, with stacks of information. It boasts a powerful search engine which will give you all your accommodation options, but doesn't handle bookings.

# Eating

These two towns are walk-in gourmet treats. Vincent St in Daylesford has a great range of food joints, and when you've tried them all, go around the side streets for more, or head to the lake. Daylesford is the setting for two (yes two) of Victoria's handful of Michelin-starred restaurants: the Lake House and Farmers Arms.

Wholesome Food Cafe ( ☎ 5348 1030; 11 Howe St, Daylesford; mains $10-15; ○ breakfast & lunch Tue-Sun) This tiny place produces homemade comfort food, gluten-free and highly praised.

Boat House Café ( ☎ 5348 1387; 1 Leggatt St; mains $16-24) In an old boatshed with views of ducks and swans.

Lake House ( ☎ 5348 3329; www.lakehouse.com.au; King St, Daylesford; mains $36-38; ○ breakfast, lunch & dinner) Glorious dining room, picture windows showing Lake Daylesford, food to dream about and impressive service. An express lunch on the deck costs $35 for two courses and wine.

Farmers Arms ( ☎ 5348 2091; www.farmersarms.com .au; 1 East St, Daylesford; mains $26-36; ○ dinner nightly, lunch Sat & Sun) Modern and classical meld tastefully here, both in the surroundings and the food.

# Sleeping

This is tourist heaven, so many places charge more on weekends and stipulate a two-night stay. Budget accommodation is limited, so book ahead.

Daylesford Wildwood Youth Hostel ( ☎ 5348 4435; www.mooltan.com.au/ww/wildwood.htm; 42 Main Rd, Hepburn Springs; dm/s/d from $27/40/48) In a charming cottage with a grand lounge room, you'd never know it was a youth hostel (except for the members discount). Some rooms have grand bathtubs and garden views.

Continental House ( ☎ 5348 2005; www.continental house.com.au; 9 Lone Pine Ave, Hepburn Springs; dm/s/d $30/40/70) This rambling, timber guesthouse has a laid-back alternative vibe, a superb veranda with views over the hills and a music room. BYO linen. Concession rates available.

## TAKING TO THE WATERS

Communities have always enjoyed bathing in sensual ways – consider the gorgeous bathhouse ruins in Pompeii and Ephesus – so why break the tradition? Simply come to Daylesford and Hepburn Springs, and enter a world of calm and sensual indulgence. Wrap yourself in a fluffy white dressing gown, slip your feet into a hydrotherapy sandals, sit back and relax. You're about to be bubbled and scrubbed, oiled and steamed – your every whim attended to before you've even thought of it.

At Salus ( ☎ 5348 3329; www.lakehouse.com.au; King St, Daylesford) the magic starts as you walk through a small rainforest to your exotic jasmine flower bath in a cedar-lined tree house overlooking the lake.

Daylesford Day Spa ( ☎ 5348 2331; www.daylesforddayspa.com.au; 25 Albert St, Daylesford) might start you off with a vitamin-rich mud coat and steam in a Neoqi cocoon.

Or try Mineral Spa Wellness Retreat ( ☎ 5348 2100; www.mineralspa.com.au; Peppers Springs Retreat, 124 Main Rd, Hepburn Springs), where you can have an algae gel wrap, based on an ancient Chinese treatment, then move into the lavender steam room.

The Hepburn Spa Resort ( ☎ 5348 2034; www.hepburnspa.com.au; Hepburn Mineral Springs Reserve, Hepburn Springs), where it all began in 1896, has been revamped and was due to reopen by the end of 2008. It will have plunge pools, floatation tanks, saunas, a swimming pool, salt pool and aero spa – every way of taking to the waters. Contact the resort for opening times.

The waters in the underground cavities of the area have been absorbing minerals and carbon dioxide for a million years. They're as pure as can be. Take a container and fill it at the public springs in the parks. After a drink, you'll sparkle both inside and out.

There are other boutique providers, and taking to the waters doesn't cost too much. Start with an outdoor sundeck hot tub ($15 per hour), graduate to a treatment (from $85 per hour) then extend your holiday so you can try them all. Enjoy!

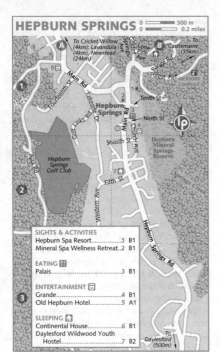

**HEPBURN SPRINGS**

SIGHTS & ACTIVITIES
Hepburn Spa Resort....................1 B1
Mineral Spa Wellness Retreat...2 B1

EATING
Palais......................................3 B1

ENTERTAINMENT
Grande....................................4 B1
Old Hepburn Hotel...................5 A1

SLEEPING
Continental House....................6 B1
Daylesford Wildwood Youth
Hostel.................................7 B2

On Saturday a vegan buffet dinner is served ($15).

**Daylesford Hotel** ( ☎ 5348 2335; mev31112@bigpond .net.au; cnr Albert & Howe Sts, Daylesford; r from $66) This old pub has small rooms upstairs that are prettily painted. Bathrooms are tiny but crisp, and there's a cosy guest TV room. The balcony is fantastic.

**Daylesford Central Motor Inn** ( ☎ 5348 2029; www .daylesfordcentralmotorinn.com; 54 Albert St, Daylesford; s/d/f from $75/85/120; ✷ ) Just an easy stroll from everything, the inn is comfortable and pretty.

**Lake House** ( ☎ 5348 3329; www.lakehouse.com.au; King St; B&B d from $320; ✷ ) You can't talk about Daylesford without mentioning the Lake House, set in rambling gardens with bridges, waterfalls and every service.

There are so many charming guesthouses, cottages and B&Bs that are bookable through agencies:

**Daylesford Accommodation Booking Service (DABS;** ☎ 5348 1448; www.dabs.com.au; 94 Vincent St, Daylesford)

**Daylesford Cottage Directory** ( ☎ 5348 1255; www.the spacountryholidayshop.com.au; 86 Vincent St, Daylesford)

**Daylesford Getaways** ( ☎ 5348 4422; www.dayget.com .au; 123 Vincent St, Daylesford)

# KYNETON

### pop 4300

Finding nuggets wasn't the only way to prosper during the gold rush. Kyneton was the main coach stop between Melbourne and Bendigo, and the centre for the farmers who were supplying the diggings with fresh produce. Piper St is a historic precinct lined with buildings made of local bluestone that are now tearooms, antique shops, museums and restaurants. There's a major street party here in November to start off Budburst ( ☎ 1800 244 711; www.budburst.com), a wine and food festival hosted throughout the region over several days. The old bank building (1855) is now Kyneton Historical Museum ( ☎ 5422 1228; 67 Piper St; adult/child $3/1; ☉ 11am-4pm Fri-Sun) housing a display of local history items – the upper floor is furnished in period style.

Kyneton Fine China & Wattle Ceramics ( ☎ 5422 3337; www.wattleceramics.com.au; ☉ 9.30am-4.30pm Mon-Fri) has a studio gallery where you can see artists at work or buy fine bone-china figurines and flowers.

Kyneton is famous for its daffodils. The annual Kyneton Daffodil & Arts Festival (www.kynetondaffodil arts.org.au) is held each September, with 10 days of gala evenings, markets, concerts, fairs, art shows and, of course, flower shows.

Don't miss the Botanic Gardens (Clowes St), beside the Campaspe River, that Baron Ferdinand von Mueller established in the 1860s.

## Information

Kyneton visitors centre ( ☎ 5422 6110; 127 High St; ☉ 9am-5pm) Situated just off High St, on the southeastern outskirts of town. Ask for the brochures Town Walks, Self Drive Tour and Campaspe River Walk. You'll discover heaps here, including a barbecue area and rotunda at the start of the river walk.

## Eating & Sleeping

The café scene in Kyneton will totally delight you and keep you eating out for days.

Glamorous one-hat Royal George ( ☎ 5422 1390, www.royalgeorge.com.au; 24 Piper St; mains $27-32; ☉ lunch Thu-Sun, dinner Wed-Sat) is a great addition to the town. Check out the stylish Rockville accommodation upstairs.

Kyneton and the surrounding areas are dotted with B&Bs and self-contained cottages, each one more elegant, peaceful and luxurious than the last. Check out www.travelvictoria .com.au/kyneton, or the staff at the visitors centre can give you the details.

# CASTLEMAINE
## pop 7250

Kick back and relax – you're in Castlemaine, a town where artists live amidst splendid architecture and gardens. Besides, this is where (surprise, surprise) Castlemaine XXXX beer-brewing company (now based in Queensland) and Castlemaine Rock, a hard-boiled lolly dating back to the gold rush days, began. It's also the 'Street Rod Centre of Australia', where hotrods have been built since 1962.

Farmers first moved into the district in the 1830s. But that all changed when gold was discovered at Specimen Gully in 1851. The Mt Alexander Diggings had 30,000 diggers working there and Castlemaine became the thriving marketplace for the goldfields. The town's importance waned as the surface gold was exhausted by the 1860s but, fortunately, the centre of town was well established by then and remains relatively intact.

A superb Art Deco building houses the Castlemaine Art Gallery & Historical Museum ( ☎ 5472 2292; www.castlemainegallery.com; 14 Lyttleton St; adult/student/family $4/2/8; ☯ 10am-5pm Mon-Fri, noon-5pm Sat & Sun), which features colonial and contemporary Australian art, including work by well-known Australian artists such as Frederick McCubbin and Russell Drysdale. The museum, in the basement, provides an insight into local history, with costumes, china and gold mining relics.

At Buda Historic Home & Garden ( ☎ 5472 1032; www.budacastlemaine.org; cnr Hunter & Urquhart Sts; adult/child/family $9/4/20; ☯ noon-5pm Wed-Sat, 10am-5pm Sun) there's an interesting mix of architectural styles: the original Indian-villa influence, and later Edwardian-style extensions dating from 1861. Home to a Hungarian silversmith and his family for 120 years, the house has permanent displays of the family's extensive art and craft collections, furnishings and personal belongings.

The imposing sandstone building of Old Castlemaine Gaol ( ☎ 5470 5311; www.oldcastlemainegaol.com.au; cnr Bowden & Charles Sts; adult/child $11/5; cafe ☯ 11am-3pm Mon-Fri) looks down on the town, with panoramic views from the car park. Arrange a tour at the café and soak up the eerie atmosphere.

An institution in itself, the Restorers Barn ( ☎ 5470 5669; www.restorersbarn.com.au; 129-133 Mostyn St; ☯ 10am-5.30pm) is chock-full of interesting bric-a-brac and collectables.

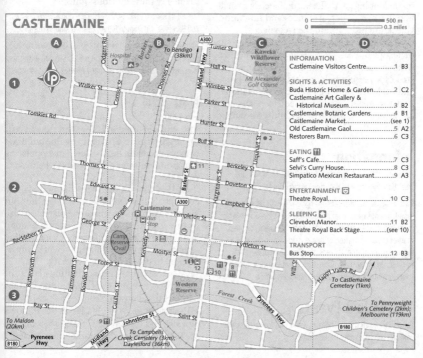

## CASTLEMAINE

0 — 500 m
0 — 0.3 miles

**INFORMATION**
Castlemaine Visitors Centre...............1  B3

**SIGHTS & ACTIVITIES**
Buda Historic Home & Garden...........2  C2
Castlemaine Art Gallery &
　Historical Museum.........................3  B2
Castlemaine Botanic Gardens............4  B1
Castlemaine Market.......................(see 1)
Old Castlemaine Gaol.......................5  A2
Restorers Barn...............................6  C3

**EATING**
Saff's Cafe....................................7  C3
Selvi's Curry House..........................8  C3
Simpatico Mexican Restaurant...........9  A3

**ENTERTAINMENT**
Theatre Royal...............................10  C3

**SLEEPING**
Clevedon Manor............................11  B2
Theatre Royal Back Stage............(see 10)

**TRANSPORT**
Bus Stop.....................................12  B3

## LOOKING FOR ...

The cemeteries in central Victoria provide people with a chance to trace their past.

- Castlemaine Cemetery (Colles Rd, Castlemaine) brings researchers most weekends.
- Campbells Creek Cemetery (Cemetery Rd, Campbells Creek) has many old gravestones.
- Goldfields Historical Chinese Cemetery (Holdsworth Rd, Bendigo) is the oldest and most significant one in Australia, with a prayer oven where paper money for the spirits of the dead was burnt.
- Pennyweight Children's Cemetery (Chewton) is a small cluster of tiny graves of children who died during the gold-rush years.
- Maryborough Cemetery (Argyle St, Maryborough) has an old mausoleum and Chinese section.
- Maldon Cemetery (Nuggetty Rd, Maldon) has very old gravestones, and there's a whisper of ghosts.

Historic Theatre Royal ( ☎ 5472 1196; www.theatre royal.info; 30 Hargreaves St; ☺ from 1.30pm daily, to 3am Fri & Sat) is a cinema with a difference. Patrons can dine while the movie is showing, then don their clubbing gear afterwards. There's a small bar, live bands, performances and functions. Check the program on the website.

When you've seen enough buildings, go to majestic Castlemaine Botanic Gardens (cnr Downes Rd & Walker St), amongst the oldest in Victoria, which strikes a perfect balance between sculpture and wilderness among awe-inspiring National Trust–registered trees. Electric barbecues are available, along with a children's plastic playground.

## Information

Accommodation Booking Service ( ☎ 1800 171 888; free) Bookings essential during festival times.

Castlemaine visitors centre ( ☎ 5470 6200; www .maldoncastlemaine.com; Mostyn St; ☺ 9am-5pm) In the magnificent old Castlemaine Market, the town's original market building fronted with a classical Roman-basilica façade with a statue of Ceres, the Roman goddess of the harvest, on top. Ask about historic town walks, vehicle tours and buy yourself a gold-panning kit for $8.

## Festivals & Events

Browse through the calendar at www.maldoncastlemaine .com for all the events in the shire.

State Festival (www.castlemainefestival.com.au) One of Victoria's leading arts events, featuring theatre, music, art and dance; held in April in odd-numbered years.

Festival of Gardens (www3.visitvictoria.com) Over 50 locals open their properties to the public; held in November in odd-numbered years

## Eating & Sleeping

There are many neat eating places spread around town.

Saff's Cafe ( ☎ 5470 6722; 64 Mostyn St; mains $14-24; ☺ breakfast & lunch daily, dinner Wed-Sat) A fun place with friendly people, local artwork on the walls, the best coffee in town and an interesting menu.

Selvi's Curry House ( ☎ 5470 5345; 81 Forest St; mains $15-21; ☺ dinner Wed-Sun) Set in the lovely 1850s Globe Hotel with its superb garden courtyard. Bookings essential.

Simpatico Mexican Restaurant ( ☎ 5472 5222, 0448-695 162; 32 Johnstone St; mains $13-26; ☺ dinner) Fab family-friendly Mexican, with delicious meals and fun music. You'll love it even if you don't love Mexican. The courtyard Cactus Bar opens till 1am and has live music Friday and Saturday.

There's stacks of accommodation around town. Try these glorious options:

Clevedon Manor ( ☎ 5472 5212; clevedon@netcon.net.au; 260 Barker St; s/d from $70/100) Nestled among the antiques.

Theatre Royal Back Stage ( ☎ 5472 1196; www.theatre royal.info; 30 Hargreaves St; B&B d $195) In bed with the stars, where rates include as many movies as are screening.

## MALDON
**pop 1200**

The whole of Maldon is a well-preserved relic of the gold-rush era, with many fine buildings constructed from local stone. The population is a scant reminder of the 20,000 who used to work the local goldfields.

In 1966 the National Trust named Maldon Australia's first 'notable town', an honour given only to towns where the historic architecture is intact and valuable. In fact Maldon is so important in the history of Victoria that special planning regulations were implemented to preserve it for posterity.

All along High St are fascinating places: the Maldon, Kangaroo and Grand Hotels; the old marketplace that's now the Historical Museum ( ☎ 5474 1633; oldsdyle@aapt.net.au; ☺ 1.30-4pm Mon-Fri, to 5pm Sat & Sun); and the Old Post Office (95 High St), built in 1870, that was the childhood home of Henry

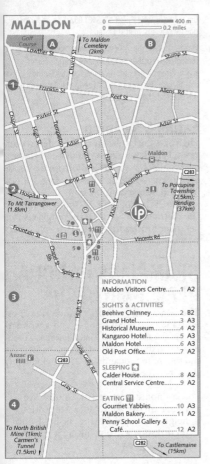

## MALDON

INFORMATION
Maldon Visitors Centre........1 A2

SIGHTS & ACTIVITIES
Beehive Chimney................2 B2
Grand Hotel.......................3 A3
Historical Museum.............4 A3
Kangaroo Hotel..................5 A3
Maldon Hotel.....................6 A3
Old Post Office...................7 A2

SLEEPING
Calder House......................8 A2
Central Service Centre.........9 A2

EATING
Gourmet Yabbies..............10 A3
Maldon Bakery..................11 A3
Penny School Gallery &
Café.............................12 A2

.au; return rides adult/child/family $27/13/60; rides 10.30am, 1 & 3pm Wed & Sun) along the original track through the Muckleford Forest to Castlemaine. For a little extra, go first class (adult/child/family $40/23/93, Sunday only) in an oak-lined viewing carriage. Magical!

Porcupine Township ( 5475 1000; www.porcupine township.com.au; cnr Bendigo & Allens Rds; adult/child/family $9/56/25; 10am-5pm) is a quaint, recreated gold-mining village (1835 to 1851) with old slab buildings, built on the site of the original township.

## Information

Maldon visitors centre ( 5475 2569; www.maldon castlemaine.com; 95 High St; 9am-5pm) Has internet access. Pick up the *Information Guide* and *Historic Town Walk* brochure, which guides you past some of the most historic buildings, or the *Taste of Gold food and wine trail* pamphlet (if you dare).

## Festivals & Events

Twilight Food & Wine Festival (www.tasteofgold.com) Fine food, lanterns, live music and wine tasting in early January. Arrive by steam train: www.vgr.com.au.

Maldon Easter Fair (www.maldon.org.au/EasterFair) Held March or April.

Maldon Folk Festival (www.maldonfolkfestival.com) Maldon's main event, held in early November, is this fun festival, featuring a wide variety of world music.

## Eating & Sleeping

Lots of cafés and tearooms line Main St, each with an interesting feature.

Gourmet Yabbies ( 0419-102 723; 44 Main St; meals $7-12; lunch Wed-Sun) Features yummy yabby pies. Yabbies are farmed in the area.

Penny School Gallery & Café ( 5475 1911; www.penny schoolgallery.com.au; 11 Church St; mains $20-30; lunch & dinner Fri-Sun) Exhibitions of well-known artists' work look splendid against the original old school walls, with wood-lined ceilings.

Central Service Centre ( 5475 2216, 0418-166 353; cnr Main & High Sts; s/d $50/85; ) For a bed in the centre of town, head to the petrol station. Don't worry, you're not bedded between oil drums, but in sweet cottagey rooms with views of the main street through the lace curtains.

Calder House ( 5475 2912; www.calderhouse.com.au; 44 High St; s/d from $90/110) If you're in the mood for grand, you'll step back in time at this formal yet very inviting place.

Handel Richardson. She (yes, she!) writes about it in her autobiography, *Myself When Young* (1950). On Main St, the Maldon Bakery ( 5475 2519; 51 Main St; pies from $3.30; 7am-4pm) uses the original oven at the site of a bakery which opened around 1854.

You'll soon notice the 24m-high Beehive Chimney, just east of Main St, and it's worth taking the short trip south along High St to the North British Mine. Keep going south to Carmen's Tunnel ( 5475 2656; carmanstunnel@maldon.vicmail.net; off Parkin's Reef Rd; adult/child $5/2; tours 1.30, 2.30 & 3.30pm Sat & Sun). The 570m-long tunnel, excavated in the 1880s, took two years to dig, yet produced only $300 worth of gold.

Maldon train station was built in 1884. Harry Potter types can go by steam with the Victorian Goldfields Railway ( 5470 6658, 5475 2966; www.vgr.com

There are plenty of self-contained cottages and charming B&Bs in restored buildings around town. Many are managed by these services:

Heritage Cottages of Maldon ( ☎ 5475 1094; www .heritagecottages.com.au; 41 High St).

Mount Alexander Accommodation Booking Service ( ☎ 1800 171 888, 5470 5866; www.maldoncastlemaine.com)

## MARYBOROUGH

### pop 7700

The district around Charlotte Plains was already an established sheep run, owned by the Simson brothers, when gold was discovered at White Hills in 1853 and Four Mile Flat in 1854. A police camp established at the diggings was named Maryborough. By the time gold mining had stopped being economical, Maryborough had developed a strong manufacturing base. Its alluvial goldfields still attract prospectors.

The town boasts plenty of impressive Victorian-era buildings, but Maryborough Railway Station (38 Victoria St; ☽ 10am-5pm, till 11pm Thu & Fri, closed Tue) leaves them all for dead. Built in 1892, the magnificent and inordinately large station was described by Mark Twain as 'a train station with a town attached'. Now, with a grand renovation, it houses a mammoth antique emporium, a regional wine centre and a café that specialises in savoury and sweet crepes ($12 to $14). Dinner and live music Thursday and Friday.

Built in the 1894, Worsley Cottage ( ☎ 5461 2800; www.vicnet.net.au/~mbhs; 3 Palmerston St; adult/child $3/ free; ☽ 10am-noon Tue & Thu, 2-4pm Sun) is the local historical society museum. Every room is furnished with pieces from the times, often donated by local people, and there's a large photographic collection. Records held here are used in family history research.

Maryborough Paramount Theatre ( ☎ 5460 5434; www.yourmovies.com.au; 56 Nolan St; adult/child $13/9; ☽ 10.30am-9pm) screens the latest movies.

## Information

Maryborough visitors centre ( ☎ 1800 356 511, 5460 4511; www.visitmaryborough.com.au; cnr Alma & Nolan Sts; ☽ 9am-5pm) Loads of helpful maps and friendly staff.

## Festivals & Events

Highland Gathering (www.maryboroughhighlandsociety .com) Have a fling at Maryborough's Scottish festival, with races, stalls etc, held every New Year's Day since 1857.

Great Pacific Bike Ride ( ☎ 5461 0621) An endurance ride for veterans; held at Easter.

Energy Breakthrough Festival (www.racvenergybreak through.net) Focusing on alternative energy sources, school groups bring their inventive vehicles for the 24-hour and 16-hour (for juniors) RACV Energy Breakthrough grand prix; held late November.

## Eating & Sleeping

High St is the foodie area, with cafés, restaurants, bakeries, takeaways, pubs and clubs.

Legenz Café Wine Bar ( ☎ 5460 4033; 190 High St; mains $12-21; ☽ breakfast & lunch Mon-Wed, dinner Thu & Fri) This will help you hit the spot.

There's lashings of accommodation in the district. Contact Maryborough visitors centre or browse its website (www.visitmary borough.com.au).

# GRAMPIANS NATIONAL PARK (GARIWERD)

The Grampians are one of Victoria's most outstanding natural features and a wonderland of flora and fauna. Major Thomas Mitchell named the ranges the Grampians after the mountains in Scotland. In 1836 he eloquently described them as:

> …a noble range of mountains, rising in the south to a stupendous height, and presenting as bold and picturesque an outline as a painter ever imagined.

It's really something to be surrounded by these spectacular shapes. Other attractions include an incredibly rich diversity of wildlife and plant species, glorious wild-flower displays, unique and unusual rock formations, Aboriginal rock art, fine bushwalking, an extensive network of creeks, streams, cascades and waterfalls (after rain!), and excellent abseiling and rock climbing.

Over 900 species of native trees, shrubs and wild flowers have been recorded here, with everything from fern gullies to red-gum forests. There are almost 200 species of bird, 35 different mammals, 28 reptiles, 11 species of amphibian and six types of freshwater fish; so you never know what you might see in your wanderings. It's worth visiting at any time of year, but it's best in spring when the wild flowers (including 20 species that don't exist

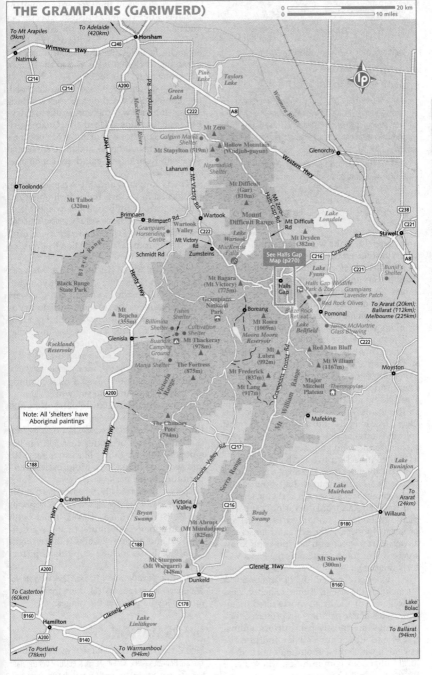

# THE GRAMPIANS (GARIWERD)

0 — 20 km
0 — 10 miles

To Mt Arapiles (9km)
To Adelaide (420km)
Horsham
Wimmera Hwy
C240
Natimuk
C214
C214
A200
Grampians Rd
Pine Lake
Taylors Lake
Green Lake
C222
A8
Wimmera River
Mt Zero
Gulgurn Manja Shelter
Hollow Mountain (Wudjub-guyun)
Mt Stapylton (519m)
Glenorchy
Western Hwy
Laharum
Ngamadjidj Shelter
MacKenzie River
Mt Talbot (320m)
Mt Difficult (Gar) (810m)
Brimpaen
Brimpaen Rd
Wartook
Mount Difficult Range
Mt Difficult Rd
Lake Lonsdale
C238
C221
Toolondo
Black Range
Mt Victory Rd
Wartook Valley
Grampians Horseriding Centre
C222
Mt Difficult
Mt Dryden (382m)
Stawell
A8
Schmidt Rd
Mt Victory Rd
Zumsteins
Lake Wartook
MacKenzie Falls
See Halls Gap Map (p270)
Grampians Rd
C216
Lake Fyans
C221
Bunjil's Shelter
Black Range State Park
Mt Bagara (Mt Victory) (775m)
Halls Gap
Halls Gap Wildlife Park & Zoo
Grampians Lavender Patch
Red Rock Olives
To Ararat (20km); Ballarat (112km); Melbourne (225km)
Mt Bepcha (355m)
Fishes Shelter
Grampians National Park
Boreang
Mt Rosea (1009m)
Blaze Rock Retreat
Pomonal
Rocklands Reservoir
Billimina Shelter
Cultivation Shelter
Buandik Camping Ground
Mt Thackeray (978m)
Moora Moora Reservoir
Lake Bellfield
James McMurtrie Glass Blowing
C222
Glenisla
Manja Shelter
The Fortress (875m)
Victoria Range
Mt Lubra (992m)
Mt Frederick (837m)
Red Man Bluff
Mt William (1167m)
Moyston
A200
Mt Lang (917m)
Grampians Tourist Rd
Major Mitchell Plateau
Thermopylae
Mt William Range
Mafeking
Note: All 'shelters' have Aboriginal paintings
The Chimney Pots (794m)
C217
Serra Range
C188
Cavendish
Victoria Valley Rd
Lake Buninjon
To Ararat (24km)
Henty Hwy
Bryan Swamp
Victoria Valley
C216
Brady Swamp
Lake Muirhead
B180
Willaura
A200
Mt Abrupt (Mt Murdadjoog) (825m)
C188
Glenelg Hwy
B180
Mt Sturgeon (Mt Wurgarri) (448m)
Mt Stavely (300m)
Lake Bolac
To Casterton (60km)
B160
Dunkeld
Glenelg Hwy
B160
To Ballarat (94km)
Hamilton
A200
B140
B160
C178
Lake Linlithgow
To Warrnambool (94km)
To Portland (78km)

## TRANSPORT: GRAMPIANS NATIONAL PARK (GARIWERD)

**Distance from Melbourne** Halls Gap 260km

**Direction** Northwest

**Travel times** Halls Gap 2½ hours

**Bus & Train** V/Line ( ☎ 13 61 96; www.vline.com.au) runs a train/bus service between Melbourne (Southern Cross station) and Halls Gap (return $57, four hours, one daily) with connections at Ballarat and Stawell.

**Car** Take the Western Hwy past Ballarat to Ararat, then the scenic country road through Pomonal. It may be quicker to go to Stawell, then west to Halls Gap. A beautiful route is to head west to Dunkeld (from north Ballarat) then enjoy a dramatic entry into the ranges on Grampians Tourist Rd.

anywhere else in the world) are at their peak. Sadly, bushfires recently destroyed some areas, so ask Parks Victoria which roads, walks or camping grounds are open, as recovery continues. Years of very low rainfall means water is limited; you need to take your own supplies of water to picnic and camping grounds (and drinking water on walks, of course).

The four greatest mountain ranges are the Mt Difficult Ranges in the north, Mt William Ranges in the east, Serra Ranges in the southeast and Victoria Ranges in the southwest. They spread from Ararat to the Wartook Valley and from Dunkeld up almost to Horsham. Halls Gap lies in the Fyans Valley. The smaller Wonderland Range, close to Halls Gap, has some of the most splendid and accessible outlooks, scenic drives, picnic grounds and gum-scented walks, such as to the Pinnacle or to Silverband Falls.

There are more than 150km of well-marked walking tracks, ranging from half-hour strolls to overnight treks through difficult terrain. The walks all start from the various car parks, picnic grounds and camping areas. Wear appropriate footwear, take a hat and sunscreen, always carry water and let someone know where you're going (preferably the Parks Victoria rangers).

An extensive collection of Aboriginal Rock Art includes the site in Bunjil's Shelter, near Stawell, one of Victoria's most sacred indigenous sites. These paintings, in protected rock overhangs, are mostly hand prints, animal tracks and stick figures. They indicate the esteem in which these mountains are held by local indigenous communities, whose name for the region is Gariwed.

Zumstein Reserve in the Western Grampians is named after Walter Zumstein, a beekeeper and naturalist who settled in the area in 1910 and developed it into a wildlife reserve. There are picnic facilities, free electric barbecues and a walking track that takes you to the base of the spectacular MacKenzie Falls.

Mt Stapylton and Hollow Mountain in the north are renowned as abseiling and rock climbing spots. Along the way there are walks to Briggs Bluff and the ruins of Heatherlie Quarry (origin of the sandstone in many of Melbourne's Victorian-era buildings), and there are several sites with Koorie rock paintings, canoe trees and middens.

The Grampians and Mt Arapiles region are the best in Victoria for rock climbing and abseiling, set up for people of any age. Member companies of the Australian Climbing Instructors Association (ACIA; ☎ 5387 1332; www.acia.com.au) offer everything from basic instruction to advanced guided climbs.

Hangin' Out ( ☎ 5356 4535, 0407-684 831; www.hangin out.com.au; rock climbing from $65) will get you onto the cliff faces with Earl, who gives a lively interpretation of the surrounding country as you go. His adventure walk (full day $125) includes rock climbs and abseils – an exhilarating Grampians experience.

The Grampians Mountain Adventure Company (GMAC; ☎ 5383 9218, 0427-747 047; www.grampiansadventure .com.au; half-day from $60) tailors a rock climbing or abseiling adventure to suit you.

Bush walk, abseil, go wildlife-spotting and mountain biking with Absolute Outdoors Australia ( ☎ 5356 4556; www.absoluteoutdoors.com.au; Shop 4, Stony Ck, Halls Gap). Most activities cost $35 for beginners, more for things like canoeing ($40) and rock climbing ($65). Motorcycles aren't permitted in the park.

Grampians Personalised Tours & Adventures ( ☎ 5356 4654, 0429-954 686; www.grampianstours.com; tours/walks from $59/15) has a range of 4WD tours (with off-road options), adventures (half-day abseiling $69) and discovery walks (full day/night $125/15). Tours include stop-offs at picturesque locations.

Stawell Aviation Services ( ☎ 5357 3234; www.stawell aviation.com.au; per 3 people $180) offers thrilling 40-minute joy flights over the ranges.

## INFORMATION

Parks Victoria ( ☎ 13 19 63, 5361 4000; www.parkweb.vic .gov.au; Brambuk – the National Park & Cultural Centre, Halls Gap; ☼ 9am-4.30pm) Has an office in Halls Gap. There are plenty of maps and brochures, and the rangers can advise you about where to go, where to camp and what you might see. They also issue camping permits and fishing permits ($12) required for fishing in local streams.

## CAMPING

Parks Victoria maintains more than 10 camp sites ( ☎ 5356 4381; camp sites per vehicle or 6 people $12.50), with toilets, picnic tables and fireplaces (BYO water). Permits are required; you can register and pay at the office. Bush camping is permitted, except in the Wonderland Range area, around Lake Wartook and in parts of the Serra, Mt William and Victoria Ranges. Other areas, including Rosea camping ground and sites on the Major Mitchell Plateau, have recently closed due to bushfire damage – check with the rangers about what's off limits.

Pay close attention to fire restrictions – apart from the damage you could do to yourself and the bush, you can be jailed for lighting *any* fire, including fuel stoves, on days of total fire ban. For more information see p355.

If you like your camping luxurious, Parkgate Resort ( ☎ 1800 810 781, 5356 4215; www.grampians.com; Grampians Tourist Rd, Halls Gap; sites per 2 people from $32, cabins/cottages d from $75/105; ⚅ ⚇ ) is fabulous. It has everything for the kids, including a jumping pillow and playground. For adults there are tennis courts, a camp kitchen, games and lounge rooms and free barbecues.

## HALLS GAP

### pop 7700

This small township in the heart of the Grampians is a popular base. It has some shops, adventure activity offices, restaurants, cafés and a wide range of accommodation. The Halls Gap general store and post office has an ATM and Eftpos.

You'll be drawn to the amazing buildings of Brambuk – the National Park & Cultural Centre ( ☎ 5361 4000; www.brambuk.com.au; Grampians Tourist Rd; ☺ 9am-4.30pm), 2.5km south of Halls Gap.

The Cultural Centre (the back building) is run by five Koorie communities. Its flowing orange roof represents the open wings of the cockatoo; the curved seat is the caring embrace of Bunjil, the creator spirit; the ramp is the eel dreaming. The ceiling of the Gariwerd Dreaming Theatre (adult/child $5/3) represents the southern right whale (totem of the Gundjitmara people). Here you can see Dreamtime stories of Gariwerd and informative films about the region. Displays in the centre of Koorie art, clothes, weapons and tools help raise visitors' awareness of their history. Also on offer are Koorie music and dance, a bushtucker walk (adults $6), boomerang throwing (adult/family $4/10), painting (boomerang/message stone $7/3), and holiday programs. Planted outside are native plants used for food and medicine. A two-hour rock art tour (adult/child $25/10) to Bunjil's Shelter leaves at 9.30am; bookings essential.

The roof of the front building represents eel-fishing nets. There's an information desk here and a Parks Victoria office (opposite), plus interesting educational displays covering the natural features and the history of the Grampians, a souvenir shop and Brambuk Bush Tucker Café (meals $8-19; ☺ 9am-4pm) that spills out onto a lovely deck overlooking the gardens.

Keep on towards Lake Bellfield to the world-class Grampians Adventure Golf ( ☎ 5356 4664; www.grampiansadventuregolf.com.au; Grampians Tourist Rd; adult/child/family $12/9/38; ☺ 10am-5pm Wed-Mon). This is not to be missed – a hectare of 18-hole minigolf with fairways such as 'Grand Canyon' where you squeeze down between bushes. There's a licensed café (lunch around $7) in which to recover after your kids have trounced you.

## Information

Accommodation Booking Service ( ☎ 1800 065 599; free) Rates vary with season.

Halls Gap visitors centre ( ☎ 1800 065 599, 5356 4616; www.grampianstravel.com, www.visithallsgap.com.au; Centenary Hall, Grampians Tourist Rd; ☺ 9am-5pm) The staff here are great, and can book tours, accommodation and activities for you.

Parks Victoria (opposite)

## Festivals & Events

Halls Gap is the focal point for local festivities:

Grampians Jazz Festival (www.grampiansjazzfestival .com.au) Held in early February.

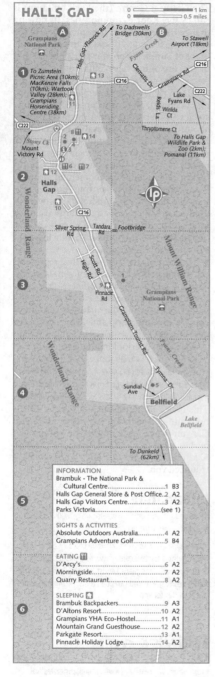

## HALLS GAP

**INFORMATION**
| | |
|---|---|
| Brambuk - The National Park & Cultural Centre | 1 B3 |
| Halls Gap General Store & Post Office | 2 A2 |
| Halls Gap Visitors Centre | 3 A2 |
| Parks Victoria | (see 1) |

**SIGHTS & ACTIVITIES**
| | |
|---|---|
| Absolute Outdoors Australia | 4 A2 |
| Grampians Adventure Golf | 5 B4 |

**EATING**
| | |
|---|---|
| D'Arcy's | 6 A2 |
| Morningside | 7 A2 |
| Quarry Restaurant | 8 A2 |

**SLEEPING**
| | |
|---|---|
| Brambuk Backpackers | 9 A3 |
| D'Altons Resort | 10 A2 |
| Grampians YHA Eco-Hostel | 11 A1 |
| Mountain Grand Guesthouse | 12 A2 |
| Parkgate Resort | 13 A1 |
| Pinnacle Holiday Lodge | 14 A2 |

---

**Grampians Gourmet Weekend** (www.grampiansgreat escape.com.au) On the first weekend in May.

**Halls Gap Wildflower Exhibition** (www.visithallsgap.com .au) Held in October.

**Halls Gap Film Festival** ( ☎ 5356 4616) Held in November.

## Eating

Eateries are mostly along Grampians Tourist Rd and beside the boardwalk along pretty Stony Creek, where the bakery makes the best vanilla slices ever, and the fudge factory can bring your diet undone.

**Morningside** ( ☎ 5356 4222; Grampians Tourist Rd; continental/cooked $10/14; ☺ breakfast) A quiet spot, perfect for early morning coffee and a heap of breakfast bacon.

**Quarry Restaurant** ( ☎ 5356 4858; Stony Ck; mains $18-32; ☺ breakfast & dinner daily, lunch Fri-Mon) It's in a good position to watch the creek gurgling past, except the creek's been dry for a while. Never mind – there's a lovely casual atmosphere and good food.

**D'Arcy's** ( ☎ 5356 4344; Grampians Tourist Rd; mains $20-33; ☺ dinner) An elegant burgundy-and-white restaurant, D'Arcy's has a good reputation, an interesting menu and a wide range of wines from the Grampians and Pyrenees wineries.

## Sleeping

There are several backpacker places in town, all shiny, clean and welcoming.

**Brambuk Backpackers** ( ☎ 5356 4250; www.bram buk.com.au; Grampians Tourist Rd; B&B dm/d/family from $19/55/80; ▣ ) Across from the cultural centre, and recently redecorated to give a sense of nature and Koorie art. Rooms all have en suites and the lounge is utterly comfortable.

**Grampians YHA Eco-Hostel** ( ☎ 5356 4544; www.yha .com.au; cnr Grampians Tourist Rd & Buckler St; dm/s/d/f $23/52/57/77) Designed to use less power and water, with lots of light, views, interesting spaces and a very smart kitchen. Keep an eye on the kitchen bench: your host puts out freshly-laid eggs and other eco-goodies for free.

**Mountain Grand Guesthouse** ( ☎ 5356 4232; www .mountaingrand.com; Grampians Tourist Rd; B&B s/d $98/128) It's a gracious, old-fashioned timber guesthouse, peaceful and friendly, with welcoming guest lounges. Bedrooms are fresh and colourful, with their own spacious bathrooms. Ask about dinner and getaway packages; the restaurant is grand.

lonelyplanet.com

REGIONAL VICTORIA **GOLDFIELDS & GRAMPIANS**

Pinnacle Holiday Lodge ( ☎ 5356 4249; www.pinnacle holiday.com.au; 21-45 Heath St; d $92-151; 🌐 🐾 ) Right in the centre of Halls Gap, this gorgeous property sits stylishly behind the Stony Creek shops. It has everything: indoor pool, tennis courts and spacious modern units including self-contained units and two-bedroom family units (from $142 for four people).

D'Altons Resort ( ☎ 5356 4666; www.daltonsresort.com .au; 48 Glen St; studio/deluxe cottages from $100/140) These delightful timber cottages, with their little verandas, spread up the hill between the gums and kangaroos. They have cosy fires and big lounge chairs.

## AROUND HALLS GAP

Southeast of Halls Gap on Pomonal Rd, set in natural bush, is the Halls Gap Wildlife Park & Zoo ( ☎ 5356 4668; www.hallsgapwildlife.com; Pomonal Rd; adult/child/family $12/6/30; 🕙 10am-5pm Wed-Mon). Wallabies, grey kangaroos, deer and peacocks get up close and personal – very interested in having you feed them (all tickly on your fingers). Animals like wombats, possums and spider monkeys are behind barriers. There are free tours of the property (book ahead), a kiosk and playground.

Further down the Ararat–Halls Gap road there's a lot of pampering happening. Blaze Rock Retreat ( ☎ 5356 6171; www.blazerock.com.au; 3757 Ararat-Halls Gap Rd; treatments from $45) will treat your body. Take a Tasmanian peat mud bath (30 minutes $75) or have a hot rock massage (90 minutes $120).

Across the road, Jocelyn at Grampians Lavender Patch ( ☎ 5356 6285; www.glp.net.au; 3616 Ararat-Halls Gap Rd; 🕙 10am-5pm Sep-May) will feed you lavender ice cream. Sample the honeys, jams and jellies then look around the farm.

Next door, Red Rock Olives ( ☎ 0401-700 868; www.redrockolives.com.au; cnr Ararat-Halls Gap Rd & Tunnel Rd; 🕙 10am-5pm Sat & Sun) has olive products to sample and buy, or just wander around the olive groves.

Just past Pomonal is James McMurtrie Glass Blowing ( ☎ 0427-949 921; www.jamesmcmurtrie.com .au; 163 Springwood Hill Rd; 🕙 10am-4pm most days). See glassware being formed and admire or buy the artistic pieces.

Lush Wartook Valley runs down the Grampians' western foothills: enjoy spectacular views of the mountains as you travel through. The unsealed roads and tracks lead past little creeks, thundering (well, tinkling) waterfalls and idyllic picnic spots. The Grampians Horseriding Centre ( ☎ 5383 9255; www.grampianshorseriding.com.au; 430 Schmidt Rd, Brimpaen, Wartook Valley; 2hr rides $65; 🕙 10am & 2pm) will give you a horse riding adventure around a grand property with sweeping views, lakes and wandering bush tracks. Ask about the elegant accommodation.

Down south, the Grampians Tourist Rd from Dunkeld gives you a glorious passage into the Grampians; the cliffs and sky opening up as you pass between Mt Abrupt and Mt Sturgeon. Dunkeld has a good hotel, café scene, craft shops and many accommodation options. The town was established in the 1860s, but much of it was destroyed by bushfires in 1944. The bright Historical Society Museum (cnr Wills & Templeton Sts, Dunkeld; admission $2; 🕙 1-5pm Sun) in an old bluestone church has a local history collection, including Aboriginal artefacts and old photographs. The Dunkeld visitors centre ( ☎ 5577 2558; www.sthgrampians.vic.gov.au; Parker St, Dunkeld; 🕙 9am-5pm) has useful information.

# LITTLE DESERT NATIONAL PARK

It you're expecting rolling sand dunes, you are in for a surprise: the soil here is sandy, but the park is rich in flora and fauna that thrive in the dry environment. There are over 670 indigenous plant species here, and in spring and early summer the landscape is transformed into a colourful wonderland of wildflowers. Over 220 species of birds have been recorded here, and you may also see possums, kangaroos and reptiles such as bearded dragons and stumpy-tailed lizards. The best-known resident is the mallee fowl, an industrious bird that can be seen in an aviary at the Little Desert Lodge.

The park covers a huge 132,000 hectares, and the vegetation varies substantially due to the different soil types, climate and rainfall in each of its three blocks (central, eastern and western). The rainfall often reaches 600mm per year, but summers are dry and very hot.

In the late 1960s the state government announced a controversial plan to clear the area for agriculture. Conservationists and environmentalists protested, and the Little Desert became a major conservation issue. Finally, it was declared a national park and was expanded to its present size in 1986.

The Nhill road into the park is sealed and the road from Dimboola is gravel, but in the park the tracks are mostly sand – only suitable

## TRANSPORT: LITTLE DESERT NATIONAL PARK

Distance from Melbourne **Dimboola 360km, Nhill 398km**

Direction **Northwest**

Travel times **Dimboola 3¾ hours, Nhill four hours**

Bus & Train V/Line ( ☎ 13 61 96; www.vline.com.au) services start with trains between Melbourne (Southern Cross station) and Geelong/Ballarat or Bendigo, then coach direct or via Ararat or Horsham: to Dimboola (return $58, four to seven hours, five daily); to Nhill ($60; 4½ to eight hours, five daily). Times depend on route and changeovers. The *Overland* train will stop, by request when you buy your ticket, at Dimboola at about 2.30am.

Car Dimboola and Nhill are a leisurely drive up the Western Hwy from Melbourne, past Ballarat. They offer easy access to the park.

for 4WD vehicles or walking. Some are closed to 4WDs in the wet season (July to October).

If you want a brief introduction to the park there are several well-signposted walks: south of Dimboola is the Pomponderoo Hill Nature Walk, south of Nhill is the Stringybark Nature Walk and south of Kiata is the Sanctuary Nature Walk. Other longer walks leave from the camping ground south of Kiata, including a 12km trek south to the Salt Lake. Always carry water and notify the rangers at Parks Victoria ( ☎ 5389 1204) before you set out. The rangers will also give you advice on where to go and what to look for at different times of the year.

There's camping grounds (camp sites per 2 people $12) with drinking water, toilets, picnic tables and fireplaces. Or you can bush camp in the central and western blocks; see the rangers first.

A welcoming retreat on the northern edge of the desert, Little Desert Lodge ( ☎ 5391 5232; www .littledesertlodge.com.au; B&B s/d $90/115; ❄ ) is run by Whimpey Reichelt (one of Victoria's 'living treasures'). It includes a camping ground (powered site $18.50), bunk rooms (bed $20, BYO linen), restaurant open for all meals (set dinner $25), barbecue and mallee fowl aviary (tours adult/child $10/5). Whimpey takes visitors on 4WD tours (½-/¾-day $50/75) and evening spotlight walks.

## INFORMATION

Wail Park Office ( ☎ 5389 1204; www.parkweb.vic.gov .au; Nursery Rd, Dimboola) Off the Western Hwy south of Dimboola.

## GATEWAY TOWNS

The delightful town of Nhill, 16km north of the Little Desert Lodge, is an interesting place

## A RARE OLD BIRD

The rare mallee fowl is one of Australia's most fascinating birds. The mature birds are about the size of a small turkey, with wings and backs patterned in black, white and brown, which helps to camouflage them in the mallee scrub. They can fly short distances if necessary. Until the establishment of the Mallee's national parks, the mallee fowl was threatened with extinction.

The life cycle of the mallee fowl is an amazing story of survival and adaptation. It is the only one of the world's 19 mound-building birds that lives in an arid area, and it has developed incredibly sophisticated incubation methods to maintain its egg mounds at stable temperatures until the eggs hatch.

The male bird spends up to 11 months preparing the mound for the eggs. First he digs a hole, or opens up an old mound, fills it with leaves, bark and twigs, and covers the lot with sand to create the main egg chamber. When the mound has been saturated by rain so the organic material starts to decompose, he covers it all with more sand – by now it can be up to 1m high and 5m in diameter – and tests the core temperature daily by sticking his beak inside. Once the temperature is stable at 33°C, he lets the female know that she can start laying her eggs.

The female lays between 15 and 20 eggs, which hatch at various stages over spring and summer. The male continues to check the mound temperature daily, and if it varies from 33°C he adjusts it by covering the mound or removing sand.

After hatching, the chicks dig their way up to the surface, can run within a few hours and fly on their first day out. However, the mortality rate is very high. The parents don't recognise or help their own young and, while an average pair of mallee fowl will produce around 90 chicks in their lifetimes, only a few will survive to reproduce.

to base yourself. Producing ducks for Victorian gourmet experiences is the town's big industry. It's also a wheat industry centre – you'll see huge grain silos and flour mills around town. Nhill visitors centre ( ☎ 5391 3086; www.hindmarsh.vic.gov.au; Victoria St; ☒ 9am-5pm; ☐ ) is by the rotunda. The Nhill-Harrow Rd heads south through the centre of the Little Desert National Park.

On the eastern edge of the Little Desert, beside the Wimmera River, Dimboola offers another base that's got loads to offer. Riverside Host Farm ( ☎ 5389 1550; www.visitvictoria.com/riverside hostfarm; 150 Riverside Rd; unpowered sites $18; cabins from s/d $55/77; ☒ ) is a working farm that spreads along the riverbank. When the river is flowing you can take a boat tour from here into the Little Dessert (per person $8 an hour) or paddle the farm's canoes. Just out of town towards the park is Pomponderoo Bush Retreat ( ☎ 5389 1957, 0419-824 618; www.pomponderoobush retreat.com; 345 Horseshoe Bend Rd; d/tr from $110/125; ☒ ☒ ), very natural but with all the luxuries in timber cottages. The owners also run tours into the desert (per person $20) and are busy producing Pomponderoo Boosh

Produce like wattle-seed coffee from their native food forest.

Horsham, first settled in 1841, makes a good base for exploring local national and state parks. The main shopping strip has postal and banking facilities, supermarkets and plenty of other shops and eateries. Horsham visitors centre ( ☎ 1800 633 218, 5382 1832; www.grampianslittledesert .com.au; 20 O'Callaghan's Pde; ☒ 9am-5pm) has information on the surrounding areas.

While you're in town, visit the Horsham Regional Art Gallery ( ☎ 5362 2888; www.horshamartgallery; 80 Wilson St; adult/child $2/free; ☒ 10am-5pm Tue-Fri, 1-4.30pm Sat & Sun), which houses the Mack Jost Collection of significant Australian artists, including works by Rupert Bunny, Sir Sidney Nolan, John Olsen and Charles Blackman. Horsham's Botanic Gardens (Firebrace St) were established in the 1870s and designed by the curator of Melbourne's Royal Botanic Gardens, William Guilfoyle. The Wool Factory ( ☎ 5382 0333; 134 Golf Course Rd; tours adult/child $5/1.50; ☒ 8.30am-4.30pm, tours 10.15am, 11am, 1.30pm & 2.30pm) produces ultrafine Merino wool; there's a walk-through sheep shed and shop where you can buy wool products.

Gippsland is home to some of the most diverse, unspoilt and beautiful wilderness areas and beaches in the state. The region sprawls from just outside Melbourne right along the coast to the New South Wales border, edged by the imposing Great Dividing Range. You'll find towns with strong identities, isolated beaches, and more wildlife and bush then you'll see anywhere else in Victoria. You can get a taste of it just over an hour from Melbourne along Grand Ridge Rd, a sensational day-long drive along a mostly gravel road, punctuated by a winery and a brewery, and ending with the splendour of Tarra-Bulga National Park – a feast for the eyes with towering mountain ash and valleys of giant tree ferns.

Two hours from Melbourne is the popular South Gippsland beachside town of Inverloch, and the rugged and spectacular Bunurong Marine Coastal Park – perfect for indulging your surfing, snorkelling or diving passions, or just having fun swimming, rock-pool rambling or hanging out in cafés. Not much further on is the iconic Wilsons Promontory National Park, where you can immerse yourself in the carefully preserved pristine wilderness, with walking tracks ranging from easy strolls with prams to tough terrain for the intrepid.

Within two to three hours' drive of Melbourne are some quirky little towns like alternative Koonwarra, with its organic cooking school, day spa, and delightful general store/café, the increasingly upmarket fishing village of Port Albert, and the historic gold-mining township of Walhalla.

In the centre of the region are the huge Gippsland Lakes, dotted with coastal towns with jetties full of bobbing boats. The Lakes District is Australia's largest inland waterway system, a rich haven for birds, and a favourite for boating, fishing and swimming. It's separated by coastal dunes from the long stretch of Ninety Mile Beach, which has some superbly isolated beaches.

Beyond the Lakes it's a four-hour drive into East Gippsland, home to a third of Victoria's forests. Here you'll find fabulous and varied camping opportunities, modest cabins and lodges and the occasional lighthouse to stay in. One of the most accessible parks from Melbourne is Cape Conran Coastal Park, a fabulous park for wildlife spotting, nature walks, swimming, diving and fishing. Once you're past Cape Conran there are surprisingly few travellers. This wilderness coast is one of the most beautiful regions of the state, with the rugged mountains, raging river and deep ravines and gorges of the Snowy River National Park, pristine old-growth rainforests in Errinundra National Park, and isolated beaches, calm inlets and endless bush in the internationally recognised Croajingolong National Park.

## NATURE

If you've only got time for one nature experience, make it Wilsons Promontory National Park (p278), with its extensive walking trails that can take any time from less than an hour to up to a few days. Here you'll find mountains, swamps, forests, squeaky white-sand beaches, pristine bushland teeming with wildlife, fern valleys and coastal vistas. Some of the finest walks include the 45km Great Prom Walk and the 7km ascent to Mt Oberon Summit (see p281 for more information on these and other walks). One day will give you a taste of the Prom, but at least two or three is ideal.

With more time you could visit Cape Conran Coastal Park (p294), with its abundance of pristine white-sand beaches, surf- and river-swimming, walking trails and Aboriginal cultural heritage. There's bush camping here, as well as cosy wooden huts, luxury safari tents and upmarket eco-cottages close by.

To really immerse yourself in the bush, travel further into the rugged Snowy River National Park (p292). If you have time and the inclination do a four-day white-water rafting trip down the river, otherwise check out the Little River Falls, camp at McKillops Bridge and travel through the park to Errinundra National Park (p293) for some driving and walking trips in this eco-wilderness.

Internationally renowned Croajingolong National Park (p296) has great camping options – Thurra River and Wingan Inlet are the best – or stay at Point Hicks Lighthouse.

If you're able, spend at least two days in each park to get a feel for them.

## TOWNS

The tiny township of Koonwarra (p278), right on the South Gippsland Hwy, is a rejuvenating spot to spend the day – try a short cooking course at the organic cooking school, some indulgence time at the day spa, or perhaps a little wine tasting. Whatever, be sure to enjoy some slow food and take in the gardens at the legendary Koonwarra General Store.

Continue further up the South Gippsland Hwy to visit Port Albert (p281), a fishing village with a proud maritime history, all on display at the town's small museum. Don't leave town without trying some fish and chips, allegedly the best in the state, or checking out the general store with its gourmet café and eclectic shop. You could stay overnight and do a loop back to Melbourne via Walhalla (p283), once a prosperous gold-mining town, now one of Victoria's most scenic historic townships, built on a precipitous hillside. Walk around the township, tour an old mine, or stay longer and take in a ghost tour or a 4WD adventure around the area.

Heading further east to the Gippsland Lakes, there are numerous small townships to stop in, but the pick of them is Metung (p286). A few minutes drive off the highway, the road sweeps around the lake into the village, perched on a tiny spit of land. Hire a boat for an afternoon, take a cruise, and enjoy the café scene or a meal at the lakeside pub overlooking the water.

## BEACHES

Just about any Gippsland beach is perfect if you want an expanse of white, sandy beach. Ninety Mile Beach (p285) offers just that – ninety miles of secluded beaches, with a few small towns dotted along the way. Inverloch (right) and Lake Tyers Beach (p289) are favourites with the bucket-and-spade brigade, with calm, safe swimming beaches, plus surf beaches for the grown-ups where you can take lessons if you're new to the game.

Further afield, Cape Conran (p294) and Mallacoota (p295) are beautiful beach spots offering inlet- or river-swimming, as well as some fantastic surf, both in idyllic bush settings.

## DIVING

This region isn't famous for its diving but there are a few great dive sites here. The un-assuming Bunurong Marine & Coastal Park (p277) in South Gippsland provides some of Australia's best diving opportunities, and close by, there's the opportunity to experience Wilsons Promontory National Park (p278) from a different angle.

In both these parks, local operators organise dives for certified divers and run courses for those interested in learning to dive.

Further up the coast at Cape Conran Coastal Park (p294), dives are offered most weekends for experienced divers.

## INVERLOCH

### pop 4140

Inverloch's proximity to Melbourne and its fabulous surf, calm inlet beaches and out-standing diving, snorkelling, restaurants and cafés make it a popular destination. It expands to bursting point during the Christmas school holidays, when visitors descend on the town's inlet beaches and the ocean surf beaches along the road to Cape Paterson, but somehow the town manages to maintain a down-to-earth vibe. Inverloch also draws the crowds when it hosts the popular Inverloch Jazz Festival ( ☎ 5674 3141; www.inverlochjazzfest.org.au) on the Labour Day long weekend each March.

If you want to learn to catch a wave, the Learn to Surf Offshore Surf School ( ☎ 5674 3374; 32 Park St; www.surfingaustralia.com.au; 2hr lesson $45) offers lessons at the main town surf beach. Alternatively, find some solitude on the Screw Creek Nature Walk (40 minutes return), which starts from the Inver-loch Foreshore Camping Reserve car park – an easy walk via dunes, swamps and grasslands with expansive views from the bluff.

## INFORMATION

Bunurong Environment Centre & Shop ( ☎ 5674 3738; www.sgcs.org.au; cnr The Esplanade & Ramsey Blvd; ☼ 10am-4pm Fri-Mon, daily during school holidays) An abundance of books and brochures on environmental and

---

### TRANSPORT: INVERLOCH

Distance from Melbourne 145km

Direction Southeast

Travel time Two hours

Car Take the M1 (CityLink/Monash Fwy) then exit at the South Gippsland Hwy and travel to Korumburra. From there take the Inverloch-Korumburra Rd.

Train & Bus V/Line ( ☎ 13 61 96; www.vline.com .au) trains depart daily (twice on Saturdays) from Melbourne's Flinders St and Southern Cross stations for Dandenong, connecting with buses to Inverloch ($13, 2¾ hours).

# GIPPSLAND & WILSONS PROMONTORY

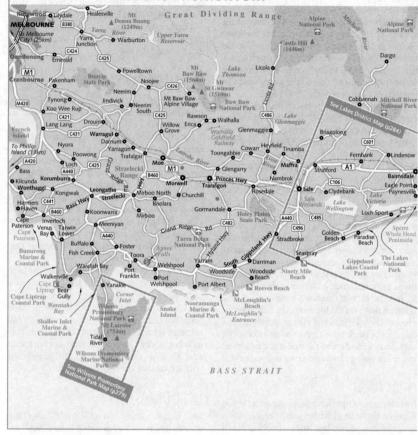

sustainable-living topics. Environmental tours organised during school holidays.

Inverloch visitors centre ( ☎ 1300 762 433; www.visit basscoast.com; 39 A'Beckett St; ☒ 9am-5pm; 💻 ) Helpful staff can make accommodation bookings for free. Internet access $1.50 per hour.

Sandsford Antiques ( ☎ 5674 3339; 13 A'Beckett St; ☒ 9am-5pm Mon-Sat, 10am-5pm Sun; 💻 ) Wireless internet access $4 per 30 minutes. Great coffee and light lunches available.

## EATING

Kiosk ( ☎ 5674 3611; 2-4 Abbott St; meals $4-18; ☒ breakfast & lunch) This is a local favourite and the perfect breakfast spot. Just across from the beach, about a kilometre from the town centre, it's a little red shack turning out generous breakfasts, enormous muffins and tasty smoothies and juices.

Cafe Pajez ( ☎ 5674 1516; 27 A'Beckett St; lunch $5-12, dinner $17-22; ☒ lunch & dinner Wed-Sun) The wafting aroma of speciality curries will entice you into this warm, earthy café, festooned with rugs. Choose your own level of heat with their five-star curry-rating system.

Cafe Gabriel (5674 1178; 9a A'Beckett St; mains $21-32; ☒ lunch Sat & Sun, dinner Thu-Sun) Adding an upmarket option to the Inverloch scene is this classy restaurant and bar. The tone here is refined.

## SLEEPING

Inverloch Foreshore Camping Reserve ( ☎ 5674 1236; www .inverlochholidaypark.com.au; cnr The Esplanade & Ramsay Blvd; unpowered/powered sites $21/24) There's shade and privacy here and it's only a short toddle

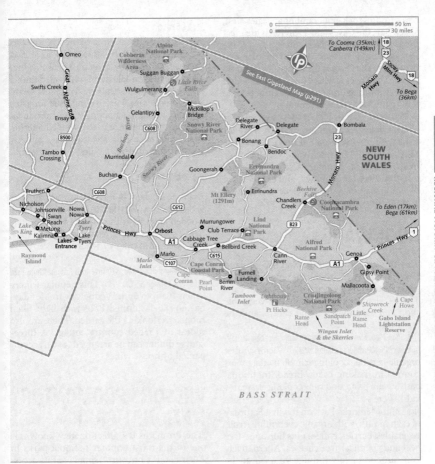

over the scrub-covered dunes to the beach. The reserve is managed by the neighbouring Inverloch Holiday Park.

**Moilong Express** ( ☎ 0439-842 334; www.basscoast.info /moilong; 405 Inverloch-Venus Bay Rd; d $100) These railway guards' vans, complete with traditional wood panelling and an old railway station clock, have been converted into very comfortable accommodation with a kitchen and a palatial queen-sized bed. With views over Anderson's Inlet, the carriages accommodate up to five people.

**Lofts** ( ☎ 1300 762 433; www.theloftapartments.com .au; Scarborough St; apt from $150; 🌀 ) Spread yourself out in these sleek, multilevel apartments with high ceilings and name-sake lofts. They're handily adjacent to the park, beach and shops. Some of these designer apartments have water views and most have a spa. They're managed

by several real estate agents, so it's easiest to book through the local visitors centre.

# BUNURONG MARINE & COASTAL PARK

This surprising little marine and coastal park offers some of Australia's best snorkelling and diving, and a stunning, cliff-hugging drive between Inverloch and Cape Paterson. It certainly surprised the archaeological world in the early 1990s when dinosaur remains dating back 120 million years were discovered here (at the time it was thought that dinosaurs had become extinct about 40 millions years earlier than that).

Head down from the car parks along the Cape Paterson-Inverloch Rd to the well-signposted coves for fun rock-pool rambling. Eagles Nest, Shack Bay, the Caves and Twin Reefs are great for snorkelling; Eagles Nest, Shack Bay, Cape Paterson and Flat Rocks are also popular scuba diving sites. The Oaks is the locals' favourite surf beach. The Caves is where the dinosaur dig action is; the Bunurong Environment Centre & Shop (p275) runs tours here in January.

SEAL Diving Services ( ☎ 5174 3434; www.sealdiving services.com.au; 7/27 Princes Hwy, Traralgon; PADI 4-day course $575, 1-day double dive $80, introductory dive $99) SEAL offers PADI open-water dive courses in Inverloch in summer. Also available are one-day dives for beginners and experienced divers, and weekend trips for certified divers at Bunurong Marine & Coastal Park.

# KOONWARRA

## pop 750

This tiny township on the South Gippsland Hwy has built itself around the reputation of its general store, renowned for its fabulous café. There's also an organic fruit-and-vegetable shop and sustainable-living centre, and the inspiring Peaceful Gardens Organic Cooking School ( ☎ 5664 2480; www.peacefulgardens.com.au; Koala Dr; half-/full-day $75/100, children's half-day $35) – Victoria's first organic-certified cooking school. It offers short courses in making cakes, bread, traditional pastries and pasta, and runs cooking classes for kids. There's a Farmers Market ( ☎ 6569 8208; ⊗ 8am-1pm Sat) at Memorial Park on the first Saturday of each month, with organic everything (fruit, vegetables, berries, coffee) plus hormone-free beef and chemical-free cheeses. Alternatively you can completely indulge yourself at the Koonwarra Day Spa ( ☎ 5664 2332; www.koonwarraspa .com.au; 9 Koala Dr; most 30min treatments $50), a new centre offering spas, saunas and body treatments ranging from a 30-minute mineral spa ($30) to a six-hour pamper package ($465).

---

**TRANSPORT: KOONWARRA**

Distance from Melbourne 142km

Direction Southeast

Travel time Two hours

Bus V/Line ( ☎ 13 61 96; www.vline.com.au) buses depart Melbourne's Southern Cross station for Leongatha ($11, 2½ hours, five daily), five minutes' drive from Koonwarra.

Car Take the M1 (CityLink/Monash Fwy) and exit at the South Gippsland Hwy.

---

# EATING

Koonwarra Food, Wine & Produce Store ( ☎ 5664 2285; cnr South Gippsland Highway and Koala Drive; mains $6-34; ⊗ breakfast & lunch daily, dinner Fri) Local produce and wines are on sale in this renovated timber building. Inside is a renowned café that serves simple food with flair, priding itself on using organic, low-impact suppliers and products. Soak up the ambience in the wooded interior, or relax at a table in the shaded cottage gardens, home to the Outside Bit, a quirky little nursery.

# SLEEPING

Koonwarra Cottages ( ☎ 5664 2488; hayward@dcsi.net.au; South Gippsland Hwy; s & d $110; ⊠ ) These timber-lined, wooden cottages with spas and wood heaters have a cosy, country-kitchen feel. They're spotlessly clean and run by friendly owners.

Lyre Bird Hill Winery & Guest House ( ☎ 5664 3204; www.lyrebirdhill.com.au; 370 Inverloch Rd; guesthouse s/d $100/175, cottage d $120; ⊠ ) This popular winery (open 10am to 5pm Wednesday to Monday) has an old-fashioned B&B with light-filled rooms overlooking the garden. There are also rooms in a faded country cottage. A three-course dinner can be arranged ($60), accompanied by house wines.

# WILSONS PROMONTORY NATIONAL PARK

'The Prom', as it's affectionately known, is one of the most popular national parks in Australia. It's not surprising given its accessibility from Melbourne, more than 80km of walking tracks, wonderful beaches for swimming and surfing, and abundant wildlife. The park caters to day-trippers looking for short walks, experienced hikers wanting a wilderness experience, and everyone in between.

Tidal River is the hub, and home to the Parks Victoria office, a general store, café and accommodation. The wildlife around Tidal River is incredibly tame: kookaburras and rosellas lurk expectantly (but you're not allowed to feed them), and wombats nonchalantly waddle out of the undergrowth.

There's an extensive choice of walking tracks here, taking you through swamps, forests, marshes, valleys of tree ferns and along beaches lined with sand dunes. The Parks Victoria office has brochures with details of walks, from 15-minute strolls to overnight and longer

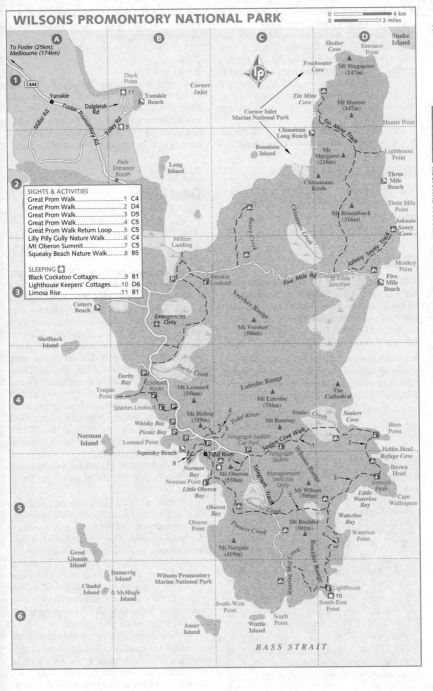

# WILSONS PROMONTORY NATIONAL PARK

0 ━━━━━ 4 km
0 ━━━━━ 2 miles

**SIGHTS & ACTIVITIES**
Great Prom Walk...................1  C4
Great Prom Walk...................2  D4
Great Prom Walk...................3  D5
Great Prom Walk...................4  C5
Great Prom Walk Return Loop...5  C5
Lilly Pilly Gully Nature Walk.....6  C4
Mt Oberon Summit.................7  C5
Squeaky Beach Nature Walk.....8  B5

**SLEEPING**
Black Cockatoo Cottages.........9  B1
Lighthouse Keepers' Cottages...10  D6
Limosa Rise.........................11  B1

To Foster (25km);
Melbourne (174km)

C444

Yanakie

Millar Rd

Foster–Promontory Rd

Dalgleish Rd

Edley Rd

Duck Point

Yanakie Beach

Corner Inlet

Snake Island

Shelter Cove

Entrance Point

Freshwater Cove

Mt Singapore (147m)

Tin Mine Cove

Mt Hunter (347m)

Hunter Point

Tin Mine Track

Corner Inlet Marine National Park

Chinaman Long Beach

Lighthouse Point

Mt Margaret (218m)

Park Entrance Booth

Long Island

Bennison Island

Chinamans Knob

Three Mile Beach

Three Mile Point

Mt Roundback (316m)

Johnnie Souey Cove

Barry Creek

Chinaman Creek

Johnny Souey Track

Monkey Point

Millers Landing

Vereker Lookout

Five Mile Rd

St Kilda Junction

Five Mile Beach

Cotters Beach

Vereker Range

Mt Vereker (586m)

Emergencies Only

Shellback Island

Darby Creek

Darby Bay

Lookout Rocks

Tongue Point

Sparkes Lookout

Mt Leonard (556m)

Latrobe Range

Mt Latrobe (754m)

The Cathedral

Mt Bishop (319m)

Tidal River

Mt Ramsay

Sealers Creek

Sealers Cove

Horn Point

Whisky Bay

Picnic Bay

Telegraph Saddle Car Park

Sealers Cove Walk

Hobbs Head

Refuge Cove

Norman Island

Leonard Point

Squeaky Beach

Tidal River

Telegraph Saddle

Wilsons Range

Brown Head

Kersops Peak

Cape Wellington

Norman Bay

Mt Oberon (558m)

Management Vehicles Only

Mt Wilson (705m)

Little Waterloo Bay

Norman Point

Little Oberon Bay

Telegraph Track

Growler Creek

Waterloo Bay

Oberon Bay

Mt Boulder (581m)

Waterloo Point

Oberon Point

Fresers Creek

Roaring Meg Creek

Boulder Range

Mt Norgate (419m)

Great Glennie Island

Dannevig Island

Citadel Island

McHugh Island

Wilsons Promontory Marine National Park

Lighthouse

South-East Point

South-West Point

South Point

Anser Island

Wattle Island

BASS STRAIT

279

hikes. For some serious exploration, buy a copy of *Discovering the Prom* ($15).

The northern area of the park is much less visited. Most walks in this wilderness area are overnight or longer, and mainly for experienced bushwalkers; permits are required. For those into diving or surfing, SEAL Diving Services (p278) offer dives for certified divers, and Learn to Surf Offshore Surf School (p275) runs surfing lessons here.

Day entry to the park is $10 per car (included in the overnight charge if you're camping).

## INFORMATION

Parks Victoria ( ☎ 1800 350 552, 13 19 63; www.park web.vic.gov.au; Tidal River; ☯ 8am-4.30pm) This office books all park accommodation, including permits for camping away from Tidal River.

## TOURS

Bunyip Tours ( ☎ 1300 286 947, 9650 9680; www.bunyip tours.com; tours 1-/3-days $110/160) Proudly carbon-neutral Bunyip Tours offers a one-day guided tour to the Prom from Melbourne, with the option of staying on another two days to explore by yourself. Camping costs and gear are included in the three-day trip. YHA members get a discount.

First Track Adventures ( ☎ 5634 2761; www.firsttrack .com.au) This Gippsland-based company organises customised bushwalking, canoeing and abseiling trips to the Prom for individuals and groups. Prices vary with group size and activity.

Hiking Plus ( ☎ 9431 1050; www.hikingplus.com; 5-day tours $1420-1712) This tour company organises hikes to the Prom from nearby Foster, where it has comfortable

guesthouse accommodation (including spa) for the start and end of each trip. Packages include a two- to three-day hike, meals, a massage and spa.

## EATING

Stock up in Foster, which has supermarkets and a fruit shop, on your way to the Prom. In Tidal River the general store has supplies of all the basics, there's a takeaway, and the recent addition of a café ( ☯ breakfast, lunch & dinner; mains $12-19) serving light lunches and bistro-style meals.

## SLEEPING
### Tidal River

Tidal River accommodation is incredibly popular. Book well in advance through Parks Victoria ( ☎ 1800 350 552, 13 19 63; www.parkweb.vic.gov .au). Bookings can be made up to 12 months ahead.

Camp Sites (unpowered sites per car & 3 adults or 2 adults & 2 children $21.50, extra adult/child/car $5/2.50/6.50) Tidal River has 480 camp sites. For the Christmas school holiday period there's a ballot for sites (apply online by 31 July at www.parkweb.vic .gov.au). For this peak time Parks Victoria reserves some sites for overseas and interstate visitors; there's a two-night maximum stay, and the sites can be booked in advance. There are another 11 bush-camping areas around the Prom, all with pit or compost toilets, but no other facilities; you need to carry in your own drinking water. Overnight hikers need camping permits (adult/child $7.50/3.50 per night), which should be booked ahead through Parks Victoria.

Huts (4-/6-bed $60/92) These cosy wooden huts have bunks and kitchenettes, but no bathrooms.

Timber Cabins (d $158) These spacious and private self-contained cabins have large, sliding glass doors and decking, and overlook the bush or river. They're simple but ultra-comfortable, with the luxury of a bathtub.

Safari Tents (d/f $240/280) Nestled in bushland at Tidal River, these plush tents (which sleep up to four) are the latest addition to the park's accommodation. Besides comfortable queen-size beds, they also have bathrooms, and there's a shared tent kitchen.

Lighthouse Keepers' Cottages (8-12-bed cottages per person $47-74) Magnificent, heritage-listed 1850s cottages with thick stone walls, on a pimple of land that juts out into the wild ocean. Kick back after the 19km hike here and watch ships

## TOP FIVE PROM WALKS

The Prom's delights are best discovered on foot. Times and distances include walking back.

### Sealers Cove Walk

This is the best overnight walk at the Prom. Start from the Telegraph Saddle car park and walk down Telegraph Track (it's better than returning uphill via this gnarly track) and stay overnight at beautiful Little Waterloo Bay (12km, 4½ hours). The next day, walk on to Sealers Cove via Refuge Cove and return to Telegraph Saddle car park (24km, 7½ hours).

### Great Prom Walk

This is the most popular long-distance hike, a moderate circuit (45km, two or three days) across to Sealers Cove, down to Refuge Cove, Waterloo Bay, the lighthouse and back. Coordinate your walk with tide times, as creek crossings can be hazardous. It's possible to visit or stay at the lighthouse by prior arrangement with Parks Victoria (see Sleeping).

### Lilly Pilly Gully Nature Walk

An easy walk (5km, two hours) through heathland and eucalypt forests, with lots of wildlife. Alternatively, take the longer route through stringy-bark forests (6km, two or three hours).

### Mt Oberon Summit

This moderate-to-hard walk (7km, 2½ hours) starts from Telegraph Saddle car park, your efforts rewarded by excellent panoramic views from the summit. From November to Easter a free shuttle bus operates between Tidal River car park and Mt Oberon car park – a gentle way to start the Great Prom Walk.

### Squeaky Beach Nature Walk

Another easy stroll (5km, two hours) returning through coastal tea trees and banksias to a sensational white-sand beach. Go barefoot on the beach and find out where the name comes from!

or whales passing by. You can usually visit the lighthouse itself, depending on ranger availability. Prices increase 50% on Saturday nights.

## Around Tidal River

Limosa Rise ( ☎ 5687 1135; www.limosarise.com.au; 40 Dalgleish Rd, Yanakie; d $200-270; ❀ ) This new, luxury, self-contained accommodation has already won regional and state awards with its contemporary design of the three tastefully-appointed cottages. Full-length glass windows take complete advantage of sweeping views across Corner Inlet and the Prom's mountains.

Black Cockatoo Cottages ( ☎ 5687 1306; www.blackcockatoo.com; 60 Foley Rd, Yanakie; d $140) These cottages are in Yanakie, the nearest settlement to the Prom. You can take in glorious views of the national park without leaving your very comfortable bed in these private, stylish, black-timber, self-contained cottages.

Prom Coast Backpackers ( ☎ 5682 2171; www.yha.com.au; 40 Station Rd, Foster; dm/d/f from $25/60/80; 🖵 ) There are no hostels in the park, but nearby Foster has this cosy, renovated cottage with contemporary wooden furnishings that sleeps 10. It's close to the shops and across the road from a good

playground. The friendly owners can usually organise a lift to the Prom for $20. Prices are about 10% higher for non-YHA members.

Warrawee Holiday Apartments ( ☎ 5682 2171; www.gippsland.com/web/warraweeholidayapartments; 38 Station Rd, Foster; d/f $120/130; ❀ ) Next door to Prom Coast Backpackers and under the same management are these comfortable, two-bedroom apartments, some with air-conditioning.

## PORT ALBERT

### pop 250

Quaint old fishing village Port Albert is galloping into the 21st century with new upmarket accommodation, cafés and a gallery opening. It's lost none of its charm, with the town's old buildings being carefully restored for more contemporary uses. The Port Albert town sign proudly pronounces itself as Victoria's first established port. The many historic timber buildings in the main street dating from its busy 1850s port days bear a brass plaque, detailing their age and previous use. Find out more about the town's heyday at the Maritime Museum ( ☎ 5183 2520; Tarraville Rd; adult/child $5/1; ☼ 10.30am-4pm daily Sep-May, Sat & Sun Jun-Aug), where the lovely volunteer staff will give you some quick highlights of Port Albert's maritime history, before leaving you to check out stories of shipwrecks, the town's whaling and sealing days and local Aboriginal legends.

## EATING

General Store ( ☎ 5183 2291; 71 Tarraville Rd; mains $10-22; ☙ breakfast & lunch Tue-Sun) This café/gallery in the 1856 general store has fast attracted a following. People travel a long way for the (limited) gourmet menu complemented with Gippsland wines (try the cheese platter with crusty bread, marinated olives and fig relish,). The Asian-influenced gallery has unexpected treasures such as Chinese peasant chairs and wooden croaking frogs, while the shop sells an eclectic range of books and gourmet local produce.

Port Albert Wharf Fish & Chips ( ☎ 5183 2434; Port Albert Wharf; meals from $6; ☙ lunch & dinner) The fish and chips here are renowned, and fresh as can be.

## SLEEPING

Port Albert Hotel/Motel ( ☎ 5183 2212; fax 5183 2429; 37 Wharf St; s/d $55/75; ☒ ) Victoria's oldest continually-licensed pub still draws the crowds, with its friendly staff, down-to-earth vibe, quality bistro food (mains $15 to $30) and takeaway fish and chips (just ring the bell at the outdoor counter). The motel rooms are clean but faded.

Rodondo ( ☎ 5183 2688; susan333@optusnet.com.au; 74 Tarraville Rd; cottage $75, B&B d/f $140/160) The contemporary blends seamlessly with the historic in this renovated 1871 home. The rooms have a homely but luxurious feel, and the friendly hospitality adds to the satisfaction of staying here. There's also a cosy, self-contained cabin in the former wash house.

# WALHALLA

**pop 18**

This is one of the state's best-preserved and most charming historic towns. In its gold-mining heyday, Walhalla's population was 5000; now there are just 18 people. There's still plenty to see in Walhalla, and the windy drive up to the town is beautiful. Stringers Creek runs through the centre of the township – an idyllic valley encircled by a cluster of historic buildings set into the hillsides. Many of Walhalla's attractions are open year-round, but there's more happening on weekends, during high season and (oddly enough) on Wednesdays.

The best way to see the town is on foot – take the circuit walk (45 minutes) anticlockwise from the information shelter as you enter town. The trail passes the main sights before climbing up the hill to follow the old timber tramway then heading back down to the car park. There's a group of restored shops along the main street, including Walhalla Post Office & Museum ( ☎ 5165 6250; www.walhalla.org.au; admission $2; ☷ 10am-4pm) which offers ghost tours ($22, 1¼ hours) on the first three Saturdays of each month (7.30pm April to October, 8.30pm October to April).

Guided tours of the Long Tunnel Extended Gold Mine ( ☎ 5165 6259; off Walhalla-Beardmore Rd; tours adult/child/family $15/12/36; ☷ tours 1.30pm Mon-Fri, noon, 2pm & 3pm Sat & Sun, public & school holidays) give you a look at Cohens Reef, once one of Australia's top reef-gold producers. Almost 14 tonnes of gold came out of this mine.

You can take a very scenic 20-minute ride between Thomson Station (on the main road, 3.5km before Walhalla) and Walhalla on the Walhalla Goldfields Railway ( ☎ 9513 3969; rides adult/child/family $17/12/37; ☷ from Thomson Station 11.40am, 1.40pm & 3.40pm Wed, Sat & Sun, public holidays, from Walhalla station 12.10pm, 2pm & 3.50pm). The train snakes along Stringers Creek Gorge, passing lovely, forested gorge country and crossing a number of trestle bridges.

Back in town, steps lead up a steep hillside to Walhalla Cricket Ground. Walhalla Cemetery gives a more sombre insight into the history of the area. The terrain here is so steep that some folk were buried vertically!

For some seriously rugged mountain adventuring, Mountain Top Experience ( ☎ 5134 6876; www.mountaintopexperience.com; trips adult & child $20, family $60) operates an 1½-hour 4WD Copper Mine Adventure trip most weekends and Wednesdays, along old coach roads to a disused mine.

## TRANSPORT: WALHALLA

**Distance from Melbourne** 181km

**Direction** Southeast

**Travel time** 2½ hours

**Car** Take the M1 (CityLink/Monash Fwy/Princes Hwy) and exit at Moe. Take the Moe-Rawson Rd and then Walhalla Rd.

## EATING

**Walhalla Lodge Family Hotel** ( ☎ 5165 6226; Main St; mains $14-22; ☷ lunch & dinner Wed-Mon) A cosy, one-room pub decked out with prints of old Walhalla and serving reasonable pub meals.

**Parker's** ( ☎ 5165 6262; www.starhotel.com.au; Main Rd; mains $25-27; ☷ dinner) Housed in the rebuilt historic Walhalla Star Hotel, Parker's is an upmarket restaurant. No children under 12.

## SLEEPING

**Walhalla Star Hotel** ( ☎ 5165 6262; Main Rd; s & d/tr $199/229) The Star Hotel offers stylish, boutique-hotel accommodation with sophisticated designer décor and king-sized beds.

**Camping** (free) Walhalla's camp sites are free, and there are good bush camping areas along Stringer's Creek, as well as the designated North Gardens camping ground (with toilets) at the top of the town.

## SALE

Sale is the gateway to the Lakes District, the largest inland waterway system in Australia. There's not a lot in the way of sights in Sale itself, but there's some fabulous accommodation, some classy restaurants and bars, and a striking entertainment centre here. It's an upmarket base from which to explore Ninety Mile Beach.

The Sale Wetlands Walk (4km, 1½ hours), close to the Princes Hwy, is a pleasant walk around the town lakes and incorporates an Indigenous Art Trail commemorating the importance of the wetlands to the local Gunai/Kurnai population.

Sale Common, a 300-hectare wildlife refuge with bird hides, an observatory, waterhole, board-walks and other walking tracks is part of an internationally recognised wetlands system. The wildlife refuge is 2km south of Sale on the South Gippsland Hwy. The best time to visit is early morning or late evening (wear some mosquito repellent) when you'll see lots of bird life.

The Gippsland Art Gallery ( ☎ 5142 3372; www.wellington.vic.gov.au/gallery; Civic Centre, 68 Foster St; adult/child $3/1.50; ☻ 10am-5pm Tue-Fri, 1-5pm Sat & Sun) is always worth a look, exhibiting work by locally and nationally renowned artists and hosting touring exhibitions.

## INFORMATION

Central Gippsland visitors centre ( ☎ 5144 1108; www .tourismwellington.com.au; 8 Foster St; ☻ 9am-5pm; ☐ ) Internet facilities and a free accommodation booking service.

Parks Victoria ( ☎ 13 19 63; www.parkweb.vic.gov.au; 1 Lacey St; ☻ 9.30am-noon & 1-3.30pm Tue & Fri) Turn right at Foster St into Guthridge St, then right into Lacey St.

## EATING

Relish@the Gallery ( ☎ 5144 5044; Gippsland Art Gallery, 68-70 Foster St; meals $4-30; ☻ breakfast & lunch daily, dinner Wed-Sat) Take a table by the window and check out the old port of Sale while you tuck into dishes like the salmon, spinach, capers, red onion and goat's cheese omelette in this bustling café. There's also an extensive kids menu.

bis cucina ( ☎ 5144 3388; Wellington Entertainment Centre, 100 Foster St; breakfast & lunch $6-22, dinner $19-34; ☻ breakfast Sat & Sun, lunch daily, dinner Tue-Sat) Relaxed and attentive service combined with carefully chosen modern Australian cuisine makes this a fine choice for both serious foodies and theatre-goers wanting a quick meal preshow. bis has the most sumptuous children's menu in Gippsland, with offerings such as organic chicken.

## SLEEPING

minnies ( ☎ 5144 3344; www.minnies.com.au; 202 Gibsons Rd; s/d $150/160; 🏊 ) It takes some flair to make an

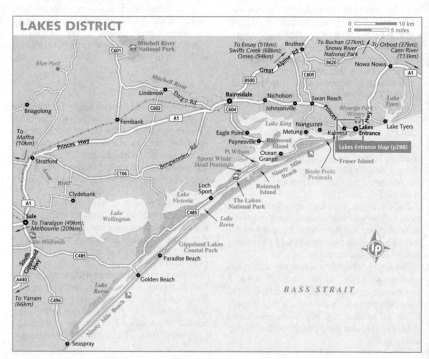

outlandish purple-and-green colour scheme not only work but look inspired, and indeed it does in the huge lounge area of this modern B&B. Choose between the funky green room and the more traditional rose room, with its antique-look bed head complete with rose imprints.

Cambrai Hostel ( ☎ 5147 1600; www.maffra.net.au/hostel/backpackers.htm; 117 Johnson St, Maffra; dm/d incl breakfast $25/60; 🖥 ) There's no backpackers in Sale, but in nearby Maffra this place is a budget haven. It's in a 120-year-old building that was once a doctor's residence, and is now a relaxed hostel with licensed bar, open fire and pool table in the cosy lounge, tiny self-catering kitchen and clean, cheerful rooms.

# NINETY MILE BEACH

Isolated Ninety Mile Beach is a long, narrow strip of beach backed by dunes, swamplands and lagoons. The area is great for surf-fishing and walking, though the beaches can be dangerous for swimming, except where patrolled at Seaspray, Woodside and Lakes Entrance.

Between Seaspray and Lakes Entrance is the Gippsland Lakes Coastal Park, with oodles of low-lying coastal shrub, banksias and tea trees, and bursts of native wild flowers in spring. If you're interested in the challenge of hiking the length of the Ninety Mile Beach, permission for remote camping can be obtained from Parks Victoria ( ☎ 13 19 63; www.parkweb.vic.gov.au).

One of the main access roads to Ninety Mile Beach is from Sale to Seaspray, Golden Beach and Loch Sport, a small, bushy town sprawling along a narrow spit of land. It's the entry point to the Lakes National Park, a narrow strip of coastal bushland surrounded by lakes and ocean. It's a beautifully quiet little spot to set up camp, except in January when everyone else has the same idea. Banksia and eucalypt woodland abound with areas of low-lying heathland and some swampy salt-marsh scrub. In spring the park is carpeted with native wildflowers and has one of Australia's best displays of native orchids. You're likely to spot kangaroos, as well as wallabies, possums, emus and possibly

koalas. A loop road through the park provides good car access, and there are well-marked walking trails, including some short walks, and several picnic areas (BYO water). Point Wilson, at the eastern tip of the mainland section of the park is the best picnic spot and a popular gathering place for kangaroos (no feeding them of course). There's plenty of bird life too – more than 190 species have been sighted.

## EATING

Marina Hotel ( ☎ 5146 0666; Basin Blvd, Loch Sport; mains $15-23 🕒 lunch & dinner) Perched by the lake, this pub has a friendly vibe and superb sunset views. There's standard bistro food, featuring fish.

## SLEEPING

Emu Bight Camp Site ( ☎ 13 19 63; www.parkweb.vic.gov.au; Lakes National Park; sites per 6 people $12) This camp site is nestled in bushland, with pit toilets and fireplaces available. BYO water.

Seaspray/Golden Beach Camp Sites (Seaspray-Golden Beach Rd; free) These shady sites on the Ninety Mile Beach foreshore are idyllically close to the beach and hugely popular over summer. Some sites have barbecues and pit toilets, but you need to bring your own water or firewood. Hot showers are available at Golden Beach ($2).

90 Mile Beach Holiday Retreat ( ☎ 5146 0320; www.90milebeachholidayretreat.com; Track 10, off Golden Beach-Loch Sport Rd; unpowered/powered sites $26/28, caravans/bunk rooms d $60/75, lodge & cottage d & f $155-165) On a huge chunk of land a few kilometres from Loch Spot, this retreat has 2.4km of pristine beach frontage. It's separated from the rest of the world by 6km of dirt track. There are plenty of shady grassy areas for camping, small ex-Melbourne Olympic Village bunkrooms, and spacious, light-and-airy lodges. The comfortable self-contained cottage is nestled into the dunes, just a minute from the beach.

Gary Powers Real Estate ( ☎ 5146 0411; www.garypowersrealestate.com; Lot 217, Lake St, Loch Sport; houses per night $110-250) This Loch Sport real-estate agent manages 40 holiday houses, ranging from ordinary to luxury, available for nightly or weekly rental.

## BAIRNSDALE

**pop 11,290**
Bairnsdale is East Gippsland's commercial hub, with a bustling main street and a sprinkling of attractions.

**TRANSPORT: NINETY MILE BEACH**

Distance from Melbourne 240km

Direction East

Travel time 3¼ hours

Car Take the M1 (CityLink/Monash Fwy/Princes Hwy) to Sale, then the C496 south to Seaspray.

Krowathunkoolong Keeping Place ( ☎ 5152 1891; 37-53 Dalmahoy St; adult/child $3.50/2.50; ✆ 9am-5pm Mon-Fri) is a stirring Koorie cultural exhibition space that explores Gunai/Kurnai life from the Dreamtime until after white settlement. The exhibition traces the Gunai/Kurnai clan from their Dreamtime ancestors, Borun the pelican and his wife Tuk the musk duck, and covers life at Lake Tyers Mission, east of Lakes Entrance, now a trust privately owned by Aboriginal shareholders. The massacres of the Kurnai during 1839–49 are also detailed. The Keeping Place is signposted from the highway.

East Gippsland Aboriginal Arts Corporation ( ☎ 5153 1002; www.australiacouncil.gov.au; 222 Nicholson St; admission free; ✆ 9am-5pm Mon-Fri) is an art gallery featuring the work of local Aboriginal artists. The East Gippsland Art Gallery ( ☎ 5153 1988; www .eastgippslandartgallery.org.au; 2 Nicholson St; admission free; ✆ 10am-4pm Tue-Fri, to 2pm Sat) is a bright, open space that has regular exhibitions, mostly the work of East Gippsland artists.

On the edge of town (signposted from the highway at the roundabout as you arrive in Bairnsdale from the west) is the MacLeod Morass Boardwalk, an internationally recognised wetland reserve with walking tracks and bird hides – a peaceful change of pace.

## INFORMATION

Bairnsdale visitors centre ( ☎ 1800 637 060, 5152 3444; www .lakesandwilderness.com.au; 240 Main St; ✆ 9am-5pm; 🖳 )

East Gippsland Shire Library ( ☎ 5152 4225; 22 Service St; ✆ 10am-5pm Mon, 10am-1pm Tue, 9am-6pm Wed & Fri, 9am-7pm Thu, 9.30am-12pm Sat; 🖳 ) Free internet access.

## EATING

Peppers ( ☎ 5152 3217; 222 Main St; fish & chips $8; ✆ 8.30am-8.30pm) This contemporary fish-and-chip shop adds flair to the usual offerings. Try its popular fish souvlaki smothered with tzatziki.

---

### TRANSPORT: BAIRNSDALE

**Distance from Melbourne** 282km

**Direction** East

**Travel time** Four hours

**Car** Take the M1 (CityLink/Monash Fwy/Princes Hwy) to Bairnsdale.

**Train** V/Line ( ☎ 13 61 96; www.vline.com.au) runs trains between Melbourne and Bairnsdale ($25, 3½ hours, three daily).

---

Gourmet Deli ( ☎ 5152 1544; 144 Main St; dishes $6-10; ✆ lunch Mon-Fri) Stop by here for the best coffee and herbal tea in town. Gourmet sandwich ingredients are on display in their deli and served up in thick, crusty bread.

River Grill ( ☎ 5153 1421; 2 Wood St; mains $27-36; ✆ lunch & dinner Mon-Sat) The newest addition to East Gippsland's culinary scene, River Grill offers contemporary fine dining with Mediterranean flair.

## SLEEPING

Riversleigh Country Hotel ( ☎ 5152 6966; www.riversleigh .info; 1 Nicholson St; s/d incl breakfast from $112/122; ✦ ) This Victorian-era boutique hotel offers elegant rooms with heritage furnishings. Breakfast is served in the sunny conservatory, and there's also a formal restaurant here (mains $10 to $33, open for lunch and dinner Monday to Saturday), maximising the use of local ingredients in inventive, modern cuisine.

Mitchell Gardens Holiday Park ( ☎ 5152 4654; www .mitchellgardens.com.au; unpowered/powered sites $20/23, cabins d $50-86; ✦ ) East of the town centre on the banks of the Mitchell River, this is a friendly park with plenty of shade for cabins and a little for tents. The deluxe cabins have a lovely outlook over the Mitchell River.

## METUNG

### pop 730

Metung (www.metungtourism.com.au) is the nicest town on the Gippsland Lakes – the unhurried charm of this picturesque village on Bancroft Bay is contagious. It's an upmarket base for boating and fishing, and its shoreline is dotted with jetties and small wooden craft. Boats and yachts for cruising, fishing and sailing on the Gippsland Lakes are available from Riviera Nautic ( ☎ 5156 2243; www.rivieranautic.com.au; 185 Metung Rd; motor boat per day $175, yachts per 3 days 4-/8-berth $1170/1980). Fuel and a boating lesson are included – a fabulous way of exploring the lakes. There are countless islands, jetties and stretches of beach to moor your boat at night. If you prefer someone else to drive, take an afternoon cruise to Lakes Entrance onboard the Director ( ☎ 5156 2628; 2½hr cruise adult/child $42/free; ✆ 3pm Tue, Thu & Sat). Drinks and local cheeses are included. The owners of The Director also hire out sea kayaks (per 1/4hr from $25/65) for checking out the quiet waters of the lakes.

Opposite Metung Yacht Club on the edge of Bancroft Bay is Legend Rock, a sacred Aboriginal site. According to Aboriginal oral histories, the rock represents a hunter who was turned to stone for not sharing the food he had caught. The road into town shaves past the rock.

Providing a new focus for the energetic local art scene is Nu Art Metung ( ☎ 5156 2909; www.nuartmetung .com; 69a Metung Rd; admission free; 10am-5pm Thu-Mon), a contemporary gallery hosting fine-art exhibitions and showcasing the work of local artists.

## INFORMATION

Metung visitors centre ( ☎ 5156 2969; www.metung accommodation.com.au; 3/50 Metung Rd; ☿ 9am-5pm) Accommodation booking and boat-hire services.

## EATING

Metung Galley ( ☎ 5156 2330; 3/59 Metung Rd; lunch $10-18, dinner $19-29; ☿ breakfast & lunch daily, dinner Wed-Mon) Felicity and Richard's city hospitality experience shines through in this friendly, efficient café, serving up beautifully presented, quality food. The smoked trout, organic goat's cheese and rocket tart is delicious.

Metung Hotel ( ☎ 5156 2206; 1 Kurnai Ave; meals $18-30; ☿ lunch & dinner) On the edge of the lake, and with an outdoor deck, Metung Hotel has had a makeover since top local restaurateur Archie was installed as manager. The bistro food is superb – the best you'll find in a Gippsland pub.

Nina's ( ☎ 5156 2474; 3/51 Metung Rd; dishes $4-12; ☿ breakfast & lunch Wed-Sun) Don't miss the organic coffee and Mindy's divine home-cooked brownies.

## SLEEPING

Anchorage B&B ( ☎ 5156 2569; www.anchoragebedand breakfast.com.au; 11 The Anchorage; d $150; ☒ ) You'll receive a warm welcome here. Enjoy a sumptuous gourmet breakfast in the sunny guest breakfast room, then kick back in the bush garden and take in the water views. Fluffy towels, crisp sheets and soothing autumn tones make these rooms a very comfortable place to stay. Closed mid-June to mid-August.

McMillans of Metung ( ☎ 5156 2283; www.mcmillans ofmetung.com.au; 155 Metung Rd; cottages/villas d $165/245; ☒ ☒ ) This lakeside resort has won stacks of tourism awards for its complex of English-country-style cottages, set in three hectares of manicured gardens, and has expanded with some modern villas.

Moorings at Metung ( ☎ 5156 2750; www.themoorings .com.au; 44 Metung Rd; r $140-270; ☒ ☒ ) In the heart

### TRANSPORT: METUNG

Distance from Melbourne 312km

Direction East

Travel time 4¼ hours

Car Take the M1 (CityLink/Monash Fwy/Princes Hwy) to Swan Reach then take the Metung turn-off.

Taxi Metung Taxis ( ☎ 5156 2005) Swan Reach to Metung ($20, 5km).

Train & Bus V/Line ( ☎ 13 61 96; www.vline.com.au) runs from Melbourne to nearby Swan Reach ($26, four hours, two daily), from where you can catch a taxi.

of Metung village, this large, contemporary apartment complex has motel rooms and self-contained units, all with water views. It's a luxuriously comfortable option with stylish rooms and a tennis court, indoor and outdoor pools and spa.

Metung Holiday Villas ( ☎ 5156 2306; www.metungholi dayvillas.com; cnr Mairburn & Stirling Rds; cabins $100-150; ☒ ☒ ) Metung's former caravan park has reinvented itself as a minivillage of luxury cabins. The landscaped bush gardens around them provide some privacy. Linen provided.

## LAKES ENTRANCE
pop 4100

Lakes Entrance is the region's main tourist town and is popular. It's in a picturesque location on the gentle waters of Cunninghame Arm, backed by sand dunes and fishing boats, just a stroll from a magnificent stretch of ocean beach. It's probably best to focus on these virtues, rather than the town's enormous crop of caravan parks and graceless strip of motels, souvenir shops and minigolf courses lining the Esplanade.

In summer it's packed out, and you'll find businesses catering to every water-related whim you may have. A footbridge crosses the Cunninghame Arm inlet from the east of town to the ocean and Ninety Mile Beach. From December to Easter, paddle boats, canoes and sailboats can be hired by the footbridge on the ocean side. This is also where the Eastern Beach Walking Track (2.3km, 45 minutes) starts, taking you through coastal scrub to the entrance itself, artificially created in 1889 to provide ocean access from the lakes system. From here you can loop back along Ninety Mile Beach.

To explore the lakes, three companies along Marine Pde offer boat hire (hire per 4/8hr $90/150).

Several companies offer cruises on the lakes, including the following:

**Corque** ( ☎ 5155 1508; Post Office Jetty, The Esplanade; 4½hr cruise incl lunch & wine tasting adult $50, child under/over 6 $6/25) Popular daily lunch cruise to Wyanga Park Winery, and weekend dinner and Sunday brunch cruises.

**Mulloway Fishing Charters** ( ☎ 0427-943 154, 5155 3304; 3hr cruise adult/child $40/20) Fishing cruises on the lake departing the jetty opposite 66 Marine Pde. Rods, tackle, bait and morning or afternoon tea provided.

**Peels Tourist & Ferry Services** ( ☎ 5155 1246; Post Office Jetty, The Esplanade; 2hr cruise adult/child $34/17, 4hr Metung cruise with/without lunch $44/12.50) These folks have been running cruises for almost a century. There's a lake cruise at 2pm daily, plus a longer cruise to Metung at 11am Wednesday to Monday.

Surfing lessons (gear provided) are run by the **Surf Shack** ( ☎ /fax 5155 4933; 507 The Esplanade; 2hr lesson $45) at nearby Lake Tyers Beach. The **Fisherman's Co-op Viewing Platform** ( ☎ 5155 1688; Bullock Island) provides a mesmerising view of fishing boats unloading their catch. There's often a boat there but you can phone ahead to check. The Co-op is just off the Princes Hwy: turn at the roundabout at the west end of Lakes Entrance. Also on

**TRANSPORT: LAKES ENTRANCE**

**Distance from Melbourne** 317km

**Direction** East

**Travel time** 4¼ hours

**Car** Take the M1 (CityLink/Monash Fwy/Princes Hwy) to Lakes Entrance.

**Train & Bus** V/Line ( ☎ 13 61 96; www.vline.com .au) runs between Melbourne and Lakes Entrance ($28, 4¼ hours, two daily).

the Princes Hwy on the western side of town is Kalimna Lookout, a popular viewing spot. For an even better view of the ocean, lake and entrance (and a quieter location), take the road directly opposite Kalimna Lookout; you'll almost immediately see a sign to Jemmy's Point Lookout.

Lakes' newest offering is the blissfully indulgent Illuka Day Spa ( ☎ 5155 3533; www.esplanaderesort .com.au/dayspa; 1 The Esplanade; ☺ 9am-5pm Sat-Mon & Wed-Thu, to 8pm Tue, to 7pm Fri), where therapies range from a 30-minute aromatherapy tub ($60) to the 3¼-hour 'Illuka Dreaming' – a foot treatment, sea wrap (with pearl-and-kelp body mud) and head-to-toe massage ($350).

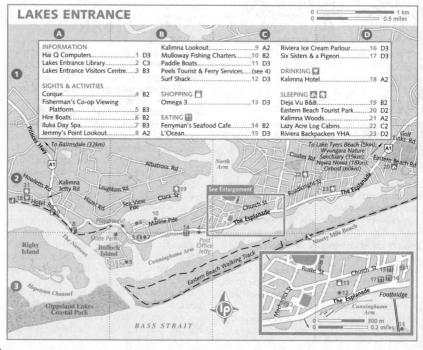

**LAKES ENTRANCE**

0 — 1 km
0 — 0.5 miles

| INFORMATION | | |
|---|---|---|
| Hai Q Computers | 1 | D3 |
| Lakes Entrance Library | 2 | C3 |
| Lakes Entrance Visitors Centre | 3 | B3 |

| SIGHTS & ACTIVITIES | | |
|---|---|---|
| Corque | 4 | B2 |
| Fisherman's Co-op Viewing Platform | 5 | B3 |
| Hire Boats | 6 | B2 |
| Iluka Day Spa | 7 | B3 |
| Jemmy's Point Lookout | 8 | A2 |

| | | |
|---|---|---|
| Kalimna Lookout | 9 | A2 |
| Mulloway Fishing Charters | 10 | B2 |
| Paddle Boats | 11 | D3 |
| Peels Tourist & Ferry Services | (see 4) | |
| Surf Shack | 12 | D3 |

| SHOPPING | | |
|---|---|---|
| Omega 3 | 13 | D3 |

| EATING | | |
|---|---|---|
| Ferryman's Seafood Cafe | 14 | B2 |
| L'Ocean | 15 | D3 |

| | | |
|---|---|---|
| Riviera Ice Cream Parlour | 16 | D3 |
| Six Sisters & a Pigeon | 17 | D3 |

| DRINKING | | |
|---|---|---|
| Kalimna Hotel | 18 | A2 |

| SLEEPING | | |
|---|---|---|
| Deja Vu B&B | 19 | B2 |
| Eastern Beach Tourist Park | 20 | D2 |
| Kalimna Woods | 21 | A2 |
| Lazy Acre Log Cabins | 22 | C2 |
| Riviera Backpackers YHA | 23 | D2 |

To Bairnsdale (32km)

Princes Hwy

To Lake Tyers Beach (5km);
Wyangara Nature
Sanctuary (15km);
Nowa Nowa (18km);
Orbost (60km)

Coates Rd

Eastern Beach Rd

Golf Links Rd

Albatross Rd

North Arm

Howletts Rd

Kalimna Jetty Rd

Laughtons Rd

Hazel Rd

Sea View Pde

Clara St

Hotel Rd

Roadknight St

The Esplanade

See Enlargement

Church St

The Esplanade

Playground

Marine Pde

Skate Park

The Narrows

Bullock Island

Post Office Jetty

Cunninghame Arm

Ninety Mile Beach

Rigby Island

Eastern Beach Walking Track

Hopetoun Channel

Gippsland Lakes Coastal Park

BASS STRAIT

Rowe St

Church St

The Esplanade

Mechanics St

Footbridge

Cunninghame Arm

0 — 300 m
0 — 0.2 miles

Guided walks to spot nocturnal wildlife, in the company of an experienced naturalist, are run by Wildlife at Night ( ☎ 5156 5863; Wyungara Nature Sanctuary, Veldens Rd; walks adult/child/family $22/13/55; ☺ departs sunset Sat), signposted off the Princes Hwy 15km east of Lakes Entrance.

## INFORMATION

Hai Q Computers ( ☎ 5155 4247; cnr Myer St & The Esplanade; ☺ 9.30am-5pm Mon-Fri, 10am-2pm Sat; ▣ ) A computer business with a quirky gift shop, offering internet access ($7 per hour, including wireless).

Lakes Entrance Library ( ☎ 5153 9500; 18 Mechanics St; ☺ 8.30am-5pm Mon-Fri; ▣ ) Free internet access.

Lakes Entrance visitors centre ( ☎ 1800 637 060, 5155 1966; www.lakes-entrance.com; cnr Princes Hwy & Marine Pde; ☺ 9am-5pm) Free accommodation and boat-trip booking service.

## EATING & DRINKING

L'Ocean ( ☎ 5155 2253; 19 Myer St; ☺ lunch & dinner) With one of Australia's largest commercial fishing fleets, Lakes Entrance is a great place for fresh fish and chips ($8). One of the local favourites is the award-winning L'Ocean, which also caters for the gluten-free crowd and serves delicious fried pumpkin.

Riviera Ice Cream Parlour ( ☎ 5155 2972; 583 The Esplanade; ice creams $4; ☺ 9.30am-5pm) Organic ice cream – the perfect follow-up to fresh fish and chips.

Six Sisters & a Pigeon ( ☎ 5155 1144; 567 The Esplanade; meals $6-17; ☺ breakfast & lunch Tue-Sun) On a sunny day, join the locals street-side or by the large open window with your newspaper or magazine. This licensed café adds style to standard café offerings. Try the eggs Atlantic with egg, smoked salmon, baked mushrooms and spinach on Turkish bread. You'll find the best coffee in town here, which goes nicely with the chocolate almond torte.

Ferryman's Seafood Cafe ( ☎ 5155 3000; Middle Harbour, The Esplanade; mains $10-39; ☺ brunch, lunch & dinner) Propped in the harbour among a flotilla of fishing boats is this café, serving fish with flair. The salmon fillet, encrusted in pistachio nuts, with pomegranate sauce, is divine. It's child-friendly, with high chairs, a toy box and friendly staff. During business hours you can also buy fresh fish from the shop on the deck below.

Omega 3 ( ☎ 5155 4344; Shop 5, Safeway Arcade, Church St; ☺ 9am-5pm) This is the shop front for the local Fishermen's Co-op – the best place to buy fish in East Gippsland.

Kalimna Hotel ( ☎ 5155 1202; 1 Hotel Rd, Kalimna; 11am-1am Mon-Sat, to 11pm Sun) For a drink with views, you can't beat this hotel, signposted off the highway on the Melbourne side of Lakes Entrance.

## SLEEPING

Goat & Goose B&B ( ☎ 5155 3079; www.goatandgoose.com; 16 Gay St; d $140-210) Bass Strait views are maximised at this wonderfully unusual, multistorey, timber-pole-framed house. The owners are friendly, and all the gorgeously quaint rooms have spas.

Deja Vu B&B ( ☎ 5155 4330; www.dejavu.com.au; Clara St; d $150-250; ▨ ) This imposing, sandstone-coloured, modern home has been built on the slope of a hill to maximise water views, and the bushy garden ensures privacy. After a sumptuous breakfast, canoe across the North Arm to town. Two-night minimum on weekends.

Kalimna Woods ( ☎ 5155 1957; www.kalimnawoods.com.au; Kalimna Jetty Rd; d $115-155, f $145-185; ▨ ) Retreat 2km from the town centre to Kalimna Woods, set in a large rainforest-and-bush garden, complete with friendly resident possums and birds. These country-style cottages with either spa or wood fire are spacious and comfortable.

Eastern Beach Tourist Park ( ☎ 5155 1581; www.eastern beach.com.au; 42 Eastern Beach Rd; unpowered/powered sites $23/27; ▣ ) Close to the beach, this park is refreshingly old-style. It has a bush setting by the Eastern Beach Walking Track (30 minutes into town) and free wireless internet.

Lazy Acre Log Cabins ( ☎ 5155 1323; www.lazyacre.com; 35 Roadknight St; d/f $105/125; ▨ ▣ ) These small, self-contained timber cabins are shaded with old gum trees, and it's a friendly, relaxed place to stay. There's bicycle hire and a babysitting service, and disabled access is available.

Riviera Backpackers YHA ( ☎ 5155 2444; www.yha.com.au; 660-71 The Esplanade; YHA members dm/s/d/f $19/30/44/86; ▣ ▣ ) Part of the Beaches Family Holiday Units complex, these YHA rooms are in old-style brick units, each with two or three bedrooms and a bathroom. There's a big communal kitchen, and lounge with pool table and internet access ($2 for 15 minutes). Bike and fishing-rod hire are available. Non-YHA members pay a few dollars more.

## LAKE TYERS BEACH

**pop 550**

This is a quiet alternative to Lakes Entrance, popular with surfers for the good surf breaks at Red Bluff, and with families for the calm lake waters and ocean beaches. Two-hour boat cruises ( ☎ 5156 5492; cruises adult/child/family $25/15/70; ☺ departs 2pm Mon, Wed, Thu & Sat, 6.30pm Fri) aboard the electric-powered *MV Rumbeena* with the friendly and knowledgeable Bernie are a peaceful way to spend the afternoon. Surfing lessons are offered at Red Bluff by the Surf Shack (p288).

## EATING

Waterwheel Tavern ( ☎ 5156 5530; 557 Lake Tyers Beach Rd; mains $19-35; ☺ lunch & dinner) The Waterwheel has an inspired bistro menu and brilliant views over the lake. See if you can get through the sumptuous seafood platter for two.

## SLEEPING

Lake Tyers Beach House ( ☎ 5156 5995; www.lakes-entrance .com/beachhouse/house.htm; 3 Larkins Pl; up to 4 people $200) This sunny, four-bedroom house has a fabulous, artistically-inspired, hot-pink, retro-chic living area. Wander down the bushy garden path to a quiet stretch of ocean beach, or next door to the yoga studio to stretch out, take a class or have some private tuition. Two-night minimum stay.

Lakes Beachfront Holiday Retreat ( ☎ 5156 5582; www .holidayretreats.com.au; 430 Lake Tyers Beach Rd; unpowered/ powered sites $30/34, cabins d $95-135, f $119-149, beach cottages d/f $170/184, villas $350; ☺ ☺ ) These camp sites are the best you'll find outside of the area's national parks. Vegetation offers shade and privacy, and it's just a short stroll to the ocean beach. The park is almost totally surrounded by native bush, protecting local flora and fauna. Cabins are spotlessly clean and the luxury cabins are like mini motel rooms, complete with irons and hairdryers. Villas with all mod cons are the latest addition.

# BUCHAN
pop 330

The sleepy town of Buchan in the foothills of the Snowy Mountains is famous for the spectacular limestone cave system at the Buchan Caves Reserve, open to visitors for almost a century. Underground rivers cutting through ancient limestone rock carved the caves and caverns, and local Aboriginal people lived in them more than 18,000 years ago. Parks Victoria ( ☎ 5162 1900; www.parks.vic.gov.au; tours adult/child/family $13/7/33) runs several guided caves tours daily, alternating between Royal and Fairy caves. They're both impressive: Royal has more colour, a higher chamber and extinct kangaroo remains; Fairy has more delicate decorations and fairy sightings have been reported(!). The rangers also offer hard-hat guided tours to the less developed Federal Cave during the high season. The reserve itself is a pretty spot with shaded picnic areas, walking tracks and grazing kangaroos. Invigoration is guaranteed when taking a dip in the icy rock pool (admission free; ☺ 9am-5pm).

## INFORMATION

Buchan General Store ( ☎ 5155 9202; 57 Main St; ☺ 8am-6pm Mon-Sat, 9am-5pm Sun) Local information.

Buchan Neighbourhood House ( ☎ 5155 9216, 6 Centre Rd, ☺ 9am-4.30pm Mon-Fri) Internet access $4 per hour.

Buchan Valley Roadhouse ( ☎ 5155 9484; 52 Main St, ☺ 7am-6pm Mon-Fri, 8am-5pm Sat, 9am-5pm Sun) Sells petrol.

## EATING

Caves Hotel ( ☎ 5155 9203; 49 Main St; mains $15-24; ☺ lunch & dinner) This century-old timber pub has quality bistro meals and some wicked desserts (like the Mars Bar cheesecake).

## SLEEPING

Buchan Caves Reserve ( ☎ 5162 1900; www.parks.vic.gov .au; Buchan Caves Reserve; unpowered/powered sites $13/18, cabins d & f from $58, wilderness retreats s/d $100/120; ☺ ) Edged by state forest, the camp ground within this reserve offers plenty of shady sites. There are a couple of standard cabins, plus new safari-style tents providing a luxury wilderness experience (think comfortable queen-size bed) without having to pitch your own tent. It's ideal for those who'd love to camp, if only it wasn't so uncomfortable.

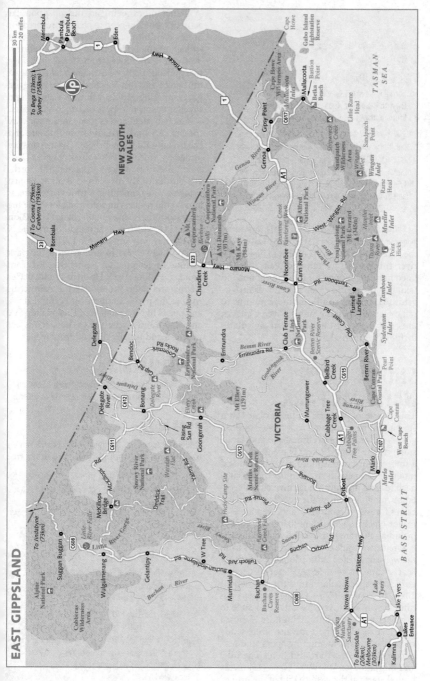

EAST GIPPSLAND

**Buchan Lodge Backpackers** ( ☎ 5155 9421; www.buchan lodge.com; 9 Saleyard Rd; dm $25) A short walk from the caves and the town centre, and just by the river, this friendly, rough-and-ready, timber-lined building is great for lounging about and taking in the country views. Staff will also organise a transport shuttle for those wanting to raft or canoe down the Snowy River. Children under 14 can stay by arrangement only. Rates include continental breakfast.

# SNOWY RIVER NATIONAL PARK

This is one of Victoria's most isolated and spectacular national parks, dominated by deep gorges carved through limestone and sandstone by the Snowy River. The entire park is a smorgasbord of unspoiled, superb bush and mountain scenery. It covers more than 95,000 hectares and includes a huge diversity of vegetation, ranging from alpine woodlands and eucalypt forests to rainforests and even areas of mallee-type scrub. It is home to loads of wildlife, including the rare brush-tailed rock wallaby.

On the west side of the park, the views from the well-signposted clifftop lookouts over Little River Falls and Little River Gorge, Victoria's deepest gorge, are spectacular. From there it's about 20km to McKillops Bridge, a huge bridge spanning the Snowy River, making it possible to drive across the park to Errinundra National Park (see opposite). There are also some sandy river beaches and swimming spots, and several good short walks around here. The hilly and difficult Silver Mine Walking Track (15km, six hours) starts at the eastern end of the bridge.

Walking and canoeing are the most popular activities, but you need to be well prepared for both – conditions can be harsh and subject to sudden change. The classic canoe or raft trip down the Snowy River from McKillops Bridge to a pull-out point near Buchan takes at least four days, and offers superb scenery: rugged gorges, raging rapids, tranquil sections and excellent camping spots on broad sand bars.

The two main access roads to the park are the Buchan-Jindabyne Rd from Buchan, and the Bonang Rd from Orbost. These roads are joined by McKillops Rd (also known as Deddick Valley Rd), which runs across the northern border of the park from Bonang to just south of Wulgulmerang. Various access roads and scenic routes run into and alongside the park from these three main roads. The 43km Deddick Trail, which runs through the middle of the park, is only suitable for 4WDs.

Good scenic drives in and around the park include McKillops Rd, Rising Sun Rd from Bonang, Tullock Ard Rd from just south of Gelantipy, and Yalmy Rd, which is the main access road to the park's southern and central areas, and places like Waratah Flat, Hicks Camp Site and Raymond Creek Falls. These roads are unsealed and usually closed during winter.

## INFORMATION

**Parks Victoria** ( ☎ 13 16 93; www.parkweb.vic.gov.au) Provides information about camping and road conditions.

## SLEEPING

**McKillops Bridge Camp Site** (free) This is the park's main camp site, though there are other free sites throughout the park. It's a beautiful spot and has toilets and fireplaces.

Karoonda Park ( ☎ 5155 0220; www.karoondapark.com; 3558 Gelantipy Rd; dm/d $28/56, cabins per 6-10 people $110; ⊠ 💻 🐾 ) At Gelantipy, 40km north of Buchan on the road to Snowy River National Park, this cattle-and-sheep property has comfortable backpacker and cabin digs. Rates include breakfast; other meals are available. Activities available include abseiling ($25 per hour), horse riding ($35 per hour), wild caving ($35 per hour) and white-water rafting (see p294).

# ERRINUNDRA NATIONAL PARK

Errinundra National Park contains Victoria's largest cool-temperate rainforest and is one of East Gippsland's most outstanding natural areas. The forests surrounding the park are a constant battleground between loggers and environmentalists who are trying to protect old-growth forests.

The national park coves an area of 25,600 hectares and has three granite outcrops that extend into the cloud, resulting in high rainfall, deep, fertile soils and a network of creeks and rivers that flow north, south and east. The park has several climatic zones – some areas of the park are quite dry, while its peaks regularly receive snow. This is a rich habitat for native birds and animals, which include many rare and endangered species such as the potoroo.

Errinundra is one of the best examples in the world of 'mixed forest' vegetation – it's dominated by southern sassafras and black oliveberry, with tall eucalypt forests providing a canopy for the lower rainforests. Some of the giant trees are many hundreds of years old.

You can explore the park by a combination of scenic drives, and short and medium-length walks. Mt Ellery has spectacular views; Errinundra Saddle has a rainforest boardwalk; and from Ocean View Lookout there are stunning views down the Goolengook River as far as Bemm River. The park also has mountain plum pines, some of which are more than 400 years old, which are easily accessible from Goonmirk Rocks Rd.

Nestled by the edge of the national park is tiny Goongerah (population 50), where there's a thriving community with two active community environmental organisations. Goongerah Environment Centre ( ☎ 5154 0156; www.geco.org.au) organises ongoing protests and blockades in the forest surrounding the park and has detailed information about park drives and walks on its website. The other community group, Environment East Gippsland ( ☎ 5154 0145; www.eastgippsland.net .au), lobbies extensively on forest issues. It also provides people with the chance to explore the forests under the guidance of environmental experts at the Forests Forever Ecology Camp ( ☎ 5154 0145; www.eastgippsland.net.au; adult/child/teenager per day $20/free/10) held each Easter at Ellery Creek camp site in Goongerah. Ecologists guide you through the forest, hoping you'll be awed by their beauty and complexity, outraged by their destruction, and will spread the word. You need to bring your own camping gear and food.

The main access roads to the park are Bonang Rd from Orbost and Errinundra Rd from Club Terrace. Bonang Rd passes along the western side of the park, while Errinundra Rd passes through the centre. Road conditions are variable and the roads are often closed or impassable during the winter months or after floods (check Parks Victoria in Orbost or Bendoc first) and watch out for logging trucks. Roads within the park are all unsealed, but are 2WD accessible. Expect seasonal closures between June and November, though roads can deteriorate quickly at any time of year after rain.

## INFORMATION

Parks Victoria ( ☎ 13 16 93, Orbost 5161 1222, Bendoc 02-6458 1456; www.parkweb.vic.gov.au) Information about camping and road conditions in the park.

## SLEEPING

Frosty Hollow Camp Site (sites free) This is the only camping area within the national park, on the eastern side. There are also free camping areas on the park's edges – at Ellery Creek in Goongerah, and at Delegate River.

Jacarri ( ☎ 5154 0145; www.eastgippsland.net.au /jacarri; cnr Bonang Hwy & Ellery Creek Track, Goongerah; s & d/f $80/90) This gorgeous little cottage, made from recycled and plantation timber, is on Jill

---

### TRANSPORT: ERRINUNDRA NATIONAL PARK

Distance from Melbourne 474km

Direction East

Travel time Seven hours

Car Take the M1 (CityLink/Monash Fwy/Princes Hwy) to Orbost and follow the signs from there.

---

## OFF THE BEATEN TRACK

You can't access most of the Snowy River or Errinundra National Parks with a 2WD, and sections of Croajingolong are only open to a limited numbers of walkers. However, there are a few companies providing organised trips into these beautiful wilderness areas.

An eco-tourism award winner, Gippsland High Country Tours ( ☎ 5157 5556; www.gippslandhighcountrytours .com.au; 5-/7-day tour $1190/1970) is an East Gippsland-based company running easy, moderate and challenging five- to seven-day hikes in Errinundra, Snowy River and Croajingolong National Parks. The Croajingolong trips include three nights accommodation in the Point Hicks Lighthouse. There's also a five-day bird-watching tour in Snowy River country.

A Goongerah-based organisation, Rainforest Adventure Services ( ☎ 5154 0174; www.rainforestadventures.com .au; 2-day walk incl meals $120) runs weekend forest walks in Errinundra National Park, with overnight camping.

Snowy River Expeditions ( ☎ 5155 9353; www.karoondapark.com/sre; Karoonda Park, Gelantipy; tours per day $135) is an established company, running adventure tours including one-, two- or four-day rafting trips on the Snowy. Half- or full-day abseiling or caving trips are also available. Costs include transport, meals and camping gear.

A mostly volunteer-run organisation, Wilderness Bike Ride ( ☎ 5154 6637; www.wildernessbikeride.com.au; 3-day ride incl meals & camp fees $310) runs a finely-organised three- or four-day mountain-bike ride in April each year, usually through the wilds of Errinundra National Park.

Redwood's organic farm. It's solar-powered, has a slow combustion stove for heating and cooking, and sleeps four.

# CAPE CONRAN COASTAL PARK

This is one of the most beautiful spots in the state. It's a blissfully undeveloped part of the coast, with long stretches of remote white-sand beaches. The 19km coastal route from Marlo to Cape Conran is particularly pretty, bordered by banksia trees, grass plains, sand dunes and the ocean.

Cape Conran is a fabulous spot for walking – Parks Victoria has a brochure detailing the many options. One favourite is the nature trail which meets up with the East Cape Board-walk, where signage gives you a glimpse into how indigenous people lived in this area. Following an indigenous theme, take the West Cape Rd off Cape Conran Rd to Salmon Rocks, where there's an Aboriginal shell midden dated at more than 10,000 years old.

For some relaxed swimming, canoeing and fishing go to the Yeerung River. There's good surfing at West Cape Beach, where you can take lessons through the Surf Shack (see p288). For qualified divers, Cross Diving Services ( ☎ 5153 2010, 0407-362 960; per dive $50) offers dives on most weekends (equipment hire available).

If you're staying in the park, keep an eye out for bandicoots and potoroos, whose numbers have increased in recent years following the introduction of the park's fox management program. Check out Cabbage Tree Palms, which can

be accessed from a number of points, and is a short detour off the road between Cape Conran and the Princess Hwy. This is Victoria's only stand of native palms – a tiny rainforest oasis.

## SLEEPING

Parks Victoria ( ☎ 51548438; www.conran.net.au) manages the following three accommodation options in Cape Conran Coastal Park.

Cape Conran Cabins (cabin $109) These self-contained cabins, which can sleep up to eight people, are surrounded by bush and are just 200m from the beach. Built from local timbers, the cabins are like oversized cubby houses with lofty mezzanines for sleeping. BYO linen. Rain water on tap.

Banksia Bluff Camping Area (unpowered sites $17) This camping ground is right by the foreshore, with generous sites surrounded by banksia wood-lands offering shade and privacy. The camping ground has toilets, cold showers and a few fire-places, but you'll need to bring drinking water (or purchase it from the park office).

Cape Conran Wilderness Retreats (d/f $120/150) Nestled in the bush by the sand dunes are these classy safari tents. All the simplicity of camping, but with comfortable beds and a deck outside your fly-wire door. Two-night minimum stay.

West Cape Cabins ( ☎ 5154 8296; www.westcapecabins .com.au; 1547 Cape Conran Rd; s & d/f $175/205) Crafted from locally grown or recycled timbers, these self-contained cabins a few kilometres from the national park are a work of art. The timbers are all labelled with their species, and even the queen-size bed bases are made from tree trunks. The eight-seater outdoor spa adds to the joy. It's a 15-minute walk through coastal bush to an isolated beach.

# MALLACOOTA
**pop 980**

Relaxed Mallacoota is completely surrounded by the internationally acclaimed Croajingolong National Park, and is one of the nicest towns in the state. Its long, empty ocean beaches, tidal river mouths and vast inlet are a paradise for swimmers, surfers, anglers and boaties. At Christmas and Easter it's a crowded family holiday spot, but most of the year it's pretty quiet.

One of the best ways to experience the beauty of Mallacoota is by boat. The calm estuarine waters of Mallacoota Inlet have more than 300km of shoreline. There are many public jetties where you can tie your boat up and come ashore for picnic tables, toilets or to take a dip. Mallacoota Hire Boats ( ☎ 0438-447 558; Main Wharf, cnr Allan & Buckland Drs; motor boats per half-/full day $85/145, canoes per hr $17) is centrally located and hires out canoes and boats. No licence required; cash only. You can take a cruise aboard MV Loch-Ard ( ☎ 5158 0764; Main Wharf, cnr Allan & Buckland Drs; 2hr cruise adult/child $25/10), which has been plying the lakes for almost a century. This old wooden boat also does two- and three-hour trips, including one to the far side of the lake where the original Mallacoota settlement once was.

Wilderness Coast Ocean Charters ( ☎ 0418-553 809; Gabo Island $60, Skerries $120) runs trips to the Skerries seal colony to view these delightful creatures. Whales are sometimes spotted on trips from September to November. It also runs trips to Gabo Island from Bastion Point, leaving early in the morning with pick-up in the afternoon. On Gabo Island, the windswept 154-hectare Gabo Island Lightstation Reserve, 14km from Mallacoota, is home to sea birds and one of the world's largest colonies of little penguins. Whales, dolphins and fur seals are regularly sighted off shore. The island has an operating lighthouse (tours adult/child $10/5), built in 1862, which is the tallest in the southern hemisphere. Accommodation is also available here (see p296). Mallacoota Air Services ( ☎ 0408-580 806; www .mallacootaairservices.com; return per 3 adults or 2 adults & 2 children $200) also provide access to the island.

There are plenty of great short walks around the town, the inlet, and in the bush, ranging from a half-hour stroll to a four-hour walk. The easy Bucklands Jetty to Captain Creek Jetty Walk (one way 5km, 1½ hours) starts about 4km north of the town and follows the shoreline of the inlet past the Narrows. The walk can be extended from Captains Creek via eucalypt forests to either Double Creek (3km) or the Mallacoota-Genoa Rd (3km). The Mallacoota Town Walk (7km, five hours) loops round Bastion Point, and combines five different walks, is also popular. Walking notes with maps are available from Parks Victoria and the visitors centre.

For good surf, head to Bastion Point or Tip Beach. There's swimmable surf and some sheltered waters at Betka Beach, which is patrolled during Christmas school holidays. There are also good swimming spots along the beaches of the foreshore reserve, at Bastion Point and Quarry Beach.

## INFORMATION

Lucy's ( ☎ 5158 0666; 64 Maurice Ave; ☺ 8am-9pm; ☐ ) Have coffee and cake or Lucy's homemade rice noodles while you access the internet ($2 per 15 minutes).

Mallacoota Newsagency ( ☎ 5158 0888; 14 Allan Dr; ☺ 8am-5pm Mon-Sat, to noon Sun; ☐ ) Internet access $2.50 per 15 minutes. You can also plug in your own computer here.

Mallacoota visitors centre ( ☎ 5158 0800; Main Wharf, cnr Allan & Buckland Dr; ⏰ 10am-4pm) Operated by friendly volunteers.

Parks Victoria ( ☎ 5161 9500; www.parkweb.vic.gov.au; cnr Buckland & Allan Drs) An information centre opposite the main wharf with excellent outdoor displays and information on Croajingolong and Mallacoota.

## EATING

Croajingolong Cafe ( ☎ 5158 0098; Shop 3, 14 Allan Dr; mains $5-13; ⏰ breakfast & lunch Tue-Sun) Overlooking the inlet, this is a great place for a coffee. Grab your newspaper and settle down to pancakes and wild berries or the enormous Veggie Brekky. No credit cards.

Mallacoota Hotel Motel ( ☎ 5158 0455; 51-55 Maurice Ave; mains $15-29; ⏰ lunch & dinner) The pub bistro provides hearty meals on its varied menu, with reliable favourites like chicken Kiev and vegetable risotto. Bands play at the pub regularly in the summer.

Tide Restaurant ( ☎ 5158 0100; 70 Maurice Ave; mains $17-29; ⏰ dinner) The service is attentive at Mallacoota's most upmarket dining option, with a prime lakeside setting. The menu features well-presented seafood. No credit cards.

## SLEEPING

There are plenty of options here, though during Easter and Christmas school holidays you'll need to book well ahead and expect prices to be significantly higher.

Karbeethong Lodge ( ☎ 5158 0411; www.karbeethong lodge.com.au; 16 Schnapper Point Dr; d/f $120/150) It's hard not to be overcome by a sense of serenity as you rest on the broad verandas of this early 1900s timber guesthouse, with uninterrupted views over Mallacoota Inlet. The large guest lounge and dining room have an open fire and period furnishings, and there's a mammoth kitchen if you want to prepare meals. The pastel-toned bedrooms are small but neat and tastefully decorated. The Lodge is signposted from the Genoa-Mallacoota Rd.

Mallacoota Foreshore Caravan Park ( ☎ 5158 0300; camppark@vicnet.net.au; cnr Allan Dr & Maurice Ave; unpowered/powered sites $17/21, caravans d $65; 🖳 ) Hundreds of grassy sites extend along the foreshore and have sublime views of the lake, with its resident population of black swans and pelicans. The sunsets and sunrises here are superb, and there's free internet access for campers.

Gabo Island Lighthouse ( ☎ Parks Victoria 13 19 63, 5161 9500; www.parkweb.vic.gov.au; up to 8 people $169) Accommodation is available in the three-bedroom Assistant Lighthouse Keeper's residence. Enjoy the extreme isolation (well, along with the 300-plus local animal species) and watch for migrating whales in autumn and late spring. Pods of dolphins and seals basking on the rocks are also regular sightings. Two-night minimum stay.

Mallacoota Houseboats ( ☎ 5158 0775; Karbeethong Jetty; 3-night minimum $850) These houseboats are a divine way to explore Mallacoota's waterways. The clean and cosy boats sleep up to six and have a kitchen, toilet, shower and barbecue. Prices almost double in peak season.

Adobe Mudbrick Flats ( ☎ 5158 0329; www.adobe holidayflats.com.au; 17 Karbeethong Ave; flats $80) These 1970s-built, eco-friendly, comfortable mudbrick flats are about 5km from the town centre. They're particularly fun for families, with birds to feed, a farmyard of ducks, and kangaroos and a lyrebird to look out for. Check out the gorgeous inlet views from the comfort of your hammock. You're encouraged to recycle, compost and conserve water. Linen costs extra.

Mallacoota Hotel, Motel & Backpackers ( ☎ 5158 0455; inncoota@bigpond.net.au; 51-55 Maurice Ave; dm $22, motel s/d from $65/80; 🚫 🖳 ) The backpackers rooms here are a bit shabby, but there's a good shared kitchen, use of the motel pool and it's conveniently next door to the pub. Motel and family units overlook the lawn and pool.

# CROAJINGOLONG NATIONAL PARK

Croajingolong is one of Australia's finest national parks, recognised by its listing as a World Biosphere Reserve by Unesco (one of 12 in Australia). This coastal wilderness park covers 87,500 hectares, stretching for about 100km from Bemm River to the NSW border. Magnificent, unspoiled beaches, inlets, estuaries and forests make this an ideal park for camping, walking, swimming and surfing. The five inlets – Sydenham, Tamboon, Mueller, Wingan and Mallacoota (the largest and most accessible) – are popular canoeing and fishing spots.

Two sections of the park have been declared Wilderness Areas (which means no vehicles, access to a limited number of walkers only and permits required): the Cape Howe Wilderness Area, between Mallacoota Inlet and the NSW border, and the Sandpatch Wilderness Area, between Wingan Inlet and Shipwreck Creek. The Wilderness Coast Walk, only for the well-prepared and

## TRANSPORT: CROAJINGOLONG NATIONAL PARK

**Distance from Melbourne** 450-525km (depending on entry point)

**Direction** East

**Travel time** 6 ½-7 ½ hours

**Car** Take the M1 (City Link/Monash Fwy/Princes Hwy) to Cann River and turn right for Thurra River and Mueller Inlet. Continue along the Princes Hwy past Cann River to take Wingan Inlet turn-off. Travel along the Princes Hwy to Genoa, turn right for Mallacoota for Shipwreck Creek.

intrepid, starts at Sydenham Inlet by Bemm River and heads along the coast to Mallacoota (you can start anywhere in between). Thurra River is a good starting point, making the walk an easy-to-medium hike (59km, five days) to Mallacoota. Tony Gray runs a car shuttle (☎ 5158 0472, 0408-516 482; up to 6 people $212) to Thurra River from Mallacoota (leave your car at Mallacoota airport). Lonely Planet's *Walking in Australia* has an excellent detailed description of the walk from Thurra River to Mallacoota.

Croajingolong is a bird-watcher's paradise, with more than 300 recorded species (including glossy black cockatoos and the rare ground parrot), while the inland waterways are home to myriad water birds, such as the delicate azure kingfisher and the magnificent sea eagle. There are also many small mammals here, including possums, bandicoots and gliders, and some huge goannas.

Park vegetation ranges from typical coastal landscapes to thick eucalypt forests, with areas of warm-temperate rainforest. The heathland areas are filled with impressive displays of orchids and wildflowers in the spring.

Point Hicks was the first part of Australia to be spotted by Captain Cook and the *Endeavour* crew in 1770, and was named after his first Lieutenant, Zachary Hicks. There's a lighthouse here which is open for tours (see right), recanting tales of dark, stormy nights filled with ghosts and shipwrecks. You can still see remains of the SS *Saros*, which ran ashore in 1937, on a short walk from the lighthouse.

Access roads of varying quality lead into the park from the Princes Hwy. Apart from Mallacoota Rd, all roads are unsealed and can be very rough in winter, so check road conditions with Parks Victoria before venturing on, especially during or after rain.

## INFORMATION

Parks Victoria (☎ 13 19 63, Cann River 5158 6351, Mallacoota 5161 9500; www.parkweb.vic.gov.au) Contact offices in Cann River or Mallacoota for information on road conditions, overnight hiking, camping permits and track notes.

## SLEEPING

The park's main camping areas are listed below. Given their amazing beauty, these camping grounds are surprisingly quiet, and bookings only need to be made for the Christmas and Easter holiday periods. Wingan and Shipwreck can be booked through Parks Victoria (☎ 13 19 63); Thurra and Mueller through Point Hicks Lighthouse (☎ 5158 4268).

Wingan Inlet (unpowered sites $15.50) This serene and secluded site has superb sandy beaches and great walks. The Wingan River Walk (5km, 2½ hours return) through rainforest has great waterholes for swimming.

Shipwreck Creek (unpowered sites $15.50) Only 15km from Mallacoota, this is a beautiful camping ground set in forest above a sandy beach. It's a small area with just five sites, and there are lots of short walks to do here.

Mueller Inlet (unpowered sites $16) The calm waters here are fantastic for kayaking and swimming, and the camp sites are only a couple of metres from the water (not ideal for toddlers). It has eight sites, three of them walk-in, but it's the only camping ground without fireplaces. There's no vegetation providing privacy, but outside Christmas and Easter holidays it's usually quiet.

Thurra River (unpowered sites $16) This is the largest of the park's camping grounds, with 46 well-designed sites stretched along the foreshore from the river towards the lighthouse. Most of the sites are separated by bush, and there are communal fireplaces and pit toilets. Both Thurra River and Mueller Inlet camping grounds are less than 5km from the lighthouse.

Bush Camping (unpowered sites per person $5) Several other bush-camping sites lie along the Wilderness Coast Walk. BYO drinking water. Permits required.

Point Hicks Lighthouse (☎ 5158 4268, 5156 0432; www.gippslandlakesescapes.com.au/Properties/PointHicks Lighthouse; up to 6 people $250-295) This remote lighthouse has two comfortable, heritage-listed cottages that originally housed the Assistant Lighthouse Keepers. The cottages have sensational ocean views and wood fires.

# THE HIGH COUNTRY

Let's go where the air is clear, the scenery spectacular and there's a thousand different ways to enjoy yourself. The High Country's greatest asset is its unspoilt, natural beauty, but an action-packed trip awaits, if you dare. Go downhill or cross-country skiing and snowboarding; horse ride or walk the mountain trails; paraglide over and kayak down pristine, icy streams; idle along a bike trail, or puff up an alpine trail. It's all happening in a diverse, fragile and beautiful environment at the southern end of the Great Dividing Range. Mt Bogong, the highest point at 1986m, squats in the Alpine National Park. Mt Buffalo does its buffalo look-alike sprawl in Mt Buffalo National Park. Mt Baw Baw sits prettily in Mt Baw Baw National Park. And for winter playgrounds, there's the magic three: Mt Hotham, Mt Buller and Falls Creek.

Just driving along the High Country roads is as thrilling as their names suggest. The Great Alpine Rd takes a stately run beside creeks, wooded areas, farm lands and mountains till it reaches the sea. The Snow Rd tempts you to vineyards and gourmet food spots. The Omeo Hwy speeds through valleys a range or two away from Kiewa Valley Hwy, both offering glorious scenery and picnic spots, while down south, the Goulburn Valley Hwy tracks the tinkling Goulburn River.

Former gold-mining towns such as Beechworth and Yackandandah are well-preserved historical encounters, while towns at the foothills of the mountain resorts such as Mansfield, Bright and Mt Beauty are all-season holiday spots, with stacks of activities, exciting restaurants and fab accommodation. The thriving Milawa gourmet region has acclaimed wineries and impressive local produce.

Away from the mountains, Lake Eildon National Park is a water sports paradise. Spend a few days on a houseboat, do some fly-fishing or just take in the gorgeous surroundings from the veranda of one of the many attractive B&Bs.

## SNOWSHOE SHUFFLE

This is winter playground territory: skiers, snowboarders and snow-kiters are all out there, breaking bits of the old bod. If that's not your scene, embrace the air and the scenery on a snowshoe walk where your guide takes you through snow drifts, along snow-capped ridges, through snow-dusted snowgum forests and along icy, crackly little creeks. You'll find snowshoe walks at Mt Buffalo (p313) and Mt Buller (p300), Falls Creek (p304) and Mt Hotham (p302). Love it? Take a three-day adventure on snowshoes up on the Bogong High Plains (p319).

## TRAILS

Winter is for snow sports, but summer also makes the most of the cross-country ski trails. Every mountain has a network of short, long and in-between trails which delight nature-lovers and completely win-over doubters who hadn't realised how magnificent this region is when the blanket of white has melted away. For seriously dedicated hikers, the Australian Alps Walking Track (p310) is well-marked and supported.

For cyclists, the Murray to the Mountains Rail Trail (p308) is a blast, or hire a mountain bike and take to the trails above Bright (p307). Take your bike up the chairlift to the top of Mt Buller and blast your way back down, or go with a group along the trails of Dinner Plain (p302) and Mt Hotham (p302), walking, biking or on a horse. Breeze along the rich-green trails around Marysville (p314).

Biking not for you? Take to the trails in a 4WD or on a tag-along tour. No? Then the Brewery Trail (p308) must be a goer . Whatever you enjoy, the High Country has a trail waiting.

## GOURMET INDULGENCE

It's the air. Everything here grows better, tastes better, looks better. Local produce includes meats, game, cheese, fruits, berries, nuts, honey, jams, sauces and preserves. Freshwater fish and crustaceans bred in the King, Ovens and Murray rivers include trout, Chinook salmon, Murray cod, yellow perch and yabbies. Indulge every taste bud.

Start with the Gourmet Food Trail (p317) around Milawa. Head up to Beechworth (p315), down to Marysville (p314) or out to Mt Beauty (p309), stopping at the vineyards along every way, or at roadside stalls selling apples, chestnuts, mushrooms, asparagus and berries when in season.

For the ultimate wickedness, go on a gourmet hike (p319) where there's a reward for every step taken.

## THE BEAST WITHIN

Mountains and horses belong together, and the High Country is renowned for its horsemen. Start by exploring the real *Man From Snowy River* scenery up in Corryong (p315). Staying out back, go by horse down the road to Omeo (p319) and check out the wildest goldfield of Victoria. Or head east to Beechworth (p315) and check out our Ned's horse-thieving ways. Time your visit to see the Golden Horseshoe Festival; the gold was so plentiful in Beechworth that a local politician's horse wore golden horseshoes.

Have the total countryside experience and get in touch with your inner beast on a trail-ride up at Dinner Plain (p302), or down around beautiful Mt Beauty (p309). If you head to Mansfield (p305) you can join a horse-riding group and tackle the cliff-face where *The Man From Snowy River* was filmed in 1981. Continuing the film theme, you can also take a horse ride through the Rubicon Valley (p312) just south of Bonnie Doon ('How's the serenity?').

## BEING THERE

In this alpine environment, weather conditions can change dramatically and without warning any time of year. In winter, most of the higher mountains are snow-capped and frosts are frequent. A fine, sunny day can deteriorate into blizzard conditions, so make sure you have access to protective clothing on the slopes.

In the height of summer, you can walk or bike all day in the heat without finding water, then face temperatures below freezing at night. Bushwalkers should have a tent, fuel stove, warm clothes, a sleeping bag and plenty of water.

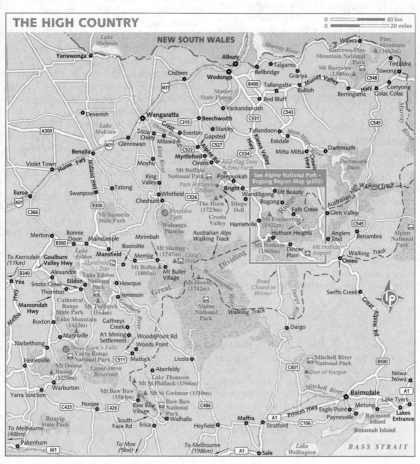

THE HIGH COUNTRY

Sunburn is also a serious problem, even on cloudy days, so slap on a high-SPF sunscreen and wear sunnies. March flies are also a problem in summer. Take a healthy supply of insect repellent and avoid wearing dark-coloured clothing.

If you are driving up to the snowfields in winter, you are required by law to carry snow chains even if there's no snow – heavy penalties apply if you don't. Chains can be rented from local service stations and ski-hire shops. Take care as roads can be slick with ice and snow, and some can become impassable. Check road conditions with the Official Victorian Snow Report ( 1902 240 523; www.vicsnowreport.com.au) before heading out. The website features daily snow-condition reports, information, accommodation links and 'snow cams'.

If travelling in a diesel-powered vehicle, it's a good idea to purchase 'Alpine Mix' (diesel with antifreeze) at either Omeo (p319) or Harrietville (p318) – it could save you a call to the Royal Automobile Club of Victoria (RACV; 13 11 11; www.racv.com.au).

# MOUNTAIN PLAYGROUNDS
## MT BULLER
**elevation 1805m**

Victoria's largest and busiest ski resort has an extensive lift network, including the Horse Hill chairlift that begins in the car park and ends in the middle of the ski runs. The downhill skiing area is 180 hectares (snow-making covers 44 hectares) with a vertical drop of 400m. Runs are 25% beginner, 45% intermediate, 30% advanced. Cross-country trails link Mt Buller and Mt Stirling.

It's a well-developed resort with a buzzing village atmosphere all year and a complete range of facilities. In winter there's night skiing on Wednesday and Saturday night. If you're not skiing, there's a scenic chairlift (adult/child $20/12) and tobogganing, or go snowtubing in the snowtube park. If you're freestyling, there's a rail park, halfpipe and other terrain parks. Snowshoeing here is fantastic, especially if you're not wild about skiing. Join the Snowshoe Guru ( 1800 039 049; www.snowshoeguru.com.au; half-day from $78) on a Back Country Experience.

Year-round staff at the Australian Alpine Institute (AAI; 5777 6000; www.alpineinstitute.com.au; Level 1, Community Centre, Summit Rd) run a variety of outdoor adventures, including rock climbing, abseiling and fly-fishing. Its sports hall (Level 2) and gym (Level 1) have fab indoor activities (casual visit $10) and massages (per 30 minutes $55).

There are art works and artefacts on display around the mountain. Ask at a visitors centre for a leaflet to see them on a self-guided walk. High Country Scenic Tours ( 5777 5101; www.highcountryscenictours.com.au) runs Alpine 4WD tours to historic sites and wineries.

The only Alpine museum in Australia, the National Alpine Museum of Australia (NAMA; 5777 7235; www.nama.org.au; Level 1, Community Centre, Summit Rd; admission free; 10am-1pm & 4-6pm Mon-Fri, 9am-6pm Sat & Sun in summer, 9am-6pm in winter), highlights the fascinating history of this area.

Breathtaker on High Spa Retreat ( 1800 088 222; www.breathtaker.com.au; massage per hr from $110) offers the chance to soak and revive with a range of luxurious treatments, a 20m lap pool and a hydrotherapy 'geisha tub' ($45 per 15 minutes in aromatic bath milk).

In summer, mountain biking is big, big, big, with the Horse Hill chairlift operating on weekends lifting you and your bike up to the plateau (all-day lift and trails access $45). Pick up the *Mountain Biking Guide & Maps* from a visitors centre. Bike hire is available from Altitude ( 5777 7560; Village Centre; 1hr/half-/full-day $20/40/60). Or forget the bike and just ride the chairlift all day (adult/child $18/10).

## ON THE SLOPES

If you like your skiing and boarding with sun, blue skies and gum trees, head to the High Country and hope you don't get a whiteout. You'll also find impressive resorts and a rocking *après*-ski scene. The ski season officially launches (with or without snow) on the Queen's Birthday long weekend in June and runs until mid-September. The best deals are to be found in June and September (shoulder season), with late July to August (high season) the busiest and most expensive time. The resorts have their own Alpine Resort Management Boards, with information offices (open year-round) on the mountains. There are no dedicated banks, but Eftpos is widely available.

In October the ski trails transform into fine walking and mountain-biking environments. Go to www.visitalpinevictoria.com.au for a High Country calendar of events. Several lodges and cafés remain open if you're heading up for summer activities, or just to enjoy the crisp alpine air.

## TRANSPORT: MOUNTAIN PLAYGROUNDS

**Distance from Melbourne** Mt Buller 228km, Mt Hotham 377km, Falls Creek 386km

**Direction** Northeast

**Travel Time** Mt Buller three hours, Mt Hotham 4½ hours, Falls Creek 4½ hours

**Air** Altitude Aviation ( ☎ 1800 747 300, 9351 0311; www.helicoptercharterflights.com.au; Moorabbin Airport, Melbourne; return per 4/6 people $3300/4600). Flights take less than an hour from Melbourne – the ultimate rockstar arrival!

**Bus** Mansfield-Mt Buller Buslines ( ☎ 5775 2606, winter 5777 6070; www.mmbl.com.au) runs buses between Mt Buller and Melbourne ($140, four hours, three weekly) and Mansfield (return $47, one hour, daily). Trekset ( ☎ 9370 9055; www.snowballexpress.com.au) runs between Mt Hotham and Melbourne ($155, 5½ hours, daily) and Bright (return $47,1½ hours, daily). Falls Creek Coach Service ( ☎ 5754 4024; www.pyles.com.au) operates between Falls Creek and Melbourne (return $140, 6 hours, daily) and Mt Beauty ($40, one hour, daily). Reduced summer services.

**Car** For Mt Buller, take the Maroondah Hwy through Alexandra and Bonnie Doon to Mansfield. Alternatively, head up Melba Hwy to Yea then Bonnie Doon. Mt Hotham can be reached via either the Hume Fwy (M31) and the Great Alpine Rd to Bright, or the Princes Hwy (A1) to Bairnsdale then north up Great Alpine Rd. In winter contact Mount Hotham Resort Management Board ( ☎ 5759 3550) to check road conditions before deciding which route to take. For Falls Creek, take the Hume Fwy and Great Alpine Rd to Mt Beauty then Bogong High Plains Rd.

## Information

The Mt Buller Resort Management Board ( ☎ 5777 6077; www.mtbuller.com.au; Level 5, Community Centre, Summit Rd; ⏰ 8.30am-5pm) also opens an information office in the village square in winter. Entrance fees to the Horse Hill day car park in winter are $32 per car. You can take the quad chairlift from here into the skiing area – ski hire and lift tickets are available at the base of the chairlift. There's a free day-tripper shuttle bus service into and around the village. If you have luggage, a 4WD taxi service is available around town (adult/child $8.50/6.50) and from the overnight car park ($12/8). Lift tickets cost $94/50 per adult/child. Combined lift-and-lesson packages start at $94. University students get discounted tickets; age a bit (over 65) and you get a 50% discount; 70-year-olds ski for free!

## Festivals & Events

Mt Buller holds an array of event weekends throughout the year. Check the calendar on www.mtbuller.com.au or contact the Mansfield visitors centre (p306). Highlights include the Buller Beerfest, in mid-January, and Kids' Weekend, held on the Australia Day weekend.

## Eating

You'll find plenty of great dining experiences here in summer, and in winter the choice is endless. Year-round eateries include the following:

Cattleman's Café ( ☎ 5777 7942; base of Bourke St; mains $9-17; ⏰ breakfast & lunch Mon-Fri Oct-May, breakfast, lunch & dinner daily Jun-Sep) A top spot using local produce.

Uncle Pat's Lounge Café ( ☎ 5777 6494; Cow Camp Plaza; mains $8-30; ⏰ dinner Thu-Sat Oct-May, breakfast, lunch & dinner daily Jun-Sep) A family-friendly restaurant that serves pasta, burgers and stir-fries.

Supermarket ( ☎ 5777 6133; Athletes Walk; ⏰ 10am-1pm & 4-6pm Mon-Fri, 9am-6pm Sat & Sun summer, 9am-6pm winter) The licensed supermarket carries all the usual stuff, gourmet items, a full range of fresh produce and newspapers.

Mt Buller Chalet ( ☎ 5777 6566; lunch from $8.50, mains $26-38; Summit Rd; ⏰ breakfast, lunch & dinner) There's a slew of restaurants, bars and cafés at this stunning chalet.

Arlberg Hotel ( ☎ 5777 6260; 189 Summit Rd; lunch from $8, mains $24-30; ⏰ lunch & dinner) There's a full range of eats from fry-ups to fine dining at this much-loved hotel.

Breathtaker ( ☎ 5777 6377; 8 Breathtaker Rd) Pizzas (from $15) after 4pm, a café/tapas (from $7.50) range of eats from 10.30am till late, and fine dining (mains $30-50) at its Signature Restaurant.

## Drinking & Entertainment

There's no shortage of entertainment here in winter, but in summer you might have to make your own fun, or just kick back at the Chalet.

Mt Buller Village Cinema ( ☎ 5777 6077, 5777 6000; Level 4, Community Centre, Summit Rd; adult/child $12.50/8.50). Australia's highest cinema shows latest releases twice a week in summer, twice a day in winter.

Kooroora Hotel ( ☎ 5777 6050; Village Square; ☿ 5pm-midnight in summer, 7am-3am in winter) Rocks hard and late. There's live music on Wednesday night and most weekends, with the occasional top-line act.

Ski Club of Victoria ( ☎ 1300 554 709; Summit Rd; ☿ 7am-midnight in winter) The 'Whitt' (Ivor Whittaker Memorial Lodge) has bands playing during winter, and there are pool tables, a bar and restaurant.

Moosehead Bar ( ☎ 5777 6091, 5777 7899; Summit Rd; ☿ 5pm-1am in winter) This downstairs bar has plenty of atmosphere, snazzy cocktails and tapas.

## Sleeping

There are over 7000 beds on the mountain, with rates varying with summer/winter seasons. Mt Buller Central Reservations ( ☎ 1800 285 537; www.mtbuller .com.au) books accommodation; there's generally a two-night minimum stay on weekends.

Monash University Alpine Lodge ( ☎ 5777 6577; www .sport.monash.edu.au/alpine-lodge.html; 84 Stirling Rd; dm summer/winter from $35/65) Right near the ski-lift ticket office, this grand lodge has four bunks to a room, a pleasant lounge, kitchen, TV room and drying room.

Andre's at Buller ( ☎ 5777 6966; www.andresatbuller .com; Cobbler Ln; d incl breakfast summer/winter from $240/250) A useful ski-in/ski-out position and glorious sunsets at this luxurious chalet.

Mt Buller Chalet ( ☎ 5777 6566; www.mtbullerchalet.com .au; Summit Rd; d incl breakfast summer/winter from $195/335; ☒ ) Famous for its splendid appearance, the Chalet offers a range of suites, a library with billiard table, well-regarded eateries, an impressive sports centre and heated pool.

YHA Mt Buller ( ☎ 5777 6181; www.yha.com.au; The Ave; dm $60-70) In winter this famous little YHA offers good facilities and friendly staff. Check out its colourful history.

## MT HOTHAM
### elevation 1868m

If you're serious about your hiking, mountain biking and skiing, you can't do better than Mt Hotham, with stunning alpine trails from November to May, and 245 hectares of downhill ski runs. About 80% of the ski trails are intermediate or advanced, with many double-black-diamond runs. The 'Big D' lift opens for night skiing every Wednesday and Saturday in

winter; the village chairlift opens for summer fun from late December to early January and at Easter. Dinner Plain (www.visitdinnerplain.com), just down the road, is a year-round village.

You can also off-piste ski in steep and narrow valleys here, and cross-country ski along 35km of trails winding through snowgum glades, or across the Bogong High Plains to Falls Creek. Below Mt Hotham village is a series of trails to Dinner Plain.

If you're on a bike, get the *Conquer the Seven Peaks* booklet and hit those mountain tops. The most popular trail in summer is to Mt Feathertop (1922m). This crosses the Razorback Ridge starting at the Diamantina Hut (2.5km from Mt Hotham village). It's 22km return and requires sound walking shoes (and strong knees and ankles!).

Don't venture out alone. Adventures with Altitude ( ☎ 5159 6608; www.adventureswithaltitude.com.au; Great Alpine Rd, Dinner Plain) runs fabulous hiking, biking ($15/60/90 per hour/half-/full day) and horse riding ($80/150/200) jaunts. You won't get lost, and you'll see all the good bits: trout-filled rivers, historic huts, snowgum forests, gold mines, wildlife and views. And you get fed! Bike hire ($15/40/60) is also available.

Fairly new in Hotham is snow-kiting. If you like some extreme action, contact Australian Adventure Experience ( ☎ 5759 3550, 0417-028 004; www .ausadventures.com; 2hr $90) and get some air with the help of a little parachute.

When the agony ends, head to Onsen Retreat and Spa ( ☎ 5150 8880; www.onsen.com.au; massage/treatment from $65/135; ☿ 11am-7pm summer, 7am-9pm winter), a totally divine Japanese-influenced, indoor-outdoor experience where the body gets to feel beautiful. Ritual onsen bathing plus swim, sauna and gym is $40.

Once the snow melts, fly-fishing begins, with Flytrek Fly Fishing ( ☎ 5159 1680, 0418 591 475; www.flytrek. com.au; 1-/2-day $175/465). Rod (that's his name) will teach you how to handle a rod. Prices include accommodation and everything you need.

## Information

The ski-season admission fee is $26 per car. Lift tickets per adult/student/child cost $94/80/47. Lift-and-lesson packages are $142 for adults. Lift tickets also cover Falls Creek. A free shuttle runs frequently around the resort from 7am to 3am; the free 'Zoo Cart' takes skiers from their lodges to the lifts between 8am and 6pm. A separate shuttle runs to Dinner Plain.

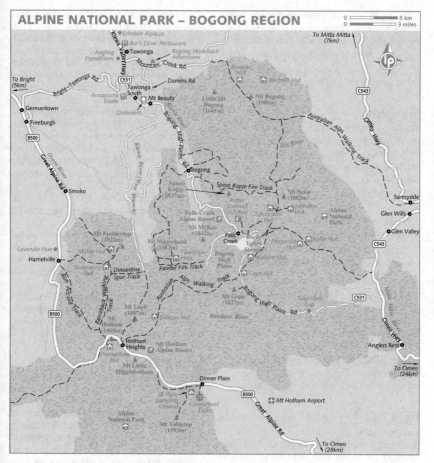

## ALPINE NATIONAL PARK – BOGONG REGION

**Helicopter Lift Link** ( ☎ 1800 204 424; return flight $69)
On clear days fly between Mt Hotham and Falls Creek in
six minutes.

**Mt Hotham Alpine Resort Management Board**
( ☎ 5759 3550; www.mthotham.com.au; ⏱ 8am-4pm
Mon-Fri Oct-May, daily Jun-Sep) At the village administration centre. Collect a range of brochures with maps for
short, eco, heritage and village walks.

## Festivals

**Cool Summer Festival** ( ☎ 1300 734 365; www.coolsum
merfestival.com.au) Three days of music in the middle of
nowhere; held in February or March.

**Mountain Fresh Festival** ( ☎ 5759 3550; www.mountain
fresh.com.au) A week of food and wine with altitude; held
in mid-July.

## Eating

In winter, there are plenty of great eating
choices here. In summer a couple of places
serve meals and the small supermarket at
General is open.

**General** ( ☎ 5759 3523; Great Alpine Rd; meals $7-25;
⏱ lunch & dinner) This pub does pizzas and
counter meals; it's a popular watering hole,
summer and winter, offering internet access,
a post office and ATM.

**Zirky's** ( ☎ 5759 3542; Great Alpine Rd; meals $10-14;
⏱ breakfast & lunch Wed-Sun) The café here opens
all year, while the Austrian-inspired restaurant (open for dinner in winter) is loved for
its fine food.

Only open in winter, but with excellent
reputations:

Swindlers ( ☎ 5759 3436; Hotham Central; mains $16-40; ☖ breakfast, lunch & dinner) Features an impressive Mod Oz menu, a lovely deck and grand bar that rocks till 2am.

White Room ( ☎ 5759 3456; Hotham Central; mains $28-36; ☖ lunch & dinner) Fine dining and an atmospheric cocktail bar where you can chill till late.

## Sleeping

Ski-season accommodation generally has a minimum two-night stay. Booking agencies:

Mt Hotham Accommodation Service ( ☎ 1800 032 061, 5759 3636; www.mthothamaccommodation.com.au; Lawlers Apartments) Books mountain accommodation during the ski season.

Mt Hotham Central Reservations ( ☎ 1800 657 547, 5759 3522; www.mthotham-centralres.com.au) Books on- and off-mountain accommodation throughout the year.

Mt Hotham Reservation Centre ( ☎ 1800 354 555; www.hotham.net.au; Hotham Central) Operates all year.

Summer accommodation includes the following:

Asgaard Alpine Club ( ☎ 1300 767 434; www.asgaard .com.au; Great Alpine Rd; s summer/winter $55/59) The price includes breakfast and linen.

Gravbrot Ski Club ( ☎ 5759 3533; www.gravbrot.com; Great Alpine Rd; s summer/winter $90/100) The price includes breakfast and dinner; bring your own linen.

## FALLS CREEK
### elevation 1780m

Australia's upmarket, fashion-conscious resort, Falls Creek combines a picturesque Alpine setting with impressive skiing and infamous *après*-ski entertainment. Skiing is spread over two main areas – the Village Bowl and Sun Valley – with 19 lifts and a vertical drop of 267m. Falls is also the freeride snowboard capital, with four parks and lessons on jumping berms, jibbing rails and riding boxes. The best cross-country skiing in Australia is also here. Night skiing in the Village Bowl operates several times a week. The Summit chairlift also runs over the Christmas and Easter breaks.

The best local hiking trails include the walk to Wallace Hut, built in 1889, and said to be the oldest cattleman's hut in the High Country.

A great summer program ( ☎ 1800 232 557) includes an outdoor cinema and guided tours: climb Mt McKay at sunset ($25) with some bubbly and canapés; cruise over the top with Heli Link ($99); take a giant swing, high-rope or climbing-wall climb ($35); or have a blast on the new skate ramp in the Village Bowl (free).

In winter the Activities Hotline ( ☎ 1800 204 424) snowsports program includes snocce (bocce on snow), snowshoe walks and dragon performances. Operators can set you up with a double-black-diamond rush with Kat Skiing/Boarding (half-day $69) where you hitch a lift on a heated Kassbohrer (snow cat) up Mt McKay.

Falls Creek Ski Lifts ( ☎ 5758 1000, 0438-458 726) offers a bungy trampoline experience, scenic chairlift rides and tennis (court hire $10 per hour). Parks Victoria ( ☎ 13 19 63; www.parkweb.vic.gov .au) can give you info on boating and canoeing at adjacent Rocky Valley Lake. At the end of the day (or in the middle) go to Endota Huski Day Spa ( ☎ 5758 3848; www.endota.com.au; Huski Lodge) for the body beautiful.

The High Country is famous for its horsemen. Join in the fun with Packers High Country Horse riding ( ☎ 5159 7241; www.horsetreks.com; 1½hr/half-/full-day $80/120/180), riding through river valleys and snowgum forests, down the road to Omeo.

Don't forget mountain biking ( ☎ 1800 232 557). There are downhill trails, lift-accessed trails, spur fire trails, aqueduct trails, road circuits and bike rental.

## Information

The free booklet *fallscreek* has stacks of info; the ☎ 1800 232 557 number will hook you up with accommodation and activities. Ski season daily resort entry is $30 per car. Lift tickets cost $94/80/47 per adult/student/child. Combined lift-and-lesson packages cost $142/120/96. Lift tickets also cover Mt Hotham. An over-snow taxi service operates between the car parks and the lodges ($31 return) from 8am to midnight daily (to 2am Friday night). Car parking for day visitors is at the base of the village, next to the ski lifts.

Helicopter Lift Link ( ☎ 1800 204 424; return flight $69) On clear days fly between Falls Creek and Mt Hotham in six minutes.

Resort Management ( ☎ 1800 033 079, 5758 3224; www.fallscreek.com.au; bottom of Gully chairlift; ☖ 9am-5pm) Has informative pamphlets including *crosscountry* (about ski trails which are also good for summer walking).

## Festivals & Events

Taste of Falls Creek Festival ( ☎ 1800 232 557; www .fallscreek.com.au/tasteoffallscreek) A food and wine festival in early January.

Mile High Dragon Boat Festival ( ☎ 1800 232 557; www.fallscreek.com.au/dragonboats) Gorgeous, glorious dragon boats race on Rocky Valley Lake held 26 to 27 January.

Easter Festival ( ☎ 1800 232 557; www.fallscreek.com .au/easterfestival) A giant Easter-egg hunt.

Kangaroo Hoppet ( ☎ 5754 1045; www.hoppet.com.au) Australia's premier long-distance cross-country ski race; held in August.

## Eating

Most accommodation places make you feed yourself – quality kiosks, cafés and restaurants abound. The following are open all year:

Winterhaven Restaurant ( ☎ 5758 3888; 7 Schuss St; mains $18-35; � dinner Wed-Sun Oct-May, lunch & dinner Jun-Sep) Great menu; bookings essential; bar open nightly from 5pm till late.

Gateway Café & Bar ( ☎ 5758 3646; 1 Bogong High Plains Rd; meals $8-14; � breakfast & lunch Mon-Fri Oct-May, breakfast & lunch daily & dinner Tue-Thu Jun-Sep) Busy, busy, busy. Join the fun!

Falls Creek Licensed Supermarket ( ☎ 5758 3355; Hub Complex, Falls Ck Rd; � 10am-5.30pm Oct-May, 8.30am-7pm Jun-Sep) Feeding yourself is not so difficult!

In winter, favourites include the following two options.

Café Max ( ☎ 5758 3347; 27 Falls Creek Rd; � breakfast, lunch & dinner) A very social café in the Village Bowl serving tasty Mod Oz dishes and *après* drinks.

Summit Ridge ( ☎ 5758 3800; 8 Schuss St; mains $18-34; � dinner) A rustic restaurant offering fine dining with crisp Asian flavours and an extensive wine list; feel free to scan the shelves. Bookings essential.

## Entertainment

Man ( ☎ 5758 3362; www.fallscreek.com.au/themanhotel; 20 Slalom St; � 5pm-1.30am) 'The Man' hotel has been around forever, is open all year and is a top nightspot. In winter it becomes a club, cocktail bar and live-music venue featuring popular Aussie bands. Very good pub dinners and pizzas are available ($11 to $28).

Milch Cafe Wine Bar ( ☎ 5758 3770; Schuss St; mains $12-18; � from 11.30am) The café here is open all year, until 1am in winter.

Cinema Glo ( ☎ 5758 3407; www.fvfalls.com.au; Schuss St; tickets $5; � noon-6pm) Downstairs from Milch, this cinema shows movies on a wide screen.

## Sleeping

All accommodation at Falls is above the snow-line, so in winter the lodges are truly ski-in, ski-out. The following two options are open year-round.

Alpha Lodge ( ☎ 5758 3488; www.alphaskilodge.com.au; 5 Parallel St; dm summer/winter from $56/130) A spacious lodge set up with a sauna, a large lounge with panoramic views and a communal kitchen.

Frueauf Village ( ☎ 1300 300 709; www.fvfalls.com .au; d summer from $150, winter 2-nights from $470; ☐ ) These luxurious, architect-designed apartments have everything, with private outdoor hot tubs, plus the funky Milch Cafe Wine Bar and Cinema Glo on hand.

Accommodation may be booked via several agencies, including the following:

Falls Creek Central Reservations ( ☎ 1800 033 079; www.fallscreek.com.au/centralreservations)

Falls Creek Reservation Centre ( ☎ 1800 453 525; www .fallscreek.com.au/reservationcentre)

# MOUNTAIN BASES
## MANSFIELD
### pop 2850

This is an all-seasons destination that outdoor enthusiasts get really excited about. There's stacks to do, from skiing at Mt Buller to horseback rides through the mountains, to spending the night at a zoo.

The three Mansfield police officers killed at Stringybark Creek by Ned Kelly and his gang in 1878 rest in Mansfield Cemetery. There's also a monument (1879) to the slain officers in the centre of the roundabout in High St.

Mansfield Zoo ( ☎ 5777 3576; www.mansfieldzoo .com.au; 1064 Mansfield Woods Point Rd; adult/child/family $15/8/44; � 10am-evening) is a fabulous surprise. Hand-reared animals and birds look healthy and eager for you to feed them from your bucket of bits. Two sleepy lions regard you earnestly, but decide the fence is too high. If you're older than eight, you can sleep in the paddocks in a swag (adult/child $65/45) and wake to the dawn chorus.

If the adrenalin is still flowing, let it rush with Adrenalin White Water Rafting ( ☎ 0438-298 288; www.whitewaterrafting.com.au; 1092 Upper King River Rd, Cheshunt; big-boat rafting from $155), which will take you out on the King River. Try the indulgence package (raft, wine, dine) and stay the night for $295.

Want to get off-road? Join a High Country Scenic Tour ( ☎ 5777 5101; www.highcountryscenictours.com.au;

🕑 Nov-May), which has exciting 4WD day-tours from $120 per person.

Alpine Helicopter ( ☎ 0428 376 619; www.alpineheli .com.au; flights from $150) runs themed helicopter flights, such as 'Cattlemen's Huts', 'Ned Kelly Country' and 'Rivers & Waterfalls'.

Take yourselves and the little tackers on a trail ride with one of the local horse riding companies:

High Country Horses ( ☎ 5777 5590; www.highcountry horses.com.au; Mt Buller Rd, Merrijig; 2hr/half-day rides $65/80, overnight from $435; 🕑 summer only) Takes you to the top of the world, or just splash across a creek and feel the serenity.

McCormacks Mountain Valley Trail Rides ( ☎ 5775 2886; www.mountainvalleytrailrides.com; 12 Reynolds St, Mansfield; 2hr/half-day $55/80, 4-day getaway $890; 🕑 summer only) Heads off to the King or Howqua Valleys, or wherever you like.

Watson's Mountain Country Trail Rides ( ☎ 5777 3552; www.watsonstrailrides.com.au; Three Chains Rd, Boorolite; 1/2hr $35/60; 🕑 daily) A peaceful property where you can learn or just take off. One of the highlights is the downhill area featured in *The Man from Snowy River*.

## Information

Mansfield & Mt Buller High Country visitors centre ( ☎ 5775 2518, 1800 039 049; www.mansfield-mtbuller .com.au; Maroondah Hwy; 🕑 9am-5pm Oct-May, 8am-9pm Jun-Sep) In the Old Railway Station. Displays include a felt mural of pioneer women and screens featuring local personalities. The centre books general accommodation for the region (including Eildon), ski accommodation and sells lift tickets.

## Festivals & Events

There are festive occasions throughout the year, plus regular café concerts and theatre productions backed by the Performing Arts Centre. Festival highlights:

High Country Autumn Festival (www.mansfield-mtbuller .com.au) Markets, picnics and a rodeo in early March.

Upper Goulburn Wine Region Vintage Celebrations ( ☎ 5777 3447; www.uppergoulburnwine.org.au) Local wines, musicians and chefs make for three fun days in April.

Mansfield–Mt Buller High Country Spring Arts Festival ( ☎ 1800 039 049; www.artsmansfield.com) Rodeo, Melbourne Cup-day picnic races, art exhibitions and bush markets in the first week of November.

## Eating

This is an arty area, and the ski crowd passes through feeling ravenous – a recipe for many pleasant eating spots. High St has an annual Food & Wine on High festival over a weekend in late February.

FORTY one ( ☎ 5775 2951; 41 High St; mains $8-17; 🕑 breakfast & lunch) Enjoy gourmet surprises in a sunny courtyard.

Mansfield Regional Produce Store ( ☎ 5889 1404; 68 High St; mains $12-19; 🕑 breakfast & lunch Tue-Sun, dinner Fri) This rustic store sells an array of local produce and artisan breads, giftware out the back and excellent meals.

Mansfield Hotel ( ☎ 5775 2101; 86 High St; mains $13-25; 🕑 lunch & dinner) Yes, it's a pub, but walk through to the attractive dining area and Mediterranean courtyard where kids play equipment is tucked into a large corner. The food is truly good.

Deck on High ( ☎ 5775 1955; 15 High St; mains $18-33; 🕑 lunch & dinner) There's a relaxed vibe at this striking bar, with its red couches and dining area up on the deck. The food is Asian fusion.

## Sleeping

Mansfield Backpackers' Inn & Travellers Lodge ( ☎ 5775 1800; www.mansfieldtravellodge.com; 116 High St; dm $25, s/d/f from $85/95/185; ❀ ) Perfectly placed in the centre of town, with spacious dorms in a restored heritage building and large, spotless motel rooms.

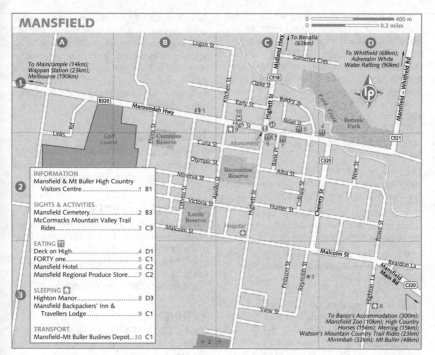

**MANSFIELD**

0 ——— 400 m
0 ——— 0.2 miles

To Maindample (14km);
Wappan Station (23km);
Melbourne (190km)

To Benalla
(63km)

To Whitfield (68km);
Adrenalin White
Water Rafting (90km)

Logan St
Somerset Cres
Clarke St
C518
Baldry St
Early St
High St
Nolan St
Botanic
Park
Maroondah Hwy
Kitchen St
Highett St
Midland Hwy
Ford Creek
Whitfield Rd – Mansfield
C521

INFORMATION
Mansfield & Mt Buller High Country
    Visitors Centre.........................1 B1

SIGHTS & ACTIVITIES
Mansfield Cemetery....................2 B3
McCormacks Mountain Valley Trail
    Rides.......................................3 C3

EATING 🍽
Deck on High.............................4 D1
FORTY one.................................5 C1
Mansfield Hotel..........................6 C2
Mansfield Regional Produce Store.....7 C2

SLEEPING 🛏
Highton Manor............................8 D3
Mansfield Backpackers' Inn &
    Travellers Lodge.....................9 C1

TRANSPORT
Mansfield-Mt Buller Buslines Depot...10 C1

Links Rd
Golf
Course
Elvins St
Cummins
Reserve
Curia St
Monument
Olympic St
Minerva St
Apollo St
Victoria St
Tilting St
Highett St
Malcolm St
Lords
Reserve
Hospital
Recreation
Reserve
Ailsa St
Hunter St
Bank St
Collopy St
Chenery St
New St
C320
Malcolm St
Reardon La
Mansfield
Main Rd
C320
Fintison St
Reynolds St
View St
Highton La
Rowe St

To Banjo's Accommodation (300m);
Mansfield Zoo (10km); High Country
Horses (15km); Merrijig (15km);
Watson's Mountain Country Trail Rides (23km)
Mirimbah (32km); Mt Buller (48km)

There's a kitchen, table tennis and discount coupons for local restaurants and activities.

Highton Manor ( ☎ 5775 2700; www.hightonmanor.com.au; 140 Highton Ln; dm $60, d stable/manor/tower $130/$200/365 incl breakfast; 🔊 ) Built in 1896 for Francis Highett, who sang with Dame Nellie Melba, this stately two-storey manor has beds in a group/party room, modern rooms in the stables, and lavish period-rooms in the main house.

Banjo's Accommodation ( ☎ 5775 2335; www.banjos mansfield.com.au; cnr Mt Buller Rd & Greenvale Ln; d/tr/q from $90/110/130; 🔊 ) Looking great on the edge of town, these units are self-contained, modern and spacious.

Wappan Station ( ☎ 5778 7786; www.wappanstation .com.au; Royal Town Rd, Maindample; shearers' quarters adult/ child $30/15, cottages d from $150; 🔊 ) Watch farm activities from your deck at this sheep-and-cattle property on the banks of Lake Eildon. There's a two-night minimum stay, but bring some friends and the price will hardly change – charges for extra people are minimal.

## BRIGHT
### pop 2100
Most spectacular in autumn when its leafy avenues and gardens are really showing their colours, this picturesque holiday town in the foothills of the Alps is a popular base year-round. Bright (www.brightvictoria.com.au) is perfectly placed to provide access to the wonders of the Alpine National Park, the Falls Creek and Mt Hotham ski resorts, and a wide range of outdoor adventure activities. To top it off, the abundance of local produce, coupled with the savvy ski tourists passing through, has made for a sophisticated restaurant scene.

Trails around Bright include the 3km loop Canyon Walk, 4km Cherry Walk and a 6km track to Wandiligong that follows Morses Creek. Collect the brochure *Short Walks around Bright* from the visitors centre.

### CRAIG'S HUT

Cattlemen built huts throughout the High Country from the 1850s on, but most iconic is Craig's Hut, built in 1981 for the film *The Man From Snowy River*. It was changed from a film set into a more substantial visitors centre 10 years later, then rebuilt in 2003. In 2006 it was totally burnt down by bushfires. Rebuilt (again) in 2007, people also go to the site for the breath-taking views.

If you're cycling, the Murray to the Mountains Rail Trail (below) starts behind the old train station. Bikes, tandems and baby trailers can be rented from Cyclepath Adventures ( ☎ 5750 1442; 74 Gavan St; per hr/half-/full-day $16/20/28; ⏲ 9am-5pm Mon-Fri, 10am-4pm Sat & Sun). Cyclepath also leads bike tours through the hills around Bright.

Alternatively, get off your bike and get airborne:

Active Flight ( ☎ 0428-854 455; www.activeflight.com.au) Introductory paragliding ($130) or extended scenic flights (from $180).

Alpine Paragliding ( ☎ 5755 1753; www.alpineparagliding.com; 100 Gavan St; ⏲ Oct-Jun) Offers 10-minute high-glides from Mystic ($130) or 30-minute thermalling flights ($180).

Bright Microflights ( ☎ 5750 1555; brightmicroflights@swiftdsl.com.au) Takes you on powered hang-glider flights over Porepunkah ($70) or Mt Buffalo ($155).

Eagle School of Microlighting & Hang Gliding ( ☎ 5750 1174; www.eagleschool.com.au; flights from $70) Will make you feel like a bird.

Back on the ground, take a yummo food-and-wine tour in a stretch limo with Elm Lodge Limousine Tours ( ☎ 5755 1144; tours $75; ⏲ 1.30-5.30pm by arrangement) or try its country pub tour on Saturday night ($90). Speaking of pubs, Bright Brewery ( ☎ 5755 1301; www.brightbrewery.com.au; 121 Gavan St; ⏲ from noon) produces a range of beers (sample five for $9) and runs tours (ring to book a time). Love it? Be a 'Brewer for the Day' ($320) or ask for the *High Country Brewery Trail* brochure and head off to the microbreweries at Rutherglen, Beechworth, Porepunkah, Buffalo and Jamieson.

Try abseiling ($185 per day) or visit a glow-worm river-cave (from $99) with Adventure

Guides Australia ( ☎ 5755 1851; www.adventureguidesaustralia.com.au), or join 5 Star Adventures ( ☎ 5759 2555; www.5staradventure.com.au; 120 Great Alpine Rd) for a half-day kayaking ($115), an alpine dinner tour ($60), or just a coffee in their office/café. North East Off-road Tours ( ☎ 0418-579 218; www.neoffroadtours.com.au) offers alpine 4WD and tag-along tours.

## Information

Bright visitors centre ( ☎ 1300 551 117; www.brightescapes.com.au; 119 Gavan St; ⏲ 9am-5pm) Has an accommodation-booking service and Parks Victoria information.

## Festivals & Events

Bright Autumn Festival ( ☎ 5755 2275; www.brightautumnfestival.org.au) Open gardens, scenic convoy tours and a popular gala day; held April or May.
Bright Spring Festival ( ☎ 5755 2275; www.brightspringfestival.org.au) Celebrate all things Bright and beautiful in October or November.

## Eating

Riverdeck Cafe ( ☎ 5755 2199; Great Alpine Rd; dishes $9-16; ⏲ breakfast & lunch) Sit on the deck overlooking the park and enjoy the wide outdoors.

Liquid Am-Bar ( ☎ 5755 2318; 8 Anderson St; mains $19-25; ⏲ dinner Thu-Tue) Locals and visitors pack into this cosy shopfront with great pasta choices and robust mountain fare.

Cosy Kangaroo ( ☎ 5750 1838; 93 Gavan St; mains $19-25; ⏲ dinner Thu-Tue) Truly a family restaurant, with a play cubby for kids, fab coffee and a menu that includes local trout cooked to perfection.

Simone's Restaurant ( ☎ 5755 2266; 98 Gavan St; mains $32-35; ⏲ dinner Tue-Sat) Outstanding Italian food

### GET ONYA BIKE

The Murray to the Mountains Rail Trail ( ☎ 5751 1283; www.railtrail.com.au) is one of the best ways to experience the High Country as you ride (or walk) through stunning rural scenery, enjoying river gums, mountain ash, spring blossoms and snow-capped ranges. The 94km trail follows the path of disused railways between the townships of Wangaratta, Beechworth, Myrtleford, Porepunkah and Bright.

Break up the journey and explore the area: stop off for a cold beer in a country pub, feast on some regional produce, or spend a day or two in one of the many comfortable local B&Bs.

Aficionados say the 16km between Everton and Beechworth is the best part of the trail (despite a challenging uphill section), as you're cycling through the bush. When you reach the highest point traditional vineyard Pennyweight ( ☎ 5728 1747; www.pennyweight.com.au; off Diffey Rd; ⏲ 10am-5pm) is ready to offer sustenance. The landscapes and views along all the sections are tremendous. There's good signage, several toilet and water stops and all the towns en route have bike-hire facilities. If you're car-free and don't want to return via the same route, think about catching the train to Wangaratta then the local bus to Bright or Beechworth, then riding back to Wang. Bus-a-Bike ( ☎ 5752 2974) carries up to 11 people and their bikes to wherever, from wherever, along the trail. Ring to arrange your pick-up.

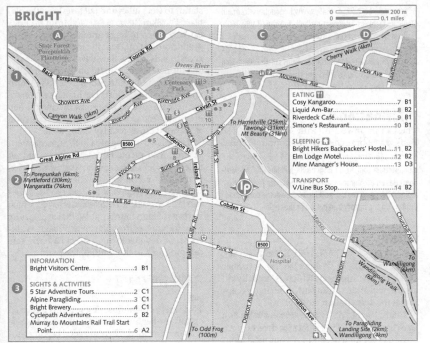

## BRIGHT

EATING 🍴
Cosy Kangaroo..................................7  B1
Liquid Am-Bar...................................8  B2
Riverdeck Café...................................9  B1
Simone's Restaurant.........................10  B1

SLEEPING 🛏
Bright Hikers Backpackers' Hostel.....11  B2
Elm Lodge Motel...............................12  B2
Mine Manager's House......................13  D3

TRANSPORT
V/Line Bus Stop.................................14  B2

INFORMATION
Bright Visitors Centre..........................1  B1

SIGHTS & ACTIVITIES
5 Star Adventure Tours.........................2  C1
Alpine Paragliding................................3  C1
Bright Brewery......................................4  C1
Cyclepath Adventures...........................5  B2
Murray to Mountains Rail Trail Start
    Point...............................................6  A2

---

in a heritage-listed house, with a focus on local
ingredients and seasonal produce.

## Sleeping

There's an abundance of accommodation here,
but rooms are scarce during the holiday seasons – book ahead. There are several caravan
and camping grounds along the Ovens River.

Bright Hikers Backpackers' Hostel ( ☎ 5750 1244; back
packers@brighthikers.com.au; 4 Ireland St; dm/s/tw $21/30/44;
🖵 ) This little gem in the middle of town justi-
fies the good reports. There's a cosy lounge for
winter nights, and a huge veranda for summer
lazing in the hammock.

Elm Lodge Motel ( ☎ 5755 1144; www.elmlodge.com.au;
2 Wood St; s/d from $65/75; 🛋 ) There are rooms to
suit all budgets in this restored 1950s pine mill
set in a gorgeous garden. The friendly owners
can help you plan your activities.

Odd Frog ( ☎ 5755 2123; www.theoddfrog.com; 3 Mc-
Fadyens Ln; d from $190) Expect to be impressed
with these contemporary, eco-friendly studios
with fabulous outdoor decks.

Mine Manager's House ( ☎ 5755 1702; 30 Coronation
Ave; d $205) Restored to its 1892 glory, this grace-
ful guesthouse has a gorgeous English-style
garden.

## MT BEAUTY
### pop 1700

Nestled at the foot of Mt Bogong (Victoria's
highest mountain), Mt Beauty is a handy base
for Falls Creek. The pretty 2km Tree Fern Walk
and slightly longer Peppermint Walk both start
from Mountain Creek Picnic & Camping Reserve on Mountain Creek Rd, off Kiewa Valley
Hwy. Find out about bushwalking, boating
and swimming spots at the visitors centre.

Bike rides through the mountains are organised by Rocky Valley Bikes ( ☎ 5754 1118; www.rockyvalley
.com.au; Kiewa Valley Hwy; rides beginner/advanced $25/95).
Bike hire is available from $20 per half-day.

Annapurna Estate ( ☎ 5754 4517; www.annapurna
estate.com.au; Simmonds Creek Rd, Tawonga South; meals $12-
28; ⏲ 10am-5pm Wed-Sun) is a stunning vineyard.
So is the food, served all day on a lovely deck
looking over the vines. Stay on for dinner on
Saturday.

This is a world-renowned trout-fishing area,
and fly-fishing trips are run by Angling Expeditions ( ☎ 5754 1466; www.anglingvic.com.au; 82 Kiewa Valley
Hwy, Tawonga; trips per 1/2/3/4 people from $205/110/90/70).
Sleep over at the Tawonga Fishing Lodge (B&B
from $25), then experience this beautiful area
on the back of a horse with Bogong Horseback

Adventures ( ☎ 5754 4849; www.bogonghorse.com.au; Mountain Creek Rd, Tawonga; 2hr/half-/full-day $70/80/160).

Just 5km north of Tawonga you can handfeed the alpacas at picturesque Erindale Alpacas ( ☎ 5754 5330; www.erindale-alpacas.com.au; Reids Ln; ☻ 10am-5pm Wed-Sun & school holidays). To get here, turn off Kiewa Valley Hwy onto Red Bank Rd.

## Information

The Commonwealth (with ATM) and ANZ Banks have branches in the shopping centre. Mt Beauty visitors centre ( ☎ 1800 111 885; www.visit alpinevictoria.com.au; 31 Bogong High Plains Rd; ☻ 9am-5pm) Has an accommodation-booking service (enquiries@ alpineshire.vic.gov.au), a working hydroelectric model and displays on the history and nature of the region.

## Eating

Roi's Diner Restaurant ( ☎ 5754 4495; 177 Kiewa Valley Hwy, Tawonga; mains $18-25; ☻ dinner Thu-Sun) A timber shack on the highway which is actually an award-winning restaurant, offering exceptional modern-Italian cuisine.

Bogong Hotel ( ☎ 5754 4449; 169 Kiewa Valley Hwy, Tawonga; mains $16-27; ☻ lunch Sat & Sun, dinner daily) An obvious spot for a beer. Enjoy your meal looking out over the snow-capped mountains.

## Sleeping

There's camping along the Kiewa River and several good-looking motels along the highway.

Braeview ( ☎ 5754 4756; www.braeview.com.au; 4 Stewarts Rd; B&B from $120) Has traditional rooms with scrumptious country breakfasts served on the balcony, and a self-contained cottage with spa and white, fluffy bathrobes.

Dreamers ( ☎ 5754 1222; www.dreamers1.com; Kiewa Valley Hwy, Tawonga South; d from $200; ☒ ) An enchanting collection of timber-and-stone cottages built around a peaceful lagoon.

# NATIONAL PARKS & GATEWAYS

## BAW BAW NATIONAL PARK

All walks are rewarding in Baw Baw National Park, an offshoot of the Great Dividing Range encompassing the Baw Baw Plateau and the forested valleys of the Thomson and Aberfeldy Rivers. Walk along marked tracks through sub-alpine vegetation, ranging from open eucalypt stands to wet gullies and tall forests on the plateau. The 3km Mushroom Rocks Walk from Mt Erica car park leads to huge granite tors (blocks of granite broken off from the massif). The main access roads are the Baw Baw Rd from Noojee and the new South Face Rd off Thomson Valley Rd. The highest points are Mt St Phillack (1566m) and Mt Baw Baw (1564m). The higher sections of the park are covered with snow in winter, when everyone heads for Baw Baw Village ski resort and Mt St Gwinear cross-country skiing area.

There is a camping area in the northeastern section, with picnic tables, fireplaces and pit toilets. Dispersed bush camping (unpowered sites free) is also allowed on the Baw Baw Plateau (fuel stove only). A section of the Australian Alps Walking Track (p310; www.netc.net.au/bushwalking/alpswalk), which starts its 655km journey at Walhalla, passes by a few kilometres from Baw Baw Village. Walkers have a designated camp site at Eastern Tyers camping area in the south of the park.

## BAW BAW VILLAGE
### pop 11

This small, downhill-skiing resort is a relaxed option for beginners and families, and is seldom overcrowded. There are good beginner-to-intermediate runs and a couple of harder runs. The downhill skiing area is 35 hectares with a vertical drop of 140m. Baw Baw is also a base for cross-country skiing, with plenty of trails, including one that connects to the Mt St Gwinear trails on the southern edge of the plateau. Ski patrols operate during the season, and Mt Baw Baw Ski Hire ( ☎ 1800 629 578, 5165 1120; www.bawbawskihire.com.au; Currawong Rd) hires skis and ski gear. The day car park costs $35 per car if the ski lifts are operating ($25 if they're not). Lifts per adult/child cost $71/41 per day; lift-and-lesson packages are $95/70. There's a new Cactus Rail Park for freestyle riders (or anyone who's cactus?), a toboggan park and snowplay area.

In the centre of the village, Mt Baw Baw Alpine Resort Management ( ☎ 5165 1136; www.mountbawbaw .com.au) runs things, offering general tourist information and an accommodation service ( ☎ 1300 651 136). Lodges and eateries are open year-round.

Kelly's Cafe ( ☎ 5165 1120; 11 Frosti Ln; mains $16-24; ☻ breakfast, lunch & dinner) This rustic favourite is a ski-in in winter. Its pizzas are famous, but you can't really go past the bangers and mash for $10 at lunchtime. If you're too exhausted from hiking and skiing, it will deliver.

Village Central Sea2Sky Restaurant ( ☎ 5165 1123; Alpine Resort, Currawong Rd; mains $18-25; ☻ lunch Fri-Mon &

## TRANSPORT: NATIONAL PARKS & GATEWAYS

**Distance from Melbourne** Marysville 95km, Eildon 170km, Baw Baw Village 170km, Myrtleford 290km

**Direction** Northeast and East

**Travel times** Marysville one hour, Eildon two hours, Baw Baw Village 2½ hours, Myrtleford three hours

**Bus & Train** McKenzie's Tourist Services ( ☎ 5962 5088, 9853 6264; www.mckenzies.com.au) has a service to Marysville (return $28, 2½ hours, daily) and Eildon (return $46, 3½ hours, daily). V/Line ( ☎ 13 61 96; www.vline .com.au) takes you to Myrtleford ($51, 4½ hours, daily) with a change from train to coach at Wangaratta. V/Line trains to Warragul ($16.50, 1½ hours, daily) connect with Baw Baw Betty Transport Service (www.mountbawbaw .com.au/location.aspx) coaches. Country Touch Tours ( ☎ 5963 3753; www.countrytouch.com.au) shuttles between Marysville and Lake Mountain (return $30, 30 minutes most days in winter).

**Car** Travel up Maroondah Hwy, turning off at Lilydale for Yarra Junction and Baw Baw; at Narbethong for Marysville; or at Alexandra for Eildon. Myrtleford is an easy drive up Hume Fwy to the Snow Rd, taking you through the Milawa Gourmet region.

dinner by appointment Oct-May, lunch & dinner daily Jun-Sep) Look out over the village or west Gippsland while you enjoy Mod Oz meals specialising in local produce.

**Kelly's Lodge B&B** ( ☎ 5165 1129; www.kellyslodge .com.au; 11 Frosti Ln; r summer/winter $120/275) A super-friendly place in the centre of everything, with comfortable rooms and a cosy lounge. You can cook in the shared kitchen or go through to Kelly's Cafe.

**Alpine Hotel** ( ☎ 1300 651 136; Currawong Rd; dm summer/winter from $25/30, d $90/120) The pub has motel-style accommodation as well as a backpacker dorm on the top floor. In winter the bar-café is a good spot to hang while local bands belt-out rock covers.

## LAKE EILDON NATIONAL PARK

Surrounding most of Lake Eildon, Lake Eildon National Park covers over 27,000 hectares and provides excellent opportunities for walking and camping. Various 4WD tracks lead off the road into the park and across to the lake. There are walking tracks throughout, including Candlebark Nature Walk. From the 1850s, the areas around Lake Eildon were logged and mined for gold, so much of the vegetation is regrowth eucalypt forest. There are several busy lakeside camping areas (unpowered sites per 4 people $15) at Coller Bay in the Fraser section that are equally popular with kangaroos. Showers and pit toilets are available; no bookings are taken. A kiosk sells basic supplies at the gate to Coller Bay; admission is $8 per car.

There's an established camping ground with toilets and showers, café and licensed grocery store at Jerusalem Creek Marina & Camping Ground ( ☎ 5774 2585; www.jerusalemcreekmarina.com.au;

501 Jerusalem Creek Rd, Eildon; unpowered sites adult/child $10/5). You can hire a picnic boat (per two hours/day $70/250) or a luxury 'boatel' (per night from $100) from the marina.

If you prefer to bush camp, set up along the Eildon–Jamieson road. This road is steep, winding and unsealed in sections, but particularly scenic.

Lake Eildon was created as a massive reservoir for irrigation and hydroelectric schemes. Originally called Sugarloaf Reserve, the lake was constructed between 1915 and 1929 and flooded the town of Darlingford and surrounding farm homesteads. Today the lake covers 14,000 hectares. Recent drought years turned the area into a moonscape, but recent rain has improved this. Behind the dam wall the pondage spreads below Eildon township.

On the northern arm of the lake is Bonnie Doon, a popular weekend base, which reached icon status as the nondescript spot where the family in the satirical 1997 Australian film *The Castle* enjoyed the serenity.

## EILDON

### pop 740

This small, one-pub town is a popular recreation and holiday base, built in the 1950s to house Eildon Dam project workers. Drive across the top of the dam's massive retaining wall to a lookout point, boat-launching ramps and Lake Eildon National Park. A road leads around the lake to Jerusalem Inlet.

There are quiet walking and cycling trails along the pondage shores, which also give easy access to the best fishing spots. Ask at the visitors centre for the *Future Fish Eildon Fishing Trails* brochure with map.

Kids will love the touch-and-feel tanks and aquariums at the Freshwater Discovery Centre ( ☎ 5774 2208;Goulburn Valley Hwy, Snobs Creek; adult/child/family $7/4.50/20; ⏰ 11am-4pm Fri-Mon), a trout farm and hatchery that releases over one million fish each year. Alternatively, take them fishing at Eildon Trout Farm ( ☎ 5773 2377; www.eildontroutfarm.com.au; 460 Back Eildon Rd, Thornton; entry/fishing $1/2; ⏰ 9am-5pm) where you'll definitely catch a trout or salmon. Have it cleaned then buy it – you'll know it's fresh!

The lake and local rivers offer plenty of action to keep you wet all day long. Hooked on the Goulburn Fishing Tours ( ☎ 5772 2626, 0428-345 366; 1/2 people from $35/40) takes you fishing or sightseeing on selected sections of the Goulburn River. If you'd like to try fly-fishing, or are already hooked, go to Goulburn Valley Fly-Fishing Centre ( ☎ 5773 2513; www.goulburnvlyflyfishing.com.au; 1270 Goulburn Valley Way; fishing introductory/5hr $45/198). Stay over in the cottages (single/double from $105/140), which includes fishing in the private lake.

Mystic Mountains Outdoors (p314) is the only place in the area that rents out kayaks.

Stay relatively dry on a horse trail-ride through beautiful valleys, into the Great Divide and along the Rubicon Valley. Rubicon Valley Horse-riding ( ☎ 5773 2292; www.rubiconhorseriding.com.au; Rubicon Rd, Thornton; rides introductory/2hr/half-day $45/65/90; ⏰ 10am & 2pm) caters for all levels and runs overnight safaris, as does nearby Stockman's Reward ( ☎ 5774 2322; Goulburn Valley Hwy; rides 1/2hr $35/65) towards Eildon. Tiny tots can ride ponies ($10 to $20 depending on age) in the yard here, or around the property.

If you prefer extreme water action, contact Australian Adventure Experience ( ☎ 5772 1440, 0417-028 004; admin@ausadventures.com) for canoeing, rafting, or rock-climbing (from $88).

A trip further west past Yea to the Kerrisdale Mountain Railway & Museum ( ☎ 5797 0227; www.kerrisdalemtnrailway.com.au; 7523 Goulburn Valley Hwy, Kerrisdale; adult/child $15/10; ⏰ 10am-5pm Thu-Mon) is an absolute must. Countless cute trains chuff around a panoramic wildlife reserve.

The best way to experience Lake Eildon is to be on it. Hire a luxurious houseboat from one of the following operators, who set you up with a 10- or 12-berth houseboat (minimum hire per weekend from $1100):

Eildon Houseboat Hire ( ☎ 0438-345 366; www.eildonhouseboathire.com.au)

Lake Eildon Marina & Houseboat Hire ( ☎ 5774 2107; www.houseboatholidays.com.au)

## Information

Eildon visitors centre ( ☎ 5774 2909; www.lakeeildon.com; Main St; ⏰ 10am-2pm) Opposite the shopping centre. Book accommodation and houseboats through Mansfield & Mt Buller High Country visitors centre (p306).

## Eating

Vicki & Alberts Restaurant ( ☎ 5774 2865; 5 Hillside Ave; mains $16-26; ⏰ dinner Thu-Mon) You'll be served a tasty home-cooked meal here.

Taste of Eildon ( ☎ 5774 2642; 1 Riverside Dr; mains $12-19; ⏰ breakfast & lunch Thu-Mon, dinner Fri & Sat) This café-cum-gallery in the old general store sells gourmet food, wine and giftware.

## Sleeping

Eildon Parkview Motor Inn ( ☎ 5774 2165; www.cute.com.au/parkview; 5 Hillside Ave; s/d from $75/85) Right in the centre of town, yet with stacks of space both inside and out.

Robyn's Nest B&B ( ☎ 5774 2525, 0409-932 724; www.visitvictoria.com.au/robynsnest; 13 High St; d $120-160) This magnificent B&B has private balconies looking over the Eildon Valley and Mt Torbreck. When you want to get active, hire one of Don's mountain bikes.

See left for details on hiring a houseboat.

## ALPINE NATIONAL PARK

This park is a spectacular and fragile environment with diverse vegetation. Eucalypt forests range from stringybark and peppermint in the lower reaches, to blue gum, mountain ash, alpine ash and snowgum in the higher areas. In spring and summer the areas above the snowline are carpeted with beautiful wild flowers. More than 1100 plant species have been recorded in the park, including 12 that are unique to Australia.

Declared a national park in December 1989, its 646,000 hectares covers most of the High Country of the Great Dividing Range, and joins High Country areas of New South Wales (NSW) and the Australian Capital Territory (ACT).

There are plenty of access roads to and through the park, although in winter a number are closed. The opportunities for recreation and eco-tourism in the area are outstanding. Bush camping (unpowered sites free) is allowed; visitors should use designated camping grounds and observe fire bans. The area's many walking tracks include a major stretch of the Australian

## CATTLE COUNTRY

When the National Trust bluntly stated in 2004 that mountain cattlemen are not as culturally important as the environment, which their activities damage, the High Country graziers were hoofing mad. In May 2005 the state government then announced a permanent ban on cattle grazing in the Alpine National Park – there was a major outcry. The Mountain Cattlemen's Association of Victoria (www.mcav.com.au) is trying to preserve the 170-year-old practice of grazing. It argues that the tradition is important for all Australians, and are currently gaining scientific evidence to back their claim that grazing reduces fires and that sustainable alpine grazing is possible and sensible. They are determined to keep the heritage alive.

It's a romantic bush idyll, but the cattle grazing here each summer puts huge pressure on an environment already stressed from drought and bushfires. The damage has long been recognised. Cattle grazing has dramatically increased the spread of weeds, and caused massive erosion of moss-beds, bogs and stream banks from cattle trampling the fragile peaty soils. The National Parks Association says that about 20 plants and animals are listed as threatened by grazing in northeastern Victoria. If this complex, fragile environment has a future it will be based on sustainable management and not romantic tales of the past.

Cattle grazing in areas such as Mt Feathertop, Mt Hotham and Mt Bogong was phased out during the 1960s, and the state government has made a transitional payment to licence holders to take their cattle into the state forests. But anyone who has been to the High Country rodeos will empathise with this desire to maintain a tradition, at least in a controlled manner that the mountain men have proposed. And without their controlling presence, bushfires have recently raged through the area.

Perhaps governments need to look at the whole picture, consider the damage done by other users, find ways to get rid of the wild goats and brumbies, and perhaps join the cattlemen one summer day.

Alps Walking Track (p310) on its 655km way from Walhalla to the outskirts of Canberra.

Visitors centres can provide Parks Victoria notes, while Parks Victoria has a number of offices in the region for more specific queries.

## MT BUFFALO NATIONAL PARK

Always one of the state's best-loved and most popular spots, spectacular Mt Buffalo National Park (31,000 hectares) was declared back in 1898. It was named in 1824 by the explorers Hume and Hovell on their trek from Sydney to Port Phillip; they thought its bulky shape resembled a buffalo. The main access road is out of Porepunkah.

The mountain is surrounded by huge granite boulders. There's abundant plant and animal life, many streams and waterfalls, and over 90km of walking tracks. The Big Walk, an 11km, five-hour ascent of the mountain starts from Eurobin Creek Picnic Area, north of Porepunkah, and finishes at the Gorge Day Visitor Area. Self-guided walks include the 2.5km-return Gorge, the 4km-return View Point and the 4km-return Dickson's Falls Nature Walks. A road leads to just below the summit of the Horn (1723m), the highest point on the massif.

In winter many roads and tracks here are closed, so always check. There are 14km of groomed cross-country ski trails starting out from the Cresta Valley car park. There may not be any downhill lifts operating, but hey, take a snowshoe shuffle!

The Larder Café ( ☎ 5755 1590; Dingo Dell; snacks $7-15; ❂ 9am-5pm) has light meals, refreshments, a few supplies and some gear for hire, both in summer and winter.

In summer Mt Buffalo is a hang-gliding paradise, and the near-vertical walls of the Gorge provide some of Australia's most challenging rock-climbing. Check out the adventure companies in Bright (p307) for abseiling, caving, hang-gliding and rock-climbing opportunities, alpine-style (the more rain and snow the better!).

Nearby Lake Catani is good for swimming and canoeing, and has 54 camp sites.

## Information

Mt Buffalo Entrance Station ( ☎ 5756 2320, 13 19 63; www.parkweb.vic.gov.au; Mt Buffalo Tourist Rd; ❂ 8.30am-3.30pm) A Parks Victoria office where you pay the $10 per car entry fee and can get track information and camping permits. Collect the colourful Mount Buffalo Plateau Vegetation Map which shows trails and lookouts clearly.

## MYRTLEFORD

### pop 2700

Known as the 'Gateway to the Alps', Myrtleford is more than just an overnight stop en route to the snowfields. Ask for the Myrtleford Discovery Trail Guide at the visitors centre and check out the town's history as you stroll past labelled landmarks detailing each site's story.

The Murray to the Mountains Rail Trail (p308) follows a path close to the Great Alpine Rd from Gapsted (northwest of Myrtleford) south to Bright. Myrtleford Cycle Centre ( ☎ 5752 1511; 59 Clyde St; rental per day/weekend $25/40; ☼ 10am-5.30pm Mon-Fri, 9am-1pm Sat) rents bikes and helmets.

Holiday Air Adventures ( ☎ 5753 5305; www.haa.com .au; 849 Happy Valley Rd, Rosewhite; flights from $60) flies you over spectacular gorges and lakes in a Cessna Hawk XP.

## Information

Myrtleford visitors centre ( ☎ 5752 1044; www.visit myrtleford.com.au; 38 Myrtle St; ☼ 9am-5pm) Information and a booking service for the alpine valley area ski fields.

## Eating

Alpine Gate Restaurant ( ☎ 1800 991 044; 38 Myrtle St (Great Alpine Rd), Myrtleford; mains $9-18; ☼ breakfast & lunch) A lovely spot in front of the visitors centre, with an airy ambience, chilled music and fab food.

## Sleeping

Myrtleford Hotel ( ☎ 5752 1001; myrtleford.hotel@bigpond .com; 67 Standish St; s/d/f $35/50/80) It's shiny-clean, spacious and there's a grand veranda.

Myrtle Creek Farmstay Cottages ( ☎ 5753 4447; www .myrtlecreekcottages.com; 5 Myrtleford-Stanley Rd; d $128, child $15) Feed alpacas and horses at this hands-on farm accommodation. The log cabins have spas and well-equipped kitchens.

## LAKE MOUNTAIN

Part of Yarra Ranges National Park, Lake Mountain (1433m) has world-class facilities, with 37km of trails and several toboggan runs. It is renowned as the premier cross-country ski resort in Australia. In winter, ski patrols operate daily, and both summer and snow camping are allowed – there's no fee, but you *must* notify the Alpine visitors centre (see Information) of your intentions before heading out.

Walkers and mountain bikers make use of the ski trails in summer. Take the 4km Summit Walk (two hours return), which crosses alpine bogs and granite rock faces. It starts from Gerraty's car park.

## Information

The daily admission fee is $27 per car; the trail fee is from $10/5.50 per adult/child.

Alpine visitors centre ( ☎ 5963 3288; www.lakemoun tainresort.com.au; Snowy Rd; ☼ 8am-4.30pm Mon-Fri Oct-May, 7am-6pm daily Jun-Sep) Has ski hire, a ski school, a café and undercover barbecue areas.

## MARYSVILLE
### pop 520

Sleepy Marysville was a private mountain retreat back in 1863, and by the 1920s was known as Melbourne's honeymoon capital. Today its beautiful mountain setting attracts nature-lovers, and it's the main base for the cross-country ski fields at Lake Mountain. Cross-country ski and toboggan hire is available at several places on Murchison St.

Lady Talbot Drive, which starts in Marysville, is a stunning 48km loop past some of the area's prettiest spots, camp sites and most spectacular features, including Phantom Falls. Popular walks along the drive include the 2km return Keppel Falls Walk and the 4km Beeches Rainforest Walk. The road is unsealed, but should be fine for 2WD vehicles in the dry months.

Spectacular Steavenson's Falls is Victoria's highest waterfall (82m). A short walk from the car park (parking $2) leads to the falls, which are floodlit until midnight. There are several bushwalks from here, many quite steep, including those to Nicholl's Lookout and Keppel's Lookout.

Cumberland Scenic Reserve, with numerous walks and the Cora Lynn and Cumberland Falls, is 16km east of Marysville.

This is Mystic Mountains territory, a notion which perhaps inspired the following fun places. Check out Bruno's Art & Sculptures Garden ( ☎ 5963 3513; 51 Falls Rd; adult/child $5/free; ☼ garden 10am-5pm daily, gallery 10am-5pm Sat & Sun), where there's hundreds of fantasy terracotta statues in an otherworldly rainforest setting. In a similar vein is Crystal Journey of Marysville ( ☎ 5963 4373; 883 Buxton Rd; ☼ 10am-5pm Wed-Sun); have a reading, wander through the garden, or take a farm tour (ring first). Equally out-there are the 40 Meccano-based exhibits at Manical Mechanicals ( ☎ 0417-739 9072; www.manicalmechanicals.com.au; 2 Murchison St; adult $2; ☼ 9am-4pm).

The Steavenson, Taggerty and Acheron Rivers have excellent fishing and magnificent settings. Pick up the *10 Best Fishing Spots* notes from the visitors centre, or fish the easy way at one of the trout and salmon farms at Buxton or Marysville.

If you just want to play, Mystic Mountains Outdoors ( ☎ 5963 7029; 631 Maroondah Hwy, Narbethong;

## THE MAN FROM SNOWY RIVER

You've seen the film and probably read Banjo Paterson's famous poem, but out at Corryong they live the legend. It looked like so much fun in the film that the locals just had to try it – mountain horse-racing where 'the hills are twice as steep and twice as rough'. Yes, it's the Country Wide Challenge, Australia's ultimate test of horse-riding prowess! The race is a feature of the Man From Snowy River Bush Festival ( ☎ 6076 1992; www.manfromsnowyriverbushfestival .com.au; ☼ Mar) – four days of whip-cracking and yarn-spinning fun.

Corryong is a pretty township ringed by mountains – a natural playground for trout fishing, canoeing, cycling and bushwalking. The Man From Snowy River Museum ( ☎ 6076 1114; 105 Hanson St; adult/child $4/50c; ☼ 10am-noon & 2-4pm) is actually a local history museum, featuring a set of snow skis from 1870 and the Jarvis Homestead, a 19th-century slab-timber hut.

Corryong visitors centre ( ☎ 6076 2277; www.towong.com; 50 Hanson St; ☼ 9am-5pm) has info on the region, including Jack Riley's Grave (Corryong Cemetery) which is inscribed with the words, 'In memory of the Man from Snowy River, Jack Riley, buried here 16th July 1914.'

☼ 9am-6pm Oct-May, 7.30am-6pm Jun-Sep) hires kayaks (per day $40, including a soft car rack). You can hire skis and ski gear here too.

## Information

Marysville visitors centre ( ☎ 5963 4567; www.marys villetourism.com; Murchison St; ☼ 9am-5pm) Info on the area's natural attractions and walks.

## Eating

Fraga's Café ( ☎ 5963 3216; 19 Murchison St; mains $18-27; ☼ lunch Thu-Tue, dinner Fri & Sat) Enjoy creative meals and good coffee in an art-filled dining room or out on the deck.

Terracotta Room ( ☎ 5963 4004; Village Walk, Murchison St; mains $12-18; ☼ lunch Wed-Sun) New and inviting with a range of salads and platters using local produce.

Gilberts at Fruit Salad Farm ( ☎ 5963 3232; Aubrey-Couzens Dr; mains $22-35; ☼ dinner Fri-Mon, lunch by arrangement) In the rainforest, Gilberts offers fine, intimate dining in enchanting grounds. Their self-contained B&B cottages between the trees cost from $110 per double.

## Sleeping

Keppels Hotel ( ☎ 5963 3207; www.keppels.net; Murchison St; s/d $60/70) Fresh bedrooms look out over splendid gardens.

Nanda Binya Lodge ( ☎ 5963 3433; www.virtual.net .au/~nandabinya; 29 Woods Point Rd; B&B s/d $100/110-125) Guests' rooms and the large lounge open onto a deck with magnificent views over a charming garden.

Delderfield B&B ( ☎ 5963 4345; www.delderfield.com .au; 1 Darwin St; d from $215) You'll see Delderfield's gorgeous garden from down the street and get excited! The whole place displays the creativity of the owners. Total luxury just one street back from Marysville's centre.

See also Gilberts at Fruit Salad Farm (see Eating).

# BEECHWORTH

### pop 2650

The National Trust rated Beechworth as one of Victoria's two 'notable' towns, and you can see why. It's a living legacy of the gold-rush era. In the historical and cultural precinct, the buildings (built in the 1850s) are built from a distinctive honey-coloured local granite – you can feel the past as well as learn about it. There are many attractive shops along Ford St, for every type of shopping spree, and the scenic countryside is just made for picnics, walking, cycling and tours of the region's superb vineyards.

Visit the honey-coloured buildings on a tour of the fascinating Historic & Cultural Precinct ( ☎ 1300 366 321; tours adult/child/family $12.50/6/25, less for just one site). First is the Beechworth Courthouse, where the trials many key historical figures took place (including Ned Kelly and his mother). Ned was committed to trial for the murders of constables Scanlon and Lonigan here in August 1880. Ned's cell is behind the Shire Hall; his mother's is behind the courthouse. Send a telegram to anywhere in the world from the Telegraph Station on Ford St, the original Morse-code office. Just like old times! Next door, the new Chinese Cultural Centre ( ☎ 5728 2866; www.beechworthchinese.com.au; ☼ 10am-5pm Wed-Mon) displays the history of the 6000 Chinese gold seekers from Guangdong province who arrived here in the 1850s, hoping to strike it rich. Walk through to Loch St where your tour ticket will get you into the Burke Museum

( ☎ 5728 8067; www.beechworth.com/burkemus; adult/child $5/3.50; Loch St; ۩ 9am-5pm). It's named after the hapless explorer Robert O'Hara Burke, who was Beechworth's superintendent of police before he set off on his historic trek north with William Wills. Also here are gold-rush relics and an arcade with 16 shopfronts preserved as they were 150 years ago.

Daily guided walking tours (adult/child/family $7.50/5/15) leave from the visitors centre and feature lots of gossip and interesting detail. The Ned Kelly–themed tour leaves at 10.30am; the Gold Rush tour at 1pm. Come twilight (mystical, mysterious twilight) join Adam on Beechworth Ghost Tours ( ☎ 1300 366 321, 5720 8050; Bailedup@gmail.com.au; Sambell's Bistro, Albert Rd; tours adult/child/family $17/7/45; ۩ 8.30pm Oct-May, 7pm Jun-Sep) and explore by lantern-light. *Whooo…*

Two-hour Historic Town Bus Tours (adult/child/family $12.50/7.50/37.50) run twice a day (departing 11am and 1.30pm), or buy the self-guided tour map for $1 and follow the 46 labelled pioneer sites.

Old brewery paraphernalia is on display at MB Historic Cellars ( ☎ 5728 1304; 29 Last St; admission $1; ۩ 10am-4pm), a former brewery that now produces traditional cordials like ginger beer. In the same premises is the Carriage Museum, displaying gorgeous old horse-drawn carriages. The work of local potters features at the folksy Potters of Beechworth ( ☎ 5728 2636; www.onetreehillpottery .com.au; 56 Ford St; ۩ 10am-5pm).

The Golden Horseshoes Monument (cnr Sydney Rd & Gorge Scenic Dr) is where, in 1855, a horse was shod with golden shoes and ridden into town by candidate Donald Cameron on the nomination day of Victoria's first parliamentary elections. The Victorian-era PR stunt seemed to work – Cameron was duly elected to parliament.

If you walk behind the historic precinct you'll find the Chinese Gardens, a tribute to the Chinese gold miners. Behind them is pretty Lake Sambell. If a swim beckons, you'll find that the surrounding hills look even prettier from the water.

On the northern outskirts of town lies Beechworth Historic Park, an area that was once potholed with gold-mining activity. The Gorge area has 12km of walking tracks, and most points of interest have self-guided information. Also within the park is the Gorge Scenic Drive, a 5km driving or walking tour (with a swim if you feel like it) to Newtown Falls.

The Murray to the Mountains Rail Trail (p308), from Wangaratta to Bright, detours east to Beechworth at Everton. An extension northwest to Wahgunyah is about to happen. If you need your bicycle repaired head to Beechworth Cycles ( ☎ 5728 1402; 17 Camp St).

For extreme activities contact Beechworth Adventures ( ☎ 5728 1804, 0419-280 614; www.adventure guidesaustralia.com.au; activities per day from $165), which will take you abseiling and rock climbing around the area's stunning cliffs and crags.

Seen and done enough? Kick back at Bridge Road Brewers ( ☎ 5728 2703; www.bridgeroadbrewers.com .au; Old Stable House, Ford St; meals $8-17; ۩ 11am-6pm Wed-Mon). It's a happy little spot behind the Commercial Hotel, with an interesting range of boutique beers and a great lunch menu. Sunday night is pizza-and-movie night (from 8pm).

## YACKANDANDAH

### pop 660

The beautiful hills and valleys around here will blow you away. The entire town of Yackandandah has been classified by the National Trust, which could explain why it still has a 'drapery' store! The Yackandandah visitors centre ( ☎ 02-6027 1988; www.uniqueyackandandah.com.au; 27 High St; ۩ 9am-5pm) is in the grand, 1878 Athenaeum building. Pick up the free *A Walk in High Street* brochure, which details the history of the shops, and the helpful *Yackandandah – Unveil the Mystery* booklet.

The Yackandandah Folk Festival ( ☎ 02-6027 1447; http://folkfestival.yackandandah.com; ۩ mid-Mar) is three days of music, parades, workshops and fun.

When you finish curio-shopping in the fascinating local shops, try trout fishing on Yackandandah Creek; visit the Lavender Patch ( ☎ 02-6027 1603; www.lavenderpatch.com.au; 461 Yackandandah Rd (Beechworth Rd); ۩ 9am-5.30pm) for some lavender ice cream; or check out the studio-gallery Kirby's Flat Pottery ( ☎ 02-6027 1416; www .johndermer.com.au; 225 Kirby's Flat Rd; ۩ 10.15am-5.30pm Sat & Sun), 4km south of Yackandandah.

An exciting new attraction is the extraordinary tour of Karrs Reef Goldmine ( ☎ 02-6027 1988; tours adult/child $18.50/16.50; ۩ 10am, noon, 2pm & 4pm). For 1½ hours you're guided through the hard-dug tunnel to see the way it all worked. Departs from the visitors centre.

The unsealed 14km Yackandandah Scenic Forest Drive begins at Bells Flat Rd and travels over former gold-mining territory, much of which is now Stanley State Forest. There are also 4WD tracks in the area.

## Information

Beechworth visitors centre ( ☎ 1300 366 321; www .beechworthonline.com.au; 103 Ford St; ☼ 9am-5pm) In the Old Shire Hall. Staff run an accommodation and activity booking service, sell tour tickets, and have information on local walks and wineries. Pop in to look through the glossy photo albums!

## Festivals & Events

Golden Horseshoe Festival ( ☎ 1300 366 321) Donald Cameron's ride on a gold-shod horse is re-enacted in a grand parade at this Easter event. Food stalls, Easter-egg hunt, music and fun.

Harvest Celebrations (www.harvestcelebration.com.au) Food and wine workshops take to the streets in May.

Chinese Moon Festival (www.beechworthchinese.com) Feasting, Chinese-dragon dancing and lantern displays in early October.

Celtic Festival (www.beechworthcelticfestival.com.au) Art, entertainment, food, music and mayhem in mid-November.

## Eating

Beechworth Pantry ( ☎ 5728 2456; 77 Ford St; mains $8-19; ☼ breakfast & lunch) Exciting sandwiches, plus stacks of other gourmet meals.

Green Shed ( ☎ 5728 2360; 37 Camp St; mains $27-28; ☼ lunch Fri-Sun, dinner Wed-Sun) A former printery, now a cosy place where the meals are a pure delight.

Beechworth Provender ( ☎ 5728 2650; 18 Camp St; sandwiches from $7; 9am-5pm) Crammed with delectable local produce, such as Milawa cheeses, antipasto, and everything you need for a gourmet bush-picnic.

Wardens ( ☎ 5728 1377; 32 Ford St; mains $26-35; ☼ breakfast, lunch & dinner Wed-Sun) Simply the best!

## Sleeping

There are oodles of B&Bs and self-contained cottages in the area; see www.beechworth .com/accommodation.

Tanswells Commercial Hotel ( ☎ 5728 1480; tanscom@ bigpond.net.au; 50 Ford St; s/d incl breakfast $45/65) Neat rooms above an interesting old pub.

La Trobe at Beechworth ( ☎ 5720 8050; www.latrobeat beechworth.com.au; Albert Rd; s/d/ste incl breakfast from $75/110/160, self-contained cottages from $170) This was the Beechworth Lunatic Asylum for over 130 years – there's a walking tour (collect the map) through the heritage gardens. The Art Deco buildings are now full of pleasant rooms.

Freeman on Ford ( ☎ 5728 2371; www.beechworth .com/freemanonford; 97 Ford St; d/deluxe incl breakfast from $165/250) In the 1876 Oriental Bank, this glorious place offers Victorian luxury, right in the centre of town. The owner, Heidi, will make you feel very special.

# HIGH COUNTRY ROAD TRIPS

## MILAWA GOURMET REGION ALONG THE SNOW ROAD

Forget skiing. Take the Snow Rd and follow your senses! Good food and wine is a normal part of life here: there are so many small-scale, local, hands-on specialists that you just have to stop, taste and graze. Events during the year (www.milawagourmet.com) showcase the talents of local chefs and producers.

To get started, head off the Hume Fwy near Glenrowan and you'll eventually (hours, days later) drive out onto the Great Alpine Rd near Myrtleford. The highpoints are around Oxley and Milawa. At Oxley, wineries include John Gehrig Wines ( ☎ 5727 3395; www.johngehrigwines.com .au; Gehrig's Ln; ☼ 10am-5pm) with its rare varieties like verjuice. Don't drive too fast or you'll miss the old general store, which is now King River Cafe ( ☎ 5727 3461; Snow Rd; mains $11-26; ☼ lunch Mon & Wed-Sun, dinner Wed-Sun), where local wines from producers like Pizzini, Chrismont and Moyhu are served with scrumptious food.

In Milawa, Milawa Mustard ( ☎ 5727 3202; www .milawamustard.com.au; Old Emu Inn, The Cross Roads; ☼ 10am-5pm) has tastings of its handmade seeded mustards, herbed vinegars and preserves, while the Olive Shop ( ☎ 5727 3887; www .theoliveshop.com.au; 1605 Snow Rd; ☼ 10am-5pm Thu-Mon) is an olive 'gallery' with oils and tapenades for sampling. A few metres west over Factory Rd, try about eight different honeys at Walkabout Apiaries ( ☎ 5727 3468; Snow Rd; ⏰ 10am-5pm).

Next stop is the famous Brown Brothers Vineyard ( ☎ 5720 5547; www.brownbrothers.com.au; Bobbinawarrah Rd, Milawa; ⏰ 9am-5pm). The winery's first vintage was in 1889, and the winery has remained in the hands of the same family ever since. As well as the tasting room, there's an attractive restaurant, gorgeous garden, kids play equipment and picnic and barbecue facilities.

The Milawa Cheese Company ( ☎ 5727 3589; milawacheese@netc.net.au; Factory Rd; ⏰ 9am-5pm) is 2km north of Milawa. From humble origins, it now produces a mouth-watering array of cheeses to sample or buy. It excels at soft farmhouse brie and pungent washed-rind cheeses. Blow your taste buds over in the old butter room at Milawa Chocolates ( ☎ 5727 3500; ⏰ 11am-4pm Fri-Wed), or pop around the back to the Muse Gallery of Milawa ( ☎ 5727 3599; www.musegallery.com.au; ⏰ 10am-5pm Thu-Mon) to heighten a few other senses.

Rose Hill Estate Wines ( ☎ 5727 3930; jo@rosehillestate wines.com.au; 1400 Oxley Flats Rd; ⏰ 10am-6pm Fri-Mon) is where specialist Kevin enthuses about his latest wines as you taste them.

Further north is EV Olives Groves ( ☎ 5727 0209; www.evolives.com; 203 Everton Rd, Markwood; ⏰ 10am-5pm), where the fruity taste of the oils, olives and tapenades will have you buying your next year's supplies.

Wood Park Wines ( ☎ 5727 3367; Whorouly Rd, Whorouly; ⏰ 10am-5pm Wed-Mon) has wine tastings at its picturesque vineyard, but ring first as it's a bit of a hike (signposted off the Snow Rd).

Some of the area's gorgeous food and wine producers have restaurants attached, or try Milawa Gourmet Hotel ( ☎ 5727 3208; cnr Snow Rd & Factory Rd, Milawa; mains $16-27; ⏰ lunch & dinner) – a traditional country pub serving meals with gourmet flair.

There are charming B&Bs, country houses, old inns and boutique hotels in the region. Stay if you dare – you may never go home! Find your nest at www.milawagourmet.com /v5/accommod.htm.

## GREAT ALPINE ROAD

Australia's well-loved Great Alpine Road (www .greatalpineroad.info) flows through the Ovens Valley past the mountain playgrounds on a 308km route from Wangaratta to Bairnsdale. It's Australia's highest year-round-accessible sealed road. If you're not hurtling along it hell-bent on arriving at the ski slopes, you'll notice it winds past forests, rivers, vineyards and farms on its scenic way over Mt Hotham down almost to the Tasman Sea. Along the way there's farm produce, cafés and a range of accommodation.

Two wineries you'll pass are Michelini Wines ( ☎ 5751 1990; www.micheliniwines.com.au; Myrtleford; ⏰ 10am-5pm) and Gapsted ( ☎ 5751 1383; www.vic torianalpswinery.com.au; Gapsted; ⏰ 10am-5pm). Both offer tastings in beautiful surroundings.

Look out for dusty old Ovens Hotel ( ☎ 5751 1628; Ovens; mains $12-26; ⏰ lunch Tue-Sun, dinner Wed-Sun) hiding behind the vines. It's a popular place for a drink, especially when a blues band jams in the beer garden.

Between Myrtleford and Bright, stop at the Red Stag Deer & Emu Farm ( ☎ 5756 2365; www .alpinelink.com.au/redstag; Hughes Ln; ⏰ 10am-4.30pm). You may get to bottle-feed a baby deer, or be fed yourself – the lunches are delicious and the views amazing.

One of the cutest little towns en route is Harrietville at the base of Mt Hotham, where you'll see Lavender Hue ( ☎ 5759 2588; www.alphalink.com .au/lavenderhue; Harrietville; ⏰ open 10am-4pm Thu-Mon) spread along the Ovens river. Stop and visit for a total sensory experience.

## OMEO HIGHWAY

Stretching almost 300km on its journey from the Murray River to the coast, the Omeo Hwy (C543) passes through the heart of the High Country, and takes in some of Victoria's most scenic and diverse countryside. The highway is unsealed in several sections (between Anglers Rest and Mitta Mitta), and snow often makes it difficult to pass in winter, but at any time it is a memorable drive.

The first section of the road from Tallangatta follows the flatlands of the Mitta Mitta River between wooded mountains. It's a totally serene section. Mitta Mitta is an old gold-mining settlement, and a track leads from the highway to the former Pioneer Mine site, one of the largest hydraulic sluicing operations in Victoria, yielding some 15,000oz (425.25kg) of gold over 16 years. For unique accommodation, head to Bharatralia Jungle Camp ( ☎ 02-6072 3621; cgotto@msn .com; Omeo Hwy, Mitta Mitta; tents per person $25) just 2km north of town The luxurious tents are set in a charming animal retreat, and there's a camp kitchen, barbecues and meals are available.

At Anglers Rest, beside the Cobungra River, is the Blue Duck Inn ( ☎ 5159 7220; www.blueduckinn.com .au; Omeo Hwy; mains $18-27; ⏰ lunch & dinner Wed-Sun), popular with anglers, canoeists and bush-

## ALPINE TOURS

Here are a few more high-altitude tours to tempt you. Most 4WD tours or walking tours only run from November to late May.

Hedonistic Hiking ( ☎ 5755 2307; www.hedonistichiking.com.au; 1-/5-day tours $120/1600) runs walks ranging from dead-easy to challenging, always including a gourmet food experience, a glass of wine and a lively chat about the culture, nature and history of the area.

Epicurious ( ☎ 0407-261 510; www.epicurioustravel.com.au; 3-/5-day tour $1290/1590) offers luxury, all-inclusive cycling and walking holidays that combine spectacular High Country scenery with fine food and accommodation.

Mountain Top Experience ( ☎ 5134 6876; www.mountaintopexperience.com) can provide food-parcel drop-offs and car shuttles (from $30) for walkers on the Australian Alps Walking Track (p310). It also has a range of 4WD tag-along tours (per day $100) and 4WD hire.

River Mountain Guides ( ☎ 0414-989 134; www.rivermountainguides.com.au; per day from $350) runs snowsports and treks around the Bogong High Plains. Four people can take a three-day snowshoe shuffle with food and camping gear provided for $370 per person. Go, go, go!

walkers for its hearty meals and barbecue area by the river. Self-contained units here sleep up to eight people (from $120 a double).

Finally, 30km south of Anglers Rest, is pretty little Omeo, a town where you co-exist with history. Omeo's origins date back to the gold-rush days of the 1850s when it was Victoria's wildest, remotest goldfield. It attracted many Chinese gold diggers who built a Chinatown in the area behind the Omeo Service Station.

Omeo offers the only all-weather access to Dinner Plain and Mt Hotham, a 30-minute climb with amazing views. You must carry chains in winter – hire them at Omeo Service Station (BP; ☎ 5159 1312; www.omeoskihire.com.au; Main St, Omeo).

You'll find tea rooms, cafés and top-quality pub food in town. The stunning Art Deco Golden Age Motel & Bar ( ☎ 5159 1344; www.omeoregion .com.au/goldenage; Day Ave; s/d/f $85/99/175) includes the James Washington restaurant (mains $14 to $29, open for dinner daily). Stay over in the top-quality rooms and enjoy the grand veranda. Another good choice is the historic Omeo Bank House ( ☎ 5159 1405; www.omeoregion .au/bankhouse; 154 Day Ave; d/tr $130/150). Its rooms hold a mix of queen-size, king-single or bunk beds. Check out other accommodation options at www.omeoregion.com.au or contact Omeo visitors centre ( ☎ 5159 1552; www.omeoregion.com .au; 199 Day Ave; ⊙ 9am-5pm). Pick up a brochure to the *Historical Gold Mining Site*, the Oriental Claims. These days the site is a monument to the pioneers, and is full of wildlife (if not gold).

## THE BEST ROAD OF ALL

Well, the best and the worst! The spectacular 165km drive south from Jamieson to Baw Baw Village should not be undertaken lightly. The first section to Woods Point is delightfully rough, snaking alongside the Goulburn River. You'll pass forests, hills and a series of derelict gold-mining settlements, many of which were destroyed by the 1939 bushfires (or finished off in the 2007 fires). About 20km south of Jamieson, Tunnel Bend Reserve has a camping ground (unpowered sites free) with picnic facilities, and some good swimming spots in the Goulburn River.

Woods Point, 55km south of Jamieson, is a tiny, historic gold-mining town in a deep valley on the upper reaches of the Goulburn River. The friendly old Commercial Hotel ( ☎ 5777 8224; 1 Bridge St; B&B per person $50) is a dusty pub filled with travellers who don't want to take the road out of town. Why? The next section is a narrow, twisting track strewn with sharp rocks and potholes. Road verges piled with loose gravel drop away into deep, wooded valleys. The dispute over who owns this section of road has left it unmaintained for yonks. Don't expect to hurry as you rattle and jolt the 55km to Aberfeldie, shocking your shock absorbers and tracking the crystal creek which eventually grows into the Goulburn River.

Finally, you cross the wide, smooth concrete dam wall over Thomson Dam. Stunning! Whiz along the sealed Thomson Valley Rd to the fabulous new South Face Rd, a gravel road that was cut through in 2008 to give access to the Baw Baw ski resort. South Face Rd runs for 30km through bush over Western Tyers River Bridge and Christmas Creek Bridge to Baw Baw Tourist Rd, just higher than the entrance box. Another 8km to the village, and yes, the drive may have been worth it!

# NORTH TO THE MURRAY

The magic of the Murray, Australia's largest river, sweeps you away in a tourist heaven of balmy weather, water sports, paddle steamers and, of course, wineries. Australia's most important waterway flows from the mountains of the Great Dividing Range in northeastern Victoria to Encounter Bay in South Australia – more than 2700km. It's also an unusual river: for very long stretches it collects no water from the country it passes through.

Many of the river towns carry evocative reminders of past riverboat days, including historical museums, old buildings and well-preserved paddle steamers. The Murray Valley Hwy links them all, but is separated from the river by flood plains, subsidiary waterways and forests of red gum. However, you can take advantage of the fairly frequent tracks (often marked 'River Access') that lead you to the banks.

Those magnificent red gum forests have made the Murray River famous, and provide plentiful bird and animal life plus leisurely riverbank camping. There's almost always 'twin' towns along here: back in the days before Federation (1901), all major river crossings had customs houses on each bank, from which the two states (Victoria and New South Wales) levied tariffs on goods carried across their borders.

Whichever road you take north from Melbourne, the air grows warmer as the country rolls away. By the time you reach the mighty Murray, you are in endless summer (well, it feels like that…). Travel up through the wide spaces of the Mallee, or up the Hume, Victoria's busiest freeway, past pleasant country towns, wineries, galleries, fine food outlets and adventure sports opportunities. Or there's the Hume's little sister, the Goulburn Hwy, which leads you through Victoria's fruit bowl, the Goulburn Valley, a rich agricultural district. The wineries here include the well-respected Tahbilk and Mitchelton.

## WATER WONDERLAND

Have your swimwear and sunscreen ready, your body trimmed and tanned (or not-so-trim and healthily pale), and muster up loads of energy – a plethora of water sports is waiting for you. There's water-skiing, wake-boarding, kayaking, swimming, or even just floating, regardless of which direction you're headed. And if the rivers and lakes are a bit too *au naturale,* from Wangaratta to Wodonga, Mildura to Nagambie, there are state-of-the-art aquatic centres with slides, wave pools, spas and saunas.

Love the water but prefer to stay dry? Paddle steamers are steamed-up and ready to burble you along the magic Murray; canoes tempt you out onto the Goulburn River; river launches transport you to wineries or wetlands; and houseboats await for you to stay in, anywhere from Rutherglen to Mildura. Just follow your divining stick and sniff the air – you're headed for water!

## TAKE TO THE SKY

You don't need to feel earthbound, water-bound or bound at all. This is fun country, holiday time, sporting heaven – take to the skies and totally embrace your freedom! If you're adventurous, the air currents around Nagambie, Euroa and Benalla mean stacks more days available for skydiving and hot-air ballooning (p340). Reliable weather further north encourages small aircraft to offer you seats for scenic joyflights. Everywhere you go there'll be a sky-bound experience waiting for you.

If you prefer your feet on the ground, visit the Lake Boga Flying Boat Museum (p328).

## PIONEER EXPLORATIONS

Amidst all this leisure, it's surprising to find such a treasure-trove of history. Of course, Echuca (p329) is renowned for its historic wharf and living-history walk along the Esplanade; but homesteads like Byramine (p333) also take you back to the past in a truly emotional way.

Learn about the engineering and personal struggles involved in building the irrigation scheme in Mildura (opposite). Fascinating! See the river ports where pioneers built punts and fords, bars and stores to assist the transport of produce throughout the region. Be totally immersed in the past at ancient little towns like Chiltern (p335) and Rushworth (p338), or recall your youth at the costume museum (if you're over 15!) in Benalla (p340). Surely the ultimate relationship with the past can be found at the very many B&Bs that offer dream-filled nights in stunning old banks, grand estates, princely farmhouses and towered homesteads.

## WINE, WOMEN & SONG

Well, forget the women and song. This is wine, wine, wine country! Head off on Swan Hill's Golden Mile Wine Trail (p328). Check out Mildura's wineries (p323), where most of Australia's export wine is produced. Settle in for the long haul at Rutherglen (p334), where you can catch a festival or two and roll from one gourmet experience to the next. On all sides on your way north, vineyards with cellar-door sales and gorgeous, scrumptious food await to distract you from your journey.

## MILDURA

**pop 30,000**

After crossing windswept deserts and pale-golden wheat fields, you reach a thriving regional centre. Mildura (pronounced 'Milld-yoo-ra', meaning 'red soil') is a true oasis: a town ready to take you back to the grand old pastoralist era.

Mildura makes full use of the Murray, one of the state's great water-sports playgrounds, where activities include fishing, swimming, canoeing, water-skiing, houseboat holidays and paddle steamer cruises. The Murray region is also a golfer's paradise, with plenty of excellent riverside courses.

Mildura is an amazing tourist destination for people in search of endless blue skies. Foodies, clubbers, shoppers and lazeabouts delight in the resorts, wineries, markets, boutique or budget shopping, and the fabulous eateries known for their famous chefs. The main road, Deakin Ave, is a wide boulevard impressively lined with palms and gum trees, lit-up at night by the neon signs of motels and restaurants. Langtree Ave, one block north, is a shopping mall between Eighth and Ninth Sts. The Centro Plaza is an ultramodern, one-stop retail-therapy spot.

The irrigation schemes of northern Victoria support dairy farms, vineyards, market gardens, orchards and citrus groves that provide fresh fruit and supply the thriving dried-fruit industry. The area is also the biggest producer of wine in Australia (most of which is exported). In fact, Mildura is one of the richest agricultural areas in the country. It's easy to forget you're in the midst of Victoria's arid region when you see the lush green golf courses, endless orange groves, orchards and vineyards for which Mildura is renowned.

Sadly, after years of irrigation, soil salinity has become a major problem, one that poses a long-term threat to the economic viability of much of this area.

Mildura owes its existence to the Chaffey brothers and their irrigation systems (see below). The visitors centre has a brochure called *The Chaffey Trail*. Pick up a copy and follow the Chaffey story.

Stops on the Chaffey Trail include the Old Mildura Homestead ( ☎ 5018 8322; Cureton Ave, Old Mildura House Heritage Park; adult/child $2/free; ☒ 9am-6pm), a cottage that was the first home of William B Chaffey. On the banks of the Murray, it's in a pleasant heritage park which contains a few other historic buildings and has picnic and barbecue facilities.

Nearby is Chaffey's grand homestead, the historic Rio Vista (part of the Mildura Arts Centre; see p322). The house has been beautifully preserved; restorers peeled back the walls to the original wallpaper then reproduced it. The interior is set up as a series of historical displays depicting life in the 19th century, with period furnishings, costumes, photos and a collection of letters and memorabilia.

Also emerging from the Chaffey vision were the Mildura Wharf, the weir and the lock.

---

### THE CHAFFEY BROTHERS

Canadian brothers George and William Chaffey were famous 19th-century irrigation engineers who set up an irrigation colony at Mildura.

Their promotional scheme was launched in 1887 and attracted more than 3000 settlers to the area. They cleared scrub, dug irrigation channels and built fences, and two massive pumping-station engines were shipped from England.

The early years of the settlement were tough and full of frustrations. There was an economic collapse in the 1890s, rabbit plagues and droughts, and clearing the mallee scrub was a nightmare. George became disillusioned, and in 1896 returned to North America.

In 1889 William built Rio Vista, a grand riverside homestead, to express his confidence in the new settlement. But his wife, Hattie, died during childbirth before it was finished, and their newborn son died five months later. William later married his deceased wife's niece, also named Hattie, and lived in Mildura until he died in 1926 at the age of 70. Happily, he was there to see the Melbourne–Mildura railway line finally open in 1902, meaning the town's future was assured.

## NORTH TO THE MURRAY

The lock is operated at 11am, 12.30pm, 2pm and 3.30pm daily.

The Old Psyche Bend Pump Station ( ☎ 5024 5637; off Cureton Ave; adult/family $3/8; ☼ 1-4pm Tue & Thu, 10am-noon Sun) is where Chaffey set up his system to supply irrigation and drainage over 115 years ago. The system is still used, except the pumps are electric now and placed a bit further up the river. You can walk around the old centrifugal pumps and Chaffey's triple-expansion steam-engine pump. The old pumps run on special occasions; ask at the visitors centre.

Mildura Arts Centre ( ☎ 5018 8322; www.milduraarts.net.au; 199 Cureton Ave; adult/child $3/free; ☼ 10am-5pm), at the Rio Vista complex, combines a modern-art gallery and a theatre. The gallery has a large collection which includes *Woman Combing Her Hair at the Bath* by French Impressionist Edgar Degas in the European section. Australian paintings include works by Fred McCubbin

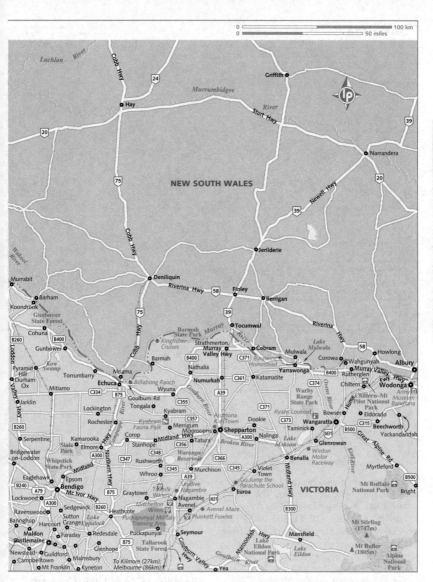

and Arthur Streeton, and there's an interesting Australian sculpture collection too.

Chateau Mildura ( ☎ 5024 5901; www.chateaumildura .com.au; 191 Belar Ave, Irymple; adult/child $10/free; ☼ 10am-4pm), established in 1888 and still producing table wines, is a living wine and horticultural museum with wine tasting to help your cultural experience.

Cruises depart from the Mildura Wharf, and most go through a lock: watch the gates open-ing and the water levels changing. A favourite cruise is on PS Melbourne ( ☎ 5023 2200; Mildura Wharf; 2hr cruise adult/child $24/8; ☼ cruises 10.50am & 1.50pm), one of the original paddle steamers, and the only one still driven by steam power. Watch the operator stoke the original boiler with wood. Another popular choice is PV Rothbury ( ☎ 5023 2200; Mildura Wharf; dinner or winery cruise adult/child $56/26, lunch cruise $26/10). The fastest of the riverboats, it

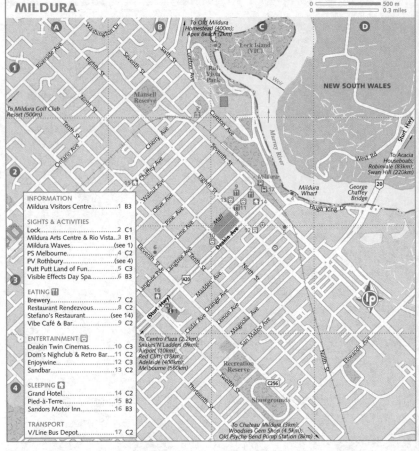

# MILDURA

0 — 500 m
0 — 0.3 miles

**INFORMATION**
Mildura Visitors Centre...............1 B3

**SIGHTS & ACTIVITIES**
Lock..........................................2 C1
Mildura Arts Centre & Rio Vista...3 B1
Mildura Waves.....................(see 1)
PS Melbourne............................4 C2
PV Rothbury.........................(see 4)
Putt Putt Land of Fun.................5 C3
Visible Effects Day Spa................6 B3

**EATING**
Brewery.....................................7 C2
Restaurant Rendezvous................8 C2
Stefano's Restaurant..............(see 14)
Vibe Café & Bar.........................9 C2

**ENTERTAINMENT**
Deakin Twin Cinemas.................10 C3
Dom's Nightclub & Retro Bar....11 C2
Enjoywine................................12 C3
Sandbar...................................13 C2

**SLEEPING**
Grand Hotel..............................14 C2
Pied-à-Terre.............................15 B2
Sandors Motor Inn.....................16 B3

**TRANSPORT**
V/Line Bus Depot.....................17 C2

offers a dinner or winery cruise on Thursday and a lunch cruise on Tuesday. The winery cruise visits Trentham Estate Winery.

Sunraysia Helicopters ( ☎ 5023 5255, 0409-555232; www.sunraysiahelicopters.com.au; 20min flight per person $135) offers a range of stunning scenic flights; see the spectacularly red Perry Sandhills, the wayward Kings Billabong and more.

Kayaking is big on the Murray. Take a guided kayak adventure tour with Moontongue Eco-Adventures ( ☎ 5024 3721, 0427-898 317; moontongue@bigpond.com; tours from $25; ☼ sunset Sat & Sun). Ian will tell you about the landscape and bird life as you work those muscles in magnificent, peaceful surroundings.

There's a fun range of outdoor activities available with Wild Side Outdoors ( ☎ 5024 3721; www.wildsideoutdoors.com.au; sunset canoe tours adult/child

$25/10), which runs a six-hour 4WD tour into the Hattah-Kulkyne National Park (adult/ child $75/35). It also has canoe/kayak/mountain bike hire ($30/20/20 per hour).

The Mildura Golf Club ( ☎ 5023 1147; www.mildura golfclub.com.au; Twelfth St; 18 holes $22, club hire $16) has a well-maintained course, open to the public, and also offers motel rooms, a pool, barbecue and bistro, all in a beautiful setting. The Riverside Golf Club ( ☎ 5023 1560; www.visitmildura.com.au/golf; Park St, Nichols Pt; 18 holes $18) is a good course by the river, with a licensed clubhouse.

If your golf swing fails you, try a hot-air balloon trip with Mildura Ballooning ( ☎ 5021 2876; www .milduraballooning.com.au; 40min from $255; ☼ dawn daily), weather permitting. The price includes champagne afterwards to celebrate your dream trip. Alternatively, drown your problems at Mildura Waves ( ☎ 5023 3747; www.mildurawaves.com.au; cnr Deakin Ave & 12th St; adult/child from $5/2.50; ⏱ 6am-9pm Mon-Thu, to 7pm Fri, 8am-6pm Sat & Sun), a modern complex with an artificial wave pool among other facilities. If you are swimming in the mighty, muddy Murray, be careful of snags and deep holes, and never jump into water when you can't see what's below the surface. Apex Beach is a favourite swimming spot.

Grab a few hours at Visible Effects Day Spa ( ☎ 5022 8000; www.visibleeffects.com.au; 157 Lime Ave; ⏱ 9am-5pm Mon, Tue & Fri, to 8pm Wed & Thu, to 1pm Sat). Try the Vitamin A facial ($55) followed by a hot-stone massage ($135) in a cocoon of music and aromatherapy.

Other stuff to do includes tenpin bowling and For- mula K Go Karts – both somehow irresistible when you're taking a break. Check with the visitors centre for details, or perhaps head off to Putt Putt Land of Fun ( ☎ 5023 3663; cnr 7th St & Orange Ave; ⏱ 10am-7.30pm), which has to be good with a name like that. Other play-places are Snakes 'N' Ladders ( ☎ 5025 3575; Seventeenth St, Cabarita; admission $8; ⏱ 9am-4.30pm) – 6 hectares of fun, with a playground, vineyard and museum, and Woodsies Gem Shop ( ☎ 5024 5797; cnr Morpung & Cureton Ave, Nichols Pt; admission free; ⏱ 9am-5.30pm), which has a huge garden maze (adult/child $2/1) covered in pretty vines and flowers, a sparkly Aladdin's Cave and a workshop where gems are cut and polished.

## INFORMATION

Mildura visitors centre ( ☎ 1800 039 043, 5018 8380; www.visitmildura.com.au; cnr Deakin Ave & 12th St; ⏱ 9am-5.30pm Mon-Fri, to 5pm Sat & Sun) In the Alfred Deakin Centre. There's a free accommodation-booking service, interesting displays, local produce and very helpful staff who book tours and activities.

## TOURS

Famous, extraordinary Mungo National Park (in NSW) is within striking distance of Mil-dura. Several operators run tours out there, concentrating on its culture, 45,000 years of history, and wildlife:

Discover Mildura Tours ( ☎ 5024 7448; www.discovermil dura.com.au; tours adult/child $89/30) Takes you out at 10am to see the river and the land, and through gourmet food experiences. Add a scenic helicopter flight for an extra $70.

Harry Nanya Tours ( ☎ 5027 2076; www.harrynanyatours .com.au; tours adult/child $130/55) The best-known Mungo tour. Guide Graham Clarke keeps you enchanted with Dream-time stories and his deep knowledge and understanding of the region. In summer, there's a spectacular sunset tour.

Sunraysia Discovery Tours ( ☎ 5023 5937; www.sunray siadiscoverytours.com.au; all-day tours from adult/child $95/45) Takes you to Mungo daily ($105/45), and to pioneer sites or on nature tours twice a week.

## FESTIVALS & EVENTS

Mildura Wentworth Arts Festival (www.visitmildura .com.au/major-events;r) Magical concerts by the river, in the sandhills, and all around; held in March.

Easter Power Sports (www.milduraevents.com.au) In-cludes the Mildura 100 Ski Race, drag racing and motocross.

Mildura Country Music Festival (www.milduracountry music.com.au) Ten days of free concerts during the September school holidays.

Jazz, Food & Wine Show (www.mrimf.com.au/jazz) Traditional bands, great food, good wine; held in October or November.

Mildura Show (www.mildura.vic.gov.au) One of the larg-est festivals in rural Victoria; held mid-October.

## EATING

Mildura's café and restaurant precinct runs along Langtree Ave and around the block, between the mall and the river. Many local motels have well-respected restaurants; many local vineyards offer picnic and barbecue fa-cilities in beautiful surroundings, with wine-tasting thrown into the mix.

### BIG LIZZIE

Red Cliffs, 18km southeast of Mildura, is the final resting place of *Big Lizzie*, a huge steam-engine tractor. Mr Frank Bottrill designed it to cart wool from the outback sheep stations around Broken Hill in central NSW.

Lizzie was built in 1915 in a backyard factory in Richmond, Melbourne, but she wasn't made for city living. She had a travelling speed of 1.6km per hour and a turning circle of 60m. Undaunted, Frank and his family set out; two years later they reached the Murray River but the river was in flood. Lizzie couldn't get across. So she was put to work in the Mallee where she cleared scrub and trees for many years.

Lizzie was saved from rusty oblivion and brought to Red Cliffs in 1971, and now stands proudly in a small park on the Calder Hwy, where a taped commentary tells her story.

## TRANSPORT: MILDURA

Distance from Melbourne **570km**

Direction **Northwest**

Travel time **Seven hours**

Air Regional Express Airlines (Rex; ☎ 13 17 13; www.regionalexpress.com.au) flies daily between Melbourne and Mildura, as does Qantas ( ☎ 13 13 13; www.qantas.com.au), with return fares from $252.

Bus V/Line ( ☎ 13 61 96; www.vline.com.au) runs direct overnight buses from Melbourne (return $70, 9½ hours, nightly Sunday to Friday), and train/bus services with changes at Bendigo or Swan Hill (return $70, seven to eight hours, several daily). V/Line's Murraylink service connects towns along the Murray River from Mildura: Swan Hill (return $42, 2¾ hours, four weekly), Yarrawonga ($54, six hours, four weekly), Wodonga ($61, seven hours, four weekly).

Car See p336.

Vibe Café & Bar ( ☎ 5023 1555; 29 Langtree Ave; mains $12-24; ☽ lunch & dinner) New in town, this place buzzes as it makes its mark on the street.

Brewery ( ☎ 5022 2988; www.mildurabrewery.com.au; 16 Langtree Ave; snacks $6-14, meals $14-28; ☽ lunch & dinner Tue-Sun) This microbrewery is still the 'in' place, set amongst fabulous stainless steel vats, pipes and brewing equipment. Take a tour, have a taste, buy a few ales, kick back, eat and be merry.

Restaurant Rendezvous ( ☎ 5023 1571; 34 Langtree Ave; mains $28-33; ☽ lunch Mon-Fri, dinner Mon-Sat) A local favourite with fine dining in a warm, casual atmosphere (alfresco if you'd rather), and many Sunraysia wines from which to choose.

Stefano's Restaurant ( ☎ 5023 0511; Grand Hotel, 7th St; set menu $95; ☽ dinner Mon-Sat) Down in the old cellars of the Grand Hotel is this candle-lit experience: five delightful northern Italian courses using local produce, with extras like mouth-freshening sorbets. Bookings essential.

## ENTERTAINMENT

Mildura has a small but lively nightlife scene. All the nightclubs are about two minutes' walk apart, so it's easy to find a change of scene or band.

Sandbar ( ☎ 5021 2181; www.thesandbar.com.au; cnr Langtree Ave & Eighth St; ☽ noon-late Tue-Sun) Hang out in the only licensed beer garden in town. Local, national, original and mainstream bands play on Thursday to Sunday nights.

Dom's Nightclub & Retro Bar ( ☎ 5021 3822; 28 Langtree Ave; meals $5-22; ☽ lunch & dinner Tue-Fri, nightclub till 2am Fri & Sat) Enjoy a luscious snack, then go upstairs (cover $7) to where the music is mostly dance.

Enjoywine ( ☎ 5023 7722; www.enjoywine.com.au; 120 Eighth St; ☽ 7am-late Mon-Sat, 7-10.30am Sun) In the lovely old Hotel Mildura you can taste the local wines until you decide which one to buy for dinner. It could take a while – there are 32 vineyards represented. Tastings are free (or wines per glass cost $5 to $7.50).

Deakin Twin Cinemas ( ☎ 5023 4452; movie hotline 1900 937 179; www.deakincinema.com.au; 93 Deakin Ave; tickets $9; ☽ from 1pm) Shows the latest mainstream films.

## SLEEPING

There are nearly 30 camping grounds and caravan parks around Mildura. It really is a holiday destination!

Staying on a houseboat is bliss. Over 20 companies hire houseboats that range from two- to 12-berth and from modest to luxurious. Most have a minimum hire of three days and prices increase dramatically in summer and during school holidays. Contact the visitors centre for details, or try these operators:

Acacia Houseboats ( ☎ 0428-787 250; www.acaciaboats .com.au; 3 nights from $580) Has many gorgeous houseboats (including the *Love Boat*) with everything supplied except food and drink.

Willandra Houseboats ( ☎ 5024 8867; www.willandra houseboats.com.au; 3 nights from $660) Has gourmet and golf getaways, or complete packages including airfares.

Sandors Motor Inn ( ☎ 1800 032 463, 5023 0047; www .sandorsmotorinn.com; 179 Deakin Ave; B&B s/d from $95/105; ☒ ☒ ) If you're driving into town hot and weary, turn into this attractive motel for a warm welcome, spacious rooms and cooling pool.

Mildura Golf Club Resort ( ☎ 1300 366 883; www.mildura golfclub.com.au, Twelfth St; s/d/f from $80/85/135; ☒ ☒ ) This is the place for golf enthusiasts, or those who enjoy lazing comfortably while others chase little white balls around. The rooms look out over the course, there's a barbecue area, great pools, abundant bird life, and a bar and bistro.

Grand Hotel ( ☎ 5023 0511; www.milduragrandhotel .com; Seventh St; B&B std/grand/ste $100/160/230; ✕ 📧 ) The different architectural styles of the Grand reflect Mildura's development. Although it's a gambling venue, there are pleasant rooms upstairs and many suites (like the Grand Suite; $280) open onto a delightful courtyard garden. There are bars and dining areas to suit every taste, including award-winning Stefano's down in the cellar.

Pied-à-terre ( ☎ 5022 9883; 97 Chaffey Ave; d $180, extra adult/child $30/10) *Pied-à-terre* is French for a home-away-from-home, but we doubt home ever looked this good! Five-bedroom, stylish and luxurious accommodation with all amenities, boat and car parking, barbecue area and holiday vibes. Ask about discounts.

# SWAN HILL
## pop 9700

Back in 1836, Major Mitchell, explorer and surveyor, was kept awake all night by swans on the nearby lagoon. So he named the spot Swan Hill. The area was settled by sheep graziers soon after, and the original homesteads of the two major properties in the area, Murray Downs and Tyntyndyer, are still looking magnificent. Swan Hill is a major regional centre surrounded by fertile irrigated farms that produce grapes and other fruits, yet it maintains the easy pace of a country town.

Swan Hill's major attraction is the Pioneer Settlement Museum ( ☎ 5036 2410; www.pioneersettle ment.com.au; Horseshoe Bend; adult/child/family $22/12/53; ⏱ 9.30am-4pm), a re-creation of a riverside port town of the paddle steamer era The settlement's displays include PS *Gem*, one of Australia's largest riverboats, a great collection of old carriages and buggies, and an old-time photographic parlour. The paddle steamer PS *Pyap* makes short cruises (adult/child/family $16/9.50/40.50) along the Murray at 10.30am and 2.30pm. Other attractions include vintage-car and wagon rides. Every night at dusk the 45-minute sound-and-light show (adult/child/family $16/9.50/40.50) entails a dramatic journey through the settlement in an open-air transporter.

Tyntyndyer Homestead ( ☎ 5030 2754; Murray Valley Hwy, Beverford; adult/child/family $8/4/20; ⏱ tours 10am-4pm Tue & Thu), 16km north of town, has a small museum and many reminders of the hardships of colonial life, such as the wine cellar! Visit at other times by appointment.

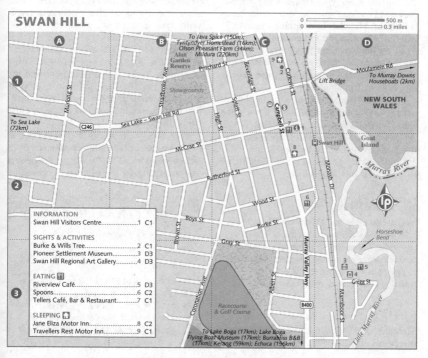

## THE BURKE & WILLS TREE

This magnificent Moreton Bay fig tree, the largest in the southern hemisphere, was planted in 1860, possibly by Burke himself. It was to commemorate the visit by Burke and Wills as they passed through Swan Hill on their ill-fated journey to the Gulf of Carpentaria. The planting was held at the home of Dr Gummow, who hosted the explorers and their party. Everyone expected the explorers to see the progress of their tree on their return visit, but they never made it back. The tree is on Curlewis St opposite the bowling green.

The Swan Hill Regional Art Gallery ( ☎ 5036 2430; www.swanhill.vic.gov.au/gallery; Horseshoe Bend; admission by donation; ⏰ 10am-5pm Tue-Sun), opposite the Pioneer Settlement Museum, concentrates on the works of contemporary artists.

The famous Catalina flying boat *A24-30* is on display, outside a secret communications bunker, just 16km away at Lake Boga Flying Boat Museum ( ☎ 5037 2850; www.oldcmp.net/lake_boga .html; Catalina Park; adult/child/family $6/2.50/12; ⏰ 9.30am-4pm). Flying boats were repaired at Lake Boga during WWII.

The Golden Mile Wine Trail is a section along the Murray River where major wine companies and boutique wineries offer cellar-door tastings and lunches overlooking the river. It will indeed make you feel golden! Wine festivals are held here every October, including the Australian Inland Wine Show (www.inlandwine.com; ⏰ 3rd weekend Oct). The region's motto: 'Life is too short to drink bad wine.'

For one fabulous jaunt, get a map and drive out to Olson Pheasant Farm ( ☎ 5030 2648; www.game birds.com.au; 2167 Chillingollah Rd; adult/child/family $7/4/18; ⏰ 10am-4pm), where game birds are reared, native birds are on display and peacocks wander around looking gorgeous. Take a picnic or ring ahead if you'd like lunch.

## INFORMATION

Swan Hill visitors centre ( ☎ 1800 625 373, 5032 3033; www.swanhillonline.com; cnr McCrae & Curlewis Sts; ⏰ 9am-5.30pm Mon-Fri, to 5pm Sat & Sun; 🖳 ) Crammed with helpful maps and brochures. Book tickets for concerts, and find out where to go to taste olives, pistachios, orchard produce and, of course, wines.

## EATING

The café scene is on Campbell St where everyone heads on Sunday morning.

Spoons ( ☎ 5032 2601; 387 Campbell St; meals $6-16; ⏰ breakfast & lunch) A small, award-winning deli with inside/outside eating areas, and delicious risottos, salads, curries and couscous dishes.

Riverview Café ( ☎ 5032 1231; Monash Dr; meals $9-14; ⏰ breakfast & lunch Tue-Sun) Sit at big log tables and watch the mighty Murray zap past. The food is good and the service quick.

Tellers Café, Bar & Restaurant ( ☎ 5033 1383; 223 Campbell St; mains $14-28; ⏰ lunch & dinner Mon-Sat) Named 'Tellers' because it's inside an old bank, this friendly place uses all-local produce.

Java Spice ( ☎ 5033 0511; 17 Beveridge St; mains $19-25; ⏰ lunch Thu-Fri, dinner Tue-Sun) New and exciting, set-up as a southeast Asian village and getting an amazing reputation for its cuisine.

## SLEEPING

There are no grand hotels or quaint B&Bs right in town, but you'll find plenty of very pleasant places to stay.

Jane Eliza Motor Inn ( ☎ 5032 4411; jeliza@swanhill.net .au; 263 Campbell St; s/d/f $86/100/190; ✂ 🐕 ) The lady is getting old, but the position is excellent and the staff friendly.

Travellers Rest Motor Inn ( ☎ 5032 9644; www.bestwest ern.com.au/travellersrest; 110 Curlewis St; s/d/f $99/109/125) Sits gloriously in the shade of the Burke & Wills Tree, giving you a good feeling, as do the comfortable rooms.

Burrabliss B&B ( ☎ 5037 2527; www.burrabliss.com .au; 169 Lakeside Dr, Lake Boga; d/ste $115/150) It's only 10 minutes' drive out to Lake Boga and the luxury of the fabulous B&B. Go with your hosts to see their ultra-fine-wool sheep, birdwatch in the wetlands, or walk by the lake and enjoy the gardens.

Murray Downs Houseboats ( ☎ 5032 2160, 0428-500 066; www.murrayriver.com.au/houseboats/murraydowns; 8-/12-berth per 3 nights from $700/1950). This is the perfect way to experience the Murray. High-season

## TRANSPORT: SWAN HILL

Distance from Melbourne 337km

Direction Northwest

Travel times 3½ hours

Bus & Train V/Line ( ☎ 13 61 96; www.vline.com .au) runs trains between Melbourne and Swan Hill (return $57, four hours, three daily), and some train/coach services with a change at Bendigo.

Car See p336.

## ECHUCA

**pop 12,400**

Echuca (pronounced 'E-*choo*-ka', meaning 'the meeting of the waters') is where three great rivers meet – the Goulburn, Campaspe and the Murray. There's history in these waters. Some of Australia's earliest explorers, including Thomas Mitchell, Charles Sturt and Edward Eyre travelled along the Murray. Long before roads and railways crossed the land, the Murray's paddle steamers carried supplies and carted wool to and from remote sheep stations and homesteads, travelling for hundreds of miles along the Murray's winding waterways, and up and down the Murrumbidgee, Goulburn and Darling Rivers.

The town was founded in 1853 by ex-convict Harry Hopwood. He settled on the banks of the Murray, converted some rough sheds into an inn and store, then established punt and ferry crossings over the Murray and Campaspe Rivers. With his transport monopoly and the gold rush in full swing, he profited handsomely! Hopwood built the Bridge Hotel in 1858, and lived his remaining years in Echuca as a wealthy man, watching his town grow into the busiest inland port in Australia.

At the peak of the riverboat era there were more than 100 paddle steamers carting wool, timber and other goods between Echuca and the outback sheep stations. Lined with shops and hotels, the famous red-gum wharf was just over 1km long.

It was too good to last: the Melbourne–Echuca railway line opened in 1864, and within a decade the boom years of the riverboat trade had ended.

These days Echuca has some fascinating tourist attractions plus water-skiing, swimming, paddle steamer cruises and houseboat holidays.

The most wonderful thing about Echuca is its Historic Port (cnr Leslie St & Murray Esp; passport adult/child/family $12/8/35, with paddleboat cruise $27/13.50/72; 9am-5pm, tours 11.15am). Attractions are spread along the waterfront, and you buy a passport at the entrance that admits you to the three main sections: Echuca Wharf, the Star Hotel and the Bridge Hotel. Everything is original – you're exploring living history as you walk along the pedestrian-only Murray Esplanade. Complimentary (and very entertaining) guided tours with Buster and Rocky the cocky set out from the gift shop.

Behind the entrance is Echuca Wharf. In the wharf's cargo shed, there's a surprisingly interesting audiovisual presentation and dioramas depicting life on the riverboats. Walk along the various levels of the massive wharf and onto the restored historic paddle steamers: PS *Pevensey* (built in 1911) and PS *Adelaide* (1866), which are moored alongside. The wharf was built with three tiers because of the changing river levels. There are gauges marking the highest points.

Back on the Esplanade, stop in at the Star Hotel (1867) and escape through the underground tunnel, which helped drinkers avoid the police during the years when the pub was a 'sly grog shop'. Hang about for breakfast or lunch in the café, or come to hear live music on Friday and Saturday nights.

On Hopwood Pl at the far end is the Bridge Hotel, where your ticket admits you to a historic upstairs gallery. The pub now operates as a restaurant and bistro.

Sharp's Magic Movie House & Penny Arcade ( ☎ 5482 2361; www.sharpsmoviehouse.com.au; Murray Esp; adult/child/family $15/10/45; 9am-5pm) has authentic and fully restored penny-arcade machines – you're given a fist-full of pennies. Free fudge tasting is another blast from the past. The movie house shows old movies such as Buster Keaton or Laurel & Hardy classics using original equipment. Your ticket is valid all day so you can come and go; nick through the back door to the Olive Company ( ☎ 5482 2361; 622 High St; 9am-5pm) to see a range of local products.

Other port-area sights include Red Gum Works (Murray Esp; admission free; 9am-4pm), a historic sawmill that recreates old timber-milling days. Watch wood-turners and blacksmiths work with traditional equipment, and purchase red-gum products.

A paddle steamer cruise (Murray Esp; 45min cruise adult/child/family $16/7.50/43.50, 1hr cruise $19.50/8/50) here is almost obligatory. Buy tickets from the port entrance or along the Esplanade, and ask for the brochure on the boats' histories. Check out the timetable for lunch and dinner, twilight and sunset cruises. At least six paddle steamers offer cruises:

PS Adelaide ( ☎ 5482 4248) The oldest wooden-hulled paddle steamer still operating anywhere in the world.

PS Alexander Arbuthnot ( ☎ 5482 4248)

PS Canberra ( ☎ 5482 2711)

PS Emmylou ( ☎ 5480 2237) Fully restored and driven by an original engine.

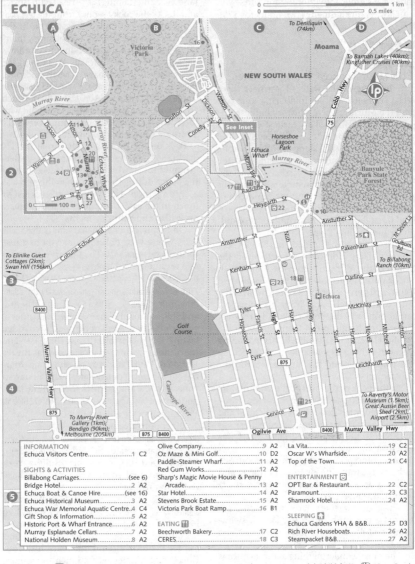

ECHUCA

| INFORMATION | | |
|---|---|---|
| Echuca Visitors Centre | 1 | C2 |
| **SIGHTS & ACTIVITIES** | | |
| Billabong Carriages | (see 6) | |
| Bridge Hotel | 2 | A2 |
| Echuca Boat & Canoe Hire | (see 16) | |
| Echuca Historical Museum | 3 | A2 |
| Echuca War Memorial Aquatic Centre | 4 | C4 |
| Gift Shop & Information | 5 | A2 |
| Historic Port & Wharf Entrance | 6 | A2 |
| Murray Esplanade Cellars | 7 | A2 |
| National Holden Museum | 8 | A2 |
| Olive Company | 9 | A2 |
| Oz Maze & Mini Golf | 10 | D2 |
| Paddle-Steamer Wharf | 11 | A2 |
| Red Gum Works | 12 | A2 |
| Sharp's Magic Movie House & Penny Arcade | 13 | A2 |
| Star Hotel | 14 | A2 |
| Stevens Brook Estate | 15 | A2 |
| Victoria Park Boat Ramp | 16 | B1 |
| **EATING** 🍴 | | |
| Beechworth Bakery | 17 | C2 |
| CERES | 18 | C3 |
| La Vita | 19 | C2 |
| Oscar W's Wharfside | 20 | A2 |
| Top of the Town | 21 | C4 |
| **ENTERTAINMENT** 🎭 | | |
| OPT Bar & Restaurant | 22 | C2 |
| Paramount | 23 | C3 |
| Shamrock Hotel | 24 | A2 |
| **SLEEPING** 🛏 | | |
| Echuca Gardens YHA & B&B | 25 | D3 |
| Rich River Houseboats | 26 | A2 |
| Steampacket B&B | 27 | A2 |

PS Pevensey ( ☎ 5482 4248)

PS Pride of the Murray ( ☎ 5482 5244)

MV Mary Ann ( ☎ 5480 2200; Murray Esp; 1½hr cruise adult/child $45/10) is a cruising restaurant. Prices include a two-course meal and entertainment. Call ahead for dining times.

Breeze around the port in style in a horse-drawn coach with Billabong Carriages ( ☎ 5483 5122; www.justhorses.com.au; adult/child $6/5; ⏱ 10am-2pm). Get your tickets on the coach. Love it? Then take a scenic wine tour ($65) out to Cape Horn Vineyard for the day.

There are free tastings of local wines at Murray Esplanade Cellars ( ☎ 5482 6058; Old Customs House, Murray Esp; ⏱ 10am-5.30pm) and at Stevens Brook Estate ( ☎ 5480 1916; www.stevensbrookwines.com; 620 High St; ⏱ 10am-6pm) around the corner.

Echuca Historical Museum ( ☎ 5480 1325; 1 Dickson St; adult/child $3.50/1; ⊙ 11am-3pm) is in the old police station, classified by the National Trust. It has a collection of local history items, charts and photos from the riverboat era, and early records.

Murray River Gallery ( ☎ 5482 3608; 8774 Northern Hwy; entry free; ⊙ 10am-5pm Thu-Mon), an Aboriginal fine-art gallery, helps you read the message in each piece (art was used for story-telling in the past).

Car buffs should check out the National Holden Museum ( ☎ 5480 2033; www.holdenmuseum.com.au; 7 Warren St; adult/child $6/3; ⊙ 9am-5pm), which has over 40 beautifully restored Holdens and associated memorabilia. Then head off to see Raverty's Motor Museum ( ☎ 5482 2730; 33 Ogilvie Ave; adult/child $5/1; ⊙ 9.30am-5pm), where vehicles date from 1900.

A spot of real culture is at the Great Aussie Beer Shed ( ☎ 5480 6904; www.greataussiebeershed.com.au; 337 Mary Ann Rd; adult/child/family $9.50/3.50/20; ⊙ 9am-5pm Sat & Sun). Expect wall-to-wall beer cans (one dating back to Federation), guided tours and an interesting display of old equipment.

To get out on the Murray, Echuca Boat & Canoe Hire ( ☎ 5480 6208; www.echucaboatcanoehire.com; Victoria Park Boat Ramp) hires out tinnies ($40/60 per one/two hours), 'barbyboats' (10 people $100/135), kayaks ($16/26) and canoes ($20/30). Multiday hires also available. Around on the Goulburn River are canoe safaris or canoe hire with River Country Adventours ( ☎ 0428-585 227; www.adventours.com.au; half-/full-/2-day safaris $55/88/125).

Several operators offer water-skiing trips and classes. Very popular is Brett Sands Watersports ( ☎ 5482 1851; www.brettsands.com; half/full day $140/220), which will teach you skills behind a boat on skis, wake board, knee board or barefoot.

Magnificent Barmah Lakes offers something totally different. Head out to the visitors area where Kingfisher Cruises ( ☎ 5480 1839; www.kingfisher cruises.com.au; adult/child/family $25/18/82; ⊙ Sun, Mon, Wed, Thu & Sat) glides you along in a flat-bottom boat through Australia's largest river red-gum forest and Barmah's World Heritage–listed wetlands. Your captain points out bird and mammal species along the way. Ring for departure times and bookings.

For horse riding along rivers or through the bush, contact Billabong Trail Rides ( ☎ 0428-507 828; www.justhorses.com.au; per hr/half-day $35/80), which also has rides for kids and a pub ride. Go out to the Billabong Ranch ( ☎ 5483 5122; www.just horses.com.au; 2831 Tehan Rd; adult/child/family $25/22/75; ⊙ 10am-3pm Mon-Fri, 9am-5pm Sat & Sun) for a fun day. There's minigolf, pedal boats, an animal nursery, tenpin bowling, a playground, a café,

## TRANSPORT: ECHUCA

**Distance from Melbourne** 220km

**Direction** North

**Travel times** 2½ hours

**Bus & Train** V/Line ( ☎ 13 61 96; www.vline.com .au) has direct Melbourne–Echuca train and bus services (return $40, 3½ hours, seven daily), plus combo train/bus services with changes at Bendigo, Murchison or Shepparton.

**Car** See p336.

bar and pony rides, amongst other things like off-road buggies ($30 per 15 minutes).

The Echuca War Memorial Aquatic Centre ( ☎ 5480 2994; cnr High & Service Sts; adult/child/family $5/3.50/11.50; ⊙ 6am-8pm Mon-Fri, 9am-6pm Sat & Sun) is crystal-bright, with heated pool, spa, sauna and gym.

Take to the air with Aus-Air ( ☎ 5480 3100; www .ausair.com; Echuca Airport; flights from $110), which offers all sorts of fun trips over the rivers. Air Nostalgia ( ☎ 0428-991 309; www.airnostalgia.com.au) flies you to Echuca from Melbourne in a 1940s DC3, takes you for a cruise on an old paddle steamer, then flies you back to Melbourne.

Just to ground you, try to find your way around Oz Maze & Mini Golf ( ☎ 5480 2220; www.ozmaze .com.au; cnr Heygarth & Annesley Sts; maze or golf adult/child/family $8.50/7.50/30, maze & golf $15/14/54; ⊙ 10am-4pm Wed-Mon).

## INFORMATION

Echuca visitors centre ( ☎ 1800 804 446, 5480 7555; www.echucamoama.com; 2 Heygarth St; ⊙ 9am-5pm) Has an accommodation booking service.

Murray River website (www.murrayriver.com.au) Stacks of useful information.

## TOURS

It's holiday time up here, so relax and be looked after.

Echuca Limo Tours ( ☎ 0418-509 493; www.echucalimo tours.com.au; tours per person 2½/4hr $69/99) Visit wineries and enjoy cheese platters or lunch.

Echuca Moama Wine Tours ( ☎ 5480 1839; www.echuca moamawinetours.com.au; tours $75) Winery visits and a cruise along the Murray. Reduced tour prices for children.

Happy Hookers ( ☎ 0427-466 547; half-day adult/child/family $95/60/260) Helps you feed the fish.

Murray River Fishing Tours ( ☎ 0418-576 526; www
.geocities.com/fishforcod; half-day adult/child/family
$80/40/240) Takes you out in a shaded boat.

# FESTIVALS & EVENTS

There are many events and activities in
Echuca. Check the online calendar at www
.echucamoama.com/html/whatson.htm.

Club Marine Southern 80 (www.southern80.com.au) The
world's largest water-skiing race; held in February.

Riverboats Jazz Food & Wine Festival (www.echuca
moama.com/jazz) Music, food and wine by the Murray;
held in late February.

Steam, Horse & Vintage Rally (www.echucasteamrally
.com.au) On the Queen's Birthday weekend in June; classic
and historic vehicles powered by all imaginable methods.

# EATING

High and Hare Sts both have a collection of bakeries, cafés, restaurants, pubs and takeaways.

Beechworth Bakery ( ☎ 5480 1057; 513 High St; meals
$5-12; ☽ breakfast & lunch) An open, cheerful place
with delicious sandwiches and home-baked
goodies. Find a seat on the deck overlooking
the rippling Campaspe River.

La Vita ( ☎ 5482 6688; 554 High St; mains $16-38; ☽ lunch
Sat & Sun, dinner nightly) A sparkling Italian place with
a great atrium and award-winning dishes.

CERES ( ☎ 5482 5599; Nish St; tapas $3-10, mains $27-
39; ☽ lunch & dinner) An atmospheric place with
an innovative menu, top chef, all-day coffee
and tapas and a lounge bar, all in an historic
1881 flour mill.

Oscar W's Wharfside ( ☎ 5482 5133; 101 Murray Esp;
mains $28-35; ☽ lunch & dinner) Enjoy the only res-
taurant in the whole world that overlooks the
Murray! Maybe not true, but still, the view is
magic. The food here is delicious, the prices
reasonable and the wine list extensive.

Top of the Town ( ☎ 5482 4600; cnr High & Service Sts;
fish & chips $11; ☽ 10am-8pm) This claims to be the
best fish-and-chip shop in the state. It has a
good range including river fish (redfin, yellow-
belly), crays and oysters.

# ENTERTAINMENT

Shamrock Hotel ( ☎ 5482 1036; 583 High St; ☽ 10am-
11pm Mon-Fri, 10-2am Sat & Sun) There are quite a
few good pubs in town. This one has a big
welcome, Guinness and live music.

OPT Bar & Restaurant ( ☎ 5480 0150; 272 Hare St; ☽ bar
from 5pm Tue-Sat, nightclub to 4am Fri & Sat) This is the

place to be, with its mezzanine dining and live
music on weekends. Downstairs is a dance
band, upstairs a DJ.

Paramount ( ☎ 1900 931 166; 392 High St; adult/child
$13.50/9.50; ☽ from 10.30am) Has daily screen-
ings of mainstream movies and occasional
live shows.

# SLEEPING

Echuca has accommodation everywhere, from
quaint B&Bs to spacious caravan parks, huge
brick motels and old lace-trimmed hotels. Alternatively, experience river life on a houseboat – they sleep from four to 12, and are fully
equipped with facilities including sundecks and
TVs. Rates vary according to season and size of
boat; the visitors centre has full details.

Echuca Gardens YHA & B&B ( ☎ 5480 6522; echucagar
dens@iinet.net.au; 103 Mitchell St; dm/d $30/70, B&B d 1/2
nights $130/195) A 145-year-old workers' cottage
with tiny bedrooms, smart bathrooms, country kitchen and TV room. The garden has
ponds, statues, chooks and fruit trees. There's
also an exotic B&B where rooms are works
of art and breakfast is served amongst potted
plants. Owner Kym can tell you where to go
and entertain you with local anecdotes.

Steampacket B&B ( ☎ 5482 3411; fax 5482 3408; cnr
Murray Esplanade & Leslie St; B&B s/d from $98/135) Right
by the old port in a National Trust–classified
building, the rooms here have views of the
activities on the wharf, taking you right back in
time. The lounge room is cosy and breakfast is
served on fine china. It's even kid-friendly.

Elinike Guest Cottages ( ☎ 5480 6311; www.elinike.com
.au; 209 Latham Rd; B&B d 1/2 nights $185/320) Quaint
cottages set in rambling gardens on the
Murray River, totally private and gorgeous,
blending old-world romance with modern
conveniences like double spas. The lilac cottage ($195) has a glass-roofed garden room.

Rich River Houseboats ( ☎ 1800 032 643; www.rich
riverhouseboats.com.au; Riverboat Dock; 4 nights from $660)
Right in town, with a range of beautiful boats.
Packages include a stay-put deal (sleeping at
the dock) for $200 per couple. Now that's
easy, and the views are spectacular!

# YARRAWONGA

## pop 5700

If you like sunny weather, activities like wind-
surfing, swimming, power boating and water-
skiing, lots of parks and a laid-back, slightly
surreal atmosphere, then Yarrawonga is for

you. It has more sunshine hours than almost anywhere else in Australia.

When Elizabeth Hume's husband was killed by bushrangers, she moved here and built Byramine Homestead ( ☎ 5748 4321; Murray Valley Hwy; adult/child/family $4.50/2.50/14; lunch $15; ☺ 10am-4pm Sun-Thu) in 1842 – a safe haven which saw her become the first permanent European settler in the area. The homestead is shaped like a fortress and is set in magnificent grounds, just 14km west of town. Enjoy a ploughman's lunch or Devonshire tea under a very grand old tree.

Back in town, the Clock Museum ( ☎ 5744 1249; 21 Lynch St; admission $4.50; ☺ 10am-4.30pm Sat-Thu) has hundreds of clocks simultaneously ticking and tocking – encouraging or ominous, your life ticking away…

Lake Mulwala, the centre of much activity and entertainment, has great parks along its shores, with picnic and barbecue areas. The lake was formed during the project to harness the waters of the Murray for irrigation. Every few years the lake is drained for weir maintenance purposes – the empty lake is an eerie sight.

Two cruise boats – the Lady Murray ( ☎ 0412-573 460) and the Paradise Queen ( ☎ 0418-508 616) – take you cruising along the lake and the Murray River, pointing out historic spots and bird life. Both have 1½-hour barbecue cruises ($20) at noon, scenic cruises ($12) at 2pm, and dinner cruises during summer.

Yarrawonga Outdoors ( ☎ 5744 3522; www.yarrawongaoutdoors.com.au; 21 Belmore St; ☺ 9am-5.30pm Mon-Fri, to 12.30pm Sat, open some Sun) hires out kayaks ($45), wake-board gear ($50) and bikes ($20). To really discover the lake and river, take one of their half-day guided kayak tours ($80). Ask about romantic overnight B&B paddles.

Wander along the foreshore to see where the cruise boats leave. There's a pool and waterslide here to tempt you, and Ski Rides ( ☎ 0419-211 122; www.skirides.com.au; per 30min $50) which runs water-skiing lessons and sessions. Other boat-towed thrills include tubing, or hire a canoe ($40 per half-day) or fishing boat ($60).

Feeling a bit up in the air? Take a scenic flight with Jarden Aviation ( ☎ 5743 3636, 0409-008 960; www.jardenaviation.com.au; Yarrawonga Airport; flights 15/25min $45/65) to see vineyards, snowfields and the mighty Murray. Good deals for children travelling with adults.

## INFORMATION

Yarrawonga visitors centre ( ☎ 1800 062 260, 5744 1989; www.yarrawongamulwala.com.au; Irvine Pde; ☺ 9am-5pm) By the lake; you can book accommodation and tours here for no charge.

## EATING

There's a fantastic café scene on Belmore St, with lots of outdoor seating from which to enjoy the sunshine and people-watching while modern, fresh food is prepared for you.

Nosh Deli ( ☎ 5744 1756; 42 Belmore St; meals $7-12; ☺ breakfast & lunch) Busy, bright and beautiful. Good coffee too.

Four Winds ( ☎ 5743 3533; cnr Murray Valley Hwy & Woods Rd; mains $15-20; ☺ dinner Tue-Sun) New in town and all the rave, this Thai restaurant is in an old house next to Pistols Sports Tavern. Essential eating.

Coops Restaurant & Wine Bar ( ☎ 5743 1922; 137 Belmore St; mains $15-31; ☺ breakfast & lunch daily, dinner Wed-Sun) Great for dining, quick snacks or just a leisurely drink at the bar. On Wednesday and Thursday there's a $20 two-course special.

## SLEEPING

There are lots of caravan parks, motels and time-share resorts in Yarrawonga.

Terminus Hotel ( ☎ 5744 3025; fax 5743 2725; 95 Belmore St; s/d from $50/65) This popular old pub has spacious rooms, a grand balcony and fresh bathrooms, and the lounge area has a TV and kitchen appliances. Downstairs, there's lunch and dinner available in the bistro.

Lakeview Motel ( ☎ 5744 1555; fax 5743 1327; 1 Hunt St; s/d/f $85/95/130; ☒ ☒ ) It looks out onto the lake, has spacious attractive rooms and the rates are very reasonable. Large pool, cable TV. Top spot.

Coghill Cottages ( ☎ 5744 2271; www.coghill.com.au; 6 Coghill St; d/f $95/150; ☒ ☒ ) It's close to the lake and the cottages are smart and modern.

---

**TRANSPORT: YARRAWONGA**

Distance from Melbourne 290km

Direction North

Travel times 3¼ hours

Bus/Train V/Line ( ☎ 13 61 96; www.vline.com.au) train/coach services run between Melbourne and Yarrawonga (return $46, four hours, three daily) with a change at Benalla.

Car See p336.

Murray Valley Resort ( ☎ 5744 1844; www.murrayvalley resort.com.au; Murray Valley Hwy; s/d from $120/145; 🅿 🅿 ) The amazing facilities here include a gym, indoor and outdoor pools, tennis courts, billiard tables and spas. The accommodation is modern with soft colours and lots of space.

# RUTHERGLEN

**pop 2000**

A food-and-wine buff's paradise, Rutherglen is at the centre of one of Victoria's major wine-growing districts. As well as being a popular base for touring the wineries, the town has a Main St that is an historic precinct, lined with weathered timber buildings, antique and bric-a-brac shops, tearooms and veranda-fronted pubs.

The Common School Museum ( ☎ 1800 622 871, 02-6033 6300; 57 Main St; admission $2; 🕙 1-4pm Sun) has an amazing range of weights and measures, local inventions, period pieces and school equipment.

A great way to take a winery tour is with Rutherglen Stretch Limousine ( ☎ 02-6032 7317; www .rutherglenlimousines.com.au). The limo takes up to 11 passengers, picnic hampers can be provided, and half- or full-day tours arranged.

Head out of town to the stunning All Saints Estate ( ☎ 02-6035 2222; www.allsaintswine.com.au; All Saints Rd, Wahgunyah; 🕙 9am-5.30pm). There's an atmospheric cellar-door in a 120-year-old castle, and in the front building Indigo Cheese Co offers tastings of gourmet cheeses and other produce from the region. Between them, The Terrace ( ☎ 02-6033 1922; meals $28-32; 🕙 lunch daily, dinner Sat) serves meals showcasing local produce.

Return to town along Hopetoun Rd and call into the Wicked Virgin ( ☎ 02-6032 7022; www.the wickedvirgin.com; Calico Town, 165 Hopetoun Rd; lunch $8-15; 🕙 10am-4pm Thu-Mon) to taste their delicious fresh olives and oils and enjoy a light lunch (soups

## TRANSPORT: RUTHERGLEN

Distance from Melbourne 290km

Direction Northeast

Travel time Three hours

Bus/Train V/Line ( ☎ 13 61 96; www.vline.com.au) has a train/coach service between Melbourne and Rutherglen with a change at Wangaratta (return $50, four hours, four weekly).

Car See p336.

and platters). It's at Calico Town, a picturesque vineyard producing an exclusive range of wines including an award-winning shiraz.

A few blocks south of Main St is Scion ( ☎ 02-6032 8844; www.scionvineyard.com; 74 Slaughterhouse Rd; 🕙 10am-5pm Sat & Sun), a cellar-door with an art exhibition and a small range of boutique wines.

## INFORMATION

Rutherglen visitors centre ( ☎ 1800 622 871, 02-6033 6300; www.rutherglenvic.com.au; 57 Main St; 🕙 9am-5pm) A fun place where you'll get all the info you need.

## FESTIVALS & EVENTS

There are special events on almost every weekend here, all featuring a wide range of activities, especially focussed around eating and drinking. For details on the following events see www.rutherglenvic.com/events.

Tastes of Rutherglen Two weekends of total indulgence with food-and-wine packages at dozens of vineyards and restaurants; held in March.

Winery Walkabout Weekend Australia's original wine festival – there's music, barrel racing and probably some wine; held in June.

---

### DETOUR: WAHGUNYAH

Just northeast of Rutherglen on the Murray River is the idyllic little township of Wahgunyah (population 800). At the height of the riverboat era, Wahgunyah was a thriving port town and trade depot. Now, renowned wineries such as All Saints Estate (above), St Leonards and Pfeiffers surround it – wining and dining here is fantastic.

In town is the fabulous old Wahgunyah Empire Hotel ( ☎ 02-6033 1094; 6 Foord Street), where Fairy's (mains $14-23; 🕙 lunch & dinner daily) serves traditional fare with fresh veggies. The perfect place to stay is Riverside Waterfront Motel ( ☎ 02-6033 1177; www.riversidemotel.com.au; Cadel Tce; s/d $85/95; 🅿 ), where sparkling units lead out onto the grassy banks of the Murray. Rates include a light breakfast, plus there's a communal kitchen and barbecue – and a courtesy car!

While you're here, visit the Cofield winery for tastings and a pleasant meal in the Pickled Sisters Café ( ☎ 02-6033 2377; Distillery Rd, Wahgunyah; mains $19-28; 🕙 lunch Wed-Mon year-round, dinner Fri & Sat Dec-Feb).

**Rutherglen Agriculture & Wine Show** Don't miss this late-September show: a cowbell is rung at 7am to signal a mad rush as all wines are $8.

**Tour de Rutherglen** A cycling event with a purpose; held in early October.

**Winemakers' Legends Weekend** The new generation of winemakers mix it with the legends to provide picnics, markets, feasts and wine; held in late October.

## EATING

There are cafés all along Main St, and takeaway places to fill a picnic hamper.

**Rendezvous Courtyard** ( ☎ 02-6032 9114; 68 Main St; mains $24-27; ☾ dinner) A traditional menu where the décor is pleasantly casual.

**Tuileries Restaurant** ( ☎ 02-6032 9033; 13 Drummond St; mains $25-32; ☾ dinner) Lots of glass around a fountain, and fine dining in an attractive restaurant. On the other side of the fountain, the café has equally exciting lunches ($10 to $16) and top-quality breakfasts. Around the vineyard here, luxury B&B units cost from $175 for two.

**House at Mount Prior** ( ☎ 02-6026 5256; www.house atmountprior.com.au; 1194 Gooramadda Rd; mains $12-25; ☾ lunch & dinner) On a hill above the Mt Prior winery, this homestead even has a tower. Have drinks at dusk on the veranda then move into the elegant dining room for a delicious three-course set meal ($55). Stay the night in a stun-

ning room with soaring ceilings from $110 per double.

## SLEEPING

Accommodation here is likely to be tight during major festivals when rates are, of course, higher. They're also seriously higher on weekends and public holidays.

**Victoria Hotel** ( ☎ 02-6032 8610; www.victoriahotel rutherglen.com.au; 90 Main St; s $35 d with/without bathroom $65/40) This beautiful National Trust–classified place has several little, old rooms. Grab a front room with bathroom and views over Main St, and live like a king. The wide, lace-trimmed balcony is the perfect spot to discuss wine.

**Motel Woongarra** ( ☎ 02-6032 9588; www.motelwoon garra.com.au; cnr Main & Drummond Sts; s/d/f $77/88/104; ☒ ☒ ) You'll love the special touches, like the carafe of port on your dresser.

**Carlyle House** ( ☎ 02-6032 8444; www.carlylehouse .com.au; 147 High St; B&B r/ste from $155/185) Spread your wings in a garden apartment, or nestle amongst the antiques inside the beautifully restored house. The breakfast is excellent.

# THE WAY NORTH
## UP THROUGH THE MALLEE

Coming from the south where the trees are tall, the Mallee appears as flat horizon and

---

### CHILTERN

Tiny Chiltern (population 1100) is one of Victoria's most historic and charming colonial townships. The streetscape is so authentic that the town is often used as a film set for period pieces, including the early Walt Disney classic *Ride a Wild Pony*. Originally called Black Dog Creek, it was established in 1851 and prospered when gold was discovered here in 1859.

Ask Beryl at the Chiltern visitors centre ( ☎ 5726 1611; www.chiltern.com.au; 30 Main St; ☾ 10am-4pm) about bird-watching in the nearby Chiltern-Mt Pilot National Park, and pick up the *Chiltern Touring Guide*, which walks you around 14 labelled sites (or go to www.albury.net.au/~tim/chwalk.htm). The following National Trust–classified buildings (www.nattrust.com.au; adult/child $2/free) you'll pass on this route are staffed by volunteers who open them most days, but ring and make an appointment to be sure:

Athenaeum Library & Museum ( ☎ 5726 1467; www.chilternathenaeum.com.au; Conness St), in the former Town Hall (1866), has a collection of memorabilia, art, photos and equipment from the gold-rush days.

Dow's Pharmacy ( ☎ 5726 1597; Conness St) has lotions and potions from the early days; it's been a chemist since 1859.

Lake View Homestead ( ☎ 5726 1317; Victoria St) was built in 1870 and overlooks Lake Anderson. It was the home of Henry Handel (Florence Ethel) Richardson, who wrote about life here in the book *Ultima Thule* (1929), the third part of her trilogy *The Fortunes of Richard Mahony* (1930).

Star/Grapevine Theatre ( ☎ 5726 1395; cnr Main & Conness Sts), once used for plays and dances, was the centrepiece of Chiltern's social and cultural life. It's now a museum filled with memorabilia. The grapevine in the courtyard is the largest in Australia.

When you've explored the town, check out the surrounding countryside on a friendly horse with Mt Pilot Trail Rides ( ☎ 5726 1655; mtpilotfarm@hotmail.com; Toveys Rd; 1hr rides $35).

## TRANSPORT: THE WAY NORTH

Distance from Melbourne Ouyen/Mallee Hwy 460km, Shepparton 180km, Wodonga 300km

Direction Northwest, north, northeast

Travel times Six hours, two hours, 3½ hours

Air Regional Express Airlines (Rex; ☎ 13 17 13; www.regionalexpress.com.au) flies between Melbourne and Albury-Wodonga (return from $200, 45 minutes, daily).

Bus & Train V/Line ( ☎ 13 61 96; www.vline.com.au) runs a coach through the Mallee to Mildura ($70, 9¾ hours, one daily). Trains run between Melbourne and Shepparton, stopping at Seymour (return $34, 2½ hours, two daily). V/Line train/coach services to Wodonga (return $39, three hours, daily) follow the Hume Fwy, stopping at Seymour, Euroa, Benalla and Wangaratta. CountryLink ( ☎ 13 22 32; www.countrylink.info) trains have an XPT (express) service to Albury-Wodonga ($134, 3¼ hours, two daily); reservations required.

Car Heading north through the Mallee is a fast drive on open roads: take the Calder Hwy through Bendigo, or the Western Hwy to Ballarat then the Sunraysia Hwy. The Hume Fwy takes you over the Great Divide to Seymour. Exit the Goulburn Hwy 10km from Seymour for the Goulburn Valley, Shepparton and Echuca, or continue north on the Hume Fwy to Wodonga. The Northern Hwy from Kilmore is a smooth run to Echuca.

endless, undulating, twisted mallee scrub. A mallee is a hardy eucalypt with multiple slender trunks. Its roots are twisted, gnarled, dense chunks of wood, famous for their slow-burning qualities and much sought after by wood-turners. Mallee gums are canny desert survivors – root systems over 1000 years old are not uncommon – and are part of a diverse and rich biosystem with waterbirds, fish in the huge (but unreliable) lakes, kangaroos and other marsupials, emus, and the many edible plants that thrive in this environment.

When the railway line from Melbourne to Mildura was completed in 1902, much of the region was divided into small blocks for farming. The first Europeans had terrible problems trying to clear the land. They used mullenising (crushing the scrub with heavy red-gum rollers pulled by teams of bullocks, then burning and ploughing the land). But after rain, the tough old mallee roots regenerated and flourished. Farmers also had to deal with rabbit and mouse plagues, sand drifts and long droughts. Today the Mallee is a productive sheep-grazing and grain-growing district, with more exotic crops, such as lentils, also appearing.

You know you've reached the northwest when the land extends forever, skies are vast, rivers lazy and the sun is always meltingly hot. It's dry here, although the creeks and lake beds did fill three times in the last 100 years. The attractions (other than huge horizons and friendly little towns) are the semi-arid wilderness areas, such as Wyperfeld National Park, Big Desert Wilderness Park and Murray-Sunset National Park. Collectively these parks cover over 750,000 hectares, and are particularly notable for their abundance of native plants, spring wild flowers and birds. This is 'Sunset Country', the one genuinely empty part of the state. Nature-lovers might delight in it, but it's frighteningly inaccessible, except to experienced bushmen with wide hats and wider water bottles, in their high-clearance 4WDs.

## Hattah-Kulkyne National Park

The vegetation of the beautiful and diverse Hattah-Kulkyne National Park ranges from dry, sandy mallee-scrub country to the fertile riverside areas closer to the Murray, which are lined with red gum, black box, wattle and bottlebrush.

When the area was proposed as a park in 1976, it was the most rabbit-infested part of the state. The rabbits were largely eradicated, but now the 20,000-odd local population of kangaroos are wrecking the fragile environment – they can't be culled because the issue is too politically sensitive.

The Hattah Lakes system fills when the Murray floods, which is great for waterbirds. The many hollow trees here are perfect for nesting, and more than 200 species of birds have been recorded. There are many native animals, mostly nocturnal desert types and wetland species, such as the burrowing frog, which digs itself into the ground and waits until there's enough water to start breeding. Reptiles here include the mountain devil, the inspiration for the Aussie saying 'flat out like a lizard drinking' because it draws surface water into its mouth by lying flat on the ground. Over 1000 plant species have been recorded here, 200 of which are listed as rare or endangered.

The main access road is from Hattah, 70km south of Mildura on the Calder Hwy. There are two nature drives, the Hattah and the Kulkyne, and a network of old camel tracks which are great for cycling, although you'll need thorn-proof tubes. Tell the rangers where you're going, and carry plenty of water, a compass and a map.

You can camp (unpowered sites $12) at Lake Hattah and Lake Mournpoul, but there's limited water and the lake water (when there is any) is undrinkable. Camping is also possible anywhere along the Murray River frontage.

### INFORMATION

Hattah-Kulkyne National Park visitors centre ( ☎ 5029 3253; 5km into the park) A cool building with posters, tables and chairs. Ring the ranger to find out if the tracks are passable.

Parks Victoria ( ☎ 13 19 63; www.parkweb.vic.gov.au) For more information.

## Murray-Sunset National Park

If you've packed your hat and filled your water bottle you're ready to enjoy the stunning 633,000 hectares of mallee woodland of Murray-Sunset National Park, reaching from the river red gums of Lindsay Island down to Underbool. Don't go exploring in a 2WD; one hour's driving equals one day's walking, and you won't see any water or passing traffic. Move slowly in your 4WD to catch glimpses of rare animals, especially at dusk. The park was established to save unique native fauna, which suffered greatly from the clearing of 65% of the mallee scrub.

The Pink Lakes, near Underbool, get their colour from millions of microscopic organisms in the lake, that concentrate an orange pigment in their bodies. From Linga, on the Mallee Hwy, there's a signed, unsealed road that was built when salt was harvested from the lakes. Nearby is a basic camping ground, but beyond that you need a 4WD.

It you go for walks along the tracks, leave before dawn and be out of the sun before noon. As the wide sky turns pink at dusk, venture out again to watch the bird life and the magic of the night sky.

You can go fishing and yabbying in the billabongs and creeks around Lindsay Island, and marvel at the snow-white sand dunes. On the western side of the park, the Shearer's Quarters ( ☎ 5028 1218; off Settlement Rd; groups $55) has hostel-type accommodation. It's pretty basic (hot and cold water and a fridge are supplied) and accessible only by 4WD.

In Underbool, the old Underbool Hotel ( ☎ /fax 5094 6262; Cotter St; s/d $45/83) has basic rooms and serves dinner on Wednesday and Saturday. In Murrayville near the South Australian border, the Mallee Fowl Hotel ( ☎ /fax 5095 2120; Mallee Hwy, Murrayville; B&B s/d $70/83; ☒ ) has en suite rooms, motel units and a bistro serving lunch and dinner from Monday to Saturday.

### INFORMATION

Parks Victoria ( ☎ 13 19 63, Underbool 5094 6267, Werrimull 5028 1218; www.parkweb.vic.gov.au) For more information and to let someone know your whereabouts contact the rangers in Underbool on the Mallee Hwy, or north at Werrimull.

## THROUGH THE GOULBURN VALLEY

The beautiful Goulburn River, the irrigation source that makes intensive agriculture possible, was once a complex of rivers, creeks and billabongs. It's been tamed by dams, levees and channels, although you can still find pockets of riverine ecology.

The 'Food Bowl of Australia' is an important centre for fruit, dairy, food processing and some of Australia's oldest and best wineries. The waterways – the Goulburn, Broken and Murray Rivers – are the lifeblood of the region and their wetlands are the habitat for diverse wildlife.

To get here, leave the Hume Fwy after Seymour and head north on its little sister road, the Goulburn Valley Hwy.

## Nagambie
### pop 1400

First stop, Nagambie, is on the shores of pretty Lake Nagambie, which was created by the construction of the Goulburn Weir back in 1887. The weir is now popular for water sports such as water-skiing, rowing, canoeing, sailing, fishing and swimming. The World Masters Rowing ( ☒ March) competition is held on the lake; school rowing camps do much splashing around year-round. The town provides a useful base for touring local wineries, wetlands, horse studs and the Strathbogie Ranges.

Two of the best-known wineries in Victoria are just south of town: Tahbilk Winery ( ☎ 5794 2555; www.tahbilk.com.au; off Goulburn Valley Hwy; ☒ 9am-5pm Mon-Sat, 11am-5pm Sun) and Mitchelton Wines ( ☎ 5794

2710, 5736 2222; www.mitchelton.com.au; Mitchellstown Rd; 10am-5pm). Visit both these wineries on a cruise with Goulburn River Cruises ( 5794 2877; rivercruise@bigpond.com; per person $19; Sep-May), a delightful way to go. Floodlit evening cruises and meals are available; group cruises can be arranged.

Nagambie is also the place to try skydiving (see p340). Afterwards you'll deserve a gourmet dining experience at one of the excellent restaurants around town, and a bed in one of the many accommodation options (contact the visitors centre or visit their website).

## INFORMATION

Nagambie visitors centre ( 1800 444 647, 5794 2647; www.nagambielakestourism.com.au; 319 High St; 9am-5pm) Staff are passionate about their lake, their town and their region. Enjoy a coffee at the adjacent café while you consider your next move.

# Shepparton
## pop 45,000

Where the Goulburn and Broken Rivers meet is Shepparton, the regional centre of the Goulburn Valley. It's a modern town at the junction of the Midland and Goulburn Valley Hwys.

'Shepp' started out in 1850, when McGuire's punt and inn were built beside the Goulburn River. In 1912 irrigation technology came to the Goulburn Valley, leading to a sudden influx of settlers and a steady growth in the local agricultural industries. You'll know you've arrived here when you see the extraordinary

cows alongside the road. So colourful! Perhaps they produce flavoured milk…

Make sure your stay here includes a visit to the Shepparton Art Gallery ( 5832 9861; www .sheppartonartgallery.com.au; Eastbank Centre, 70 Welsford St; 10am-4pm). Its permanent collection of Australian art includes Goulburn River near Shepparton (1862) by Eugene von Guèrard, depicting McGuire's punt crossing the river. A separate gallery houses temporary and touring exhibitions.

Bangerang Cultural Centre ( 5831 1020; Parkside Dr; 9am-4pm Mon-Fri) is always a place to visit. Check out its unique collection of Koorie art and artefacts.

Just south of town beside beautiful and popular Victoria Park Lake (Wyndham St) is Aquamoves ( 5832 9400; www.aquamoves.com.au; Tom Collins Dr; adult/child $4.50/3; 6am-8pm Mon-Fri, 8.30am-5pm Sat & Sun), a health and fitness extravaganza with several pools (including a rapid-river simulation pool), a hydrotherapy pool and gym. Take a swim, spa and sauna for $7.50.

Ardmona KidsTown ( 5831 4213; www.kidstown .org.au; Midland Hwy/Mooroopna Causeway; admission gold coin; dawn-dusk) is for kids under 98 years old, with flying fox, miniature railway, giant playground, barbecues, café and more, just a few minutes east out of Shepparton.

## INFORMATION

Shepparton visitors centre ( 1800 808 839, 5831 4400; www.greatershepparton.com.au/visitors/vic; Wyndham St; 9am-5pm) At the southern end of the Victoria Park Lake. Staff provide info and make bookings for you.

## GOLD, WITH A DUSTING OF BROWN

Famous old Rushworth (population 1000), a spread-out little town that lazes dustily in the sun, was a stopover for travellers between the Beechworth and Bendigo gold diggings, until some local Koories took a couple of travellers to see a local gold deposit. By the 1880s there were more than 50 gold reefs being mined around here.

Rushworth's High St, classified an historic precinct, is divided by a central plantation and a Victorian band rotunda. You hardly need to visit the Historical Museum ( 58561951; rushworthmuseum@hotmail.com; High St; admission by donation; 10am-noon Sat, 11am-3pm Sun) in the old Mechanics Institute to get a feel for the past.

The surrounding box ironbark country is known as 'golden ironbark', since it provided wealth after the gold ran out. At one stage these forests supported seven sawmills. Ironbark gums are scruffy, but let your eyes adjust to their raggedy-tag limbs and you'll grow to love this harsh bush.

South of Rushworth is Whroo Historic Reserve (pronounced 'Roo'), an old gold-mining ghost town with relics aplenty: old mine shafts, cyanide vats (used for separating the gold from quartz), puddling machines, and the Balaclava open-cut mine – walk through the tunnel. Whroo visitors centre ( 5856 1561; wmr46@hotmail.com; 9am-5pm) has a café and a newly produced DVD and history book for sale; see the area as it was and trace the local history. The town once had over 130 buildings, but the ironbarks have reclaimed much of it. There are walking tracks and signed nature trails twisting through the scrub, and the evocative cemetery nearby on Spring Hill. Headstone inscriptions indicate that life was hard for the diggers and their families.

## AN EARLY STOP

Kilmore (population 4700) was the first coach stop on the Melbourne-to-Sydney route, reaching its prime during the gold-rush years. Impressive old bluestone and brick buildings from the era include three pubs and the courthouse buildings (1863). The Old Post Office & Museum (cnr Powley & Foote Sts) will soon house a café, and the old mill sells antiques and coffee.

There's trash-and-treasure and produce markets ( ☎ 5781 1319; www.mitchellshire.vic.gov.au) around the district on some weekends, and an Agriculture Show in December on East St, complete with showbags.

Whitburgh Cottage ( ☎ 5782 1118; Piper St; admission free; ☾ 2-4pm Sun) was built in 1857. This simple and solid bluestone cottage, with twin-peaked slate roof, has been preserved as an historic museum.

The friendly Kilmore visitors centre ( ☎ 5781 1319; msls@vicnet.net.au; 12 Sydney St; ☾ 9am-5pm) is in the central library.

## Kyabram
pop 5600

Kyabram, from a local Koorie word meaning 'dense forest', is a bustling commercial centre, with modern retail facilities for the surrounding farming communities. Kyabram Fauna Park ( ☎ 5852 2883; Lake Rd; adult/child/family $14/7/35; ☾ 9.30am-5.30pm) is respected throughout the region for its devotion to native species. Kangaroos, koalas, Tasmanian devils and dingoes live here in natural habitats. There's a large number of bird species in aviaries and a variety of waterbirds in the wetlands section.

River Country Adventours ( ☎ 5852 2736; www.adventours.com.au; 57 Lake Rd; half-/full-/2-day safaris $55/88/125) takes you frolicking on the beautiful Goulburn River. Rent a canoe if you'd rather.

The indigenous peoples of this area called the Murray River *tongala*. Northwest of Kyabram, the town of Tongala boasts the Golden Cow Centre ( ☎ 5859 1100; cnr Henderson & Finlay Rds; adult/child/family $9/5.50/25; ☾ 10.30am-4pm Wed-Fri & Sun-Mon, tours & milking 11am), a working dairy with amazing, interactive displays on the dairy industry (milk a tin cow!) and the best milkshakes in Australia.

## UP THE HUME

This used to be a track to Sydney, with bullock wagons piled with wheat waiting for those ahead to make the next river crossing. Even 40 years ago, heading north was a jostle of sedans, caravans and trucks on a narrow, potholed road. If they could see us now! Powering north on a broad band of bitumen, the Hume Fwy runs along the eastern edge of the Goulburn Valley, separating the valley from the foothills of the High Country in Victoria's northeast. Wangaratta and Benalla are the main centres.

Off the freeway, the minor roads and flat terrain make this the perfect region for leisurely cycling. The many country clubs boast excellent golf courses, and race-meetings are held throughout the region.

## Seymour to Benalla

Come off the freeway to stroll along the banks of the Goulburn River at Seymour (population 6000), passing the historic New Crossing Bridge, vineyards, majestic old gums and abundant native wildlife. Seymour is known for industry and agriculture. It's also central to many activities. The Seymour visitors centre ( ☎ 5799 0233; Emily St; ☾ 9am-5pm) will set you up with fun activities which won't disappoint – like walking up Mt Disappointment!

Riddy's Trawool Valley Tours ( ☎ 5792 3641, 0419-168 918; riddys@eck.net.au; 8366 Goulburn Valley Hwy; adult/child $40/20) offers 4WD scenic tours of Trawool Valley, its waterfalls, reservoir and granite mine.

Seymour Railway Heritage Centre ( ☎ 5799 0515; www.srhc.org.au; Victoria St; admission $2; ☾ 10am-3pm Tue, Thu, Sat & Sun) has a fantastic collection of heritage Victoria Railway locomotives and carriages.

The RAAC Tank Museum ( ☎ 5735 7285; www.armytankmuseum.com.au; Hopkins Barracks, Puckapunyal; adult/child/family $7.50/3/15; ☾ 10am-5pm Tue-Fri, to 4pm last weekend of the month) is 18km west of Seymour. It houses vintage armoured vehicles and tanks (including the *Vicker MKII*), antitank weapons and historic army displays. From here you can start the 107km Military Heritage Trail along Tourist Drive 65 to Murchison, which takes in points like the Graytown War Camps and the Italian Ossario Memorial.

Back on the freeway heading north, turn into Plunkett Fowles ( ☎ 5796 2150; www.plunkettfowles.com.au; Lambing Gully Rd, Avenel; ☾ 9am-5pm). The wines made here are full and fresh, and from the stunning café (lunch $15-27; ☾ breakfast & lunch) you look across the vineyard to the Strathbogie Ranges. If you sit out in the courtyard you may be serenaded!

A little further north, Upton Rd takes you through beautiful countryside to Avenel Maze

## MITCHELL, WHERE THE FUN BEGINS

A small shire that includes places like Kilmore, Seymour and Tallarook State Forest, Mitchell (www.mitchell shire.vic.gov.au) is just an hour's easy drive north of Melbourne. You'll find action-packed activities up here, varied and exquisite crafts, superb food and wine, and a countryside that's flush with rivers, plantlife, wildlife and sweeping plains. The special events here are fantastic – everything from Celtic festivals and classic-car days to spring racing carnivals and wine-and-food festivals. Check out the Events Calendar on the shire's website, or contact any regional visitors centre for details.

( ☎ 5796 2667; Upton Rd, Avenel; ☺ 10am-5pm Thu-Mon). There are five amazing mazes here; the hedge mazes smell fantastic but you'll be totally bamboozled, so try the rock labyrinth where you can see where you're going. There's also minigolf, a licensed café and barbecue area.

Continue up the freeway to Euroa (population 2800; see also below), a pretty town at the foot of the Strathbogie Ranges. Here you'll find late-Victorian and Edwardian redbrick buildings, the Farmers Arms museum, many parks, and the Seven Creeks which run through town. Euroa's Miniature Steam Train ( ☎ 5759 3000; www.euroaonline.com.au; Turnbull St; rides $1.50) steams up on the fourth Sunday of the month. On any day, call into Jumping Jumbuck ( ☎ 5795 1181; Old Hume Hwy; mains $10-14; ☺ breakfast & lunch daily, dinner Fri-Sun). The quick-service meals and heady coffee will set you happily back onto the freeway and on to Benalla.

Benalla (population 9000) has associations with the Ned Kelly legend: Ned made his first court appearance here in 1869 when, aged

14, he was charged with robbery and assault. In 1877 he was again being escorted to the Benalla court when he escaped and hid in a saddle-and-boot maker's shop on Arundel St. It was here he told police trooper Thomas Lonigan that if ever he shot a man, it would be Lonigan, which he did a year later (see p342).

Benalla visitors centre ( ☎ 5762 1749; www.benalla.vic .gov.au; Mair St; ☺ 9am-5pm), by the lake, is in the Costume & Pioneer Museum (www.benallamuseum.org; adult/child $3/2), which has fascinating exhibits and a delightful miniature house. The centre has all the info you'll need to explore the town and its culture, full accommodation listings, and the brochures *A Self-guided Heritage Tour*, *Benalla Lake Walk* and *Benalla Ceramic Mural Guide*.

Across the lake, Benalla Art Gallery ( ☎ 5762 3027; www.benallaartgallery.com; Bridge St; ☺ 10am-5pm) has a collection of Australian art, including paintings from the Heidelberg School, and a café that spreads onto a deck overlooking the lake. Outside is the very moving Weary Dunlop Memorial.

Northeast of Benalla, the Winton Motor Raceway ( ☎ 5766 4235; www.wintonmotorraceway.com.au; Fox St, Winton) is one of Victoria's main motorracing circuits. It's website also lists local accommodation.

## Glenrowan
### pop 350
Ned Kelly's legendary bushranging exploits came to their bloody end here in 1880. The story of Ned and his gang has been preserved in Glenrowan, a town of legend and tourist attraction. All the sites are signed – collect a walking map and become immersed in the Glenrowan Affair.

## COME FLY WITH ME

From the coast, head north over the Great Divide to where the weather patterns don't change and calm air-currents enable far more days suitable for skydiving. Euroa and Nagambie are really into this most exhilarating of sports. Don't believe us? Go out to the airfields, lie in the sun, and watch people of all ages and fitness floating down from above.

Go Jump the Parachute School ( ☎ 1300 302 907; www.skydivingassoc.com.au; Drysdale Rd, Euroa) has 150 hectares of open acres in Euroa and bunk houses where you can stay for free. Start with an introductory scenic flight with a tandem jump ($345), or take a weekend course ($516) where you end up freefalling with two instructors and pull your own ripcord.

Skydive Nagambie ( ☎ 1800 266 500, 5794 2626; www.skydivenagambie.com; 1232 Kettles Rd, Nagambie) offers tandem dives ($340) or a two-day package with three jumps ($865).

Benalla, known worldwide for its fabulous thermal activity, is more into gliding. The Gliding Club of Victoria ( ☎ 5762 1058; www.gliding-benalla.org; Samaria Rd Aerodrome; flights from $175) has a base at Benalla airport. Go softly, quietly, into a timeless space…

The highlight is the living museum, Kellyland-Animated Theatre ( ☎ 5766 2367; Gladstone St; adult/child/family $10/14/60; ⏰ 9.30am-4.30pm, shows every 30min). Move through different rooms, like the bar of McDonell's Tavern, while the story acts out around you courtesy of life-like computerised characters (it may be too scary for young children). Original props include a hand gun owned by Ned, Sgt Kennedy's hitching post and a rare copy of the findings of the Royal Commission into the Kelly manhunt. Also ask for the brochure titled *Glenrowan – Ned Kelly's Last Stand*.

Nearby, underneath Kate's Cottage, a museum ( ☎ 5766 2448 www.nedkellyworld.com.au; Gladstone St; adult/child $2/50c; ⏰ 9am-5pm) holds Kelly memorabilia and artefacts gathered from all over the district.

# Warby Range State Park

The 400-million-year-old Warby Range extends about 25km north of Glenrowan and probably provided Ned Kelly and his gang with many vantage points. It's a low range of steep, granite slopes, preserved as a state park because of its scenic value (and, probably, because it wasn't farmable). Features include fast-flowing creeks and waterfalls after rain, wildflowers in spring, some great picnic spots and an abundance of bird life.

The views from Ryan's Lookout are exceptional. There are good sealed roads (a short trip starts at Ryan's Lookout, goes along Gerrett Rd, links up with Adam's Track and then Thoona Rd), and also good walking tracks, picnic areas and a camp site. Ask for a map and brochure at the Wangaratta visitors centre (right).

# Wangaratta

**pop 15,500**

Wangaratta (just plain old 'Wang' to the locals) means 'resting place of the cormorants'. The town is at the junction of the Ovens and King Rivers, and the first buildings, in the 1840s, were based around a punt service which operated until 1855. The Wangaratta Woollen Mills (Australian Country Spinners) and Bruck Mills, established after WWII, are both still operating. These days, Wangaratta is an industrial and textile centre. It's also the turn-off point for the Great Alpine Rd, which leads to the northern ski resorts of the Victorian Alps (see p300).

At the Wangaratta Cemetery, south of town, is the grave of Dan 'Mad Dog' Morgan, a notorious bushranger. It contains most of Morgan's remains – after he was fatally shot at nearby Peechelba Station in April 1865, his head was taken to Melbourne for a study of the criminal mind, and his scrotum was supposedly fashioned into a tobacco pouch.

Head 20km east of Wangaratta to Eldorado, which has a signed walk around 31 mining and commercial sites from the 1850s on. The main feature is Cock's Eldorado Dredge. This mining monstrosity has a belt with 110 steel buckets that can dig down to 30m. It dredged for gold and tin in Reedy Creek for 18 years.

## INFORMATION

Wangaratta visitors centre ( ☎ 1800 801 065, 5721 5711; www.visitwangaratta.com.au; 100 Murphy St; ⏰ 9am-5pm; 🖳 ) In the old library, with displays, internet access and videos depicting local rail trails, a Ned Kelly debate, and snippets from the annual Wangaratta Jazz Festival. Pick up informative brochures like *Official Visitors Guide* and *Murray to the Mountains Rail Trail* (which starts in Bowser, 8km northeast of Wangaratta), and *Wangaratta Cemetery Self-guided Tour*.

## FESTIVALS & EVENTS

Wangaratta Sports Carnival ( ☎ 5721 8708) An athletics meeting featuring the Wangaratta Gift foot race; held in late January.

Wangaratta Jazz Festival (www.wangaratta-jazz.org.au) First held in 1990, this is one of Australia's premier music festivals, featuring traditional, modern and contemporary jazz. It's held on the weekend before the Melbourne Cup in November, with hundreds of musicians and acts, and many awards and workshops.

## EATING

The café scene is all happening along Murphy St and Reid St, in the centre of town.

Hollywood's ( ☎ 5721 9877; 87 Murphy St; mains $23-36; ⏰ breakfast, lunch & dinner Tue-Sun) This friendly spot spreads itself around the pavement.

Café Martini ( ☎ 5721 9020; 1 Murphy St; mains $13-26; ⏰ lunch & dinner Mon-Sat, dinner Sun) Choose a table on the veranda and look down on the town.

Vine Hotel ( ☎ 5721 2605; Detour Rd; mains $12-24; ⏰ lunch & dinner Wed-Sun) Ned Kelly and his gang used to hang out here; these days the food's better! Go underground to the small museum and cellars. The Vine is about 3km north of town, on the road to Eldorado.

## SLEEPING

There's all sorts of accommodation here, which you can book online at www.visitwangaratta.com.au.

## THE KELLY GANG

Ned Kelly is probably Australia's greatest folk hero. His life and death have been embraced as a part of the national culture – from Sidney Nolan's famous paintings to Peter Carey's Booker Prize–winning novel *True History of the Kelly Gang*. Ned himself has become a symbol of the Australian rebel character.

Before he became a cult hero, Edward 'Ned' Kelly was labelled a horse thief. Born in 1855, Ned was first arrested when he was 14 and spent the next 10 years in and out of jails. In 1878 a warrant was issued for his arrest for stealing horses, so he and his brother Dan went into hiding. Their mother and two friends were arrested, sentenced and imprisoned for aiding and abetting. The Kelly family had long felt persecuted by the authorities, and the jailing of Mrs Kelly was the last straw.

Ned and Dan were joined in their hide-out in the Wombat Ranges, near Mansfield, by Steve Hart and Joe Byrne. Four policemen – Kennedy, Lonigan, Scanlon and McIntyre – came looking for them, and, in a shoot-out at Stringybark Creek, Ned killed Kennedy, Lonigan and Scanlon. McIntyre escaped to Mansfield and raised the alarm.

The government put up a £500 reward for any of the gang members, dead or alive. In December 1878 the gang held up the National Bank at Euroa, and got away with £2000. Then, in February 1879, they took over the police station at Jerilderie, locked the two policemen in the cells, and robbed the Bank of New South Wales wearing the policemen's uniforms. By this time the reward was £2000 a head.

On 27 June 1880, the gang held 60 people captive in a hotel at Glenrowan. A train-load of police and trackers was sent from Melbourne. Ned's plan to destroy the train was foiled when a schoolteacher warned the police. Surrounded, the gang holed up in the hotel and returned fire for hours, while wearing heavy armour made from ploughshares. Ned was shot in the legs and captured, and Dan Kelly, Joe Byrne and Steve Hart, along with several of their hostages, were killed.

Ned Kelly was brought to Melbourne, tried, then hanged on 11 November 1880. He met his end bravely; his last words are famously quoted as, 'Such is life.'

His death mask, armour and the gallows on which he died are on display in the Old Melbourne Gaol (see p56).

Pinsent Hotel ( ☎ 5721 2183; 20 Reid St; s/d $35/60) The charming old rooms upstairs here are quite swish.

Billabong Motel ( ☎ 5721 2353; 12 Chisholm St; s/d from $40/55; 🐾 ) A homely warren of fresh little rooms, with very old but clean bathrooms.

Hermitage Motor Inn ( ☎ 5721 7444; www.hermitagemotorinn.com.au; cnr Cusack & Mackay Sts; s/d/f/spa $98/115/135/140; 🐾 🛏 ) You'll see the sign to this place as you come into town from the south; it's a great place to stay.

## Wodonga
pop 30,000
Wodonga looks out on the lovely Sumsion Gardens and a lake formed by Wodonga Creek. It's a commercial centre, also know for its sporting and aquatic facilities and bike trails. The Lincoln Causeway runs from the city centre across Wodonga Creek to the border at the Murray River. The Gateway shopping area, along the Causeway, has art and craft shops where you can watch timber pieces being carved, or buy fine china, dolls or whatever takes your fancy.

There are signed trails for the many walking and bike trails around Gateway Island, along the Murray River and to the beautiful wetlands of Sumsion Gardens.

The Army Museum Bandiana ( ☎ 6055 2525; www.defence.gov.au/army/awma_mus; Murray Valley Hwy, Bandiana; adult/child/family $5/2/10; 🕤 9.30am-5pm) displays a variety of war weaponry, items from missions, and documents. The old cars are magnificent. There's Buick and Holden staff cars, Chevrolet and Dodge trucks, carriages, motorbikes.

### INFORMATION
Wodonga visitors centre (Gateway visitors centre; ☎ 1300 796 222, 6051 3750; www.destinationalbury wodonga.com.au; Hume Hwy, Gateway Is; 🕤 9am-5pm) Has 24-hour touch-screen information and an accommodation-booking service.

# TRANSPORT

Melbourne's city centre is a delight for pedestrians, with trams at the ready when you're fatigued or in a hurry. Surrounding neighbourhoods can be reached easily via the extensive tram, train and bus network. All three methods of transport are overseen by Metlink ( ☎ 131 638; www.metlinkmelbourne.com.au).

In this book, the nearest tram/train/bus route or station is noted after the 🚋 🚆 🚌 symbols in each listing.

Flights, tours and rail tickets can all be booked online at www.lonelyplanet.com/travel_services.

## AIR
### Airlines

You can fly into Melbourne from most international hubs and from all major cities and tourist destinations in Australia. Not all international flights are direct and you may need to change planes and terminals in Sydney. Frequent, and often discounted, domestic flights are offered by Qantas ( ☎ 13 13 13; www.qantas.com.au) and its budget/leisure subsidiary Jetstar ( ☎ 13 15 38; www.jetstar.com.au), as well as competitors Virgin Blue ( ☎ 13 67 89; www.virginblue.com.au) and Tiger Airlines ( ☎ 9335 3033; www.tigerairways.com), which flies out of Melbourne to all state and territory capitals, plus a variety of regional resort destinations, at rock-bottom prices. Tiger also flies to Singapore and connects through to a variety of destinations in Indonesia, China, Vietnam, India and Malaysia.

Because of the state's compact size, scheduled internal flights are limited and often

ludicrously expensive. Airlines that fly to regional centres around the state and other country destinations:

QantasLink ( ☎ 13 13 13; www.qantas.com) Flies to Mildura and Mt Hotham, as well as Burnie and Devonport. Book through Qantas.

Regional Express ( ☎ 13 17 13; www.regionalexpress.com.au) Regional Express, better known as Rex, flies to Albury, Mildura and Portland. It also offers flights to Burnie, Devonport, King Island and Mt Gambier.

## Airports
### MELBOURNE AIRPORT

The city's major airport, Melbourne Airport ( ☎ 9297 1600; www.melair.com.au), often referred to as Tullamarine or Tulla, is around 25km northwest of the city centre. All international and domestic terminals are within the same complex. There are no direct train or tram services linking it with the city (don't get us started on this pet beef for Melbourne's frequent flyers). See the boxed text below for transport options.

## CLIMATE CHANGE & TRAVEL

Climate change is a serious threat to the ecosystems that humans rely upon, and air travel is the fastest-growing contributor to the problem. Lonely Planet regards travel, overall, as a global benefit, but believes we all have a responsibility to limit our personal impact on global warming.

### Flying & Climate Change

Pretty much every form of motor transport generates $CO_2$ (the main cause of human-induced climate change) but planes are far and away the worst offenders, not just because of the sheer distances they allow us to travel, but because they release greenhouse gases high into the atmosphere. The statistics are frightening: two people taking a return flight between Europe and the US will contribute as much to climate change as an average household's gas and electricity consumption over a whole year.

### Carbon Offset Schemes

Climatecare.org and other websites use 'carbon calculators' that allow travellers to offset the greenhouse gases they are responsible for with contributions to energy-saving projects and other climate-friendly initiatives in the developing world – including projects in India, Honduras, Kazakhstan and Uganda.

Lonely Planet, together with Rough Guides and other concerned partners in the travel industry, supports the carbon offset scheme run by climatecare.org. Lonely Planet offsets all of its staff and author travel.

For more information check out our website: www.lonelyplanet.com.

### AVALON AIRPORT

Most Jetstar flights to and from Sydney and Brisbane use Avalon Airport ( ☎ 1800 282 566, 5227 9100; www.avalonairport.com.au), around 55km southwest of the city centre. The Sunbus ( ☎ 9689 6888; www.sunbusaustralia.com.au) meets all flights at Avalon Airport and picks up or drops off at Southern Cross Station and Franklin St ($20/36 one way/return). Hotel pick-ups can be booked 48 hours prior to departure. The trip takes around 40 minutes.

## BICYCLE

Melbourne's bike-friendly terrain is endowed with many dedicated bike lanes and paths. One note of caution: tram tracks can cause havoc for cyclists. See p171 for further information, including bike hire.

Bicycles can be taken onto trains for free, but commuters with bikes are requested to travel during off-peak times (between 9.30am and 4pm Monday to Friday; no restriction on weekends). Bikes are not permitted on trams and buses.

Bicycles are carried free on all V/Line regional services provided you check in 30 minutes before departure. The system of rail trails (disused train lines adapted as bike paths) is growing in country Victoria, and provides scenic, hassle-free cycling. Some routes connect with V/Line train stations. See www.railtrails.com.au for details. V/Line bus services do not carry bicycles.

## BOAT

The slow but scenic Melbourne Water Taxis ( ☎ 9686 0914; www.melbournewatertaxis.com.au) services the Yarra and Maribyrnong Rivers, from Richmond to Williamstown – great for arriving at the Australian Open in style.

The Spirit of Tasmania ( ☎ 1800 634 906; www.spiritoftasmania.com.au), a car and passenger ferry, sails nightly to Devonport on Tasmania's northern coast from Station Pier in Port Melbourne, with additional day sailings during summer. The crossing takes around 11 hours. A wide variety of fares are available, from basic seats to private en suite cabins.

## BUS

Melbourne's red and yellow buses are usually of more use if travelling out into the suburbs, but can provide shortcuts or more direct routes than trams on some inner routes. These include the 220, (which runs from the city to Doncaster, and takes in Carlton, Fitzroy, Collingwood and Abbotsford), the 220 Sunshine–City–Gardenvale (which Gardenvale bound takes you via Southbank, St Kilda Rd, Prahran, Hawksburn and East St Kilda) and the 250 Garden City–City–La Trobe University (running through Port Melbourne, South Melbourne, the city, Carlton, Carlton North, Fitzroy North and Northcote). Many, but not all, buses are wheelchair- and stroller-accessible 'bendy' buses. Call Metlink for more information about accessibility.

## PLAYING HOOKIE

Melbourne has a peculiar road rule known as the hook turn. In the city centre many intersections require that you make a right-hand turn from the left lane so as not to block oncoming trams. They also appear along Clarendon St, South Melbourne. These intersections are marked with a 'Right Turn from Left Only' sign and are affectionately known as a 'hookie'. You're required to veer off to the left and wait in the front of the line of traffic at the red light. When the traffic light turns green (for the street you're about to turn in to) hook right and complete your turn. It sounds scarier than it is.

Melbourne City Council runs a free hop-on, hop-off tourist shuttle from 9.30am and 4.30pm daily. The grey and red buses intersect with the City Circle Tram and travel beyond the grid to the Shrine of Remembrance, Carlton and the Arts Centre. The Federation Square visitors centre (www.thatsmelbourne.com.au) has details.

Based at Southern Cross Station in Melbourne, Victoria's regional bus network V/Line (☎ 9697 2076; www.vline.com.au) is a relatively cheap and reliable services, though it can require planning if you intend to do more than straightforward city-to-city trips. Most buses are equipped with air-con, toilets and DVDs, and all are smoke-free zones. The smallest towns eschew formal bus terminals for a single drop-off/pick-up point, usually outside a post office, newsagent or shop.

## CAR & MOTORCYCLE

Congestion on the city's roads and the high price of fuel makes the city's public transport network very attractive for visitors. However, many of Victoria's national parks, remote beaches and mountain regions are not readily accessible by public transport.

### Driving

Foreign driving licences are valid as long as they are in English or accompanied by a translation. An International Driving Permit, obtainable from your local automobile association, must be supported by your own licence, so bring both to Australia.

In Australia, you must drive on the left-hand side of the road. The speed limit in residential areas is 50km/h, rising to 70km/h or 80km/h on some main roads and dropping to 40km/h in specially designated areas such as school zones. On highways the speed limit is generally 100km/h, while on some sections of freeway it rises to 110km/h.

Wearing seat belts is compulsory, and small children must be belted into an approved safety seat. Motorcyclists must wear crash helmets at all times. The police strictly enforce Victoria's blood-alcohol limit of 0.05% with random breath testing (and drug testing) of drivers.

### Hire

All the big car-hire firms have offices in Melbourne. Apart from the many companies in the city, you'll find Avis (☎ 13 63 33; www.avis.com.au), Budget (☎ 1300 362 848; www.budget.com.au), Europcar (☎ 1300 131 390; www.europcar.com.au), Hertz (☎ 13 30 39; www.hertz.com) and Thrifty (☎ 1300 367 227; www.thrifty.com.au), which all have desks at the airport. Car-hire offices tend to be at the northern end of the city centre or in North Melbourne.

The major companies all offer unlimited-kilometre rates. One-day hire rates for fully licensed drivers over 25 years of age vary between $40 and $60, depending on the vehicle. The longer the hire period, the cheaper the daily rate.

The Yellow Pages (www.yellowpages.com.au) lists lots of other firms that rent new and used vehicles of all shapes and sizes.

If you suddenly decide you'd like to take on the undulating curves of the Great Ocean Rd on a Harley Davidson, or explore the city on a zippy 100cc, then the option is there. Garner's Hire-Bikes (☎ 9326 8676; www.garnersmotorcycles.com.au) has a large range of bikes for hire. Prices range from $100 a day for a Vespa to $275 a day for a Harley Davidson Softail Custom.

### Parking

Parking spaces in the city are metered. Check parking signs for restrictions and times, and watch out for clearway zones that operate during peak hours. There are more than 70 parking garages in the city; check www.iconparking.com.au for the locations of off-street car parks, plus maps and rates.

### Toll Roads

Melbourne's CityLink (☎ 13 26 29; www.citylink.com.au) tollway road system has two main routes: the Southern Link, which runs from the southeastern suburb of Malvern to Kings Way on the southern edge of the city centre; and the Western Link, which runs from the

## PUBLIC TRANSPORT TICKETING

Melbourne's public transport system, also called the Met ( ☎ 13 16 38; www.victrip.com.au), incorporates buses, trains and trams; the same ticket allows you to travel on all three. The most common tickets are based on a specific period of travelling time (eg two hours, one day, one week) and allow unlimited travel during that period and within the relevant zone. You must validate your ticket in the validating machine when boarding a tram or bus or entering a train station.

The metropolitan area is divided into two zones, with the price of tickets (Metcards) dependant on which zone(s) you will be travelling in and across. Zone 1 covers the city and inner suburbs and most travellers are unlikely to venture beyond it; adult fares follow.

| Zone(s) | Two hours ($) | All day ($) | Weekly ($) |
| --- | --- | --- | --- |
| 1 | 3.50 | 6.50 | 28 |
| 2 | 2.70 | 4.60 | 19.20 |
| 1 & 2 | 5.50 | 10.10 | 47.40 |

A daily Metcard ($6.50), which can be used on trams, trains and buses, is good value if you will be travelling throughout the day. Otherwise a two-hour ticket ($3.50) will suffice for a return journey within two to 2½ hours, depending on the time of purchase. There are also City Saver tickets ($2.60), which allow for a one-way journey in a limited city radius. An alternative to a weekly ticket is the five x daily or 10 x two-hour Metcards, which offer the flexibility of not having to travel on consecutive days and are slightly cheaper than individual fares.

Buying a ticket is as simple as feeding your coins into a machine at the train station or on the tram, or paying the driver on a bus. Most machines are coin-only, including those on trams, so make sure you have sufficient loose change. Many small businesses, such as newspaper kiosks and newsagents, milk bars (corner shops) and 7-Elevens sell Metcards; look for the sign. You can also buy Metcards at the MetShop (Map pp52–3; ☎ 13 16 38; www.metlinkmelbourne .com.au; cnr Little Collins & Swanston Sts) under the Melbourne Town Hall or from the online store (http://store .metlinkmelbourne.com.au).

For timetables, maps and further fare details on all services, contact Metlink ( ☎ 13 16 38; www.metlinkmelbourne .com.au).

Calder Fwy intersection with the Tullamarine Fwy south to the West Gate Fwy, on the western edge of the city centre.

CityLink 24-hour passes are generally the best option for visitors. A day pass for the entire system costs $11.55 and is valid for 24 hours from your first entry through a tollway. A 24 hour Tulla pass for unlimited travel between Bulla and Flemington Roads only is $4.10. To buy a day pass, go to an Australia Post office (anywhere in Australia), a newsagent, Shell service station, a CityLink customer service centre or the CityLink website. Alternatively, you can pay by credit card by telephoning CityLink.

If you accidentally find yourself on the CityLink toll road (and it's very easy to do), don't panic as there's a three-day grace period. Passes are not required for motorbikes.

## TAXI

Melbourne's yellow taxis can be hailed or look for one of the taxi ranks around the city, usually outside major hotels or at Flinders Street and Southern Cross Stations. A shining rooftop light means the taxi is free. Finding one is not often a hassle, except on rainy Friday nights or New Year's Eve. The flag-fall is a standard $3.10, plus $1.47 per kilometre. There's a surcharge from midnight to 5am, and a fee for telephone bookings. Tipping is not obligatory but welcomed by the poorly paid drivers. The main players are Silver Top Taxis ( ☎ 13 10 08), 13 CABS ( ☎ 13 22 27), Arrow ( ☎ 13 22 11) and Embassy Taxis ( ☎ 13 17 55).

## TRAIN

Imposing Flinders Street Station is the main terminal for all suburban trains. There are four other stations on the underground City Loop: Southern Cross, Flagstaff, Melbourne Central and Parliament. Handy for crossing the city, the loop stops form part of other routes; see station displays for details. Trains begin around 5am and finish at midnight and run between every 10 and 30 minutes, depending on the time of day. Sunday services begin a little later. For train routes, see the Metlink site: www.metlinkmelbourne.com.au. Suburban trains are run by Connex (www.connex

its website lists facilities at given stations.

Southern Cross Station is Melbourne's main terminus for all regional V/Line rail services and Countrylink and Overland trains to Sydney and Adelaide respectively. The rail network is fairly limited, so you will often need to rely on buses (see p344). See individual destination entries for details about train services within regional Victoria.

## TRAM

Both iconic and useful, Melbourne's trams criss-cross the city and travel into the suburbs. They run from around 5am in the morning until midnight. Timetables are variable; expect a tram to rattle along in anything between five and 20 minutes. Travel in peak hour can require patience (and on some routes, a sense of the absurd) as delays are not uncommon. Light rail routes, such as the 96 to St Kilda, are spared traffic snarls. As the tram lines tend to radiate outwards from the city, travel between suburbs is usually tricky (buses fill these gaps).

Tickets can be purchased on board, but you'll need coins to do so. Unless you've just purchased your ticket from the machine, make sure you validate your ticket every trip. Don't be tempted to go without a ticket even on the shortest of rides; plainclothes inspectors are as stealthy as they are merciless. Fines for 'fare avoidance' currently sit at $162. Tram stops in the city centre are often purpose built and in the middle of the road, but further out stops are street-side. You'll need to hail trams from there and exercise caution when getting on and off (traffic is obliged to give way to passengers).

Free City Circle trams travel the perimeter of Melbourne's central business district every day between 10am and 9pm, except Christmas Day and Good Friday. The service takes in many of Melbourne's landmarks and runs every 12 minutes. The entire route takes around 45 minutes to complete and is usually plied by maroon vintage W class trams.

## BUSINESS HOURS

Businesses, including post offices, are generally open between 9am and 5pm, Monday to Friday, with some larger branches also open on Saturday mornings. Banks open at 9.30am and shut their doors at 4pm, or 5pm on Fridays. A few banks open on Saturday morning, though this tends to be in suburban shopping centres. Retail businesses tend to open a little later, usually 10am to 6pm. Late night trading is on a Friday; shops stay open until between 7pm and 9pm. Most shops also open on Saturdays from 10am to 5pm and on Sundays from 11am or midday to at least 4pm.

Pubs open from 11am to 1am; bars from 4pm to late. Restaurants open around noon to 3pm for lunch and then for dinner from 6pm to 10pm, and often close either on a Sunday or a Monday. That said, Melbourne bars, restaurants and cafés often blur their boundaries and many are all-day affairs, serving coffee and croissants at 7am and still mixing cocktails come midnight.

Banks, businesses and many shops are closed on public holidays (see p350). Museums and other attractions are closed on Christmas Day and Boxing Day.

## CHILDREN

Melbourne's status as a great city for visitors extends to little travellers, who'll appreciate the city's easy pace and multitude of sights and activities. Pick up a free copy of Melbourne's Child (www.melbourneschild.com.au) magazine from libraries and some cafés; it includes an events calendar and ideas for local activities. The *Entertainment Guide (EG)*, published in Friday's *Age*, has a 'Children's Activities' section that details what's on for children each weekend, such as pantomimes, animal nurseries and museum programs. Kids activities are also listed in the Saturday and Sunday editions of the paper. The free *Melbourne Events* guide available from the Melbourne Visitor Information Centre (Map pp52–3) also has a children's section.

See For Children (p51) for some of the city's better places for kids. Try also: the Aquarium (p57), any of the city's public swimming pools (p174) and *Puffing Billy* (p211), a vintage steam train that runs through the Dandenong Ranges. The city's glorious parks are always great options for keeping kids amused when the weather's cooperating. A map of the city's playgrounds is available from the City of Melbourne (www.melbourne.vic.gov.au).

The Melbourne City Council runs a childminding centre (Map p52-3; ☎ 9329 9561; 104 A'Beckett St; ☺ 9am-5pm) for children up to five years old. It charges $10.50 per hour; book a week in advance if possible.

## Babysitting

Most larger hotels will offer a babysitting service, usually drawing on the resources of a reputable agency. There are a large number of agencies that provide casual babysitting, such as Dial An Angel (www.dialanangel.com). These services should be booked well ahead. For long-term visitors, the Find a Babysitter (www.findababysitter.com.au) service is simple and easy to use, and can provide casual babysitting, nannies or after-school care.

## CLIMATE

Melbourne has four distinct seasons. In summer, average temperatures range from a high of 26°C to a low of 14°C; the average winter maximum is 13°C and the minimum 6°C; in spring and autumn average highs and lows range from around 20°C to 7°C. In Australia, summer begins in December, autumn in March, winter in June and spring in September.

Of course, averages never tell the whole story. You are just as likely to wake to shocking blue skies in winter and Dublin-style drizzle in summer. As Crowded House once sang, it's be four seasons in one day. If that's a touch too poetic, the other saying goes: if you don't like the weather in Melbourne, just wait a couple of minutes.

Summer is the most popular time for visitors, although packing for this time of year can be a fraught task. Expect good beach weather but be prepared for the occasional heat wave when the mercury bubbles past 40°C for days at a time. Scorchers are often followed by the

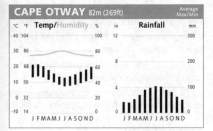

**CAPE OTWAY** 82m (269ft)  
Average Max/Min  
°C °F **Temp/**Humidity % in **Rainfall** mm

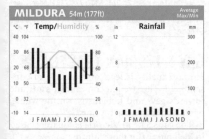

**MELBOURNE** 31m (101ft)  
Average Max/Min  
°C °F **Temp/**Humidity % in **Rainfall** mm

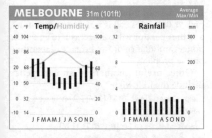

**MILDURA** 54m (177ft)  
Average Max/Min  
°C °F **Temp/**Humidity % in **Rainfall** mm

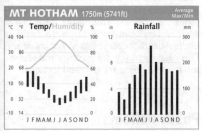

**MT HOTHAM** 1750m (5741ft)  
Average Max/Min  
°C °F **Temp/**Humidity % in **Rainfall** mm

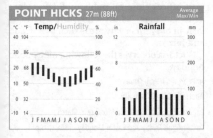

**POINT HICKS** 27m (88ft)  
Average Max/Min  
°C °F **Temp/**Humidity % in **Rainfall** mm

welcome relief of a 19°C day. Nights can be hot but are usually not as balmy as those of the northern states. Melbournians love the crisp autumn months when the days are warm and the light is staggeringly beautiful. Winters are chilly, especially on windy days, but are far from extreme. Spring is glorious, gusty and grey in turn.

There are three climatic regions in Victoria: the southern and coastal areas, the alpine areas, and the areas north and west of the Great Dividing Range.

Rainfall is spread fairly evenly throughout the year, although mid-January to mid-March tends to be the driest period. Victoria's wettest areas are the Otway Ranges and the High Country. With exposure to frequent cold fronts and southerly winds, the coastal areas are subject to the most changeable weather patterns.

The weather is generally more stable north of the Great Dividing Range. It snows during the alpine high-country winter; the closest viable cover to Melbourne is on Mt Donna Buang, though falls are often reported in the Dandenong Ranges and on Mount Macedon.

## COURSES

The CAE (Centre for Adult Education; Map pp52–3; ☎ 9652 0611; www.cae.edu.au; 253 Flinders Lane) runs a wide variety of courses. On offer is everything from languages, literature, visual arts and music to computer studies, cooking, history and philosophy. Its summer program usually has day-long activities of interest to travellers, although there are one-day weekend sessions all year round. Fees vary according to the number of sessions and the type of course. Course guides are available online or from the centre.

See the Eating chapter for more on cooking courses (p127), and the Arts (p164) for more on dance classes.

## CUSTOMS REGULATIONS

Cash amounts of more than $A10,000 and foodstuffs, goods of animal or vegetable origin must be declared at customs. This includes seemingly innocuous things such as wooden carvings, straw hats and woven baskets, which can carry unwanted seeds and other nasties. Bags are screened specifically for these items. If you fail to declare quarantine items on arrival and are caught, you risk an on-the-spot fine of $220, or prosecution, which can result in fines over $60,000, as well as up to 10 years imprisonment. The authorities are keen to protect Australia's unique environment and the country's important agricultural industries by preventing weeds, pests or diseases getting into the country (Australia's isolation means that it is free of those prevalent elsewhere in the world).

There are also restrictions on taking fruit, vegetables, plants or flowers across state borders. Many Australians have amusing stories about being force-fed fruit when approaching state borders on childhood road trips. There is a particularly strict fruit-fly exclusion zone which takes in an area along Victoria's northeast border, stretching into NSW and SA. This includes most fruit (except pineapple), fruits of ornamentals, tomatoes, cucumbers, capsicums, chillies and zucchinis. Penalties do apply. For more details on quarantine regulations contact the Australian Quarantine and Inspection Service (AQIS; www.daffa.gov.au/aqis), or for questions about state quarantine contact the Department of Natural Resources & Environment Plant Standards Centre ( ☎ 9687 5627; 1800 084 881).

Most goods can be brought in free of duty, provided that customs are satisfied they are for personal use. Travellers over 18 have a duty-free quota of 2.5L of alcohol, 250 cigarettes and dutiable goods up to the value of $900 (or $450 for those under 18). Contact Australian Customs ( ☎ 1300 363 263; www.customs.gov .au) for more information.

## ELECTRICITY

Power supply is 240V 50Hz. Plugs are three-pin, but different to the larger British sort. Universal adaptors are available from the airport, luggage and outdoor supply shops, department stores and some chemists.

## EMBASSIES & CONSULATES

Most foreign embassies are in Canberra but some countries have diplomatic representation in Melbourne. Their hours are usually from 8.30am to 12.30pm and 1pm to 4.30pm Monday to Friday, but these can vary.

Canada (Map pp52–3; ☎ 9653 9674; www.canada.org .au; Level 50, 101 Collins St, Melbourne, Vic 3000)

France (Map pp52–3; ☎ 9602 5024; www.ambafrance-au .org; Suite 805, Level 8, 150 Queen St, Melbourne, Vic 3000)

Germany (Map pp84–5; ☎ 9828 6888; www.german embassy.org.au; 480 Punt Rd, South Yarra, Vic 3141)

Indonesia (Map pp92–3; ☎ 9525 2755; www.kjri -melbourne.org; 72 Queens Rd, Melbourne, Vic 3004)

Japan (Map pp52–3; ☎ 9639 3244; www.melbourne.au .emb-japan.go.jp; 360 Elizabeth St, Melbourne, Vic 3000)

Netherlands (Map pp52–3; ☎ 9670 5573; Level 4, 118 Queen St, Melbourne, Vic 3000)

UK (Map pp52–3; ☎ 9650 4155; http://bhc.britaus.net; Level 17, 90 Collins St, Melbourne, Vic 3000)

USA (Map pp84–5; ☎ 9526 5900; http://melbourne.uscon sulate.gov/melbourne; 553 St Kilda Rd, Melbourne, Vic 3004)

## EMERGENCY

In the case of a life-threatening emergency, dial ☎ 000. This call is free from any phone, and the operator will connect you to either the police, ambulance or fire brigade, depending on the problem.

Other useful numbers in an emergency include the following:

Lifeline Counselling ( ☎ 13 11 14) A 24-hour service available in six languages.

Poisons Information Centre ( ☎ 13 11 26)

Police (Map pp52–3; ☎ 9247 5347; 228-232 Flinders Lane)

Translating & Interpreting Service ( ☎ 13 14 50) Available 24 hours.

## GAY & LESBIAN TRAVELLERS

Homosexuality is legal and the age of consent is 17. The straight community's attitude towards gays and lesbians is, on the whole, open-minded and accepting.

The gay scene in Victoria is squarely based in Melbourne (for more information, see p178), where there are exclusive venues and accommodation options. Around the state, places such as Daylesford and Hepburn Springs, Phillip Island, the Mornington Peninsula and Lorne have a strong gay presence and accommodation catering for gays and lesbians.

## HOLIDAYS
### Public Holidays

Government departments, banks, offices and post offices close on public holidays. Most cafés stay open, as do some stores, particularly in busy inner-city areas such as St Kilda and Fitzroy.

Victoria observes the following nine public holidays:

New Year's Day 1 January

Australia Day 26 January

Labour Day First or second Monday in March

Easter Good Friday and Easter Monday in March/April

Anzac Day 25 April

Queen's Birthday Second Monday in June

Melbourne Cup Day First Tuesday in November (Melbourne only)

Christmas Day 25 December

Boxing Day 26 December

When a public holiday falls on a weekend, the following Monday is declared a holiday (with the exception of Anzac Day and Australia Day).

## School Holidays
The school year is divided into four terms. Holidays are generally as follows: Christmas holidays from late-December until the end of January; and three two-week holiday periods that vary from year to year, but fall approximately from late March to mid-April, late June to mid-July and mid-September to early October. The Victorian Department of Education's website (www.education.vic.gov.au) has a full listing of upcoming dates.

## INTERNET ACCESS
There's no shortage of internet cafes in Melbourne, and wi-fi access is increasingly common, both in public places as well as hotels. Several websites keep track of free wi-fi hotspots: Only Melbourne (www.only melbourne.com.au) has a comprehensive list, though we can't vouch for its accuracy. Melbourne Airport offers wi-fi for a pay-as-you-go fee. Hotels will at least offer broadband access, but often wi-fi. Rates vary from complimentary access to ludicrously expensive daily fees, so it's best to check when booking.

If you don't have a laptop, most backpacker hostels have a terminal or two where you can access the internet. Expect to pay around $2 per hour at an internet café. Public libraries, including the State Library of Victoria, usually offer a free service but you'll often need to book. Access charges range from $4 to $9 an hour. If you're concerned that public terminals may contain nasties such as key-stroke-capturing software, set up a separate on-the-road email address.

## LEGAL MATTERS
Most travellers won't have any contact with the Victorian police or any other part of the legal system. Those that do are likely to experience these while driving. There is a significant police presence on the region's roads, with the power to stop your car and ask to see your licence (you're required by law to carry it), to check your vehicle for road-worthiness, and also to insist that you take a breath test for alcohol. Needless to say, drink-driving offences are taken very seriously.

If you are arrested, it's your right to telephone a friend, relative or lawyer before any formal questioning begins. Legal Aid (www.legalaid.vic.gov.au) is available only in serious cases and only to the truly needy (for details see the website). However, many solicitors do not charge for an initial consultation.

## MAPS
The Melbourne Visitor Information Centre (Map p52-3; Federation Sq) and information booth (Map p52-3; Bourke St Mall) hand out the free *Melbourne Visitors Map,* which covers the city and inner suburbs.

Comprehensive street directories are produced by Melway, UBD and Gregory's, and are available at bookshops and newsagents. The *Melway Greater Melbourne Street Directory* is such a Melbourne institution that places often give their location by simply stating the relevant Melway page and grid reference, and people often refer to their home's map number with affection.

Local tourist offices around Victoria can usually be relied upon to dole out a free map, though the quality can vary. For more detailed maps, try the Royal Automobile Club of Victoria (RACV; www.racv.com.au), which has a stack of road maps available (including free downloadable route maps). For a serious guide to the states roads, pick up a copy of RACV's *Vicroads Country Street Directory of Victoria* (members/nonmembers $45/50).

Map Land (Map pp52–3; ☎ 9670 4383; 372 Little Bourke St) is the city's best source for a wide range of maps.

## MEDICAL SERVICES
Visitors from Finland, Italy, the Republic of Ireland, Malta, the Netherlands, New Zealand, Sweden and the UK have reciprocal health rights, which means they are eligible for a subsidy on medical bills; register at any Medicare office ( ☎ 13 20 11; www.medicareaustralia.gov.au).

## Alternative Therapies

A huge variety of natural therapists practice throughout Melbourne and regional Victoria. This includes naturopathy, acupuncture and traditional Chinese medicine (TCM) and homeopathy. See the Natural Therapy Pages (www.naturaltherapypages.com.au) or Yellow Pages (www.yellow pages.com.au) for listings.

The Southern School of Natural Therapies (Map pp74–5; ☎ 9416 1448; www.southernschool.com; 39 Victoria St, Fitzroy) offers natural health care at a reduced rate. Final-year students under professional supervision staff the college's clinic.

Vitamins, herbal medicines and other supplements are widely available at supermarkets, health food stores, pharmacies and specialist retailers.

## Clinics

See the Yellow Pages (www.yellowpages.com.au) for a list of medical practitioners, general and specialist.

Carlisle Contemporary Health Practice (Map pp88–9; ☎ 9537 3600; 30 Carlisle St, St Kilda) General practitioners; bookings advised.

Carlton Clinic (Map pp78–9; ☎ 9347 9422; 88 Rathdowne St, Carlton) General practitioners; gay and lesbian-friendly clinic.

City Medical Centre (Map pp52–3; ☎ 9650 3122; Level 5, 313 Little Collins St) General practitioners.

Travellers' Medical & Vaccination Centre (TMVC; Map pp52–3; ☎ 9602 5788; www.traveldoctor.com.au; Level 2, 393 Little Bourke St) Specialists in travel-related medical advice such as inoculations.

## Emergency Rooms

Public hospitals with 24-hour accident and emergency departments include the following:

Alfred Hospital (Map pp84–5; ☎ 9276 2000; Commercial Rd, Prahran)

Royal Melbourne Hospital (Map pp78–9; ☎ 9342 7000; Grattan St, Parkville)

St Vincent's Hospital (Map pp74–5; ☎ 9288 2211; 41 Victoria Pde, Fitzroy)

## Pharmaceutical Supplies

Over-the-counter medications are widely available at privately owned chemists throughout Australia. These include painkillers, antihistamines for allergies and skincare products.

You may find that medications readily available over the counter in some countries are only available in Australia by prescription. These include the oral contraceptive pill, topical hydrocortisone and all antibiotics. If you take medication on a regular basis, bring an adequate supply, a prescription and ensure you have details of the generic name as brand names may differ between countries.

## MONEY

Australia uses the decimal system. Its currency is the Australian dollar, which is made up of 100 cents. There are 5c, 10c, 20c, 50c, $1 and $2 coins, and $5, $10, $20, $50 and $100 notes. Although 5c is the smallest coin in circulation, prices are often still marked to the single cent. Shops should round prices to the nearest 5c on your total bill.

## ATMs

Most bank branches have 24-hour ATMs and will accept debit cards that are linked to international network systems, such as Cirrus, Maestro, Barclays Connect and Solo. There is a limit on the daily withdrawal amount, which is usually around $1000. Almost all retail outlets have Eftpos, which allows you to pay for purchases electronically.

## Changing Money

Changing foreign currency is no problem at most larger banks. There are foreign-exchange booths at Melbourne Airport's international terminal, which are open to meet all arriving flights, as well as in the city and at large shopping centres. Most large hotels will also change currency (or travellers cheques) for their guests, but the rate might not be as good as from other outlets.

For an approximate guide to the exchange rate see the inside front cover of this guidebook.

## Credit Cards

The most commonly accepted credit cards are Visa, MasterCard, American Express and, to a lesser extent, Diners Club. For lost or stolen card services call the following:

American Express ( ☎ 1300 132 639)

Diners Club ( ☎ 1300 360 060)

MasterCard ( ☎ 1800 120 113)

Visa ( ☎ 1800 450 346)

# NEWSPAPERS & MAGAZINES

Melbourne's broadsheet newspaper is The Age (www.theage.com.au), which covers local, national and international news. It has various supplements during the week, including the food & wine focussed Epicure on Tuesdays, Friday's *Entertainment Guide (EG)* listings and arts coverage on Saturdays. It also carries the Saturday and Sunday magazines shared with its sister newspaper, *The Sydney Morning Herald,* and a monthly city magazine, the (melbourne)magazine. The Herald Sun (www.heraldsun .com.au) does what tabloids do well: several editions per day, scads of sensationalism and a whole lotta sport. The Australian (www.theaus tralian.news.com), a national daily, is also widely available.

Most magazine publishing in Australia needs the numbers that only national circulation can provide; several attempts to establish a Melbourne city magazine have failed. Some of this slack has been taken up by online ventures such as Three Thousand (www.threethousand.com .au). However, the current affairs and culture magazine, the Monthly (www.themonthly.com.au), the Australian Book Review (www.australianbookreview .com.au) and the charitable Big Issue (www.bigissue .org.au) are published locally so tend to be less Sydney-centric than some.

The excellent Gourmet Traveller and Vogue Entertaining and Travel magazines often have Melbourne restaurant news, features and reviews. *Gourmet Traveller* shares a restaurant critic with the *Age,* so there tends to be a bit of overlap. The free Melbourne's Child newspaper has listings of children's activities.

Music listings can be found in the free Beat (www.beat.com.au) and Inpress (http://streetpress.com .au) magazines.

Big newsagents and bookshops stock magazines suited to all interests and hobbies. Try Mag Nation (Map pp52–3; ☎ 9663 6559; 88 Elizabeth St), McGills (Map pp52–3; ☎ 9602 5566; 187 Elizabeth St), Readings (Map pp78–9; ☎ 9347 6633; www.readings.com.au; 309 Lygon St, Carlton) or Borders (Map pp84–5; ☎ 9824 2299; 500 Chapel St, South Yarra).

# ORGANISED TOURS & WALKS

The free *Melbourne Events* guide, which is updated monthly, is available at visitors centres, hotels and newsagents, and has an extensive section on tours. Ask at the visitors centre in Federation Square if you've got something particular in mind. The National Trust publishes the *Walking Melbourne* ($20) booklet, which is particularly useful if you're interested in Melbourne's architectural heritage. Also see the Eating (p127) and Shopping (p106) chapters for special interest tours.

AAT Kings ( ☎ 9663 3377; www.aatkings.com/au) This multinational offers the full range of standard sightseeing tours both around Melbourne and to popular destinations like the 12 Apostles, Puffing Billy, Healesville Sanctuary and Phillip Island. They also do lunch tours to Yarra Valley wineries.

Aboriginal Heritage Walk (Map p82; ☎ 9252 2429; www.rbg.vic.gov.au; Royal Botanic Gardens; adult/concession/child/family $18/14/9/50; ⊙ 11am Thu & Fri, 10.30am alternate Sun) The Royal Botanic Gardens are on a traditional camping and meeting place of the original owners, and this tour takes you through their story – from song lines to plant lore, all in 90 fascinating minutes. The tour departs from the visitors centre.

Balloon Sunrise ( ☎ 9427 7596; www.hotairballooning .com.au; adult/child $345/240) Although perhaps not fully awake (the tour leaves before dawn), you'll certainly feel dreamy floating above the building tops and peering into backyards from a hot-air balloon. This tour includes an hour's air time, plus a champagne breakfast at the Langham Hotel Melbourne (p188), from where tours depart. Balloons go up every morning (weather permitting) except Christmas and New Year's Day, though you'll need to book a few weeks ahead. Children must be over six years old. They also go up in the Yarra Valley.

Chinatown Heritage Walk (Map p55; ☎ 9662 2888; http://chinatownmelbourne.com.au/attractions_walk .htm; 22 Cohen Pl; adult/concession from $8-34) Be guided through historic Chinatown, with its atmospheric alleys and bustling vibe. You can opt in for lunch.

City Circle trams (www.metlinkmelbourne.com.au/city _circle/routes.html) A free service operating from 10am to 6pm daily. This tram travels around the city centre, along Flinders, Spring and Latrobe Sts, and then back along Harbour Esplanade (there are also trams running in the opposite direction). Designed primarily for tourists, and passing many city sights along the way, the trams run every 10 minutes or so. Eight refurbished W-class trams operate on this route. Built in Melbourne between 1936 and 1956, they have all been painted a distinctive deep burgundy and gold. You can even dine on board a tram (www.tramrestau rant.com.au) while taking a scenic night cruise around Melbourne's streets (although this one isn't free).

Hidden Secrets Tours ( ☎ 9329 9665; www.hiddensecrets tours.com) Walking tours of around three hours that cover laneways, art and design or wine with small groups and knowledgeable guides.

Maribyrnong River Cruises ( ☎ 9689 6431; www.black birdcruises.com.au; Wingfield St, Footscray; adult/child from $8/5) One- or two-hour cruises are available. The longer cruise goes up the Maribyrnong River to Avondale Heights (you'll see the Lonely Planet head office on the way). The one-hour cruise heads down to the West Gate Bridge and the docklands. Departures are from the end of Wingfield St in Footscray. Cruises run on Tuesday, Thursday, Saturday, Sunday and public holidays.

Melbourne River Cruises ( ☎ 9681 3284; www.melb cruises.com.au; Berth 5 & 6, Southbank Lower Promenade, Southgate; adult/child from $14/7.50) Take a one-hour cruise upstream or downstream, or a 2½-hour return cruise. Regular cruises along the Yarra River depart from a couple of locations – check with the company for details. It also operates a ferry between Southgate and Gem Pier in Williamstown. There are three to six sailings daily, depending on the season.

Walkin' Birrarung ( ☎ 8622 2600; www.koorieheritage trust.com/education; $13) This unique two-hour walk is a journey back through time. It explores both the landscape of the Yarra as well as the dramatic and irrevocable changes to both the people and the place. Its impact on all senses evokes memories that lie beneath the modern city. Highly recommended.

Walk to Art ( ☎ 9419 5848; www.walktoart.com.au; $98 per person, including an art 'starter pack', wine and cheese) These walking tours take you to galleries, artists' studios and artist-run spaces hidden in Melbourne's buildings and laneways. The tour itinerary, around the CBD and inner neighbourhoods, is always changing and revealed on the day of the walk. The tours operate Wednesday and Saturday, in all weather conditions and last for three hours with wine and cheese afterwards.

White Hat Tours ( ☎ 9329 6055; www.whitehat.com.au) White Hat loves Melbourne and offers a range of quirky tours including the Melbourne General Cemetery and Melbourne by Lamplight.

If you want to venture further a field but don't feel like travelling solo, or are time-poor, there are literally dozens of tours through Victoria to suit all tastes and budgets. Recommended operators such as Autopia Tours ( ☎ 1800 000 507 or 9419 8878; www.autopiatours.com.au), Go West ( ☎ 9828 2008; www.gowest.com.au) and Wild-Life Tours ( ☎ 9741 6333; www.wildlifetours.com.au) offer day trips to similar popular destinations, including the the Grampians, the Great Ocean Road, and the Phillip Island Penguin Parade.

Activity-based tours are increasing in both number and popularity; the following is just a sample of the countless options on offer. For a more comprehensive list, contact Tourism Victoria ( ☎ 13 28 42; www.visitvictoria.com.au).

Echidna Walkabout ( ☎ 9646 8249; www.echidnawalk about.com.au) Runs nature ecotrips (from day trips to five-day expeditions) featuring bushwalking and koala spotting.

Eco Adventure Tours ( ☎ 5962 5115; www.ecoadventure tours.com.au) Offers fascinating guided night walks in the Yarra Valley and the Dandenong Ranges. Ideal for animal lovers. See p215.

Ecotrek: Bogong Jack Adventures ( ☎ 08-8383 7198; www.ecotrek.com.au) Runs a wide range of cycling, canoeing and walking tours through the Grampians, Murray River and High Country regions.

Steamrail Victoria ( ☎ 9397 1953; www.steamrail.com.au) For steam-train devotees, Freudians and those who are looking for an unusual day out, this not-for-profit puts old trains back on the tracks for jaunts to various country destinations around the state.

# POST

Australia's postal services are efficient and inexpensive. It costs 50c to send a standard letter or postcard within Australia. Australia Post (http://auspost.com.au) divides international destinations into two zones: Asia Pacific and Rest of the World. Airmail letters cost $1.35 and $2 respectively. Postage for postcards ($1.30) is the same to any country. You can send and receive faxes from any post office for around $1 per page. Generally, post offices are open from 9am to 5pm Monday to Friday. You can also buy stamps from most newsagents.

The Melbourne GPO (Map pp52–3; ☎ 13 13 18; cnr Little Bourke & Elizabeth Sts; ☼ 8.30am-5.30pm Mon-Fri, 9am-4pm Sat, 10am-4pm Sun) offers a poste restante service. You'll need to provide some form of photo ID to collect your mail.

# RADIO

Melbourne has a huge number of radio stations broadcasting everything from hits-and-memories to talkback. The Australian Broadcasting Corporation (ABC) offers four national and one local station.

ABC Classic FM (105.9FM) Classical music.

Nova (100.3FM) Old and new music targeting the 20- and 30-somethings.

Radio National (621AM) Thoughtful analysis and fascinating features, with a 10-minute world-news service every hour on the hour.

Radio for the Print Handicapped (1179AM) Readings of daily newspapers; between 11.05pm and 6am broadcasts the BBC World Service.

3AW (693AM) Top-rating commercial talkback station.

3JJJ (107.5FM) The ABC's national youth network. Specialises in alternative music and young people's issues; streaming online.

3LO (774AM) Local ABC station with regular talkback programs, an excellent news service on the hour and a world-news feature at 12.10pm every weekday.

3PBS (106.7FM) Independent subscriber-based station, with alternative music programs; streaming online.

3RRR (102.7FM) Excellent subscriber-based station featuring independent music, current affairs and talk-show programs; streaming online.

3SBS (93.1FM) Multilingual station.

3JOY (94.9FM) Gay, lesbian, bisexual, transgender and intersex community station.

3MBS (103.5FM) Classical community station that features local performers.

# SAFETY
## Animal Bites & Stings
### FLIES & MOSQUITOES
For four to six months of the year, you'll have to cope with those two banes of the Australian outdoors: the fly and the mosquito ('mozzie'). Flies aren't too bad in the city but they start getting out of hand in the country, and the farther out you go the more numerous and persistent they seem to be. A March fly looks like a bigger, uglier version of the common fly – its bite is painful for an instant, but the aftermath is much like a mosquito bite. Widely available repellents such as Aerogard and Rid may also help to deter the little bastards, but don't count on it.

Mozzies are a problem in summer. Try to keep your arms and legs covered as soon as the sun goes down and use insect repellent liberally.

### SNAKES
Australian snakes have a terrible reputation that is justified in terms of the potency of their venom, but unjustified in terms of the actual risk to travellers and locals. Snakes are usually quite timid in nature, and in most instances will move away if disturbed. They only have small fangs, making it easy to prevent bites to the lower limbs (where 80% of bites occur) by wearing protective clothing (such as gaiters, boots, socks and long trousers) around the ankles when bushwalking. Snakes are quite common in country Victoria. If you see one, leave it alone.

In all confirmed or suspected bites, preventing the spread of toxic venom can be achieved by applying pressure to the wound and immobilising the area with a splint or sling before seeking medical attention. Firmly wrap an elastic bandage (you can improvise with a T-shirt) around the entire limb, but not so tight as to cut off the circulation. Along with immobilisation, this is a life-saving first-aid measure. Don't use a tourniquet, and *don't* try to suck out the poison!

### SPIDERS
Victoria's most dangerous spider is the redback. It has a very painful, sometimes lethal, bite. Bites cause increasing pain at the site followed by profuse sweating and generalised symptoms (including muscular weakness, sweating at the site of the bite, nausea). First aid includes application of ice or cold packs to the bite, then transfer to hospital.

White-tail spider bites may cause a painful ulcer that is very slow and difficult to heal. Clean the wound thoroughly and seek medical assistance.

### TICKS & LEECHES
The common bush-tick (found in the forest and scrub country all along Australia's east coast) can be dangerous if left lodged in the skin, as the toxin excreted by the tick can cause partial paralysis and, in theory, death. Check your body for lumps every night if you're walking in tick-infested areas. Remove the tick by dousing it with methylated spirits or kerosene and levering it out, but make sure you remove it intact. After a walk in the bush, remember to check children and dogs for ticks.

Leeches are common, and while they will suck your blood, they are not dangerous and are easily removed by the application of salt or heat.

## Bushfires & Blizzards
Bushfires happen every year in Victoria. In hot, dry and windy weather, be extremely careful with any naked flame – cigarette butts thrown out of car windows have started many fires. On a total-fire-ban day it's forbidden even to use a camping stove in the open. Locals will not be amused if they catch you breaking this particular law; they'll happily dob you in, and the penalties are severe.

If you're unfortunate enough to find yourself driving through a bushfire, stay inside your car and try to park in an open space, away from trees, until the danger passes. Lie on the floor under the dashboard, covering yourself with a wool blanket if possible. The front of the fire should pass quickly, and you will be much safer than if you were out in the open. It is very important to cover up with a wool blanket or wear protective clothing, as heat radiation is the big killer in bushfire situations.

Bushwalkers should seek local advice before setting out – be careful if a total fire ban is in place, or delay your trip. If you're out in the bush and you see smoke, even a long way away, take it seriously – bushfires move very quickly and change direction with the wind. Go to the nearest open space, downhill if possible. A forested ridge is the most dangerous place to be.

More bushwalkers actually die of cold than in bushfires. Even in summer, temperatures can drop below freezing at night in the mountains and Victorian weather is notoriously changeable. Exposure in even moderately cool temperatures can sometimes result in hypothermia. Always take suitable spare clothing and adequate water and carbohydrates.

## Swimming & Boating

Popular Victorian beaches are patrolled by surf life-savers in summer and patrolled areas are marked off by a pair of red and yellow flags. Always swim between the flags if possible.

Victoria's ocean beaches often have treacherous waves and rips. Even if you're a competent swimmer, you should exercise extreme caution and avoid the water altogether in high surf. Children should be watched closely and kept out of the water if conditions are rough. If you happen to get caught in a rip when swimming and are being taken out to sea, try not to panic. Raise one arm until you have been spotted, and then swim parallel to the shore – *don't* try to swim back against the rip.

A number of people are also paralysed every year by diving into shallow water and hitting a sandbar; check the depth of the water before you leap.

Melbourne's Port Phillip Bay is generally safe for swimming – the closest you're likely to come to a shark is in the local fish-and-chip shop. The small blue-ringed octopus is sometimes found hiding under rocks in rockpools on the foreshore. Its sting can be fatal, so don't touch it under any circumstances.

Boating on Port Phillip Bay can be hazardous, as conditions can change dramatically and without warning.

## Theft

Victoria is a relatively safe place to visit, but you should still take reasonable precautions. Don't leave hotel rooms or cars unlocked, and don't leave money, wallets, purses or cameras unattended, in full view through car windows, for instance. Most accommodation places have a safe where you can store your valuables. If you are unlucky enough to have something stolen, immediately report all details to the nearest police station.

## Trams

In Melbourne, be *extremely* cautious when stepping on and off trams. Don't step off without looking both ways. Pedestrians in Bourke St Mall should watch for passing trams too, though you are more likely to be embarrassed by the driver's persistant 'tinging' than be run over.

Car drivers should treat Melbourne trams with caution. Cyclists should be careful not to get their wheels caught in tram tracks, and motorcyclists should take special care when tram tracks are wet.

## TAXES & REFUNDS

Australia has a 10% Goods and Services Tax (GST) automatically applied to most purchases, though some fresh food items are exempt. Visitors who purchase goods with a total minimum value of $300 from any one supplier within 30 days of departure from Australia are entitled to a GST refund. You can get a cheque refund at the designated booth located beyond Customs at the airport. Contact the Australian Taxation Office ( ☎ 13 28 66; www.ato.gov.au) for details.

## TELEPHONE

The area code for Melbourne and Victoria is ☎ 03; if dialling into Melbourne drop the zero from the area code. The country code for dialling into Australia is ☎ 61; and the international access code for dialling out is ☎ 0011. Toll-free numbers start with the prefix ☎ 1800, while numbers that start with ☎ 1300 charge the cost of a local call no matter where you're calling from.

The increasingly elusive public payphone is either coin- or card-operated; local calls are unlimited and cost 50c, calls to mobile phones are timed and attract higher charges. Some accept credit cards; many don't work at all.

## Mobile Phones

All Australian mobile phone numbers have four-digit prefixes beginning with 04. Australia's digital network is compatible with GSM 900 and 1800 handsets. Quad-based US phones will also work. Prepaid SIM cards are available from providers such as Telstra (www.telstra.com), Optus (www.optus.com.au), Virgin (www.virginmobile.com.au) and Vodafone (www.vodafone.com.au).

## Phonecards

There's a wide range of local and international phonecards available from most newsagents and post offices for a fixed dollar value (usually $5 to $50). These can be used with any public or private phone by dialling a toll-free access number and then the PIN number on the card.

## TELEVISION

The Melbourne region has six free-to-air TV stations. The three commercial networks – Channels Seven, Nine and Ten – are just like commercial channels anywhere, with a varied but not particularly adventurous diet of sport, soap operas, lightweight news and sensationalised current affairs, plus plenty of sitcoms. Channel Ten differentiates itself by producing youth-oriented programs. See p33-4 for a rundown on locally produced shows.

Channel Two is the government-funded, commercial-free ABC station. They have had a recent rebranding due to the introduction of a free digital-only station. The regular channel is now called ABC1, while the digital channel is called ABC2. ABC TV produces some excellent current affairs shows, documentaries and a news service, and screens its fair share of sport and, mainly British, sitcoms and drama. The ABC also has a knack for producing comedy and drama that, if successful, gets snaffled up by the cheque-book wielding commercials.

The most thorough international news service is broadcast at 6.30pm daily on the publicly funded Special Broadcasting Service (SBS, Channel 28, UHF). SBS has a multicultural mandate and screens some of the most diverse programs shown on TV, including current affairs, documentaries, soap operas, and foreign language films. (Hence the expression 'like SBS without the subtitles', used to describe someone so drunk you cannot understand what they are saying.)

## TIME

Victoria (along with Tasmania, NSW and Queensland) keeps Eastern Standard Time, which is 10 hours ahead of GMT/UTC. That means that when it's noon in Melbourne it's

9pm the previous day in New York, 2am in London and 11am in Tokyo. For quick timezone calculations, go to Time and Date (www.timeanddate.com/worldclock).

Daylight-saving time, when clocks are put forward an hour, is between the last Sunday in October and the last Sunday in March.

## TICKETS & RESERVATIONS

Moshtix ( ☎ 1300 438 849; www.moshtix.com.au) A local outfit that sells tickets to smaller and independent concerts, theatre and other performances.

Ticketek (Map pp52–3; ☎ 132 849; www.ticketek.com.au; 225 Exhibition St) The main booking agency for theatre, concerts and sports. Book by phone, online or in person at outlets listed on the website.

Ticketmaster (Map pp52–3; www.ticketmaster.com.au; Myer, Level 5, 275 Lonsdale St, City) Another large agency for music, performing arts and sports, including games at the MCG and Telstra Dome. They have outlets at larger venues and around the city and suburbs.

## TIPPING

Tipping isn't mandatory in Melbourne, but 10% is expected at restaurants, with more for notable service. Taxi drivers also welcome tips, though a generous rounding up is usually ok in lieu of a more rigid percentage calculation. For hotel porters, $2 to $5 should suffice.

## TOILETS

Public toilets are a rapidly disappearing institution. In the city, department stores are your best bet. There are safe and clean facilities underneath the Melbourne Town Hall (Map pp52–3) on Collins St in the city. Pubs are worth a try but often frown on 'casual' visitors.

## TOURIST INFORMATION

Melbourne's government-run Visitor Information Centre (Map pp52–3; www.visitmelbourne.com; Federation Sq; ✆ 9am-6pm) provides an accommodation and tour service and internet access. Their website is translated into several languages and offers some very comprehensive information. Its parent organisation Tourism Victoria ( ☎ 13 28 42; www.visitvictoria.com.au) has a phone service and website that are equally thorough. Their online travel planner offers maps, travel ideas and a route planner that you can tailor to your specific tastes.

There are additional information booths located in the Bourke St Mall and in the international terminal at Melbourne Airport. Melbourne City Council's That's Melbourne (www.thatsmel bourne.com.au) is also an excellent resource.

All visitor's centres carry the free Melbourne: Official Visitors Guide. This publication has all sorts of helpful information, including a calendar of events, transport maps, and attraction and accommodation listings.

Regional centres throughout the state will usually have a visitor's centre or tourist information booth in a central location. These are listed throughout this book.

Parks Victoria ( ☎ 13 19 63; www.parkweb.vic.gov.au) has an information service and will also mail out brochures; its website is loaded with useful information on state and national parks.

The Melbourne Design Guide (edited by Viviane Stappmanns & Ewan McEoin), available from http://melbournedesignguide.com, is a great reference for visitors interested in the city's unique aesthetic. The Slow Guide Melbourne (Martin Hughes), available from http://slowguides .com.au, celebrates the intimate, natural, traditional and sensory (of which there is plenty in Melbourne).

## TRAVELLERS WITH DISABILITIES

Many of Melbourne's attractions are accessible for wheelchairs. Trains and newer trams have low steps to accommodate wheelchairs and people with limited mobility. Access Cabs ( ☎ 13 62 94) and Silver Top Taxis ( ☎ 8413 7202) have wheelchair accessible taxis; both should be booked ahead. Australian visitors can use their M50 cards and reciprocal taxi vouchers. Many car parks in the city have convenient spaces allocated for disabled drivers. All pedestrian crossings feature sound cues and accessible buttons.

The Melbourne Mobility Centre (Map pp52–3; ☎ 9650 6499, TTY 9650 9316; www.accessmelbourne .vic.gov.au; 1st fl car park, Federation Sq; ☺ 9am-6pm Mon-Sat, 10am-4pm Sun) offers TTY phone and web services, equipment hire and general information including a mobility map, which can also be downloaded from the website. The Traveller's Aid Centres ( ☎ 9654 2600; 2nd floor, 169 Swanston St & 9670 2873; Lower Concourse, Southern Cross Railway Station) are particularly helpful to those with special needs and offer a variety of facilities to travellers, including showers, baby-change facilities, toilets, lounge area, public telephone, lockers, stroller and wheelchair hire, ironing facilities, meeting room hire and tourist information.

## Organisations

Access Foundation (www.accessibility.com.au/melbourne /melmain.htm) City guide to Melbourne's accessible sites.

Access Melbourne (www.accessmelbourne.vic.gov.au) Online mobility map and information.

National Information Communication & Awareness Network (Nican; ☎ 1800 806 769; www.nican.com.au) An Australia-wide directory providing information on access issues, accommodation, sporting and recreational activities, transport and specialist tour operators.

Vision Australia ( ☎ 1300 84 74 66.; www.visionaustralia .org.au) The Royal Victorian Institute for the Blind has become part of this national organisation. Its services can be accessed through the centralised phone number. The Victorian head office remains in Kooyong.

VicRoads ( ☎ 13 11 71; www.vicroads.vic.gov.au) Supplies parking permits for disabled drivers.

VicDeaf ( ☎ 9657 8111; www.vicdeaf.com.au) Auslan interpreter service available.

## VISAS

Visas are required for all overseas visitors except for New Zealand nationals, who receive a 'special category' visa on arrival. Visa application forms are available from diplomatic missions, travel agents, the Department of Immigration and Multicultural Affairs ( ☎ 13 18 81; www .immi.gov.au). Some visitors are eligible to apply for an online Electronic Travel Authority (www.eta .immi.gov.au).

## WOMEN TRAVELLERS

Victoria is generally a safe place for women travellers, although the usual sensible precautions apply. It's best to avoid walking alone late at night. And if you're out for a big night on the town, always keep enough money aside for a taxi back to your accommodation. Alcohol-fuelled violence is becoming more common in Melbourne's city centre. The same applies to rural towns, where there are often a lot of unlit, semideserted streets. Lone women should also be wary of staying in basic pub accommodation unless it looks safe and well managed.

Aussie male culture does sometimes manifest in sexist bravado, and sexual harassment isn't uncommon, especially when alcohol is involved.

We do not recommend that women hitchhike alone.

The following organisations offer advice and services for women:

Royal Women's Hospital Health Information Service
( ☎ 9344 2007)

Royal Women's Hospital Sexual Assault Unit
( ☎ 9344 2201)

Women's Health Information Service ( ☎ 1800 133 321)

# WORK

If you come to Australia on a 12-month working-holiday visa, you can officially work for the entire 12 months, but you can only stay with any one employer for a maximum of three months. Working on a regular tourist visa is strictly prohibited.

To receive wages you must have a Tax File Number (TFN), issued by the Australian Taxation Office. Application forms are available at all post offices, and you are required to show your passport and visa. Short-term job opportunities usually exist in factories, the hospitality industry, fruit picking, nannying and telephone sales. Saturday's *Age* has extensive employment listings, or try online at www .mycareer.com.au or www.seek.com.au.

## Doing Business

The Melbourne Convention and Visitors Bureau (www .mcvb.com.au) is an industry organisation that promotes Melbourne as a city for convention and business events. The *Age* has a daily pull-out section dealing with business issues. Business- and finance-specific publications to look out for include the *Australian Financial Review* and *Business Review Weekly (BRW)*.

## Volunteer Work

Good Company (www.goodcompany.com.au) is a not-for-profit organisation that matches professionals, skilled in all areas, with community organisations needing short-term projects fulfilled on a pro-rata basis. Otherwise, contact your preferred organisation directly while you're in town.

# BEHIND THE SCENES

## THIS BOOK

This guidebook was commissioned in Lonely Planet's Melbourne office, and produced by the following:

Commissioning Editor Emma Gilmour

Coordinating Editors Sasha Baskett, Averil Robertson, Gina Tsarouhas

Coordinating Cartographers Hunor Csutoros, Anthony Phelan

Coordinating Layout Designer Indra Kilfoyle

Managing Editor Geoff Howard

Managing Cartographer David Connolly

Managing Layout Designer Celia Wood

Assisting Editors Monique Choy, Daniel Corbett, Peter Cruttenden, Penelope Goodes, Rosie Nicholson, Charlotte Orr, Charles Rawlings-Way

Assisting Cartographers Corey Hutchison, Erin McManus, Mandy Sierp

Assisting Layout Designer Jacqui Saunders

Cover Designer Pepi Bluck

Cover Artwork Pablo Gastar

Project Manager Sarah Sloane

Thanks to Lisa Knights, Trent Paton, Adam McCrow, Katy Murenu, Maryanne Netto, Laura Jane, Lauren Hunt, Darren O'Connell, Mik Ruff

Cover photographs The Twelve Apostles at dusk, Jon Barter/Auscape International (top); Bond bar interior, Melbourne, Shania Shegedyn/Lonely Planet Images (bottom)

Internal photographs p3 Daniel New; p7 (#2) Michael Ruff All other photographs by Lonely Planet Images: p8 (#3) John Banagan; p4 (#3) Glenn Beanland; p5 (#1) , p6 (#2) , p7 (#3) James Braund; p2 Tom Cockrem; p5 (#2) Juliet Coombe; p6 (#1) Michael Coyne; p4 (#1) Patrick Horton; p8 (#2) Richard I'Anson; p5 (#3) Gerard Walker; p4 (#2) Phil Weymouth; p7 (#1) Dallas Stribley; p8 (#1) Glenn van der Knijff

All images are copyright of the photographer unless otherwise indicated. Many of the images in this guide are available for licensing from Lonely Planet Images: www.lonelyplanetimages.com.

## THANKS
### DONNA WHEELER

Thanks to Emma Gilmour without whose support, patience and enthusiasm there would be no book, and to my fellow authors who did a wonderful job out on the road. New contributors Kristen Otto, Richard Watts and George Dunford have enriched the text, as has everyone who generously shared their Melbourne intelligence or a glass of wine with me. Special thanks to my families: Mum and Debbie for fielding terse and tired phone calls; Antonia and John for the pickups and the plates of pasta forno; Rumer and Biba for their unfailing sweetness; and finally Joe Guario (to yet again paraphrase Stevie: I was made to love you). This book is also in memory of Ron Wheeler, whose curiosity about the world inspired my own.

### THE LONELY PLANET STORY

Fresh from an epic journey across Europe, Asia and Australia in 1972, Tony and Maureen Wheeler sat at their kitchen table stapling together notes. The first Lonely Planet guidebook, *Across Asia on the Cheap*, was born.

Travellers snapped up the guides. Inspired by their success, the Wheelers began publishing books to Southeast Asia, India and beyond. Demand was prodigious, and the Wheelers expanded the business rapidly to keep up. Over the years, Lonely Planet extended its coverage to every country and into the virtual world via lonelyplanet.com and the Thorn Tree message board.

As Lonely Planet became a globally loved brand, Tony and Maureen received several offers for the company. But it wasn't until 2007 that they found a partner whom they trusted to remain true to the company's principles of travelling widely, treading lightly and giving sustainably. In October of that year, BBC Worldwide acquired a 75% share in the company, pledging to uphold Lonely Planet's commitment to independent travel, trustworthy advice and editorial independence.

Today, Lonely Planet has offices in Melbourne, London and Oakland, with over 500 staff members and 300 authors. Tony and Maureen are still actively involved with Lonely Planet. They're travelling more often than ever, and they're devoting their spare time to charitable projects. And the company is still driven by the philosophy of *Across Asia on the Cheap*: 'All you've got to do is decide to go and the hardest part is over. So go!'

## JOCELYN HAREWOOD

To everyone I met in Regional Victoria, your enthusiasm is contagious. Down here in the big smoke we hear of dry riverbeds, bushfires, salination, doom and gloom, but drive into any country town and the good feelings, pride and busy buzz, along with the gourmet produce and fun, wild or extreme activities, lets you know Australia is alive and well. To staff and volunteers at visitors centres along the way, thanks heaps, you are great. Thanks too to my travelling companions Caryn, Peregrine, Ern and Anne. And thanks to Emma, David and Errol in at Lonely Planet.

## CATH LANIGAN

A big thanks to Gippslanders who shared their local knowledge: Amanda Hack, Andrew Sharpe, Daya Jepsen, Fiona Maud, Gavin van Eede, Joel Orenstein, Kate McAnergney, Kathryn Goller, Kerrianne Crane, Kylie Greenaway, Liz Cook, Noel Maud, Phil Sewell, Shannyn van der Nol and Uli Hasel. Thanks to Parks Victoria staff Andrew Schulze, Carla and Josh Puglisi, Daryl Burns, Drue Shultz, Graeme Baxter and Wing Hagger; and to LP commissioning editor Emma Gilmour and co-author Rowan McKinnon for help and support. Special thanks to my family: John for all the driving and Zoe and Jarno for beach research.

## ROWAN MCKINNON

Thanks to Sue McKinnon (my mum), Vicky Shackley, the cleaner at the Twelve Apostles carpark display centre and Paul Kelly for the onion. Thanks too to my commissioning editor Emma Gilmour and cartographic guru David Con-

## SEND US YOUR FEEDBACK

We love to hear from travellers – your comments keep us on our toes and help make our books better. Our well-travelled team reads every word on what you loved or loathed about this book. Although we cannot reply individually to postal submissions, we always guarantee that your feedback goes straight to the appropriate authors, in time for the next edition. Each person who sends us information is thanked in the next edition – and the most useful submissions are rewarded with a free book.

To send us your updates – and find out about Lonely Planet events, newsletters and travel news – visit our award-winning website: www.lonelyplanet.com/contact.

Note: We may edit, reproduce and incorporate your comments in Lonely Planet products such as guidebooks, websites and digital products, so let us know if you don't want your comments reproduced or your name acknowledged. For a copy of our privacy policy visit www.lonelyplanet.com/privacy.

nolly. To my family – Jane Hart and my kids Lewis, Eadie, Lauren and Wesley – thanks for everything, always.

## OUR READERS

Many thanks to the travellers who used the last edition and wrote to us with helpful hints, useful advice and interesting anecdotes:

Janika Bischof, Christopher Brumby, Will Denby, Tim Evans, Frances Rowland, Keith Shaw, Monica Sharma

BEHIND THE SCENES

# Notes

INDEX

## ARTS
### MELBOURNE

## REGIONAL VICTORIA

## DRINKING
### MELBOURNE

000 map pages
**000** photographs

INDEX

# SIGHTS
## MELBOURNE
### Amusement Parks

### Aquariums

INDEX

INDEX

# SPORTS & ACTIVITIES

## MELBOURNE

## REGIONAL VICTORIA

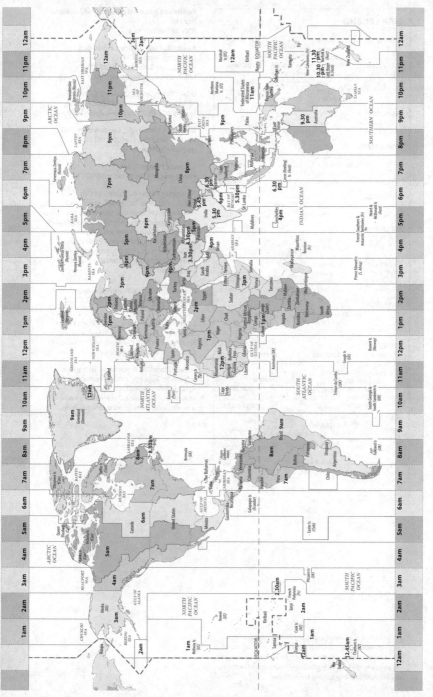

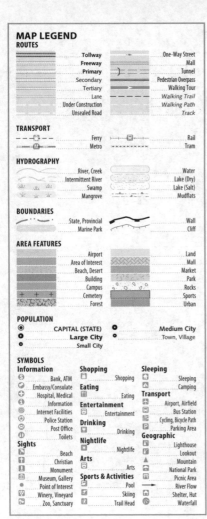

## MAP LEGEND
### ROUTES

| | |
|---|---|
| Tollway | One-Way Street |
| Freeway | Mall |
| Primary | Tunnel |
| Secondary | Pedestrian Overpass |
| Tertiary | Walking Tour |
| Lane | Walking Trail |
| Under Construction | Walking Path |
| Unsealed Road | Track |

### TRANSPORT

| | |
|---|---|
| Ferry | Rail |
| Metro | Tram |

### HYDROGRAPHY

| | |
|---|---|
| River, Creek | Water |
| Intermittent River | Lake (Dry) |
| Swamp | Lake (Salt) |
| Mangrove | Mudflats |

### BOUNDARIES

| | |
|---|---|
| State, Provincial | Wall |
| Marine Park | Cliff |

### AREA FEATURES

| | |
|---|---|
| Airport | Land |
| Area of Interest | Mall |
| Beach, Desert | Market |
| Building | Park |
| Campus | Rocks |
| Cemetery | Sports |
| Forest | Urban |

### POPULATION

| | |
|---|---|
| CAPITAL (STATE) | Medium City |
| Large City | Town, Village |
| Small City | |

### SYMBOLS

**Information**
Bank, ATM
Embassy/Consulate
Hospital, Medical
Information
Internet Facilities
Police Station
Post Office
Toilets

**Sights**
Beach
Christian
Monument
Museum, Gallery
Point of Interest
Winery, Vineyard
Zoo, Sanctuary

**Shopping**
Shopping

**Eating**
Eating

**Entertainment**
Entertainment

**Drinking**
Drinking

**Nightlife**
Nightlife

**Arts**
Arts

**Sports & Activities**
Pool
Skiing
Trail Head

**Sleeping**
Sleeping
Camping

**Transport**
Airport, Airfield
Bus Station
Cycling, Bicycle Path
Parking Area

**Geographic**
Lighthouse
Lookout
Mountain
National Park
Picnic Area
River Flow
Shelter, Hut
Waterfall

**Published by Lonely Planet Publications Pty Ltd**
ABN 36 005 607 983

**Australia** Head Office, Locked Bag 1, Footscray, Victoria 3011,
☎03 8379 8000, fax 03 8379 8111,
talk2us@lonelyplanet.com.au

**USA** 150 Linden St, Oakland, CA 94607,
☎510 250 6400, toll free 800 275 8555,
fax 510 893 8572, info@lonelyplanet.com

**UK** 2nd fl, 186 City Rd, London, EC1V 2NT,
☎020 7106 2100, fax 020 7106 2101,
go@lonelyplanet.co.uk

Printed by Hang Tai Printing Company.
Printed in China.